B-104

PRINCIPLES OF ACCOUNTING
INTRODUCTORY

PRENTICE-HALL ACCOUNTING SERIES

H. A. Finney, Editor

PRINCIPLES
OF ACCOUNTING

——INTRODUCTORY——

by

H. A. FINNEY, Ph.B., C.P.A.

and

HERBERT E. MILLER, Ph.D., C.P.A.

Professor of Accounting, University of Michigan

FIFTH EDITION

Englewood Cliffs, N. J.

PRENTICE-HALL, INC.

FIFTH EDITION

Library of Congress
Catalog Card No.: 57-8350

First printing .... April, 1957
Second printing .... January, 1958
Third printing .... February, 1958
Fourth printing .... June, 1959
Fifth printing .... May, 1960
Sixth printing .... February, 1961

PRINTED IN THE UNITED STATES OF AMERICA

70381—C

Preface

In keeping with the policy adopted in preceding revisions, the authors have requested teachers to make suggestions for improvements in the text from the standpoint of both majors and non-majors. Many responded and we wish to express our obligation to them. Their names appear following the Preface.

Some of the similarities and differences between this edition and the preceding one are mentioned below.

Corporate, non-trading approach. The first edition of this text introduced two innovations:

(1) Beginning with the corporation instead of the individual proprietorship, to avoid the student's difficulty in distinguishing between the proprietorship equity in a business and the total net worth of the proprietor.

(2) Basing the first illustrations of the accounting cycle on the accounts of a service business, to avoid the inventory complication in the first explanation of the procedure of closing the books.

These features seem to have been widely approved, and they are retained in this edition.

Easier initial treatment of accounting cycle. This edition has been made easier where a textbook should be most easy: in the early chapters. This has been accomplished in two ways:

(1) In the preceding edition, the first presentation of the accounting cycle was covered in four chapters; in this edition, five chapters are used, thus making the presentation less concentrated.

(2) In the preceding edition, adjustments for accruals and apportionments were presented in Chapter 3, and working papers involving all such adjustments were presented in Chapter 4; in this edition, adjustments for accruals, and working papers involving accruals, are presented in Chapter 4; adjustments for apportionments, and working papers involving such adjustments, are presented in Chapter 5. It is believed that this arrangement will make the nature of the two major classes of adjustments more readily understandable, and that devoting por-

v

tions of two chapters, instead of one full chapter, to working papers will be helpful to the student.

Extensive revision.   Every chapter in the text has received the most painstaking attention, recognition being given to the suggestions of those who made recommendations for improvements, with the objective of perfecting the text content and the simplicity and clarity of expression.

Modern terminology.   In the past, the authors have been reluctant to abandon long-established terminology in favor of suggested alternatives until they were rather generally adopted; such alternatives were mentioned, however.   It now appears that the trend toward such expressions as *stockholders' equity, retained earnings, accumulated depreciation,* and *allowance for doubtful accounts* has become sufficient to warrant regarding them as generally accepted while mentioning the older terms so that students will not be unacquainted with them.

Increased emphasis on theory.   The fourth edition was stronger on theory than its predecessors; this edition is even stronger.   A greater effort has been made to weave in the "why" throughout the book, particularly in the early chapters, thus improving the balance between theory and procedure.

Chapter sequence.   Some changes have been made in chapter sequence to make the text more teachable.   This was done largely in two ways:

(1) By postponing some specialized material, such as perpetual inventories, departmental operations, and manufacturing accounts, to the latter part of the book.

(2) By bringing into sequence the material on notes, the material on partnerships, and the chapters on manufacturing accounts and manufacturing costs.

Additional subject matter.   This edition contains some new material dealing in an elementary way with such subjects as installment sales and branch accounting; process cost accounting; the nature of a budget; the uses of accounting data in the making of policy decisions; and the nature and purposes of the statement of application of funds and consolidated statements.   This material has been added in recognition of the current trend toward placing greater emphasis on the managerial aspects of accounting.   It is believed that it will be of benefit to:

(1) Majors.   The addition of this material is an extension of the long-standing policy of the authors of this series: the development of a subject on a spiral—that is, elementary

coverage in the Introductory text to make the going easier when the student faces an extensive treatment of the subject in a later course.

(2) Non-majors, who otherwise would not be exposed to certain fields of accounting knowledge that would be beneficial to them.

(3) Students in liberal arts colleges where a limited number of accounting courses are given but where teachers would like their students to get somewhat more than the traditional first course.

It is believed that the enrichment of the introductory course by the addition of this material, rudimentary though it may be, will stimulate an increased interest in the accounting curriculum on the part of all students in the first-year course. These chapters and the related assignment material have been developed as optional chapters. They are not substitutes for material dropped from the previous edition; little of consequence has been dropped. Some teachers may omit one or more of these chapters, depending on the objectives of the introductory course, the kind of advanced courses offered, and the number of hours of credit granted for the first course in accounting.

The long practice set in the latter part of the book does not require a knowledge of any of these added subjects; any or all of them may be omitted without interfering with the assignment of that set.

Assignment material. Although the assignment material has been thoroughly revised, its general nature remains unchanged. The new edition has as many problems of the *A* and *B* variety as the preceding edition, and forms for their solution are similar to those accompanying that edition. The two principal practice sets have been somewhat shortened. There are also questions and a workbook.

Reference to Institute bulletins. Accounting research bulletins of the American Institute of Certified Public Accountants are copyrighted by the Institute. Quotations in this text are by its permission.

H. A. FINNEY
HERBERT E. MILLER

Acknowledgments

We are deeply grateful to the following teachers who made valuable suggestions for improvements in this new edition:

Conley R. Addington, University of Miami
Wilton T. Anderson, University of Colorado
Wilmer Baer, State College of Washington
D. L. Barnes, University of Oklahoma
Ralph F. Beckert, Ohio University
D. M. Beights, Stetson University
Walter F. Behler, Xavier University
Martin L. Black, Jr., Duke University
Peter C. Briant, University of Michigan
Thomas A. Budd, University of Pennsylvania
A. R. Burton, Arizona State College
Edwin Carey, Flint Junior College
Frances Clark, University of Akron
Norman B. Clark, Woodbury College
Robert G. Cox, University of Pennsylvania
Dudley W. Curry, Southern Methodist University
Howard Daniels, University of Houston
Glee Duncan, Long Beach City College
Tom Dickerson, Western Reserve University
Merrill Dilley, Drake University
Clarence L. Dunn, Louisiana State University
Donald J. Emblen, Montana State University
William H. Fenzel, Ohio University
James Finnie, Sir George Williams College
Theodore Fitzgerald, Temple University
Edward A. Gee, Michigan State University
Paul W Glennon, Becker Junior College
Dennis Gordon, University of Akron
W. Rogers Hammond, Georgia State College of Business Administration
Sib O. Hansen, Los Angeles State College
Robert D. Haun, University of Kentucky
H. M. Heckman, University of Georgia
Samuel R. Hepworth, University of Michigan
E. J. Hilkert, Arizona State College
Roderick L. Holmes, Baylor University
Delmer P. Hylton, Wake Forest College

Hugh Jackson Jr., San Jose State College
Frank S. Kaulbach, Jr., University of Virginia
Hazen W. Kendrick, University of Colorado
Fred L. Kistler, University of Michigan
Frank Lee, Boston College
T. M. Leland, Texas A. & M. College
William C. McGrew, University of Oklahoma
Louis W. Matusiak, University of Detroit
Stuart B. Mead, Michigan State University
Robert B. Mitchell, University of Pennsylvania
Arthur B. Moss, University of Michigan
Louis A. Myers, University of Arizona
Carl Nelson, University of Minnesota
Colin Park, Haskins & Sells, Buffalo
W. H. Reininga, Ohio University
Harry Rosenthal, The American University
Raymund Ross, University of Connecticut
Earl A. Russell, Bryant-Stratton Business Institute
Alton Sadler, University of North Carolina
George C. Selzer, Xavier University
Warren Slagle, University of Tennessee
Mary Vernon Slusher, University of Akron
Robert J. Smith, Brigham Young University
Dan Sweeney, State University of Iowa
Clayton Tidyman, Long Beach State College
Vern A. Vincent, University of Tennessee
William F. Vendley, Purdue University
Harry H. Wade, University of Miami
Kenneth J. Weller, Hope College
Howard A. Zacur, University of Miami

Contents

Office Routines; Documents· Duties of the accounting department; Internal control. Purchase Routine: Purchase requisitions; Purchase order; Invoice; Purchaser's verification of invoice; Payment of the invoice; Checks, advices, and receipts. Sales Routine: Sales; Statements.

general ledger accounts and perpetual inventories; Underabsorbed and
overabsorbed overhead. Process Cost Accounting: Illustration—No
goods in process at beginning or end of period; Illustration—Goods in
process at end of period; Illustration—Goods in process at beginning and
end of period; Management statistics; Applicability of process cost procedure; General ledger accounts and perpetual inventories.

PRINCIPLES OF ACCOUNTING
INTRODUCTORY

CHAPTER 1

Assets, Liabilities, and Owners' Equity

Description of accounting. The nature of accounting and its significance in the business world can be described by noting the variety of work performed by persons trained in the field of accounting.

(1) *Installation of accounting systems:* As a general rule, the first accounting work performed for any business involves the development of an accounting system. The accountant studies the nature of the business, determines the types of transactions that probably will occur, and plans or selects the necessary forms and records in which the transactions of the business may be recorded. As a business grows, it is customary to review the accounting system from time to time and to initiate any desirable amplifications or modifications.

(2) *Record keeping:* After the accounting system has been designed and installed, the results of business transactions are recorded in the accounting forms and records.

(3) *Preparation of financial statements:* At regular intervals the accountant, using the financial data accumulated in the accounting records, prepares statements showing the financial position of the business and the results of its operations. Such statements furnish important information to management, owners, investors, bankers, and governmental agencies.

(4) *Auditing:* Auditing is a procedure by which experts examine the accounting records and statements to safeguard against fraud and error and to give assurance that these records and statements have been prepared in accord with accepted accounting principles. Auditing is of two general classes:

    (a) Continuous internal audit. Large businesses usually have on their own payroll a staff of accountants whose duty it is to make continuous checks of the work performed by the accounting department.

    (b) Periodic audit by public accountants. To give added assurance to the management and to outsiders, a business may engage the services of an outside, independent accountant to determine whether the statements present fairly the financial position of the business and the results of operations in accordance with generally accepted accounting principles, and to express, in his audit report, an opinion on these matters.

It should be mentioned that auditing is not the only service performed by public accountants. They may, among other things, install accounting systems, prepare or review tax returns, and make special studies for their clients.

(5) *Tax accounting:* Most accountants have some contact with tax matters, and many accountants specialize in this field.

(6) *Budgeting:* Although the preparation of budgets (plans and forecasts for the future) may not be his exclusive responsibility, the accountant's understanding of the accounting records and procedures and of the information previously recorded makes him an important participant in budget preparation.

(7) *Cost accounting:* Many accountants specialize in the field of cost accounting. If a business manufactures the goods which it sells, it is essential that it keep adequate detailed records showing the cost of material, labor, and other items used in the production of the various kinds of goods. Cost records may also be maintained for the selling or distribution phases of the business. The cost accountant participates in determining how cost data shall be accumulated in the records and generally is charged with the responsibility of interpreting cost information for management.

(8) *Controllership:* The controller is the chief accounting officer of a business and one of the financial advisors to its management. Controllership is a specialized field of accounting calling for broad and thorough training in accounting and business management.

(9) *Special investigations:* Frequently, special investigations requiring a thorough knowledge of accounting principles and procedures must be made for such purposes as establishing a price for the sale of an entire business, a department thereof, or merely one of its products, deciding whether a given activity is or might be profitable, or determining the feasibility of retirement or bonus plans.

Accounting is now recognized as one of the very important professions. Employment opportunities are varied and numerous, and the compensation to be expected compares very favorably with that in other professions. There is always an opportunity for qualified accountants to obtain satisfactory employment with government agencies, private business, and public accounting firms.

As in any other honorable calling, the person who practices accounting should be a person of integrity; he must also be possessed of a high degree of analytical ability; he must not be averse to dealing with vast amounts of detail; he must be tactful; and he should maintain a personal appearance consistent with his professional status.

The importance of accounting procedures. From the above discussion of the work of the accountant, it is apparent that record keeping is only one part of this broad field of activity. This phase of accounting is frequently referred to as the procedural part of accounting. Whether a business is large or small, and whether the procedures are simple or complex, the work of record keeping is extremely important, because the satisfactory accomplishment of most of the other accounting activities depends, to a great extent, upon the accuracy and completeness of the accounting records.

However, from the point of view of the accounting student, a knowledge of procedures is important for an additional reason: with such a background, accounting theory will be more easily understood. In turn, a good foundation in accounting theory will better enable the student to see that the accounting records are in conformity with accepted accounting principles and to understand and interpret financial statements.

The importance of understanding financial statements and of being able to interpret them is well recognized. Anyone faced with the necessity of making business decisions, whether as corporation officer, individual proprietor, sales manager, plant engineer, credit manager, purchasing agent, investor, or accountant, should find accounting data useful. Too often business executives, investors, and others who need the information contained in accounting statements have had insufficient training in accounting to enable them wholly to grasp the significance of such reports prepared for their guidance.

Forms of business organization. Business operations may be conducted by an individual proprietorship, a partnership, or a corporation. An individual may start a business with almost no preliminary legal formalities, perhaps only a local license being required. For a partnership to come into existence, an agreement between the partners is required. A corporation is not so easily formed, since authorization by the state must be obtained. Such authorization is sought by filing an application with a designated state official. If the application is approved, the state will issue a charter which evidences the fact that the corporation has been legally organized and is authorized to issue capital stock and to conduct business.

The balance sheet.   One of the major purposes of accounting is to provide the information required for the preparation of a statement showing the financial position of a business on a stated date. This statement, called a *balance sheet*, shows the assets of the business, its liabilities, and the owners' equity.   Following is a simple illustrative balance sheet.

COMMUNITY TELEVISIONS
Balance Sheet
August 31, 19—

Assets		Liabilities and Stockholders' Equity		
Cash	$2,795.00	Liabilities:		
Accounts receivable	1,250.00	Accounts payable		$1,200.00
Installation and repair		Stockholders' equity:		
parts	3,800.00	Capital stock	$8,000.00	
Land	1,500.00	Retained earnings	145.00	8,145.00
	$9,345.00			$9,345.00

Observe that the heading of the balance sheet shows (1) the name of the business, (2) the name of the statement, and (3) the date.   Observe also that the above illustration is a balance sheet of a corporation.   The owners of a corporation are its stockholders; hence, the owners' equity in the business is referred to as *stockholders' equity*.   If the business had been organized as a partnership, *partners' equity* would be a suitable caption for the owners' equity.   The words *proprietor's equity* would be appropriate in a balance sheet of a business owned and operated by an individual proprietor.   *Owners' equity* is suitable as a general term but not as a balance sheet caption for a particular business.

It will help us to understand the balance sheet if we consider the nature of its elements: assets, liabilities, and owners' equity.

Assets.   Assets are things of value owned.   Cash, accounts and notes receivable (amounts owed to the business as a result of credit transactions), merchandise, office supplies, land, buildings, machinery and other equipment, and patents are some of the assets that may be owned by a business.

Things may have value for several reasons; for instance:

(1) Because the asset may be used as purchasing power.
    Cash is an example.   It has value because other things can be acquired with it.
(2) Because the asset is a money claim.
    Accounts receivable, notes receivable, and United States savings bonds are examples, the holder or claimant being entitled to receive money for them, usually at some specified date.

(3) Because the asset can be sold and thereby converted to cash or to a money claim.

Merchandise held for sale by a merchant is an example.

(4) Because the asset offers some potential benefits, or rights, or services to the owner.

A building is an example. It provides shelter or a place in which business activities may be conducted. Land, machinery, equipment, patents, and supplies are other examples.

Assets of the type described under (4) are acquired by a business with the expectation of earning something from their use. The fact that it might be possible to sell them is not of major importance to the accountant under normal circumstances: they are acquired because of their potential benefits or services.

Liabilities. Liabilities are debts; they are amounts owed to creditors. Accounts payable, notes payable, mortgages payable, wages payable, and taxes payable are some of the liabilities that may be owed by a business.

Owners' equity. The excess of the assets over the liabilities of a business is the owners' equity.

For instance,

If a business has assets in the amount of...................	$9,345.00
And has liabilities of.....................................	1,200.00
The owners' equity is.....................................	$8,145.00

Sources of owners' equity. The owners' equity in a corporation may come from the following sources:

From stockholders' investments—Shown in the illustrative balance sheet on page 4 as Capital Stock.

From earnings—Shown in the illustrative balance sheet on page 4 as Retained Earnings.

In this chapter, we shall deal only with the portion of the owners' equity produced by stockholders' investments. Retained earnings will be dealt with in the next chapter.

The balance sheet equation. The assets of a business are always equalled by the sum of the liabilities and the owners' equity. This fact can be expressed in the form of an equation, thus:

$$\text{ASSETS} = \text{LIABILITIES} + \text{OWNERS' EQUITY}$$
$$\$9,345 = \$1,200 + \$8,145$$

The illustrative balance sheet on page 4 is an expression of this equation.

Continuing balance sheet equality. The totals of the two sides of a balance sheet are always equal, because, no matter what business transactions occur, the assets of a business are always equalled by the rights of the creditors and the owners. To demonstrate this fact, let us consider a number of transactions of a business, prepare a balance sheet after each transaction, and observe the equality of the two sides of each balance sheet.

Issuance of capital stock. J. C. White, Henry Dobson, and J. B. Hudson organized a corporation called Community Televisions. The charter obtained from the state authorized the corporation to issue 800 shares of capital stock of $10 par value per share; this gave the corporation an authorized capital stock of $8,000.

We shall assume that White invested $4,000, and that each of the other men invested $2,000.

Investments in a corporation are evidenced by stock certificates. An illustration of a stock certificate appears below.

Certificate No.____1____   ____200____ Shares

CAPITAL STOCK $8,000.00
800 Shares of $10.00 Par Value

THIS CERTIFIES That_____Henry Dobson_____is the

owner of_____Two hundred_____Shares of the Capital Stock of

COMMUNITY TELEVISIONS

transferable only on the books of the Corporation by the holder hereof in person or by attorney upon the surrender of this Certificate properly endorsed.

IN WITNESS WHEREOF, the said Corporation has caused this Certificate to be signed by its duly authorized officers, and to be sealed with the seal of the Corporation at Chicago, Illinois this____20th____day of ____July____, 19 —

J. B. Hudson
Secretary

J. C. White
President

Stock Certificate

As evidence of his investment, Dobson received this certificate for 200 shares of stock, with a total par value of $2,000. Certificates were issued to the other incorporators for their investments.

After the issuance of $8,000 par value of capital stock for cash on July 20, the company's balance sheet appeared as follows:

COMMUNITY TELEVISIONS
Balance Sheet
July 20, 19—

Assets		Stockholders' Equity	
Cash................	$8,000.00	Capital stock..........	$8,000.00
	$8,000.00		$8,000.00

Purchase of land. The company planned to erect its own shop building, and purchased two adjoining pieces of land on July 22 for $1,500 each, paying cash. As a result of this transaction, the company acquired a new asset (land) and decreased its cash. After this transaction, the company's balance sheet appeared as follows:

COMMUNITY TELEVISIONS
Balance Sheet
July 22, 19—

Assets		Stockholders' Equity	
Cash................	$5,000.00	Capital stock..........	$8,000.00
Land................	3,000.00		
	$8,000.00		$8,000.00

Sale of land. The management decided that more land had been purchased than was needed, and one of the lots was sold to G. E. Dutton on July 27 for $1,500, the amount it had cost the company. No cash was received from Dutton on this date. This transaction produced an accounts receivable asset of $1,500, and correspondingly decreased the land asset. After this transaction, the balance sheet appeared as follows:

COMMUNITY TELEVISIONS
Balance Sheet
July 27, 19—

Assets		Stockholders' Equity	
Cash................	$5,000.00	Capital stock..........	$8,000.00
Accounts receivable....	1,500.00		
Land................	1,500.00		
	$8,000.00		$8,000.00

Purchase of installation and repair parts. To conduct its operations, the company will need a considerable quantity of antennas and other installation and repair parts. Mr. White found a dealer, O. E. Maltby, who was going out of business, and purchased the dealer's entire stock of such parts for the company on July 28. Mr. Maltby said that he thought he could easily obtain at least $4,000 for the parts by selling them at auction, but was willing to accept $3,800 for them at a quick sale. It is a generally recognized accounting principle that the accounting basis for assets, at the date of their acquisition, is the cost thereof, regardless of possible value; therefore, the parts are shown in the following balance sheet at their $3,800 cost. Delivery was postponed until the company acquired or rented a building. No cash payment was made to Maltby on this date.

By this transaction, the company acquired a new asset (installation and repair parts) and incurred an accounts payable liability. After this transaction, the balance sheet appeared as follows:

COMMUNITY TELEVISIONS
Balance Sheet
July 28, 19—

Assets		Liabilities and Stockholders' Equity	
Cash	$ 5,000.00	Liabilities:	
Accounts receivable	1,500.00	Accounts payable	$ 3,800.00
Installation and repair parts	3,800.00		
Land	1,500.00	Stockholders' equity:	
		Capital stock	8,000.00
	$11,800.00		$11,800.00

Collection on an account receivable. On July 29, $1,000 in cash was received from G. E. Dutton, in partial settlement of his account. This transaction increased the cash asset and decreased the accounts receivable asset. The balance sheet after this transaction appeared as follows:

COMMUNITY TELEVISIONS
Balance Sheet
July 29, 19—

Assets		Liabilities and Stockholders' Equity	
Cash	$ 6,000.00	Liabilities:	
Accounts receivable	500.00	Accounts payable	$ 3,800.00
Installation and repair parts	3,800.00		
Land	1,500.00	Stockholders' equity:	
		Capital stock	8,000.00
	$11,800.00		$11,800.00

Payment on an account payable. On July 31, the company paid $2,600 to O. E. Maltby to apply on account. This transaction decreased the accounts payable liability and also decreased the cash. After this transaction, the balance sheet appeared as follows:

COMMUNITY TELEVISIONS
Balance Sheet
July 31, 19—

Assets		Liabilities and Stockholders' Equity	
Cash	$3,400.00	Liabilities:	
Accounts receivable	500.00	Accounts payable	$1,200.00
Installation and repair parts	3,800.00		
Land	1,500.00	Stockholders' equity:	
		Capital stock	8,000.00
	$9,200.00		$9,200.00

There is a customary order in which assets are listed in balance sheets. This matter is discussed in some detail in Chapter 8. For the present, it is sufficient to say that assets may be listed in the following order: cash, receivables, and supplies (such as installation and repair parts), with land, buildings, and machinery and equipment as the last items.

Cost and value. In the discussion of the purchase of installation and repair parts, the statement was made: "It is a generally recognized accounting principle that the accounting basis for assets, at the date of their acquisition, is the cost thereof, regardless of possible value." The primary reason for the preference of cost over value as an accounting basis for assets acquired by purchase is the indefinite nature of value. Value is subjective. Frequently, it is merely someone's opinion—often affected by optimism or pessimism. Value is something that people often argue about. It may be quite difficult to find several businessmen who would agree on the value of a building, or a patent, or a complicated machine. In contrast, cost is objective; it is the result of a bargained transaction. Cost is a fact, not an opinion. Furthermore, the cost basis of reporting has the merit of showing on subsequent balance sheets what management paid in acquiring various assets. Thus, the balance sheet enables those interested in the financial position of the business to judge to some extent the ability of its management by the record of its past decisions regarding asset purchases.

As an example, suppose that a banker has received a request for a loan from A Corporation. In most cases the banker would want to investigate the financial affairs of the corporation before granting the loan, and one of the things examined would be the balance sheet. The assets shown in the balance sheet would reveal the cash position, the claims to cash, and the cost of assets purchased for resale or acquired for use in carrying on business activities, the latter being for the most part the physical plant or facilities of the business. Thus, accounting provides through the balance sheet a report of what management has done with the resources available to the business.

In most cases it would be wrong to conclude from the above that cost and value differ greatly at acquisition date. Under normal conditions, cost is a reliable indication of value at the date the transaction is completed, because, as a general rule, a seller would not sell an asset for an amount less than its worth, nor would a purchaser pay more than an asset is worth. In a sense, the two amounts (cost and value) can be said to coincide, at least approximately, at acquisition.

What happens with the passage of time? No predictions can be offered regarding the trend of values. It may develop in some cases that acquisition cost and value will remain close together. It is just as likely that "old" costs will become a poor indication of "current" values. An important point to remember is that a balance sheet may not disclose current values for the assets shown thereon. Whether original cost will closely approximate current value depends on the nature of the asset and the economic changes that have occurred since the asset was acquired.

Does the above observation destroy the usefulness of balance sheets? Generally, a negative answer can be justified. Even when a disparity exists between old costs shown in the balance sheet and current values, the usefulness of the balance sheet is not destroyed, because in most cases the assets in question will have been acquired to be used and not to be resold. In such cases current values often are of slight significance to the "going concern" (an established business which is being conducted with the expectation of continuing indefinitely), because the assets will continue to be used until they wear out or expire. There is also the point noted above, that the balance sheet has some merit by providing a report of past decisions in terms of the amounts spent for various assets.

Owners' equity and net worth. For many years, Net Worth was used as a balance sheet caption; in recent years there has been a decided shift to such captions as Stockholders' Equity. This shift was caused by accountants' fears that the word "worth" might mislead balance sheet readers who were not trained accountants—that such readers might believe that the amount shown as net worth was what the owners would get if the business were closed up.

Such a misunderstanding might arise from a belief that assets are shown in the balance sheet at their realizable values, or at what they are worth; it would then follow that the total of the assets at realizable values minus the liabilities would be the amount that the owners would receive if the business were liquidated.

But, as stated in the preceding comments on cost and value, showing assets at their *value* is not one of the objectives of accounting. It follows that, if the total shown for assets does not represent realizable value, the difference between assets and liabilities does not represent what the owners would receive upon liquidation.

Because the word "equity" seems less conducive to misunderstanding than the word "worth," "equity" captions have come into extensive use.

CHAPTER 2
Basic Accounting Procedures

Accounts. In Chapter 1 a balance sheet was prepared after each business transaction. This was done to illustrate the continuing equality of assets with liabilities and owners' equity, and to show the effects of some common transactions on the assets, liabilities, and owners' equity. Actually, it would be impracticable to prepare a balance sheet for a business after each transaction. Instead, the transactions are recorded in the accounting records, and the information accumulated in these records is used for the preparation of balance sheets at periodic intervals.

Transactions cause increases and decreases in the assets, the liabilities, and the owners' equity. These increases and decreases are recorded in *accounts*. The following illustration shows an account form:

SHEET NO.___				*Account Title*			ACCOUNT NO.___	
DATE	EXPLANATION	REF.	AMOUNT	DATE	EXPLANATION	REF.	AMOUNT	

Accounts usually are kept in a loose-leaf binder or in a file. The binder or the file, together with the accounts therein, is called a *ledger*.

A separate account is kept for each type of asset, each type of liability, and each element of the owners' equity. The July 31 balance sheet of Community Televisions on page 8 shows that, in order to record the July transactions, the accounts listed on page 12 were needed. The accounts should be arranged in the ledger in the order in which they will appear in the balance sheet, and they should be numbered. The following list shows that some numbers have not been assigned to any accounts; these numbers have been reserved for other accounts which can be added in balance sheet sequence later if required.

Account Number

Assets:
Cash................................. 1
Accounts receivable.................... 2
Installation and repair parts........... 10
Land................................. 15
Liabilities:
Accounts payable...................... 20
Stockholders' equity:
Capital stock......................... 50

You will observe that the account form has two sides, with identical columns. The column headings (*Date, Explanation, Ref.,* and *Amount*) shown in the preceding illustration may not appear in accounts, but are included in the illustration to indicate the purpose of each column.

The *Date* column shows the date of the transaction.

The *Explanation* column may contain some short comment indicating the reason for the entry. This column is used only on rare occasions when it may be desirable to describe some unusual transaction.

Ref. is an abbreviation of *Reference.* The use of this column is explained later in the chapter.

The *Amount* column shows the dollar amount of the entry.

To simplify illustrations and problem assignments, ledger accounts often take the form of a large capital T, thus eliminating some of the rulings common to the complete ledger account form. Such accounts are referred to as "T-accounts" or "skeleton accounts." An example follows:

Debit and credit. The left side of an account is called the *debit* side; the right side is called the *credit* side. An entry on the left side of an account is called a *debit entry,* or merely a *debit;* an entry on the right side is called a *credit entry,* or a *credit.* The words *debit* and *credit* are also used as verbs. When you make an entry on the left side of an account, you are *debiting* the account. When you make an entry on the right side, you are *crediting* the account.

Many non-accountants seem to think that *debit* means something unfavorable and *credit* means something favorable. This is not the case. The words merely refer to the two sides of an account.

The difference between the total debits and the total credits in an account is called the *balance.* If the dollar total of the debits exceeds the dollar total of the credits, the account has a debit balance; if the dollar total of the credits exceeds the dollar total of the debits, the account has a credit balance.

Debit and credit entries in accounts.   As previously stated, transactions cause increases and decreases in assets, in liabilities, and in owners' equity.   Accounts have two sides so that increases can be recorded on one side and decreases can be recorded on the other side.   The nature of the account determines the side to be used for increases and the side to be used for decreases.

Asset accounts.   Assets are shown on the left side of the balance sheet.   Consistency suggests that asset accounts should therefore have balances on the left, or debit, side.   For an asset account to have a debit balance, it is necessary that increases and decreases in the asset be recorded thus:

Any Asset Account

Increases	Decreases

Liability and owners' equity accounts.   Since the liabilities and the owners' equity are shown on the right side of the balance sheet, consistency also suggests that increases and decreases in liabilities and increases and decreases in owners' equity be recorded in the manner indicated below:

**Any Liability Account or
Any Owners' Equity Account**

Decreases	Increases

Summary statement of debit and credit procedure.   The procedures stated above may be summarized as follows:

In ASSET accounts:
   Increases are recorded by debits.
   Decreases are recorded by credits.

In LIABILITY and OWNERS' EQUITY accounts:
   Increases are recorded by credits.
   Decreases are recorded by debits.

Recording transactions.   To illustrate the debiting and crediting of accounts, let us review the transactions of Community Televisions mentioned in Chapter 1, analyze each transaction to see what increases or decreases occurred, and observe the debit and credit entries which record these increases and decreases.   To simplify the illustration, T-accounts are used and only the amounts of the debits and credits are shown.   To help you identify the entries, the debit and credit for each successive transaction are shown in italics.   Asset accounts are shown at the left; liability and owners' equity accounts are shown at the right.

Capital stock was issued for cash, $8,000.

The cash asset was increased—Debit Cash.

The owners' equity was increased—Credit Capital Stock.

Cash		Capital Stock	
8,000			8,000

Land was purchased for cash, $3,000.

The land asset was increased—Debit Land.

The cash asset was decreased—Credit Cash.

Land	
3,000	

Cash	
8,000	3,000

Land was sold to G. E. Dutton on account for $1,500—its cost.

An accounts receivable asset was acquired—Debit Accounts Receivable.

The land asset was decreased—Credit Land.

Accounts Receivable	
1,500	

Land	
3,000	1,500

Installation and repair parts were purchased from O. E. Maltby on account, $3,800.

A new asset (installation and repair parts) was acquired—Debit Installation and Repair Parts.

An accounts payable liability was incurred—Credit Accounts Payable.

Installation and Repair Parts		Accounts Payable	
3,800			3,800

Cash was collected from G. E. Dutton to apply on account, $1,000.

The cash asset was increased—Debit Cash.

The accounts receivable asset was decreased—Credit Accounts Receivable.

Cash	
8,000	3,000
1,000	

Accounts Receivable	
1,500	1,000

Cash was paid to O. E. Maltby to apply on account, $2,600.
  The accounts payable liability was decreased—Debit Accounts Payable.
  The cash asset was decreased—Credit Cash.

Cash		Accounts Payable	
8,000	3,000	*2,600*	3,800
1,000	*2,600*		

Accounts receivable and payable.   In the foregoing illustration, there was only one individual indebted to Community Televisions and only one creditor.   The Accounts Receivable and Accounts Payable accounts will be used regardless of the number of debtors and creditors.   The Accounts Receivable account will show the total amount receivable, and the Accounts Payable account will show the total amount payable.   Chapter 10 describes additional records that show the amount receivable from each debtor and the amount payable to each creditor.

Journal and ledger.   Although transactions *could be* recorded directly in the ledger accounts, it is customary (for reasons stated later) to use at least two bookkeeping records:

(1) *A Journal.*
    The first record of a transaction is made in a journal.
    The procedure of recording transactions in the journal is called *journalizing*.   A journal is called a *book of original entry*.
    The entry for each transaction shows what accounts will later be debited and credited in the ledger.

(2) *A Ledger.*
    The debits and credits to the various accounts, as shown by the journal entries, are entered in the accounts by a process called *posting*.

Journalizing.   On page 16 are journal entries recording, in chronological order, the transactions of Community Televisions previously mentioned.   Following is the procedure for journalizing:

Analyze each transaction by asking yourself the question:
    In what ways were the assets, the liabilities, or the owners' equity of the business increased or decreased by this transaction?   The answer to this question will indicate the accounts to be debited and credited.
After each transaction is analyzed, it is recorded in the journal in the following manner:
    Write the date of the transaction in the Date column: the year, month, and day of the month should be written in the first

journal entry on each page; entries on the same page for subsequent transactions in the same year and month need show
only the day of the month.

Write the name of the account to be debited, and enter the
amount of the debit in the left money column.

On the next line, write the name of the account to be credited,
and enter the amount of the credit in the right money column.
The name of the account credited should be indented somewhat to the right of the name of the account debited.

Write an explanation of the transaction.

Leave a blank line after each journal entry.

The account names written in journal entries should be the
exact names of the accounts as they appear in the ledger.

The journal of Community Televisions appears below. The
words at the head of the journal (*Date, Account Debited,* and so
forth) are included in the illustration for instructional purposes
only. The transactions have been journalized, but the journal
entries have not been posted.

Journal   (*Page 1*)

DATE	ACCOUNT DEBITED	ACCOUNT CREDITED	L.F.	DEBIT AMOUNT	CREDIT AMOUNT
July 20	Cash			8000 00	
		Capital stock			8000 00
		Issuance of 800 shares of stock at $10 par value.			
22	Land			3000 00	
		Cash			3000 00
		Purchase of two building lots for $1,500 each; paid in cash.			
27	Accounts receivable			1500 00	
		Land			1500 00
		Sale to G. E. Dutton of one lot at the price it cost the company. Sale made on account			
28	Installation and repair parts			3800 00	
		Accounts payable			3800 00
		Purchase of installation and re-pair parts on account			
29	Cash			1000 00	
		Accounts receivable			1000 00
		Collection on account.			
31	Accounts payable			2600 00	
		Cash			2600 00
		Payment on account			

Advantages of the journal. The journal serves three useful purposes. In the first place, it reduces the possibility of error. If transactions were recorded directly in the ledger, there would be considerable danger of omitting the debit or the credit entry, or of making two debit entries or two credit entries. This danger is reduced to a minimum by using the journal. In the journal, the debits and credits for each transaction are recorded together, where such errors would be readily observed.

In the second place, the journal shows offsetting debit and credit entries for each transaction, and thus provides a complete record of the transaction in one place. Also, the journal provides ample space for an explanation of the transaction.

In the third place, the journal shows all of the pertinent facts about the transactions in their *chronological order*.

Posting. *Posting* is the process of recording in the ledger accounts the debits and credits indicated by the journal entries.

The procedure of posting consists of the steps stated below:

First post the debit member of the entry:
  Turn to the account to be debited.
  Enter on the debit side of the account:
    In the Date column—the date.
    In the Reference column—the number of the journal
      page *from* which the entry was posted.
    In the money column—the amount of the debit.
  Turn to the journal and, in the "L.F." (which means *ledger
    folio* or page or account number) column at the left of
    the money column, enter the number of the account *to*
    which the entry was posted.
  Post the credit member of the journal entry in a similar
    manner.

Entering the journal page number in the ledger and the account number in the journal serves two purposes:

While the bookkeeper is posting, it shows how much of the
  posting has been done. Thus, if the bookkeeper is called
  away before the posting is completed, he knows that the work
  should be taken up again with the first journal entry showing
  no account number in the L.F. column.

After the posting has been completed, the numbers serve as
  cross references between the journal and the ledger. This is
  particularly helpful if the bookkeeper, when looking at some
  account, wishes to find the journal entries from which the
  postings were made.

The first journal entry is repeated below to show how the account numbers are entered in the ledger folio column.

Journal   (Page 1)

19—					
July 20	Cash...	1	8,000 00		
	Capital stock............................	50			8,000 00
	Issuance of 800 shares of stock at $10 par value.				

After this journal entry is posted, the accounts affected appear as follows:

Cash   (Account No. 1)

July 20		1	8,000 00			

Capital Stock   (Account No. 50)

				19— July 20		1	8,000 00

After the completion of the posting of all of the journal entries, the accounts appear as follows:

Cash   (Account No. 1)

19— July 20		1	8,000 00	19— July 22		1	3,000 00
29		1	1,000 00	31		1	2,600 00

Accounts Receivable   (Account No. 2)

19— July 27		1	1,500 00	19— July 29		1	1,000 00

Installation and Repair Parts   (Account No. 10)

19— July 28		1	3,800 00				

Land   (Account No. 15)

19— July 22		1	3,000 00	19— July 27		1	1,500 00

Accounts Payable   (Account No. 20)

19— July 31		1	2,600 00	19— July 28		1	3,800 00

Capital Stock   (Account No. 50)

				19— July 20		1	8,000 00

Computing balances of accounts. Account balances may be computed, and shown in the accounts, in the manner described and illustrated below:

Add the debit column of the account, and enter the total in small pencil figures at the bottom of the column.

Add the credit column of the account, and enter the total in small pencil figures at the bottom of the column.

Enter the balance in small pencil figures in the Explanation column: on the line of the last debit entry, if the account has a debit balance; on the line of the last credit entry, if the account has a credit balance.

Cash   (Account No. 1)

19—					19—				
July	20			1	8,000 00	July	22		1	3,000 00
	29	3,400.00		1	1,000 00		31		1	2,600 00
					9,000 00					5,600 00

If only one entry appears on either side of an account, a pencil total of that side is, of course, unnecessary. If an account contains only one entry, the amount of that entry is the balance of the account, and it is unnecessary to write the balance again in the Explanation column.

If an account contains only debit entries or credit entries, the pencil total of the column shows the balance of the account, and it is unnecessary to enter the balance in the Explanation column.

The trial balance. Double-entry bookkeeping derives its name from the fact that the recording of each transaction requires debit and credit entries of equal amount. Since the debit and credit entries for each transaction are equal, it is obvious that the total debit entries in all of the accounts should be equal to the total credit entries. It is equally true that the total of the debit balances in the accounts should be equal to the total of the credit balances.

It is customary to check the equality of the debit and credit balances in a ledger by listing and totaling them. Such a list is called a *trial balance*. Following is the July 31 trial balance of Community Televisions:

COMMUNITY TELEVISIONS
Trial Balance
July 31, 19—

Cash..	3,400.00	
Accounts receivable...........................	500.00	
Installation and repair parts....................	3,800.00	
Land...	1,500.00	
Accounts payable..............................		1,200.00
Capital stock.................................		8,000.00
	9,200.00	9,200.00

Uses of the trial balance.   A trial balance is useful in checking the *mathematical* correctness of the ledger.   But it should be understood that a trial balance proves nothing more than the equality of the debit and credit entries.   The trial balance will still "balance" even though a transaction was not journalized, or though a wrong account was debited or credited in the journal, or though a debit or credit was posted to a wrong account in the ledger, or though there was a failure to post both the debit and credit of a journal entry.

A trial balance is also useful to an accountant whenever periodic statements are to be prepared.   Although it is possible for the accountant to prepare such statements by working directly from the ledger, it is much easier to use the account balances shown by a trial balance.   For example, the above trial balance would furnish the information for the preparation of a balance sheet such as the one shown on page 8.

Compound journal entries.   Sometimes the recording of a transaction requires more than a single debit and credit.   For instance, assume that land which cost $10,000 was sold at cost, and that U. S. Government bonds worth $6,000 and cash in the amount of $4,000 were received in settlement; the entry to record the transaction is:

U. S. Government bonds	6,000.00	
Cash	4,000.00	
Land		10,000.00
Sale of land.		

Such entries, having more than one debit and/or more than one credit, are called *compound journal entries*.

Punctuating numbers.   When numbers are written on columnar-ruled paper, it is unnecessary to indicate decimal locations by using commas and periods; the rulings accomplish this purpose. Numbers written on paper which does not have money-column rulings should be punctuated, thus: 2,356,457.87.

Use of zeros and dashes.   In books of original entry, ledger accounts, and trial balances, the use of two zeros or a dash in the cents column is a matter of choice.   Thus, an amount may be written 1 257 00 or 1 257 —.   Many bookkeepers feel that a dash is more easily written than two zeros, and that the use of dashes facilitates the addition of the cents column.

In balance sheets and other statements it is preferable, for the sake of appearance, to use zeros.

Dollar signs.   Dollar signs need not be written in books of original entry, ledger accounts, and trial balances.   They should be used in balance sheets and other formal statements. In such statements, a dollar sign should be written:

Beside the first amount in each column. Look at the balance sheet on page 28 and observe the dollar signs in $2,795.00, $1,200.00, and $8,000.00.

Beside each amount appearing below an underline. Look at the same balance sheet and observe the dollar sign in $9,345.00.

CHAPTER 3

Changes in Owners' Equity.   Closing the Books

Causes of changes in owners' equity.   The principal causes of increases and decreases in the owners' equity in a corporation are stated below:

Discussed in Chapters 1 and 2:
Investments by stockholders.
Discussed in this chapter:
Revenues.
Expenses.
Dividends to stockholders.

As an introduction to the accounting for revenues, expenses, and dividends, we shall continue the Community Televisions illustration through the month of August.

Revenue.   Revenue is an inflow of assets in the form of cash, receivables, or other property from customers or clients, and is related to the rendering of services and the disposal of goods. Revenue also can be earned from investments; for instance, interest may be earned on bonds or on savings deposits.

Revenue results in an increase in the owners' equity; therefore, an inflow of assets that is offset by an increase in liabilities is not revenue.

It should also be noted that the owners' equity may be increased from sources other than revenue.   For instance, an inflow of capital funds from stockholders investing in the corporation increases the owners' equity, but it is not revenue.

Community Televisions has a contract with George Sloan, a television dealer, under which it expects to earn revenue in the following ways:

Selling television sets on a commission basis.
Installing television sets and antennas.
Making inspections of television sets within thirty days from the date of sale.
Repairing television sets.

Because of the time required for setting up its shop, the only revenue earned by Community Televisions during August consisted of commissions on the sale of television sets.

Expense. Expense is the cost of the use of things or services for the purpose of generating revenue. A businessman advertises with the expectation of attracting customers, he engages employees so that customers may be served, and he rents space so that he will have a place to conduct the operations of the business; in all such activities, he is utilizing things or services for the purpose of generating revenue, and hence is incurring expenses.

Although expenses decrease the owners' equity, they are incurred in the hope that the revenues they generate will increase the owners' equity more than it is decreased by the expenses.

Community Televisions incurred two kinds of expense during August:

Salaries expense—Two of the stockholders, White and Hudson, were employed by the corporation. A third man, an expert in television, was also engaged by the corporation. Their salaries, totaling $900 per month, were expenses.

Office expense—Pending the time when the company could move into its own quarters, Mr. White arranged with an acquaintance for telephone, stenographic, and other office services at a monthly cost of $125.

Income or loss. If the revenues of a business exceed the expenses, income is earned and the owners' equity will have increased. If the expenses exceed the revenues, a loss results and the owners' equity will have decreased.

Dividends. Dividends are distributions of assets to stockholders. Such distributions usually are made in cash. Dividends reduce the owners' equity, but they are *not* an expense: they are not paid for the purpose of generating revenue.

The company paid an $80 dividend at the end of August.

Debit and credit procedure. The previous chapter stated a general rule for recording increases and decreases in the owners' equity. This rule was:

In OWNERS' EQUITY accounts:
  Increases are recorded by credits.
  Decreases are recorded by debits.
In accordance with this general rule,
  Revenues, which increase the owners' equity, are credited to revenue accounts.
  Expenses, which decrease the owners' equity, are debited to expense accounts.
  Dividends, which decrease the owners' equity, are debited to a Dividends account.

To provide detailed information about the operating activities of a business, accountants customarily use a separate revenue account for each class of revenue and a separate expense account for each class of expense.

Illustrative entries. The transactions of Community Televisions during August are stated and journalized below.

Revenue. On August 16, Community Televisions collected $500 cash from George Sloan for commissions on television sales made during the first half of the month. The journal entry to record this transaction was:

Aug.	16	Cash...................................		500	00		
		Commissions earned......................				500	00
		Commissions for first half of August.					

On August 31, the company billed Sloan $750 for commissions earned during the last half of August; no cash was received on this date. The journal entry for the transaction was:

Aug.	31	Accounts receivable.........................		750	00		
		Commissions earned......................				750	00
		Commissions for second half of August.					

Expenses. The salaries and office expense previously mentioned were paid on August 31. The journal entries were:

Aug.	31	Salaries expense.............................		900	00		
		Cash..				900	00
		Salaries for August.					
	31	Office expense.............................		125	00		
		Cash..				125	00
		Use of office facilities during August.					

Dividend. The dividend payment was made on August 31, and was recorded as follows:

Aug.	31	Dividends..................................		80	00		
		Cash......................................				80	00
		Payment of dividend to stockholders.					

Complete journal. Following is Community Televisions' journal containing entries for all of its August transactions:

Journal (Page 2)

19—							
Aug.	16	Cash...............................		500	00		
		Commissions earned......................				500	00
		Commissions for first half of August.					
	31	Accounts receivable..		750	00		
		Commissions earned......................				750	00
		Commissions for second half of August.					

	Journal	(Page 2 Concluded)

31	Salaries expense.............................	900 00	
	Cash..		900 00
	Salaries for August.		
31	Office expense..............................	125 00	
	Cash..		125 00
	Use of office facilities during August.		
31	Dividends...................................	80 00	
	Cash..		80 00
	Payment of dividend to stockholders.		

Ledger. Following is the ledger of Community Televisions after the posting of the August entries. The August entries are shown in italics. Balances have been computed in all accounts containing more than one entry.

Cash   (1)

19—					19—				
July	20		1	8,000 00	July	22		1	3,000 00
	29		1	1,000 00		31		1	2,600 00
Aug.	*16*	*2,795.00*	*2*	*500 00*	*Aug.*	*31*		*2*	*900 00*
				9,500 00		*31*		*2*	*125 00*
						31		*2*	*80 00*
									6,705 00

Accounts Receivable   (2)

19—					19—				
July	27		1	1,500 00	July	29		1	1,000 00
Aug.	*31*	*1,250.00*	*2*	*750 00*					
				2,250 00					

Installation and Repair Parts   (10)

19—									
July	28		1	3,800 00					

Land   (15)

19—					19—				
July	22	1,500.00	1	3,000 00	July	27		1	1,500 00

Accounts Payable   (20)

19—					19—				
July	31		1	2,600 00	July	28	1,200.00	1	3,800 00

Capital Stock   (50)

					19—				
					July	20		1	8,000 00

Dividends   (52)

19—									
Aug.	*31*		*2*	*80 00*					

Commissions Earned   (61)

		19—			
		Aug.	16	2	500 00
			31	2	750 00
					1,250 00

Salaries Expense   (71)

19—				
Aug. 31	2	900 00		

Office Expense   (72)

19—				
Aug. 31	2	125 00		

Trial balance. The following trial balance was taken from the foregoing ledger.

COMMUNITY TELEVISIONS
Trial Balance
August 31, 19—

Cash..	2,795.00	
Accounts receivable.........................	1,250.00	
Installation and repair parts...................	3,800.00	
Land.......................................	1,500.00	
Accounts payable...........................		1,200.00
Capital stock...............................		8,000.00
Dividends..................................	80.00	
Commissions earned.........................		1,250.00
Salaries expense............................	900.00	
Office expense..............................	125.00	
	10,450.00	10,450.00

Income statement. Most businesses are engaged in a continuing "stream" of operations which are conducted with the object of earning income. The success of a business is largely judged by its earnings—not only by the amount of the income, but by its trend and by comparing it with the income of comparable businesses. In the income statement, the excess of revenues over expenses traditionally has been called "net income" rather than merely "income."

The income statement of Community Televisions for August is on page 27. It was prepared by using the balances of the revenue and expense accounts shown in the trial balance.

Observe that the heading of the statement shows: (1) the name of the business, (2) the name of the statement, and (3) the period covered. The heading of a balance sheet and the heading of an income statement differ in this important particular: the heading of a balance sheet shows the *date* on which the stated financial condition existed; the heading of the income statement shows the *period* covered by the statement.

COMMUNITY TELEVISIONS
Income Statement
For the Month of August, 19—

Revenue:		
Commissions earned..................................		$1,250.00
Expenses:		
Salaries expense..............................	$900.00	
Office expense................................	125.00	1,025.00
Net income...		$ 225.00

Not until a business has ceased to function as a going concern and has disposed of its assets and paid its liabilities is it possible to compute, *with absolute accuracy*, the amount of its entire net income or net loss. But it obviously would be unsatisfactory to make no attempt to measure the results of the operations of a business until its life span had been completed. To get an idea of the success of a business, it is customary to prepare periodic income statements. Such statements usually are prepared at least once a year; they may be prepared more frequently.

Some of the common uses of income statements are set forth below:

They may be included in a report to stockholders and used by the stockholders in forming an opinion regarding the progress of the business and the effectiveness of the management group.

They may be submitted to banks in support of a request for a loan, for the banks' use in judging the earnings prospects of the corporation.

They may be used by investors in reaching decisions whether to acquire, to continue to hold, or to dispose of securities issued by the corporation, for example, the corporation's capital stock.

They may be used by management to judge the effectiveness of their past policies and decisions, to detect unfavorable trends and developments, and to provide data upon which to base decisions regarding a wide variety of matters, such as whether to expand production, whether to change advertising policy, whether to introduce a new product, whether to alter selling prices, and whether to merge with another corporation.

For many of the above uses, the balance sheet also will be examined. The balance sheet and the income statement may be thought of as companion statements, each supplementing the other.

Retained earnings. The *retained earnings* of a corporation is the portion of the owners' equity derived from income. It is the excess of the company's aggregate income since organization over all dividends distributed to stockholders.

For many years, the words "earned surplus" were used to describe the portion of the owners' equity derived from earnings. Accountants and businessmen continue to use "earned surplus" in their vocabulary and probably will continue to do so for many years. The terms "retained earnings" and "earned surplus" are synonymous. However, "retained earnings" is favored over "earned surplus" by many accountants who believe that the words "retained earnings" are more descriptive and less subject to misunderstanding. The trend of usage appears to support such preference, and the American Institute of Certified Public Accountants recommends it.

It is important to make a distinction between capital stock and retained earnings, and to maintain this distinction in the statements and accounts, because the amount of the retained earnings usually has a bearing on the amount of dividends which a corporation can legally distribute. Furthermore, statement users consider it helpful to know how much of the owners' equity resulted from investments by stockholders and how much is attributable to the retention of income.

Illustrative statement. The statement of retained earnings covers the same time period as the companion income statement, and the period is shown in the heading of the statement.

COMMUNITY TELEVISIONS
Statement of Retained Earnings
For the Month of August, 19—

Net income for the month—per income statement..............	$225.00
Deduct dividends..	80.00
Retained earnings, August 31, 19—.........................	$145.00

If a company had any retained earnings at the beginning of the period for which the statement is being prepared, this beginning-of-period balance should be shown in the statement. See the illustration on page 48.

Balance sheet. Using information presented in the trial balance and the statement of retained earnings, the following balance sheet may be prepared.

COMMUNITY TELEVISIONS
Balance Sheet
August 31, 19—

Assets		Liabilities and Stockholders' Equity		
Cash....................	$2,795.00	Liabilities:		
Accounts receivable.......	1,250.00	Accounts payable..........		$1,200.00
Installation and repair parts	3,800.00	Stockholders' equity:		
Land....................	1,500.00	Capital stock.....	$8,000.00	
		Retained earnings.	145.00	8,145.00
	$9,345.00			$9,345.00

Closing the books. An income statement and a statement of retained earnings are prepared at annual intervals. To provide the information required for the preparation of statements for a year, the revenue, expense, and dividend accounts must contain the required data for that year and for that year only.

To achieve this, it is necessary that the revenue, expense, and dividend accounts have zero balances at the beginning of each year. Such zero balances are produced by a procedure called "closing the books."

Closing the books not only leaves the revenue, expense, and dividend accounts with zero balances, but also produces in the Retained Earnings account a balance representing the amount of retained earnings at the end of the year.

Although it is customary to close the books only at the end of the accounting year, we shall close the books of Community Televisions at the end of August, to illustrate the procedure.

Closing revenue accounts. Revenue accounts are closed by making and posting journal entries which transfer their credit balances to the credit side of a new account called Revenue and Expense Summary.* Community Televisions has only one revenue account; it is closed by the following journal entry:

Journal (Page 3)

19—				
Aug.	31	Commissions earned.......................... 61	1,250 00	
		Revenue and expense summary............ 55		1,250 00
		To close the revenue account.		

The account numbers in the folio column of the journal show that the postings have been made. Following are the two accounts affected by this journal entry. In the following ledger accounts, the debit and credit of each successive journal entry are shown in italics, as an aid in identifying them.

Commissions Earned (61)

19—					19—				
Aug.	31	3	1,250 00	Aug.	16		2	500 00
					31		2	750 00
			1,250 00					1,250 00

When an account is ruled, any small pencil totals or balances placed in the accounts when computing balances for trial balance purposes may be erased.

---

* This account is sometimes called Profit and Loss.

Revenue and Expense Summary (55)

			19—				3	1,250	00
			Aug.	31					

The Commissions Earned account has now been closed; that is, it has no balance.   This fact is indicated by the totals and rulings. The closing entry transferred the credit balance of the Commissions Earned account to the credit of Revenue and Expense Summary.

Closing expense accounts.   Expense accounts are closed by transferring their debit balances to the debit side of the Revenue and Expense Summary account.   Community Televisions has two expense accounts; they are closed by making and posting the following journal entries:

Journal (Page 3 Continued)

31	Revenue and expense summary................	55	900	00		
	Salaries expense..........................	71			900	00
	To close the Salaries Expense account.					
31	Revenue and expense summary................	55	125	00		
	Office expense............................	72			125	00
	To close the Office Expense account.					

The accounts affected by these closing entries are shown below.

Salaries Expense (71)

19—			2	900	00	19—			3	900	00
Aug.	31					Aug.	31				

Office Expense (72)

19—			2	125	00	19—			3	125	00
Aug.	31					Aug.	31				

Revenue and Expense Summary (55)

19—			3	900	00	19—			3	1,250	00
Aug.	31					Aug.	31				
	31		3	125	00						

The two expense accounts are closed.   Revenue and Expense Summary has a credit balance of $225, which is the amount of the net income; the balance of this account should, and does, agree with the net income shown by the income statement on page 27.

Ruling closed accounts.   You should observe the method of ruling closed accounts.   In the Commissions Earned account, note the single rulings on the same line in the debit and credit money columns, the totals, and the double rulings in three places on the line below the totals.   Since the expense accounts contain only one entry on each side, totals are unnecessary, and the accounts are ruled with double lines only.

Single rulings extend across the money columns only, whereas the double rulings extend across the date, reference, and money columns.

Graphic summary. The effect of these closing entries is shown graphically below. The amounts of the closing entries are shown in italics. The numbers in parentheses indicate the sequence in which the closing entries are made.

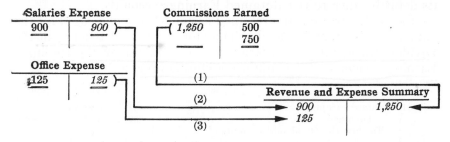

Closing the Revenue and Expense Summary account. The retained earnings were increased by the $225 of net income earned during August. Therefore, the Revenue and Expense Summary account is closed by transferring its $225 credit balance to the Retained Earnings account.

Journal				(Page 3 Continued)	
31	Revenue and expense summary..................	55	225	00	
	Retained earnings........................	51			225	00
	To close the Revenue and Expense Summary account and credit Retained Earnings with the net income for August.				

The two accounts affected are shown below:

			Revenue and Expense Summary						(55)	
19—					19—					
Aug.	31	3	900	00	Aug.	31		3	1,250	00
	31	3	125	00						
	31	*3*	*225*	*00*						
			1,250	00					1,250	00

			Retained Earnings						(51)	
					19—					
					Aug.	31		3	*225*	*00*

The nature and purpose of the Revenue and Expense Summary account should now be clearly apparent. The account is used only when the books are closed. It has no balance before the closing procedure is begun, and it has no balance after the closing procedure is completed. It is used to assemble, in the ledger, the data required for the computation of the net income, and it is closed when the net income is transferred from Revenue and Expense Summary to Retained Earnings.

Closing the Dividends account. Since dividends are not an expense, the Dividends account should not be closed to Revenue and Expense Summary. But dividends do reduce the retained earnings; therefore, the Dividends account is closed by transferring its debit balance to the Retained Earnings account.

In the illustration, the retained earnings were decreased by the payment of an $80 dividend. Therefore, the debit balance in the Dividends account is transferred to the debit side of the Retained Earnings account by the following closing entry:

<table>
<tr><td colspan="5" align="center">Journal</td><td colspan="2" align="right">(Page 3 Continued)</td></tr>
<tr><td>31</td><td>Retained earnings............................</td><td>51</td><td>80</td><td>00</td><td></td><td></td></tr>
<tr><td></td><td>   Dividends................................</td><td>52</td><td></td><td></td><td>80</td><td>00</td></tr>
<tr><td></td><td>   To close the Dividends account.</td><td></td><td></td><td></td><td></td><td></td></tr>
</table>

The two ledger accounts affected by this closing entry appear below:

<table>
<tr><td colspan="6" align="center">Dividends</td><td align="right">(52)</td></tr>
<tr><td>19—</td><td></td><td></td><td></td><td>19—</td><td></td><td></td></tr>
<tr><td>Aug.</td><td>31</td><td>2</td><td>80 00</td><td>Aug. 31</td><td>3</td><td>80 00</td></tr>
</table>

<table>
<tr><td colspan="6" align="center">Retained Earnings</td><td align="right">(51)</td></tr>
<tr><td>19—</td><td></td><td></td><td></td><td>19—</td><td></td><td></td></tr>
<tr><td>Aug.</td><td>31</td><td>3</td><td>80 00</td><td>Aug. 31</td><td>3</td><td>225 00</td></tr>
</table>

The Retained Earnings account now has a credit balance of $145, the amount of the retained earnings on August 31, 19—, as shown by the statement of retained earnings on page 28 and in the balance sheet on the same page.

Summary of closing entries. The procedure of closing the books (that is, closing the revenue, expense, and dividend accounts) is summarized as follows:

Close the revenue and expense accounts to the Revenue and Expense Summary account. The balance of the Revenue and Expense Summary account then shows the net income *for the period.*

Close the Revenue and Expense Summary account and the Dividends account to Retained Earnings. The balance of the Retained Earnings account then shows the accumulated, undistributed earnings *at the end of the period.*

The complete closing procedure is shown graphically on page 33.

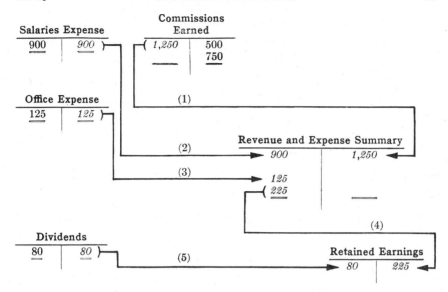

Journal with closing entries. The journal page containing all of the closing entries, with posting references included, follows:

		Journal				(Page 3)	
19—							
Aug.	31	Commissions earned...........................	61	1,250	00		
		Revenue and expense summary.............	55			1,250	00
		To close the revenue account.					
	31	Revenue and expense summary.................	55	900	00		
		Salaries expense..........................	71			900	00
		To close the Salaries Expense account.					
	31	Revenue and expense summary.................	55	125	00		
		Office expense............................	72			125	00
		To close the Office Expense account.					
	31	Revenue and expense summary.................	55	225	00		
		Retained earnings........................	51			225	00
		To close the Revenue and Expense Summary account and credit Retained Earnings with the net income for August.					
	31	Retained earnings............................	51	80	00		
		Dividends................................	52			80	00
		To close the Dividends account.					

Ledger. To indicate as clearly as possible the effect of closing the books, the accounts of Community Televisions are shown on the following pages. They are arranged in two principal groups:

Accounts which remain open after the books are closed:
    Accounts showing assets, liabilities, and owners' equity at the end of the period.

Accounts which have no balances after the books are closed: Revenue, expense, and dividend accounts, showing the changes in retained earnings during the period.

Accounts which remain open after the books are closed.

Asset Accounts

Cash (1)

19—					19—			
July	20		1	8,000 00	July	22	1	3,000 00
	29		1	1,000 00		31	1	2,600 00
Aug.	16	2,795.00	2	500 00	Aug.	31	2	900 00
				9,500 00		31	2	125 00
						31	2	80 00
								6,705 00

Accounts Receivable (2)

19—					19—			
July	27		1	1,500 00	July	29	1	1,000 00
Aug.	31	1,250.00	2	750 00				
				2,250 00				

Installation and Repair Parts (10)

19—				
July	28		1	3,800 00

Land (15)

19—					19—			
July	22	1,500.00	1	3,000 00	July	27	1	1,500 00

Liability Account

Accounts Payable (20)

19—					19—			
July	31		1	2,600 00	July	28	1,200.00	1	3,800 00

Owners' Equity Accounts

Capital Stock (50)

				19—			
				July	20	1	8,000 00

Retained Earnings (51)

19—				19—			
Aug.	31	3	80 00	Aug.	31	3	225 00

Accounts which have no balances after the books are closed.

Dividends (52)

19—				19—			
Aug.	31	2	80 00	Aug.	31	3	80 00

Revenue and Expense Summary (55)

19—				19—			
Aug.	31	3	900 00	Aug.	31	3	1,250 00
	31	3	125 00				
	31	3	225 00				
			1,250 00				1,250 00

Commissions Earned　　　　　(61)

19— Aug. 31		3	1,250 00	19— Aug. 16 31		2 2	500 00 750 00
			1,250 00				1,250 00

Salaries Expense　　　　　(71)

19— Aug. 31		2	900 00	19— Aug. 31		3	900 00

Office Expense　　　　　(72)

19— Aug. 31		2	125 00	19— Aug. 31		3	125 00

Trial balance after closing. After the books are closed, it is advisable to take an *after-closing* trial balance (sometimes called a *post-closing* trial balance), to be sure that the equality of debits and credits in the ledger has not been destroyed by errors made in closing the books. The trial balance of Community Televisions after closing on August 31 is shown below:

COMMUNITY TELEVISIONS
After-Closing Trial Balance
August 31, 19—

Cash...	2,795.00	
Accounts receivable.............................	1,250.00	
Installation and repair parts.....................	3,800.00	
Land..	1,500.00	
Accounts payable................................		1,200.00
Capital stock....................................		8,000.00
Retained earnings................................		145.00
	9,345.00	9,345.00

Before the books are closed:

The balance in the Retained Earnings account shows the retained earnings, if any, at the beginning of the period.
The balances in the revenue, expense, and dividend accounts show the changes in retained earnings during the period.

After the books are closed:

The balance in the Retained Earnings account shows the retained earnings at the end of the period.
The revenue, expense, and dividend accounts have no balances. They are therefore ready for recording the changes in retained earnings during a subsequent period.

Sequence of accounting procedures. The various accounting procedures thus far explained are performed in the sequence shown on the following page.

Journalize.

Post.

Take a trial balance.

Prepare an income statement for the period.

Prepare a statement of retained earnings for the period.

Prepare a balance sheet showing the financial position at the end of the period.

Make and post the journal entries necessary to close the books.

Take an after-closing trial balance.

Ruling the open accounts. When the closed accounts are being ruled, the bookkeeper may "rule up" the open accounts and "bring down their balances." This practice is illustrated below:

Cash (1)

19—						19—				
July	20		1	8,000	00	July	22		1	3,000	00
	29		1	1,000	00		31		1	2,600	00
		3,400.00		9,000	00					5,600	00
							31	To balance		3,400	00
				9,000	00					9,000	00
19—						19—					
Aug.	1	Balance		3,400	00	Aug.	31		2	900	00
	16	2,795.00	2	500	00		31		2	125	00
				3,900	00		31		2	80	00
										1,105	00
							31	To balance		2,795	00
				3,900	00					3,900	00
19—											
Sept.	1	Balance		2,795	00						

Such rulings serve to separate the transaction data recorded in the balance sheet accounts by accounting period. The practice is not required.

Locating errors. If a trial balance does not balance, the amount of the difference should be determined; the following steps may be taken to locate the error:

(1) Refoot the trial balance.

(2) See that the balances have been carried correctly from the ledger to the trial balance. Watch for:

    (a) Differences between the balances in the accounts and the balances shown in the trial balance.

    (b) Debit balances in the accounts entered on the credit side of the trial balance, and vice versa.

    (c) Ledger balances omitted from the trial balance.

(3) Recompute the ledger balances; this will involve the following steps:

    (a) Refooting the debit side and the credit side of each account.

    (b) Recomputing the difference between the two sides of each account.

(4) Check the postings from the journal to the ledger. Beginning with the first journal entry, see whether each debit and credit has been correctly posted. Watch for:

    (a) Errors in amounts.

    (b) Postings to wrong accounts.

    (c) Posting a journal debit to the credit side of the ledger, or a journal credit to the debit side of the ledger.

As each entry in the journal is traced to the ledger, place a check mark ($\sqrt{}$) beside the amount in the journal and also beside the amount in the ledger. A check mark usually is placed at the right of an amount. After the checking of the postings has been completed, look for:

    (a) Unchecked entries in the journal—see whether these items have been posted.

    (b) Unchecked entries in the ledger—see whether these items belong in the ledger; it is possible that a journal entry has been posted twice, that one ledger entry has been checked, and that the unchecked ledger entry is a duplicate posting.

(5) See that the debit and credit amounts in each journal entry are equal.

In looking for errors, be constantly on the watch for:

Transpositions—such as $79.85 posted as $78.95.
Slides—such as $.75 posted as $75.00.

Erasures should not be made in accounting records. When an error is discovered, the incorrect amount or other item in the entry should be struck out by drawing a line through it, and the correct entry should be inserted above the incorrect one.

CHAPTER 4

Adjustments for Accrued Revenue and Expense. Working Papers

Transactions and adjustments. The statements prepared at the end of the accounting period should reflect, as correctly as possible, the revenues earned and the expenses incurred during the period and the assets, liabilities, and owners' equity at the end of the period. To attain this objective it often is necessary, in addition to recording the transactions of the business, to make "adjusting entries" at the end of the period. This chapter deals with adjusting entries for:

Accrued expenses: Expenses that have been incurred but have not been recorded by transaction entries.

Accrued revenues: Revenues that have been earned but have not been recorded by transaction entries.

For purposes of explanation, we shall continue the Community Televisions illustration through September.

September transactions. Following is a list of the company's transactions during the month. The journal entries that would be made to record the September transactions are indicated below the data for each transaction.

September 1—The company rented a building and paid the September rent of $250.

Building rent expense	250.00	
Cash		250.00
Payment of rent for September.		

September 3—The company collected from George Sloan the $750 for which he was billed on August 31 for commissions on sales during the last half of August.

Cash	750.00	
Accounts receivable		750.00
Collection of commission billing for last half of August.		

September 10—The company, at the request of O. E. Maltby, converted the account payable to a note payable by giving him the note appearing on the following page.

Chicago, Illinois, __September 10,__ 19--

__Thirty days__ _____after date the undersigned promises to pay

to the order of_____O. E. Maltby_____ $ 1,200.00

One thousand two hundred and no/100 _____ Dollars

Value received with interest at _6_ per cent after date.

Due _October 10, 19--_ No. _1_　　　　COMMUNITY TELEVISIONS

By _J. C. White, President_

The parties to the above note are:

The maker, Community Televisions.
The payee, O. E. Maltby.

Every promissory note is a liability from the standpoint of the maker, because he has a legal obligation to pay money. He credits Notes Payable when he issues the note, and debits Notes Payable when he pays it.

Every promissory note is an asset from the standpoint of the payee, because he has a legal right to receive money. He debits Notes Receivable when he receives a note, and credits Notes Receivable when he collects it.

Community Televisions' entry for the issuance of the note is:

Accounts payable.............................. 1,200.00
　　Notes payable.............................　　　　1,200.00
　　Conversion of an account payable to a note payable
　　in favor of O. E. Maltby.

September 12—The company abandoned the idea of building a plant and sold the land. It received $500 in cash and took a mortgage for $1,000.

Cash..　 500.00
Mortgage receivable................... ....　1,000.00
　　Land............................ ....　　　　1,500.00
　　Sale of land.

September 16—Cash in the amount of $625 was received from Sloan for commissions on sales during the first half of September.

Cash... 625.00
　　Commissions earned.......................　　　 625.00
　　Collection of commissions for first half of September.

September 30—Sloan was billed $1,000 for commissions on sales during the last half of September.

Accounts receivable............................ 1,000.00
    Commissions earned..........................   1,000.00
    Commission billing for last half of September.

September 30—Salaries for the month were paid, in the amount of $900.

Salaries expense................................ 900.00
    Cash......................................   900.00
    Payment of salaries for the month.

September 30—A dividend of $80 was paid.

Dividends...................................... 80.00
    Cash......................................   80.00
    Payment of dividend.

Trial balance after posting transaction entries. The following trial balance shows the balances of the accounts after the completion of the posting of the entries for the September transactions.

COMMUNITY TELEVISIONS
Trial Balance
September 30, 19—

Cash...	3,440.00	
Accounts receivable..........................	1,500.00	
Installation and repair parts...................	3,800.00	
Mortgage receivable..........................	1,000.00	
Notes payable................................		1,200.00
Capital stock.................................		8,000.00
Retained earnings.............................		145.00
Dividends.....................................	80.00	
Commissions earned...........................		1,625.00
Salaries expense..............................	900.00	
Building rent expense.........................	250.00	
	10,970.00	10,970.00

Adjustments for accruals. The words *accrued* and *accrual* are applied to revenues that have been earned or expenses that have been incurred but for which no transaction entries have been recorded.

Accrued revenue. When the company sold its land on September 12, it received $500 in cash and a $1,000 mortgage. The mortgage bore 6% interest, payable semiannually. Although no interest was *collected* during September, interest for eighteen days, or $3 ($1,000 × .06 × $18/360$), was *earned* during the month. Therefore, the following adjusting entry was required at the end of September:

Accrued interest receivable...................... 3.00
    Interest earned............................   3.00
    Eighteen days' interest on mortgage.

The debit balance in the Accrued Interest Receivable account will be shown in the balance sheet as an asset.   The credit balance in the Interest Earned account will be shown in the income statement.

The following general rule may be stated for making adjusting entries for accrued revenues: *If a company has earned revenue for which no transaction entry has been made, debit an asset account and credit a revenue account.*

Accrued expense.   The company rented a truck at a rate of ten cents a mile.   The rent for each month was payable on the second day of the following month.   The company drove the truck 2,150 miles during September, and thus incurred a rent expense of $215 during the month; but, since the rent was not paid during the month, the expense was not recorded by a transaction entry. Therefore, the following adjusting entry was required:

<pre>
Truck rent expense.............................   215.00
    Accrued truck rent payable...................   215.00
    Expense and liability for use of truck during Sep-
    tember.
</pre>

The debit balance in the Truck Rent Expense account will appear as an expense item in the income statement; the credit balance in the Accrued Truck Rent Payable account will appear as a liability in the balance sheet.

Although the company *paid* no interest during September, twenty days' interest expense, or $4 ($1,200 $\times$ .06 $\times$ $^{20}/_{360}$), was incurred by the end of the month on the note issued to O. E. Maltby.   When the note matures on October 10 and is paid, Community Televisions will pay the face of the note plus interest for the thirty-day period.   However, it would be incorrect to regard the interest for the entire thirty-day period as an expense of October, the month during which the interest payment was made. Rather, the interest should be divided between September and October on a time-elapsed basis.   Therefore, the following adjusting entry was required at the end of September:

<pre>
Interest expense.................................   4.00
    Accrued interest payable.....................   4.00
    Twenty days' interest on the note payable.
</pre>

The debit balance in the Interest Expense account will appear as an expense item in the income statement; the credit balance in the Accrued Interest Payable account will appear as a liability in the balance sheet.

The following general rule may be stated for making adjusting entries for accrued expenses: *If a company has incurred an expense for which no transaction entry has been made, debit an expense account and credit a liability account.*

Working papers. Working papers are a columnar device employed by accountants as a convenient and orderly way of organizing the accounting data to be used in the preparation of adjusting entries, periodic statements, and closing entries.

If the ledger contains only a few accounts and there are few adjusting entries, working papers are not necessary; if the ledger contains numerous accounts or if there are numerous adjustments, working papers are very useful.

Illustrative working papers. The account balances of Community Televisions at the end of September and the related adjustment data presented in the preceding portion of this chapter will be used to illustrate the preparation of working papers. There are so few accounts and adjustments that an experienced accountant probably would not consider it worth while to prepare working papers, but in a textbook it is desirable to begin with a relatively simple illustration.

The steps in the preparation of working papers are stated and illustrated on the following pages.

First step.   Headings were written; the account balances before adjustments were entered in the Trial Balance columns; and these columns were totaled to determine their equality.

COMMUNITY TELEVISIONS
Working Papers
For the Month of September, 19—

	Trial Balance		Adjustments	Adjusted Trial Balance	Income Statement	Retained Earnings Statement	Balance Sheet
Cash.....................	3,440						
Accounts receivable.......	1,500						
Installation and repair parts....	3,800						
Mortgage receivable.......	1,000						
Notes payable...........		1,200					
Capital stock............		8,000					
Retained earnings........		145					
Dividends...............	80						
Commissions earned......		1,625					
Salaries expense.........	900						
Building rent expense.....	250						
	10,970	10,970					

Second step. The required adjustments were entered in the Adjustments columns. These adjustments are the same as those already mentioned in this chapter. Observe that the nature of each adjustment is stated at the bottom of the working papers, with a key letter referring to the debit and credit entries in the Adjustments columns. (These letters may be placed at either the left or the right of the dollar amounts.) These letters not only key the debit and credit entries in the Adjustments columns to the explanatory data at the bottom of the working papers but also make it easier to match an entry in the Adjustments debit column with its related credit—a matter of considerable importance if two or more adjustments happen to be of the same amount. Read the explanation of each adjustment at the bottom of the working papers and observe the related debit and credit entries in the Adjustments columns. Also observe that the names of accounts not appearing in the trial balance were entered in the working papers below the trial balance. The Adjustments columns were totaled as a check against errors. The account balances after adjustments were entered in the Adjusted Trial Balance columns, and these columns were totaled as a test of accuracy.

COMMUNITY TELEVISIONS
Working Papers
For the Month of September, 19—

	Trial Balance		Adjustments		Adjusted Trial Balance		Income Statement	Retained Earnings Statement	Balance Sheet
Cash...........................	3,440				3,440				
Accounts receivable...........	1,500				1,500				
Installation and repair parts..	3,800				3,800				
Mortgage receivable...........	1,000				1,000				
Notes payable.................		1,200				1,200			
Capital stock.................		8,000				8,000			
Retained earnings.............		145				145			
Dividends.....................	80				80				
Commissions earned............		1,625				1,625			
Salaries expense..............	900				900				
Building rent expense.........	250				250				
	10,970	10,970							
Accrued interest receivable...			3a		3				
Interest earned...............				3a		3			
Truck rent expense............			215b		215				
Accrued truck rent payable....				215b		215			
Interest expense..............			4c		4				
Accrued interest payable......				4c		4			
			222	222	11,192	11,192			

Adjustments
a—Accrued interest receivable.
b—Accrued truck rent.
c—Accrued interest payable

Third step. Each account balance appearing in the Adjusted Trial Balance columns was entered in a column at the right corresponding to the statement in which it should appear. Debit balances were entered in debit columns; credit balances were entered in credit columns.

COMMUNITY TELEVISIONS
Working Papers
For the Month of September, 19—

	Trial Balance Dr	Trial Balance Cr	Adjustments Dr	Adjustments Cr	Adjusted Trial Balance Dr	Adjusted Trial Balance Cr	Income Statement Dr	Income Statement Cr	Retained Earnings Statement Dr	Retained Earnings Statement Cr	Balance Sheet Dr	Balance Sheet Cr
Cash	3,440				3,440						3,440	
Accounts receivable	1,500				1,500						1,500	
Installation and repair parts	3,800				3,800						3,800	
Mortgage receivable	1,000				1,000						1,000	
Notes payable		1,200				1,200						1,200
Capital stock		8,000				8,000						8,000
Retained earnings		145				145				145		
Dividends	80				80				80			
Commissions earned		1,625				1,625		1,625				
Salaries expense	900				900		900					
Building rent expense	250				250		250					
	10,970	10,970										
Accrued interest receivable			3a		3						3	
Interest earned				3a		3		3				
Truck rent expense			215b		215		215					
Accrued truck rent payable				215b		215						215
Interest expense			4c		4		4					
Accrued interest payable				4c		4						4
			222	222	11,192	11,192						

Adjustments
a—Accrued interest receivable.
b—Accrued truck rent.
c—Accrued interest payable.

Fourth step. The net income for the month, amounting to $259, was determined by computing the balance of the Income Statement columns. This computation was facilitated by totaling the items in these two columns. The $259 was entered in the Income Statement debit column as a balancing figure; and, since the net income increases the retained earnings, it was also entered in the Retained Earnings Statement credit column. The Income Statement columns were then totaled.

COMMUNITY TELEVISIONS
Working Papers
For the Month of September, 19—

	Trial Balance		Adjustments		Adjusted Trial Balance		Income Statement		Retained Earnings Statement		Balance Sheet	
Cash	3,440				3,440						3,440	
Accounts receivable	1,500				1,500						1,500	
Installation and repair parts	3,800				3,800						3,800	
Mortgage receivable	1,000				1,000						1,000	
Notes payable		1,200				1,200						1,200
Capital stock		8,000				8,000						8,000
Retained earnings		145				145				145		
Dividends	80				80				80			
Commissions earned		1,625				1,625		1,625				
Salaries expense	900				900		900					
Building rent expense	250				250		250					
	10,970	10,970										
Accrued interest receivable			3a 3		3						3	
Interest earned				3a 3		3		3				
Truck rent expense			215b 215		215		215					
Accrued truck rent payable				215b 215		215						215
Interest expense			4c 4		4		4					
Accrued interest payable				4c 4		4						4
			222	222	11,192	11,192	1,369	1,628				
Net income							259			259		
							1,628	1,628				

Adjustments
a—Accrued interest receivable.
b—Accrued truck rent.
c—Accrued interest payable.

Fifth and final step. The retained earnings balance at the end of the month, in the amount of $324, was determined by computing the balance of the two Retained Earnings Statement columns. The $324 was entered as a balancing figure in the Retained Earnings Statement debit column; and, since the retained earnings also appear in the balance sheet, the $324 was also entered in the Balance Sheet credit column.

The Retained Earnings Statement columns were totaled.

The two Balance Sheet columns were totaled and found to be in agreement. If the Balance Sheet columns did not have the same totals, an error some place in the working papers would be indicated.

COMMUNITY TELEVISIONS
Working Papers
For the Month of September, 19—

	Trial Balance		Adjustments		Adjusted Trial Balance		Income Statement		Retained Earnings Statement		Balance Sheet	
Cash	3,440				3,440						3,440	
Accounts receivable	1,500				1,500						1,500	
Installation and repair parts	3,800				3,800						3,800	
Mortgage receivable	1,000				1,000						1,000	
Notes payable		1,200				1,200						1,200
Capital stock		8,000				8,000						8,000
Retained earnings		145				145				145		
Dividends	80				80				80			
Commissions earned		1,625				1,625		1,625				
Salaries expense	900				900		900					
Building rent expense	250				250		250					
	10,970	10,970										
Accrued interest receivable			3a		3						3	
Interest earned				3a		3		3				
Truck rent expense			215b		215		215					
Accrued truck rent payable				215b		215						215
Interest expense			4c		4		4					
Accrued interest payable				4c		4						4
			222	222	11,192	11,192						
							1,369	1,628	80	404		
Net income							259			259		
							1,628	1,628				
Retained earnings, September 30, 19—									324			324
									404	404	9,743	9,743

Adjustments

a—Accrued interest receivable.
b—Accrued truck rent.
c—Accrued interest payable.

Statements prepared from working papers. The working papers furnish in a convenient form the information required for the periodic statements.

Income statement. The following statement shows the amounts which appear in the Income Statement columns of the working papers.

COMMUNITY TELEVISIONS
Income Statement
For the Month of September, 19—

Revenues:
Commissions earned................................. $1,625.00
Interest earned....................................... 3.00
  Total... $1,628.00
Deduct expenses:
Salaries expense............................. $900.00
Building rent expense......................... 250.00
Truck rent expense........................... 215.00
Interest expense............................. 4.00
  Total... 1,369.00
Net income... $ 259.00

Statement of retained earnings. The following statement shows the amounts which appear in the Retained Earnings Statement columns of the working papers.

COMMUNITY TELEVISIONS
Statement of Retained Earnings
For the Month of September, 19—

Retained earnings, August 31, 19—....................... $ 145.00
Add net income for the month—Per income statement....... 259.00
  Total... $ 404.00
Deduct dividends....................................... 80.00
Retained earnings, September 30, 19—................... $ 324.00

Balance sheet. The following statement was prepared from data which appear in the Balance Sheet columns of the working papers.

A balance sheet customarily is prepared showing the assets at the left and the liabilities and stockholders' equity at the right. If space limitations make it desirable, the liabilities and stockholders' equity may be presented below the assets, as in the following illustration.

COMMUNITY TELEVISIONS
Balance Sheet
September 30, 19—
Assets

Cash... $3,440.00
Accounts receivable....................................... 1,500.00
Accrued interest receivable............................... 3.00
Installation and repair parts............................. 3,800.00
Mortgage receivable....................................... 1,000.00
$9,743.00

Liabilities and Stockholders' Equity

Liabilities:
Notes payable.............................. $1,200.00
Accrued truck rent payable...................   215.00
Accrued interest payable 4.00
    Total... $1,419.00

Stockholders' equity:
Capital stock............................. $8,000.00
Retained earnings—Per statement of retained
    earnings...............................   324.00
    Total...   8,324.00
                                                    $9,743.00

Adjusting entries. The adjusting entries are shown below.

Accrued interest receivable......................   3.00
    Interest earned............................   3.00
Eighteen days' interest on mortgage.

Truck rent expense.............................   215.00
    Accrued truck rent payable.................   215.00
Expense and liability for use of truck during September.

Interest expense...............................   4.00
    Accrued interest payable....................   4.00
Twenty days' interest on the note payable.

Closing entries.
The closing entries can be prepared from the data in the Income Statement columns and the Retained Earnings Statement columns of the working papers.

	Journal			(Page 6)	
19—					
Sept. 30	Commissions earned...........................		1,625|00		
	Interest earned...............................		3|00		
	Revenue and expense summary............			1,628	00
	To close the revenue accounts.				
30	Revenue and expense summary.................		1,369|00		
	Salaries expense...........................			900	00
	Building rent expense......................			250	00
	Truck rent expense........................			215	00
	Interest expense...........................			4	00
	To close the expense accounts.				
30	Revenue and expense summary...............		259|00		
	Retained earnings.........................			259	00
	To close the Revenue and Expense Summary account.				
30	Retained earnings...........................		80|00		
	Dividends.................................			80	00
	To close the Dividends account.				

In Chapter 3, a separate journal entry was made for the closing of each revenue and expense account. This was done for purposes of clear explanation. The closing procedure can be simplified by making compound journal entries, as illustrated above.

The Revenue and Expense Summary and Retained Earnings accounts after the posting of the closing entries will appear as shown below.

Revenue and Expense Summary (55)

19—						19—				
Sept.	30		6	1,369	00	Sept.	30		6	1,628 00
	30		6	259	00					
				1,628	00					1,628 00

Retained Earnings (51)

19—						19—				
Aug.	31		3	80	00	Aug.	31		3	225 00
Sept.	30		6	80	00	Sept.	30		6	259 00

Trial balance after closing. The following trial balance was taken from the ledger after the completion of the posting of the adjusting and closing entries.

COMMUNITY TELEVISIONS
After-Closing Trial Balance
September 30, 19—

Cash...	3,440.00	
Accounts receivable...........................	1,500.00	
Accrued interest receivable.....................	3.00	
Installation and repair parts.....................	3,800.00	
Mortgage receivable...........................	1,000.00	
Notes payable..................................		1,200.00
Accrued truck rent payable......................		215.00
Accrued interest payable........................		4.00
Capital stock..................................		8,000.00
Retained earnings..............................		324.00
	9,743.00	9,743.00

The accounting cycle. The accounting procedures are performed in the following order:

Make and post the entries for transactions.
Take a trial balance (usually entered directly on the working papers, if they are prepared).
Complete working papers.
Prepare the income statement, the statement of retained earnings, and the balance sheet.
Make and post adjusting and closing entries.
Take an after-closing trial balance.

These procedures, in total, constitute an *accounting cycle*. In actual business, the complete cycle usually is performed only once a year, because the books ordinarily are not closed more frequently. In the illustrations and problems in this text it is often assumed, for convenience and simplicity, that the cycle is completed monthly.

CHAPTER 5

Adjustments for Revenue and Cost Apportionments. Working Papers (Continued)

Purpose of the chapter. The preceding chapter dealt with adjustments for accruals of revenues that had been earned but had not been recorded by transaction entries, and adjustments for accruals of expenses that had been incurred but had not been recorded by transaction entries.

This chapter deals with adjustments that are required when transaction entries related to revenues are made before the revenues are earned, and when transaction entries affecting expenses are made before the expenses are incurred.

Revenue apportionments. A business may acquire assets from a revenue-producing transaction before the revenue is earned. This may happen when cash is received for services to be rendered in the future, or when a business, pursuant to an agreement, bills a customer in advance. The accounting procedures to be used in such cases are stated below:

If the service will be completely performed, and the total revenue thereby earned, during the accounting period in which the transaction occurs, a revenue account should be credited at the time the transaction is recorded.

If the service will not be completely performed during the accounting period in which the transaction occurs:

The entire amount of the billing or collection should be credited to an account with a title clearly indicating that its content is revenue received in advance.

At the end of the period, the portion of the revenue earned during the period by the performance of service should be transferred, by an adjusting entry, from the revenue-received-in-advance account to a revenue account.

Cost apportionments. An expenditure is a payment, or the incurring of an obligation to make a future payment, for a benefit received or to be received. The amount of the expenditure is the cost of the benefit.

If an expenditure benefits only the period in which it is made, the cost should be debited to an expense account. This was the case with the expenditures for monthly building rental and salaries in the preceding chapter.

If an expenditure will benefit more than one period, it is properly chargeable to an asset account; but at the end of each period, it is necessary to determine how much of the cost should be charged as an expense of the period and what portion of the cost should still be shown in the balance sheet as an asset. The accounting procedure to be used in such cases is stated below:

> At the date of the expenditure, debit the entire cost to an asset account.
>
> At the end of each period benefited by the expenditure, transfer, by an adjusting entry, an appropriate portion of the cost from the asset account to an expense account.

Illustrative transactions. For purposes of illustration, the operations of Community Televisions are continued through the month of October. Following is a description of the transactions and the journal entries to record them. If a transaction gives rise to an adjusting entry at the end of the month for an income or cost apportionment, that fact is indicated.

Payment of building rent. Building rent for the month, in the amount of $250, was paid on October 1.

Since the expenditure will benefit the current month only, it is debited to an expense account.

Building rent expense............................	250.00	
Cash.....................................		250.00
Payment of rent for October.		

Collection for repair work. As part of the sales agreement, George Sloan promises each customer that he will provide, free, all repair work required on any set for a period of six months. George Sloan has contracted with Community Televisions to carry out this pledge on the following terms: $200 per month, payable in advance on the first day of each month. The fee for October was received on October 1.

Since the revenue will all be earned during the current accounting period, it is credited immediately to a revenue account.

Cash...	200.00	
Repair service revenue........................		200.00
Fee for repair service to be rendered in October.		

Payment for insurance policy. A cash payment of $120 was made on October 1 for a one-year fire insurance policy.

Since this expenditure will benefit more than one monthly accounting period, it is charged to an asset account.

Unexpired insurance............................ 120.00
    Cash......................................   120.00
    Premium on one-year fire insurance policy.

An adjusting entry will be required at the end of October transferring one-twelfth of the premium cost from Unexpired Insurance to Insurance Expense.

Purchase of equipment. Equipment was purchased on October 1 at a cost of $2,400; payment was made in cash.

The equipment has an expected useful life of ten years; accordingly, it is properly chargeable to an asset account.

Equipment.................................... 2,400.00
    Cash......................................   2,400.00
    Purchase of equipment.

It is expected that the equipment will be worthless at the end of ten years. Since the equipment will be used during its ten-year use-life to assist in the business activities carried on to earn (or "generate") revenue, a portion of the cost should be transferred to expense during each accounting period. This is achieved by a monthly adjusting entry.

Payment of truck rent. The truck rent accrued at the end of September, in the amount of $215, was paid on October 2.

This transaction merely removes the liability for truck rent payable; the expense was applicable to, and reported in the income statement for, September.

Accrued truck rent payable..................... 215.00
    Cash......................................   215.00
    Payment of truck rent accrued at the end of September.

Collection of an account receivable. Cash was received on October 3 from George Sloan in settlement of the commission billed him on September 30.

This revenue was earned and reported as earned in September; this transaction is merely a collection of a previously recorded receivable.

Cash... 1,000.00
    Accounts receivable........................   1,000.00
    Collection of commission previously billed to George Sloan.

Payment of matured note. The 30-day note in favor of O. E. Maltby matured and was paid on October 10.

The amount of the disbursement was computed as follows:

Face of note... $1,200
Interest ($1,200 × .06 × $^{30}/_{360}$)..........................   6
Cash disbursement... $1,206

The cash disbursement affected the following accounts:

Notes Payable—the liability for the face of the note was settled. . $1,200
Accrued Interest Payable—the interest accrual as of September 30
    was paid.   4
Interest Expense—the interest expense for the period October 1
    through October 10 was paid.   2
                                                        $1,206

Notes payable. 1,200.00
Accrued interest payable. 4.00
Interest expense. 2.00
    Cash. 1,206.00
    Paid note maturing today in favor of O. E. Maltby.

Collection for inspection service.   When a television set is sold, Sloan agrees to have it inspected within thirty days from the date of sale.   Starting October 1, Community Televisions is to do this work.   At the end of each month Sloan is to pay the company, at the rate of $5 per set, for inspection service on all sets sold during the month, regardless of whether the inspection has yet been made. On October 31, cash was received from George Sloan, in the amount of $250, for the inspection of television sets sold during October.

Since the company has thirty days from the date of sale to make the inspection, the amount collected each month presumably will not be completely earned during the month; therefore, the collection should be credited to a revenue-received-in-advance account, thus:

Cash. 250.00
    Inspection revenue received in advance. 250.00
    Received cash for inspection service on 50 sets sold
    during October.

At the end of the month, an adjusting entry will be made for the portion of the $250 earned by making inspections.

Commissions earned.   On October 31, $2,075 was received from Sloan for commissions on television sales during October.

Since the commissions have been earned, the credit is to a revenue account.

Cash. 2,075.00
    Commissions earned. 2,075.00
    Commissions on television sales during October.

Installation revenue.   When a television set is sold, Community Televisions is given the job of installing the set and installing an outside antenna if one is required.   The company is to be paid by Sloan at the end of each month for all such work done during the month.   The company received $825 on October 31 for such work.

Since the work has been performed, a revenue account is credited.

```
Cash........................................    825.00
   Installation revenue.........................              825.00
   For television set and antenna installations during
   October.
```

Payment of salaries.　Salaries were paid on October 31 in the amount of $1,450.

Since the expenditure relates to the current month only, it is debited to an expense account.

```
Salaries expense.............................  1,450.00
   Cash.......................................             1,450.00
   Paid salaries for October.
```

Payment of dividend.　An $80 dividend was paid on October 31.

```
Dividends....................................    80.00
   Cash.......................................               80.00
   Payment of dividend.
```

Trial balance after posting transaction entries.　The following trial balance shows the balances of the accounts after completion of the posting of the entries for the October transactions.

COMMUNITY TELEVISIONS

Trial Balance

October 31, 19—

```
Cash........................................   2,069.00
Accounts receivable.........................     500.00
Accrued interest receivable.................       3.00
Installation and repair parts...............   3,800.00
Unexpired insurance.........................     120.00
Mortgage receivable.........................   1,000.00
Equipment...................................   2,400.00
Inspection revenue received in advance......                  250.00
Capital stock...............................                8,000.00
Retained earnings...........................                  324.00
Dividends...................................      80.00
Commissions earned..........................                2,075.00
Repair service revenue......................                  200.00
Installation revenue........................                  825.00
Salaries expense............................   1,450.00
Building rent expense.......................     250.00
Interest expense............................       2.00
                                             ─────────  ─────────
                                             11,674.00  11,674.00
```

Adjustments for accruals.　The two following adjusting entries for accrued revenue and accrued expense are similar to those made at the end of September.

Accrued interest on mortgage.　An adjusting entry is required for the mortgage interest accrued during October.

```
Accrued interest receivable......................    5.00
   Interest earned..............................               5.00
   October accrual of interest on mortgage receivable
   ($1,000 × .06 × 1/12).
```

After this entry is posted, the two accounts affected will appear as follows:

Accrued Interest Receivable

19—						
Sept.	30		5	3 00		
Oct.	31		8	5 00		

Interest Earned

19—					19—				
Sept.	30		6	3 00	Sept.	30		5	3 00
					19—				
					Oct.	31		8	5 00

Accrued truck rent. The company drove the rented truck 2,800 miles during October, thus incurring a rent expense of $280.

Truck rent expense...............................	280.00	
Accrued truck rent payable..................		280.00
Expense and liability for use of truck during October.		

Adjustment for revenue apportionment. One adjustment is required at the end of October for an apportionment of revenue.

Inspection service. On October 31 the company collected $250 to be earned by inspection of television sets at $5 per set. The amount collected was credited to Inspection Revenue Received in Advance. By the end of October, the company had inspected 12 sets and therefore had earned $60. This $60 is transferred from the revenue-received-in-advance account to a revenue account by the following adjusting entry:

Inspection revenue received in advance............	60.00	
Inspection service revenue...................		60.00
Amount earned by inspection of 12 sets.		

After this entry is posted, the accounts affected will appear as follows:

Inspection Revenue Received in Advance

19—					19—				
Oct.	31		8	60 00	Oct.	31		7	250 00

Inspection Service Revenue

					19—				
					Oct.	31		8	60 00

The $60 credit balance in the Inspection Service Revenue account will be shown in the income statement. The $190 credit balance in the Inspection Revenue Received in Advance account (sometimes called a deferred revenue or deferred income account) will be shown on the liability side of the balance sheet; it represents an obligation to render inspection service in the future.

Adjustments for cost apportionments.   Three adjustments are required for cost apportionments.

Insurance.   The $120 cost of the fire insurance policy purchased on October 1 was charged to an asset account—Unexpired Insurance.   One-twelfth of this asset expires each month.   The cost expiration is an expense; the adjusting entry is:

```
Insurance expense.............................     10.00
     Unexpired insurance.........................              10.00
Insurance expense for the month.
```

After this entry is posted, the accounts will appear as follows:

Unexpired Insurance

19—					19—					
Oct.	1		7	120 00	Oct.	31		8	10 00	

Insurance Expense

19—						
Oct.	31		8	10 00		

The $10 debit balance in the Insurance Expense account will appear in the income statement.   The $110 debit balance in the Unexpired Insurance account will be shown on the asset side of the balance sheet.

Installation and repair parts.   In July the company purchased antennas and other parts at a cost of $3,800, which was debited to an asset account called Installation and Repair Parts.   In its installation and repair work during October, some of these antennas and parts were used.   To determine the amount thus disposed of (expense) and the amount remaining on hand (asset), the employees counted the installation and repair parts at the close of business on October 31 and determined that such items had cost the company $3,530.   With this information, the cost of the installation and repair parts used was computed as follows:

```
Cost of installation and repair parts available.................  $3,800
Cost of such parts remaining on hand October 31.............   3,530
Cost of installation and repair parts chargeable as October expense  $  270
```

To give recognition to the expense and the reduction in the asset resulting from the use of some of the antennas and other parts during October, the adjusting entry on the following page is required.

Installation and repair parts expense.............   270.00
  Installation and repair parts.................   270.00
  Expense for the month.

After this entry is posted, the accounts affected will appear as follows:

Installation and Repair Parts

19— July	28		1	3,800	00	19— Oct.	31		8	270	00

Installation and Repair Parts Expense

19— Oct.	31		8	270	00						

The $3,530 debit balance in the Installation and Repair Parts (asset) account will appear on the asset side of the balance sheet. The $270 debit balance in the Installation and Repair Parts Expense account will appear in the income statement.

Depreciation of equipment.   Since the equipment purchased on October 1 has a ten-year use life, there is a monthly cost expiration of $\frac{1}{120}$ of $2,400, or $20.   This cost expiration, which is called *depreciation,* is recorded by an adjusting entry.   If depreciation were ignored, periodic net income would be overstated.

The monthly adjusting entry for depreciation includes a debit to an expense account: Depreciation Expense—Equipment.   The credit *might* be made to the Equipment (asset) account, but it is desirable to have the balance of such an account continue to show the cost of the asset.   Therefore, it is customary to credit a separate account.   "Reserve for Depreciation" has long been used as the title of this account, and it continues to be used, although with declining frequency.   Some accountants prefer the account title "Allowance for Depreciation."   Current usage favors the account title "Accumulated Depreciation," which is used here.

Following is the October 31 adjusting entry:

Depreciation expense—Equipment................   20.00
  Accumulated depreciation—Equipment........   20.00
  Depreciation for October.

After this entry is posted, the accounts will appear as follows:

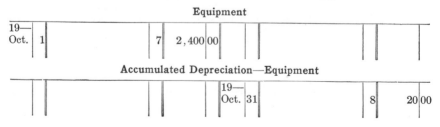

Equipment

19— Oct.	1		7	2,400	00						

Accumulated Depreciation—Equipment

						19— Oct.	31		8	20	00

Depreciation Expense—Equipment

19—							
Oct. 31		8	20 00				

The asset and its contra account for accumulated depreciation will appear in the balance sheet thus:

```
Equipment................................... $2,400.00
   Less accumulated depreciation...............   20.00 $2,380.00
```

The depreciation expense account balance will appear as an expense in the income statement.

It should be noted that the balance of the depreciation expense account is transferred to Revenue and Expense Summary when the books are closed, but the contra account for accumulated depreciation remains open and its balance is increased by the periodic adjusting entries for depreciation.

Depreciation for fractional periods. If assets subject to depreciation are acquired during an accounting period, depreciation must be computed and recorded for a fractional period. Since depreciation is an estimate, it seems unnecessary to compute fractional-period depreciation in terms of days. Depreciation is not that precise. As a general rule, fractional-period depreciation is computed in terms of months or fractions of months. This procedure is illustrated below, where it is assumed that the company's accounting period ends on December 31.

	Delivery Equipment	Office Machine
Date asset acquired..................	March 31	September 17 (treated as Sept. 15 for fractional-period purposes)
Cost of asset.......................	$4,000	$1,200
Depreciation rate per annum..........	20%	10%
Annual charge for depreciation........	$ 800	$ 120
Months that asset was in use first year..	9	3½ (7 half-months)
Fraction of year....................	9/12	7/24
Depreciation charge applicable to first accounting period.................	$ 600	$ 35

Determining when adjustments are required and the amounts thereof. In accounting courses, the data required for adjusting entries are usually given in the text. In business, the required information comes from many sources. As a first step, the accountant usually reviews the trial balance. The mere appear-

ance of some accounts in the trial balance may suggest the necessity
for certain adjustments.   For instance, an Equipment account suggests provisions for depreciation; a Mortgage Receivable account
suggests the possibility of a required adjustment for accrued
interest receivable; a Notes Payable account suggests the need for
an adjustment for accrued interest payable.

If any prepaid expense accounts (for example, Unexpired Insurance) or deferred revenue accounts (for example, Inspection
Revenue Received in Advance) appear in the trial balance, they
should immediately draw the accountant's attention to the fact
that adjustments for cost or revenue apportionments may be
required.

The accountant is well advised to consider each revenue
and each expense account and ask himself whether there is any
possibility that an adjustment may be in order, either for an
accrual or for an apportionment.   Often a reference to the prior
period's adjusting entries will disclose adjustments that are again
appropriate.

Although an inspection of the trial balance and a review of
earlier adjusting entries may suggest the *nature* of the required
adjustments, it usually is necessary to have recourse to other
sources of information to determine the *amounts* of the adjustments.   For instance, insurance-premium apportionments may be
determined by an inspection of the policies; interest adjustments
may be determined by an examination of notes or other documents.
In some cases, for example, installation and repair parts, the dollar
amount of the adjustment will be based on a physical count of the
items remaining on hand.   Thus, an accountant may refer to the
accounting records and to a variety of business documents, or he
may count and list things in the process of developing the information that he needs for adjusting entries.

Working papers.   Working papers for the month of October are
on pages 61 and 62.   They differ as follows:

Page 61: A pair of Adjusted Trial Balance columns is included,
as in the illustration in Chapter 4.

Page 62: The Adjusted Trial Balance columns have been
omitted.   To save time and labor, many accountants prefer
to extend the trial balance amounts, as modified by the data
in the Adjustments columns, directly to the statement
columns.

Observe that, when an account affected by an adjusting entry
appears in the trial balance, it is not necessary to write the account
title again below the trial balance.

COMMUNITY TELEVISIONS
Working Papers
For the Month of October, 19—

	Trial Balance Dr	Trial Balance Cr	Adjustments Dr	Adjustments Cr	Adjusted Trial Balance Dr	Adjusted Trial Balance Cr	Income Statement Dr	Income Statement Cr	Retained Earnings Statement Dr	Retained Earnings Statement Cr	Balance Sheet Dr	Balance Sheet Cr
Cash	2,069				2,069						2,069	
Accounts receivable	500				500						500	
Accrued interest receivable	3		5a		8						8	
Installation and repair parts	3,800			270e	3,530						3,530	
Unexpired insurance	120			10d	110						110	
Mortgage receivable	1,000				1,000						1,000	
Equipment	2,400				2,400						2,400	
Inspection revenue received in advance		250	60c			190						190
Capital stock		8,000				8,000						8,000
Retained earnings		324				324				324		
Dividends	80				80				80			
Commissions earned		2,075				2,075		2,075				
Repair service revenue		200				200		200				
Installation revenue		825				825		825				
Salaries expense	1,450				1,450		1,450					
Building rent expense	250				250		250					
Interest expense	2				2		2					
	11,674	11,674										
Interest earned				5a		5		5				
Truck rent expense			280b		280		280					
Accrued truck rent payable				280b		280						280
Inspection service revenue				60c		60		60				
Insurance expense			10d		10		10					
Installation and repair parts expense			270e		270		270					
Depreciation expense—Equipment			20f		20		20					
Accumulated depreciation—Equipment				20f		20						20
			645	645	11,979	11,979	2,282	3,165				
Net income							883			883		
							3,165	3,165	80	1,127		1,127
Retained earnings, October 31, 19—									1,127	1,207	9,617	9,617
									1,207			

Adjustments

a—Accrued interest on mortgage receivable.
b—Accrued truck rent.
c—Portion of inspection service revenue earned during October.
d—Portion of insurance cost expired during October.
e—Cost of installation and repair parts used during October.
f—Depreciation of equipment for October.

COMMUNITY TELEVISIONS
Working Papers
For the Month of October, 19—

	Trial Balance		Adjustments		Income Statement		Retained Earnings Statement		Balance Sheet	
Cash..........................	2,069								2,069	
Accounts receivable...........	500								500	
Accrued interest receivable....	3		5a						8	
Installation and repair parts...	3,800			270e					3,530	
Unexpired insurance...........	120			10d					110	
Mortgage receivable...........	1,000								1,000	
Equipment....................	2,400								2,400	
Inspection revenue received in advance......		250	60c							190
Capital stock.................		8,000								8,000
Retained earnings.............		324						324		
Dividends....................	80						80			
Commissions earned...........		2,075				2,075				
Repair service revenue........		200				200				
Installation revenue..........		825				825				
Salaries expense..............	1,450				1,450					
Building rent expense.........	250				250					
Interest expense..............	2				2					
	11,674	11,674								
Interest earned...............				5a		5				
Truck rent expense...........			280b		280					
Accrued truck rent payable....				280b						280
Inspection service revenue.....				60c		60				
Insurance expense............			10d		10					
Installation and repair parts expense......			270e		270					
Depreciation expense—Equipment....			20f		20					
Accumulated depreciation—Equipment....				20f						20
			645	645						
Net income...................					883			883		
					3,165	3,165				
Retained earnings, October 31, 19...							1,127			1,127
							1,207	1,207		
									9,617	9,617

The description of the adjustments would be the same as on page 61.

Statements. Statements were prepared as follows:

COMMUNITY TELEVISIONS
Income Statement
For the Month of October, 19—

Revenues:		
Commissions earned.................................		$2,075.00
Repair service revenue...............................		200.00
Installation revenue.................................		825.00
Inspection service revenue...........................		60.00
Interest earned.....................................		5.00
Total..		$3,165.00
Deduct expenses:		
Salaries expense............................	$1,450.00	
Building rent expense........................	250.00	
Truck rent expense...........................	280.00	
Insurance expense............................	10.00	
Installation and repair parts expense...........	270.00	
Depreciation expense—Equipment.............	20.00	
Interest expense.............................	2.00	
Total..		2,282.00
Net income...		$ 883.00

COMMUNITY TELEVISIONS
Statement of Retained Earnings
For the Month of October, 19—

Retained earnings, September 30, 19—....................	$ 324.00
Add net income for the month—Per income statement.......	883.00
Total...	$1,207.00
Deduct dividends.....................................	80.00
Retained earnings, October 31, 19—.....................	$1,127.00

COMMUNITY TELEVISIONS
Balance Sheet
October 31, 19—
Assets

Cash..		$2,069.00
Accounts receivable..................................		500.00
Accrued interest receivable............................		8.00
Installation and repair parts...........................		3,530.00
Unexpired insurance..................................		110.00
Mortgage receivable..................................		1,000.00
Equipment...................................	$2,400.00	
Less accumulated depreciation................	20.00	2,380.00
		$9,597.00

Liabilities and Stockholders' Equity

Liabilities:		
Accrued truck rent payable..................	$ 280.00	
Inspection revenue received in advance........	190.00	
Total..		$ 470.00
Stockholders' equity:		
Capital stock.............................	$8,000.00	
Retained earnings—Per statement of retained		
earnings................................	1,127.00	
Total..		9,127.00
		$9,597.00

Closing entries.   The following closing entries were prepared from the working papers:

Journal   (Page 9)

19—				
Oct.	31	Commissions earned..........................	2,075 00	
		Repair service revenue.......................	200 00	
		Installation revenue.........................	825 00	
		Inspection service revenue...................	60 00	
		Interest earned.............................	5 00	
		Revenue and expense summary.............		3,165 00
		To close the revenue accounts.		
	31	Revenue and expense summary.................	2,282 00	
		Salaries expense............................		1,450 00
		Building rent expense.......................		250 00
		Interest expense............................		2 00
		Truck rent expense..........................		280 00
		Insurance expense...........................		10 00
		Installation and repair parts expense.........		270 00
		Depreciation expense—Equipment...........		20 00
		To close the expense accounts.		
	31	Revenue and expense summary.................	883 00	
		Retained earnings..........................		883 00
		To transfer the net income to Retained Earnings.		
	31	Retained earnings...........................	80 00	
		Dividends..................................		80 00
		To close the Dividends account.		

After-closing trial balance.   The following trial balance was taken after the completion of the posting of the adjusting and closing entries.

COMMUNITY TELEVISIONS
After-Closing Trial Balance
October 31, 19—

Cash..	2,069.00	
Accounts receivable...........................	500.00	
Accrued interest receivable....................	8.00	
Installation and repair parts...................	3,530.00	
Unexpired insurance...........................	110.00	
Mortgage receivable...........................	1,000.00	
Equipment....................................	2,400.00	
Accumulated depreciation—Equipment...........		20.00
Accrued truck rent payable....................		280.00
Inspection revenue received in advance...........		190.00
Capital stock.................................		8,000.00
Retained earnings.............................		1,127.00
	9,617.00	9,617.00

Accrual and cash bases of accounting.   The accounting process described thus far is known as the *accrual basis* of accounting, the objective of which is to report revenue in the income statement for the period when it is earned (regardless of when it is collected) and to report expense in the period when it is incurred (regardless of when the cash disbursement is made). The accrual basis will continue to be the primary concern of this text. However, in some instances, generally among small businesses and professional practices, a type of accounting known as the *cash basis* is used. It is desirable to note the contrasting features of these two bases.

The *cash basis* means that revenue is reported in the period when the related cash collection is made, and that expenses are reported in the period when the cash disbursements are made. The cash basis does not mean that all cash receipts are regarded as revenue and that all cash disbursements are regarded as expenses. It is obvious, for instance, that cash received in connection with the issuance of capital stock is not revenue, and that a dividend payment is not an expense.

The fundamental difference between the cash and accrual bases is in the matter of "timing." Accountants often describe the process of periodical net income determination as a proper "matching" of revenue and expenses by periods. This is achieved by the accrual basis of accounting; it is not achieved by the cash basis of accounting except to the extent that revenue is earned in the same period that the related cash collection is received, and that expense is incurred in the same period that the related cash disbursement is made. This frequently is not the case; consider the following typical business situations:

$500 worth of coal is purchased and paid for in July; the coal will be used during the winter for heating.

$500 is the correct measure of expense, but the expense is not incurred in July. The expense is incurred when the coal is consumed.

$80 worth of office supplies are purchased on account in July; the supplies are used in August, and the liability for the supplies is settled by a cash payment in October.

Again, the amount of the cash disbursement is the measure of the total expense. However, the expense is an August expense. The month of acquisition and the month of the cash disbursement are incorrect periods for reporting the expense.

In December a customer inquired about the price that would be charged to remove a tree from his premises. When the businessman informed the customer that he would remove the tree for $90, the customer ordered it done, provided that the work would be completed before June 1. The tree was removed in April and the customer was billed on May 1. On June 15, $90 was received from the customer.

On the accrual basis, the man who removed the tree would include the $90 in his income statement for April, the month when the service was performed.   Any expenses incurred by him in removing the tree would be treated as an April expense.   On the cash basis, the income would be included in the June statement.

Although adjusting entries such as those described in this and the preceding chapters are often essential to place the accounts on a *complete* accrual basis, it does not follow that the accounts will be on a cash basis if the adjustments are not made.   For instance, revenue may have been earned during a month and recorded by a debit to Accounts Receivable instead of to Cash; no adjustment is required to place the accounts on an accrual basis, but they are not on a cash basis.   Similarly, an expense may have been incurred during a month and recorded by a credit to Accounts Payable rather than to Cash; again, no adjustment is necessary to place the accounts on an accrual basis, but they are not on a cash basis.   Adjusting entries are required only to the extent that the transaction entries do not assign revenue and expenses to the periods to which they are properly applicable.

Net loss for the period.   If the expenses exceed the revenues for the period, the income statement will report a net loss, as illustrated below:

THE *AB* CORPORATION
Income Statement
For the Year Ended December 31, 19—

Revenues:
Commissions earned.................................. $8,950.00
Interest earned....................................... 90.00
   Total.. $9,040.00
Deduct expenses:
Salaries expense............................ $6,310.00
Rent expense.............................. 1,200.00
Advertising expense......................... 960.00
Office expense.............................. 670.00
Depreciation expense—Equipment............ 180.00
   Total.. 9,320.00
Net loss.. $ 280.00

Since the operations resulted in a loss, the Revenue and Expense Summary account will have a debit balance after the revenue and expense accounts have been closed, and will in turn be closed by an entry debiting Retained Earnings and crediting Revenue and Expense Summary.

Deficit.   The occurrence of net losses may cause the Retained Earnings account to have a debit balance.   A debit balance in the

Retained Earnings account is called a deficit in the balance sheet, and is deducted from the capital stock as follows:

Stockholders' equity:
    Capital stock............................. $40,000.00
    Deduct deficit........................... 10,000.00
        Net...................................... .... $30,000.00

CHAPTER 6

Merchandise Operations

Illustrative income statement. In the illustrations in the preceding chapters, the business operations consisted of rendering services. Many businesses, however, derive all or a large portion of their earnings from selling merchandise. An income statement for a company whose entire income is derived from selling merchandise is presented below.

THE MORTON COMPANY
Income Statement
For the Month of April, 19—

Sales..			$3.600.00
Deduct cost of goods sold:			
Inventory, March 31, 19—...................	$1,200.00		
Purchases.................................	3,000.00		
Cost of goods available for sale............	$4,200.00		
Deduct inventory, April 30, 19—............	1,500.00		
Cost of goods sold................................		2,700.00	
Gross profit on sales....................................		$ 900.00	
Deduct expenses:			
Advertising expense.........................	$ 25.00		
Rent expense...............................	85.00		
Salaries expense............................	500.00		
Total..		610.00	
Net income..		$ 290.00	

Gross profit on sales. Notice the new feature introduced by the merchandising operations: namely, the appearance in the income statement of the "gross profit on sales." The gross profit is the excess of the selling price over the cost of the goods sold.

Some accountants, perhaps because of the appearance of the "gross profit," prefer to give the above statement the heading "Statement of Profit and Loss" or "Profit and Loss Statement." All of these statement headings are acceptable, and all are used in this text in order to familiarize the student with such variations.

Accounting for sales. A sale of merchandise is recorded in the same way as a "sale" of service—that is, by a credit to a revenue account. The Sales account is used for this purpose. One sale occurred during April:

April 18—Nine air-conditioning units were sold to Bailey Apartments on account, for $400 each.

The journal entry to record the sale was:

```
Accounts receivable............................ 3,600.00
    Sales......................................              3,600.00
        Sale of nine units on account to Bailey Apartments.
```

After this entry was posted, the Sales account appeared as follows:

Sales   (50)

		19—			
		April 18		1	3,600 00

Cost of goods sold. As shown in the income statement of The Morton Company, the cost of goods sold is determined as follows:

```
Inventory of merchandise at beginning of period............ $1,200.00
Add purchases during the period..........................    3,000.00
Total goods available for sale............................   $4,200.00
Deduct inventory of merchandise at end of period...........   1,500.00
Cost of goods sold.......................................    $2,700.00
```

The above computation is not based on a new concept. In the Community Televisions illustration for October, the installation and repair parts expense was determined in the same manner:

```
Total parts available.................................... $3,800.00
Deduct inventory of parts at end of period................   3,530.00
Cost of parts used.......................................  $  270.00
```

The sources of the information for the computation of the cost of goods sold are discussed below.

Inventory at beginning of period. The Morton Company was organized on March 31. The stockholders invested $3,800 cash and air-conditioners that cost $1,200. The investment was recorded as follows:

```
Cash......................................... 3,800.00
Inventory....................................  1,200.00
    Capital stock...........................              5,000.00
        Stockholders' investments.
```

After this entry was posted, the Inventory account appeared as follows:

Inventory   (5)

19—			1	1,200 00				
March 31								

Purchases. The Purchases account is used to record all acquisitions of merchandise in which the business deals; purchases are debited to the account. One purchase transaction occurred during April, as stated on the following page.

April 3—Ten air-conditioning units costing $300 each were purchased from White Company on account.

The journal entry to record this transaction was:

```
Purchases....................................  3,000.00
    Accounts payable...........................        3,000.00
    Purchased ten air-conditioning units on account
    from White Company.
```

After this entry was posted, the Purchases account appeared as follows:

Purchases   (100)

19—								
April	3		1	3,000 00				

Inventory at end of period.   The end-of-period inventory was determined by counting and listing all merchandise on hand held for sale, pricing such merchandise at cost, and totaling the money amounts.   The inventory of The Morton Company on April 30 was $1,500.

Other April transactions.   In addition to the transactions already mentioned, the following transactions occurred in April:

April 1—The rent for the month, $85, was paid in cash.
     15—Newspaper advertising, $25, was paid in cash.
     26—A cash payment of $1,500 was made to White Company, to apply on account.
     27—A cash collection of $1,750 was received from Bailey Apartments, to apply on account.
     30—Salaries for the month, $500, were paid in cash.
     30—A cash dividend of $50 was declared and paid.

Trial balance.   The trial balance in the working papers on page 71 shows the balances that would appear in the ledger as of April 30 after all journal entries were posted.   Note that the inventory figure shown is the beginning-of-period inventory.

Working papers.   Working papers in various stages of completion appear on pages 71, 73, and 75.   They are based on the data of The Morton Company shown on the preceding pages of this chapter.   Adjustments have been omitted for simplicity; any required adjustments would be made in the manner illustrated in Chapters 4 and 5.

Stage 1.   The working papers identified as Stage 1 (see page 71) show the condition of the papers after the following steps:

(1) All working paper headings entered.
(2) The trial balance entered.

Stage 1.

THE MORTON COMPANY
Working Papers
For the Month of April, 19—

	Trial Balance		Income Statement		Retained Earnings Statement		Balance Sheet	
Cash....................	3,390							
Accounts receivable.....	1,850							
Inventory, March 31, 19—..	1,200							
Accounts payable		1,500						
Capital stock............		5,000						
Dividends...............	50							
Sales...................		3,600						
Purchases...............	3,000							
Advertising expense......	25							
Rent expense............	85							
Salaries expense.........	500							
	10,100	10,100						

Stage 2.   Page 73 shows how the working papers appear after the completion of the following additional steps (shown in italics):

(1) The balances of the Inventory (beginning of period) and Purchases accounts have been extended to the Income Statement debit column.   The sum of these two debits, $4,200, is the cost of goods which were available for sale during the period.

(2) The end-of-period inventory, $1,500, which does not appear in the trial balance, has been entered in the working papers in two places:

   (a) In the Income Statement credit column, because it will appear in the income statement as an element of the computation of the cost of goods sold.   It is entered in the working papers in the Income Statement credit column because it is a deduction from the opening inventory and the purchases, which are debits.   The Income Statement columns now have a debit balance of $2,700, the cost of goods sold.

   (b) In the Balance Sheet debit column, because the ending inventory will be shown in the balance sheet as an asset.

Stage 2.

THE MORTON COMPANY
Working Papers
For the Month of April, 19—

	Trial Balance		Income Statement	Retained Earnings Statement	Balance Sheet
Cash............................	3,390				
Accounts receivable...........	1,850				
Inventory, March 31, 19—......	1,200		1,200		
Accounts payable..............		1,500			
Capital stock.................		5,000			
Dividends.....................	50				
Sales.........................		3,600	3,000		
Purchases.....................	3,000				
Advertising expense...........	25				
Rent expense..................	85				
Salaries expense..............	500				
	10,100	10,100			
Inventory, April 30, 19—.....			1,500		1,500

Stage 3. The completed working papers are on page 75. The following steps were taken to complete the papers:

(1) The $3,600 balance of the Sales account was extended to the Income Statement credit column. At this point, the Income Statement columns have a credit balance of $900, the gross profit on sales.

(2) The balances of the three expense accounts were extended to the Income Statement debit column. At this point, the Income Statement columns have a credit balance of $290, the net income for the period.

(3) The $290 net income was entered as a balancing figure in the Income Statement debit column, and also in the Retained Earnings Statement credit column. The Income Statement columns were totaled and ruled.

(4) The dividends amount was extended to the Retained Earnings Statement debit column.

(5) The amount of the retained earnings at the end of April, $240, was entered in the Retained Earnings Statement debit column, and also in the Balance Sheet credit column.

(6) Balance sheet items were extended from the trial balance to the Balance Sheet columns.

(7) The Retained Earnings Statement and Balance Sheet columns were footed and ruled.

Statements prepared from working papers. The income statement is on page 68. The other statements appear below:

THE MORTON COMPANY
Statement of Retained Earnings
For the Month of April, 19—

Net income for the month—Per income statement.............	$290.00
Deduct dividends..	50.00
Retained earnings, April 30, 19—.......	$240.00

THE MORTON COMPANY
Balance Sheet—April 30, 19—

Assets		Liabilities and Stockholders' Equity		
Cash......................	$3,390.00	Liabilities:		
Accounts receivable.........	1,850.00	Accounts payable.........		$1,500.00
Inventory.................	1,500.00	Stockholders' equity:		
		Capital stock...	$5,000.00	
		Retained earnings—Per statement of retained earnings.........	240.00	5,240.00
	$6,740.00			$6,740.00

Stage 3.

THE MORTON COMPANY
Working Papers
For the Month of April, 19—

	Trial Balance		Income Statement		Retained Earnings Statement		Balance Sheet	
Cash	3,390						3,390	
Accounts receivable	1,850						1,850	
Inventory, March 31, 19—	1,200		1,200					
Accounts payable		1,500						1,500
Capital stock		5,000						5,000
Dividends	50				50			
Sales		3,600		3,600				
Purchases	3,000		3,000					
Advertising expense	25		25					
Rent expense	85		85					
Salaries expense	500		500					
	10,100	10,100						
Inventory, April 30, 19—				1,500			1,500	
			4,810	5,100				
Net income			290			290		
			5,100	5,100				
Retained earnings, April 30, 19—					240			240
					290	290	6,740	6,740

(Note that the items in the Income Statement and Retained Earnings columns were footed to facilitate the computation of the $290 and $240 balances.)

Closing entries. The closing entries for a merchandising concern, in this case The Morton Company, are presented below. Observe that the beginning inventory is removed from the Inventory account by a credit in the second closing entry, and that the ending inventory is recorded on the books by a debit to Inventory in the first entry. Otherwise, the closing-entry procedure is identical with the method presented for a service enterprise.

		Journal		(Page 2)	
19— April	30	Sales...	3,600 00		
		Inventory....................................	1,500 00		
		Revenue and expense......................		5,100 00	
		To close the Sales account and set up the ending inventory.			
	30	Revenue and expense..........................	4,810 00		
		Inventory..................................		1,200 00	
		Purchases.................................		3,000 00	
		Advertising expense.......................		25 00	
		Rent expense..............................		85 00	
		Salaries expense..........................		500 00	
		To close the expense accounts and to remove the beginning inventory from the Inventory account.			
	30	Revenue and expense..........................	290 00		
		Retained earnings.........................		290 00	
		To close the Revenue and Expense account.			
	30	Retained earnings.............................	50 00		
		Dividends.................................		50 00	
		To close the Dividends account.			

Note that the account title Revenue and Expense Summary has been shortened by dropping the word "summary." From now on, either title will be acceptable.

After the above entries are posted, the Inventory account will appear as follows:

			Inventory					(5)	
19— March	31	1	1,200 00	19— April	30		2	1,200 00	
April	30	2	1,500 00						

The Inventory account is a peculiar account in that it is inactive except when the accounts are being closed at the end of each accounting period. During the closing process, the Inventory account is credited to remove the beginning inventory and debited to record the ending inventory.

Special note regarding a newly organized business. A newly organized business may start operations without a beginning inventory.   The cost of goods sold during its *first* accounting period will be computed by simply deducting the ending inventory from the purchases.

Two principal sources of revenue.   If a company has two principal sources of revenue, one from merchandising operations and the other from rendering services, its income statement may be presented as follows:

THE *M N* COMPANY
Condensed Income Statement
For the Month of August, 19—

Sales..	$8,000.00
Deduct cost of goods sold.............................	5,000.00
Gross profit on sales.................................	$3,000.00
Revenue from services.................................	2,000.00
Total...	$5,000.00
Deduct expenses.......................................	4,000.00
Net income..	$1,000.00

Office Routines; Documents

Duties of the accounting department.   The work of the accounting department includes:

(1) Writing up various documents, such as sales invoices, checks, and notes.   Most of these documents are delivered to the parties with whom the company does business; duplicates of some of them (duplicate sales invoices, for instance) may be retained in the company's files for future reference and as evidence of the propriety of the entries for the transactions.

(2) Checking similar documents received from the parties with whom the company does business, to determine whether or not they have been prepared in accordance with the facts of the transactions.   After having been checked, the documents are filed as evidence of the transactions.

(3) Recording the transaction facts indicated by the documents written up in the office or received from other parties.

Internal control.   The office and accounting procedure should be so organized that errors will be prevented so far as possible, and that, if errors are made (by the company's employees or in documents received from people with whom the company does business), they probably will be discovered.   Moreover, the work of the various members of the organization should be so interrelated and checked that fraud cannot be committed and concealed without the collusion of two or more persons. The method of effecting these safeguards is called the *system of internal check* or *internal control*.

It should be understood that the discussion in this chapter relative to office routines is intended to indicate methods which *may be* used to provide for internal control. It is not intended to describe procedures used in every business.

The number of copies of each document prepared in any given business may be more or less than the number stated in the following comments. Also, the office routines depend on the size of the business and on the ideas of the company's accountant regarding the relative advantages of different procedures.

Purchase Routine

Purchase requisitions. All purchases may be made by the purchasing agent, who obtains information concerning requirements from purchase requisitions sent to him by other members of the organization. Requisition forms are of various kinds; the following is illustrative.

R. E. JOHNSON & COMPANY

Requisition No. __M135__   Date __July 2, 19--__

Please purchase for delivery __before July 6__

Quantity	Description
10 cases	XXXX Strawberry preserves
15 cases	Acorn Peanut butter
10 cases	Acorn peas

Requisitioned by __C. E. Walters__   Approved by __J. E. White__

Purchasing Agent's Memorandum of Order

Purchase Order No. __1705__   Issued to __The Osborne Co.__

Date of Order __July 2__   __Chicago__

Purchase Requisition

Purchase requisitions may be filled out by various persons, depending on the nature and size of the business.

In the case of staple merchandise, the merchandise manager may fix a minimum quantity below which the stock must not be allowed to fall without reordering. When the stock is reduced to the minimum quantity determined by the merchandise manager, the stock clerk enters the description of the article on a requisition; he may also enter the quantity to be ordered (if a standard quantity to be purchased has been established), or the quantity may be entered on the requisition by the merchandise manager.

In the case of non-staple merchandise, the requisition may be prepared in the office of the merchandise manager after consultation with the sales manager regarding quantities which probably will be required.

Purchase order. The purchasing agent places the order by filling out a purchase order. Purchase orders vary in form; the following is illustrative.

Purchase Order   No. 1705

R. E. JOHNSON & COMPANY
2913 North Western Avenue
Chicago

To **The Osborne Company**   Date __July 2, 19--__

                        Deliver __Before July 6__

215 West Canal Street   Ship via __Your truck__

                        F. O. B. _____

Chicago   Terms __1/10; n/30__

Quantity	Description	Price
10 cases	XXXX Strawberry Preserves	27.80
15 cases	Acorn Peanut Butter	9.20
10 cases	Acorn Peas	12.40

R. E. Johnson & Company

Req. No. __M135__   By __L. K. Bacon__

                              Purchasing Agent

Purchase Order

Three copies of the purchase order may be made, and disposed of as follows:

Original—sent to the supplier from whom the goods are being purchased.

First carbon—retained in the purchasing department files.

Second carbon—sent to the receiving department.

The uses subsequently made of the first and second carbon copies of the purchase order are described in a subsequent section of this chapter.

Invoice. The purchaser receives an invoice from the seller. The invoice describes the merchandise shipped, shows the amount charged therefor, and gives other important information. An illustrative invoice appears below.

THE OSBORNE COMPANY
215 West Canal Street
Chicago, Illinois

Invoice No. __2397__

Customer's Order No. __1705__

Date of Order __7/2/19--__   Invoice Date __July 3, 19--__

Sold to __R. E. Johnson & Company__   Terms __1/10; n/30__

__2913 North Western Ave.__

__Chicago, Ill.__   F. O. B. _____

Shipped to __Same__   Date Shipped __July 3__

How Shipped __Truck__

Car. No. & Initials _____

Quantity	Description	Unit Price	Amount
10 cases	XXXX Strawberry Preserves	27.80	278.00
15 cases	Acorn Peanut Butter	9.20	138.00
10 cases	Acorn Peas	12.40	124.00
			540.00

Invoice

Purchaser's verification of invoice. When the invoice is received, it is sent to the purchasing department, where a check sheet in the following general form is attached to it, or a rubber stamp imprint of the same form is made on it.

Goods checked to invoice   _____
Invoice checked to purchase order for:
    Merchandise   _____
    Prices   _____
    Discount terms   _____
    Freight terms   _____
Invoice footings and extensions checked   _____
Approved for payment   _____
Paid by Check No._____Date_____

Check Sheet

Before the purchase is recorded, the purchasing company should know that:

(1) The goods invoiced have been received.
    The second carbon of the purchase order was sent to the receiving department. When the goods are received, the receiving clerk:

        Inspects the merchandise to see that it is in good condition.
        Counts, weighs, or otherwise determines the quantities received, and enters these quantities on his copy of the purchase order. This copy was made with a narrow carbon, so that the quantities ordered were not typed on it; such a practice assures a careful count by the receiving clerk instead of a perfunctory checking of typed quantities.
        Initials the copy of the purchase order and sends it to the purchasing department, where it is filed in a binder called a *receiving record*.

    A clerk in the purchasing department compares the quantities received (shown by the receiving record) with the quantities billed (shown by the invoice). If they agree, he initials the check sheet on the "Goods checked to invoice" line.

(2) The invoice agrees with the purchase order.
    The first carbon of the purchase order was retained in the purchasing department files. A clerk checks the invoice against this carbon of the purchase order to see that the

merchandise invoiced is the same as the merchandise ordered, and that the prices, the discount terms, and the freight terms are correct. He indicates the accuracy of these matters by initialing the check sheet on the four lines provided therefor.

(3) The extensions and footings of the invoice are correct.

The computations are checked by a clerk in the accounting department, and their accuracy is indicated by his initials on the "Invoice footings and extensions checked" line of the check sheet.

After the invoice has been checked, an entry is made to record the purchase.

Payment of the invoice. The terms of the invoice received from The Osborne Company were 1/10; n/30. This is read as follows: *1% in 10 days; net 30**. It means that 1% cash discount will be allowed if the invoice is paid within ten days from its date, July 3, and that the invoice is due in thirty days without discount.

To be sure that all invoices are paid within the discount period, they may be filed in a *tickler*, which is a card file with index cards bearing dates. The Osborne invoice will be filed in front of the card for July 12, the date on which the check should be mailed to reach the creditor before the expiration of the discount period.

When the payment date arrives, the invoice is taken from the tickler and sent to the treasurer. If funds are available for the payment of the invoice, the treasurer signs or initials the check sheet on the "Approved for payment" line and sends the invoice to the cashier, who:

(1) Draws a check;

(2) Enters the check number and date of payment on the check sheet attached to the invoice;

(3) Sends the check to the treasurer for his signature. The check is clipped to the invoice so that the treasurer can be sure that the check he is signing is in payment of an approved invoice.

The treasurer signs the check and sees that it is mailed to the creditor. The invoice is sent to the bookkeeper, who records its payment. The invoice is then filed for future reference as evidence of the propriety of the entries for the purchase and the payment.

Checks, advices, and receipts. When a remittance is sent to a creditor, it is important that the creditor be given information which will indicate the particular invoice which is being paid. A debtor may owe several bills; he has a legal right to specify that

---

* The expression *net* is a misnomer, because the gross amount of the invoice (not the net amount) is payable after 10 days.

his remittance shall apply to a certain bill or certain bills, and the
debtor's and the creditor's records should show which bills are
being paid.   It is also desirable to obtain a receipt from the
creditor.   Several methods may be used to accomplish these purposes; two methods in common use are described below:

(1) The check form may be a simple one, similar to the fol-
    lowing illustration:

FIRST NATIONAL BANK 2-1	No. _1668_
	Chicago, ___July 12,___ 19 --
Pay to the order of _____The Osborne Company_____	$ 534.60
EXACTLY $534 AND 60 CTS. _____	Dollars
	R. E. Johnson & Company
	Peter Oldham Treasurer

Check

When the purchaser sends the seller the check, he may send
with it a letter, stating that the check is sent in payment of
the creditor's invoice 2397 of July 3, in the amount of $540,
less 1% cash discount.

This method has two disadvantages:

(a) It necessitates writing a letter.
(b) Although the creditor's endorsement of the check is a
    receipt for $534.60, it is not an acknowledgment of the
    payment of a particular invoice.

(2) Data with respect to the invoice that is being paid may be
    shown in a space provided for that purpose at the left
    of the check, as illustrated below.

Date	Invoice	Amount	
			FIRST NATIONAL BANK 2-1 No. _1668_
7/3/19--	2397	540.00	Chicago, ___July 12,___ 19 --
			Pay to the order of ___The Osborne Company___ $ 534.60
			EXACTLY $534 AND 60 CTS. ___ Dollars
Total		540.00	
Discount		5.40	R. E. Johnson & Company
Net		534.60	_Peter Oldham_
			Treasurer

Check with Space for Data at Left

The back of the left end of the check may contain the following or similar words: "Endorsement of this check by the payee shall constitute a receipt for the items described on the face thereof." A receipt for specific items is thus obtained from the creditor.

Sales Routine

Sales. The office and accounting procedures with respect to sales differ in retail and wholesale businesses; they also depend on the nature and size of the business. The procedures described in the following paragraphs are typical and illustrative; but you should understand that, although they are indicative of methods of establishing internal control, other procedures may be used with equal effectiveness.

In retail stores, where the orders in most cases are oral, the clerk may merely ring up the sale on the cash register. If it is a charge sale, the salesman may make out a sales ticket in duplicate, showing the name and the address of the customer and the items purchased; one copy will be given to the customer, and the other copy will be sent to the bookkeeping department for entry in the records. If the order is to be filled from stock in the storeroom, a third copy may be made for use in filling the order.

In wholesale businesses, most orders are received in written form from the company's salesmen or customers, the sales are made on account, and the goods are shipped or otherwise delivered to the customers. The procedure may be somewhat as follows:

(1) The order goes to the credit department for approval of the customer's credit rating. If the approval is given,

(2) The order goes to a billing clerk who types an invoice in triplicate. The three copies are used as follows:

The second carbon is sent to the stock room for order filling, and thence (with the merchandise) to the shipping room for packing and shipment. After the goods have been shipped, this copy of the invoice is initialed by the shipping clerk and sent to the accounting department, where it is filed, in invoice-number sequence, in a binder which serves as a shipping record. Maintaining a record relative to the shipment of goods is important. In the first place, it serves as evidence of the propriety of the entry debiting Accounts Receivable and crediting the Sales account; in the second place, if the goods are delayed or lost in transit, it furnishes information which may be of assistance in tracing the shipment or in substantiating a claim for loss.

The first carbon remains in the accounting department, where it is checked to determine that it is in agreement with the order, and that the prices, terms, and computations are correct. After the second carbon is returned to the accounting department (thus showing that the goods have been shipped), the first carbon is filed in a sales binder and used by the bookkeeper in making his entries.

The original is mailed to the customer after the goods are shipped.

Statements. In many lines of business, merchants send their customers monthly statements. Such statements show:

(1) The balance owed by the customer at the beginning of the month.

(2) Charges to the customer during the month, for sales.

(3) Credits to the customer during the month, for cash remittances, returns and allowances, and so forth.

(4) The balance owed by the customer at the end of the month.

STATEMENT

R. E. JOHNSON & COMPANY

2913 NORTH WESTERN AVENUE   Telephone: NOrmandy 1-1111

CHICAGO, ILLINOIS_____ July 31,_____ 19 --

IN ACCOUNT WITH

           J. K. Larson

           Whitney, Oklahoma

DATE	INV. NO.	CHARGES	CREDITS	BALANCE
June 30		BALANCE FORWARDED		39.85
July 7	7-456	47.88		87.73
9			39.85	47.88
18	7-890	40.50		88.38

Accounts Are Payable on Tenth of Month Following Delivery

CHAPTER 7

Miscellaneous Operating Matters

Purpose of the chapter. This chapter deals with a number of miscellaneous matters that are customarily encountered in merchandise accounting. Some of them also arise in the accounting for concerns that earn their income by rendering services. Although they are somewhat diverse in nature, it seems desirable to deal with them in a single chapter, rather early in the text, so that the student will be introduced as soon as practicable to comprehensive and realistic statements.

Expense classification. The expense accounts kept by each business depend upon the kinds of expenses which the business incurs and the amount of detailed information desired by the management. Frequently it is possible to distinguish between those expenses that are incurred in connection with selling activities and those that are incurred in the general administration of the business. Whenever such a classification can be made, it may increase the informative value of the income statement to so classify them.

Partial Income Statement

Gross profit on sales			$29,000.00
Deduct expenses:			
Selling:			
Salesmen's salaries	$9,000.00		
Store rent	5,000.00		
Advertising	3,250.00		
Depreciation expense—Store fixtures	410.00		
Total selling expenses		$17,660.00	
General:			
Office salaries	$5,760.00		
Insurance	450.00		
Taxes	550.00		
Depreciation expense—Office equipment	280.00		
Total general expenses		7,040.00	
Total selling and general expenses			24,700.00

Transportation charges. Freight, express, and other transportation costs applicable to merchandise purchased are part of the cost of obtaining the goods. They should be debited to an account with some title such as Transportation In or Freight In and should be added to the purchases in the income statement, as illustrated on the following page.

Partial Income Statement

Sales..			$60,500.00
Deduct cost of goods sold:			
Inventory, June 30, 19—....................		$115,700.00	
Purchases....................	$50,100.00		
Transportation in.............	525.00	50,625.00	
Cost of goods available for sale...........		$166,325.00	
Deduct inventory, July 31, 19—............		117,320.00	
Cost of goods sold.................................			49,005.00
Gross profit on sales....................................			$11,495.00

Freight, express, and other expenses incurred in delivering goods to customers should be debited to an account such as Transportation Out or Freight Out, and should be shown in the income statement under the Selling Expenses caption.

Transportation terms. Transportation terms are expressed thus:

> *F.o.b. destination.* This means free on board cars (or other means of transportation) at destination. In other words, the seller bears the transportation charges.
>
> *F.o.b. shipping point.* This means that the seller bears the cost of putting the merchandise on board the cars (or other means of transportation), but the purchaser bears the transportation charges.

Transportation charges may be paid by the party to a transaction who, according to the terms of sale, does not have to bear them. Thus, a seller shipping merchandise f.o.b. shipping point may prepay the freight as a matter of convenience to his customer and add the freight charges to his bill. To illustrate such a case, assume that transportation charges amounting to $17 on an order for $300, f.o.b. shipping point, are paid by the seller.

Seller's books:

Accounts receivable............................	300.00	
Sales.......................................		300.00
Sale of merchandise, f.o.b. shipping point.		
Accounts receivable............................	17.00	
Cash.......................................		17.00
Payment of transportation charges for convenience of customer.		

Purchaser's books:

Purchases....................................	300.00	
Transportation in..............................	17.00	
Accounts payable.........................		317.00
Receipt of bill for merchandise and prepaid transportation charges.		

A situation somewhat comparable to the above would exist if the purchaser paid the transportation company for the freight charges on merchandise shipped to him f.o.b. destination. He would then deduct the amount paid for transportation from the bill for merchandise received from the seller. The entries would be:

Purchaser's books:

Purchases......................................	1,000.00	
Accounts payable...........................		1,000.00
Merchandise purchased.		
Accounts payable..............................	20.00	
Cash.......................................		20.00
Paid transportation company freight charges on goods shipped f.o.b. destination.		
Accounts payable..............................	980.00	
Cash.......................................		980.00
Paid for merchandise less transportation charges paid locally.		

Seller's books:

Accounts receivable............................	1,000.00	
Sales......................................		1,000.00
Sale on account, f.o.b. destination.		
Cash...	980.00	
Transportation out............................	20.00	
Accounts receivable........................		1,000.00
Collection of account, less freight paid by customer on shipment f.o.b. destination.		

Sales returns and allowances. Customers, after receiving merchandise sold to them, may:

(1) Return the goods because they are not of the kind or quality ordered. When the returned goods are received, the selling company should make entries as follows:

If the customer has paid for the goods, and cash is returned to him:

Sales returns and allowances......................	500.00	
Cash.......................................		500.00

If the customer is given credit for the returned goods:

Sales returns and allowances......................	500.00	
Accounts receivable........................		500.00

(2) Request and receive an allowance on the price. If the allowance is granted, the seller should make entries as follows:

If cash is sent to the customer for the amount of the allowance:

Sales returns and allowances......................	40.00	
Cash.......................................		40.00

If the customer is given credit for the allowance:

Sales returns and allowances...................... 40.00
    Accounts receivable........................ 40.00

The notice sent to the customer that his account has been credited for a return or an allowance may be in the form of a letter, or a credit memorandum may be issued to him. A form for a credit memorandum is illustrated below:

R. E. JOHNSON & COMPANY

2913 North Western Avenue

Chicago

Credit Memo No. __ _____

Date _____

We credit your account as follows:

Reason for Credit	Amount

R. E. Johnson & Company

Per_____

Credit Memorandum

At least two copies should be made of credit memorandums. The original is usually signed by an officer or an employee of the company and is sent to the customer. As evidence that the credit was properly authorized, a copy should be initialed by the person who signed the original; this copy should be filed in a credit memo binder to give the bookkeeper the information he will need in recording the allowance. The initialed copies of the credit memorandums also serve as evidence of the propriety of the entries crediting Accounts Receivable and debiting Sales Returns and Allowances.

The debit balance in the Sales Returns and Allowances account should be shown in the income statement as a deduction from the gross sales, as illustrated in the partial income statement on the following page.

Partial Income Statement

Gross sales...	$5,000.00
Deduct sales returns and allowances.......................	350.00
Net sales..	$4,650.00

Purchase returns and allowances. Goods purchased may be found unsatisfactory and may be returned. Or the goods may be kept if the concern from which they were purchased grants an allowance from the purchase price. Entries for purchase returns or allowances are illustrated below:

Accounts payable...............................	375.00	
Purchase returns and allowances..............		375.00
To charge Davis and Company for goods returned.		

or,

Cash..	50.00	
Purchase returns and allowances..............		50.00
To record return of goods to Osborne Corporation		
and cash received therefor.		

The credit balance of the Purchase Returns and Allowances account should be deducted in the income statement from the debit balance of the Purchases account, as illustrated below:

Cost of goods sold:		
Inventory, August 31, 19—.........................		$ 6,900.00
Add net cost of purchases:		
Purchases..............................	$3,215.00	
Deduct purchase returns and allowances....	122.00	
Net purchases..........................	$3,093.00	
Add transportation in...................	275.00	3,368.00
Cost of goods available for sale.......................		$10,268.00

Trade discounts. Trade discounts are deductions from the list price allowed for various reasons, such as:

(a) To avoid frequent publication of catalogues; the prices can be changed merely by changing the discount rates.

(b) To allow dealers a deduction from an advertised retail price; this practice is followed, for instance, by publishers whose advertisements state the retail prices of their books, dealers being allowed a discount from the published, or list, price.

Trade discounts may be stated as a single rate or as a series of rates. For instance, assume that the list price of merchandise is $1,200 and that a trade discount of 35% is allowed; the sale price is computed as follows:

List price..	$1,200
Less trade discount—35% of $1,200..........................	420
Sale price...	$ 780

Or, assume that the list price is $2,000, and that trade discounts of 30% and 10% are allowed; the sale price is computed as follows:

List price...	$2,000
First discount—30% of $2,000...............................	600
Remainder after first discount.............................	$1,400
Second discount—10% of $1,400..............................	140
Sale price...	$1,260

No entries are made in the accounts for trade discounts; entries for sales and purchases are made at the sale price. For instance, assume that Wharton and Company sold goods to James Benton at a list price of $2,000, subject to trade discounts of 30% and 10%. Wharton and Company would make the following entry:

Accounts receivable...........................	1,260.00	
Sales.....................................		1,260.00

and Benton's entry would be:

Purchases......................................	1,260.00	
Accounts payable...........................		1,260.00

Cash discounts.   Cash discounts are deductions allowed to customers to induce them to pay their bills within a definite time. Cash discount terms are stated on the invoice in the following manner: 2/10; n/30. This means that a 2% discount will be allowed if the invoice is paid within ten days from its date, and that the purchaser, by foregoing the discount, can postpone payment of the invoice until thirty days from its date.

Purchase discounts.   Referring to the above entry recording Benton's purchase of goods, and assuming that he paid the invoice within a ten-day discount period, his entry would be:

Accounts payable..............................	1,260.00	
Purchase discounts...........................		25.20
Cash.......................................		1,234.80
To record payment of Wharton and Company invoice of June 19, less 2% cash discount.		

For many years, purchase discounts were shown in the income statement as a separate item of revenue. This was done on the theory that purchase discounts, like interest earnings, were related to the use of money. It is coming to be recognized that purchase discounts are not revenue, but are a reduction in the cost of goods purchased. Treating them as revenue is based on an absurdity: it assumes that, by purchasing merchandise and paying for it within the discount period, revenue is earned regardless of whether or not the goods have been sold.

The treatment of purchase discounts in the income statement is illustrated on the following page.

Partial Income Statement

Net sales..			$22,998.00
Deduct cost of goods sold:			
Inventory, May 31, 1958............................		$ 5,450.00	
Add net cost of purchases:			
Gross purchases.........................	$17,500.00		
Deduct:			
Purchase returns and allowances.....................	$235.00		
Purchase discounts...........	315.00	550.00	
Net purchases......................	$16,950.00		
Add transportation in.................	415.00	17,365.00	
Cost of goods available for sale......................		$22,815.00	
Deduct inventory, May 31, 1959....................		7,815.00	
Cost of goods sold...			15,000.00
Gross profit on sales......			$ 7,998.00

Sales discounts. Referring to the preceding illustration, the entry to be made by Wharton and Company for the collection of the invoice, less the cash discount, would be:

Cash.................................	1,234.80	
Sales discounts.................................	25.20	
Accounts receivable.........................		1,260.00
To record collection from James Benton of invoice		
of June 19, less 2% cash discount.		

Since sales discounts reduce the amount received for sales, they are shown in the income statement as a deduction from sales, thus:

Partial Income Statement

Gross sales... ...		$23,560.00
Deduct:		
Sales returns and allowances...................	$365.00	
Sales discounts..............................	197.00	562.00
Net sales...		$22,998.00

Accounting for bad debts. At the end of 1958, the first year of operations, a company prepared the following statements:

THE *X Y* COMPANY
Balance Sheet
December 31, 1958
Assets

Cash..		$ 6,000.00
Accounts receivable..................................		13,000.00
Inventory..		19,000.00
		$38,000.00

Liabilities and Stockholders' Equity

Accounts payable....................................		$ 5,000.00
Stockholders' equity:		
Capital stock............................	$25,000.00	
Retained earnings........................	8,000.00	33,000.00
		$38,000.00

THE *X Y* COMPANY
Condensed Income Statement
For the Year Ended December 31, 1958

Sales...	$100,000.00
Deduct cost of goods sold.............................	80,000.00
Gross profit on sales....................................	$ 20,000.00
Deduct expenses...	12,000.00
Net income...	$ 8,000.00

Both the income statement and the balance sheet are probably incorrect because no consideration has been given to losses that will arise if some of the accounts receivable prove to be uncollectible.

The balance sheet shows that there are $13,000 of accounts receivable on the books. But it is a rare thing for businessmen to collect all of their accounts receivable; some losses are almost certain to occur. Therefore, if the balance sheet is fairly to present the financial position of the company, it should show the *net* amount that probably will be collected from the accounts receivable; this will be less than $13,000.

Moreover, the income statement for each period should include all losses and expenses applicable to the period. Losses from uncollectible accounts should therefore be deducted in the statement for the period in which the losses are incurred. In what period are bad debt losses incurred? Bad debt losses result from selling merchandise to customers who do not pay their accounts; such losses are therefore incurred in the period in which the sales are made. If goods were sold in 1958 to customers whose accounts were found in 1959 to be worthless, the loss was *incurred* in 1958. The loss was not incurred in 1959; it was merely *discovered* in that year.

Thus it is evident that both the balance sheet and the income statement will be incorrect unless recognition is given to the probable losses on accounts receivable.

If it is estimated that only $12,000 will be collected from the receivables totaling $13,000, the loss is estimated at $1,000, and the following adjusting journal entry should be made at the end of 1958:

Bad debts expense.................................	1,000.00	
Allowance for doubtful accounts..............		1,000.00
Estimated loss on uncollectible accounts.		

In a statement in which the expenses are classified, the debit balance of the Bad Debts Expense account may be shown in the general expenses section, because passing on credit is usually an administrative function rather than a function of the sales force. Like other expense accounts, this account should be closed to Revenue and Expense.

Nature of allowance account. The estimated loss from uncollectible accounts cannot be credited to Accounts Receivable, because this account should show the gross amount owed by all customers. Therefore, we credit Allowance for Doubtful Accounts, which is an *offset* or *contra* account to Accounts Receivable. The balances of the two accounts are shown in the balance sheet as follows:

```
Accounts receivable......................... $13,000.00
    Less allowance for doubtful accounts......   1,000.00  $12,000.00
```

Writing off uncollectible accounts. After the adjusting journal entry shown above is posted, the ledger contains the following balances:

```
Accounts receivable ......................... $13,000.00
Allowance for doubtful accounts...............             $1,000.00
```

Let us now assume that it has been found impossible to collect $75 owed by P. K. Lane; this amount should be removed from the accounts receivable by the following journal entry:

```
Allowance for doubtful accounts.................   75.00
    Accounts receivable.........................            75.00
    Amount owed by P. K. Lane found to be uncollect-
    ible.
```

It should be noted that the write-off is charged to the allowance account and not to Bad Debts Expense. If we debited the expense account when the *estimated* loss was recorded and later with *ascertained* losses, a double charge to expense would result.

Estimating bad debts expense. The amount to be debited to Bad Debts Expense and credited to Allowance for Doubtful Accounts at the end of a period is frequently computed as a percentage of the net sales for the period. For instance, assume that a ledger contains the following balances on December 31:

```
Accounts receivable......................... $20,000.00
Allowance for doubtful accounts.............              $    315.00
Sales.......................................               215,000.00
Sales returns and allowances................    1,500.00
```

Assume, further, that experience shows that the allowance account should be credited with a provision for losses equal to ½ of 1% of the sales for the year less returns and allowances. The provision is computed as follows:

```
Sales..................................................... $215,000.00
Less sales returns and allowances.........................    1,500.00
Sales less returns and allowances......................... $213,500.00
    Loss provision = ½ of 1% of $213,500 = $1,067.50.
```

This amount is debited to Bad Debts Expense and credited to Allowance for Doubtful Accounts.

The allowance account is now $315.00 + $1,067.50, or $1,382.50, and the accounts receivable will be shown in the balance sheet as follows:

```
Accounts receivable........................  $20,000.00
    Less allowance for doubtful accounts......   1,382.50 $18,617.50
```

Payroll and Sales Taxes

Payroll taxes and employees' income taxes withheld.   The subject of payroll taxes is presented in considerable detail in Appendix 1.   The subject is introduced here in an abbreviated form; the objective is to present the basic debit-credit procedures for recording such taxes.   Since we are concerned in this text with taxes and withholdings applicable to business payrolls, consideration is nct given to taxes on, and withholdings from, the wages of domestic employees.   For the same reason, no treatment is given of social security taxes levied on self-employed persons.

Old-Age and Survivor Insurance Taxes.   The Social Security Act of 1935, as amended, provides for monthly retirement benefits, disability benefits, supplementary monthly benefits to wives, husbands, and dependent children, and death and survivor benefits. At one time, only a relatively few classes of employees and their dependents were eligible for social security benefits.   Over the years, coverage has been extended to an increasing number of employment classifications.   It is estimated that in 1955 nine out of every ten jobs were covered by social security.

The following taxes are levied under the Federal Insurance Contributions Act (F.I.C.A.) to finance the federal social security program:

Employee's tax: If covered by social security, employees are subject to a tax of $2\frac{1}{4}$* per cent of the first $4,200* of wages or salaries received each calendar year.   The taxes levied on employees are withheld by the employers.

Employer's tax: The employer's tax is equal to the amount of tax withheld from the employees' pay.

Several abbreviations are in use which identify these taxes. The initials *F.I.C.A.* refer to the Federal Insurance Contributions Act, the latest (at this writing) act under which the taxes are levied; the initials *O.A.S.I.* are sometimes used, since they serve as an abbreviation of *old-age and survivor insurance*, which words describe the federal social security program; *O.A.B.* or *F.O.A.B.* refer to *old-age benefits* or *federal old-age benefits*, also used frequently as

---

* At the date of this writing.

descriptive of the federal social security program; and the initials *S.S* are used to abbreviate *social security*.

Unemployment Insurance Taxes. Taxes are levied against employers (but not against employees) under the Federal Unemployment Tax Act to obtain funds required to meet the provisions of the Social Security Act relative to unemployment insurance. sometimes called *unemployment compensation.*

The federal unemployment insurance tax rate is 3 per cent; wages in excess of $3,000 paid to any one individual during any one calendar year are not subject to the tax. Although the tax rate is 3 per cent, the employer is entitled to a credit for taxes paid to the states and territories under their unemployment compensation laws This credit cannot be more than 90 per cent of the tax assessed by the federal government at the 3 per cent rate. Because of this provision in the federal law, the states have generally established a 2.7 per cent unemployment compensation tax rate. Since taxable wages are generally (although subject to some minor exceptions) computed in the same manner for both federal and state taxes, the tax rates are usually considered to be as follows:

```
Federal tax—Payable after close of year.........................  .3%
State tax—Payable after close of quarter......................  2.7
   Total.......................................................  3.0%
```

Income taxes withheld. As a general rule, employers are required to withhold federal income taxes when wages and salaries are paid to employees. The amount withheld is affected by a number of factors, such as the length of the pay period, the amount of pay, and the number of dependents claimed by the employee.

Summary. The various payroll deductions and taxes are summarized as follows:

Deducted from employees' wages, and paid to the government by the employer:

> Income taxes of employees.
> Employees' share of F.I.C.A. taxes: 2¼% of first $4,200 of employee's wages.

Payroll tax expense of employer:

> Employer's share of F.I.C.A. taxes—same as employees' share.
> Unemployment compensation taxes:
> > Federal—.3% of first $3,000 of wages earned by each employee.
> > State—2.7% of first $3,000 of wages earned by each employee.

Entries.   The entries in connection with withholding and payroll taxes are presented below.

Entries for the payroll.

If the payroll liability is computed and recorded one or more days prior to payment:

Salesmen's salaries............................	400.00	
Office salaries.................................	600.00	
F.I.C.A. tax liability........................		22.50
Income tax withholding liability..............		120.00
Accrued payroll..............................		857.50
Salaries and withholding taxes thereon.		
Accrued payroll................................	857.50	
Cash..		857.50
Payment of payroll.		

If the two steps above are combined:

Salesmen's salaries............................	400.00	
Office salaries.................................	600.00	
F.I.C.A. tax liability........................		22.50
Income tax withholding liability..............		120.00
Cash..		857.50
Salaries and withholding taxes thereon.		

Entry for employer's payroll taxes.

Payroll taxes expense..........................	52.50	
F.I.C.A. tax liability........................		22.50
Federal unemployment tax liability............		3.00
State unemployment tax liability..............		27.00
Liability for payroll taxes.		

Statement presentation.   The following accounts are liability accounts and their balances are shown in the balance sheet: F.I.C.A. Tax Liability, Income Tax Withholding Liability, Federal Unemployment Tax Liability, State Unemployment Tax Liability.

Since the withheld amounts and the employer's share of the F.I.C.A. tax are reported on the same form and remitted to the same agency of the federal government, it is acceptable to use one liability account in place of the two noted above, as shown below:

F.I.C.A. Tax Liability   } Withholding and F.I.C.A.
Income Tax Withholding Liability }   Tax Liabilities

The tax expense is presented in the income statement either classified as a general expense or apportioned among the expense classifications according to the payroll apportionment.   In other words, the payroll tax on a salesman's salary may be classified as a selling expense and the payroll tax on a bookkeeper's salary may be classified as a general expense.

Entries when taxes are paid. When the taxes are paid and the amounts withheld are remitted to the federal or state government, the liability accounts are debited and Cash is credited.

Payroll tax accruals. Although payroll taxes (old-age and survivor insurance taxes and unemployment insurance taxes) are based on wages and salaries *paid* to employees, a proper allocation of expenses to periods seems to require an accrual accounting procedure with respect to them.

For example, assume that an adjusting entry is made on December 31 for wages earned by employees during December but not payable to them until January 5. The cost of the employees' services in December includes the wages that will be paid to them on January 5, plus the taxes that will be assessed against these wage payments. To correctly state the December cost of services, accrual entries should be made for both elements of this cost: the wages and the taxes thereon.

No similar adjusting entries are required for social security and income tax withholdings to be made from January 5 wage payments, because the withholdings are not expenses of the business.

Sales taxes. A number of taxes that are levied on the consumer are collected by the businessman. The businessman, in turn, remits such collections to the unit of government levying the tax. Such taxes include sales taxes, luxury taxes, transportation taxes, and gasoline taxes. The accounting for such taxes can be illustrated by an example based on a 2% retail sales tax.

Entries for sales include credits to Liability for Sales Taxes for the amount of the tax collected or charged to the customer, thus:

Cash	102.00	
Sales		100.00
Liability for sales taxes		2.00
Cash sale.		

When the tax is remitted to the government, the liability account is debited and Cash is credited. If the tax law specifies that the amount to be remitted is to be computed by multiplying the sales for the period by 2%, the amount due may differ from the amount collected from customers and credited to Liability for Sales Taxes. Any excess due is a tax expense; if the amount due is less than the amount collected, a miscellaneous revenue is realized.

A variant of the above procedure is described below. The merchant buys sales tax coupons from the state, debiting Sales Tax Coupons (an asset account) and crediting Cash. When sales are made, coupons are given to the customer for the amount of the tax charged him, and entries are made debiting Cash (or Accounts Receivable) and crediting Sales and Sales Tax Coupons.

CHAPTER 8

Statement and Ledger Organization.   Classified Statements

Introduction.   Many financial statements are widely circulated.   Stockholders, banks, stock brokers, investment dealers, governmental agencies, and investors are frequent users of financial statements.   Members of the management group of a business review and analyze a considerable number of accounting statements in the regular course of their work.   Consider the confusion and inconvenience that statement users might suffer if every business followed its own preference of account arrangement in financial statements.

To minimize the misunderstanding and annoyance that would be likely to prevail if no uniformity existed relating to the form and content of financial statements, accountants and businessmen have developed some account groupings and presentation techniques that have become rather widely used in practice.   The balance sheet of The Potter Company illustrates some of these conventional statement practices.

<table>
<tr><td colspan="4" align="center">THE POTTER COMPANY</td><td align="right">Exhibit A</td></tr>
<tr><td colspan="4" align="center">Balance Sheet</td><td></td></tr>
<tr><td colspan="4" align="center">December 31, 1958</td><td></td></tr>
<tr><td colspan="4" align="center">Assets</td><td></td></tr>
<tr><td colspan="5">Current assets:</td></tr>
<tr><td>Cash...</td><td></td><td>$18,325.00</td><td></td><td></td></tr>
<tr><td>Temporary investments............................</td><td></td><td>8,000.00</td><td></td><td></td></tr>
<tr><td>Accounts receivable....................</td><td>$16,120.00</td><td></td><td></td><td></td></tr>
<tr><td>Less allowance for doubtful accounts....</td><td>620.00</td><td>15,500.00</td><td></td><td></td></tr>
<tr><td>Notes receivable.................................</td><td></td><td>3,000.00</td><td></td><td></td></tr>
<tr><td>Accrued interest receivable.........................</td><td></td><td>100.00</td><td></td><td></td></tr>
<tr><td>Inventory.......................................</td><td></td><td>26,000.00</td><td></td><td></td></tr>
<tr><td>Prepaid rent....................................</td><td></td><td>500.00</td><td></td><td></td></tr>
<tr><td>Unexpired insurance..............................</td><td></td><td>50.00</td><td>$ 71,475.00</td><td></td></tr>
<tr><td colspan="5">Sundry assets:</td></tr>
<tr><td>Land (Held for future use).........................</td><td></td><td>$15,000.00</td><td></td><td></td></tr>
<tr><td>Long-term investments............................</td><td></td><td>12,000.00</td><td>27,000.00</td><td></td></tr>
<tr><td colspan="5">Fixed assets:</td></tr>
<tr><td>Parking lot......................................</td><td></td><td>$13,000.00</td><td></td><td></td></tr>
<tr><td>Store fixtures...........................</td><td>$10,000.00</td><td></td><td></td><td></td></tr>
<tr><td>Less accumulated depreciation..........</td><td>4,400.00</td><td>5,600.00</td><td></td><td></td></tr>
<tr><td>Delivery equipment.....................</td><td>$ 3,000.00</td><td></td><td></td><td></td></tr>
<tr><td>Less accumulated depreciation..........</td><td>1,500.00</td><td>1,500.00</td><td>20,100.00</td><td></td></tr>
<tr><td></td><td></td><td></td><td>$118,575.00</td><td></td></tr>
</table>

Liabilities and Stockholders' Equity

Current liabilities:

Accounts payable.................................	$ 6,113.00	
Notes payable.....................................	1,000.00	
Accrued interest payable...........................	20.00	
Accrued salaries...................................	400.00	
Estimated income tax payable......................	3,200.00	
Liability for sales taxes............................	600.00	
Withholding and F.I.C.A. tax liabilities..............	300.00	
Federal unemployment tax liability..................	36.00	
State unemployment tax liability.....................	81.00	$ 11,750.00

Long-term liability:

Mortgage payable...		15,000.00

Stockholders' equity:

Capital stock......................................	$60,000.00	
Retained earnings, per Exhibit B....................	31,825.00	91,825.00
		$118,575.00

Balance sheet classifications. The balance sheet illustrated above is called a *classified* balance sheet. The classifications used in a balance sheet depend upon the nature of the business and the types of balance sheet accounts appearing in the ledger. The principal balance sheet categories are stated below.

Assets:

Current assets: Cash and other assets, such as temporary investments in securities, accounts and notes receivable, inventory, and prepaid expenses, that presumably will be converted into cash or used during a normal operating cycle. Such items are held to be indicative of short-run debt-paying ability.

An operating cycle can be described as follows: business operations consist of a round of conversions—cash to inventories, to receivables, to cash; the average time required to complete this round is an *operating cycle*. The time period of an operating cycle depends on the nature of the business.

The current assets are customarily listed in the following order: cash, securities, receivables, accrued receivables, inventories, and short-term expense prepayments. Short-term expense prepayments are regarded as current assets because a company with, say, $18,325 of cash and a $500 rent prepayment for one month is in essentially the same position as a company with $18,825 of cash but faced with the necessity of immediately spending $500 for rent.

Sundry assets: Any assets, such as land held for future use or long-term investments in securities, which do not fall into the other classifications.

Fixed assets: Property of a relatively permanent nature used in the operations of the business and not intended for sale.

Tangible fixed assets, such as land, buildings, furniture and fixtures, office equipment, and delivery equipment, are customarily listed according to their use-life, assets with the longest use-life being listed first, assets with the shortest use-life being listed last. Intangibles, such as patents and franchises, also shown under the Fixed Assets caption, are usually listed after the tangible assets.

Liabilities and stockholders' equity:

Current liabilities: The debts or obligations that, according to reasonable expectations, are to be satisfied within the operating-cycle period or one year, whichever is longer. Items of revenue collected in advance, which are to be earned by the future performance of services or delivery of merchandise within the operating cycle, are properly classifiable as current liabilities, because the earning of such revenue normally requires the utilization of current assets.

The excess of the current assets over the current liabilities is called *working capital.*

Long-term liabilities: Bonds, mortgages, and other debts not classified as current liabilities.

Stockholders' equity: The capital stock and retained earnings.

Additional illustrative statements. The statement of retained earnings and the income statement of The Potter Company are shown below. Notice that many of the accounts introduced in the preceding chapter are included in the illustration. Notice also the additional matters illustrated in the statements.

Income tax. The Income Tax account should be debited for the estimated income tax in the period in which the taxable income was earned. As a general rule, the balance of the Income Tax account is shown as the last item in the income statement in the manner illustrated on page 102.

Other revenue. Businesses sometimes earn incidental revenues in addition to those derived from their principal operations. Such earnings may be shown in the income statement under the caption "Other Revenue," after the net operating income. Examples include revenues from interest, rent, and dividends on shares of stock owned by the business.

Other expense. Expenses may be incurred which cannot properly be classified either as selling expense or as general expense. Interest expense is an example. Such expenses are presented in the income statement under the caption "Other Expense," as illustrated on page 102.

THE POTTER COMPANY   Exhibit B

Statement of Retained Earnings
For the Year Ended December 31, 1958

Retained earnings, December 31, 1957............................	$28,950.00
Add net income, per Exhibit C....................................	6,875.00
Total..	$35,825.00
Deduct dividends..	4,000.00
Retained earnings, December 31, 1958............................	$31,825.00

THE POTTER COMPANY   Exhibit C

Income Statement
For the Year Ended December 31, 1958

Gross sales..			$103,500.00
Sales returns and allowances........................	$ 900.00		
Sales discounts....................................	1,800.00	2,700.00	
Net sales...			$100,800.00
Cost of goods sold:			
Inventory, December 31, 1957......................	$25,000.00		
Purchases............................. $65,000.00			
Purchase returns and allow-			
ances.................... $1,000.00			
Purchase discounts.......... 1,200.00	2,200.00		
Net purchases......................	$62,800.00		
Transportation in...................	2,000.00	64,800.00	
Cost of goods available for sale.......................	$89,800.00		
Inventory, December 31, 1958......................	26,000.00	63,800.00	
Gross profit on sales..			$ 37,000.00
Selling expenses:			
Store rent............................... $ 6,000.00			
Advertising............................. 1,800.00			
Depreciation expense—Store fixtures...... 400.00			
Depreciation expense—Delivery equipment 500.00			
Other delivery expense.................... 2,200.00			
Freight out............................. 1,800.00			
Salesmen's salaries..................... 8,000.00			
Miscellaneous selling expenses............ 600.00	$21,300.00		
General expenses:			
Office expenses......................... $ 2,130.00			
Taxes, other than income and payroll..... 596.00			
Bad debts expense...................... 504.00			
Office salaries......................... 3,000.00			
Payroll taxes expense.................... 495.00			
Insurance expense...................... 300.00	7,025.00	28,325.00	
Net operating income..			$ 8,675.00
Other revenue:			
Rent of land........................... $ 1,200.00			
Interest earned......................... 930.00	$ 2,130.00		
Other expense:			
Interest expense....................................	730.00	1,400.00	
Net income before income tax...................................			$ 10,075.00
Income tax..			3,200.00
Net income...			$ 6,875.00

Exhibit letters. Refer to the balance sheet of The Potter Company. It will be noted that it is identified as *Exhibit A.* The additional illustrative statements are likewise identified as *Exhibit B* and *Exhibit C,* respectively.

Such identification markings are used primarily for cross-reference purposes. For example, the balance sheet shows the retained earnings at the end of the year and refers to Exhibit B, where further details regarding retained earnings can be found. In a similar fashion, the statement of retained earnings shows the net income for the year and refers to Exhibit C, where details of revenue and expense can be found.

Unusual and nonrecurring items. For many years it was standard accounting procedure to show in the income statement only the results of *regular operations* for the *current period,* and to show in the statement of retained earnings any corrections of the net income or loss of prior periods and any unusual, extraordinary, or nonrecurring gains and losses, such as those resulting from sales of investments and fixed assets. Statements prepared in this manner are said to be in accordance with the *current operating concept* of net income; they are illustrated below.

THE JONES CORPORATION	Exhibit C

Income Statement
For the Year Ended December 31, 1958

Net sales..	$1,204,960.00
Deduct cost of goods sold..........................	826,940.00
Gross profit on sales..............................	$ 378,020.00
Deduct expenses...................................	261,290.00
Net income..	$ 116,730.00

THE JONES CORPORATION	Exhibit B

Statement of Retained Earnings
For the Year Ended December 31, 1958

Retained earnings, December 31, 1957.................		$ 326,215.00
Add:		
Net income for the year—per Exhibit C..............		116,730.00
Correction of net income for 1956 and 1957 for excess depreciation provided in error...................		19,600.00
Total...		$ 462,545.00
Deduct:		
Loss on sale of abandoned plant..........	$15,325.00	
Dividends............................	90,000.00	105,325.00
Retained earnings, December 31, 1958.................		$ 357,220.00

At the present time many accountants advocate the *all-inclusive* or *clean surplus concept;* that is, they believe that corrections of the net income or loss of prior periods and extraneous gains and losses should be shown in the income statement. Statements prepared in accordance with the all-inclusive concept of net income are shown below.

THE JONES CORPORATION	Exhibit C

Income Statement
For the Year Ended December 31, 1958

Net sales...............................		$1,204,960.00
Deduct cost of goods sold...............		826,940.00
Gross profit on sales...................		$ 378,020.00
Deduct expenses........................		261,290.00
Net operating income...................		$ 116,730.00
Add—deduct*:		
Correction of net income for 1956 and 1957 for excess depreciation provided in error......................	$19,600.00	
Loss on sale of abandoned plant........	15,325.00*	4,275.00
Net income............................		$ 121,005.00

THE JONES CORPORATION	Exhibit B

Statement of Retained Earnings
For the Year Ended December 31, 1958

Retained earnings, December 31, 1957.................	$ 326,215.00
Add net income for the year—per Exhibit C.........	121,005.00
Total.................................	$ 447,220.00
Deduct dividends.......................	90,000.00
Retained earnings, December 31, 1958.......	$ 357,220.00

Some of the arguments presented by the two schools of thought are briefly stated below.

Current operating concept. The proponents of the current operating concept of net income support their position by the following arguments:

Investors are more interested in the net income of a business than in any other one figure shown by the annual statements. And the net income in which they are interested is that which resulted from normal operating transactions. If extraneous gains and losses and corrections of the reported net income of prior periods are included, it is difficult to determine the trend of a company's operations.

If the stated net income of one year is affected by a material correction of the net income of a prior year, the error is compounded—the current year's net income is overstated or understated to the extent that the net income of the past was understated or overstated. Indicated trends are therefore misleading.

Because of the danger that some readers of accounting reports are likely to assume that the income statement tells all that is to be told about profits and losses and are not aware of the significance of matters disclosed in the statement of retained earnings, a combined statement of income and retained earnings is sometimes advocated. Such a statement, prepared in accordance with the current operating concept, is shown below:

THE JONES CORPORATION

Statement of Income and Retained Earnings

For the Year Ended December 31, 1958

Net sales...		$1,204,960.00
Deduct cost of goods sold............................		826,940.00
Gross profit on sales..................................		$ 378,020.00
Deduct expenses.....................................		261,290.00
Net income...		$ 116,730.00
Add:		
Retained earnings, December 31, 1957...............		326,215.00
Correction of net income for 1956 and 1957 for excess depreciation provided in error....................		19,600.00
Total...		$ 462,545.00
Deduct:		
Loss on sale of abandoned plant..........	$15,325.00	
Dividends.............................	90,000.00	105,325.00
Retained earnings, December 31, 1958................		$ 357,220.00

All-inclusive concept. The proponents of the all-inclusive concept present the following arguments:

> The total of the amounts shown as net income in the statements for a series of years should be the aggregate net income for those years; this will not be the case if corrections of the reported net income of prior periods are shown in the statement of retained earnings.
>
> When an accountant charges retained earnings with a loss because he considers it extraordinary or extraneous, he implies that it is nonrecurring. But a study of business history indicates that such losses do recur.
>
> The line of demarcation between operating items and extraordinary and extraneous items is not clear-cut and is often a matter of opinion. Studies of annual reports have shown many inconsistencies in classifications between income and retained earnings made by different companies, and by the same company in different years. Wide variations in net income can be caused by such inconsistencies.
>
> Many so-called extraordinary or extraneous charges and credits are closely related to operations—not to the operations of a single year, but to those of a series of years.
>
> They may be regarded as corrections of the stated net income of a number of prior years; for instance, a gain or loss

on the disposal of a fixed asset may be regarded as a correction of prior years' charges for depreciation.

Or extraordinary charges may relieve future periods of operating charges which otherwise would be required; this is the case when fixed assets are written down or written off and future years are thereby relieved of depreciation charges that otherwise would be required.

Concluding note.   Accountants have not yet arrived at a unanimity of opinion with respect to these conflicting concepts of net income.   Differences exist in practice.   The American Accounting Association, in its official publications, has taken a strong position in favor of the clean surplus concept.   The Committee on Accounting Procedure of the American Institute of Certified Public Accountants has taken a somewhat modified position; in its Bulletin No. 43, the committee stated:

> "It is the opinion of the committee that there should be a general presumption that all items of profit and loss recognized during the period are to be used in determining the figure reported as net income. The only possible exception to this presumption relates to items which in the aggregate are material in relation to the company's net income and are clearly not identifiable with or do not result from the usual or typical business operations of the period."

In view of the fact that practice and authoritative opinion leave this matter still in a somewhat controversial state, it is perhaps undesirable for a textbook to take a firm, definite position on the question.   An accounting student should be familiar with both points of view, and should be adaptable enough to follow either approach, as directed.

Until the issue is more clearly resolved, an instructor is justified in suggesting the adoption of either point of view, if for no other reason than to achieve class uniformity.

Ledger Organization

Account numbers.   Most ledgers are kept on cards or in loose-leaf binders.   Each account is given a number, and the cards or sheets are kept in numerical order.

It is advisable to number accounts in a systematic manner so that the account numbers indicate classifications and relationships. Numbering systems differ, but the following chart of accounts illustrates the general principle.

Observe that each account number contains four digits, and that the first digit at the left indicates a main classification, as shown on the following page.

1---   Assets and related contra accounts.
2---   Liabilities.
3---   Stockholders' equity.
4---   Sales and related accounts.
5---   Purchases and related accounts.
6---   Selling expenses.
7---   General expenses.
8---   Other revenue and expense.
9---   Closing account.

The second digit indicates a main subclassification, thus:

11--   Current assets and related contra accounts.
12--   Sundry assets.
13--   Fixed assets and related contra accounts.

21--   Current liabilities.
24--   Long-term liabilities.

The third and fourth digits indicate further subclassifications and relationships, thus:

2180   Withholding and F.I.C.A. Tax Liabilities.
2181   Federal Unemployment Tax Liability.
2182   State Unemployment Tax Liability.

The third digit, "8," is common to a group of liability accounts for withholding and payroll taxes. The various taxes are differentiated by the fourth digit.

The third and fourth digits in many instances are selected for reasons of consistency, or to show relationships.

As illustrations of numbers chosen for purposes of consistency, observe the following account numbers. The first digit indicates whether the account represents an asset or a liability; the fact that the item is current is indicated by the second digit; the final "30" indicates an account; the final "40" indicates a note.

1130   Accounts Receivable.
2130   Accounts Payable.

1140   Notes Receivable.
2140   Notes Payable.

Also observe that contra accounts, representing deductions from related accounts, are numbered with a final "8" or "9":

1130   Accounts Receivable.
1139   Allowance for Doubtful Accounts.

1350   Delivery Equipment.
1359   Accumulated Depreciation—Delivery Equipment.

4000   Sales.
4008   Sales Returns and Allowances.
4009   Sales Discounts.

As illustrations of account numbers assigned to show relationships, observe the following:

1191   Unexpired Insurance.
7091   Insurance Expense.

2155   Accrued Salaries.
7055   Office Salaries.

Illustrative chart of accounts.   The following chart of accounts is that of The Potter Company:

CURRENT ASSETS:

   1110   Cash.
   1120   Temporary Investments.
   1130   Accounts Receivable.
   1139   Allowance for Doubtful Accounts.
   1140   Notes Receivable.
   1154   Accrued Interest Receivable.
   1170   Inventory.
   1190   Prepaid Rent.
   1191   Unexpired Insurance.

SUNDRY ASSETS:

   1210   Land.
   1220   Long-term Investments.

FIXED ASSETS:

   1310   Parking Lot.
   1320   Store Fixtures.
   1329   Accumulated Depreciation—Store Fixtures.
   1350   Delivery Equipment.
   1359   Accumulated Depreciation—Delivery Equipment.

CURRENT LIABILITIES:

   2130   Accounts Payable.
   2140   Notes Payable.
   2154   Accrued Interest Payable.
   2155   Accrued Salaries.
   2160   Estimated Income Tax Payable.
   2170   Liability for Sales Taxes.
   2180   Withholding and F.I.C.A. Tax Liabilities.
   2181   Federal Unemployment Tax Liability.
   2182   State Unemployment Tax Liability.

LONG-TERM LIABILITIES:

2410   Mortgage Payable.

STOCKHOLDERS' EQUITY:

3510   Capital Stock.
3610   Retained Earnings.
3910   Dividends.

SALES AND RELATED ACCOUNTS:

4000   Sales.
4008   Sales Returns and Allowances.
4009   Sales Discounts.

PURCHASES AND RELATED ACCOUNTS:

5170   Purchases.
5178   Purchase Returns and Allowances.
5179   Purchase Discounts.
5200   Transportation In.

SELLING EXPENSES:

6001   Store Rent.
6002   Advertising.
6029   Depreciation Expense—Store Fixtures.
6059   Depreciation Expense—Delivery Equipment.
6070   Other Delivery Expense.
6071   Freight Out.
6080   Salesmen's Salaries.
6090   Miscellaneous Selling Expenses.

GENERAL EXPENSES:

7001   Office Expenses.
7011   Taxes, Other Than Income and Payroll.
7049   Bad Debts Expense.
7055   Office Salaries.
7085   Payroll Taxes Expense.
7091   Insurance Expense.

OTHER REVENUE:

8010   Rent of Land.
8054   Interest Earned.

OTHER EXPENSES:

8154   Interest Expense.
8160   Income Tax.

CLOSING ACCOUNT:

9000   Revenue and Expense.

Accounting Terminology Trends

Synonymous terms. A number of accounting terms are synonymous. Important examples are set forth in the following partial list:

> Allowance for uncollectible accounts—Reserve for bad debts—Provision for doubtful accounts
> Accumulated depreciation—Allowance for depreciation—Reserve for depreciation
> Stockholders' equity—Net worth—Capital—Capital stock and surplus
> Retained earnings—Earned surplus—Accumulated income
> Income statement—Statement of earnings—Profit and loss statement

Although the terms in each of the above groups are synonymous, it does not follow that they are equally popular in usage. The objective of the accountant is to use terms in financial statements that are least susceptible of being misunderstood. Therefore, a certain amount of experimentation with terminology is always present. If a substitute term appears to foster better understanding of financial statements, its usage increases.

Trends. It is probably desirable for the accounting student to become familiar with alternative terminology and to observe recent trends of usage. The following tabulations, based on a survey of annual reports of 600 companies,* show such information.

WORDS USED IN BALANCE SHEETS TO DESCRIBE THE DEDUCTION
FOR DOUBTFUL ACCOUNTS

	1955	1952	1950	1948
Most Frequently Used:				
"Allowance for"	257	210	170	88
"Reserve for"	181	213	247	337
"Provision for"	33	39	36	29

The survey shows that "doubtful" is the word which now most frequently follows the above terms, appearing in 257 of the 1955 balance sheets examined in the survey. Thus, "Allowance for Doubtful Accounts" seems to be the most widely used title for this account.

---

* *Accounting Trends and Techniques in Published Corporate Annual Reports,* 10th ed., 1956, American Institute of Certified Public Accountants, New York, New York.

WORDS USED IN BALANCE SHEETS TO DESCRIBE
ACCUMULATED DEPRECIATION

	1955	1952	1950	1948
Most Frequently Used.				
"Accumulated"	190	139	98	42
"Allowance for"	124	124	107	74
"Reserve for"	165	205	276	396

It appears that usage of "Reserve for Depreciation" is noticeably declining while "Accumulated Depreciation" is making significant gains.

WORDS USED TO DESCRIBE STOCKHOLDERS' EQUITY
SECTION IN BALANCE SHEETS

	1955	1953	1952	1951
Most Frequently Used:				
"Stockholders' (Shareholders') equity"	180	146	127	106
"Net worth"	1	5	7	8
"Capital"	67	73	76	78
"Capital stock and surplus"	139	141	150	168

TREND FROM "EARNED SURPLUS"

	1955	1952	1950	1948
Number of Companies:				
Replacing "earned surplus" (Usually changing to "retained earnings")	349	303	248	99
Retaining "earned surplus"	251	297	352	501

The above shows the marked trend away from "Earned Surplus" in favor of "Retained Earnings."

WORDS USED TO DESCRIBE "INCOME" STATEMENT

	1955	1952	1950	1948
Most Frequently Used:				
"Income"	362	336	326	332
"Earnings"	132	116	88	45
"Profit and loss"	58	97	131	170

CHAPTER 9

Notes and Acceptances

Notes

Definition. The following definition is quoted from the Negotiable Instruments Act: "A negotiable promissory note within the meaning of this act is an unconditional promise in writing made by one person to another, signed by the maker, engaging to pay on demand or at a fixed or determinable future time a sum certain in money to order or bearer."

Maturity. Notes may be drawn to mature:

(1) On a date named in the note, thus: "On June 30, 19—, I promise to pay."

(2) On demand, thus: "On demand, I promise to pay."

(3) Upon the expiration of a stated period of time; the time may be stated in several ways, as indicated below.

    (a) Years, thus: "One year after date, I promise to pay." Such notes will mature in a subsequent year on the same day of the same month as the date of issue, except that notes issued on February 29, payable in a year having only 28 days in February, will mature on February 28.

    (b) Months, thus: "Three months after date, I promise to pay." Such notes will mature in a subsequent month on the same day of the month as the date of issue, except that: (1) notes dated on the 31st of a month and maturing in a month having only 30 days will mature on the 30th of the month; and (2) notes dated on the 29th, 30th, or 31st of a month and maturing in February will mature on the last day of February.

    (c) Days, thus: "Sixty days after date, I promise to pay." The method of determining the maturity of such notes is illustrated by the following computation of the maturity of a 60-day note dated December 15, 1958:

Remaining days in December	16
Days in January	31
	47
Days in February	13 Maturity
	60

Notes Receivable

Notes Receivable account.   Since a separate account is not kept with each note, the Notes Receivable account may show details, as in the following illustration.

Notes Receivable

19—				19—			
July	3	J. B. Gates 60 da.	a 1,000 00	Aug.	1	J. F. Cole	d 1,000 00
	7	C. L. Peters 30 da.	b 1,500 00				
	18	H. N. Burt 30 da.	c 1,000 00				
	22	J. F. Cole 10 da.	d 1,000 00				

Each debit entry shows the name of the maker and the time the note is to run.   The credits are identified with the debits by names and cross-reference letters; thus, the credit records the collection of the Cole note, as evidenced by the name and the reference *d.*

The number of days shown in each entry is the number of days the note runs.   Since the note may bear a date earlier than that of the entry, the maturity of the note is not necessarily the stated number of days after the date of the entry.

Entries for note receivable transactions.   Entries for note receivable transactions are described below.

Entries for receipt of notes.   The entries for the receipt of non-interest-bearing and interest-bearing notes are the same.

> If a note is received for a cash loan, debit Notes Receivable and credit Cash.
>
> If a note is received to settle, or apply on, an account receivable, debit Notes Receivable and credit Accounts Receivable.
>
> If a note is received immediately for a sale, the entry *might be:* debit Notes Receivable and credit Sales.   However, it is considered better practice to make the two following entries: debit Accounts Receivable and credit Sales; debit Notes Receivable and credit Accounts Receivable.

Entries for collection of notes.   The entries for the collection of notes depend on whether or not they are interest-bearing.

> If the note does not bear interest, debit Cash and credit Notes Receivable.
>
> If the note bears interest, debit Cash and credit Notes Receivable and Interest Earned.   If an end-of-period adjusting entry was made for accrued interest on the note, the amount of the accrual should be credited to Accrued Interest Receivable when the interest is collected, and the remainder should be credited to Interest Earned.

Entries if note is dishonored.   If the maker of a note does not settle for it at maturity, the note is said to be *dishonored*.   It should be charged back to Accounts Receivable.

> If the note does not bear interest, debit Accounts Receivable and credit Notes Receivable.
>
> If the note bears interest, debit Accounts Receivable and credit Notes Receivable and Interest Earned.   The interest has been earned and the debtor owes the interest as well as the face of the note.

If, at the maturity of a note, we make a partial collection, only the uncollected portion should be charged back to Accounts Receivable, because the note was only partially dishonored.

Entries for a renewal note.   If a note is wholly or partially dishonored and a new note is received, the entry for the dishonor should be made as described above and the receipt of the new note should be recorded by debiting Notes Receivable and crediting Accounts Receivable.

Notes Payable

Notes Payable account.   Notes payable are also recorded in one account.   Each credit entry shows the name of the payee and the time the note is to run.   The debits recording payments are identified with the credits by writing the names of the payees and by using cross-reference letters in the manner illustrated in the Notes Receivable account on page 113.

Entries for note payable transactions.   Entries for note payable transactions are described below.   The student is already familiar with some of them.

> If a note is issued for a cash loan, debit Cash and credit Notes Payable.
>
> If a note is issued to settle, or apply on, an account payable, debit Accounts Payable and credit Notes Payable.
>
> If a note is issued immediately for a purchase, make two entries: debit Purchases and credit Accounts Payable; debit Accounts Payable and credit Notes Payable.

Entries for payment of notes.   The entries for the payment of notes without interest and with interest are stated below:

> If the note does not bear interest, debit Notes Payable and credit Cash.
>
> If the note bears interest, debit Notes Payable and Interest Expense and credit Cash.   If an end-of-period adjusting

entry was made for accrued interest on the note, the amount of the accrual should be debited to Accrued Interest Payable when the interest is paid, and the remainder should be debited to Interest Expense.

Dishonor of a note payable.   If we hold a note receivable and it is dishonored at maturity, we charge it back to Accounts Receivable so that the account will show, for credit-information purposes, that a customer has dishonored a note.   If we dishonor our note payable, there is no similar reason for transferring the amount of the note from Notes Payable to Accounts Payable.   Therefore, we shall make no entry to show that we have dishonored the note.

If the note bears interest and we do not pay it, we should debit Interest Expense and credit Accrued Interest Payable.

Entries if note is partially paid.   If, at maturity of a note payable, we pay only a portion of it, our entries should be:

If the note does not bear interest, debit Notes Payable and credit Cash for the amount of the payment.

If the note bears interest, debit Interest Expense for the amount of the interest, debit Notes Payable for the remainder of the payment, and credit Cash.

Entries for a renewal note.   A new note given for all or a portion of the principal of a dishonored note should be recorded by debiting Notes Payable and crediting Notes Payable.   The entry is required to show the elimination or reduction of the old note and the issuance of the new one.

Acceptances

Drafts.   Instead of asking a debtor to give him a promissory note, a creditor may "draw a draft" on the debtor.   Such a draft is illustrated below:

$100.00   Chicago, Illinois, June 15, 19 --

Thirty days after date _____   Pay to the order of **OURSELVES**

One Hundred-no/100--Dollars

   To___George Hill,____

           Freeport, Illinois   *Peter Rowe*

Parties to a draft.   The parties to a draft are:

The drawer—the person who draws and signs the draft.
The drawee—the person to whom the draft is addressed.
The payee—the person to whom the payment is to be made.

Although there are always three *parties* to a draft, only two *persons* may be involved.   Thus, Peter Rowe is both the drawer and the payee of the illustrative draft.   If Rowe had ordered Hill to pay Robinson, Rowe would have been the drawer, Hill the drawee, and Robinson the payee; such drafts are now rarely used.

Acceptance.   The draft illustrated above should be presented to Hill to obtain his agreement to pay it at maturity.   This agreement is called *acceptance* of the draft and is expressed in the manner illustrated below:

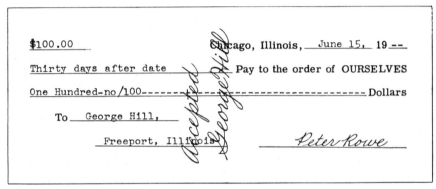

After a draft has been accepted, it is called an *acceptance.* Thus, the word *acceptance* has two meanings: the act of accepting, and an accepted draft.

Maturity of acceptances.   Acceptances may be payable:

(1) A certain period after the date of the draft; in such cases, the time is expressed thus: "Thirty days after date, pay to the order of (etc.)."

A draft drawn on June 15, payable thirty days after date, will be due on July 15, regardless of the date on which it is accepted.   Since the date of acceptance has no bearing on the maturity of the draft, the date of acceptance need not be shown.

(2) A certain period after the date when the draft is accepted by the drawee; the time may be expressed thus: "Thirty days after sight, pay to the order of (etc.)," *or* "At thirty days' sight, pay to the order of (etc.)."

A draft drawn on June 15, payable thirty days after sight, and accepted on June 20, will be due on July 20. Since the date of acceptance of such a draft determines the date of its maturity, the date of acceptance should be shown, thus:

Accepted
June 20, 19—
Drawee's signature

Accounting for acceptances. An accepted draft, like a promissory note, is a debtor's written agreement to pay a certain sum of money at a definite future date. Therefore, the accounting for acceptances is the same as the accounting for notes, previously described. Of course, no entry is made by the drawer at the time he draws the draft, because the drawee may refuse to accept.

Since a promissory note and an acceptance are similar in nature, it is customary to record both notes and acceptances in the Notes Receivable and Notes Payable accounts.

Draft for collection purposes. Drafts are occasionally used to reduce a past-due account to a written promise to pay. If a debtor will not pay his account, he may consent to give a note or accept a draft. If a draft is used, it is drawn by the creditor and sent to the debtor for acceptance. If the draft is accepted:

> The drawee debits Accounts Payable and credits Notes Payable.
>
> The drawer debits Notes Receivable and credits Accounts Receivable.

Draft per terms of sale. Sometimes the terms of sale require the purchaser of merchandise to accept a draft for the amount of the invoice.

If the purchaser has established a credit standing with the seller, the merchandise is shipped on a straight bill of lading and the draft is sent to the purchaser for acceptance.

If the purchaser has not established a credit standing, a draft with an order bill of lading attached may be sent to a bank in the purchaser's city. The purchaser cannot get the goods from the railroad without the bill of lading, and he cannot get the bill of lading from the bank without accepting the draft.

Sequence of Entries

Seller's entry at time of sale:

Accounts receivable............................	300.00	
Sales......................................		300.00
Sale of merchandise; terms, 30-day acceptance.		

Purchaser's entry at time of receipt of goods and acceptance of draft:

```
Purchases.....................................    300.00
        Accounts payable...........................           300.00
        Purchase of merchandise; terms, draft due 30 days
    after sight.

Accounts payable..............................    300.00
        Notes payable..............................           300.00
        Acceptance of 30-day draft for amount of purchase
    today.
```

Seller's entry when acceptance is received:

```
Notes receivable..............................    300.00
        Accounts receivable........................           300.00
        Acceptance received.
```

Discounting Notes

Discounting a note payable.   When a note payable is issued to a bank for a loan, the interest usually is deducted in advance.   For instance, assume that we give a bank a 60-day note for $1,000, and that the bank charges discount at 6%.   The discount is $10, and we shall receive the proceeds, $990.

Entry if note matures before the end of the accounting period:

```
Cash.........................................    990.00
Interest expense..............................     10.00
        Notes payable..............................         1,000.00
        Note due in 60 days, discounted at bank.
```

Entry if note matures after the end of the accounting period:

```
Cash.........................................    990.00
Prepaid interest expense.......................     10.00
        Notes payable..............................         1,000.00
        Note due in 60 days, discounted at bank.
```

(An adjusting entry will be required at the end of the accounting period to transfer the expense portion from the Prepaid Interest Expense account to Interest Expense.)

Discounting notes and acceptances receivable.   Instead of borrowing money from a bank by discounting our own note payable, we may obtain funds from a bank by endorsing, and transferring to the bank, any notes or acceptances receivable held by us that are acceptable to the bank.

The payee of a note or an acceptance may endorse it and transfer it to a creditor to apply on account, if the creditor is willing to take it.

To simplify the presentation in this chapter, the illustrations deal only with notes; it should be understood that the procedures and entries applicable to the discounting of acceptances are identical with those for notes.

Endorsements.   Paper that is payable to the order of a named payee must be endorsed by him if it is to be transferred to some other party.   The party who endorses a note is called an *endorser;* the party to whom the note is transferred is called an *endorsee.*

By the act of endorsement of a negotiable promissory note or acceptance, the endorser assumes an obligation (subject to certain defenses) to pay the paper to a subsequent holder if the maker fails to pay it at maturity.   This obligation is called a *contingent liability.*   For a complete discussion of the nature of the contingent liability of an endorser, and the nature of his defenses, you are referred to any good text on the law of negotiable instruments.

Paper that is payable to *bearer* can legally be transferred by delivery without endorsement; however, the party to whom it is to be transferred may require that it be endorsed in order to make the transferor contingently liable for its payment.

Endorsements are classified and illustrated below, it being assumed that F. K. Hamilton is the payee of the note.

(1) *Unqualified endorsements* (the transferor assumes the full contingent liability imposed by law upon an endorser):

> (a) In full (shows the name of the party to whom the paper is transferred):

> > Pay to the order of
> > John Smith
> > F. K. Hamilton

> The paper is still payable *to order;* that is, Smith must endorse it in order to transfer it.

> (b) In blank (does not show the name of the party to whom the paper is transferred):

> > F. K. Hamilton

> The paper is now payable to bearer and can legally be transferred without endorsement.

(2) *Qualified endorsement* (the endorser limits his contingent liability by inserting the words *Without Recourse):*

> (a) In full:

> > Pay to the order of
> > John Smith
> > Without Recourse
> > F. K. Hamilton

(b) In blank:

> Without Recourse
> F. K. Hamilton

One who endorses *without recourse* materially lessens his contingent liability as an endorser. He warrants that the paper is valid and that he has a good title to it, but he does not assume a legal obligation to pay the paper merely because the primary obligor does not do so.

(3) *Restrictive endorsement* (which must be in full):

(a) To prevent further transfers:

> Pay to John Smith only
> F. K. Hamilton

(b) To make the endorsee an agent for a special purpose:

> Pay to the order of
> First National Bank
> For collection
> F. K. Hamilton

Discounting notes receivable at the bank. Let us assume that we own two notes that are recorded in the Notes Receivable account as follows:

Notes Receivable

19—				
Aug.	1	B. Bates 60 da.	6,000	00
	1	C. Cole 60 da. 5½%	6,000	00

Let us now assume that we discount these notes at the bank on August 11. The proceeds of a discounted note or acceptance receivable are computed as follows:

First, determine the value of the receivable at maturity (this is the amount which the holder will be entitled to collect at maturity).
The maturity value of non-interest paper is the face.
The maturity value of interest-bearing paper is the face plus the interest for the full period.
Second, determine the discount period, or time from the date of discount to maturity.
Third, compute the discount at the agreed rate, on the value at maturity, for the discount period.
Fourth, deduct the discount from the value at maturity.

Let us compute the proceeds of two notes receivable discounted.

	B. Bates	C. Cole
Maker......................................	B. Bates	C. Cole
Date of note................................	August 1	August 1
Time from date of note to maturity............	60 days	60 days
Date of discount............................	August 11	August 11
Discount period—or time from date of discount to maturity..................................	50 days	50 days
Rate of interest borne by the note..............	None	5½%
Rate of discount charged......................	6%	6%
Computation of proceeds:		
Face of note..............................	$6,000.00	$6,000.00
Add interest from date of note to maturity:		
The Bates note does not bear interest.		
Interest on the Cole note at 5½% for 60 days is		55.00
Value at maturity..........................	$6,000.00	$6,055.00
Deduct discount at 6% for 50 days:		
50 days' interest on $6,000.00..............	50.00	
50 days' interest on $6,055.00..............		50.46
Proceeds.................................	$5,950.00	$6,004.54

Since we part with the notes, it may seem that the Notes Receivable account should be credited. But we should remember that, in order to transfer the notes to the bank, we must endorse them and thus render ourselves contingently liable for their payment. This contingent liability should be shown in the accounts. Therefore, we shall credit Notes Receivable Discounted, as illustrated in the following entries.

Bates note. This note does not bear interest; therefore, no interest has accrued at the date of discount, and the only asset we are disposing of is the note. The loss is the excess of the $6,000 asset disposed of over the $5,950 proceeds received.

```
Cash.........................................    5,950.00
Loss from discounting notes receivable............      50.00
    Notes receivable discounted..................            6,000.00
    Note of B. Bates discounted at bank at 6%.
```

The account Loss from Discounting Notes Receivable is shown in the same section of the income statement as Interest Expense.

Cole note. This note bears 5½% interest, and interest in the amount of $9.17 has accrued during the ten days we have held it. The following entry records the accrued interest.

```
Accrued interest receivable.......................      9.17
    Interest earned..............................            9.17
    Interest earned on Cole note.
```

We are disposing of two assets: a $6,000 note receivable and $9.17 of accrued interest, or a total of $6,009.17; since the proceeds received are only $6,004.54, the loss is $4.63. The entry is on the following page.

```
Cash.........................................  6,004.54
Loss from discounting notes receivable............     4.63
    Notes receivable discounted..................              6,000.00
    Accrued interest receivable..................                  9.17
    Note of C. Cole discounted at bank at 6%.
```

If an Accrued Interest Receivable account stands debited with an accrual on a discounted note, recorded by an adjusting entry at the close of a prior period, the amount of the credit to Accrued Interest Receivable will be the sum of this accrual and the interest subsequently accrued. For example, assume that we received from Edgar Snow a $12,000 note dated June 15, due in 60 days, and bearing 5% interest.   An adjusting entry was made on June 30 as follows:

```
Accrued interest receivable......................  25.00
    Interest earned.............................              25.00
    Accrued interest at 5% for 15 days in June on Snow
    note.
```

Assume, further, that we discounted this note at the bank on July 10. The following additional interest accrual should be recorded:

```
Accrued interest receivable......................  16.67
    Interest earned.............................              16.67
    Accrued interest for 10 days in July on Snow note.
```

The bank discounted the note at 6%. The proceeds were computed as follows:

```
Face of note..........................................  $12,000.00
Interest at 5% for 60 days............................      100.00
Value at maturity.....................................  $12,100.00
Discount: 6% of $12,100 for 35 days...................       70.58
Proceeds..............................................  $12,029.42
```

The entry to record the discounting of the note would be:

```
Cash......................................  12,029.42
Loss from discounting notes receivable...........     12.25
    Notes receivable discounted................              12,000.00
    Accrued interest receivable................                  41.67
    Discounted Snow note at 6%, 35 days before
    maturity.
```

Discounted note paid by maker at maturity. Assume that Bates and Cole paid their discounted notes at maturity. We no longer have any contingent liability, and can therefore make the following entries:

```
Notes receivable discounted......................  6,000.00
    Notes receivable............................              6,000.00
    To eliminate the Bates note and contingent liability
    from the accounts.
```

Notes receivable discounted...................... 6,000.00
    Notes receivable............................　　　　　　6,000.00
    To eliminate the Cole note and contingent liability
from the accounts.

The two ledger accounts appear as follows:

Notes Receivable

19—					19—					
Aug.	1	B. Bates 60 da.	6,000	00	Sept.	30	B. Bates		6,000	00
	1	C. Cole 60 da. 5½%	6,000	00		30	C. Cole		6,000	00

Notes Receivable Discounted

19—					19—					
Sept.	30	B. Bates	6,000	00	Aug.	11	B. Bates		6,000	00
	30	C. Cole	6,000	00		11	C. Cole		6,000	00

Discounted note dishonored by maker. An endorser cannot be held on his contingent liability for the payment of a discounted note receivable unless the holder (endorsee) has presented it to the maker at maturity, demanded and not received payment, and given proper notice of dishonor to the endorser.

Let us assume that Bates and Cole dishonored their notes at maturity and that the holder took proper steps to enforce collection from us. Our entries would be:

For payment of Bates note—which did not bear interest:

Accounts receivable............................ 6,000.00
    Cash....................................　　　　　　6,000.00
    Paid the Bates note discounted by us and dis-
honored by him.

(The payment is charged to Accounts Receivable because we have a right to enforce collection from Bates.)

Notes receivable discounted...................... 6,000.00
    Notes receivable............................　　　　　　6,000.00
    To eliminate the Bates note and the contingent lia-
bility from the accounts.

(This entry is made because there is no longer any contingent liability on the note. The contingent liability developed into a real liability, and was paid.)

For payment of Cole note—which bore interest:

Accounts receivable............................ 6,055.00
    Cash....................................　　　　　　6,055.00
    Paid the Cole note discounted by us and dishonored
by him, and 5½% interest thereon for 60 days.

Notes receivable discounted...................... 6,000.00
    Notes receivable............................　　　　　　6,000.00
    To eliminate the Cole note and contingent liability
from the accounts.

Disposition of Notes Receivable Discounted account. You should observe that the entry debiting Notes Receivable Discounted and crediting Notes Receivable is made by the endorser at the maturity of a discounted note, *regardless of whether the note is paid by the maker or by the endorser.* If the note is paid by the maker, the endorser has no further liability. If the note is dishonored, the contingent liability becomes a real liability.

Protest. In some cases, notice of dishonor can be given to the endorser informally, either orally or in writing. In other cases, protest and formal notice of dishonor are required.

Protest is a formal declaration in writing by a notary public to the effect that he has presented an instrument to the person primarily liable thereon and demanded payment, and that the instrument has been dishonored. Notice of protest is sent by the notary public to the maker and to all the endorsers.

The holder of the paper (the endorsee) engages the services of the notary public and pays his fee, which he charges to the endorser. The endorser is obligated to pay the face of the note, the protest fee, and any accrued interest.

Let us assume that the Cole note, discounted by us, was dishonored and protested, and that the protest fee was $2.04. Our entries at the time of payment will be:

```
Accounts receivable............................ 6,057.04
    Cash.......................................          6,057.04
    Paid the Cole note discounted by us and dishonored
    by him, interest, and protest fee.

Notes receivable discounted..................... 6,000.00
    Notes receivable...........................          6,000.00
    To eliminate the C. Cole note and the contingent
    liability from the accounts.
```

Purpose of Notes Receivable Discounted account. It should be understood that the Notes Receivable Discounted account is used to show the contingent liability on paper which we have owned and have transferred to other parties, thus assuming a contingent liability as a result of our endorsement.

Notes receivable and notes receivable discounted in the balance sheet. Assume that a company's accounts with notes receivable and notes receivable discounted appear as follows:

Notes Receivable

19—					19—				
June	1	Smith—30 da.	a	1,000 00	July	1	Smith	a	1,000 00
	10	Brown—30 da.	b	2,000 00		10	Brown	b	2,000 00
	20	White—60 da.	c	2,500 00					
	25	Green—60 da.	d	3,000 00					

Notes Receivable Discounted

19—				19—			
July	10	Brown	b 2,000 00	June	15	Brown	b 2,000 00
					25	White	c 2,500 00

These accounts show the following facts:

The Smith note was received on June 1 and was collected on July 1.

The Brown note was received on June 10; it was discounted on June 15; it matured on July 10, and the contingent liability was eliminated.

The White note was received on June 20; it was discounted on June 25; it has not yet matured; therefore, there is a contingent liability of $2,500.

The Green note was received on June 25; it has not yet matured, and the company therefore has an asset of $3,000.

The balance sheet should show the note receivable asset of $3,000 and the contingent liability of $2,500. The asset and the contingent liability can be determined from the balances of the two accounts, as follows:

Debit balance of Notes Receivable account.................. $5,500.00
Credit balance of Notes Receivable Discounted account—
amount to be shown as a contingent liability............. 2,500.00
Net balance of the two accounts—amount to be shown as note
receivable asset..................................... $3,000.00

The note receivable asset is shown in the balance sheet on the asset side. The contingent liability on notes receivable discounted is usually stated in a footnote. The procedure is illustrated below.

NAME OF COMPANY
Balance Sheet
July 31, 19—
Assets

Cash..	$	750.00
Accounts receivable.......................................		2,850.00
Notes receivable...		3,000.00
Inventory..		6,780.00
		$13,380.00

Liabilities and Stockholders' Equity

Liabilities:

Accounts payable.........................	$ 2,000.00	
Notes payable...........................	1,000.00	$ 3,000.00
Stockholders' equity:		
Capital stock............................	$10,000.00	
Retained earnings.......................	380.00	10,380.00
		$13,380.00

Note. On July 31, 19—, the company was contingently liable on a note receivable discounted in the amount of $2,500.

Registers

Notes receivable register. If many notes and acceptances are received, it is desirable to keep a supplementary record called a Notes Receivable Register, where spaces are provided for more detailed information about the notes and acceptances than can be entered in the Explanation columns of the Notes Receivable account. This register is a supplementary book; the entries in it do not take the place of those in the journal and the ledger, but when it is used, details can be omitted from the Explanation columns of the account.

An illustration is presented below. It shows (1) the illustrative transactions, (2) the entries to record the transactions, (3) the Notes Receivable account, and (4) the notes receivable register (page 129).

Peterson note:

On May 12, a 30-day, non-interest note for $1,000, dated May 12, payable at our office, was received from O. B. Peterson, to apply on account.

```
Notes receivable............................... 1,000.00
    Accounts receivable........................          1,000.00
```

On June 11, the note was collected.

```
Cash.......................................... 1,000.00
    Notes receivable...........................          1,000.00
```

Smith note:

On May 21, a 60-day, 6% note for $1,500, dated May 20, payable at the State Bank, was received from H. D. Smith to apply on account.

```
Notes receivable............................... 1,500 00
    Accounts receivable........................          1,500.00
```

On July 19, when the note matured, the maker dishonored it, and it was charged back to his account.

```
Accounts receivable........................... 1,515 00
    Notes receivable...........................          1,500.00
    Interest earned............................            15.00
```

On July 21, Smith paid us $315 in cash, and gave us a new 6% note, payable in three months at our office, for $1,200.

```
Cash..........................................  315.00
    Accounts receivable........................           315.00
Notes receivable............................... 1,200.00
    Accounts receivable........................          1,200.00
```

Norton acceptance:

On July 24, we drew a $900 draft on Henry Norton, payable 60 days after date. Norton accepted the draft and returned it to us. We received it on July 25.

Notes receivable.................................... 900.00
   Accounts receivable............................   900.00

The acceptance has not yet matured.

Notes Receivable

19—					19—					
May	12		1,000	00	June	11		1,000	00
	21		1,500	00	July	19		1,500	00
July	21		1,200	00					
	25		900	00					

The notes receivable register appears on page 129. The letters in the first column indicate whether the paper is a note or an acceptance. The letters *J, F, M,* and so forth, at the head of the narrow columns indicate months of maturity, and the numbers in these columns indicate the dates of maturity.

The Notes Receivable account has a debit balance of $2,100. This balance is the total of the last two items in the register.

Notes payable register. An illustration of notes and acceptances payable transactions is presented below.

Bank loan:

On March 1, we discounted at the First National Bank our 60-day note for $5,000; discount rate, 6%.

Cash... 4,950.00
Interest expense.................................   50.00
   Notes payable..............................   5,000.00

Slocum acceptance:

On March 10, we accepted a 30-day sight draft for $1,150, drawn by Frank Slocum on March 9, payable at his office.

Accounts payable.............................. 1,150.00
   Notes payable..............................   1,150.00

On April 9, the acceptance was paid.

Notes payable................................. 1,150.00
   Cash.......................................   1,150.00

Bailey note:

On March 17, we gave George Bailey a 6%, two-month note for $750. The entry is on the following page.

| Accounts payable............................. | 750.00 | |
| Notes payable............................... | | 750.00 |

Notes Payable

19—					19—				5,000	00
Apr.	9			1,150 00	Mar.	1			1,150	00
						10			750	00
						17				

The notes payable register appears on page 129.

Interest

Computing interest—General formula. The general formula for computing interest may be expressed thus:

Principal × Interest Rate × Time = Interest

Interest rates, unless specifically qualified to the contrary, are per-annum rates. If a note is described as a 6% note, the interest is at the rate of 6% per year.

If time is expressed in terms of months, interest is computed in terms of months. For example, the interest on a $1,000, 6% note for three months is computed as follows:

$$\$1,000 \times .06 \times \tfrac{3}{12} = \$15$$

If time is expressed in terms of days, the exact number of days is used in the interest computation. However, for interest-computation purposes, it is commonly assumed that there are 360 days in a year. For example, the interest on a 45-day, 6% note for $1,000 is computed as follows:

$$\$1,000 \times .06 \times \tfrac{45}{360} = \$7.50$$

In the determination of the number of days between two dates, for purposes of computing interest, exclude the first day and include the last. For instance, the time of a note dated June 17 and due August 4 would be computed as follows:

Remaining days in June.........	13
July............................	31
August.........................	4
	48

Computing interest—Short methods. There are several methods of computing simple interest. Some of the shortest are explained below. At 6% per annum,

The interest on $1.00 for 1 year is.................	$.06
The interest on 1.00 for 2 months (60 days) is......	.01 (⅙ of $.06)
The interest on 1.00 for 6 days is.................	.001 (⅒ of $.01)

Notes Receivable Register

	Date Received	Date of Paper	Maker or Drawee	Drawer or Endorser	Where Payable	Time Mo.	Time Da.	Int. Rate	When Due Year	J	F	M	A	M	J	J	A	S	O	N	D	Amount	Date Paid	Remarks
N A	19—	19—																					19—	
N	May 12	May 12	O. B. Peterson		Our office		30	—	19—						11							1,000 00	June 11	
N	21	20	H. D. Smith		State Bank		60	6 %	19—							19						1,500 00		Dishonored. See new note below.
N	July 21	July 21	H. D. Smith		Our office			6 %	19—								21					1,200 00		
A	25	24	Henry Norton	Ourselves	Our office	3	60	—	19—								22					900 00		

Notes Payable Register

	Date Given	Date of Paper	Payee	Endorser or Drawer	Where Payable	Time Mo.	Time Da.	Int. Rate	When Due Year	J	F	M	A	M	J	J	A	S	O	N	D	Amount	Date Paid	Remarks
N A	19—	19—																					19—	
N	Mar. 1	Mar. 1	First National Bk.		Bank		60	Disc.	19—				30									5,000 00		
A	10	9	Frank Slocum		His office		30	—	19—				9									1,150 00	Apr. 9	
N	17	17	George Bailey			2		6 %	19—							17						750 00		

129

It is evident that interest on $1.00 for 60 days can be computed by moving the decimal point in the principal two places to the left, and that interest on $1.00 for 6 days can be computed by moving the decimal point in the principal three places to the left. If this is true of $1.00, it is true of any principal, and a general rule may be developed in the manner shown below:

Given any principal, to find the interest at 6%:
     For   6 days, point off three places to the left
      "   60   " ,   "   "   " two   "   "   "   "
      "   600   " ,   "   "   " one   place "   "   "
      "   6,000   " , the interest is the same as the principal.

Thus,   6 days' interest on $1,230.00 is $ 1.23
         60   "   "   "   1,230.00 "   12.30
        600   "   "   "   1,230.00 "   123.00
      6,000   "   "   "   1,230.00 "   1,230.00

Multiples and fractions. The time, stated in days, may be separated into parts that are multiples or fractions of 6, 60, 600, or 6,000, and the interest for partial time periods may be added.
What is the interest on $137.65 for 15 days?

Interest for 60 days = $1.3765
     "   " 15 "   = ¼ of $1.3765, or $.3441

What is the interest on $137.65 for 88 days?

Interest for 60 days = $1.3765
     "   " 20 "   =   .4588 (⅓ of $1.3765)
     "   "   6 "   =   .13765
     "   "   2 "   =   .04588 (⅓ of $.13765)
     "   " 88 "   = $2.01883 or $2.02.

Interest for any number of days. When the time cannot easily be divided into fractions or multiples of 6, 60, 600, or 6,000,

Point off three places. (Amount is interest for 6 days.)
Multiply by the number of days. (Product is interest for 6 times the stated number of days.)
Divide by 6. (Quotient is interest for the stated number of days.)

What is the interest on $137.65 at 6% for 77 days?

Point off three places.................................... $ .13765
Multiply by..   77
Interest for 6 × 77 days................................. $10.59905
Divide by 6: $10.59905 ÷ 6 = $1.7665 = $1.77, interest for 77 days.

Interchanging principal and time. The principal and time may be interchanged if this procedure will simplify the computation.
What is the interest on $1,000 for 38 days?

Interchanging, what is the interest on $38.00 for 1,000 days?
Interest for 6,000 days   = $38.00
Divide by 6: $38.00 ÷ 6 = $ 6.33

Interest at other rates. When the rate is other than 6%, it is convenient to compute the interest at 6%, and make the adjustments for the difference between 6% and the actual rate.

What is the interest on $360 for 30 days at 7%?

> Compute the interest at 6%:
> Interest for 60 days = $3.60
> Interest for 30 days = $1.80
> Add one-sixth of $1.80   .30
> Interest at 7% $2.10

What is the interest on $3,500 for 45 days at 5½%?

> Compute the interest at 6%:
> Interest for 60 days = $35.00
> Interest for 45 days = ¾ of $35.00 $26.25
> Deduct (for ½ of 1%) ½₂ of $26.25   2.19
> Interest at 5½% $24.06

CHAPTER 10

Books of Original Entry.   Controlling Accounts

Columnar journals.   Accountants have given a great deal of attention to the development of accounting records that reduce labor.   One of the simplest labor-saving devices is a journal in which special columns are provided for accounts frequently debited or credited.   Amounts debited or credited to other accounts are entered in the Sundry columns.   Such a columnar journal is illustrated on pages 133 to 135.

Posting.   Labor is saved because, instead of posting individually the entries appearing in the special columns, only the column totals are posted.   Ledger-account numbers are entered, as posting references, below column totals to show that they have been posted, as illustrated on page 135.   Posting of column totals is usually done at the end of the month.

Before posting column totals, the bookkeeper should make sure, as a test of accuracy, that the sum of the debit-column totals agrees with the sum of the credit-column totals.   The computation, which may be made on scratch paper, is illustrated below, using the totals on the last page of the journal.

Debits	Credits
15,400	26,055
3,280	10,495
5,500	2,100
26,837	10,050
1,513	3,830
52,530	52,530

Determining this equality should never be omitted.   If the totals are not in agreement, the trial balance will not balance, and a great deal of work may have to be done before the error is discovered.

Entries in the Sundry columns, which affect accounts not frequently debited or credited, are posted individually, as shown by the ledger-account numbers in the L.F. column.   These postings may be made daily.

The purpose of the check marks in the L.F. column is explained later.

Journal (Page 1)

Purchases	Accounts Receivable	Accounts Payable	Cash	Sundry	Date	L.F.	Account	Sundry	Cash	Accounts Receivable	Accounts Payable	Sales
			25,000 00		19— May 1	30	Cash Capital stock......... Issued capital stock for cash.	25,000 00				
2,000 00					1	✓	Purchases Price and Holmes....... Invoice, May 1.				2,000 00	
5,000 00					1	1	Purchases Cash............. Cash purchase.		5,000 00			
				300 00	1	61	Store rent Cash............. Paid rent for May.		300 00			
	800 00				2	✓	R. E. West Sales............. Invoice No. 1.					800 00
			150 00		3		Cash Sales............. Cash sale.					150 00
				800 00	5	15 ✓	Notes receivable R. E. West........... Received 30-day, non-interest note for invoice of May 2.			800 00		
		1,000 00			7	✓ 21	Price and Holmes Notes payable.......... 30-day, non-interest note to apply on invoice of May 1.	1,000 00				
7,000 00	800 00	1,000 00	25,150 00	1,100 00			Totals forward........	26,000 00	5,300 00	800 00	2,000 00	950 00

(Page 2)

Journal

Date	L.F.	Item	Purchases	Accounts Receivable	Accounts Payable	Cash	Sundry	Sundry	Cash	Accounts Receivable	Accounts Payable	Sales
19— May		Totals brought forward......	7,000 00	800 00	1,000 00	25,150 00	1,100 00	26,000 00	5,300 00	800 00	2,000 00	950 00
7	✓	Price and Holmes			1,000 00							
	52	Purchase discounts......						20 00				
		Cash..........							980 00			
		Balance of invoice of May 1, less 2%.										
7	✓	G. O. Davis		450 00								
		Sales..........										450 00
		Invoice No. 2.										
9	✓	Purchases	3,500 00									
		Henderson's, Inc........									3,500 00	
		Invoice, May 8.										
12	✓	S. E. Bates		600 00								
		Sales......										600 00
		Invoice No. 3.										
13	✓	Purchases	2,600 00									
		Osborne Company.......									2,600 00	
		Invoice, May 10.										
15	42	Sales discounts					4 50					
		Cash				445 50						
	✓	G. O. Davis.........								450 00		
		Invoice, May 7, less 1%.										
16	✓	Henderson's, Inc.			3,500 00							
	52	Purchase discounts......						35 00				
		Cash..........							3,465 00			
		Invoice, May 9, less 1%.										
18	✓	R. E. West		850 00								
		Sales......										850 00
		Invoice No. 4.										
		Totals forward.........	13,100 00	2,700 00	5,500 00	25,595 50	1,104 50	26,055 00	9,745 00	1,250 00	8,100 00	2,850 00

(Page 3)

Journal

Purchases	Accounts Receivable	Accounts Payable	Cash	Sundry	Date	L.F.	Items	Sundry	Cash	Accounts Receivable	Accounts Payable	Sales
13,100 00	2,700 00	5,500 00	25,595 50	1,104 50	19— May 18		Totals brought forward	26,055 00	9,745 00	1,250 00	8,100 00	2,850 00
650 00						✓	Purchases Price and Holmes Invoice, May 16.				650 00	
	280 00				23	✓	G. O. Davis Sales Invoice No. 5.					280 00
1,300 00					24	✓	Purchases Henderson's, Inc. Invoice, May 23.				1,300 00	
			841 50	8 50	24	42 ✓	Cash Sales discounts R. E. West Invoice No. 4, less 1%.			850 00		
350 00					26	✓	Purchases Cash Cash purchase.		350 00			
	300 00				30	✓	R. E. West Sales Invoice No. 6.					300 00
			400 00		31		Cash Sales Cash sale.					400 00
				400 00	31	62	Salesmen's salaries Cash Salaries for May.		400 00			
15,400 00	3,280 00	5,500 00	26,837 00	1,513 00				26,055 00	10,495 00	2,100 00	10,050 00	3,830 00
(50)	(10)	(20)	(1)						(1)	(10)	(20)	(40)

The ledger. The following ledger accounts were produced by posting from the illustrative journal.

Cash (1)

19—					19—				
May	31		3	26,837 00	May	31		3	10,495 00

Accounts Receivable (10)

19—					19—				
May	31		3	3,280 00	May	31		3	2,100 00

Notes Receivable (15)

19—				
May	5		1	800 00

Accounts Payable (20)

19—					19—				
May	31		3	5,500 00	May	31		3	10,050 00

Notes Payable (21)

				19—				
				May	7		1	1,000 00

Capital Stock (30)

				19—				
				May	1		1	25,000 00

Sales (40)

				19—				
				May	31		3	3,830 00

Sales Discounts (42)

19—				
May	15		2	4 50
	24		3	8 50

Purchases (50)

19—				
May	31		3	15,400 00

Purchase Discounts (52)

				19—				
				May	7		2	20 00
					16		2	35 00

Store Rent (61)

19—				
May	1		1	300 00

Salesmen's Salaries (62)

19—										
May	31			3	400	00				

Subsidiary ledgers and controlling accounts. Thus far, all accounts receivable transactions with customers have been recorded in a single Accounts Receivable account. This procedure is inadequate because it is difficult to determine the amount receivable from each customer. To provide this information, an account is kept with each customer who is indebted to the business; these accounts are kept in a separate ledger, called a *subsidiary ledger.* The Accounts Receivable account previously used to show the total amount receivable from all customers is continued; it is kept in the principal ledger—usually called the *general ledger.*

The Accounts Receivable account in the general ledger is called a *controlling account* because its balance and the sum of the balances in the subsidiary ledger should be equal. The controlling account thus serves as a check on the accuracy of the subsidiary ledger.

A similar procedure may be followed with accounts payable: An Accounts Payable controlling account may be kept in the general ledger, with the individual accounts in a subsidiary ledger.

Since the controlling accounts show the total amounts receivable from trade debtors and payable to trade creditors, a trial balance can be taken of the general ledger alone, without reference to the subsidiary ledgers.

Posting to subsidiary ledgers. Subsidiary ledger accounts usually have three columns: Debit, Credit, and Balance. Balances in the accounts receivable ledger are assumed to be debits; a credit balance may be so indicated by writing "Cr." at the right of the balance. Similarly, balances in the accounts payable ledger are assumed to be credits; a debit balance may be indicated by writing "Dr." at the right of it.

The three-column form is also often used for accounts in the general ledger.

Accounts receivable ledger. The subsidiary accounts receivable ledger produced by posting from the journal appears below:

S. E. Bates

19—										
May	12			2	600	00			600	00

G. O. Davis

19—										
May	7			2	450	00			450	00
	15			2			450	00	—	
	23			3	280	00			280	00

R. E. West

19—								
May	2		1	800	00		800	00
	5		1			800	00	—
	18		2	850	00		850	00
	24		3			850	00	—
	30		3	300	00		300	00

Since the accounts in the subsidiary ledgers usually are arranged in alphabetical order and are not numbered, the bookkeeper indicates that postings have been made to these ledgers by entering check marks ($\checkmark$) in the L.F. column of the journal.

Accounts payable ledger. The accounts payable subsidiary ledger resulting from the posting of the journal appears below:

Henderson's, Inc.

19—								
May	9		2			3,500	00	3,500	00
	16		2	3,500	00			—
	24		3			1,300	00	1,300	00

Osborne Company

19—						
May	13		2		2,600	00	2,600	00

Price and Holmes

19—								
May	1		1			2,000	00	2,000	00
	7		1	1,000	00			1,000	00
	7		2	1,000	00			—
	18		3			650	00	650	00

Proving the ledgers. The equality of the debits and credits in the general ledger is established, as heretofore, by taking a trial balance. Following is the trial balance of the general ledger on pages 136 and 137.

General Ledger Trial Balance
May 31, 19—

Cash.	16,342.00	
Accounts receivable.	1,180.00	
Notes receivable.	800.00	
Accounts payable.		4,550.00
Notes payable.		1,000.00
Capital stock.		25,000.00
Sales.		3,830.00
Sales discounts.	13.00	
Purchases.	15,400.00	
Purchase discounts.		55.00
Store rent.	300.00	
Salesmen's salaries.	400.00	
	34,435.00	34,435.00

The subsidiary ledgers are proved by preparing schedules of their balances and seeing that the totals thereof are in agreement with the balances of the respective controlling accounts. Following are the schedules of the subsidiary ledgers on pages 137 and 138.

Schedule of Accounts Receivable
May 31, 19—

S. E. Bates	600.00
G. O. Davis	280.00
R. E. West	300.00
Total (per balance of controlling account)	1,180.00

Schedule of Accounts Payable
May 31, 19—

Henderson's, Inc	1,300.00
Osborne Company	2,600.00
Price and Holmes	650.00
Total (per balance of controlling account)	4,550.00

Why controlling accounts are maintained. It might seem that, when individual accounts are kept with debtors and creditors, it is a useless duplication of work to keep controlling accounts also. However, controlling accounts serve two very useful purposes.

First, Controlling accounts make it possible to determine the total accounts receivable and total accounts payable without listing the balances of the individual accounts.

Second, Controlling accounts help in locating errors. Without controlling accounts, it would be necessary to take a combined trial balance of the general ledger and the subsidiary ledgers. If they did not balance, it might be necessary to check all of the postings in search of errors. With controlling accounts, the three ledgers can be proved separately. For instance, if the general ledger is in balance, but the total of the accounts receivable ledger schedule does not agree with the balance in the Accounts Receivable controlling account, an error presumably has been made in the subsidiary ledger.

Since, with a few possible exceptions mentioned later, the controlling accounts are produced by posting column totals, very little additional work is required to obtain the above-mentioned benefits.

Special books of original entry. The previously illustrated journal with columns for accounts frequently debited and credited saves posting labor but it does not provide for a division of labor. To enable several bookkeepers to work at the same time, it is necessary to have several books of original entry. And, as we shall see, by using specially designed books of original entry for different classes of transactions, the labor of journalizing can be greatly reduced.

Books to be illustrated.   The special books to be used in any business will depend upon the nature of its operations, and upon whether transactions of a particular kind occur often enough to warrant having a special book of original entry in which to record them.

The illustration that follows is based on the transactions recorded in the preceding illustration.   Since sales, purchases, cash receipts, and cash disbursements occurred frequently, the following special books will be provided:

> Sales book.
> > For sales of merchandise on account.   (A Sales column is provided in the cash receipts book for cash sales.)
>
> Purchases book.
> > For purchases of merchandise on account.   (A Purchases column is provided in the cash disbursements book for cash purchases.)
>
> Cash receipts book.
> Cash disbursements book.

These books are sometimes called the *sales journal*, the *purchases journal*, and so forth.   Since some transactions (for instance, the receiving of a note to apply on account) cannot be recorded in the special books of original entry, it is also necessary to have a journal in which to record them; this book may be called the *general journal*, or merely the *journal*.

If a transaction is recorded in one of the special books of original entry, it is not recorded in the general journal also; only those transactions that cannot be recorded in a special book of original entry are recorded in the general journal.

Sales book.   A sales book is illustrated below.

Sales Book   (Page 1)

Date	√	Name	Invoice No.	Amount	
19—					
May 2	√	R. E. West..............................	1	800	00
7	√	G. O. Davis.............................	2	450	00
12	√	S. E. Bates.............................	3	600	00
18	√	R. E. West..............................	4	850	00
23	√	G. O. Davis.............................	5	280	00
30	√	R. E. West..............................	6	300	00
				3,280	00
				(10) (40)	

The sales book is used for recording sales of merchandise on account.   It has the following advantages:

Saving of labor:
In recording transactions:
Each entry records a debit to a customer and a credit to Sales; but the credit to Sales need not be written; it is *implied* because the entry is in the sales book.
The sales book need not contain an explanation of each entry.   A numbered invoice is given to the customer, and a copy thereof is retained and filed.   The sales book shows the number of the invoice.   Information about the kinds of merchandise sold can be obtained by referring to the filed duplicate of the invoice indicated by the number.
In posting:
A separate book of original entry for Sales, like the special Sales column in the journal on pages 133 to 135, saves posting labor because, instead of posting the amount of each sale separately to the Sales account, the bookkeeper posts the total of all of the entries to the Sales account.
The column total is also posted to the Accounts Receivable controlling account.
Division of labor:
In recording transactions:
One bookkeeper can be engaged in recording sales while other bookkeepers are recording other kinds of transactions.
In posting:
An assistant bookkeeper can post daily to the accounts receivable subsidiary ledger, and the head bookkeeper can post monthly to the general ledger.

The other special books of original entry described in this chapter have similar advantages.

Postings have been made from the illustrative sales book on page 140.   The postings of the individual debits to customers were made during the month.   The postings of the debit to Accounts Receivable controlling account (account 10) and the credit to Sales (account 40) were made at the end of the month.

Purchases book.   Savings in journalizing and posting can be effected by using a special book of original entry for recording purchases of merchandise on account.   The entries in the purchases book are equivalent to five entries debiting Purchases and crediting the parties from whom the merchandise was purchased.

Purchases Book   (Page 1)

Date	√	Name	Invoice Date	Amount
19—			19—	
May 1	√	Price and Holmes..............................	May 1	2,000 00
9	√	Henderson's, Inc...............................	8	3,500 00
13	√	Osborne Company..............................	10	2,600 00
18	√	Price and Holmes..............................	16	650 00
24	√	Henderson's, Inc...............................	23	1,300 00
				10,050 00
				(50) (20)

Postings were made as follows:

During the month, the individual entries were posted daily to the credit of the creditors' accounts in the subsidiary ledger.

At the end of the month, the column total was posted to general ledger accounts as follows:

To the debit of Purchases (50).

To the credit of Accounts Payable (20).

Cash receipts book. The illustrative cash receipts book on page 143 has the following columns:

Debits:

Cash

Sales Discounts

Provided to make it possible to record on one line of the cash receipts book a collection from a customer who takes a cash discount.

Credits:

Accounts Receivable

A controlling account column.

Sales

Provided to reduce posting.

Sundry

For credits that cannot be entered in special columns.

The cash receipts book, like the other special books of original entry, saves labor in recording transactions. Each of the entries records a receipt of cash, but the account title "Cash" does not have to be written; the debit to Cash is indicated by entering the amount in the Cash column. Similarly, the debits to Sales Discounts are indicated by the fact that the amounts are in the Sales Discounts column.

Cash Receipts Book (Page 1)

Date	Account Credited	Explanation	DEBITS		CREDITS				
			Cash	Sales Discounts	Accounts Receivable ✓ Amount	Sales	L.F.	Sundry Amount
19— May 1	Capital stock........	Investment	25,000 00				30	25,000 00
3	Sales.............	Cash sale	150 00			150 00		
15	G. O. Davis........	Invoice, May 7, less 1%	445 50	4 50	✓ 450 00			
24	R. E. West.........	Invoice, May 18, less 1%	841 50	8 50	✓ 850 00			
31	Sales.............	Cash sale	400 00			400 00		
			26,837 00	13 00	1,300 00	550 00		25,000 00
			(1)	(42)	(10)	(40) .		

Postings are made as follows:

During the month:

One bookkeeper may post the entries in the Sundry column to the credit of the general ledger accounts named under "Account Credited."

Another bookkeeper may post the entries in the Accounts Receivable column to the subsidiary ledger accounts named under "Account Credited."

At the end of the month:

Column totals are posted to general ledger accounts as follows:

Cash column—To the debit of Cash account (No. 1).

Sales Discounts column—To the debit of Sales Discounts account (No. 42).

Accounts Receivable column—To the credit of Accounts Receivable account (No. 10).

Sales column—To the credit of Sales account (No. 40).

Cash disbursements book. The cash disbursements book is on page 145. It will be observed that the two credit columns in the cash disbursements book are at the left of the debit columns. In columnar books of original entry, any column sequence may be adopted so long as the headings clearly identify the debits and credits. In both the cash receipts and the cash disbursements books, the Cash column was placed first because it is the column most frequently used.

The posting is similar to the posting from the cash receipts book.

The journal. When special journals are used, only a relatively few transactions are recorded in the general journal. For this reason, the general journal may be set up with no special columns, as is the case with the journal illustrated below.

Journal   (Page 1)

19—					
May	5	Notes receivable............................	15	800 00	
		Accounts receivable (R. E. West).........	10/√		800 00
		Received 30-day, non-interest note for balance of invoice of May 2.			
	7	Accounts payable (Price and Holmes).........	20/√	1,000 00	
		Notes payable...................	21		1,000 00
		Issued 30-day, non-interest note to apply on invoice of May 1.			

Since the above journal does not have special columns for controlling accounts, whenever a controlling account is debited or credited it will be necessary to post such debits or credits twice,

Cash Disbursements Book (Page 1)

| Date | Account Debited | Explanation | CREDITS | | DEBITS | | | |
			Cash	Purchase Discounts	Accounts Payable Amount	Purchases	L.F.	Sundry Amount
19—								
May 1	Purchases........	Cash purchase	5,000 00			5,000 00		
1	Store rent........	For May	300 00				61	300 00
7	Price and Holmes..	Invoice, May 1, less 2%	980 00	20 00	√ 1,000 00			
16	Henderson's, Inc...	Invoice, May 9, less 1%	3,465 00	35 00	√ 3,500 00			
26	Purchases........	Cash purchase	350 00			350 00		
31	Salesmen's salaries....	For the month of May	400 00				62	400 00
			10,495 00	55 00	4,500 00	5,350 00		700 00
			(1)	(52)	(20)	(50)		

once to the controlling account in the general ledger and again to an account in the subsidiary ledger.   If such double posting is not performed, agreement between the controlling account and the subsidiary ledger will not be maintained.   Thus, in the illustration on page 144, it was necessary to post the credit member of the first journal entry twice:

> To the Accounts Receivable controlling account in the general ledger, as indicated by the "10" in the L.F. column; and
> To R. E. West's account in the subsidiary accounts receivable ledger, as indicated by the check mark in the L.F. column.

Also, it was necessary to post the debit member of the second journal entry twice:

> To the Accounts Payable controlling account in the general ledger, as indicated by the "20" in the L.F. column; and
> To Price and Holmes' account in the subsidiary accounts payable ledger, as indicated by the check mark in the L.F. column.

Notice that the identity of the customer (R. E. West) and the creditor (Price and Holmes) must be included in the journal entries in order that the bookkeeper may be able to post to the subsidiary ledgers.

If many entries affecting controlling accounts and subsidiary ledgers are recorded in the general journal, it may be desirable to provide special columns for them.   A journal with such controlling account columns is illustrated on page 147.

References to books of original entry.   When several books of original entry are used, the ledger accounts must indicate the books from which the entries were posted.   Thus,

> CR 1 means cash receipts book, page 1.
> CD 1 means cash disbursements book, page 1.
> S 1 means sales book, page 1.
> P 1 means purchases book, page 1.
> J 1 means journal, page 1.

Journal

(Page 1)

DEBITS			Date	L.F.		CREDITS		
Accounts Receivable	Accounts Payable	Sundry				Sundry	Accounts Payable	Accounts Receivable
		800 00	19— May 5	15	Notes receivable			
				✓	R. E. West....................			800 00
					Received 30-day, non-interest note for balance of invoice of May 2.			
	1,000 00		7	✓	Price and Holmes			
				21	Notes payable................	1,000 00		
					30-day, non-interest note to apply on invoice of May 1.			
	1,000 00	800 00				1,000 00		800 00
	(20)							(10)

Expanded cash receipts book. Since the cash receipts book on page 143 was the first illustration of such a book, it was purposely made simple. For instance, it provided only two debit columns; thus, transactions requiring debits to accounts other than Cash and Sales Discounts could not be recorded in it. To illustrate, assume that a note payable was discounted at the bank; the record of the transaction would require debits to Cash and Interest Expense, and a credit to Notes Payable, but the cash receipts book on page 143 has no place in which to record the debit to Interest Expense.

The general journal could be used to record transactions of this nature, but it is more convenient to have all cash receipts recorded in the cash receipts book. This is made possible by providing a Sundry Accounts debit section, as shown in the following illustration. To avoid printing this illustration in extremely small type, the debit and credit portions are printed on facing pages.

Space for the names of accounts credited appears at the left of the cash receipts book on page 143; in this cash receipts book, it has been moved to the right to be close to the related amounts. The hazard of errors in posting is thus reduced.

Cash Receipts Book

(Left side)

Line No.	Date	Explanation	Cash	Sales Discounts	Sundry Accounts (DEBITS) Name	L.F.	Amount
	19—						
1	June 5	Issuance of capital stock	25,000 00				
2	6	Cash sale	120 00				
3	15	Invoice, June 5, less 2%	1,960 00	40 00			
4	18	Ten-day note payable discounted at bank	5,990 00		Interest expense	71	10 00
5	25	Refund overpayment of account	25 00				
6	30	Invoice, June 22, less 2%	784 00	16 00			
			33,879 00	56 00			10 00
			(1)	(42)			

(Right Side)

				CREDITS	
Line No.	Account Credited	Accounts Receivable Amount	Sales	Sundry Accounts L.F.	Sundry Accounts Amount
1	Capital stock..........			30	25,000 00
2	Henry Dobbs..........	2,000 00	120 00		
3	Notes payable..........			21	
4	Accounts payable (J. B. Moore).....				6,000 00
5	Dawson, Inc...........	800 00		20/✓	25 00
6		2,800 00	120 00		31,025 00
		(10)	(40)		

Expanded cash disbursements book. The cash disbursements book below makes it possible to record transactions therein which would have to be recorded in the general journal if the cash disbursements book illustrated on page 145 were being used. Observe the entry on June 13. With the Sundry Accounts credit section, such a cash disbursement transaction can be recorded in the cash book instead of the following journal entry:

Land.	5,000.00	
Buildings.	18,000.00	
Cash.		8,000.00
Notes payable.		15,000.00

Cash Disbursements Book

(Left side)

Line No.	Date	Explanation	Cash	Purchase Discounts
1	19— June 1	Paid store rent.	200 00	
2	5	Cash purchase.	2,350 00	
3	13	Bought real estate from Hudson Co. for cash and six-		
4		months note.	8,000 00	
5	22	Cash purchase.	500 00	
6	23	Invoice, June 15, less 2%.	441 00	9 00
7	30	Invoice, June 20, less 2%.	1,470 00	30 00
			12,961 00	39 00
			(1)	(52)

CREDITS

Sundry Accounts

Name	L.F.	Amount
Notes payable	21	15,000 00
		15,000 00

(Right side)

Line No.	Account Debited	Accounts Payable ✓	Amount	DEBITS Purchases	Sundry Accounts L.F.	Amount
1	Store rent..........				61	200 00
2				2,350 00		
3	Land...............				16	5,000 00
4	Buildings..........				17	18,000 00
5				500 00		
6	Holmes and Baker..	√	450 00			
7	Smith Company.....	√	1,500 00			
			1,950 00	2,850 00		23,200 00
			(20)	(50)		

Concluding note. The special books of original entry to be used in any business will depend on the nature of its operations, and upon whether transactions of a particular kind occur often enough to warrant having a special journal in which to record them. Similarly, a wide variety of columns may be used in the special journals. If an account is frequently debited or credited, a special column for that account will be useful. For instance, a small loan company probably would find it convenient to use a special column for Interest Earned and normally would have no use for a special column for Rents Earned. The reverse would be true for a business owning and renting apartments.

In many cases, special books of original entry are tailor-made devices designed to meet the needs of a particular business. They may be designed to be extremely specialized and thus capable of recording very few types of transactions, or made less specialized, the latter being achieved by the use of Sundry Accounts sections.

CHAPTER 11

Individual Proprietorships.   Partnerships

The asset, liability, revenue, and expense accounts of an individual proprietorship or a partnership may be the same as those of a corporation in the same line of business, and the revenue and expense accounts are closed to Revenue and Expense in the manner with which the student is already familiar.   The books of an individual proprietorship or a partnership necessarily differ from those of a corporation only in the owners' equity accounts.

Individual Proprietorships

Capital and drawing accounts.   In place of the Capital Stock, Retained Earnings, and Dividends accounts kept by a corporation, the books of an individual proprietor contain the following accounts:

Capital account:
>   This account is credited with the proprietor's original investment and with any additional investments; by transfer from Revenue and Expense, it is credited with the net income or debited with the net loss for the period.

Drawing account:
>   Although all changes in a proprietor's equity could be, and sometimes are, recorded in his capital account, it is a rather general custom also to have another account, variously called the *drawing* account, the *personal* account, or the *current* account.

When such an account is kept, it is debited with:
>   (a) Withdrawals of cash or other business assets.
>>   When a proprietor takes merchandise for his own use, it is customary to charge him for it at cost. Debiting the proprietor at sales price and crediting the Sales account would be illogical; a withdrawal of merchandise is not a sale.   The debit to the proprietor's drawing account is offset by a credit to Purchases.
>   (b) Disbursements of business cash for the benefit of the proprietor—as, for instance, a purchase made for him.

Other entries in the drawing account are described under the caption "Closing the books."

The following accounts are illustrative:

James White, Capital

					19—				
					Jan.	1	Investment	CR1	7,500 00
					Feb.	15	Additional		
							investment	CR2	1,500 00

James White, Drawings

19—									
Mar.	25		CD 3	900 00					
July	8		CD 7	400 00					
Sept.	5		CD 9	750 00					
Dec.	17		CD12	600 00					

Closing the books.   The procedure of closing the revenue and expense accounts to Revenue and Expense is exactly the same in an individual proprietorship as in a corporation.   Assume that the net income for the year is $4,500; the Revenue and Expense account is closed to the proprietor's capital account by the following entry:

Revenue and expense.......................... 4,500.00
    James White, capital...................... 4,500.00
    To close Revenue and Expense and transfer the net
    income for the year to the proprietor's capital
    account.

The closing procedure is completed by transferring the balance of the drawing account to the capital account by the following entry:

James White, capital.......................... 2,650.00
    James White, drawings..................... 2,650.00
    To close.

Proprietor's accounts after closing the books.   After the books are closed, the capital account and the drawing account appear as follows:

James White, Capital

19—					19—				
Dec.	31	Drawings	J12	2,650 00	Jan.	1	Investment	CR1	7,500 00
					Feb.	15	Additional		
							investment	CR2	1,500 00
					Dec.	31	Net income	J12	4,500 00

James White, Drawings

19—					19—				
Mar.	25		CD 3	900 00	Dec.	31	To capital	J12	2,650 00
July	8		CD 7	400 00					
Sept.	5		CD 9	750 00					
Dec.	17		CD12	600 00					
				2,650 00					2,650 00

Working papers. Instead of a pair of Retained Earnings columns, the working papers of an individual proprietorship contain a pair of capital columns.

The following working papers do not contain Adjustments columns; it is assumed that no adjustments are required.

JAMES WHITE
Working Papers
Year Ended December 31, 19—

	Trial Balance		Income Statement		Statement of Capital		Balance Sheet	
Cash................................	3,850.00						3,850.00	
Accounts receivable................	9,000.00						9,000.00	
Notes receivable...................	2,000.00						2,000.00	
Accounts payable...................		6,000.00						6,000.00
Notes payable......................		2,000.00						2,000.00
Sales..............................		48,000.00		48,000.00				
Sales returns and allowances.......	1,000.00		1,000.00					
Purchases..........................	35,000.00		35,000.00					
Purchase returns and allowances....		500.00		500.00				
Expenses...........................	12,000.00		12,000.00					
James White, capital...............		9,000.00				9,000.00		
James White, drawings..............	2,650.00				2,650.00			
	65,500.00	65,500.00						
Inventory, December 31, 19—........				4,000.00			4,000.00	
			48,000.00	52,500.00				
Net income—to Capital..............			4,500.00			4,500.00		
			52,500.00	52,500.00	2,650.00	13,500.00		
Capital, December 31, 19—..........					10,850.00			10,850.00
					13,500.00	13,500.00	18,850.00	18,850.00

Statements. The income statement of an individual proprietorship does not necessarily differ from that of a corporation in the same line of business.

JAMES WHITE　　　　　　　　　　　Exhibit C

Income Statement

For the Year Ended December 31, 19—

Sales...		$48,000.00
Less sales returns and allowances.........................		1,000.00
Net sales...		$47,000.00
Less cost of goods sold:		
Purchases................................	$35,000.00	
Less purchase returns and allowances........	500.00	
Net purchases.............................	$34,500.00	
Less inventory, December 31, 19—..........	4,000.00	
Cost of goods sold................................		30,500.00
Gross profit on sales..................................		$16,500.00
Less expenses...		12,000.00
Net income...		$ 4,500.00

No income tax is shown because the proprietor's total tax is usually affected by other matters not related to the business, such as income from personal investments.

Instead of the statement of retained earnings prepared for a corporation, a statement of the proprietor's capital is prepared.

JAMES WHITE　　　　　　　　　　　Exhibit B

Statement of Proprietor's Capital

For the Year Ended December 31, 19—

Investment, January 1, 19—.............................		$ 7,500.00
Add:		
Additional investment......................	$1,500.00	
Net income for the year—Exhibit C..........	4,500.00	6,000.00
Total		$13,500.00
Deduct withdrawals....................................		2,650.00
Balance, December 31, 19—.............................		$10,850.00

The investment at the beginning of the year and the additional investment during the year were determined from the capital account.

JAMES WHITE　　　　　　　　　　　Exhibit A

Balance Sheet

December 31, 19—

Assets		Liabilities and Proprietor's Equity	
Current assets:		Current liabilities:	
Cash...................	$ 3,850.00	Accounts payable........	$ 6,000.00
Accounts receivable......	9,000.00	Notes payable...........	2,000.00
Notes receivable.........	2,000.00	Total current liabilities.	$ 8,000.00
Merchandise inventory...	4,000.00	Proprietor's equity:	
		James White, capital—Exhibit B..............	10,850.00
	$18,850.00		$18,850.00

The balance sheets of an individual proprietorship and a corporation do not necessarily differ except in the owners' equity section. The balance sheet of an individual proprietorship shows the proprietor's capital in one amount, whereas the balance sheet of a corporation shows the capital stock and retained earnings.

Partnerships

Nature of a partnership. "A partnership," as defined by the Uniform Partnership Act, "is an association of two or more persons to carry on, as co-owners, a business for profit."

The partnership and the corporation are the two most common forms of organization by which two or more persons can join in a business enterprise. The partnership form is usually employed in comparatively small businesses requiring no more capital than can be contributed by a few partners; or in professional practices, such as law, medicine, and accounting, in which the relations of the firm to its clientele should involve a personal responsibility.

Some of the significant characteristics of the partnership form of business organization are briefly discussed below. For a comprehensive treatment of these matters, a text on the law of partnerships should be consulted.

No separate legal entity. Generally, a partnership has no legal status as an entity. The assets are owned, and the liabilities are owed, by the partners collectively. However, this common-law concept of the partnership has been somewhat modified by the Uniform Partnership Act, which, for instance, enables a partnership to hold real and personal property in its own name. The Uniform Partnership Act has not been adopted by all of the states.

Mutual agency. Each partner is an agent for all of the other partners in matters coming within the scope of partnership activities. Therefore, outsiders have a right to assume that the partnership is bound by the acts of any partner relative to its affairs.

Unlimited liability. Each partner is individually liable for all of the debts of a partnership incurred during his membership in the firm; he may assume a liability for debts incurred before his admission to the partnership; and, unless proper notice of withdrawal is given to the public, he may be liable for partnership debts incurred after his retirement. If a partner pays partnership debts from his personal assets, he is entitled to reimbursement.

Limited partnerships are permissible in some states. A limited partner has no personal liability to creditors, but he must maintain his investment at the amount contributed at the time of organization. There must be at least one general partner who is liable to creditors for debts which cannot be paid from firm assets.

Limited right to dispose of interest. A partner has a legal right to assign his partnership interest to another person, although he may be subject to a suit for damages for any loss incurred by his partners as a consequence of such an assignment. But he cannot compel the other partners to accept the assignee as a partner.

Division of income. Partnership income may be divided among the partners in any manner to which they agree. Consequently, the division of income is more flexible in a partnership than in a corporation.

Withdrawal of assets. Because the stockholders of a corporation generally have no personal liability for corporate debts, the law places limitations on the amounts of dividend payments or other asset distributions which may be made to corporate stockholders. There are no similar legal restrictions on partners' withdrawals of cash or other assets; however, the partners may make agreements among themselves placing limitations on the amounts which they may withdraw.

Effect of partner's death. Unless the partnership agreement provides otherwise, the death of a partner automatically dissolves the partnership of which he was a member. His heirs have a right to be paid the amount of his partnership interest, but they have no right (except by consent of the other partner or partners) to succeed him as members of the firm.

The partnership contract. The partnership relation is created by a contract. The contract may be oral, but it is much better to have it in writing, because partners have been known to forget the features of oral agreements which prove ultimately to be to their disadvantage. A partnership contract is sometimes called *the partnership agreement* and sometimes *the articles of partnership.* Among the more important things to be covered by the contract are those mentioned below.

(1) The names of the partners and the name of the partnership.
(2) The date when the contract becomes effective.
(3) The nature of the business.
(4) The place where operations are to be conducted.
(5) The amount of capital to be contributed by each partner and the assets to be invested and the valuations to be placed on them.
(6) The rights and duties of the partners.
(7) The dates when the books are to be closed and the profits ascertained and divided.
(8) The portion of the net income to be allowed to each partner.

(9) The drawings to be allowed each partner and the penalties, if any, to be imposed because of excess withdrawals.
(10) The length of time that the partnership is to continue.
(11) Conditions under which a partner may withdraw or may be compelled to withdraw; the bases for the determination of his equity in the event of withdrawal; and agreements regarding the payment of his equity in full or in installments.
(12) Procedures in the event of the death of a partner.
(13) Provision for arbitration in the event of disputes.
(14) The rights and duties of the partners in the event of dissolution.

Capital and drawing accounts. The capital and drawing accounts of a partnership are similar to those of an individual proprietorship. The following accounts are illustrative:

D. E. Snyder, Capital

				19—				
				Jan.	1	Investment	CR 1	9,000 00
				June	1	Additional investment	CR10	1,000 00

D. E. Snyder, Drawings

19—								
Apr.	15		CD 5	200 00				
Oct.	20		CD14	800 00				

J. O. Long, Capital

				19—				
				Jan.	1	Investment	CR 1	15,000 00
				July	1	Additional investment	CR11	4,000 00

J. O. Long, Drawings

19—								
Mar.	10		CD 4	500 00				
Nov.	5		CD15	700 00				

Loan accounts. A partnership may be in need of funds, which a partner is able to supply but which he is willing to furnish for a short time only. In such instances, the credit to the partner may be made in a loan account. Such loans should not be shown in the balance sheet as part of the partners' equity; they should be shown among the liabilities, but clearly distinguished from liabilities to outsiders.

On the other hand, a partner may wish to make a temporary withdrawal of funds in the form of a loan. A loan receivable

account will then appear on the partnership books.   In the balance
sheet, such a loan should be shown separately from receivables from
outsiders.

Opening the books.   If all capital contributions are in the form
of cash, no problems arise; the Cash account is debited and each
partner's capital account is credited.

If non-cash assets are invested, it is extremely important that
they be recorded at their fair values at the date of the investment.
Assume, for instance, that a partner invests land and a building
which he is carrying on his books at $20,000, which was the cost to
him less depreciation.   At the date when he invests this property
in the partnership, it is worth $25,000.   If the property were
recorded on the partnership books at $20,000 and later sold for
$25,000, all of the partners would share in the gain; this would not
be fair to the partner who invested the property and who should
have received a $25,000 credit for it.

If any liabilities of a partner are assumed by the partnership, they should, of course, be credited to liability accounts, and
the partner's capital account should be credited with the net
investment.

Goodwill.   If a partner's investment consists of a going business, it may be equitable to give the partner a capital credit for the
goodwill of the business.   A business may have goodwill if it has
exceptionally good earnings.   The valuation of the goodwill is a
matter of agreement among the partners, and should be based on
the probable future amount of profits attributable to the business
brought in by the partner.   The amount, if any, agreed upon
should be debited to a Goodwill account, with an offsetting credit
to the partner's capital account.

The profit and loss ratio.   The ratio in which partners divide
their net income or net loss is called the *profit and loss ratio*.   If
partners make no agreement regarding the division of income and
losses, the law assumes an agreement to divide them equally.   If
partners make an agreement regarding the division of income,
without any mention of losses, the agreed method for the division
of income applies also to the division of losses.

Closing the books.   After the revenue and expense accounts
have been closed to Revenue and Expense, the closing may be
completed by one of the following procedures.

(1) Close the Revenue and Expense account to the partners'
capital accounts.   Close the partners' drawing accounts to
their respective capital accounts.

This procedure is illustrated on the following page, it

being assumed that the net income of Snyder and Long for the year was $8,000, and that it was to be divided equally.

Revenue and expense............................	8,000.00	
D. E. Snyder, capital........................		4,000.00
J. O. Long, capital..........................		4,000.00
To divide the net income for the year equally.		
D. E. Snyder, capital............................	1,000.00	
D. E. Snyder, drawings......................		1,000.00
To close the drawing account.		
J. O. Long, capital..............................	1,200.00	
J. O. Long, drawings........................		1,200.00
To close the drawing account.		

(2) Close the Revenue and Expense account to the partners' drawing accounts.   Close the partners' drawing accounts to their respective capital accounts.

Revenue and expense............................	8,000.00	
D. E. Snyder, drawings......................		4,000.00
J. O. Long, drawings........................		4,000.00
To divide the net income for the year equally.		
D. E. Snyder, drawings..........................	3,000.00	
D. E. Snyder, capital.......................		3,000.00
To close the drawing account.		
J. O. Long, drawings............................	2,800.00	
J. O. Long, capital.........................		2,800.00
To close the drawing account.		

The choice of method is a matter of personal preference.   Those accountants, including the authors, who prefer the first method, like to have the capital account show details: the increase resulting from the partner's share of net income and the decrease caused by drawings.   Those who prefer the second method like to have the capital account show merely the net change resulting from income and drawings.

Working papers.   The working papers of a partnership contain a pair of columns for each partner, as shown in the illustration on page 162.

SNYDER AND LONG
Working Papers
Year Ended December 31, 19—

	Trial Balance		Income Statement		D. E. Snyder, Capital		J. O. Long, Capital		Balance Sheet	
Cash	14,800.00								14,800.00	
Accounts receivable	18,000.00								18,000.00	
Accounts payable		3,000.00								3,000.00
D. E. Snyder, capital		10,000.00				10,000.00				
D. E. Snyder, drawings	1,000.00				1,000.00					
J. O. Long, capital		19,000.00						19,000.00		
J. O. Long, drawings	1,200.00						1,200.00			
Sales		90,000.00		90,000.00						
Sales discounts	200.00		200.00							
Purchases	60,000.00		60,000.00							
Purchase discounts		700.00		700.00						
Selling expenses	13,000.00		13,000.00							
General expenses	14,500.00		14,500.00							
	122,700.00	122,700.00								
Inventory, December 31, 19—				5,000.00					5,000.00	
			87,700.00	95,700.00						
Net income—Divided equally			8,000.00			4,000.00		4,000.00		
			95,700.00	95,700.00	1,000.00	14,000.00	1,200.00	23,000.00		
Capitals at the end of the year:										
Snyder					13,000.00					13,000.00
Long							21,800.00			21,800.00
					14,000.00	14,000.00	23,000.00	23,000.00	37,800.00	37,800.00

Income statement. The income statement of a partnership will be similar to that of an individual proprietorship or a corporation in the same line of business.

SNYDER AND LONG   Exhibit C

Income Statement

For the Year Ended December 31, 19—

Sales..		$90,000.00
Less sales discounts....................................		200.00
Net sales...		$89,800.00
Less cost of goods sold:		
Purchases...............................	$60,000.00	
Less purchase discounts....................	700.00	
Net purchases..........................	$59,300.00	
Less inventory at the end of the year........	5,000.00	
Cost of goods sold................................		54,300.00
Gross profit on sales..................................		$35,500.00
Less expenses:		
Selling expenses..........................	$13,000.00	
General expenses..........................	14,500.00	27,500.00
Net income...		$ 8,000.00

This statement does not show any deduction for income taxes. A partnership, as such, does not ordinarily* pay any federal income tax, but is required to file an information return showing the results of its operations and each partner's share of the net income or net loss.   Each partner is subject to income tax on his share of the partnership net income.

Statement of partners' capitals. In order to prepare the following statement, it was necessary to refer to the capital accounts to determine the investments at the beginning of the year and the additional investments during the year.

SNYDER AND LONG   Exhibit B

Statement of Partners' Capitals

For the Year Ended December 31, 19—

	D. E. Snyder	J. O. Long	Total
Investments, January 1, 19—...............	$ 9,000.00	$15,000.00	$24,000.00
Add:			
Additional investments.................	1,000.00	4,000.00	5,000.00
Net income for the year—Exhibit C.......	4,000.00	4,000.00	8,000.00
Totals.....................................	$14,000.00	$23,000.00	$37,000.00
Deduct withdrawals......................	1,000.00	1,200.00	2,200.00
Balances, December 31, 19—...............	$13,000.00	$21,800.00	$34,800.00

Balance sheet. The balance sheet of a partnership usually shows the capital of each partner, with a reference to the statement of partners' capitals, where details can be found.

---

* Section 1361 of the Internal Revenue Code of 1954 provides that, under certain conditions, a proprietorship or a partnership can elect, for federal income tax purposes, to be taxed as if it were a corporation.

SNYDER AND LONG   Exhibit A

Balance Sheet

December 31, 19—

Assets

Current assets:

Cash... \$14,800.00

Accounts receivable................................ 18,000.00

Merchandise inventory.............................. 5,000.00

$37,800.00

Liabilities and Partners' Equity

Current liabilities:

Accounts payable.................................. $ 3,000.00

Partners' equity—Exhibit B:

D. E. Snyder, capital..................... \$13,000.00

J. O. Long, capital....................... 21,800.00   34,800.00

$37,800.00

Other methods of dividing earnings and losses.

Some of the things which should be given consideration in the determination of an equitable division of partnership earnings are:

The relative amounts of capital furnished by the partners.

The relative values of the services rendered by the partners. These may differ because of differences in business ability and/or in time devoted to partnership affairs.

Various matters, such as seniority, business contacts, profit potential of a going business contributed by a partner, and the degree of risk-taking. The degree of risk-taking depends on the dangers of loss and the relative amounts of the partners' capitals, as well as their outside assets to which the firm creditors may have recourse for the payment of partnership debts.

Various methods of dividing partnership earnings and losses are discussed below, under the following captions:

(1) In a fractional ratio.

(2) In a capital ratio.

(3) Interest on capitals, and the remainder in a fractional ratio.

(4) Salaries to partners, and the remainder in a fractional ratio.

(5) Salaries, interest, and the remainder in a fractional ratio.

Basis of illustrations. For purpose of illustration, we shall assume that the capital accounts of two partners appear as follows:

J. L. Lane, Capital

1958					1958				
June	1		CD 6	500 00	Jan.	1		CR1	10,000 00
Nov.	1		CD11	1,500 00	Aug.	1		CR8	2,000 00

D. K. Burton, Capital

1958					1958				
Apr.	1		CD 4	1,000 00	Jan.	1		CR1	20,000 00
Dec.	1		CD12	2,000 00	July	1		CR7	2,000 00

The debit balances in the drawing accounts at the end of the year were: J. L. Lane, $3,000; D. K. Burton, $4,000.

The balances in the drawing accounts represent the totals of the agreed monthly drawings; the debits in the capital accounts record withdrawals in excess of the agreed monthly drawing amounts.

The revenue and expense accounts have been closed, and the Revenue and Expense account has a credit balance of $12,000, the amount of the net income for the year.

(1) *Divisions in a fractional ratio.* The equal division of the net income of Snyder and Long on page 161 is an illustration of a division in a fractional ratio.

To illustrate another fractional-ratio division, let us assume that the partners, Lane and Burton, after consideration of the determinants of an equitable division of earnings, agree that adequate recognition can be given to all of the determinants by dividing the net income in the ratio of one-fourth to Lane and three-fourths to Burton. The entries to close the books are:

Revenue and expense...........................	12,000.00	
J. L. Lane, capital........................		3,000.00
D. K. Burton, capital......................		9,000.00
To divide the net income in the ratio of 25% and 75%.		
J. L. Lane, capital............................	3,000 00	
J. L. Lane, drawings......................		3,000.00
To close Lane's drawing account.		
D. K. Burton, capital.........................	4,000.00	
D. K. Burton, drawings....................		4,000.00
To close Burton's drawing account.		

The entries closing the drawing accounts are omitted from the remaining illustrations. They would be the same as those above.

(2) *Divisions in a capital ratio.* If the capital investments are the major source of income and the other determinants of an equitable division of earnings are not pertinent, the net income may be divided in a capital ratio. Two illustrations are given below:

Division in ratio of capitals at beginning of period. The capital accounts on pages 164 and 165 show the following balances on January 1:

J. L. Lane..	$10,000.00
D. K. Burton...	20,000.00

The net income division on this basis is shown below:

Partner	Capitals at Beginning	Fraction	Amount
Lane.............................	$10,000.00	⅓	$ 4,000.00
Burton..........................	20,000.00	⅔	8,000.00
Total.........................	$30,000.00		$12,000.00

Division in ratio of capitals at end of period. As an inducement for partners to refrain from making withdrawals of material amounts during the period for which income is being divided, and to encourage them to invest additional capital as needed, it may be preferable to divide the net income in the ratio of the capitals at the end of the period, thus:

Partner	Capitals at end	Fraction	Amount
Lane.............................	$10,000.00	1⁰⁄₂₉	$ 4,137.93
Burton..........................	19,000.00	1⁹⁄₂₉	7,862.07
Total.........................	$29,000.00		$12,000.00

(3) *Interest on capitals; remainder in fractional ratio.* Suppose that the partners agree that *some* consideration should be given to capital investments, but that consideration should also be given to other determinants of an equitable division of the net income. Therefore, they agree to divide a portion of the net income in the capital ratio by allowing 6% interest on the capitals, and to divide the remainder in some other fractional ratio—say, equally. The interest may be computed on the capitals at the beginning or at the end of the year, as agreed; in the following entries, the interest is computed on opening capitals.

```
Revenue and expense..........................  1,800.00
    J. L. Lane, capital.........................            600.00
    D. K. Burton, capital.......................          1,200.00
  To allow interest on opening capitals.
    Lane:   6% on $10,000 = $   600
    Burton: 6% on $20,000 = $1,200

Revenue and expense.......................... 10,200.00
    J. L. Lane, capital.........................          5,100.00
    D. K. Burton, capital.......................          5,100.00
  To divide remaining net income equally.
```

(4) *Salaries to partners, and remainder in a fractional ratio.* Partners may agree to make a partial division of the net income in the form of salaries in order to give recognition to the difference in the value of their services. The remaining net income may be divided equally or in any other ratio to which the partners agree. One illustration will be sufficient: salaries and an equal division of the remainder.

For purposes of illustration, assume that Lane is allowed a salary of $3,600 a year and Burton is allowed a salary of $4,800. They are permitted to draw such amounts during the year as they desire, and at the end of the year their salaries are to be credited to them.   The following entries will be made:

```
Revenue and expense...........................  8,400.00
    J. L. Lane, capital...........................              3,600.00
    D. K. Burton, capital.......................              4,800.00
    To credit the partners with their agreed salaries.

Revenue and expense...........................  3,600.00
    J. L. Lane, capital...........................              1,800.00
    D. K. Burton, capital.......................              1,800.00
    To divide the remaining net income equally.
```

(5) *Salaries, interest, and remainder in a fractional ratio.* Assume that Lane and Burton agree to make the following income division:

```
Salaries:
    Lane................................................  $3,600.00
    Burton.............................................   4,800.00
    Interest on capitals—6% on January 1 balances.
    Remainder equally.
```

Following are the entries to close the Revenue and Expense account:

```
Revenue and expense...........................  8,400.00
    J. L. Lane, capital...........................              3,600.00
    D. K. Burton, capital.......................              4,800.00
    To credit the partners with their agreed salaries.

Revenue and expense...........................  1,800.00
    J. L. Lane, capital...........................                600.00
    D. K. Burton, capital.......................              1,200.00
    To credit the partners with 6% interest on their
    January 1 capitals:
    Lane   —6% of $10,000.
    Burton—6% of $20,000.

Revenue and expense...........................  1,800.00
    J. L. Lane, capital...........................                900.00
    D. K. Burton, capital.......................                900.00
    To divide the remaining net income equally.
```

The methods of showing this division of net income in the working papers and in the statement of partners' capitals are illustrated on pages 168 and 169.   The working papers do not show all of the information required for the statement of partners' capitals.   It is necessary to refer to the partners' capital accounts on pages 164 and 165 for information about additional investments during the year and withdrawals in excess of the agreed amounts charged to the drawing accounts.

LANE AND BURTON
Working Papers
Year Ending December 31, 1958

	Trial Balance		Income Statement		J. L. Lane, Capital		D. K. Burton, Capital		Balance Sheet	
Cash	17,000								17,000	
Accounts receivable	15,000								15,000	
Accounts payable		3,000								3,000
J. L. Lane, capital		10,000				10,000				
J. L. Lane, drawings	3,000				3,000					
D. K. Burton, capital		19,000						19,000		
D. K. Burton, drawings	4,000						4,000			
Sales		90,000		90,000						
Sales discounts	200		200							
Purchases	64,000		64,000							
Purchase discounts		700		700						
Selling expenses	13,000		13,000							
General expenses	6,500		6,500							
	122,700	122,700								
Inventory, December 31, 1958				5,000					5,000	
			83,700	95,700						
Net income			12,000							
Divided as follows:										
Salaries						3,600		4,800		
Interest on capitals						600		1,200		
Balance equally						900		900		
			95,700	95,700	3,000	15,100	4,000	25,900		
Capitals at end of year:										
Lane					12,100					12,100
Burton							21,900			21,900
					15,100	15,100	25,900	25,900	37,000	37,000

LANE AND BURTON   Exhibit B

Statement of Partners' Capitals
For the Year Ended December 31, 1958

	J. L. Lane	D. K. Burton	Total
Balances, January 1, 1958.......	$10,000.00	$20,000.00	$30,000.00
Add:			
Additional investments.......	2,000.00	2,000.00	4,000.00
Net income for the year (Exhibit C):			
Salaries..................	3,600.00	4,800.00	8,400.00
Interest on capitals.........	600.00	1,200.00	1,800.00
Remainder equally.........	900.00	900.00	1,800.00
Total..................	$17,100.00	$28,900.00	$46,000.00
Deduct withdrawals............	5,000.00	7,000.00	12,000.00
Balances, December 31, 1958....	$12,100.00	$21,900.00	$34,000.00

Interest on partners' capitals and salaries to partners are not expenses but are divisions of net income; therefore, they do not enter into the computation of the net income shown by the income statement, but are shown in the statement of partners' capitals.

Salaries and/or interest in excess of net income.   The salaries and interest in the preceding illustration totaled $10,200.   Suppose that the net income had been only $9,000; how should it have been divided?

The entries for the salaries and the interest must be made in accordance with the agreement, thus:

Revenue and expense...........................	8,400.00	
J. L. Lane, capital.........................		3,600.00
D. K. Burton, capital......................		4,800.00
To credit the partners with their agreed salaries.		

Revenue and expense...........................	1,800.00	
J. L. Lane, capital.........................		600.00
D. K. Burton, capital......................		1,200.00
To credit the partners with 6% interest on their capitals.		

After these entries are posted, the Revenue and Expense account will have a debit balance of $1,200, because the salary and interest credits to the partners total $10,200, whereas the net income was only $9,000.   Because the partners agreed to an equal division of the balance after salaries and interest, the $1,200 debit balance in the Revenue and Expense account will be divided equally by the following entry:

J. L. Lane, capital.................................	600.00	
D. K. Burton, capital.............................	600.00	
Revenue and expense.........................		1,200.00
To divide the debit balance in the Revenue and Expense account equally, as agreed.		

The foregoing entries divide the $9,000 net income between the partners as follows:

	Lane	Burton	Total
Credits:			
Salaries.	$3,600.00	$4,800.00	$ 8,400.00
Interest on capitals	600.00	1,200.00	1,800.00
Total credits	$4,200.00	$6,000.00	$10,200.00
Less debit for remainder	600.00	600.00	1,200.00
Distribution of net income	$3,600.00	$5,400.00	$ 9,000.00

If partners' salaries and interest on their capitals are agreed upon, entries therefor must be made even though the operations of the business result in a loss.   For instance, assume that the operations result in a loss of $5,000, and that salaries and interest are to be allowed as in the preceding illustration; the credits to the partners for salaries and interest, and the debits to them for the final balance of the Revenue and Expense account, will be as indicated in the following tabulation:

	Lane	Burton	Total
Credits to partners:			
Salaries	$3,600.00	$4,800.00	$ 8,400.00
Interest on capitals	600.00	1,200.00	1,800.00
Total credits to partners for salaries and interest	$4,200.00	$6,000.00	
Offsetting debit to Revenue and Expense			$10,200.00
Net loss			5,000.00
Debit balance in Revenue and Expense			$15,200.00
Debits to partners to close Revenue and Expense	7,600.00	7,600.00	
Net debits to partners—equal to net loss	$3,400.00	$1,600.00	

The journal entries to close the Revenue and Expense account are as follows:

Revenue and expense	8,400.00	
J. L. Lane, capital		3,600.00
D. K. Burton, capital		4,800.00
To credit the partners with their agreed salaries.		

Revenue and expense	1,800.00	
J. L. Lane, capital		600.00
D. K. Burton, capital		1,200.00
To credit the partners with 6% interest on their capitals.		

J. L. Lane, capital	7,600.00	
D. K. Burton, capital	7,600.00	
Revenue and expense		15,200.00
To divide the debit balance in the Revenue and Expense account equally, as agreed.		

Liquidation of a partnership.   A partnership is liquidated when the business is discontinued or the assets are transferred to other parties.

Basis of illustration of liquidation. Assume the following balance sheet of a partnership:

A AND *B*

Balance Sheet

October 31, 19—

Assets			Liabilities and Partners' Equity	
Cash.......................		$ 5,000	Accounts payable.............	$ 9,000
Accounts receivable...	$25,000		*A*, loan.....................	5,000
Less allowance for			*A*, capital...................	25,000
doubtful accounts.	1,000	24,000	*B*, capital...................	20,000
Inventory............		30,000		
		$59,000		$59,000

In addition to investing $25,000, *A* has loaned the business $5,000.

Disposal of assets. Assume that *X* desires to acquire the business of *A* and *B*, and that the partners sell their inventory and accounts receivable to *X* for $52,000. *A* and *B* retain the $5,000 of cash shown in the foregoing balance sheet and are to pay the $9,000 of accounts payable. The sale of the inventory and receivables will be recorded as follows:

X..	52,000.00	
Loss on sale of business........................	2,000.00	
Allowance for doubtful accounts................	1,000.00	
Inventory................................		30,000.00
Accounts receivable......................		25,000.00
To record the sale of the assets to *X*.		
Cash..	52,000.00	
X..		52,000.00
To record collection for assets sold.		

Division of the gain or loss. Any gain or loss on the disposal of the assets should *always* be divided between the partners before any cash distribution is made to them, because the amounts of cash to which the partners are entitled cannot be determined until their shares of the gain or loss have been credited or charged to them. The gain or loss should be divided between the partners in their profit and loss ratio. Assuming that *A* and *B* share earnings equally, the $2,000 loss on the sale of the assets to *X* will be divided by the following entry:

A, capital.....................................	1,000.00	
B, capital.....................................	1,000.00	
Loss on sale of business....................		2,000.00

Distribution of cash. After the disposal of the inventory and the receivables, the collection of the cash, and the division of the loss between the partners, the balance sheet of the firm is as shown on page 172.

A AND *B*

Balance Sheet

November 3, 19—

Assets		Liabilities and Partners' Equity	
Cash.....................	$57,000.00	Accounts payable..........	$ 9,000.00
		A, loan..................	5,000.00
		A, capital...............	24,000.00
		B, capital...............	19,000.00
	$57,000.00		$57,000.00

The distribution of cash should be made in the following order:

(1) In payment of liabilities to outside creditors:

Accounts payable...........................	9,000.00	
Cash...................................		9,000.00

(2) In payment of partner's loan:

A, loan....................................	5,000.00	
Cash...................................		5,000.00

(3) In payment of partners' capitals:

A, capital.................................	24,000.00	
B, capital.................................	19,000.00	
Cash...................................		43,000.00

Partner with a debit balance. It sometimes happens that a partner has a debit balance in his capital account as a result of operating losses, drawings, and losses on the disposal of assets during liquidation. Three illustrative cases are presented.

Case 1. Assume that, after the sale of all assets and the payment of liabilities, the trial balance of a partnership shows the following balances:

Cash............................	20,000.00	
M, capital........................	5,000.00	
N, capital........................		25,000.00
	25,000.00	25,000.00

The entire cash balance should be paid to *N;* this payment would reduce his capital credit to $5,000.   He has a right to collect $5,000 from *M*.

Case 2. Assume that, after the sale of all assets and the payment of liabilities to outside creditors, the trial balance of a partnership shows the following balances:

Cash............................	25,000.00	
O, capital........................	2,000.00	
O, loan...........................		3,000.00
P, capital........................		24,000.00
	27,000.00	27,000.00

Enough of the credit in O's loan account should be transferred to his capital account to make good the debit balance in his capital account; this is accomplished by the following entry:

```
O, loan........................................  2,000.00
    O, capital.................................            2,000.00
    To apply the right of offset, by transferring $2,000
    of O's loan to his capital.
```

The payments to partners will then be made as indicated by the following entries:

```
O, loan........................................  1,000.00
    Cash......................................            1,000.00
    To record the payment of O's loan.

P, capital.....................................  24,000.00
    Cash......................................            24,000.00
    To record the payment of P's capital.
```

Case 3. In this case it is assumed that, after the sale of all assets and the payment of all liabilities, a partnership's trial balance appears as follows:

```
Cash.......................  20,000.00
R, capital.................   5,000.00
S, capital.................              15,000.00
T, capital.................              10,000.00
                            ─────────  ─────────
                            25,000.00  25,000.00
```

The profit-and-loss-sharing arrangement was as follows: R, 20%; S, 40%; T, 40%.

R should pay \$5,000 cash into the partnership to make good the debit balance in his capital account; if he does so, there will be \$25,000 cash on hand, which will be sufficient to pay S and T in full.

But suppose that it is desired to distribute the \$20,000 of cash on hand to S and T before it is known whether or not R will pay in the \$5,000. In determining how to divide the cash between S and T, we should remember that, if R fails to pay in the \$5,000, this loss will have to be borne by S and T in their profit and loss ratio. In the past, S and T each had a 40 per cent share in the net income or net loss; that is to say, their shares were equal. Therefore, if R should fail to pay in the \$5,000, S and T would share the loss equally. Accordingly, they should be paid *down to* \$2,500 each, thus leaving each of these partners with a capital balance sufficient to absorb his share of the loss if R fails to pay in the \$5,000. The entry to record the payment is:

```
S, capital.....................................  12,500.00
T, capital.....................................   7,500.00
    Cash......................................            20,000.00
    To record the distribution of cash to S and T.
```

The resulting trial balance will be:

R, capital....................	5,000.00	
S, capital....................		2,500.00
T, capital....................		2,500.00
	5,000.00	5,000.00

CHAPTER 12

Corporations

Nature of the corporation. Probably the most famous definition of the corporation is the one given in 1819 by Chief Justice Marshall in the Dartmouth College case decision, in which he described a corporation as "an artificial being, invisible, intangible, and existing only in contemplation of law."

This definition emphasizes the basic characteristic of the corporation—its separate legal entity. It is not a group of separate persons, as is the case with a partnership; it is itself a legal "person." It can make contracts in its own name; it can sue and be sued, even by its own stockholders; and it can own real estate. Within the limits of its charter, it can perform any business act which could be performed by a natural person.

Because a corporation is a legal entity, a stockholder usually is not liable for its debts unless his shares have a par value and were issued at a discount, and even under such circumstances he is liable only for the amount of the discount. Stockholders of certain classes of corporations, such as banks organized under the laws of some of the states, may have a personal liability in an amount not in excess of the par value of their shares. Although relief from personal liability is an advantage to the stockholders, it sometimes operates to the disadvantage of the corporation by limiting its borrowing power: banks frequently refuse to loan money to a corporation unless stockholders of means endorse the notes.

The separate legal entity of a corporation gives it a continuity of life. A partnership is dissolved by the death, insanity, insolvency, or withdrawal of a partner; therefore, the continued life of a partnership is constantly in jeopardy. A corporation can be dissolved only by agreement of the stockholders, by forfeiture of the charter by the state, by judicial decree, or by the expiration of the period stated in the charter. A charter may give a corporation an unlimited life; if the life is limited by the charter, a renewal usually can be obtained.

Continuity of corporate life notwithstanding changes in ownership is effected by the issuance of transferable shares. This transferability of interest gives a stockholder several advantages not enjoyed by a partner. (1) A partner cannot withdraw from a partnership or sell his interest without the consent of the other partners; if he undertakes to do so without their consent, he renders himself liable to a suit for damages. Unless there is an agreement among the stockholders to the contrary, a stockholder can sell his stock to any willing purchaser whenever he desires to do so; the consent of the other stockholders is not required. (2) If a partner dies, his heirs have a right to be paid the amount of his capital interest, but they have no right to enter the business as partners without the consent of the other partners. If a stockholder dies, his stock passes to his heirs, who thus acquire an interest in the business. (3) A stockholder can pledge his stock as collateral to a loan; a partner cannot easily pledge his partnership interest. Therefore, a stockholder is in a better position than is a partner to borrow needed funds.

These characteristics of the corporation make it an attractive form of business organization even for small enterprises. In large businesses, in which the capital requirements make it necessary to obtain funds from many investors, the adoption of the corporate form is virtually imperative. A partnership with hundreds of partners, subject to termination upon the death of any one of them, would be in an intolerable chaos of repeated dissolution and reorganization; the orderly conduct of business would be impossible, and capital could not be attracted.

On the other hand, the corporation has certain disadvantages, the chief of which are mentioned below.

Corporations are required to pay income taxes, and the stockholders are required to pay income taxes on dividends received in excess of an amount stated by the Internal Revenue Code. This "double taxation" has induced a number of small corporations to reorganize as partnerships.

The state requires the payment of a fee at the time the corporation is organized and imposes an annual franchise tax for the privilege of continuing operations. Numerous reports, not required of partnerships, must be furnished to the state of incorporation and to other states where business is transacted.

A corporation has a right to conduct only the kind of business authorized in its charter; to engage in other lines of business, it must obtain an amendment of its charter.

Each state regards corporations organized in other states as *foreign* corporations. If a corporation desires to do business in states other than the one from which it obtained its charter, it may be required to obtain licenses from those states and pay a license fee to each of them. Failure to obtain such licenses may result in losses of far greater amount than the fees. For instance, a state may refuse unlicensed foreign corporations the privilege of bringing actions in its courts, and heavy losses may be incurred because of the inability to enforce claims by actions at law.

Restrictions of various kinds are placed upon corporations by the states.   In some states, a corporation cannot own the stock of another corporation; in some states, it cannot own its own stock; in some states, its liabilities cannot exceed a certain percentage of its capital stock.   Also, corporations frequently are prohibited from owning more real estate than they require for business uses.

Organization of a corporation.   If a corporation is to be organized, an attorney should be consulted, because the laws of the various states differ regarding the rights and duties of corporations organized under their laws and the procedure for organizing corporations.   Since the procedure differs in the various states, and since the organization of corporations is the work of an attorney, the subject will not be discussed in detail here.

In general, and subject to the exceptions incident to the diversity of laws, the organization of a corporation involves steps somewhat as follows:

(1) An application, signed by a required number of incorporators, is filed with a designated state officer.   This application states, among other things:
   (a) The name of the corporation.
   (b) The nature of the business which it is desired to conduct.
   (c) The amount of the authorized capital stock, and the number of shares into which it is to be divided.
   (d) The names and the addresses of the original subscribers to the stock.
   (e) The assets paid into the corporation by these subscribers.
(2) If the application is approved, a charter (which is often the approved application itself) is received from the state officer with whom the application was originally filed. This charter evidences the fact that the corporation has been organized and is authorized to conduct business.
(3) A meeting of the incorporators (or stockholders) is held for the purpose (among other things) of electing directors.
(4) A meeting of the directors is held, and officers are elected.
(5) Capital stock certificates are issued.

Organization costs.   The organization of a corporation involves expenditures for attorneys' fees, the fee paid to the state at the time of incorporation, and other costs.

The traditional attitude of accountants toward organization costs is that they are a sheer loss and should be written off as soon as possible. However, this does not seem to be a logical attitude. The very existence of a corporation is dependent upon the incurring of organization costs, and they may be regarded as benefiting the business during its entire existence. The authors believe that management is entirely justified, from the standpoint of acceptable accounting theory, in regarding organization expenditures as the cost of an intangible asset to be shown indefinitely in the balance sheet as Organization Costs. This point of view is finding increasing acceptance among accountants.

Corporate management. If a business is organized as a corporation, the stockholders are its owners, but they have no authority to transact its business. The stockholders elect directors, to whom the general management of the business is committed. In most states, a person cannot serve as a director of a corporation unless he is one of its stockholders.

Although the directors are charged with responsibility for the general management of the business, their duties are to a considerable extent supervisory, since most of the work of management is performed by officers elected by them. The officers usually include a president, a vice-president, a secretary, and a treasurer. Sometimes one individual holds more than one office; for instance, one person may be secretary and treasurer. On the other hand, there may be several vice-presidents, an assistant secretary, and an assistant treasurer. The president usually is the ranking officer, but in some corporations there is an officer called the "chairman of the board," whose rank is superior to that of the president. The secretary is the official custodian of the corporate records and seal. The treasurer is the chief financial officer.

Elements of stockholders' equity. Corporate accounts need not differ from the accounts of other types of business organization except in the manner of reflecting the elements of stockholders' equity. In accounting for the elements of stockholders' equity of a corporation, the emphasis is placed on *source*. How much of the stockholders' equity was produced by stockholders' capital contributions? How much consists of retained earnings? How much, if any, was produced in other ways?

Proper accounting for the elements of stockholders' equity according to their source requires a knowledge of the nature of capital stock and of the various classes of surplus. These matters are discussed in this chapter and the following one.

Capital stock. The two principal classes of stock are common and preferred. Capital stock may have a par value or be without par value.

Par value stock. Although $100 is a customary par value, any par may be authorized by the charter. Thus, a corporation with an authorized capital of $100,000 might have 100 authorized shares of $1,000 par value, 1,000 shares of $100 par value, 100,000 shares of $1 par value, or its shares may have any desired par value.

No-par stock. Prior to 1912, the capital stocks of all corporations in the United States had a par value. In that year, the first American law permitting the issuance of stock without par value was enacted in New York. Other states have since passed similar laws, but, unfortunately, the laws of the several states are not uniform.

Advantages and disadvantages of no-par stock. The par value of a share of stock is usually of little significance compared to the book value and the market value. Printing a par value on a certificate has made it easy for promoters to extract money from the uninformed and the unsuspecting. There is an inevitable attraction about a $100 share of stock offered for $50, and many people find it impossible to resist such an offer. The omission of a par value may have the desirable effect of causing some prospective buyers to make inquiries regarding the issuing company's net assets and earnings.

No par value stock has another great advantage: it avoids the discount liability. If a share of stock with a par value of $100 is issued for $90, the purchaser incurs a discount liability of $10, and may be required to furnish that amount of cash for the payment of the corporation's debts. But if a no par value share is sold for $90, there is no discount liability. Discount is the difference between a par value and a lower issuing price; if there is no par value, there can be no discount and, therefore, no discount liability.

No-par stock has some disadvantages. Transfer fees, organization fees, stock taxes, fees for operation in foreign states, and other taxes may be based on an arbitrary valuation of the stock very much in excess of its fair value. Laws not uncommonly provide that no-par shares shall, for tax purposes, be assumed to have a par of $100; such a provision might entail a very inequitable expense if the shares were issued at, say, $5.

Authorized stock. The kind of stock, its basic features, and the number of shares authorized are shown by a memorandum in the capital stock account. Suppose that a corporation receives authorization to issue 1,000 shares of $100 par value common stock; this information would be recorded directly in the ledger, thus:

Common Stock	
(Authorized issue, 1,000	shares of $100 par value.)

Recording the issuance of par value shares. In the case of par value stock, the stock account is always credited with the par value of shares issued, regardless of the issuance price of the shares.

Using the stock authorization data above, if 500 shares of common stock are issued at par, the entry for the issuance is:

```
Cash......................................  50,000.00
    Common stock...........................          50,000.00
    Issuance of 500 authorized shares at their par
    value of $100.
```

When this entry is posted, the Common Stock account will appear as follows:

Common Stock

(Authorized issue, 1,000	shares of $100 par value.)
	Date 50,000.00

If stock is issued for more than par value, the excess is credited to a Premium on Common Stock account. The entry below illustrates a case where 400 shares of $100 par value common stock are issued for $110 per share.

```
Cash......................................  44,000.00
    Common stock...........................          40,000.00
    Premium on common stock................           4,000.00
    Issuance of 400 authorized shares at a premium
    of $10 per share.
```

Stock may be issued at a premium at the time of the organization of the corporation. Stock premiums are probably more common, however, when additional shares are issued at a subsequent date. For instance, assume that a company with 1,000 outstanding shares of capital stock with a total par value of $100,000 has been successful in its operations and has accumulated, over several years, retained earnings of $50,000, thus giving the stock a book value of $150 per share. It might not be fair to the old stockholders to allow new stockholders to acquire stock at par. Moreover, because of the book value of the outstanding stock and the company's earnings record and prospects, its stock might be so attractive that investors would willingly pay a premium to obtain it.

Stock may be issued for less than par; that is, at a discount. The entry below illustrates a case where 100 shares of $50 par value common stock are issued for $40 per share.

```
Cash......................................  4,000.00
Discount on common stock..................  1,000.00
    Common stock...........................          5,000.00
    Issuance of 100 authorized shares at a discount of
    $10 per share.
```

Stock is rarely issued at a discount. In many states the issuance of stock at a discount is illegal. In states where it is legal, a discount may be allowed as an inducement to prospective investors. However, such an inducement is of doubtful value because, if stock is issued at a discount and the company becomes unable to pay its debts, the holders of such stock at the time of the corporation's insolvency (whether they be the original subscribers or subsequent transferees) may be held personally liable to the corporation's creditors for amounts equal to the original discount on the shares which they hold.

Premium and discount in the balance sheet. The balances of the Premium on Common Stock and Discount on Common Stock accounts should be shown in the Stockholders' Equity section of the balance sheet in the manner illustrated below:

```
Stockholders' equity:
  Common stock—$100 par value; authorized and issued,
    1,000 shares.....................................  $100,000.00
  Premium on common stock...........................    10,000.00
  Retained earnings.................................    25,000.00
```

or thus:

```
Stockholders' equity:
  Common stock—$100 par value; authorized and issued,
    1,000 shares.....................................  $100,000.00
  Discount on common stock..........................    10,000.00*
  Retained earnings.................................    25,000.00
  * Deduction.
```

If some shares are issued at a discount while other shares are issued at a premium, the amount of discount should be shown in a discount account and the amount of premium should be shown in a premium account. They should not be offset, because the stockholder who acquired his stock at a discount is not relieved of his discount liability merely because some other stockholder acquired his stock at a premium.

Disposition of stock premium and discount accounts. Stock premiums have customarily been carried indefinitely in premium on stock accounts, and this procedure is correct. The availability of such a credit for dividends depends on the laws of the state of incorporation.

In the past, many accountants advocated writing off stock discount as rapidly as possible, by charges to Retained Earnings. This procedure was probably adopted because, although stock discount was customarily shown on the asset side of the balance sheet, it was realized that it had no valid asset status. When stock discount was recognized for what it is—not an asset, but an item to be deducted in the Stockholders' Equity section of the balance sheet to show the net amount of the funds paid in by the investors—it became apparent that there was no particular reason for writing it off. In fact, it appears definitely improper to write off stock discount. For one reason, the write-off beclouds the record of the capital investment and creates a confusion between the original investment and the accumulated earnings. For another reason, writing off the discount against Retained Earnings does not relieve the stockholders of their discount liability, but merely conceals it.

Recording the issuance of no-par stock. The methods described above for recording issuances of par value stock can be used for recording issuances of no-par stock. But, in the absence of a par, this question arises: At what amount should the shares be recorded in the capital stock accounts? The answer depends on the law of the state of incorporation and on any resolution which the directors, with the permission of the law, may have passed.

The laws of some states require that the entire amount received for no-par stock shall (like the par of par value shares) be regarded as stated, or legal, capital, not to be impaired by distributions to stockholders; if a corporation is organized in a state with such a law, the entire amount received for its no-par stock should be credited to a capital stock account.

Some states allow corporations to credit a surplus account with a portion of the proceeds of the issuance of no-par stock, and some states even allow corporations to use such surplus for dividends. If a corporation is organized in a state which permits the crediting of a surplus account with a portion of the proceeds of the issuance of no-par shares, and if the directors pass a resolution stating the amount which is to be credited to the capital stock account, the accountant should be governed by the resolution; he should credit the capital stock account with the amount stated by the resolution, and should credit a paid-in surplus account with any excess of the proceeds over the stated capital amount. If the law permits such a division of the proceeds but the directors do not pass a resolution establishing a stated value for the stock, the entire proceeds of the stock issuance should be credited to the capital stock account.

Basis of illustrations. In the following illustrations of entries recording the issuance of no-par stock, it is assumed that the corporation is authorized to issue 1,000 shares of no par value common stock. The authorization is recorded by a memorandum in the Common Stock account, in the manner previously illustrated.

First illustration. In this illustration it is assumed that the corporation was organized in a state which requires that the entire proceeds of the issuance of shares be regarded as stated capital, and that all of the authorized shares were issued at $60 per share. The entry to record the issuance is:

```
Cash......................................... 60,000.00
    Common stock.............................            60,000.00
    Issuance of 1,000 authorized shares at $60 per
    share.
```

After this entry is posted, the Common Stock account appears as follows:

Common Stock

(Authorized issue, 1,000 shares	of no par value.)
	Date 1,000 shares issued.... 60,000.00

Second illustration.   It is again assumed that all of the authorized stock was issued for $60,000, that the laws of the state of incorporation permitted the company to credit a surplus account with a portion of the proceeds, and that the directors established a $50 stated value for the shares.   The entry to record the issuance is:

```
Cash......................................... 60,000.00
    Common stock.............................            50,000.00
    Paid-in surplus..........................            10,000.00
    Issuance of 1,000 shares at $60 per share.
    Stated value of $50 per share established by the
    directors.
```

Paid-in surplus in the balance sheet.   If only a portion of the proceeds of no-par stock is credited to a capital stock account, and the remainder is credited to a paid-in surplus account, the facts may be shown in the balance sheet in the manner illustrated below.

```
Stockholders' equity:
    Common stock—No par value; authorized and
      issued, 1,000 shares at stated value........ $50,000.00
    Paid-in surplus............................  10,000.00 $60,000.00
    Retained earnings...........................            15,000.00
```

or as follows:

```
Stockholders' equity:
    Common stock—No par value; authorized and
      issued, 1,000 shares at stated value.................. $50,000.00
    Surplus:
      Paid-in surplus......................... $10,000.00
      Retained earnings......................  15,000.00  25,000.00
```

Interval between receipt and collection of subscriptions.   Time may elapse between the date when subscriptions for stock are received and the date when they are collected and the stock is issued.   Under such circumstances, the accounts to be used are as shown on the following page.

Subscriptions Receivable:
>When subscriptions are received, this account is debited with the aggregate price of shares subscribed.
>As collections are received from subscribers, the account is credited.

Common Stock Subscribed:
>When subscriptions are received, this account is credited with the par or stated value or, in the case of no-par stock without stated value, the aggregate subscription price of the shares subscribed.
>When stock certificates are issued, this account is debited and Common Stock is credited.
>The credit balance in this account shows the par or stated value or aggregate subscription price, as the case may be, of the shares subscribed for but not issued.

Common Stock:
>The number of shares authorized and the basic characteristics of the stock are shown by a memorandum entry in this account. When certificates are issued, this account is credited with the par or stated value or aggregate subscription price of the shares represented by the certificates. In other words, whatever amount was credited to the Common Stock Subscribed account when the shares were subscribed for is credited to the Common Stock account when the shares are issued.

Illustrations—Par value stock. In the three following illustrations it is assumed that the corporation has an authorized issue of 1,000 shares of common stock of $100 par value.

First illustration—All subscriptions collected in full. Subscriptions are received for 500 shares at par.

Subscriptions receivable......................	50,000.00	
Common stock subscribed..................		50,000.00
Subscriptions for 500 authorized shares at par.		

When the subscriptions are collected, the following entries are made:

Cash..	50,000.00	
Subscriptions receivable...................		50,000.00
Collection of subscriptions in full.		
Common stock subscribed.....................	50,000.00	
Common stock...........................		50,000.00
Issuance of 500 shares after collection of subscriptions in full.		

Second illustration—Some subscriptions fully, others partially, collected. Subscriptions are received for 1,000 shares at par.

```
Subscriptions receivable........................ 100,000.00
    Common stock subscribed.................          100,000.00
    Subscriptions for 1,000 authorized shares at par.
```

It is now assumed that, at a subsequent date, half of the subscriptions are collected in full.   The following entries are made:

```
Cash....................................... 50,000.00
    Subscriptions receivable....................      50,000.00
    Collection in full of subscriptions for 500 shares.

Common stock subscribed..................... 50,000.00
    Common stock...........................          50,000.00
    Issuance of 500 shares for which subscriptions
    have been fully collected.
```

It is further assumed that $10,000 is collected on the other subscriptions.   An entry is made to record the collection, but the stock certificates are not issued because the collection was only partial.

```
Cash....................................... 10,000.00
    Subscriptions receivable...................      10,000.00
    Partial collection on subscriptions for 500 shares.
```

Third illustration—Stock subscribed at a premium.   Subscriptions are received for 750 shares at a premium of $10 per share.

```
Subscriptions receivable...................... 82,500.00
    Common stock subscribed.................      75,000.00
    Premium on common stock.................       7,500.00
    Subscriptions for 750 authorized shares at $110
    per share.
```

When the subscriptions are collected, the following entries are made:

```
Cash....................................... 82,500.00
    Subscriptions receivable...................      82,500.00
    Collection of subscriptions in full.

Common stock subscribed..................... 75,000.00
    Common stock..........................          75,000.00
    Issuance of 750 shares after collection of sub-
    scriptions in full.
```

Illustrations—No-par stock.   In the two following illustrations it is assumed that the corporation has an authorized issue of 1,000 shares of common stock of no par value.

First illustration—No stated value, all subscriptions collected in full.   Subscriptions are received for 300 shares at $70 per share.

```
Subscriptions receivable...................... 21,000.00
    Common stock subscribed.................      21,000.00
    Subscriptions for 300 authorized shares at $70
    per share.
```

When the subscriptions are collected, the entries shown on the following page are made.

Cash...	21,000.00	
Subscriptions receivable.....................		21,000.00
Collection of subscriptions in full.		
Common stock subscribed......................	21,000.00	
Common stock............................		21,000.00
Issuance of 300 shares after collection of subscriptions in full.		

Second illustration—$50 stated value, some subscriptions fully, others partially, collected. Subscriptions are received for 1,000 shares at $60 per share.

Subscriptions receivable.......................	60,000.00	
Common stock subscribed.................		50,000.00
Paid-in surplus............................		10,000.00
Subscriptions for 1,000 authorized shares at $60 per share. Stated value, $50 per share.		

It is now assumed that, at a subsequent date, half of the subscriptions are collected in full and that $5,000 is received from the other subscribers in partial settlement of their subscriptions.

Cash...	35,000.00	
Subscriptions receivable....................		35,000.00
Collection from subscribers, $30,000 of which is in full settlement for subscriptions for 500 shares.		
Common stock subscribed......................	25,000.00	
Common stock............................		25,000.00
Issuance of 500 shares for which subscriptions have been fully collected.		

Uncollected subscriptions in the balance sheet. If it is expected that the subscriptions will be collected in the near future, they may be shown in the balance sheet under the Current Assets caption, but they should be clearly shown as subscriptions receivable and not combined with accounts receivable from customers.

If there is no immediate intention to call on the subscribers for the uncollected balances of their subscriptions, the subscriptions receivable may still be shown on the asset side of the balance sheet, but under the caption of Sundry Assets.

Subscribed but unissued stock in the balance sheet. Assume that a company has authorization to issue 1,000 shares of common stock of $100 par value; that 750 shares have been subscribed for; and that collections of subscriptions for 600 shares have been received in full, and the stock has been issued. The facts may be shown in the balance sheet as follows:

Stockholders' equity:
    Common stock—$100 par value; 1,000 shares authorized.

Issued, 600 shares..	$60,000
Subscribed for but not issued, 150 shares................	15,000

Notice that it is customary to set forth in the Stockholders' Equity section the basic facts regarding the capital stock of the corporation. It is considered unacceptable to use only the bare account titles of the capital stock accounts.

Stock issued for property. When capital stock is issued for property other than cash, a valuation problem may arise. If 1,000 shares of $25 par value stock are issued for a piece of property, it does not follow that $25,000, the aggregate par value of the shares issued, is the proper amount to use in recording the transaction. In accounting, the rule is that property should be recorded initially at cost. The problem is, how is cost measured when payment is made by issuing shares of stock?

Under such circumstances, accountants estimate cost by using evidence of market values as a measure of cost. For example, suppose that the stock being issued for property is actively purchased and sold by investors through an established stock exchange. If recent stock transactions show that the shares are currently worth $80 per share, it would be reasonable to infer that property acquired for 1,000 shares of stock "cost" the corporation $80,000. As an alternative, the accountant might use recent cash subscription prices, of the shares being issued for property, as an indication of the price being paid for the property.

If there are no data available regarding the value of the shares issued, the accountant will look for evidence indicative of the current value of the property acquired. Perhaps there have been recent cash sales of identical or similar property. In some instances, the appraised value of the property may be relevant. To summarize, the accountant will settle on a figure for accounting purposes by using the value of the shares issued or the value of the asset acquired, whichever is the better indicator under the circumstances of the amount "paid" for the property.

As the following illustrations show, the issuance of shares for property may require the use of stock discount or premium accounts.

Data:

A corporation acquires land for 1,000 shares of $50 par value common stock.

The common stock is actively traded on a national stock exchange; recent transactions were completed at $65 per share.

There is no recent information regarding the value of the land.

Entry:

Land..	65,000.00	
Common stock............................		50,000.00
Premium on common stock.................		15,000.00
Acquisition of land for 1,000 shares of common stock.		

Data:

A corporation acquires a patent for 1,000 shares of no-par common stock, no stated value.

The common stock is not listed on any stock exchange.

Several days ago, 1,500 shares were issued for $10 per share.

There is only meager information regarding the value of the patent.

Entry:

```
Patent...................................... 10,000.00
    Common stock............................          10,000.00
    Acquisition of patent for 1,000 shares of common
    stock.
```

Data:

A corporation acquires land for 500 shares of common stock having a stated value of $20 per share.

No shares have been issued for five years and there is no established market for the outstanding shares.

During recent weeks similar plots of land have been sold to other businesses for $12,500, cash.

Entry:

```
Land....................................... 12,500.00
    Common stock............................          10,000.00
    Paid-in surplus.........................           2,500.00
    Acquisition of land for 500 shares of common
    stock.
```

It should be mentioned that the law allows the directors of a corporation to set a valuation for accounting purposes on property acquired by the issuance of shares of stock. If the directors have exercised their prerogative in this matter, the accountant will record the property at the valuation ordered by the board of directors.

Records Peculiar to Corporations

Subscribers' ledger. If stock subscriptions are not immediately collected, the Subscriptions Receivable account in the general ledger should be supported by a subsidiary ledger containing an account with each subscriber. The subscriber's account is debited with the amount of his subscription, and is credited with the amounts collected from him.

Stock certificate and stub. Blank stock certificates are bound in books with stubs, like check books. The certificate illustrated on page 6 (Chapter 1) appears again on page 189, still attached to its stub. The certificate has been signed by the secretary and the president of the corporation, and is ready to be detached, stamped

Certificate No. 1

200 Shares

CAPITAL STOCK $8,000.00
800 Shares of $10.00 Par Value

THIS CERTIFIES That _____ Henry Dobson _____ is the

owner of _____ Two hundred _____ Shares of the Capital Stock of

COMMUNITY TELEVISIONS

transferable only on the books of the Corporation by the holder hereof in person or by attorney upon the surrender of this Certificate properly endorsed.

IN WITNESS WHEREOF, the said Corporation has caused this Certificate to be signed by its duly authorized officers, and to be sealed with the seal of the Corporation at _Chicago, Illinois_ this _20th_ day of _July___, 19 —

J.B. Hudson
Secretary

J.C. White
President

Stock Certificate with Stub

Certificate No. _1_

For _200_ Shares

Issued to

Henry Dobson

Transferred from

Original

Date _July 20, 19 —_

Original Certificate No.	Number of Original Shares	Number of Shares Transferred

with the corporation's seal, and given to Dobson. The stub, which will remain in the certificate book, shows the essential facts about the certificate.

The important facts shown by the certificate and the stub are:

	Shown by Certificate	Shown by Stub
Certificate No...................	1	1
Number of shares...............	200	200
Authorized capital...............	$8,000.00	
Number of authorized shares.....	800	
Par value per share.............	$10.00	
Issued to......................	Henry Dobson	Henry Dobson
Transferred from...............		Original
Date of issuance of certificate....	July 20, 19—	July 20, 19—

The word "Original" appearing on the "Transferred from" line means that Dobson obtained the certificate by making an investment in the corporation, and not by purchase from another stockholder.

The use of the blank spaces in the stub is explained later.

Stockholders ledger. A stockholders ledger should be kept by corporations with numerous stockholders, and may be kept by any corporation. It contains an account with each stockholder, showing the number of shares issued in his name.

The issuance of the certificate to Henry Dobson is recorded in his account in the stockholders ledger in the manner illustrated below:

Name	Henry Dobson								
Address	173 Hickory Street, Chicago 40, Illinois								
Certificates Cancelled				Certificates Issued					Balance
Date	Ref.	Certificate Number	Number of Shares	Date	Ref.	Certificate Number	Number of Shares		
				19— July 20		1	200		200

Transfer of shares. Assume that Henry Dobson wishes to sell twenty of his shares to Robert Dawson. Dobson will fill in the assignment form which is printed on the back of the certificate, as shown on page 191.

When the stock certificate is presented to the corporation for transfer of the stock, the certificate is canceled and attached to the stub from which it was originally taken. The open stubs (stubs

For Value Received,_____I_____hereby sell,

transfer and assign to___Robert Dawson_____

——————————————————Twenty—————————————————

shares of stock within mentioned and hereby authorize

_____J. B. Hudson_____

to make the necessary transfer on the books of the Corporation.

WITNESS___my___hand and seal this_____3rd_____day of

___August___, 19___—___

Witnessed by:

___Frank Heath___   ___Henry Dobson___(Seal)

Assignment Form on Back of Certificate

to which no unissued or canceled certificates are attached) will indicate the certificates still outstanding.

In accordance with the terms of Dobson's assignment, two new certificates will be issued: one certificate to Robert Dawson for the twenty shares which Dobson sold to him, and another certificate to Dobson for the one hundred eighty shares which he retained. At the right is the stub of the new certificate issued to Dawson; the stub of the certificate for one hundred eighty shares issued to Dobson would be similarly filled in.

A record of the transfer is made in the transfer journal, in the manner illustrated on page 192.

Certificate No.__5____

For_____20_____Shares

Issued to

___Robert Dawson___

Transferred from

___Henry Dobson___

Date_August 3,__19___—___

Original Certificate No.	Number of Original Shares	Number of Shares Transferred
1	200	20

Stock Certificate Stub

Stock Transfer Journal

Page 1

Date	From			To		
	Name	Certificate Number	Number of Shares	Name	Certificate Number	Number of Shares
19—						
Aug. 3	Henry Dobson	1	200	Robert Dawson	5	20
				Henry Dobson	6	180

After the entry in the transfer journal is posted, the stockholders' ledger accounts affected appear as shown below.

Name Robert Dawson

Address 1369 Fortunata Street, Chicago 61, Illinois

Certificates Cancelled				Certificates Issued				Balance
Date	Ref.	Certificate Number	Number of Shares	Date	Ref.	Certificate Number	Number of Shares	
				19— Aug.	3 TJ 1	5	20	20

Name Henry Dobson

Address 173 Hickory Street, Chicago 40, Illinois

Certificates Cancelled				Certificates Issued				Balance
Date	Ref.	Certificate Number	Number of Shares	Date	Ref.	Certificate Number	Number of Shares	
19— Aug.	3 TJ 1	1	200	19— July 20		1	200	200
				Aug.	3 TJ 1	6	180	— 180

Transfer agent and registrar.   Large corporations, particularly those whose stock is listed on a stock exchange, may (either by requirement of the stock exchange or voluntarily) engage a transfer agent and a registrar to perform the duties incident to the issuance and transfer of shares and the keeping of records showing the names and addresses of stockholders and the number of shares owned by each stockholder.   A bank or trust company usually is engaged to perform the duties of transfer agent, and another bank or trust company is engaged to perform the duties of registrar.

The employment of a transfer agent and a registrar serves as a safeguard to the stockholders.   When certificates are to be transferred, they are delivered to the transfer agent, who cancels the old certificates, signs the new certificates, and passes them to the registrar, who also signs them. Records of the stockholders are kept by the transfer agent. The registrar's chief function is to act as a control against any possible overissuance of stock, and for this purpose the registrar maintains a record showing the aggregate number of shares outstanding.

Minute book. A record of all the actions taken by the stockholders and directors at their meetings is kept by the secretary of the company in a minute book. This book does not contain debit and credit entries; it contains a record of events written in narrative form, or in the form of resolutions.

The minute book contains information which may be required by the company's accountant for purposes of making entries in the books, and by the public accountants when they audit the company's accounts. For instance, reference to the minutes may be necessary to validate the stated value of no-par stock, the amounts of officers' salaries, the valuations assigned to non-cash assets acquired for stock, and liabilities for dividends.

The minute book usually contains a copy of the company's by-laws. The rights and duties of the stockholders, directors, and officers are in general governed by the state corporation law; in many particulars, however, they are stipulated by the corporation's own by-laws. The by-laws contain other stipulations with respect to the management of the corporation, such as the dates on which the regular meetings of the stockholders and directors shall be held, the formalities to be complied with in calling special meetings, and any transactions (such as the issuance of new stock with special privileges) that require the approval of the stockholders. The by-laws are usually passed by the stockholders, but in some states they may be passed or amended by the board of directors.

CHAPTER 13
Corporations (Concluded)

Classes of stock. Shares of stock entitle their holders to four basic rights, namely:

(1) To share in the management; that is, to vote at the stockholders' meetings.

(2) To share in the earnings; that is, to receive dividends when they are declared by the directors.

(3) To share in the distribution of the assets of the corporation if it is dissolved.

(4) To subscribe to any additional issues of stock of the class held. This is known as the *pre-emptive right*.

If there is only one class of stock, these four fundamental rights are enjoyed proportionately, share and share alike, by all stockholders.

If there are two or more classes of stock, one class may enjoy more than its proportionate share of some right, or may have some right curtailed. Thus, preferred stock may enjoy special preferences in the matter of dividends or in the distribution of assets in liquidation; on the other hand, the preferred stockholders may have no right to vote, or may have a right to vote only under certain conditions, such as the failure of the corporation to pay preferred dividends for a stated period of time.

Stock preferred as to dividends. Stock which is preferred as to dividends entitles its holders to a dividend at a stipulated rate on par, or to a stipulated amount per share in the case of no-par stock, before any dividend is paid on the common stock. Preferred stockholders have no right to dividends unless the directors declare them. Directors may decline to declare dividends on preferred as well as common stock on the ground that the funds are needed in the business; the stockholders then have no recourse except to elect a board which will pay dividends, or to bring action in the courts in the hope of proving that the retention of the funds is not justifiable.

Cumulative and non-cumulative stock. Stock which is preferred as to dividends may be:

(a) Cumulative, in which case all dividends in arrears on preferred stock must be paid before dividends can be paid on the common stock.

To illustrate, assume $100,000 par value of 6% cumulative preferred stock, $100,000 par value of common stock, and retained earnings of $30,000; no dividends have been paid on the preferred stock for four years—three prior years and the current year. Since the preferred stock is cumulative, the preferred stockholders are entitled to dividends of $24,000 before any dividends can be paid to the common stockholders.

(b) Non-cumulative, in which case dividends omitted in any year are lost forever.

Non-cumulative preferred stock is not a desirable investment because of the danger that dividends may be lost. This is particularly true if the preferred stock is non-voting, or if the voting power of the common stock exceeds that of the preferred stock and the directors are elected by the common stockholders.

Participating and non-participating stock. Stock which is preferred as to dividends may be:

(a) Fully participating, or entitled to dividends at as high a rate as the dividends paid on the common stock.

To illustrate, assume $100,000 par value of 6% fully participating preferred stock, $200,000 par value of common stock, and retained earnings of $27,000.

The preferred stock is entitled to a 6% dividend, or $6,000.

A 6% dividend (or $12,000) may then be paid to the common stockholders without any additional dividend payment being made to the preferred stockholders.

But if a 9% dividend ($18,000) instead of a 6% dividend is paid to the common stockholders, an extra 3% must be paid to the preferred stockholders.

(b) Partially participating, or entitled to participate with the common stock, but only to a limited degree. For instance, the preferred may carry a 6% preference rate, with a right to participate to 8%.

(c) Non-participating, or entitled to receive its stipulated preferred dividend but no more, regardless of the rate paid on the common stock.

Rights under various conditions of preference. If the preferred stock is non-cumulative and non-participating, its holders have a right to only the stipulated rate of return, regardless of the earnings; and if a dividend is not paid in one year, the right to it is forever lost. On the other hand, if the stock is participating and cumulative, the preferred stockholders will receive as high a rate of dividend as the common stockholders receive, and the preferred dividend for every year must be paid before anything can be paid to the common stockholders.

If a corporation is successful, and its preferred stock is non-participating, the common stockholders may receive larger dividends than those paid to the preferred stockholders. As a consequence, the common stock may have a much higher market value than the preferred stock.

Stock preferred as to assets. In the event of dissolution and liquidation, stock that is preferred as to assets is entitled to payment in full (the par value of par stock or a stated liquidation value for no-par stock) before any distribution is made on the common stock.

To illustrate, assume $100,000 par value of preferred stock, $100,000 par value of common stock, and assets of only $150,000 after paying all liabilities. If the preferred stock is preferred as to assets, $100,000 should be paid to the preferred stockholders, and only $50,000 to the common stockholders. If the preferred stock is not preferred as to assets, the assets should be divided between the common and the preferred stockholders in the ratio of the par value of the two classes of stock—that is, equally.

The preference as to assets may extend only to the par of the stock, or the preferred stockholders may have a right to receive par and all dividends in arrears. Just what the preferred stockholders' rights are must be determined in each case by reference to the stock certificate or the charter.

The fact that stock is preferred as to dividends does not make it preferred as to assets also, nor is stock which is preferred as to assets necessarily preferred as to dividends also.

Reasons for classes of stocks. Different classes of stock with differing rights have been devised to meet the desires of management and to make the shares sufficiently attractive to investors. This fact can best be indicated by an illustration.

Assume that a group of men had an opportunity to buy a going business at a cost of $500,000, and that, on the basis of its past operations, the business could be expected to earn about $50,000 a year. They decided to organize a corporation to acquire the business. We shall assume that they wanted to keep their own investment down to about $250,000, perhaps because that was all they had available, or because they wanted to make other investments, or because they wanted to obtain a "leverage" on net income (this term is explained later).

If they obtained a charter which authorized the corporation to issue only common stock, they would not have control, because outsiders would have equal votes with them. They therefore decided to issue $250,000 par value of common stock and $250,000 par value of non-voting preferred stock.

The next matters which required their consideration were the rights and preferences to be given to the preferred stock. Would it be necessary to make the stock preferred as to assets as well as to dividends? Or was the business sufficiently safe to make preference as to assets unnecessary? What dividend rate would be necessary to make the stock attractive to investors? Could the stock be marketed without making it cumulative? Could it be marketed without making it participating?

We shall assume that the organizing group believed that the hazards of the business were so few and slight that preference as to assets would be unnecessary, and that a 6% cumulative preferred stock could be marketed without the participating feature. The organizing group wanted to avoid making the preferred stock participating, because non-participating preferred stock would give their common stock a leverage on the net income. To illustrate: If the preferred stock were participating and if the company earned $50,000 on the $500,000 investment, both the preferred and the common stocks would earn ten per cent; but if the preferred stock was non-participating, the allocation of earnings would be:

Total net income...	$50,000
Applicable to preferred stock—6% of $250,000................	15,000
Remainder—applicable to common stock—equal to 14% of $250,000...	$35,000

This illustration should serve to indicate the matters to which consideration is given when the capital structure of a corporation is being planned.

Accounts with various classes of stock. The methods of recording the issuance of preferred stock are the same as those applicable to common stock, previously discussed.

If several classes of stock are issued, the account title for each class should clearly indicate its nature. Thus, a ledger might contain accounts with titles similar to the following:

Subscriptions Receivable—Preferred
6% Preferred Stock
6% Preferred Stock Subscribed
Premium on Preferred Stock

Subscriptions Receivable—Common
No-par Common Stock
No-par Common Stock Subscribed
Paid-in Surplus

Common and preferred stock in the balance sheet. If there are two classes of stock, the amounts thereof should be shown separately in the balance sheet, and the special rights of the preferred stock should be described briefly. No attempt need be made to divide the surplus elements in order to show the rights of the two classes of stock therein. The balance sheet presentation of the facts may, therefore, be as follows:

```
Stockholders' equity:
  Capital stock:
    Preferred, 6% participating, cumulative;
      par value, $100; authorized and issued,
      1,000 shares......................  $100,000.00
    Common, no par value; stated value, $10;
      authorized and issued, 10,000 shares...  100,000.00 $200,000.00

  Surplus:
    Premium on preferred stock............  $  2,000.00
    Paid-in surplus.......................     10,000.00    12,000.00
    Retained earnings.................................     75,000.00
        Total.........................................   $287,000.00
```

Stock values. The following terms are used in expressing different bases for the valuation of stock:

Par value. This is a nominal value, printed on the certificate. For instance, if a corporation is authorized to issue $100,000 of capital stock, represented by 1,000 shares, the par value of each share is $100.

Book value. The book value of a share of stock of a certain class is computed by dividing the stockholders' equity applicable to the class by the number of shares of the class outstanding.

For instance, if a corporation has 1,000 shares of common stock (and no preferred stock) outstanding, and its balance sheet shows:

```
Capital stock............................  $100,000.00
Retained earnings........................     30,000.00
    Total................................                $130,000.00
```

the book value of each share is $130,000 ÷ 1,000, or $130.

If there is preferred stock outstanding, the preferred stockholders' interest in the retained earnings will depend upon whether the stock is participating, and also upon whether the preferred stock is cumulative and whether there are preferred dividends in arrears.

Market value. This is the price at which a share of stock can be sold. It depends partly on the book value of the stock and partly on the corporation's earnings record and the prospects of future earnings and dividends.

Liquidation value. This is the amount which a stockholder will be entitled to receive if the corporation goes out of business, disposes of its assets, pays its liabilities, and distributes the residue among its stockholders. If common stock only is outstanding, its liquidation value will depend only on the amount available for distribution to the stockholders after the realization of the assets and the payment of liabilities. If common and preferred stocks are outstanding, the liquidation values of both classes will also depend upon whether the preferred stock is preferred as to assets and whether the preferred stockholders are entitled to any dividends in arrears.

Redemption value. Corporations sometimes issue preferred stock with a right to redeem it. The redemption price may be stated in terms such as: *par, par and dividends in arrears,* or *par and a premium of $5 per share.*

Stated value. The concept of stated value is discussed at some length on pages 204 and 205.

The nature of surplus. Surplus may be broadly defined as the portion of the stockholders' equity not represented by its capital stock. Formerly, one surplus account was regarded as sufficient, and it was credited not only with the net income from operations, but with many other kinds of increments in net worth. During recent years, accountants have come to believe that two general classes of surplus should be recognized:

Earned surplus (now often called "retained earnings")—the portion of the owners' equity represented by retained earnings produced by operations and by extraneous transactions such as the sale of fixed assets and investments.

Paid-in surplus—including elements of the following nature:
(A) Surplus resulting from transactions in the company's own stock, such as:
   (1) Issuance of par value stock at a premium.
   (2) Issuance of no-par stock at amounts in excess of those credited to capital stock accounts.
   (3) Reissuance of treasury stock at an amount greater than its acquisition cost.
(B) Surplus resulting from stockholders' contributions:
   (1) Donations by stockholders.
   (2) Assessments on stockholders.
(C) Surplus resulting from contributions by outsiders, including gifts of assets—such as the gift of a plant to a company to induce it to locate in the donor city.

Special points on paid-in surplus. The term *paid-in surplus* is a generic term applicable to all surplus elements of the nature mentioned above, but the student should not get the impression that all paid-in surplus elements should be recorded in a single Paid-in Surplus account.　To do so would result in an inadequate classification of paid-in surplus according to source and a failure to maintain the detailed records necessary for proper accounting and statement-preparation purposes.　Therefore, the ledger may contain several paid-in surplus accounts, in which the words "paid-in" may or may not appear, such as:

Premium on Preferred Stock.
Paid-in Surplus—No-par Common Stock.
Paid-in Surplus—From Treasury Stock Transactions.

As one illustration of the importance of keeping separate accounts with the various elements of paid-in surplus, assume that preferred stock is issued at a premium of $50,000, and that common stock is issued at a discount of $20,000.　There is a net paid-in surplus of $30,000; but separate accounts should be used so that the books will show that the common stockholders are subject to a discount liability.

Another reason for setting up detailed paid-in surplus accounts is that some elements of paid-in surplus may be legally available for dividends whereas other portions are not.　Writers have sometimes expressed the opinion that dividends should never be charged to paid-in surplus.　This is incorrect.　Paid-in surplus may or may not be available for dividends, depending on how it was created and on the law of the state in which the company was incorporated. It probably would be better to say that stockholders should have a right to assume that dividends come from retained earnings unless they are informed to the contrary, and that, if dividends are charged to paid-in surplus, disclosure of that fact should be made to them. There have been instances in which a corporation has been given a false appearance of prosperity by crediting a portion of the proceeds of stock issuances to a paid-in surplus account and by charging dividends to such surplus, thus merely giving back to the stockholders a portion of their investment but creating the impression that they are receiving dividends out of earnings.

Paid-in surplus should never be charged with asset write-downs and losses which normally would be charged to income or retained earnings.　This rule was laid down in the first bulletin issued by the American Institute of Certified Public Accountants' Committee on Accounting Procedure.　Following are two illustrations of the application of the rule.　If the allowance for doubtful accounts is found to be inadequate, it should not be increased by an offsetting charge against paid-in surplus; to do so would relieve current income of a charge which normally should be made to it. Fixed assets should not be written down by charges to paid-in surplus; to do so would relieve future periods of depreciation charges which normally should be made against income.

Appropriated surplus. Corporations sometimes transfer, by journal entries, portions of their surplus to special-purpose reserves. Such appropriations or restrictions of surplus may be classified as follows:

(A) Made in compliance with contracts:
   (1) With creditors.
       For instance, bond indentures may place a limitation on the amount of dividends which can be paid while the bonds are outstanding. To reflect this limitation in the accounts, the portion of the surplus not available for dividends may be transferred to a reserve. Such a reserve is still a part of the surplus, but is temporarily not available for dividends.
   (2) With preferred stockholders.
       If, under the terms of issuance, the preferred stock of a company is to be retired (periodically or otherwise) out of funds provided by earnings, the charter provisions for the retirement of the preferred stock may require the creation of a surplus reserve. Although not available for dividends until the preferred stock is retired, such a reserve is still a part of the surplus.
(B) Made by voluntary action of the directors:
   (1) To indicate that dividends will be limited in order to permit the accumulation of funds for general purposes or for some specific purpose, such as the acquisition of additional plant assets. Such a segregation of surplus does not, of course, give any assurance that cash will be available for the expenditure to which the reserve is related.
   (2) To provide a reserve for possible losses of so uncertain and contingent a nature that the creation of a reserve by charge to income would not be justified.

If such appropriations have been made from retained earnings, the retained earnings should be detailed in the balance sheet in some manner similar to the presentation appearing on the following page.

Retained earnings:
  Appropriated:
    Bond sinking fund reserve..................... $ 60,000
    Reserve for retirement of preferred stock....... 50,000
    Reserve for plant extensions.................. 75,000
    Reserve for contingencies.................... 10,000
      Total................................. $195,000
  Free... 115,000
      Total retained earnings................... $310,000

The statement is sometimes made that appropriations of surplus should always be made from retained earnings and never from paid-in surplus. In most cases this probably is true; but, since an appropriation of surplus is usually intended to place a limitation on dividends, and since dividends are sometimes payable from paid-in surplus, occasions might arise in which an appropriation from paid-in surplus would not be improper.

The primary purpose of surplus reservations or appropriations is to communicate to persons reading the balance sheet the fact that certain amounts of surplus are restricted and not available as a basis for dividends. However, such surplus reserve accounts are frequently misunderstood. In an attempt to avoid misunderstanding, accountants are resorting to the use of footnotes to the balance sheet to communicate to the statement-user facts regarding surplus restrictions. To illustrate, suppose that a corporation is planning a large extension to its manufacturing facilities. To indicate that dividends will be limited, the directors might order a Reserve for Plant Extensions established out of retained earnings in the amount of $300,000. Thus, the trial balance would show the accounts as follows:

Reserve for plant extensions............................ 300,000.00
Retained earnings....................................... 400,000.00

However, the balance sheet could report the above facts as follows:

Retained earnings (See Note A)........................ $700,000.00

Note A:
  In view of the extensive addition to the company's manufacturing facilities now being planned, the directors have earmarked $300,000 of the retained earnings as not available for dividend purposes.

Appraisal increments. Prior to 1940, it was not an uncommon practice for companies to write up their fixed assets to appraised values. The offsetting credit frequently was made to Capital Surplus, Appraisal Surplus, or Appreciation Surplus; but many accountants, believing that the word "surplus" should not be used in connection with unrealized increments in value, preferred an account title such as "Unrealized Increment in Valuation of Fixed Assets."

In 1940 the Institute's Committee on Accounting Procedure issued a bulletin containing the following statement: "Accounting for fixed assets should normally be based on cost, and any attempt to make property accounts in general reflect current values is both impracticable and inexpedient." As a consequence of the issuance of this bulletin, the writing up of fixed assets to appraised values is now regarded as improper.

Stated capital. Among the advantages of the corporate form of business organization is that of limited liability: the stockholders are not personally liable for the debts of the corporation. Since the law gives the stockholders this protection, it is only fair that the creditors should be given some assurance that the corporation will not make payments to its stockholders, either as dividends or for the acquisition or retirement of stock, which will reduce the stockholders' equity below a stipulated amount.

Originally the corporation laws placed restrictions only on dividends. Before the advent of no-par stock, the dividend restriction usually consisted of a prohibition against any dividend payment which would reduce the stockholders' equity below the par value of the shares outstanding. With the advent of no-par stock, such a basis of restricting dividends became inapplicable; obviously it could not be applied to distributions to the holders of no-par stock.

More recently it has been recognized that the protection of creditors is inadequate unless, in addition to a restriction on dividends, there is a restriction on the amount which can be paid to stockholders for the acquisition or retirement of their stock.

For the reasons indicated above, a definition of stated capital has been included in the laws of many states. Unfortunately, the concepts of stated capital are not uniform in all states. In some states, the stated capital includes the total amount received for par or no-par shares issued, including any amount credited to a premium or paid-in surplus account. In other states, the stated capital is measured by the par value of par shares or, with respect to no-par shares, the amount per share which the directors elect to credit to a capital stock account. In some states, the amount which the directors elect to establish as stated capital per share cannot be less than a minimum fixed by law.

Since it has come to be realized that a restriction as to dividends is only a partial protection to creditors, many state statutes prescribe that the stated or legal capital must not be impaired either by the payment of dividends or by disbursements for the acquisition or retirement of shares.

Since stated capital is a legal concept, and since there is a considerable variation in the state laws with respect thereto, it is impracticable to deal exhaustively with the subject here. It must suffice to call attention to the fact that dividends and transactions in the company's stock are usually restricted by law.

Dividends. Dividends distributed by corporations to their stockholders may be classified as follows:

(A) Dividends out of surplus* (including retained earnings and paid-in surplus that is not a part of legal capital):
  (1) Decreasing stockholders' equity.
      The customary dividend of this nature is a periodical distribution of cash. However, other assets may be distributed.
  (2) Not decreasing stockholders' equity.
      This classification covers stock dividends. A stock dividend does not change the stockholders' equity; it merely decreases the surplus element and increases the capital stock element.
(B) Dividends out of legal capital:
  The principal dividends of this nature are liquidating dividends, which are intended to return all of the capital to the stockholders because the company is discontinuing operations, or to return a portion of the capital because the scope of the business is being reduced and the total capital is no longer required.

In this chapter we shall be concerned only with dividends out of surplus.

Legality of dividends out of surplus. Under what conditions does a company have a legal right to declare a dividend? It is difficult to state general rules which are not subject to exceptions because the laws of the various states differ in their regulations, especially with respect to dividends on no par value stock. In general, it may be said that a corporation has a right to pay a dividend if it has retained earnings that were produced by either operations or extraneous activities; usually, it also has a right to pay dividends from paid-in surplus that is not a part of legal capital. Dividends must not reduce the stockholders' equity below the amount of the stated capital.

Financial policy with respect to dividends. In making their decisions with respect to the amounts of dividend payments, direc-

---

* The expression "dividends out of surplus" is an abbreviation of "dividends paid out of surplus." These expressions are in common use and are therefore used in this text. However, they are subject to criticism. Since surplus is not an asset, nothing can literally be paid out of it. To avoid confusing the layman, it might be better to say "dividends which reduce surplus."

tors give consideration not only to the amount of surplus legally available for the payment of dividends, but also to matters of financial policy. A dividend payment may be undesirable because the available cash is inadequate; but if there is only a temporary shortage of cash, the directors may consider it advisable to borrow money for dividend purposes in order to maintain a continuity of dividend payments. Even when adequate cash is available, the directors may consider it advisable to pay no dividends, or to pay dividends of only limited amounts, in order to conserve the funds for expansion of the business.

Significant dates applicable to dividends, and related entries. In the case of corporations with only a few stockholders and with infrequent transfers of shares, it may be practicable to declare and pay a dividend on the same day. But for large corporations with many stockholders and frequent transfers of shares, such a procedure would be impracticable. Under such conditions there are three significant dates applicable to dividends: the date of declaration, the date of record, and the date of payment.

Date of declaration. On the date when the dividend is declared, the following entry is made:

Dividends	100,000.00	
Dividends payable		100,000.00
To record the declaration of a dividend.		

Date of record. The directors' resolution authorizing the payment of a dividend states a date as of which the corporation, by an examination of its stock records, will determine the "stockholders of record." For instance, a dividend may be declared on January 5, payable on January 30 to stockholders of record on January 20. Between January 5 and January 20, the purchaser of stock obtains a right to the dividend; after January 20, the stock is sold "ex-dividend"—that is, the seller of the stock, rather than the purchaser, is entitled to receive the dividend payment.

No entry need be made by the company on the date of record.

Date of payment. A period of time is usually required between the date of record and the date of payment because of the work involved in the determination of the stockholders of record and the preparation of the dividend checks. When the checks are mailed, the following entry is made:

Dividends payable	100,000.00	
Cash		100,000.00
Payment, to stockholders of record on January 20, of dividend declared on January 5.		

Unpaid declared dividends. After a dividend has been legally declared and notice of the declaration has been given to the stockholders, by publication or otherwise, the unpaid dividend ranks as a liability and should be shown as such in the balance sheet, usually under the Current Liability caption.   The directors may rescind the declaration of a dividend, but they can do so only if no notice of the declaration has been given to the shareholders.

Dividends in arrears on preferred stock.   Since even a preferred stockholder has no right to a dividend until it is declared, preferred dividends do not accrue; no entry for them should be made until the date of declaration.

But if dividends on cumulative preferred stock are in arrears, there is an obligation to pay these arrearages before paying dividends to the common stockholders.   The amount of the cumulative dividends in arrears should, therefore, be shown in the balance sheet.   This is usually done by adding a footnote below the balance sheet totals, thus:

> *Note:* Cumulative dividends on preferred stock were in arrears on (the balance sheet date) in the amount of $12,000.

Stock dividends.   Dividends are sometimes paid in capital stock instead of in cash.   In the usual instance, the dividend distribution is in common stock to holders of common stock.

To illustrate, assume that a company has 1,000 authorized shares of common stock of $100 par value, of which 600 shares are outstanding; also assume that a 10% stock dividend (60 shares) is declared and immediately issued.   The Committee on Accounting Procedure of the American Institute of Certified Public Accountants has taken the position that, when the shares issued as a dividend are less than about 20% of the shares previously outstanding, an amount equal to the fair value of the shares issued should be capitalized by transfer from Retained Earnings to the Common Stock and Paid-in Surplus accounts.   Assuming that the shares issued in this illustration have a fair value of $120 each, the entry to record the distribution of the stock dividend is:

Stock dividends (to be closed to Retained Earnings) .	7,200.00	
Common stock...............................		6,000.00
Paid-in surplus—From stock dividends.........		1,200.00
Issuance of a 10% dividend: 60 shares of $100 par value stock having a fair value of $120 each.		

Assume that the stock was without par value and that it had been given a stated value of $75 per share; the entry would be:

Stock dividends (to be closed to Retained Earnings) .	7,200.00	
Common stock...............................		4,500.00
Paid-in surplus—From stock dividends.........		2,700.00
Issuance of a 10% dividend: 60 shares of no-par stock (stated value, $75 per share) having a fair value of $120 each.		

If time intervenes between the declaration and payment of the stock dividend, the entries (for the dividend on par value stock, for instance) should be:

At date of declaration:

Stock dividends................................	7,200.00	
Stock dividend payable......................		6,000.00
Paid-in surplus—From stock dividends........		1,200.00
Declaration of 10% stock dividend to stockholders of record on December 31, 1958; shares to be issued February 1, 1959.		

At date of issuance:

Stock dividend payable.........................	6,000.00	
Common stock.............................		6,000.00
To record issuance of 60 shares as a stock dividend.		

If a balance sheet is prepared between the date of declaration and the date of distribution of a stock dividend, the Stockholders' Equity section should appear as illustrated below:

Stockholders' equity:			
Common stock—$100 par value; authorized, 1,000 shares.			
Issued, 600 shares.....................	$60,000.00		
To be issued February 1, 1959, as a stock dividend—60 shares................	6,000.00	$66,000.00	
Surplus:			
Paid-in—Retained earnings capitalized in connection with a stock dividend........	$ 1,200.00		
Retained earnings......................	11,000.00	12,200.00	

Treasury stock. Treasury stock is a corporation's own stock which has been issued, reacquired, and not canceled in accordance with a formal procedure specified by law. It will be noted that there are three important elements of this definition:

(1) Treasury stock must be the company's own stock; holdings of the stocks of other companies are not treasury stock.

(2) The stock must have been issued.

(3) The stock, although reacquired, must not have been canceled. Cancellation of stock is effected by a procedure prescribed by law, and places the stock in the status of unissued, or sometimes even unauthorized, shares.

Unissued and treasury stock—Purchaser's liability for discount. A stockholder who acquires unissued stock at a discount assumes a contingent liability for the amount of the discount. This means that, if the corporation is unable to pay its debts, the creditors may demand that stockholders who acquired unissued stock at a discount pay the corporation as much of the discount as is required to enable the corporation to pay its debts.

If a person acquires from a company, at a discount, par value treasury stock which was originally issued at par or more, he has no contingent liability for the discount.

Treasury stock is not an asset. Treasury shares may have a ready marketability and may be reissued; but so may unissued stock be issued; and it seems obvious that treasury stock, like unissued stock, is not an asset but is merely a possible source of additional funds.

Although treasury stock has been shown in balance sheets as an asset (sometimes even combined with securities which *are* assets, under some title such as "Government Bonds and Other Securities"), accountants now generally recognize that the acquisition of treasury stock causes a reduction in the stockholders' equity.

Treasury stock in the balance sheet. Since the acquisition of treasury stock causes a reduction of the stockholders' equity to the extent of the cost of the stock, the cost should be shown as a deduction in the Stockholders' Equity section of the balance sheet. There are several ways of showing the deduction; the method illustrated below is generally regarded as acceptable. The illustration is based on the following facts with respect to the capital stock:

The authorized issue is 1,000 shares of $100 par value common.

All the authorized stock has been issued.

The corporation has reacquired 100 shares at a cost of $12,000.

The distinction between "issued" and "outstanding" should be noted. All of the 1,000 shares have been issued, and are so shown. The number of outstanding shares is not stated in the balance sheet, but can be easily determined; there are 900 outstanding shares: the difference between the 1,000 issued shares and the 100 treasury shares.

```
Stockholders' equity:
   Common stock—$100 par value; authorized
      and issued, 1,000 shares, of which 100
      shares are in the treasury.............. $100,000.00
   Retained earnings.......................     25,000.00
         Total...........................     $125,000.00
   Deduct cost of treasury stock............     12,000.00  $113,000.00
```

If a company has a paid-in surplus as well as retained earnings, the facts may be shown in the balance sheet in this manner:

```
Stockholders' equity:
   Common stock—$100 par value; authorized
      and issued, 1,000 shares, of which 100
      shares are in the treasury.............. $100,000.00
   Paid-in surplus.........................     10,000.00
   Retained earnings.......................     25,000.00
         Total...........................     $135,000.00
   Deduct cost of treasury stock............     12,000.00  $123,000.00
```

If a company incurs a deficit after the acquisition of treasury stock, the facts may be shown as follows:

```
Stockholders' equity:
  Common stock—$100 par value;
    authorized and issued, 1,000
    shares, of which 100 shares are
    in the treasury........................ $100,000.00
  Deduct:
    Deficit.................... $ 5,000.00
    Cost of treasury stock.......  12,000.00   17,000.00 $83,000.00
```

If treasury stock is acquired by donation, there is no cost to deduct; the facts may be shown as follows:

```
Stockholders' equity:
  Common stock—$100 par value; authorized
    and issued, 1,000 shares, of which 100
    shares, acquired by donation, are in the
    treasury............................. $100,000.00
  Retained earnings......................  25,000.00 $125,000.00
```

Recording treasury stock acquisitions—Cost basis. As indicated above, the cost of treasury stock may properly be shown in the balance sheet as a deduction in the Stockholders' Equity section. To provide the information for this balance sheet presentation, it is considered proper to debit the Treasury Stock account with the cost of the stock acquired. If this procedure is adopted, an acquisition of treasury stock is recorded as follows:

```
Treasury stock................................ 12,000.00
  Cash.......................................            12,000.00
  To record the acquisition of 100 shares of $100
  par value stock at a cost of $12,000.
```

An entry of this nature should be made regardless of whether the shares have a par value or are without par value, and regardless of the amount which was received for the shares when they were issued. The treasury stock account title should indicate the nature of the stock if there is more than one class of issued stock. If the company has only one class of stock, the account title may be merely Treasury Stock; otherwise, it might be Treasury Stock—Preferred, or Treasury Stock—Common, or Treasury Stock—Common—No Par Value.

As noted, stockholders sometimes donate shares to the company; this may be done because the company is in a poor financial condition and the stockholders do not wish to invest additional funds; they, therefore, donate portions of their stock which possibly can be reissued to obtain additional funds. Since donated shares are acquired without cost, no debit and credit entries are made to

record the acquisition. A memorandum notation is made in the
Treasury Stock account, as shown below:

Treasury Stock

Date	50 shares donated								

Reissuance of treasury shares. When treasury stock is
reissued, the Treasury Stock account should be credited with the
acquisition price. Entries under various conditions are shown
below.

Reissuance at cost. Assume that the treasury stock acquired
for $12,000 is reissued for $12,000; the entry is:

```
Cash........................................ 12,000.00
    Treasury stock...........................          12,000.00
```

Reissuance at a price in excess of cost. Assume that the shares
were reissued for $13,500; the entry is:

```
Cash........................................ 13,500.00
    Treasury stock...........................          12,000.00
    Paid-in surplus—From treasury stock trans-
        actions................................           1,500.00
```

Reissuance at a price less than cost. The method of recording
reissuances of treasury stock at a price less than the original cost
depends on the law of the state of incorporation and the kinds of
surplus accounts on the company's books. Assume that shares
acquired for $12,000 are reissued for $11,500. If a paid-in surplus
exists as a result of reissuances of treasury stock of the same class
at more than cost, the entry may be:

```
Cash........................................ 11,500.00
Paid-in surplus—From treasury stock transactions.    500.00
    Treasury stock...........................          12,000.00
```

If the company has no such paid-in surplus, but has paid-in
surplus resulting from the original issuance of shares of the same
class as those acquired as treasury stock, and if this paid-in surplus
is not a part of the legal stated capital, the excess of the acquisition
price over the reissuance price of the treasury shares may be
charged to this paid-in surplus, thus:

```
Cash........................................ 11,500.00
Premium on stock (or Paid-in surplus)...........    500.00
    Treasury stock...........................          12,000.00
```

In the absence of any applicable paid-in surplus accounts, the
excess should be charged to Retained Earnings, thus:

```
Cash........................................ 11,500.00
Retained earnings..............................    500.00
    Treasury stock...........................          12,000.00
```

Reissuance of donated shares. If donated treasury stock is reissued, the entire proceeds of the reissuance should be credited to Paid-in Surplus—From Treasury Stock Transactions.

Recommended departure from the cost basis. In 1948 the executive committee of the American Accounting Association, in *Accounting Concepts and Standards Underlying Corporate Financial Statements*, expressed the following opinion:

> "An outlay by a corporation for shares of its own stock should be treated as a reduction of paid-in capital up to the pro-rata amount represented by the acquired shares, whether or not such shares are reissuable. If the outlay for the reacquired shares exceeds the pro-rata reduction in paid-in capital, the excess should be treated as a distribution of retained income. The reissue of acquired shares should be accounted for in the same manner as an original issue of corporate shares."

As an illustration of the recommended procedure, let us assume that a company's no-par stock was originally issued at $80 per share, of which $75 was credited to Capital Stock and $5 was credited to Paid-in Surplus. Also assume that a share of treasury stock is acquired at a cost of $85. If the recommended procedure is used, the entry is:

Treasury stock (Amount originally credited to Capital Stock)	75.00	
Paid-in surplus (Amount originally credited to Paid-in Surplus)	5.00	
Retained earnings	5.00	
Cash		85.00

It is believed that this procedure is followed much less frequently than the cost-basis procedure.

Surplus restrictions resulting from treasury stock acquisitions. Assume that a company has issued capital stock of $100,000 par value and has retained earnings of $25,000, but that it is holding treasury stock which it acquired at a cost of $12,000. Assume also that the law of the state of incorporation provides that dividend payments and treasury stock acquisitions, together, must not impair the stated capital*—which, in this illustration, is assumed to be the par value of the issued shares, including the treasury shares. In effect, this means that $12,000 of the retained earnings is restricted so long as the treasury stock is retained, and that, so long as this restriction exists, dividends and disbursements for

---

* The state laws differ with respect to the effect of a treasury stock acquisition on retained earnings. In at least one state, the retained earnings are reduced; more commonly, they are merely restricted.

treasury stock acquisitions must not, together, exceed the $13,000 unrestricted retained earnings. The balance sheet should be prepared in such a way as to disclose this restriction. The following Stockholders' Equity section of the balance sheet illustrates a method of making the disclosure.

```
Stockholders' equity:
  Common stock—$100 par value; authorized
    and issued, 1,000 shares, of which 100
    shares are in the treasury....................              $100,000.00
  Retained earnings:
    Not available for dividends—Equal to cost
      of treasury stock....................   $12,000.00
    Free..............................         13,000.00          25,000.00
            Total........................................       $125,000.00
  Deduct cost of treasury stock.........................         12,000.00
            Stockholders' equity........................        $113,000.00
```

Comprehensive illustration of a Stockholders' Equity section. The following illustration shows the balance sheet treatment of various matters affecting the stockholders' equity.

```
Stockholders' equity:
  Capital stock:
    Preferred stock—6% participating, cumu-
      lative; par value, $100; authorized and
      issued, 1,000 shares.................  $100,000.00
    Common stock—No par value, stated
      value, $10; authorized and issued,
      10,000 shares, of which 500 shares are
      in the treasury......................   100,000.00   $200,000.00

  Surplus:
    Paid-in:
      Premium on preferred stock..........  $  5,000.00
      Paid-in surplus—Common stock.......     27,000.00
      Paid-in surplus—From treasury stock
        transactions......................      2,000.00
      Retained earnings capitalized in con-
        nection with a stock dividend.......    3,000.00
      Donated surplus.....................      1,000.00     38,000.00
    Retained earnings:
      Appropriated:
        Reserve for contingencies..........  $ 25,000.00
        Reserve for plant extensions........   15,000.00
        Not available for dividends—Equal
          to cost of treasury stock.........    7,500.00
              Total....................  $ 47,500.00
        Free.............................    132,000.00    179,500.00
              Total.............................          $417,500.00
  Deduct cost of treasury stock—Common..............        7,500.00
              Stockholders' equity....................    $410,000.00
```

CHAPTER 14

The Voucher System

Accounting for liabilities. Most businesses purchase a wide variety of things and services on account. It is customary for the seller to submit to the purchaser a bill (invoice), which describes the transaction and shows the amount of indebtedness created by the transaction. The purchaser may pay the bill when it is received or may defer its payment, depending on credit terms, business policy, or availability of cash. In any event, well-defined procedures are needed to establish the correctness of each liability, to compare the bills received with all related documents, such as bills of lading and purchase orders, to keep track of due dates to avoid losing discounts or damaging the credit rating of the business, and finally, to preserve, in an orderly fashion, the paid bills.

In a small business the proprietor may, if he wishes, examine and verify every bill and sign every check. He is thus in a position to satisfy himself regarding each liability and each cash disbursement. In larger businesses, such work must usually be divided and assigned to several employees. The combined activity of verifying, approving, recording, and paying liabilities must be organized in a manner to give assurance that responsible employees have satisfied themselves as to the propriety of such transactions.

A common method of achieving such control over liabilities and related cash disbursements is known as the *voucher system*. The essential features of this system may be described as follows:

(1) Every liability is given an identification number.
   Thus, the first bill received in January may be identified by the numbers 1-1, the second by 1-2, and so on. February bills could be identified by the numbers 2-1, 2-2, 2-3, and so on.

(2) A form, called a *voucher*, is attached to each incoming invoice. An illustration of a voucher form is presented on page 215. As each liability is processed for payment, information is entered on the voucher by various employees. When the voucher form is complete, it describes the transaction that created the liability and shows the work done in verifying the liability and approving it for payment.

(3) Every liability, before it can be paid, must be entered in the books; the credit is made to Vouchers Payable.

R. E. JOHNSON & COMPANY
2913 North Western Avenue
Chicago, Illinois

Payee_____

_____

_____

Voucher No._____

Date_____

Terms_____

Due_____

Check No._____

Invoice Date_____   Amount $_____

Invoice No._____   Cash Discount _____
                             Net $_____

Extensions and Footings Correct:	Prices and Terms Correct:	Articles Received or Services Rendered as Ordered:

Approved_____   Passed for Payment_____
          Controller   Treasurer

Face of Voucher

Distribution	Summary
Debit:	Voucher No._____
Purchases............_____	Date_____
Transportation In...._____	Date Due_____
Freight Out........._____	Date Paid_____
Advertising........._____	Check No._____
Salesmen's Salaries...._____	Amount of Check_____
Delivery Expense....._____	To_____
Misc. Selling Expense._____	_____
Office Salaries......._____	_____
Officers' Salaries....._____	
Office Supplies......._____	Amount........ _____
Stationery & Printing._____	Discount........ _____
................_____	Net........... _____
................_____	
................_____	
Credit Vouchers Payable:	
Total............_____	
	Entered in Voucher
Distribution by_____	Register by_____

(Voucher is folded here)

Back of Voucher

When a voucher system is in use, "Vouchers Payable" is the account title commonly used instead of "Accounts Payable."

(4) Disbursements are made only by check and in each case cover previously recorded liabilities.
(Small disbursements may be made with cash from petty cash funds. Such funds are explained in Chapter 15.)

In the following pages the voucher system is described in considerable detail. It is important to recognize that the bulk of the material describes office routine. As far as accounting entries are concerned, the distinctive characteristic of the voucher system is that every cash disbursement entry results in a debit to Vouchers Payable. This is the case because checks are written only for previously recorded liabilities. This characteristic is illustrated below:

A bill covering repairs in the amount of $18 is received and paid.
Under the voucher system, the following entries are required:
Debit Repair Expense; credit Vouchers Payable.
Debit Vouchers Payable; credit Cash.

It would be incorrect under the voucher system to handle the above by one entry debiting Repair Expense and crediting Cash.

Preparing the voucher. The office procedures for the preparation of vouchers vary in different businesses. The procedures described below are indicative of the desired objectives and of an acceptable method of achieving them.

Voucher preparation begins when an invoice is received. We shall assume that the invoice shown in Chapter 6 and presented again on page 217 has been received. The voucher-preparation process is described below:

(a) A voucher clerk fills in all the required information taken from the invoice. This is shown on the voucher on page 218 as having been done with a typewriter.

(b) The voucher clerk then attaches the invoice, and any other documents related to the transaction, to the voucher. As assembled, the material is routed to the several employees performing the verification work. The employees initial the voucher when they have completed their assigned tasks. See the voucher on page 218.

(c) When the verification work is complete, the material is routed to an accountant who fills in the Distribution section on the back of the voucher in the manner illustrated on page 218. To expedite this operation, the titles (or numbers) of accounts frequently debited are printed on the voucher. Additional spaces are provided to write

THE OSBORNE COMPANY
215 West Canal Street
Chicago, Illinois

Invoice No.___2397___

Customer's Order No.___1705___

Date of Order_____7/2/19--_____   Invoice Date_July 3, 19--_

Sold to R. E. Johnson & Company   Terms___1/10; n/30___

2913 North Western Ave.

Chicago, Ill._____   F. O. B._____

Shipped to_____Same_____   Date Shipped___July 3___

How Shipped___Truck___

Car. No. & Initials_____

Quantity	Description	Unit Price	Amount
10 cases	XXXX Strawberry Preserves	27.80	278.00
15 cases	Acorn Peanut Butter	9.20	138.00
10 cases	Acorn Peas	12.40	124.00
			540.00

Invoice

the names of any other accounts debited.   Note that *all credits are made to the liability account called Vouchers Payable.*

(d) The material then reaches the controller, who examines the voucher and the documents attached to it to satisfy himself that his company (R. E. Johnson & Company, in the illustration) owes the amount shown on the voucher. He then approves the voucher by signing or initialing it.

(e) The voucher is then forwarded to the accounting department, where it is recorded in a special book of original entry called a "voucher register." The illustration on page 218 shows the voucher after it has been recorded.

R. E. JOHNSON & COMPANY
2913 North Western Avenue
Chicago, Illinois

Payee___ The Osborne Company

___ 215 West Canal Street

___ Chicago, Illinois

Voucher No.___ 7-93 ___

Date___ July 6, 19-- ___

Terms___ 1/10; n/30 ___

Due___ July 12 ___

Check No._____

Invoice Date___ July 3, 19-- ___

Invoice No._____ 2397 _____

Amount $ 540.00
Cash Discount   5.40
Net $ 534.60

Extensions and Footings Correct:	Prices and Terms Correct:	Articles Received or Services Rendered as Ordered:
L.S.	*R.W.*	*C.H.*

Approved_*G. A. Oliver*_ Passed for Payment_____
            Controller   Treasurer

Face of Voucher

Distribution	Summary
Debit:	Voucher No.___ 7-93 ___
Purchases............*540.00*	Date___ July 6, 19-- ___
Transportation In......_____	Date Due July 12, 19--
Freight Out..........._____	Date Paid_____
Advertising..........._____	Check No._____
Salesmen's Salaries...._____	Amount of check_____
Delivery Expense......_____	
Misc. Selling Expense._____	To The Osborne Company
Office Salaries........_____	215 West Canal Street
Officers' Salaries......_____	Chicago, Illinois
Office Supplies......._____	
Stationery & Printing.._____	Amount.........540.00
.................._____	Discount.........5.40
.................._____	Net............534.60
.................._____	
Credit Vouchers Payable:	
Total..............*540.00*	Entered in Voucher
Distribution by___ *W.M.* ___	Register by___ *M.M.* ___

(Voucher is folded here)

Back of Voucher

The voucher register. When a voucher system is in use, all vouchers are recorded in a special journal called a *voucher register*. The voucher register may be thought of as an expanded purchases book; the latter was described in Chapter 10. The principal difference between these two journals can be pointed out in the following way:

Purchases Book:
> A special journal used to record all purchases of merchandise on account. The entries therein are debits to Purchases and credits to Accounts Payable.

Voucher Register:
> A special journal used to record the purchase of all things and services. The entries therein debit asset or expense accounts as well as the Purchases account and credit Vouchers Payable. Occasionally, a liability account may be debited; this would be the case if a voucher was prepared authorizing the issuance of a check to pay a note.

Note the following facts with respect to the voucher register on page 220:

> Numerous explanatory columns are provided at the left for miscellaneous information about the transactions.
>
> The Vouchers Payable column is a credit column; *the amount of each voucher is recorded in this column,* and the column total is posted at the end of the month to the credit of Vouchers Payable.
>
> All the other columns are debit columns. Special columns are provided for all accounts frequently debited. (Later illustrations contain many more special columns.) Debits to accounts for which special columns are not provided are recorded by entries in the *Sundry Accounts* debit section at the right of the register, where space is provided to write the names of the accounts debited as well as the amounts.

The entry in the voucher register to record voucher No. 7-93 debits Purchases and credits Vouchers Payable.

Filing the voucher until payment. After the voucher is recorded in the voucher register, it is folded (at the line indicated in the illustration, on page 218, of the back of the voucher) with the documents inside and is filed in a tickler. A *tickler* is a file divided into sections by months, with a subdivision for each day.

The illustrative voucher shows that a 1% discount can be taken if payment is made within 10 days from the date of the invoice.

Voucher Register

| Voucher No. | Date | Payee | Explanation | Terms | Date Paid | Check No. | Credit Vouchers Payable | DEBITS | | Sundry Accounts | | |
								Purchases	Transportation In	Name of Account	L.F.	Amount
7-93	19— July 6	The Osborne Company....	Invoice, July 3	1/10; n/30			540 00	540 00				

It also shows (on the Due line) the date when payment should be made so that the remittance will reach the creditor in time to justify taking the discount. This date is July 12. Therefore, the voucher is filed in the July 12 space of the tickler so that it will receive attention on that date.

You can now see the purpose of the Summary section on the back of the voucher. This section shows most of the important facts relative to the voucher. The voucher is filed with this section facing to the front; anyone looking through the voucher file for a particular voucher can locate it without being obliged to open the folded vouchers to read from the face.

Paying the voucher. On July 12 the voucher is taken from the tickler and sent to the treasurer for approval of payment. The treasurer examines the documents and authorizes the payment by signing or initialing the voucher on the line "Passed for Payment."

The cashier then performs the following operations:

(a) Draws a check.
(b) Enters on the voucher the date of payment, the number of the check, and the amount of the check.
(c) Sends the check to the creditor.
(d) Sends the voucher to the bookkeeper, to record payment.

Recording the payment. The notations made by the cashier in the Summary section on the back of the voucher (on the lines for Date Paid, Check No., and Amount of Check) furnish the bookkeeper with all of the information he needs to record the payment. The recording of the payment includes:

(a) Making an entry in a check register—another name for the cash disbursements book.
(b) Writing notations in the Date Paid and Check No. columns of the voucher register.

The check register and voucher register on page 222 show how the payment of voucher No. 7-93 was recorded.

Filing the paid voucher. After the entry is made in the check register and the notations are made in the voucher register, the voucher is filed in a paid vouchers file. Paid vouchers usually are filed in numerical order, so that they can be found easily.

Since each voucher is signed by persons having authority to approve the expenditure and has attached to it the creditor's invoice and any other supporting documents, it furnishes evidence of the propriety of the entries in the voucher and check registers.

The entry in the following check register shows how the payment of voucher No. 7-93 was recorded. The entry shows the number of the check issued and the number of the voucher paid. Vouchers Payable is debited and Purchase Discounts and Cash are credited.

Because every voucher is recorded in the voucher register with a credit to Vouchers Payable, every entry in the check register to record the payment of a voucher includes a debit to Vouchers Payable.

Check Register

Check No.	Date	Payee	Voucher No.	Debit Vouchers Payable	CREDITS	
					Purchase Discounts	Cash
1668	19— July 12	The Osborne Company............	7-93	540 00	5 40	534 60

Observe the notations in the Date Paid and Check No. columns of the following voucher register.

Voucher Register

Voucher No.	Date	Payee	Explanation	Terms	Date Paid	Check No.	Credit Vouchers Payable	DEBITS		Sundry Accounts		
								Purchases	Transportation In	Name of Account	L.F.	Amount
7-93	19— July 6	The Osborne Company....	Invoice, July 3	1/10; n/30	July 12	1668	540 00	540 00				

Vouchers for immediate disbursements. The preceding discussion shows the procedure to be followed if some time elapses between the drawing of the voucher and its payment. The procedure is the same for transactions involving the immediate payment of a voucher except that the filing of the voucher in a tickler to await the payment date is omitted. The other steps are:

> Preparing the voucher.
> Recording the voucher in the voucher register.
> Paying the voucher.
> Recording the payment.
> Filing the paid voucher.

Observe that *an entry is made in the voucher register crediting Vouchers Payable even though the voucher is immediately paid.* There are two reasons why this is done:

(1) When a voucher system is in operation, no check can be drawn without a voucher, and each voucher should be recorded in the voucher register so that all vouchers (which are usually prenumbered) will be accounted for.
(2) It is advantageous to use the special debit columns which are provided in the voucher register.

Extended illustration. A journal, a voucher register, and a check register containing the record of a month's transactions appear on pages 225–228. To provide a large number of distributive debit columns, the voucher register extends across two facing pages. (In the illustration, the left page is printed above the right page.) Observe how the following transactions are recorded in the voucher register and in the check register.

Summary of August Transactions and Entries

Aug. 1—Received merchandise from Barnard & Co.:

Voucher Register	Check Register
Purchases	
Vouchers payable	(Later)

3—Paid C.N.W. Ry. for freight on merchandise purchased:

Voucher Register	Check Register
Transportation in	Vouchers payable
Vouchers payable	Cash

The date paid and check number are entered in the voucher register. (This should be done each time a voucher is paid.)

Aug. 4—Paid Daily News for advertising:

VOUCHER REGISTER	CHECK REGISTER
Advertising	Vouchers payable
Vouchers payable	Cash

4—Paid freight bills:

VOUCHER REGISTER	CHECK REGISTER
Transportation in	Vouchers payable
Freight out	Cash
Vouchers payable	

5—Paid Davis Supply Co. for office supplies and stationery:

VOUCHER REGISTER	CHECK REGISTER
Office supplies	Vouchers payable
Stationery and printing	Cash
Vouchers payable	

7—Paid G. E. Wilson for note and interest:

VOUCHER REGISTER	CHECK REGISTER
Notes payable	Vouchers payable
Interest expense	Cash
Vouchers payable	

The debit to Notes Payable was entered in the Sundry Accounts section.

8—Paid Barnard & Co. voucher 8-1:

VOUCHER REGISTER	CHECK REGISTER
(Notations in Date Paid and	Vouchers payable
Check Number columns)	Purchase discounts
	Cash

10—Received merchandise from L. N. Whitely:

VOUCHER REGISTER	CHECK REGISTER
Purchases	
Vouchers payable	(Later)

15—Paid store rent for the month:

VOUCHER REGISTER	CHECK REGISTER
Store rent expense	Vouchers payable
Vouchers payable	Cash

The debit was entered in the Sundry Accounts section.

17—Received merchandise from F. R. Mason & Co.:

VOUCHER REGISTER	CHECK REGISTER
Purchases	
Vouchers payable	(Later)

Aug. 19—Paid L. N. Whitely voucher 8-7:

VOUCHER REGISTER   CHECK REGISTER
(Notations in Date Paid and   Vouchers payable
Check Number columns)   Purchase discounts
     Cash

23—Paid Acme Garage for August rent:

VOUCHER REGISTER   CHECK REGISTER
Delivery expense   Vouchers payable
Vouchers payable   Cash

26—Received merchandise from George Martin:

VOUCHER REGISTER   CHECK REGISTER
Purchases
Vouchers payable   (Not paid in August)

26—Paid F. R. Mason & Co. voucher 8–9:

VOUCHER REGISTER   CHECK REGISTER
(Notations in Date Paid and   Vouchers payable
Check Number columns)   Purchase discounts
     Cash

28—Purchased postage stamps:

VOUCHER REGISTER   CHECK REGISTER
Postage   Vouchers payable
Vouchers payable   Cash

30—Received merchandise from Dalton & Doane:

VOUCHER REGISTER   CHECK REGISTER
Purchases
Vouchers payable   (Not paid in August)

31—Paid salaries for the month:

Journal

Salesmen's salaries	500.00	
Delivery expense	350.00	
Office salaries	250.00	
Officers' salaries	600.00	
Withholding and F.I.C.A. tax liabilities		341.50
Accrued payroll		1,358.50
Salaries expense, tax withholdings, and net payroll liability.		
Payroll taxes expense	89.25	
Withholding and F.I.C.A. tax liabilities		38.25
State unemployment tax liability		45.90
Federal unemployment tax liability		5.10
Employers' taxes.		

VOUCHER REGISTER   CHECK REGISTER
Accrued payroll.... 1,358.50   Vouchers payable... 1,358.50
Vouchers payable.   1,358.50   Cash...........   1,358.50

You should understand that the illustration on these two pages represents two wide facing sheets of a voucher register. The left side of the register appears at the top of pages 226 and 227. The right side of the register appears at the bottom of the two pages.

Left Page

Line No.	Voucher No.	Date	Payee	Explanation	Terms	Date Paid
		19—				19—
1	8- 1	Aug. 1	Barnard & Co........	Invoice, Aug. 1	2/10; n/30	Aug. 8
2	8- 2	3	C. N. W. Ry.........			3
3	8- 3	4	Daily News..........	Bill dated Aug. 3	Cash	4
4	8- 4	4	C. N. W. Ry.........		Cash	4
5	8- 5	5	Davis Supply Co.....	Invoice 317	Cash	5
6	8- 6	7	G. E. Wilson.........	Note dated July 8		7
7	8- 7	10	L. N. Whitely........	Invoice, Aug. 9	1/10; n/30	19
8	8- 8	15	B. N. Haines........	Rent for August		15
9	8- 9	17	F. R. Mason & Co....	Invoice 2425	2/10; n/30	26
10	8-10	23	Acme Garage........	Rent for August		23
11	8-11	26	George Martin	Invoice 1372	1/10; n/30	
12	8-12	28	Postmaster..........			28
13	8-13	30	Dalton & Doane......	Invoice 3639	2/10; n/30	
14	8-14	31	Payroll.............			31
15						
16						

Register

DEBITS

Line No.	Miscellaneous Selling Expense	Accrued Payroll		Office Supplies	Stationery and Printing	Postage	Interest Expense
1							
2							
3							
4							
5				30 00	75 00		
6							5 00
7							
8							
9							
10							
11							
12						25 00	
13							
14		1,358 50					
15		1,358 50		30 00	75 00	25 00	5 00
16		(15)		(53)	(54)	(55)	(61)

Voucher

Check No.	Credit Vouchers Payable	DEBITS						Line No.
		Purchases	Transportation In	Freight Out	Advertising	Delivery Expense		
6	1,500 00	1,500 00						1
1	18 00		18 00					2
2	150 00				150 00			3
3	35 00		20 00	15 00				4
4	105 00							5
5	1,005 00							6
8	3,500 00	3,500 00						7
7	200 00							8
10	2,600 00	2,600 00						9
9	25 00					25 00		10
	1,750 00	1,750 00						11
11	25 00							12
	1,875 00	1,875 00						13
12	1,358 50							14
	14,146 50	11,225 00	38 00	15 00	150 00	25 00		15
	(11)	(31)	(35)	(41)	(42)	(45)		16

Right page

Sundry Accounts			Remarks	Line No.
Name of Account	L.F.	Amount		
				1
				2
				3
				4
				5
Notes payable..............	12	1,000 00		6
				7
Store rent expense...........	43	200 00		8
				9
				10
				11
				12
				13
				14
		1,200 00		15
				16

Check Register

Check No.	Date	Payee	Voucher No.	Debit Vouchers Payable	CREDITS	
					Purchase Discounts	Cash
	19—					
1	Aug. 3	C. N. W. Ry.............	8- 2	18 00		18 00
2	4	Daily News.............	8- 3	150 00		150 00
3	4	C. N. W. Ry.............	8- 4	35 00		35 00
4	5	Davis Supply Co.........	8- 5	105 00		105 00
5	7	G. E. Wilson.............	8- 6	1,005 00		1,005 00
6	8	Barnard & Co............	8- 1	1,500 00	30 00	1,470 00
7	15	B. N. Haines............	8- 8	200 00		200 00
8	19	L. N. Whitely............	8- 7	3,500 00	35 00	3,465 00
9	23	Acme Garage............	8-10	25 00		25 00
10	26	F. R. Mason & Co........	8- 9	2,600 00	52 00	2,548 00
11	28	Postmaster..............	8-12	25 00		25 00
12	31	Payroll.................	8-14	1,358 50		1,358 50
				10,521 50	117 00	10,404 50
				(11)	(71)	(1)

Posting from the voucher register. The entries in the Sundry Accounts debit section should be posted during the month. At the end of the month, the columns of the voucher register are footed. The total of the footings of the debit columns should be compared with the footing of the Vouchers Payable credit column to see that the debits and the credits in the voucher register are equal. Postings are then made as follows:

Credit: Vouchers Payable—column total.
Debits: Totals of all special debit columns.

Use the letters *VR* in the ledger accounts to indicate postings from the voucher register.

Posting from the check register. At the end of the month, the columns of the check register are footed, and the total of the Vouchers Payable debit column should be compared with the sum of the totals of the two credit columns (Purchase Discounts and Cash). Postings are then made as follows:

Debit: Vouchers Payable—column total.
Credits: Purchase Discounts—column total.
Cash—column total.

Use the letters *Ch R* in the ledger accounts to indicate postings from the check register.

Elimination of accounts payable ledger. When a voucher system is in use, a subsidiary ledger with accounts payable is not required; it is possible to determine the individual liabilities at any date by merely noting the unpaid items in the voucher register. To illustrate, posting the totals of the Vouchers Payable column in the voucher register and the Vouchers Payable column in the check register in the preceding illustration will produce the following controlling account:

Vouchers Payable

19— Aug. 31	....	ChR1	10,521 50	19— Aug. 31	....	VR1	14,146 50

This account has a credit balance of $3,625. The individual liabilities making up this total are the items in the voucher register with no notations in the Date Paid and Check Number columns.

A schedule of the unpaid vouchers can be prepared as follows:

Schedule of Vouchers Payable
August 31, 19—

Voucher No.	Payee	Amount
8-11	George Martin..............................	1,750.00
8-13	Dalton & Doane............................	1,875.00
	Total............................	3,625.00

The elimination of the accounts payable subsidiary ledger is a major advantage of the voucher system, as a great deal of posting labor is thereby avoided.

Some companies like to be able to determine the purchases made from each creditor by keeping a file, with a card for each creditor, on which are listed the date and the number of each voucher payable to him. Such a card might appear as follows:

J. B. Henderson,

    1357 North Calumet Avenue,

        Chicago, Illinois

Date	Vo. No.	Date	Vo. No.	Date	Vo. No.
19 --					
Sep. 15	9-135				
Sep. 27	9-191				

This card can be referred to when it is desired to determine the numbers of the vouchers payable to each creditor, and the vouchers can be obtained from the file.

Or, carbon copies of all vouchers may be made, and carbon copies of the vouchers payable to each payee may be filed together.

Balance sheet title for liability.   When a voucher system is in use, the total liability on open vouchers is sometimes called "Vouchers payable" in the balance sheet.   The better-known title "Accounts payable" is probably preferable.

Partial payments.   If, when an invoice is received, it is known that it will be paid in installments, a separate voucher should be made and recorded for each installment.   If installment payments are decided upon after one voucher for the entire invoice has been made and recorded, a new voucher for each installment must be prepared and recorded.

To illustrate, assume that voucher number 7-20 was prepared on July 7 in the amount of $2,000, and recorded as shown in the voucher register on page 231.   On July 20 it was decided to make an installment payment of $500; two new vouchers, numbers 7-55 and 7-56, were prepared and recorded in the register with a notation "See Voucher 7-20" in the Explanation column; the credits were recorded in the Vouchers Payable column; the debit was also to the Vouchers Payable account, and it was entered in the Sundry Accounts debit section.   A notation "See 7-55 and 7-56" was made in the Date Paid and Check Number columns of the voucher register on the line for voucher 7-20, thus indicating how the liability on voucher 7-20 was cancelled.   A check (number 945) was drawn in payment of voucher 7-55; it was recorded in the check register, and the date of payment and the check number were recorded in the voucher register on the line for voucher 7-55.

The voucher and check registers are shown on page 231.

Purchase returns and allowances.   Assume that a purchase of merchandise, on invoice A1316, costing $500, with terms of 2/10; n/30, is made from Keith & Co. on November 5, and that voucher No. 11-24 is prepared and recorded in the voucher register, as shown in the first voucher register on page 232.

Assume, further, that some of the merchandise is returned to Keith & Co. and that a credit memorandum for $45 is received on November 9.   An entry in the general journal is made as follows:

Nov. 9   Vouchers payable (No. 11-24)............   45.00
             Purchase returns and allowances......   45.00
             Credit memo No. 239.

A notation is made on the face of the voucher, so that, when it is taken out of the tickler for payment, the cashier will draw a check

Voucher Register

Voucher No.	Date	Payee	Explanation	Date Paid	Check No.	Credit Vouchers Payable	DEBITS			
							Purchases	Sundry Accounts		
								Name of Account	L.F.	Amount
7-20	19— July 7	A. B. White.......	Invoice, July 6	See Vo. 7-55 & 7-56		2,000 00	2,000 00			
7-55	July 20	A. B. White.......	See Voucher 7-20	July 20	945	500 00				
7-56	20	A. B. White.......	See Voucher 7-20			1,500 00		Vouchers Payable...	11	2,000 00

Check Register

Check No.	Date	Payee	Voucher No.	DEBITS Vouchers Payable	CREDITS	
					Purchase Discounts	Cash
945	19— July 20	A. B. White.............	7-55	500 00		500 00

Voucher Register

Voucher No.	Date	Payee	Explanation	Terms	Deductions			Date Paid	Check No.	Credit Vouchers Payable	Debits	
					Date	Ref.	Amount				Purchases	Trans-portation In
11-24	19— Nov. 5	Keith & Co......	Inv. No. A1316	2/10; n/30						500 00	500 00	

Voucher Register

Voucher No.	Date	Payee	Explanation	Terms	Deductions			Date Paid	Check No.	Credit Vouchers Payable	Debits	
					Date	Ref.	Amount				Purchases	Trans-portation In
11-24	19— Nov. 5	Keith & Co......	Inv. No. A1316	2/10; n/30	19— Nov. 9	J5	45 00			500 00	500 00	

for only the net amount. The credit memo is attached to the voucher.

The list of open vouchers prepared at the end of the month should show the *net* or *revised* liability on each voucher. To make it easy for the bookkeeper to prepare the list, the voucher register may be provided with Deductions columns in which a memorandum notation (*not to be posted, because postings are made from the general journal*) may be entered in the manner illustrated in the second voucher register on page 232.

If there are enough returns and allowances to warrant it, a special purchase returns and allowances journal may be used. The entry in such a book would be made as follows:

Purchase Returns and Allowances Journal

Date		Name	Explanation	Voucher No.	Amount	
19— Nov.	9	Keith & Co..............	Cr. Memo 239	11-24	45	00

At the end of the month, the column total would be posted to the debit of Vouchers Payable and to the credit of Purchase Returns and Allowances. Memorandum notations, of the nature previously described, would be made on the face of the voucher and in the Deductions columns of the voucher register.

Notes payable. The procedure to be followed when a voucher system is in operation and a note payable is issued depends upon whether the note is issued when the liability is incurred or at a subsequent date. Illustrations covering the two situations are presented below:

Note issued when liability is incurred. Assume that a merchandise purchase is made and a note is immediately issued.

(1) Make a journal entry debiting Purchases and crediting Notes Payable.
(2) At the maturity of the note, make a voucher register entry debiting Notes Payable (and Interest Expense, if the note bears interest) and crediting Vouchers Payable.
(3) Record the payment of the note by an entry in the check register, debiting Vouchers Payable and crediting Cash.

Note issued at a date subsequent to the date of purchase. Assume that some time elapses between the date of the purchase and the date of the issuance of the note.

(1) Record the purchase in the voucher register, debiting Purchases and crediting Vouchers Payable.

(2) Record the issuance of the note by a journal entry debiting Vouchers Payable and crediting Notes Payable. In the voucher register, indicate the issuance of the note by a memorandum, "Cancelled by note," in the Deductions section, and by entering the date of the issuance of the note in the Date Paid column.

Journal entries debiting Vouchers Payable should show the number of the voucher, thus:

```
Vouchers payable (No. 5-3)............. xxx
    Notes payable ..................        xxx
```

(3) At the maturity of the note, make a new voucher and record it in the voucher register, debiting Notes Payable (and Interest Expense, if the note bears interest) and crediting Vouchers Payable.

(4) Record the payment of the note by an entry in the check register, debiting Vouchers Payable and crediting Cash.

Note that in either case the last two steps are the same.

CHAPTER 15
Cash

What is cash? In accounting usage, coin, paper money, bank balances, and other media of exchange, such as checks, bank drafts, cashier's checks, express money orders, and postal money orders, are referred to as "cash." I. O. U.'s and postage stamps, sometimes found with the contents of a cash fund, are not cash. An I. O. U. is a receivable. Postage stamps are a prepaid expense.

Although a business may have several cash accounts in its ledger, it is considered acceptable to combine the accounts for balance sheet purposes, describing the combined accounts as "Cash on hand and in banks." Or, the cash may be detailed as follows:

Cash on hand............. $ xxx
Cash in bank............. x,xxx

If some of the cash has been set aside for a special purpose or is otherwise not readily available for disbursement, such cash should be listed separately in the balance sheet.

As a general rule, cash is a current asset. There may be instances, however, where cash funds become so restricted or blocked that they should be excluded from the Current Assets section of the balance sheet. Cash in an insolvent closed bank is an example.

Internal control. The objectives of a good system of internal control, as it relates to assets, may be summarized as follows:

(1) To safeguard the assets.
(2) To achieve more accurate accounting.

The above objectives stand a better chance of being achieved if, whenever it is feasible, the custody of assets is entirely separated from the function of recording transactions affecting assets, and if the recording work is divided up in such a way that the work of one person is verified by another. An irregularity would then require collusion.

In broad outline, a basic system of internal control with regard to cash would include the following:

(1) Establishing a definite routine for accounting for cash transactions, with a division of labor which would automatically disclose errors and require collusion to effect and conceal a misappropriation of cash.

(2) Separating the handling of cash from the recording function. Persons who handle cash receipts or make disbursements should have no access to the records, and those who record cash transactions should have no access to the cash.

(3) Separating the activities which are associated with the disbursing of cash from those associated with the receiving of cash.

(4) Requiring that all cash received be deposited daily in the bank.

(5) Requiring that all disbursements be made by check.

The methods and procedures used to achieve internal control vary greatly in different organizations. The system described below is merely indicative of some of the methods and procedures in use.

Cash received. Some cash may be received *over the counter* as the proceeds of cash sales or as collections on account; cash may also come through the mail. As to the cash received for cash sales, prenumbered invoices may be made out for all cash sales, and in that case it should be the duty of some person to see that the duplicates of these cash sales invoices or tickets agree with the record of cash received, and that no invoices are missing and unaccounted for. Prenumbered receipts should be issued for all over-the-counter collections on account; if possible, these receipts should be issued by some person other than the one who receives the cash; and a third employee should compare the duplicates of the receipts with the cash record. All cash received over the counter should be recorded on a cash register, if possible. When this is done, all cash received over the counter should be counted and the total compared with the cash register tape by some person other than the one who collected the cash.

As noted above, the danger of misappropriations of cash is reduced if the system of internal control makes collusion necessary to conceal an abstraction of cash receipts. As to cash received *through the mail*, a system of internal control can be provided in which the perpetration and concealment of fraud would require the collusion of three people, whose records should be required to agree, as indicated below:

(1) All remittances received through the mail should go to an employee other than the cashier or bookkeeper for listing on an adding machine; this employee should also obtain the cash register readings so that his tape will include the total receipts for the day. After he has listed the mail

receipts, he will turn the cash over to the cashier and will send the remittance letters to the bookkeeper.

(2) The cashier will prepare the deposit tickets and will deposit the funds. Since all funds received should be deposited daily, the total of the deposit tickets for the day should equal the total of the adding machine tape prepared by the first employee. Some banks issue receipts for deposits; if the bank where a deposit is made does not do so, the cashier should prepare each deposit ticket in duplicate and request the receiving teller at the bank to receipt the duplicate; the cashier should present the bank's receipt or the duplicate deposit slip to the first employee, for comparison with his tape.

(3) The bookkeeper will record the cash receipts from information shown by the remittance letters, cash register tapes, and other papers; the total recorded receipts for the day, as shown by the cash receipts book, should equal the first employee's tape and the cashier's deposit.

With such a system of internal control, fraud cannot be practiced with the cash receipts and remain undetected without the collusion of three persons. The first employee has no access to the books and cannot falsify the records to conceal a misappropriation; he cannot expect to withhold funds received from debtors without detection, because the debtors will receive statements or letters from the credit department and will report their remittances.

If the cashier withholds any cash, his daily deposits will not agree with the first employee's list or with the bookkeeper's record of cash receipts made from the remittance letters and other sources of information. The bookkeeper, having no access to the cash, has no opportunity to misappropriate any of it, and therefore has no incentive to falsify his records unless he is participating in a three-party collusion.

Cash disbursed. Since all receipts are deposited daily in the bank, all disbursements must be made by check. The person authorized to sign checks should have no authority to make entries in the cash book; thus a fraudulent disbursement by check could not be concealed without the collusion of two persons. The collusion of a third person can be made necessary:

(1) Either by requiring that all checks shall be signed by one person and countersigned by another,

(2) Or by installing the voucher system, allowing the checks to be signed by one person, but only upon authorization evidenced by a voucher signed by some other person.

All checks should be prenumbered. All spoiled, mutilated, or voided checks should be preserved. Some companies even go so far as to require that such checks be recorded in their proper sequence in the cash disbursements record, without entry in the money column, but with a notation that the check is void.

Bank columns in the cash books. If all cash receipts are deposited daily and if all disbursements are made by check, the Cash columns of the cash books will serve as a record of the deposits in, and the withdrawals from, the bank. If several bank accounts are kept, the cash receipts book should be provided with as many columns as there are bank accounts, as shown on page 239.

Instead of a single account with Cash, there should be a separate account with each bank, and the monthly totals of the Bank columns of the cash receipts record should be posted to the debit of the respective bank accounts.

The cash disbursements book (check register) may be similarly ruled, in which case the Bank credit columns should be provided with subcolumns to show check numbers, as shown on page 239.

Instead of a cash disbursements book with several Bank columns, as in the illustration, a separate cash disbursements book may be used for each bank.

Petty cash. In the discussion of the system of internal control on cash disbursements, the statement was made that all disbursements should be made by check. How is this possible when certain disbursements of trifling amounts, for carfares and postage, for instance, frequently must be made in cash? Although such petty disbursements may not actually be made by check, their total can be covered by a check by operating a petty cash fund. The petty cash fund, which is sometimes called an "imprest fund," is operated as follows:

(1) Establishment of fund:

A check is drawn for a round amount ($10, $50, or such an amount as will provide for petty disbursements for a reasonable time) and cashed. The cash is held in the office for use in making petty disbursements. The establishment of a fund of $25 is recorded by entries indicated below.

Voucher register:
Debit Petty Cash, credit Vouchers Payable: $25.
Cash disbursements book:
Debit Vouchers Payable, credit Cash: $25.

These entries record a transfer from the general cash account to the petty cash account.

Cash Receipts Book

Date	Account Credited	DEBITS			CREDITS			
		Cash		Sales Discounts	Accounts Receivable		Sundry Accounts	
		First National Bank	First State Bank		√ Amount		L.F.	Amount
19—								
July 1	James White	1,980 00		20 00	2,000 00			
1	Notes receivable		2,000 00					2,000 00
1	F. B. Lathrop	990 00		10 00	1,000 00			
1	Sales	30 00	500 00					530 00
		3,000 00	2,500 00					

Cash Disbursements Book

Date	Payee	Vo. No.	Debit Vouchers Payable	Purchase Discounts	CREDITS			
					Cash			
					First National Bank		First State Bank	
					Check No.	Amount	Check No.	Amount
19—								
July 1	Rogers Brothers	327	1,000 00	20 00	39	980 00		
1	Victory Steel Company	321	2,500 00	50 00			317	2,450 00
1	A. R. Bell	317	1,200 00	12 00			318	1,188 00
1	City Trust Company	334	1,500 00		40	1,500 00		
						2,480 00		3,638 00

(2) Disbursements from fund:

When expenditures are made out of the petty cash fund, receipts or other memoranda are put into the petty cash box to show what the money was spent for.

In addition, memorandum entries may be made in a petty cash disbursements book, to show what accounts will be charged with the disbursements. Such a book might appear as follows:

Petty Cash Record

Date	Voucher Number	Amount	Transportation In (5172)	Transportation Out (6061)	Office Supplies (7010)	Sundry Account	Sundry Amount
19—							
July 2	1	1 15	1 15				
7	2	3 25	1 10	2 15			
13	3	7 00				Delivery expense	2 00
						Advertising	5 00
16	4	1 43		75	68		
20	5	5 70	1 20	4 00	50		
24	6	6 20	2 00	1 20		Advertising	3 00
		24 73	6 20	7 35	1 18		10 00

This is merely a memorandum book. No postings are made from it.

In many businesses, the petty cashier is required to fill out a petty cash voucher for each expenditure. An example of a completed petty cash voucher is presented below.

Petty Cash Voucher

No. *1*   Date *July 2, 19—*

Paid to *Ace Delivery Co.*

For *Transportation in*

Account No. *5172*   Amount *$1.15*

Payment Approved   Payment Received

H. Smith   *John A. Doe*

Petty cash vouchers usually provide space for the signature of the person receiving the cash from the petty cashier; thus, a receipt exists for each disbursement. Any documents received by the petty cashier supporting a petty cash disbursement can be attached to the petty cash voucher.

(3) Replenishment of fund:

Whenever the petty cash expenditures have nearly exhausted the fund, it is necessary to replenish it. In the above illustration, the petty cash book is totaled and ruled because the expenditures (which total $24.73) have nearly exhausted the fund, and it is necessary to replenish it. It is replenished by a check for the exact amount of the expenditures: $24.73. The issuance of the check is recorded as follows:

Voucher register:
Debit the various expense (or other) accounts and credit Vouchers Payable:

Transportation in	6.20
Transportation out	7.35
Advertising	8.00
Office supplies	1.18
Delivery expense	2.00
Vouchers payable	24.73

Cash disbursements book:
Debit Vouchers Payable; credit Cash: $24.73.

The expense accounts are debited when the fund is replenished, and not when the petty disbursements are made. Thus, numerous small disbursements can be recorded by one entry in the voucher register and can be covered by one check.

The foregoing procedure may be summarized as follows:

	Vouchers Payable	Cash	Petty Cash	Expense (or other) Accounts
Establishment of fund:				
Entry for voucher	25.00		25.00	
Entry for check	25.00	25.00		
Disbursements from fund: No entries, except perhaps memorandum entries.				
Replenishment of fund:				
Entry for voucher	24.73			24.73
Entry for check	24.73	24.73		

Ignoring the debits and credits to Vouchers Payable, which offset one another, we may state the procedure as follows:

Establishment of fund: Debit Petty Cash.
                                   Credit Cash.
Replenishment for
   expenditures made: Debit expense or other accounts.
                                   Credit Cash.

It will be noted that the only entry in the Petty Cash account is the one establishing the fund; other entries will be made in this account only if the established amount of the fund is increased or decreased.

The Petty Cash account is not debited for replenishments of the fund or credited for petty cash disbursements. The person in charge of the petty cash fund should always have cash or evidence of disbursements in his box equal to the balance of the Petty Cash account.

As a general rule, the petty cash vouchers covering disbursements must be presented by the petty cashier to a designated accounting officer for his review and approval. Such petty cash vouchers should equal the replenishment check, and, after being marked "cancelled," to prevent their re-use, they are filed as support for the replenishment check.

The petty cash fund should always be replenished at the end of a period before the statements are prepared and the books are closed, so that the effect of expenditures from the petty cash fund will be reflected in the accounts of the period in which the expenditures are made.

Cash over and short. In the process of handling cash receipts, making change, and making disbursements from the petty cash fund, it is possible that errors may be made, with the result that cash shortages or cash overages may develop.

Example of cash overage:

A cash register is used for cash sales. At the end of the day, the cash register shows that cash sales for the day equal $325.60. However, the cash in the drawer, when counted, amounts to $325.80. The cash overage of 20 cents is recorded in the following entry:

Cash	325.80	
Sales		325.60
Cash over and short		.20

Example of cash shortage:

A $25 petty cash fund exists.   The fund is down to $1.50 and is being replenished.   However, the petty cashier has petty cash vouchers accounting for the disbursement of only $23.00. The cash shortage is recorded in the following entry:

Various expense (or other) accounts..............	23.00	
Cash over and short...........................	.50	
Vouchers payable...........................		23.50

If the cash shortages exceed the overages during an accounting period, the Cash Over and Short account will have a debit balance. A debit balance will show the net expense arising from cash shortages and overages.   Such an expense may be treated as a general expense.   If the Cash Over and Short account has a credit balance, it may be treated as an item of miscellaneous income.

Dealings with the Bank

Opening a bank account.   When an account is opened at the bank, the persons authorized to draw checks against the account will be requested to sign cards furnished by the bank, to show the signatures which they will use on checks.

CORPORATION

To ILLINOIS NATIONAL BANK
You are hereby authorized to charge to our account all orders or obligations for payment of money drawn on or payable at, or which shall be paid or honored by, your Bank, bearing any of the signatures below. You are also authorized to recognize any of said signatures in the transaction of all other business for our account.

WILL SIGN	PRESIDENT
WILL SIGN	VICE-PRESIDENT
WILL SIGN	TREASURER
WILL SIGN	SECRETARY
WILL SIGN	ASS'T TREASURER
WILL SIGN	ASS'T SECRETARY

PLEASE SIGN FOOTNOTE
It is hereby certified that the above signatures are the duly authorized signatures of

(TITLE OF CORPORATION)

_____President_____   _____Secretary
                              (OR OTHER OFFICER)
Date_____19____

2-2-12   ORIGINAL

Signature Card

These signature cards will be filed by the bank, so that a teller who may be unfamiliar with a depositor's signature can test the authenticity of a check drawn on his account by comparing the depositor's signature on the card with the signature on the check.

If the depositor is a corporation, the bank will request that the directors pass a resolution authorizing certain officers or employees of the corporation to sign checks, and that a copy of this resolution be filed with the bank.

Deposits. Deposits should be accompanied by deposit tickets which describe the items deposited. Deposit tickets are of various forms; an illustration appears on page 245.

It was formerly a general custom for the depositor to be furnished with a pass book in which the bank teller recorded deposits; the entries in the pass book, initialed by the receiving teller, constituted receipts for the deposits.

It is now a more general custom for the bank to issue a receipt, or for the depositor to prepare deposit tickets in duplicate, and for the teller to initial the carbon copy and return it to the depositor as a receipt.

Maintaining a record of the bank balance. Cash receipts and deposits are recorded in the cash receipts book, and disbursements are recorded in the cash disbursements book. At the end of the month, totals are posted from the two books to the Cash account* in the ledger, and the resulting balance in this account should show the balance in the bank.

But, during the month, how can one ascertain the balance in the bank? The record may be kept:

(1) On the stubs of the check book, or
(2) In a bank register.

A running record on the check book stub is shown on page 245.

If many checks are drawn, the computation of the bank balance after each deposit and each check is usually regarded as unnecessary. In some cases, unbound checks are used so that carbon copies can be prepared and handed to the bookkeeper for his information in recording disbursements. For either of these reasons, it may be expedient to eliminate the running record on the check book stubs and to keep a bank register which will not show the balance after *each* deposit and *each* check, but will show the balance at the end of each day.

---

* The account title may be the name of a bank, but the account still is a cash account.

DEPOSITED WITH
ILLINOIS NATIONAL BANK
FOR ACCOUNT OF

Chicago, Illinois,_____, 19___

IN RECEIVING ITEMS FOR DEPOSIT OR COLLECTION, THIS BANK ACTS ONLY AS DEPOSITOR'S COLLECTING AGENT AND ASSUMES NO RESPONSIBILITY BEYOND THE EXERCISE OF DUE CARE. ALL ITEMS ARE CREDITED SUBJECT TO FINAL PAYMENT.

PLEASE LIST EACH CHECK SEPARATELY

CURRENCY_____

SILVER_____
CHECKS AS FOLLOWS:

TOTAL. $
SEE THAT ALL CHECKS AND DRAFTS ARE ENDORSED

Balance brought forward 8,503.75

Deposit_____ _____

Total _____

Check No._____93_____

Date____July 17, 19--

Payee__J.H. Guthrie____ 650.00

Balance 7,853.75

Deposit__7/17/-- 2,300.00

Total 10,153.75

Check No.____94____

Date____July 17, 19--

Payee__F.L. Kenyon____ 400.00

Balance carried forward 9,753.75

Deposit Ticket   **Check Book Stub**

The following is an illustration of a bank register:

Bank Register

Date	FIRST NATIONAL BANK			FIRST STATE BANK		
	Deposits	Withdrawals	Balance	Deposits	Withdrawals	Balance
19—						
June 30			5,000 00			4,850 00
July 1	3,000 00	2,480 00	5,520 00	2,500 00	3,638 00	3,712 00
2	4,500 00	3,500 00	6,520 00	4,000 00	3,200 00	4,512 00

This record is kept in the following way:

Each day enter pencil totals of the day's receipts (deposits) in the Bank debit columns in the cash receipts book (see page 239) and enter these totals in the Deposits columns of the bank register.

Similarly, enter, in pencil, daily totals of the disbursements in the Bank credit columns of the cash disbursements book, or check register (see page 239), and transfer these totals to the Withdrawals columns of the bank register.

Compute the resulting daily bank balances and enter them in the Balance columns of the bank register.

Miscellaneous transactions. In addition to providing the services of a checking account, with its benefits of a safe depository for funds and its conveniences in providing for remittances by check, the bank renders certain other services to its customers which will be merely mentioned here without discussion, since they are commented upon in other chapters. The bank will:

Through correspondent banks, collect notes and acceptances, or present time drafts to the drawees thereof for acceptance; this service may involve a collection fee.

Sell cashier's checks or bank drafts to its customers for their use in making remittances to creditors who prefer not to accept personal checks; this service may involve an exchange fee.

Loan funds to its customers on their own notes payable or on notes and acceptances receivable owned by them; this service involves an interest or a discount charge.

The bank statement. Once a month the bank will render a statement to the depositor and return the checks which it has paid and charged to his account. The statement shows the balance at the beginning of the month, the deposits, the checks paid, other debits and credits during the month, and the balance at the end of the month. A simple illustration of such a statement is shown on page 247.

The symbols on the statement require some explanation:

N.S.F.—(Not sufficient funds)—On June 27 R. M. Walker Company received a check for $63.95 from Wm. Barnes; this check was included in the deposit of June 27. It was returned to The White National Bank because Barnes did not have a sufficient balance in his bank account to cover the check. The White National Bank therefore charged it back to R. M. Walker Company.

When a returned check marked "N.S.F." is received from the bank, an entry should be made crediting Cash and debiting the party from whom the check was received. Such a check should not be regarded as cash, even if it is redeposited, until it has been paid by the maker, unless the bank gives credit for it at the time it is redeposited.

Statement of Account with
THE WHITE NATIONAL BANK
Chicago, Illinois

R. M. Walker Company
135 West State Street
Chicago, Illinois

CHECKS			DEPOSITS	DATE	BALANCES
20	Vouchers Returned		BALANCE FROM LAST STATE-MENT	May 31, 19—	3,500.17
100.00 √			310.00 √	June 1, 19—	3,710.17
96.00				June 4, 19—	3,614.17
.10 Ex.			175.00 √	June 5, 19—	3,789.07
75.00	150.50			June 6, 19—	3,563.57
			425.50 √	June 8, 19—	3,989.07
39.75				June 10, 19—	3,949.32
136.50				June 11, 19—	3,812.82
			136.75 √	June 12, 19—	3,949.57
84.20 √				June 13, 19—	3,865.37
164.19			216.80 √	June 15, 19—	3,917.98
7.25				June 18, 19—	3,910.73
			310.80 √	June 19, 19—	4,221.53
39.50				June 20, 19—	4,182.03
600.35				June 22, 19—	3,581.68
			165.00 √	June 24, 19—	3,746.68
13.75	19.50	123.80		June 26, 19—	3,589.63
.25 Col.			138.20 √	June 27, 19—	3,727.58
76.35				June 29, 19—	3,651.23
12.60	63.95 N.S.F.				
109.11				June 30, 19—	3,465.57

CC—Certified Check	Col—Collection charge	♩
EC—Error Corrected	P.S.—Payment stopped	THE LAST AMOUNT
DM—Debit Memo	N.S.F.—Not Sufficient Funds	IN THIS COLUMN IS
Ex—Exchange charge	SC—Service Charge	YOUR BALANCE.

**PLEASE EXAMINE. IF NO ERRORS ARE REPORTED
WITHIN TEN DAYS, THE ACCOUNT WILL BE CON-
SIDERED CORRECT.**

Bank Statement

The check marks are discussed later under the caption "Reconciling the bank account."

Ex. —On June 5 the bank charged $.10 exchange on a check included in the deposit of that date.

Col. —On June 27 the bank credited R. M. Walker Company with the proceeds of a note collected by the bank for the company's account, and charged a collection fee of $.25.

P.S. —(Payment stopped)—If R. M. Walker Company received and deposited with The White National Bank a check from a customer who, for some reason, stopped payment on the check, the customer's bank would refuse to pay it and would return it to The White National Bank, which would charge it back to the account of R. M. Walker Company.

S.C. —(Service charge)—Banks cannot profitably handle small accounts without making a service charge. The charge may be a fixed amount applicable to all accounts with balances averaging less than a certain minimum amount. Many banks base the service charge on a number of factors, such as the average balance of the account during the month, the number of deposits made, and the number of checks drawn.

When the bank rendered this statement, it returned all paid checks to the depositor. Accompanying the statement and the canceled checks, there were debit memoranda for all charges to the depositor not represented by checks; these included charges for exchange, collection, and the check charged back (N.S.F.).

Reconciling the bank account. The balance shown by the bank statement rarely agrees with the balance shown by the depositor's books. Items may appear on the depositor's books which have not yet been taken up on the bank's books, such as:

Outstanding checks—not presented to and paid by the bank.

Deposits not yet received by the bank—perhaps in transit in the mails.

Paper left with the bank and charged to the bank as a deposit, but taken by the bank for collection only and not credited to the depositor until collected.

Similarly, items may appear on the bank's books which have not yet been taken up on the depositor's books, such as:

Service charges.

Charges for collection and exchange.

Charges for checks returned N.S.F. Although the bank notifies the depositor immediately of such returned checks, and also of checks returned because payment has been stopped, entries may not be made immediately on the depositor's books.

Charges for protest fees.

If a company keeps funds on deposit in several banks, contra errors are sometimes made in the bank accounts on the depositor's books. Checks drawn against one bank account may be recorded as disbursements from another bank, and deposits in one bank may be charged to another bank. The banks also occasionally make errors by charging or crediting one customer with another customer's checks or deposits, particularly if the customers' names are similar. For all these reasons, the bank statement should be reconciled as soon as possible after it has been received.

Illustration. The procedure of reconciling the bank account will depend to some extent upon the system of accounting and internal control. In some cases, the bank statement will be checked against the record of deposits and checks shown by the check book stubs. If all receipts are deposited daily, the deposits shown on the bank statement may be checked against the cash receipts book.

In this illustration, we shall reconcile the June bank statement of R. M. Walker Company (page 247) with the cash books shown on pages 250 and 251.

(Page 16)

Cash Receipts Book

Date	L.F.	Account	Explanation	Cash (1111)	Sales Discount (4008)	Accounts Receivable (1120)	Sundry Accounts
19— June							
5	4001	Sales	Cash sale	175 00✓			175 00
8	✓	John Smith	Invoice, June 1	297 00	3 00	300 00	
8	✓	Wm. Barnes	Invoice, May 5	128 50		128 50	
				425 50✓			
12	4001	Sales	Cash sale	136 75✓			136 75
15	✓	D. E. McGuire	Invoice, June 8	148 50	1 50	150 00	
15	4001	Sales	Cash sale	68 30✓			68 30
				216 80✓			
19	1130	Notes receivable	E. F. Watson	250 00			250 00
19	4001	Sales	Cash sale	60 80✓			60 80
				310 80✓			
24	4001	Sales	Cash sale	165 00✓			165 00
27	1130	Notes receivable	John Smith	74 25			74 25
27	✓	Wm. Barnes	Invoice, June 1	63 95		63 95	
				138 20✓			
30	4001	Sales	Cash sale	60 50			60 50
				1,628 55	4 50	642 45	990 60
				(1111)	(4008)	(1120)	

Cash Disbursements Book   (Page 23)

Check No.	Date	Payee	Cash (1111)	Purchase Discounts (8101)	Vo. No.	Amount
	19— June					
131	1	C. R. Waterbury	75 00✓		123	75 00
132	2	O. F. Wharton	150 50✓	3 07	128	153 57
133	3	Bailey & Bayne	96 00✓		146	96 00
134	6	C. E. Whitely	136 50✓		147	136 50
135	9	R. E. Lathrop	39 75✓		130	39 75
136	13	Haines & Holmes	164 19✓	3 35	133	167 54
137	16	Geo. James	39 50✓		150	39 50
138	17	Horder & Co.	7 25✓		151	7 25
139	20	Davis & Co.	600 35✓	6 06	145	606 41
140	24	Petty cash	19 50✓		154	19 50
141	24	C. N. W. Ry.	13 75✓		149	13 75
142	26	O. F. Wharton	123 80✓	2 53	140	126 33
143	28	C. R. Waterbury	76 35✓		155	76 35
144	29	J. B. Magee	12 60✓		156	12 60
145	29	G. P. Oliver	109 11✓		158	109 11
146	30	C. E. Whitely	300 00		142	300 00
			1,964 15	15 01		1,979 16
			(1111)	(8101)		(2120)

CREDITS

The Cash account in the ledger appears as follows:

Cash
The White National Bank   (1111)

19—					19—				
May 31	Balance			3,625 97	June 30			CD23	1,964 15
June 30	3,290.37		CR16	1,628 55					
				5,254 52					

Steps in the reconciliation. The procedure of reconciling the bank account involves the following steps:

(1) Arrange in numerical order the paid checks returned from the bank.

(2) Refer to the reconciliation at the close of the preceding month; note the items which were outstanding at that date. The May 31st reconciliation appears below:

Bank Reconciliation
May 31, 19—

Balance, per books.....................................	$3,625.97
Balance, per bank statement...........................	$3,500.17
Add deposit not credited by bank.......................	310.00✓
Total...	$3,810.17
Deduct outstanding checks:	
129.................................... $100.00✓	
130.................................... 84.20✓	184.20
Adjusted balance.	$3,625.97

This reconciliation shows that $310 recorded by the company as a deposit in May had not been credited by the bank at the end of the month, and that checks for $100 and $84.20 were outstanding. Reference to the bank statement on page 247 shows that the deposit was credited by the bank on June 1, and that the checks were paid on June 1 and June 13. These items are now checked on the May 31st reconciliation and on the June 30th bank statement as follows: ✓.

(3) See whether the daily totals of receipts (as shown by the cash receipts book) agree with the entries in the Deposits column of the bank statement. Place check marks in the cash receipts book and in the Deposits column of the bank statement beside the items which are in agreement. Make a list of unchecked receipts in the cash book; these represent deposits not taken up by the bank. By reference to the cash receipts book, it will be noted that only one of the daily receipts is unchecked: the June 30 receipt of $60.50. This unchecked item

is presumably a deposit in transit and must be taken into the bank reconciliation.

Make a list of any unchecked items in the Deposits column of the bank statement, representing credits by the bank not taken up by the depositor. It will be noted that there are no unchecked items in the Deposits column of the bank statement.

(4) Compare the returned checks (which have been sorted in numerical order) with the entries in the cash disbursements book. Place a check mark in the cash disbursements book beside the entry for each check that has been returned by the bank.

Make a list of unchecked items in the cash disbursements book; these are outstanding checks. By reference to page 251, it will be noted that only one entry is unchecked: the $300 check drawn on June 30.

Make a list of any charges by the bank, as shown by the statement or by debit memos, that do not appear in the cash disbursements book. Such charges shown by the bank statement are:

Exchange..	$ .10
Collection.......................................	.25
N.S.F. check returned...........................	63.95

(5) Prepare the reconciliation statement. The following form is frequently used:

Bank Reconciliation
June 30, 19—

Balance, per books..............................			$3,290.37
Add outstanding check:			
#146..			300.00
Total...			$3,590.37
Deduct:			
Bank's charges not on the books:			
Exchange...........................	$ .10		
Collection...........................	.25		
N.S.F. check—Wm. Barnes.............	63.95	$64.30	
Deposit not taken up by the bank...............		60.50	124.80
Balance, per bank...			$3,465.57

This form of reconciliation is not entirely satisfactory because it does not show what the balance per books should be after making entries to record the items that are on the bank statement but not on the books.

The form on the following page may be preferable because it furnishes this information.

Bank Reconciliation
June 30, 19—

Balance, per books..............................		$3,290.37
Deduct bank's charges not on the books:		
Exchange....................................	$ .10	
Collection..................................	.25	
N.S.F. check—Wm. Barnes.....................	63.95	64.30
Adjusted balance...............................		$3,226.07
Balance, per bank statement......................		$3,465.57
Add deposit not taken up by the bank..............		60.50
Total..		$3,526.07
Deduct outstanding checks:		
No. 146......................................		300.00
Adjusted balance (as above).....................		$3,226.07

Certified checks. An ordinary check is deducted from the drawer's account when the check is presented to the drawer's bank for payment. In contrast, a certified check is deducted from the drawer's account when it is certified by the drawer's bank. Therefore, outstanding certified checks need not be included in the list of outstanding checks in the bank reconciliation.

Adjustments after reconciliation. The illustrative bank reconciliation discloses the fact that the bank has made certain deductions from the depositor's account which have not been taken up on the depositor's books. To take up these items, the company should debit Collection and Exchange $.35, debit Accounts Receivable (Wm. Barnes) $63.95, and credit Cash $64.30.

The book of original entry to be used for such adjusting entries depends on whether the cash journals have been footed and posted prior to the preparation of the bank reconciliation.

> Condition: Cash journals not ruled and posted prior to preparation of bank reconciliation.
> Under such a condition, any required adjusting entry can be entered in the appropriate cash journal.
> Condition: Cash journals ruled and posted prior to preparation of bank reconciliation.
> Any required adjusting entry should be recorded in the general journal.

Payroll bank account. If a company pays a large number of employees by check, it is desirable for it to open a special payroll bank account. At each pay date, a voucher is prepared for the total payroll, and a check on the regular bank account is drawn and deposited in the payroll bank account. Individual checks for the employees are then drawn on this special account, which is thus immediately exhausted. If the payroll account and the general account are kept in the same bank, different-colored checks should be used for the two accounts.

This procedure has several advantages. In the first place, one voucher against the general bank account can be drawn for the entire payroll; the checks on the payroll account can be drawn without vouchers. In the second place, the officer authorized to sign checks on the general bank account can be relieved of the work of signing numerous payroll checks; these can be signed by some other employee. In the third place, the general bank account can be reconciled without cluttering the reconciliation statement with all the outstanding payroll checks. And, in the fourth place, the labor of recording the payroll disbursements is reduced; instead of recording all payroll checks in the cash disbursements book, check numbers may be entered in a payroll record.

The payment of the payroll is recorded as follows:

> Make a voucher register entry, debiting Payroll Bank Account and crediting Vouchers Payable, for the amount needed for the payroll (say, $1,925).
>
> Draw a check on the general bank account for the amount needed for the total payroll; deposit this check in the special payroll bank account.
>
> Make a cash disbursements book entry, debiting Vouchers Payable and crediting Cash, $1,925.
>
> Make general journal entries as follows (the amounts are assumed):

Salesmen's salaries	875.00	
Office salaries	533.44	
Officers' salaries	1,055.00	
Payroll bank account		1,925.00
F.I.C.A. tax liability		55.43
Income tax withholding liability		483.01
Payroll taxes expense	129.33	
F.I.C.A. tax liability		55.43
Federal unemployment tax liability		7.39
State unemployment tax liability		66.51

Instead of making and posting a general journal entry, the payroll record may be drawn up in such a form that postings to the various expense accounts and the Payroll Bank Account can be made directly from it.

When the statement of the payroll bank account is returned from the bank, the canceled checks are arranged in numerical order and checked off against the check numbers on the payroll record. The unchecked items will represent outstanding checks, and usually will be the only items to be taken into consideration in reconciling the payroll bank account.

Dividend bank account. If a company has a large number of stockholders, a special bank account may be used for the payment of dividends. A voucher for the total amount of the dividend will be prepared, and a check for that amount will be drawn and deposited in this special bank account. Checks payable to the individual stockholders will be drawn on this account.

Bank overdrafts. An overdraft in a bank account should be shown in the balance sheet as a liability. This should be done even if there are balances in other banks that exceed the overdraft; the total of the available balances should be shown on the asset side of the balance sheet and the overdraft should be shown on the liability side.

CHAPTER 16

Receivables and Investments

Accounts Receivable

Accounts receivable in the balance sheet. The amount shown under the Current Assets caption as Accounts Receivable (without any further description) should include only amounts receivable on open account from trade debtors. Accounts receivable from stockholders, officers, or employees should be shown separately in the balance sheet unless the receivables arose from sales and are collectible in accordance with the company's regular terms; accounts with such individuals for loans or other advances may be listed under the Current Assets caption if the terms of such receivables and the company's experience with them indicate that they will be collected as soon as ordinary current receivables; otherwise, they should be shown under the caption of Sundry Assets, thus:

Sundry assets:
Accounts receivable from officers and employees............ $xx,xxx

Accounts receivable and payable with same party. If goods are purchased from and sold to the same party, it is advisable to keep two accounts: one in the accounts receivable ledger, thus:

James Smith

Date		Explanation	Folio	Debit		Credit		Balance	
19—									
Sept.	3	....	S1	500	00			500	00
	12	....	CR1			500	00	—	

and (unless a voucher system is in use) another in the accounts payable ledger, thus:

James Smith

Date		Explanation	Folio	Debit		Credit		Balance	
19—									
Sept.	7	....	P1			375	00	375	00
	15	....	CD1	200	00			175	00

If a voucher system is used, the receivable from Smith will be shown in the accounts receivable ledger, and the liability will be recorded in the voucher register.

It is recommended that such receivables and payables should not be offset when the balance sheet is prepared.

Ledger headings.   The headings of the ledger sheets or cards used for accounts receivable usually are provided with spaces in which to enter certain general information relating to the debtor which may be useful for credit or sales purposes.   The data will vary in different businesses, but may include the following:

Sheet No._____   Name_____
Rating_____   Address_____
Credit Limit_____   _____
Salesman_____   Business_____

The Sheet Number space is needed on active accounts extending over several pages kept in a loose-leaf binder; if the current sheet is number 7, it is known that six other sheets must be found, either in the current binder or the transfer binder, to include the entire account.

The Rating space is used to show the credit rating given the customer by rating agencies, such as Dun & Bradstreet, Inc.

The Credit Limit space shows the maximum amount fixed by the credit department.

The salesman's name may be desired on the account so that the sales manager can see whether the salesman appears to be neglecting his sales opportunity with the customer, and so that the credit and collection department can see which salesmen are making sales on accounts that become delinquent.

Account and statement at one impression.   Many concerns which make a practice of sending monthly statements to their customers use bookkeeping machines to keep their accounts receivable.   Such machines can be used to type the entries and compute and enter the balance after each entry.   The three-column ledger ruling with debit, credit, and balance columns is generally used with these machines.

At the beginning of the month, a statement form is inserted in the binder with each customer's ledger sheet.   When an entry is to be recorded, the account and the statement are put into the machine, with a carbon between, so that the ledger account and the statement are duplicates.   At the end of the month, the statement is removed from the binder and mailed to the customer.

C.O.D. sales.   Sales made on C.O.D. terms may be recorded in the sales book in the usual way, but a notation should be made showing that the terms are C.O.D. This can be done by merely writing *C.O.D.* after the name of the customer. From that point, custom varies. Three methods of procedure may be mentioned:

(1) The debtor's account is kept in its regular alphabetical position in the subsidiary accounts receivable ledger, with a notation in the heading of the account indicating that the customer is on a C.O.D. basis.

(2) The accounts of all customers who are on a C.O.D. basis are grouped together in one place in the ledger, where they can be more closely watched.

(3) Instead of keeping accounts with the debtors, the bookkeeper posts the amounts of all C.O.D. sales to a C.O.D. accounts receivable register. When the collection is received, it is recorded in the cash receipts book in the usual manner, and the date of the collection is entered in the Date Collected column of the register. Such a register follows:

C.O.D. Accounts Receivable Register

Date	Invoice No.	Customer	Address	Amount		Date Collected
19—						
June 1	1387	J. B. White.........	Osborne, Iowa	50	00	June 5
6	1473	R. C. Luther.........	Dayton, Minn.	75	00	
7	1489	J. Y. Ritter.........	Oliphant, Tenn.	60	00	

The open items in the register (that is, the entries with no notations in the Date Collected column) represent uncollected charges; in balancing the subsidiary records against the accounts receivable controlling account, the bookkeeper must include the open items in the register with the balances in the subsidiary ledger.

Red balances in subsidiary ledgers. The individual accounts in the accounts receivable ledger normally have debit balances; some accounts may run into credit balances because of overpayments, credits for returns and allowances after payment of the account in full, or for other reasons. Such credit balances may be entered in the accounts in red to distinguish them from the debit balances; for this reason they are sometimes called *red* balances even though written in black ink with a notation *Cr.* after them.

Assume that the debit balance in the Accounts Receivable controlling account is $6,325, which represents the subsidiary ledger balances shown on the following page.

Debit balances...........	$6,500.00
Credit balances...........	175.00
Net debit................	$6,325.00

The controlling account balance of $6,325 should not be used in the balance sheet; instead, the total debit balances and the total credit balances in the subsidiary ledger should be shown, thus:

Current assets:	Current liabilities:
Accounts receivable.. ..... $6,500.00	Credit balances in customers' accounts................ $175.00

Similarly, if the subsidiary accounts payable ledger contains some debit balances, the balance sheet should not show the balance of the controlling account but should show the total credit balances and the total debit balances of the subsidiary ledger, thus:

Current assets:	Current liabilities:
Debit balances in suppliers' accounts................ $135.00	Accounts payable......... $7,800.00

Methods of estimating bad debts provisions. Two methods of estimating the amount to be debited to Bad Debts Expense and credited to Allowance for Doubtful Accounts at the end of the period are discussed below.

Percentage of net sales. Assume that a ledger contains the following balances on December 31:

Accounts receivable............................ $20,000	
Allowance for doubtful accounts..................	$ 315
Sales...	215,000
Sales returns and allowances....................	1,500

Assume, further, that experience shows that the allowance account should be credited with a provision for bad debts equal to ½ of 1% of the sales for the year less returns and allowances. The provision is computed as follows:

Sales..	$215,000
Deduct sales returns and allowances......................	1,500
Net sales..	$213,500

Provision = ½ of 1% of $213,500 = $1,067.50.

This amount is debited to Bad Debts Expense and credited to Allowance for Doubtful Accounts.

The balance in the allowance account is now $315.00 + $1,067.50, or $1,382.50.

Estimating probable collectibility of accounts. The amount of the periodical addition to the allowance account is sometimes computed by giving consideration to the probable collectibility of each customer's account, and thereby estimating the total probable allowance account requirement. The Bad Debts Expense account is then debited and Allowance for Doubtful Accounts is credited with an amount sufficient to increase the allowance account to the required balance. For example, suppose that the management reviewed the accounts receivable, totaling $20,000 (see the preceding illustration), and decided that a $1,500 allowance account might be required. The provision required at the end of the year would be computed as follows:

Total allowance account balance required....................	$1,500
Present balance...	315
Amount to be debited to Bad Debts Expense and credited to Allowance for Doubtful Accounts........................	$1,185

Aging the receivables. The preparation of an aging schedule is one way of estimating the probable collectibility of the accounts. For example, experience may indicate that the allowance account balance computed below would be desirable, considering the age-distribution of the receivables.

Age	Accounts Receivable Balances	Estimated Per cent Uncollectible	Allowance Account Requirement
1–30 days old..................	$32,000	1	$ 320
31–60 days old..................	21,000	2	420
61–90 days old..................	14,000	8	1,120
91 days to 6 months old...........	8,000	20	1,600
Over 6 months old..........	2,000	50	1,000
	$77,000		$4,460

However, supplementary information must also be considered; some accounts which are not old may be of doubtful collectibility, whereas accounts long past due may be collectible.

The age-distribution may be obtained by preparing a schedule of the accounts receivable on columnar paper, with columns headed to indicate various ages, such as *1 to 30 days, 31 to 60 days, 61 to 90 days, 91 days to 6 months,* and *Over 6 months.* The balance of each debtor's account is analyzed to determine the age of the component elements, and the aging schedule is filled out by entries such as the following (the first item is based on the account with J. H. Boyce on page 262). After all the balances have been aged, the columns are totaled, thus completing the aging.

Accounts Receivable Aging Schedule
November 30, 19—

Name	Total	1–30 Days	31–60 Days	61–90 Days	91 Days to Six Months	Over Six Months	Credit Balances
J. H. Boyce.........	775.00	525.00		250.00			
Fred Campbell......	1,200.00		1,200.00				
G. C. Crane........	800.00				800.00		
James Dawson......	250.00					250.00	
Henry Edwards.....							50.00
Williams Company..	750.00			750.00			
Total debit balances.	77,000.00	32,000.00	21,000.00	14,000.00	8,000.00	2,000.00	
Total credit balances......							175.00

J. H. Boyce

Date		Explanation	Folio		Debit		Credit		Balance	
19—										
Sept.	15	....	S1	a	250 00				250 00	
Oct.	3	....	S2	b	500 00 ✓				750 00	
	9	....	CR1			b	500 00 ✓		250 00	
	15	....	S2	c	800 00 ✓				1,050 00	
	20	Note Receivable...........	J2			c	500 00 ✓		550 00	
	20	....	CR2			c	300 00 ✓		250 00	
	22	....	S3	d	750 00 ✓				1,000 00	
	25	....	S3	e	200 00 ✓				1,200 00	
	31	....	CR3			d, e 950 00 ✓			250 00	
Nov.	5	....	S4	f	600 00 ✓				850 00	
	7	....	S4	g	250 00				1,100 00	
	9	....	CR4			f	200 00 ✓		900 00	
	10	Note Receivable...........	J3			f	400 00 ✓		500 00	
	11	....	S4	h	375 00				875 00	
	16	....	CR5			g	100 00		775 00	

By reference to Boyce's account, it will be seen that a practice of lettering the entries in receivable accounts is very helpful in preparing the aging schedule. In this instance, the bookkeeper has also checked the offsetting items which do not enter into the balance of the account.

There are four unchecked items in the account, and these are, therefore, the only ones which enter into the balance; these items are:

Date	Debit	Credit
19—		
Sept. 15................................	(a) $250.00	
Nov. 7..................................	(g) 250.00	
11..................................	(h) 375.00	
16..................................		(g) $100.00

The $775 balance in the account consists of the $250 September item (which was between 61 and 90 days old on November 30), and two November debits and one November credit in a net amount of $525 (which was between 1 and 30 days old on November 30).

In addition to being useful in the computation of the Allowance for Doubtful Accounts requirements, data by age groups may be used by management to determine whether collections from customers are lagging. Such a trend would be revealed by a shift in the percentage relationships among the age groups, with the older balances making up a larger share of the total receivables than heretofore.

Bad debt recoveries. Suppose that an account receivable previously written off is collected. If subsequent developments indicate that the entry writing off the account was an error, the write-off should be reversed. To illustrate, assume that P. K. Lane's account in the amount of $75 had been written off. The reversing entry, at the time of the collection from Lane, will be as follows:

Accounts receivable (P. K. Lane)................	75.00	
Allowance for doubtful accounts.............		75.00
To reverse entry writing off Lane's account.		

The cash collection will then be recorded in the cash book by an entry debiting Cash and crediting Accounts Receivable (P. K. Lane).

The proper treatment of partial collections on written-off accounts is somewhat more difficult to determine because it depends upon the probability of further collections. To illustrate, assume that, after Lane's account was written off, he paid $30:

> If this collection and other facts indicate that the account may be collected in full, the entries should be:

> *In the journal:*   Debit Accounts Receivable (P. K. Lane), credit Allowance for Doubtful Accounts: $75.00.
> *In the cash book:* Debit Cash, credit Accounts Receivable (P. K. Lane): $30.00.

If no more collections are expected, the entries should be:

> *In the journal:*   Debit Accounts Receivable (P. K. Lane), credit Allowance for Doubtful Accounts: $30.00.
> *In the cash book:* Debit Cash, credit Accounts Receivable (P. K. Lane): $30.00.

Allowance accounts for returns and allowances, cash discounts, and freight. Let us assume that a company has total accounts receivable of $20,000 on December 31, and has provided an Allowance for Doubtful Accounts of $1,000. This may be an adequate provision for bad debt losses, but it does not necessarily follow that the company will collect $19,000 from the accounts. Customers may demand credits for returned merchandise and allowances on defective goods; many of the debtors will take the cash discounts to which they are entitled; and, if the goods are sold on terms which require the customers to pay the freight but allow them to deduct such payments in remitting for the merchandise, deductions will be taken for such freight.

Theoretically, all these prospective deductions should be provided for by allowance accounts, so that the accounts receivable will be stated in the balance sheet at the estimated net amount which will be collected after allowing for all such deductions. As a practical matter, however, such provisions are rarely made, for the following reasons:

(1) Such prospective deductions are difficult to estimate.
(2) The omission of such adjustments normally will have no significant effect on net income.

> This might not be the case for the first year of a new business. Its accounts would show a full year's sales with something less than a full year's deductions from sales for discounts and returns and allowances. But in the second and succeeding years, since any deductions relating to prior years' sales are recorded when taken, the accounts for discounts and returns and allowances will show deductions covering a full period.
>
> Hence, unless large fluctuations occurred in sales deductions, the failure to adjust for prospective returns and allowances and discounts affects the financial statements only in that accounts receivable will be stated at an amount slightly above their cash realizable value. Most accountants feel that this is not serious, since the amounts involved are so small. If, in a given case, it should develop that the amounts involved were significant, then no doubt the accountant would make adjusting entries of the type indicated above.

Discounts on returned sales. Assume that a customer buys merchandise for $1,000 subject to a 2% discount, and that he pays the invoice within the discount period with a check for $980. Subsequently, he returns one-tenth of the goods, which had been billed to him at $100 and which were paid for at the net amount of $98. Should he receive credit for $100 or $98?

Although this is largely a matter of policy, it would seem that the credit should be $98 if he is to be reimbursed in cash, and $100 if the credit is to be traded out. The reasoning may be made clearer by assuming that the entire shipment is returned. Allowing a credit of $1,000 to be repaid in cash would open the way to abuses of the cash discount privilege, whereas allowing a credit of only $980 payable in merchandise would cause the customer to lose the benefit of having paid his bill within the discount period.

Freight paid and discount taken by customer. Assume that a customer buys merchandise amounting to $1,000. He is to pay the freight, which amounts to $40, and is allowed to deduct it in remitting for the merchandise; he is also allowed a 2% discount for cash within 10 days.

Should the 2% discount be based on the $1,000 invoice, or on this amount less the $40 freight?

The discount should be based on the full amount of the invoice, because the customer is paying the freight for the seller, and is entitled to a cash discount for the funds so used. The settlement should, therefore, be made as follows:

Invoice...		$1,000.00
Deduct: Freight..................................	$40.00	
Discount—2% of $1,000.00................	20.00	60.00
Net amount of remittance......................		$ 940.00

Sales discount on customers' partial payments. Assume that a customer buys merchandise for $1,000 subject to terms of 2/10; n/30. Suppose that he is not able to pay the entire invoice, but does send a check for $588 in partial settlement within the ten-day discount period. Since the partial payment was made within the discount period, the seller may, as a matter of policy, allow the discount on the partial payment.

If the discount is granted on partial payments, the amount collected is the net amount, and therefore it is necessary to determine the amount of the gross obligation settled by the partial payment. This can be computed as follows:

$$\$588 \div .98 = \$600$$

In general journal form, the collection would be recorded as follows:

Cash...	588.00	
Sales discounts...............................	12.00	
Accounts receivable.......................		600.00
To record partial collection of an account receivable within the discount period.		

Uncollectible notes receivable. If a business has a large number of notes receivable, a separate allowance account (Allowance for Doubtful Notes) may be used. However, if there are only a few notes receivable, possible losses thereon are generally combined with the estimate of losses on accounts receivable. The debit to Bad Debts Expense should cover estimated losses on both accounts and notes receivable. When a note is determined to be uncollectible, it should be written off against the allowance account. If the note came from a customer, it is customary to charge it back to Accounts Receivable before writing it off against the allowance account.

Investments in Stocks and Bonds

Costs of investments.   The cost of an investment in stocks or bonds includes the purchase price, brokerage, taxes, and other expenditures incident to acquisition.

If securities are purchased through a broker on margin account, the books and the balance sheet should reflect as an asset the full cost of the securities and not merely the margin deposit, and the unpaid balance should be shown as a liability.

Assume that a dividend was declared by a corporation on December 24, payable on January 10, to stockholders of record on December 31.   If stock of this company was purchased after the declaration of the dividend and in time to have it recorded by the company in the name of the purchaser before the close of business on December 31, the purchaser would have the right to receive the dividend.   Therefore, in recording the purchase, the purchaser should debit Dividends Receivable for the amount of the dividend to which he is entitled, and debit Investment in Stocks for the remainder of the cost.

If bonds are purchased between interest dates, the purchaser's entry should debit Accrued Bond Interest Receivable for the amount of the accrued interest, and Investment in Bonds for the remainder of the cost.

Balance sheet classification and valuation.   The balance sheet classification of an investment, and its valuation at dates subsequent to acquisition, depend generally on whether the investment will presumably be held for a short or a long period.

Temporary investments.   Investments may be classified as current assets if they were purchased during a period in the operating cycle when cash requirements were low, if it is the owner's intention to convert them into cash during a period in the cycle when cash requirements will be high, and if there is a ready market for them either on an exchange or elsewhere.   The mere fact that a security is readily marketable is not sufficient justification for classifying it as a current asset; there must be an intention and probability that it will be disposed of during the operating-cycle period. Unless this rule is rigidly adhered to, there is a danger of overstating the working capital by including among current assets securities which are really permanent investments.

If securities are classified as current assets, they should be valued at the lower of cost or market for balance sheet purposes. Since losses on investments can be reported for income tax purposes only in the year of disposal, it is advisable to maintain a record of their cost in the investment account.   Therefore, entries to record market declines should not include credits to the investment account. The entry should be: debit Market Loss on Securities; credit Excess of Cost of Securities over Market Value. The investment may be shown in the balance sheet thus:

```
Stocks owned:
  Cost........................................... $50,000
  Excess of cost over market value..................   3,000
    Market value.................................... $47,000
```

or merely thus:

```
Stocks owned—at lower of cost or market.................... $47,000
```

Permanent investments. Long-term investments in securities should be shown in the balance sheet between the current and fixed assets, perhaps under a caption of Sundry Assets.

Minor declines in the market value of long-term investments need not be reflected in the accounts or the balance sheet; the market may recover before the investments are realized. But serious declines in market value, with a probable inability ultimately to recover the cost of the investments, should be recorded in the accounts and reflected in the balance sheet in the manner described in the foregoing discussion of temporary investments.

Income from securities. Dividends on stock investments declared and received in the same accounting period should be recorded as income in that period. If dividends are to be received in a period subsequent to the period of declaration, an entry debiting Dividends Receivable and crediting Dividend Income should be made in the period when they are declared, followed by an entry debiting Cash and crediting Dividends Receivable in the period when they are collected.

Bond interest earned during an accounting period should be credited to Bond Interest Earned. Illustrative entries are shown below for a company on a calendar-year basis. The bond held pays interest semiannually on May 1 and November 1.

Dec. 31, 1957	Accrued bond interest receivable....	100.00	
	Bond interest earned..........		100.00
	Accrued interest for two months.		
May 1, 1958	Cash...........................	300.00	
	Accrued bond interest receivable		100.00
	Bond interest earned..........		200.00
	Interest for six months.		
Nov. 1, 1958	Cash...........................	300.00	
	Bond interest earned......... .		300.00
	Interest for six months.		
Dec. 31, 1958	Accrued bond interest receivable...	100.00	
	Bond interest earned..........		100.00
	Accrual for two months.		

Amortization of bond premium. If the cost of a bond is in excess of par, the purchase is made "at a premium." When a bond matures, only the face amount (or par) is payable. For this reason, the value of the bond tends to decrease toward par as its maturity approaches; therefore, for balance sheet purposes, it appears proper to amortize the premium over the remaining life of the bond, and thus gradually to reduce its carrying value to par. Moreover, the net income from a bond purchased at a premium, held to maturity, and collected at par, is the total of the interest collections minus the premium lost; therefore, it appears proper to charge a portion of the premium periodically against the interest collected.

Assume that a $1,000 bond, bearing 6% interest payable semi-annually on January 1 and July 1, is purchased on January 1, 1957 (two years before maturity), for $1,017.92. Although coupons of $30 will be collected each six months, this amount cannot all be considered income; a portion of each $30 must be considered a repayment of premium. Since there are four interest periods, the premium may be written off by four semiannual entries of $17.92 ÷ 4, or $4.48. The entry to be made at each interest date would be:

Cash..	30.00	
Bond interest earned........................		25.52
Investment in bonds (for amortization of premium).................................		4.48

Or two entries may be made, thus:

Cash..	30.00	
Bond interest earned........................		30.00
Bond interest earned........................	4.48	
Investment in bonds........................		4.48

The amortization may be scheduled as follows:

Schedule of Amortization
Two-Year 6% Bond Bought for $1,017.92

Date	Debit Cash	Credit Interest Earned	Credit Investment in Bonds	Carrying Value
Jan. 1, 1957.................				$1,017.92
July 1......................	$ 30.00	$ 25.52	$ 4.48	1,013.44
Jan. 1, 1958.................	30.00	25.52	4.48	1,008.96
July 1......................	30.00	25.52	4.48	1,004.48
Jan. 1, 1959.................	30.00	25.52	4.48	1,000.00
	$120.00	$102.08	$17.92	

Thus, the amortization of the premium gradually brings the carrying value of the bond to par, spreading the premium over the period when the bond was held, as a reduction of the interest earned.

Amortization of bond discount. The value of a bond purchased at a discount tends to increase to par as the maturity approaches; hence, for balance sheet purposes, it appears proper to amortize the discount over the period between purchase and maturity, thus gradually increasing the carrying value to par. Moreover, the total income on a bond purchased at a discount, held to maturity, and collected at par, is the total of the interest collections plus the discount; therefore, it appears proper to regard a portion of the discount as earned each period.

Assume that a $1,000 bond, bearing 6% interest payable semi-annually on January 1 and July 1, is purchased on January 1, 1957 (two years before maturity), for $982.80. The discount of $17.20 may be spread over the four periods in semiannual amounts of $4.30. The entry to be made at each interest date would be:

Cash...	30.00	
Investment in bonds (amortization of discount).....	4.30	
Bond interest earned........................		34.30

Or two entries may be made, as follows:

Cash...	30.00	
Bond interest earned........................		30.00
Investment in bonds...........................	4.30	
Bond interest earned........................		4.30

The amortization may be scheduled as follows:

Schedule of Amortization
Two-Year 6% Bond Bought for $982.80

Date	Debit Cash	Debit Investment in Bonds	Credit Interest Earned	Carrying Value
Jan. 1, 1957.................				$ 982.80
July 1......................	$ 30.00	$ 4.30	$ 34.30	987.10
Jan. 1, 1958.................	30.00	4.30	34.30	991.40
July 1......................	30.00	4.30	34.30	995.70
Jan. 1, 1959.................	30.00	4.30	34.30	1,000.00
	$120.00	$17.20	$137.20	

Thus, the amortization of the discount gradually brings the carrying value of the bond up to par, spreading the discount over the period between purchase and maturity as an addition to the bond interest earned.

Amortization—Short-term investments. Amortization procedures usually are applicable only to long-term investments in bonds. If bonds are purchased as short-term investments, with no prospect of holding them until maturity, the reason for an amortization procedure does not exist. Moreover, the generally accepted basis for the valuation of short-term investments is cost or market, whichever is lower.

Sales of investment securities.   If a stock investment carried at cost is sold, an entry similar to the following would be made:

Cash..	25,500.00	
Investment in stocks......................		25,000.00
Gain on sale of stocks.....................		500.00

But assume that an entry had been made sometime in the past reducing the carrying value of the stock to $24,700 because of a decline in market value, and that the entry had not been subsequently reversed.   The entry for the sale would be:

Cash..	25,500.00	
Excess of cost of stock over market value........	300.00	
Investment in stocks......................		25,000.00
Gain on sale of stocks.....................		800.00

Similar entries would be made for the sale of a bond if no interest was accrued at the date of sale.   The credit to the Investment in Bonds account would be the amount of the balance of the account (after amortization, to date of sale, of premium or discount, if any).

If interest is accrued on the bonds at the date of sale, entries should be made as indicated below:

Accrued bond interest receivable	200.00	
Bond interest earned......................		200.00
For interest accrued at date of sale.		

Cash..	10,500.00	
Investment in bonds......................		10,000.00
Accrued bond interest receivable...........		200.00
Gain on sale of bonds.....................		300.00

Any gains or losses resulting from sales of securities are shown in the income statement below net operating income.

CHAPTER 17

Inventory Accounting

Periodical and perpetual inventory methods. There are two methods of determining the cost of inventories and, incidentally, the cost of goods sold; they are:

Periodical inventory method
Perpetual inventory method

To illustrate, assume that we are accounting for a company that deals in room air conditioners, which are purchased at wholesale for $300 and sold at retail for $400. Assume further:

Beginning inventory—4 units	$1,200
A purchase during the period—10 units	3,000
A sale during the period—9 units:	
Selling price	3,600
Cost of goods sold	2,700
Ending inventory—5 units	1,500

Periodical inventory method. The periodical inventory procedure was discussed in Chapter 6. The accounting procedure is shown below:

	Inventory	Purchases	Sales	Revenue and Expense
Beginning inventory	1,200			
Purchases		3,000		
Sales			3,600	
Closing entries:				
Beginning inventory	1,200			1,200
Purchases		3,000		3,000
Sales			3,600	3,600
Ending inventory (determined by a physical inventory)	1,500			1,500

Partial Income Statement

Sales		$3,600
Deduct cost of goods sold:		
Beginning inventory	$1,200	
Purchases	3,000	
Total goods available for sale	$4,200	
Deduct ending inventory	1,500	
Cost of goods sold		2,700
Gross profit on sales		$ 900

Perpetual inventory method. The basic characteristic of the perpetual inventory method is that it results in a running record of the inventory on hand. Changes in the inventory are shown, as they occur, by debits and credits in the Inventory account. The accounting procedure is shown below:

	Inventory	Sales	Cost of Sales	Revenue and Expense
Beginning inventory........	1,200			
Purchases.................	3,000			
Sales:				
Selling price.............		3,600		
Cost...................	2,700		2,700	
Closing entries:				
Sales...................		3,600		3,600
Cost of sales...........			2,700	2,700

The debit balance in the Inventory account is the amount of the ending inventory, $1,500. The credit balance in the Revenue and Expense account is the amount of the gross profit on sales.

Partial Income Statement

Sales..	$3,600
Cost of sales...	2,700
Gross profit on sales.....................................	$ 900

Detailed inventory records. In most instances where the perpetual inventory method is in use, a running record in terms of quantities is maintained for each of the various types of goods held for sale. Cost data may also be included. In the case just presented, such a supplementary record is illustrated as follows:

INVENTORY CARD Description <u>Room air conditioners</u>							

| | Quantities ||| Dollars |||
Date	Purchased	Sold	Balance	Debit	Credit	Balance
19——						
April 1			4			$1,200
3	10		14	$3,000		4,200
18		9	5		$2,700	1,500

As a check on the accuracy of these detailed or subsidiary records, it is advisable and customary to make counts of portions of the inventory from time to time.

Content of physical inventory. The inventory should include all goods for which the company holds title, wherever they may be located.

If a business has received an order but is holding the goods for future delivery, it is important to determine whether title has passed. The mere fact that the goods have been segregated from other merchandise may or may not mean that title has passed to the customer. If title has passed, an entry for the sale should have been made and the goods should be excluded from the inventory; if title has not passed, no sales entry should have been made and the goods should be included in the inventory.

On the other hand, goods which have been ordered but not received by the purchaser at his inventory date may properly belong in the purchaser's inventory. If the goods are in transit, the general rule as to passing of title is as follows: If the goods were shipped f.o.b. shipping point, they belong to the purchaser; if they were shipped f.o.b. destination and have not arrived at the destination, they belong to the seller. If title has passed and the goods are included in the inventory, an entry for the purchase should have been made.

A consignment is a shipment of merchandise from the owner (called the *consignor*) to another party (called the *consignee*) who is to attempt to sell the merchandise for the owner. Goods out on consignment should be included in the inventory of the consignor, who is the owner.

Importance of accuracy in taking and pricing the inventory. If the inventory is misstated, both the balance sheet and the income statement will be affected. For example, if the December 31, 1958 inventory is overstated $5,000, the current assets presented in the December 31, 1958 balance sheet will be overstated $5,000 and the net income appearing in the income statement for the year ended December 31, 1958, will be overstated the same amount. The effect on the income statement can be seen from the following illustration, in which two income statements are presented; in the first the correct ending inventory, $30,000, is used; in the second, the ending inventory is overstated $5,000.

DEUCE COMPANY

Income Statement

For the Year Ended December 31, 1958

	Correct Ending Inventory		Incorrect (Overstated) Ending Inventory	
Sales...................................		$100,000		$100,000
Cost of goods sold:				
Beginning inventory, 12/31/57...........	$20,000		$20,000	
Purchases............................	70,000		70,000	
Total..............................	$90,000		$90,000	
Deduct ending inventory, 12/31/58.......	30,000	60,000	35,000	55,000
Gross profit.............................		$ 40,000		$ 45,000
Operating expenses.......................		25,000		25,000
Net income..............................		$ 15,000		$ 20,000

Since the ending inventory of one year is the beginning inventory of the next year, a misstatement of an inventory will affect two income statements—the statement for the year in which the inventory error occurred, and the statement for the following year. This can be demonstrated by continuing the preceding illustration through 1959. It is assumed that the correct inventory for December 31, 1959, is $25,000.

DEUCE COMPANY
Income Statement
For the Year Ended December 31, 1959

	Correct Beginning Inventory		Incorrect (Overstated) Beginning Inventory	
Sales...............................		$110,000		$110,000
Cost of goods sold:				
Beginning inventory, 12/31/58...........	$30,000		$ 35,000	
Purchases...........................	65,000		65,000	
Total............................	$95,000		$100,000	
Deduct ending inventory, 12/31/59......	25,000	70,000	25,000	75,000
Gross profit...........................		$ 40,000		$ 35,000
Operating expenses.....................		27,000		27,000
Net income...........................		$ 13,000		$ 8,000

If the annual net income figures shown above are added to arrive at net income for the two-year period, it will be seen that the net income figure for the two-year period is unaffected by the inventory error.

	Net Income Computed With		
Year	Correct Inventories	An Inventory Error	Error in Net Income
1958.....................	$15,000	$20,000	$5,000 over
1959.....................	13,000	8,000	5,000 under
Total................	$28,000	$28,000	—0—

Although an inventory overstatement causes an overstatement of net income in the first year, it causes an offsetting understatement of net income in the second year. Thus, inventory errors are counterbalancing over a two-year period. The net income is misstated in each of the two years, but it is not misstated in the aggregate.

If the December 31, 1958 inventory had been understated instead of overstated, the opposite results would have occurred; the 1958 net income would have been understated and the 1959 net income would have been overstated.

The above observations are summarized on the following page.

If the ENDING inventory is: Net income for the period will be:
   Overstated   Overstated
   Understated   Understated

If the BEGINNING inventory is: Net income for the period will be:
   Overstated   Understated
   Understated   Overstated

Procedure of inventory taking.   There is no universal procedure for taking an inventory.   Probably the simplest procedure is as follows: Two people work as a team; one person counts, weighs, or otherwise measures the merchandise and calls the descriptions and quantities to the other person, who writes the information on inventory sheets.   Unit valuations are then entered on the sheets; extensions are made by multiplying unit valuations by quantities; and the sheets are footed.

Although this is a simple procedure, it does not provide safeguards against errors, because the work of one person is not checked by some other person.   There are several ways of providing such safeguards.   One such procedure is here described.

A team of two persons is assigned to a department, a section, or some other unit of space.   Each team is provided with prenumbered, two-part, perforated inventory tags, which may be printed as illustrated below:

```
Tag No.  101
Location No. _____

Article :
Identification
    number_____
    Description _____
    _____

Quantity (    ) _____
Taken by_____
- - - - - - - - - - - - - - - - - - - - - -
Tag No.  101.
Location No. _____

Article :
Identification
    number_____
    Description _____
    _____

Quantity (    ) _____
Checked by  _____
```

Each team is furnished with at least as many tags as there are different classes of articles that the team will inventory.

Each member of the team takes a complete inventory of the stock assigned to the team. One member of the team takes the tags and goes through the stock systematically, inventorying each class of merchandise and entering the data for each class on the top section of the tag, which may then appear as shown below.

```
Tag No. 101
Location No. _____  B/9 _____

Article :
Identification
   number _____  97 _____
   Description _____ _____
_____

Quantity (doz.) _____  4 _____
Taken by _____  924 _____
```

The "Description" space is used if the article does not have an identifying number. The "Taken by" line may show the person's initials or his clock number. The person who fills out the top section of the tag leaves the entire tag with the merchandise.

The second member of the team follows the first member, makes an independent identification and count of the articles, and fills out the bottom section of the tag. He compares the top and bottom sections of the tag and reports any differences to a supervisory employee. He also watches for any merchandise which the first member may have overlooked.

To deter the second member of the team from merely copying the data appearing on the top section of the tag without making a second count and without independently identifying the articles, the inventory plan frequently provides that supervisory personnel or members of the audit staff will make test checks of the tags and the items inventoried as a verification of the work of the inventory team. Such third parties should also check to see that nothing has been overlooked that should be included in the inventory.

After the inventory-taking has been completed, the bottom section of each tag is detached; the top section of the tag is left with the merchandise. The bottom sections are sent to the accounting office and are sorted in tag-number sequence. Any unused tags are sent with them, for purposes of control; if any tags are missing, they should be found, since they may contain data applicable to inventoried goods.

After the accounting department has determined that all pre-numbered tags have been accounted for, the tags are sorted by article number. This is necessary because the same kind of merchandise may be in several locations: for instance, the main department, the basement department, the display windows, the storeroom, and the receiving room. After the tags have been thus assembled, the data shown by them are entered on inventory sheets as follows:

INVENTORY

December 31, 19—

Department No. <u>B 19</u>   Sheet No. <u>1</u>

| Article No. | Tag No. | Unit of Measurement | Quantity | | Price | Amount |
			Detail	Total		
97	101	Doz.		4		
98	102	Pr.	8			
98	304	"	16			
98	419	"	31	55		

The inventory sheet shows that No. 98 articles are in three locations, as indicated by the tag numbers. The total is entered so that the total inventory valuation of all articles of this number can be computed by one multiplication and shown in one amount.

You will remember that the top half of the tag was left with the merchandise. This was done to provide a further check on the accuracy of the inventory. This is accomplished by giving all employees who handle the merchandise instructions to be on the alert, on the morning following the inventory-taking, for any merchandise not tagged or for merchandise improperly described or identified on the tag or incorrectly counted.

The unit valuations are then entered on the inventory sheets; these prices are multiplied by quantities, and the amounts are entered on the sheets; finally, totals are computed for each sheet, for each department, and for the inventory as a whole.

Inventory pricing. There are a number of acceptable bases for pricing inventories. Some are considered acceptable only under special circumstances, while others are widely applicable. The two bases most widely applicable are:

(1) Cost.
(2) Cost or market, whichever is lower.

Cost. Cost of merchandise or materials purchased includes not only the purchase price but also any additional costs necessary to put the goods into condition for sale. These incidental costs include duties, freight, cartage, storage, insurance while the goods are being transported or stored, and costs incurred during any aging period.

Incidental costs frequently are omitted for inventory-pricing purposes. Such omission is sanctioned by accountants if the incidental costs are immaterial in amount and if the effect of their exclusion on the financial statements is negligible.

From a theoretical standpoint, purchase discounts are unquestionably cost reductions. However, as a general rule, it is impractical to attempt to relate discounts taken to the merchandise on hand. Furthermore, the amount involved is relatively small. Therefore, it does not seem reasonable for accountants to insist that purchase discounts be given consideration when costs are determined for inventory-pricing purposes.

Cost selection for inventory pricing. It is a readily observable fact that prices change. Therefore, identical goods may be acquired at different costs. Consequently, accountants are faced with the problem of determining which costs apply to the goods that have been sold, and which costs apply to the goods that remain in the inventory.

Several of the more widely used methods of selecting the costs which are to be regarded as applicable to the goods in the inventory are discussed in the following paragraphs.

For purposes of illustration, assume the following facts:

	Units	Unit Cost	Total
Beginning inventory	2	$10	$20
First purchase	1	11	11
Second purchase	1	10	10
Third purchase	1	12	12
Fourth purchase	1	13	13
Cost of goods available for sale			$66
Total quantity available for sale	6		
Sold during the period	4		
Ending inventory	2		

Specific identification. If the goods on hand can be identified as pertaining to specific purchases, they may be inventoried at the costs shown by the related invoices. Assume, for instance, that the two units in the ending inventory can be identified as having been acquired by the second and fourth purchases; the cost for inventory purposes would be:

Units	Unit Cost	Total
1	$10	$10
1	13	13
Ending inventory		$23

Weighted-average method. The cost of the goods available for sale is divided by the total units available for sale. The resulting average unit cost is used for pricing the ending inventory. The computation is illustrated below.

Cost of goods available for sale.......	$66
Total units available for sale..........	6
Average unit cost...................	$11
Ending inventory, $11 × 2...........	$22

The costs determined by the weighted-average method are affected by purchases early in the period as well as toward the end of the period; therefore, on a rising market, the weighted-average unit cost will be less than current unit cost, and, on a falling market, the weighted-average unit cost will be in excess of the current cost.

First-in, first-out method. This method is based on the assumption that the first goods purchased are the first to be sold, and that the goods which remain are of the last purchases. This method, referred to as the *fifo* (initial letters of *first-in, first-out*) method, is probably the one most commonly used. Applying this method to the facts used for illustrative purposes, the two units in the ending inventory would be regarded as having been acquired by the last two purchases and would be priced as follows:

Units	Unit Cost	Total
1	$12	$12
1	13	13
Ending inventory..............		$25

The assumption that the older stock is usually the first to be disposed of is generally in accordance with good merchandising policy. There are, of course, cases in practice where the assumption does not square with the facts; for instance, the first coal dumped on a dealer's pile will be the last sold.

This method has also been considered desirable because it produces an inventory valuation which is in conformity with price trends; since the inventory is assumed to consist of the most recent purchases and is priced at the most recent costs, the pricing follows the trend of the market.

Last-in, first-out method. Under this method, referred to as the *lifo* method, the oldest costs are assumed to be applicable to the goods on hand. In the case assumed here, the two units in the ending inventory would be priced at the unit cost used in pricing the two units in the beginning inventory. Thus, the ending inventory would be computed as follows:

Units	Unit Cost	Total
2	$10	$20

If the ending inventory had been composed of three units, the third unit would be priced under *lifo* by using the unit cost applicable to the first purchase. Thus, an ending inventory of three units would total $31 under *lifo*. Graphically, the beginning and ending inventories under *lifo* can be shown as follows:

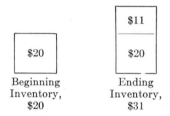

Beginning
Inventory,
$20

Ending
Inventory,
$31

If one year hence, the ending inventory should again consist of two units, the $11 unit would be dropped, since it was the last one added to the inventory, and the two units would be priced at $10 each for *lifo* inventory purposes.

Fifo—lifo and income results. The choice between *lifo* and *fifo* will have an effect on the amounts shown in a company's income statements for the cost of goods sold. This, in turn, would affect the gross profit and net income figures. To illustrate the point by a simple, and rather arbitrary, example, let us assume that a company sells one unit of a commodity each year. At the beginning of the first year it purchased one unit for $1 and marked it to sell for $1.50, since a gross profit of $.50 was considered necessary to cover expenses and leave a reasonable net income. Before any sale was made in the first year, the company purchased a second unit for $1.10, and raised its selling price of the commodity to $1.60 in order to obtain the desired $.50 gross profit under the new price situation.

By the *fifo* method, the cost of goods sold and gross profit would be computed thus:

Sale.........................	$1.60
Cost of unit sold.............	1.00
Gross profit.................	$ .60

and the ending inventory would be priced at a cost of $1.10.

By the *lifo* method, the cost of goods sold and gross profit would be computed thus:

Sale.........................	$1.60
Cost of unit sold.............	1.10
Gross profit.................	$ .50

and the ending inventory would be priced at a cost of $1.00.

Suppose that two separate companies were involved in the

above case, one using *fifo* and the other *lifo*.   Actually, the companies would be in the same position; each would have sold one unit and have one unit remaining in the inventory, but their financial statements would not be identical.

Those favoring the *lifo* method think of the expression "last-in, first-out" as not necessarily referring to an assumption regarding the flow of goods, but rather to an assumption regarding the flow of costs.   The advocates of *lifo* maintain that, during periods of changing costs and selling prices, more meaningful income statements are produced if "current" costs are assigned to cost of sales; this, in their opinion, would achieve a better matching of costs and revenues.

Cost or market, whichever is lower.   On the "cost or market, whichever is lower" basis for the valuation of inventories, cost is used except under certain conditions, described later, where market is lower than cost.   The term "market," as used here, means current replacement cost.

In making the necessary comparisons to see whether market is lower than cost, the accountant may refer to some of the following sources for information regarding market prices: current catalogues or other price lists; recent invoices; market price quotations as published in newspapers or trade journals; specific quotations furnished by suppliers for this purpose; current contracts for the purchase of like goods.

In the use of market prices for purposes of comparison with cost, if prices vary for different quantities, the accountant should use, for inventory purposes, the price for the quantity typically purchased by the business.

Application of cost or market.   There are three ways of applying the cost-or-market method:

(1) By comparing the cost and market for each item in the inventory and using the lower figure in each instance, as shown below.

Determination of Lower of Cost or Market
Item-by-Item Method

	Quantity	Unit Price Cost	Unit Price Market	Extension at Lower of Cost or Market
Men's department:				
Suits	200	$40	$37	$ 7,400
Coats	100	31	35	3,100
Ladies' department:				
Dresses	300	10	12	3,000
Coats	80	30	32	2,400
Inventory at lower of cost or market				$15,900

(2) By comparing the total cost and market for major inventory categories and using the lower figure.

Determination of Lower of Cost or Market
Category Method

	Quantity	Unit Price Cost	Unit Price Market	Extended Cost	Extended Market	Lower of Cost or Market
Men's department:						
Suits............................	200	$40	$37	$ 8,000	$ 7,400	
Coats...........................	100	31	35	3,100	3,500	
Total..........................				$11,100	$10,900	$10,900
Ladies' department:						
Dresses........................	300	10	12	$ 3,000	$ 3,600	
Coats...........................	80	30	32	2,400	2,560	
Total..........................				$ 5,400	$ 6,160	5,400
Inventory at lower of cost or market................................						$16,300

(3) By comparing the total cost and market for the entire inventory, and using the lower figure.

Determination of Lower of Cost or Market
Total Inventory Method

	Quantity	Unit Price Cost	Unit Price Market	Extended Cost	Extended Market	Lower of Cost or Market
Men's department:						
Suits............................	200	$40	$37	$ 8,000	$ 7,400	
Coats...........................	100	31	35	3,100	3,500	
Ladies' department:						
Dresses........................	300	10	12	3,000	3,600	
Coats...........................	80	30	32	2,400	2,560	
Total..........................				$16,500	$17,060	
Inventory at lower of cost or market................................						$16,500

For many years it was considered imperative to use the item-by-item method; the category and total inventory methods are now regarded as acceptable alternatives.

Recent modifications. The lower-of-cost-or-market basis of inventory valuation was adopted as one of the earliest applications of an old rule of accounting conservatism often stated as follows: Anticipate no profit and provide for all possible losses. In the days when primary emphasis was placed on balance sheet conservatism, the cost-or-market rule required that inventories be priced at market whenever market was less than cost, regardless of whether the downward trend in replacement costs had been accompanied, or would probably be followed, by a decrease in selling prices. It was merely presumed that, when market purchase prices decreased, a loss of realizable value in the inventory was inevitable; this presumptive loss was "provided for" by reducing the inventory valuation to the market replacement price.

With the increasing emphasis on the income statement and the proper matching of revenue and related costs, accountants came to realize that decreases in replacement costs are not always and inevitably accompanied by decreases in selling prices, and that, when decreases in selling prices do occur, they may be proportionately less or greater than the decreases in replacement costs. Therefore, the old cost-or-market rule was somewhat modified. The general principles now governing the application of the cost-or-market rule may be stated as follows:

Inventories may be priced at cost, even though replacement cost is lower, if it appears probable that the inventory can be disposed of at a normal profit—that is, if there has been no decline, and there is no prospect of a decline, in selling prices.

If a decline in selling prices, actual or prospective, will probably reduce, but not entirely eliminate, the margin between the cost and the selling price of the inventory, the inventory may be priced at an amount, less than cost but greater than market, which will permit the realization of a normal gross profit on its disposal. For instance, assume that goods were purchased for $100 and were marked to sell for $150; that the market replacement price dropped to $80; and that it is expected that the goods in the inventory can be sold for $145. The inventory can properly be priced at $95 per unit, because its disposal for $145 per unit would yield the normal gross profit of $50.

The inventory valuation should not exceed the prospective selling price less reasonably predictable costs of completion and disposal. For instance, assume that goods were purchased for $100; that the replacement cost is $93; that selling prices have fallen to such an extent that it is doubtful whether the goods can be sold for more than $95; and that the costs of disposal are estimated at $5. The inventory valuation should be not more than $90.

Effect of cost-or-market rule on gross profits. Although the cost-or-market rule is a conservative one and is generally accepted, the application of the rule distorts the gross profit of a period in which the market prices decline.

To illustrate, assume that a company buys goods at a cost of $10,000 and sells one-half of them for $7,500. The gross profit on the goods sold may be determined as follows:

Sales...	$7,500.00
Less cost of goods sold (½ of $10,000).....................	5,000.00
Gross profit on sales....................................	$2,500.00

But assume that the inventory valuation of the remaining half at the lower of cost or market is only $4,000. The income statement would usually be prepared thus:

```
Sales.............................................. $7,500.00
Less cost of goods sold:
    Purchases............................... $10,000.00
    Less inventory at end of period...........   4,000.00   6,000.00
Gross profit on sales.................................  $1,500.00
```

A more comprehensive statement of facts would be:

```
Sales.............................................. $7,500.00
Less cost of goods sold:
    Purchases............................... $10,000.00
    Less inventory—at cost..................   5,000.00   5,000.00
Gross profit on sales................................  $2,500.00
Less decline in replacement cost of inventory...............  1,000.00
Gross profit less inventory adjustment.....................  $1,500.00
```

Of course, to prepare a statement in the latter form illustrated, it would be necessary to price the inventory at both cost ($5,000) and the lower of cost or market ($4,000) in order to determine the reduction.

Obsolete and damaged merchandise. Regardless of the inventory-pricing basis adopted, merchandise which has become obsolete or damaged should be excluded entirely from the inventory if it is unsalable. If it can be sold at a reduced price, a conservative estimate of realizable value may be assigned to it. Thus, the loss on goods remaining unsold which have been damaged or have become obsolete is taken in the period when the loss developed, not in the period in which the goods are sold.

Valuation basis should be disclosed. Either in the balance sheet itself or in comments or footnotes accompanying the balance sheet, the basis of the inventory valuation should be stated.

Two examples of such disclosure are presented below:

```
Inventory, at cost, on a last-in, first-out basis............ $123,600.00
Inventories, on a first-in, first-out basis, at the lower of cost
    or market.......................................... $321,400.00
```

Retail inventory method. As its name suggests, the "retail" method of inventory pricing is frequently used in department and other retail stores; it is suitable for use by wholesalers also. To apply the retail method, it is necessary to maintain records of:

Purchases (and any returns thereof)—at both cost and selling price.
Sales (and any returns thereof)—at selling price.

With this information it is possible to determine a ratio of cost to retail, the uses of which are described below:

(1) To prepare an estimate of the inventory for interim financial statements without taking a physical inventory; the procedure is illustrated as follows:

	Cost	Retail
Inventory at beginning of period	$ 10,000	$ 15,000
Purchases during the period	109,000	188,000
Transportation in	3,000	
Deduct purchase returns	2,000*	3,000*
Totals	$120,000	$200,000
(Ratio of cost to retail = 60%)		
Sales		180,000
Estimated inventory at retail		$ 20,000
Estimated inventory under the retail method of inventory valuation—60% of $20,000 equals	$ 12,000	

(2) To permit pricing a physical inventory at marked selling prices and reducing the selling price valuation by applying the ratio of cost to retail, as follows:

	Cost	Retail
Determining ratio of cost to retail:		
Inventory at beginning of period	$ 22,000	$ 40,000
Purchases (none returned)	169,000	260,000
Transportation in	4,000	
Totals	$195,000	$300,000
(Ratio of cost to retail = 65%)		
Applying cost ratio to ending inventory:		
Physical inventory priced at marked selling prices	$ 50,000	
Ratio of cost to retail—See above	65%	
Ending inventory for financial statements	$ 32,500	

Using retail prices when compiling the physical inventory reduces the clerical work considerably because it eliminates the work of referring to invoices for cost data and dealing with the problem created by the fact that identical merchandise may have been acquired at several different cost figures and possibly from different suppliers.

Gross profit method of estimating inventories. It is sometimes desired to estimate an inventory. Perhaps it is desired to prepare financial statements without taking a physical inventory, or to estimate the cost of an inventory which has been destroyed by fire. The gross profit method is frequently used for such purposes.

To illustrate this method, assume that the goods on hand June 30, 1959, were destroyed by fire; no physical inventory had been taken since December 31, 1958. The books showed the following balances at the date of the fire:

Sales..		$90,000.00
Sales returns and allowances................	$ 700.00	
Inventory, December 31, 1958................	20,000.00	
Purchases...................................	65,000.00	
Purchase returns and allowances.............		1,000.00
Transportation in...........................	800.00	

Assume, further, that the company's records show that in prior years it made a gross profit of approximately 25% of net sales. Therefore, if it may be assumed that the same rate of gross profit was realized during the six months preceding the fire, the inventory at the date of the fire can be estimated as follows:

Inventory, December 31, 1958................			$20,000.00
Add net purchases:			
Purchases................................	$65,000.00		
Transportation in........................	800.00		
Total....................................	$65,800.00		
Less purchase returns and allowances........	1,000.00	64,800.00	
Total goods available for sale..............			$84,800.00
Less estimated cost of goods sold:			
Gross sales..............................	$90,000.00		
Less sales returns and allowances...........	700.00		
Net sales...............................	$89,300.00		
Less estimated gross profit—25% of $89,300.00	22,325.00	66,975.00	
Estimated inventory, June 30, 1959.........			$17,825.00

CHAPTER 18
Fixed Assets

Definitions. Fixed assets are assets of a relatively permanent nature used in the operation of the business and not intended for sale. A building used as a factory is a fixed asset; it is relatively permanent property; it is used in the operation of the business and it is not intended for sale. A factory building no longer in use is not a fixed asset because it is not used in operations. Land held as a prospective factory site is not a fixed asset; it is permanent property and not for sale, but it is not used in operations.

Fixed assets may be either tangible or intangible. An asset is tangible if it has bodily substance, like a building or a machine. An asset is intangible if, like a patent or a copyright, its value resides, not in any physical properties, but in the rights which its possession confers upon its owner.

Charging fixed asset costs to operations. Most fixed assets have a limited useful life. The cost of such an asset (less any scrap or residual value which may be realizable at the end of the asset's usefulness) should be charged off gradually against revenue during the period (known or estimated) of its useful life. The words most commonly used to describe such systematic assignment of fixed asset costs to expense are:

Depreciation, which is the systematic assignment of the cost of tangible assets other than natural resources to expense.

Depletion, which is the systematic assignment of the cost of natural resources to expense.

Amortization, which is the systematic assignment of the cost of intangible fixed assets to expense.

Classification of fixed assets. Fixed assets may be classified, with respect to their nature and the type of cost assignment to which they are subject, as follows:

(A) Tangible:
   (1) Plant property:
      (a) Subject to depreciation.
         Examples: Buildings, machinery, tools and equipment, delivery equipment, furniture and fixtures.
      (b) Not subject to depreciation.
         Example: Land.

(2) Natural resources, subject to depletion.

    Examples: Timber tracts, mines, oil wells.

(B) Intangible:

  (1) Normally subject to amortization.

    Examples: Patents, copyrights, franchises, leasehold improvements.

  (2) Not normally subject to amortization.

    Examples: Goodwill, trademarks.

These various classes of fixed assets will be discussed in the order in which they are mentioned in the foregoing classification.

Valuation of fixed assets.   Fixed assets usually are carried in the accounts on one of the following bases of valuation:

Cost.

Cost less depreciation, depletion, or amortization.

Appraised value—usually, replacement cost new less depreciation thereon.

(The use of appraisal data for accounting purposes is considered acceptable only under certain special conditions. Such conditions are encountered so infrequently that no general discussion of this valuation basis will be given in this volume; it is discussed in the authors' *Principles of Accounting, Intermediate.*)

As a general statement, it can be said that the cost of an asset is measured by, and is equal to, the cash value of the consideration parted with when acquiring the asset.   As applied to fixed asset acquisitions, cost includes all expenditures made in acquiring the asset and putting it into a place and condition in which it can be used as intended in the operating activities of the business.   Thus, the cost of machinery includes such items as freight and installation costs in addition to its invoice price.

Separate accounts should be kept with land and buildings, because the buildings are subject to depreciation, whereas the land is not.   If land and a building thereon are purchased for a lump-sum price, an appraisal may be necessary to provide a basis for dividing the cost between the land and the building.   For instance, assume that land and a building are purchased at a lump-sum price of $50,000.   An apportionment of the cost on an appraisal basis may be made as follows:

	Appraisal Valuation	Fraction	Cost Apportionment
Land........	$15,000	¼	$12,500
Building.....	45,000	¾	37,500
Total.....................	$60,000		$50,000

If, in order to obtain a desired building site, it is necessary to acquire land that has an unsuitable building thereon, the Land account should be charged with the entire purchase price. Under such circumstances, it will be necessary to demolish or remove the unsuitable building. Any costs incurred in this connection should also be charged to the Land account, since the costs were incurred to make the site suitable for building purposes. Any amounts received as salvage from the disposal of the building should be credited to the Land account.

The cost of land purchased without improvements includes the purchase price, broker's commission, fees for examining and recording title, surveying, draining, clearing (less salvage), and landscaping. Any interest accrued at the date of purchase on mortgages or other encumbrances, and paid by the purchaser and any accrued taxes paid by the purchaser are part of the cost of the land. If land and improvements are purchased, the broker's commission and any accrued interest or tax costs should be apportioned between the land and the buildings.

Expenditures for land improvements may be charged to the Land account if the expenditures result in the addition of costs which are not subject to depreciation. If depreciation must be considered in relation to such expenditures, an account with Land Improvements should be opened. Such an account would be charged with expenditures for fences, water systems, sidewalks, and paving. Special assessments for local improvements which benefit the property may be charged to the Land account.

Where a building is purchased, the Building account should be charged with any repair costs incurred to make good the depreciation prior to acquisition, and with the cost of any subsequent improvements.

The cost of a building constructed includes the payments to contractors, fees for permits and licenses, architects' fees, superintendents' salaries, and insurance and similar expenditures during the construction period. It is considered permissible to charge the Building account with interest costs incurred during the construction period on money borrowed for the payment of construction costs.

If a machine or other fixed asset is constructed by a company for its own use, it should be recorded at cost, and not at some higher price which it might have been necessary to pay if the asset had been purchased from outsiders.

Depreciation. Plant fixed assets do not last forever. They either wear out or become obsolete. The wearing out of a fixed asset is characterized by physical deterioration caused by use or the action of the elements. The nature of obsolescence is indicated by the following illustrations:

A company owns a hand machine capable of making 100 articles a day. The business has grown so that 1,000 articles must be made each day. Instead of buying nine more hand machines, it may be better to dispose of the one machine owned and buy a power machine capable of making 1,000 units a day. If so, the hand machine is obsolete.

The operation of the power machine requires the services of five men. A new automatic machine is invented. Because of the saving in labor, it may be economical business management to dispose of the recently acquired power machine and purchase the new automatic machine. If so, the power machine is obsolete.

The new automatic machine is capable of producing only one product. The market for this product suddenly ceases. The automatic machine is obsolete.

Whether the usefulness of a plant fixed asset is terminated by physical deterioration or by obsolescence, it is the objective of depreciation accounting to spread the cost of the asset over the years of its usefulness in a systematic and sensible manner. This notion of depreciation is supported by the following definition proposed by the Committee on Terminology of the American Institute of Certified Public Accountants: "*Depreciation accounting* is a system of accounting which aims to distribute the cost or other basic value of tangible capital assets, less salvage (if any), over the estimated useful life of the unit . . . in a systematic and rational manner. It is a process of allocation, not of valuation." It is important to stress the fact that depreciation, in the accounting sense, does not consist of measuring the effects of wear and tear. It is a systematic cost assignment procedure, determined primarily by the use-life expectancy of assets.

Fixed assets are, of course, subject to decreases in market value, but accountants do not consider it necessary to record such decreases, because fixed assets are not intended for sale. The market values may be up today and down tomorrow; such fluctuations in value may be ignored because the value of a fixed asset to a business normally lies in its usefulness rather than in its marketability.

Computing depreciation. There are numerous methods of estimating periodical depreciation charges. Two methods (the straight-line method and the sum of years' digits method) are discussed in this chapter. Other methods are discussed in the authors' *Principles of Accounting, Intermediate.*

The illustrations which follow are based on the following assumed data:

Cost of asset..	$3,90C
Estimated residual or scrap value—amount which it is estimated can be realized from the asset when it is no longer usable.....	300
Total depreciation to be charged to expense during the total useful life of the asset...	$3,600
Estimated useful life..	8 years

Estimates of useful life may be based on the past experience of a business with assets of the same type, or experience data may be obtained from manufacturers or trade associations. Probably the most widely used reference source reporting on commonly accepted estimates of useful life for various assets is Bulletin F, published by the Internal Revenue Service. Presented below are examples from Bulletin F.

Item	*Useful Life*
Office equipment:	
Safes..	50 years
Furniture, fixtures, and filing cases.............	20 years
Mechanical equipment.......................	8 years

Straight-line method. Giving consideration to all of the preceding assumed data, the accountant would compute the annual depreciation charge by the straight-line method as follows:

$$\$3,600 \div 8 = \$450$$

The following tabulation shows the accumulation of depreciation over the years.

Table of Depreciation
Straight-Line Method

Year	Debit Depreciation	Credit Accumulated Depreciation	Total Accumulated Depreciation	Carrying Value
				$3,900
1.................	$ 450	$ 450	$ 450	3,450
2.................	450	450	900	3,000
3.................	450	450	1,350	2,550
4.................	450	450	1,800	2,100
5.................	450	450	2,250	1,650
6.................	450	450	2,700	1,200
7.................	450	450	3,150	750
8.................	450	450	3,600	300
	$3,600	$3,600		

Sum of years' digits method. The sum of years' digits method produces a diminishing annual charge to depreciation expense. It is a device for obtaining a larger depreciation charge during the early years of the life of a fixed asset than during the later years.

Subject to certain limitations, it is acceptable for income tax purposes. The procedure is described below:

Add the numbers representing the periods of life: In the illustration, $1 + 2 + 3 + 4 + 5 + 6 + 7 + 8 = 36$.
Use the sum thus obtained as a denominator.
Use as numerators the same numbers taken in inverse order: Thus, $\frac{8}{36}$, $\frac{7}{36}$, and so forth.
Multiply the total to be depreciated (cost minus scrap value) by the fractions thus produced.

The following tabulation shows the accumulation of depreciation:

Table of Depreciation
Sum of Years' Digits Method

Year	Debit Depreciation	Credit Accumulated Depreciation	Total Accumulated Depreciation	Carrying Value
				$3,900
1.................	$ 800	$ 800	$ 800	3,100
2.................	700	700	1,500	2,400
3.................	600	600	2,100	1,800
4.................	500	500	2,600	1,300
5.................	400	400	3,000	900
6.................	300	300	3,300	600
7.................	200	200	3,500	400
8.................	100	100	3,600	300
	$3,600	$3,600		

Ignoring residual value. Theoretically, the depreciation allowances should be based on cost less residual value, as in the preceding illustrations. As a practical matter, the scrap value is often (perhaps usually) ignored and the depreciation allowances are based on cost. This procedure is probably justified because depreciation allowances are at best mere estimates; unless estimated residual values are material in amount, they may be ignored.

Recording depreciation. Depreciation is recorded by:

Debiting a depreciation account, which is an operating expense account.
Crediting either:
An accumulated depreciation account, which will have a credit balance to be deducted in the balance sheet from the debit balance of the fixed asset account; or
The fixed asset account. This is called *writing down* the asset. This method usually is not desirable for two reasons:

First, if depreciation is credited to the asset account, the cost of the fixed asset will be lost sight of.

Second, the provision for depreciation is only an estimate; by crediting it to an accumulated depreciation
account, the amount of depreciation provided can be
shown in the balance sheet, where interested parties
can get information on which to base their own
opinions as to the adequacy of the provision.

Depreciation vs. provision for replacement. The nature of
depreciation accounting is often misunderstood. The misunderstanding arises from a tendency to assume that depreciation entries
somehow produce funds for the replacement of fixed assets; this
false assumption may have been caused by a misunderstanding
of the expression "provision for depreciation" frequently used by
accountants.

Depreciation entries merely charge operations, during a series
of periods, with the cost of an asset previously acquired. Depreciation entries in no way affect the Cash account. If it is desired
to provide a fund for the replacement of the assets, cash may be
set aside in a special bank account or invested in securities to be
held until money is required for replacement purposes. The creation of such a replacement fund is very unusual, because management usually believes that the cash can be more profitably used in
regular business operations.

Expenditures during ownership. An expenditure is the payment, or the incurring of an obligation to make a future payment,
for a benefit received. Expenditures incident to the ownership of
fixed assets are of two classes:

Capital expenditures, which should be recorded by increasing
the book value of the assets. In most cases, this is done by
debiting the asset account; in some cases, it is done by debiting the Accumulated Depreciation account.
Revenue expenditures, which should be charged to expense.

A careful distinction must be made between capital and revenue expenditures if a correct accounting for fixed assets and for net
income is to be maintained. If a capital expenditure is charged
to an expense account, the book value of the fixed asset is understated, and the net income and owners' equity also are understated.
On the other hand, if a revenue expenditure is charged to an asset
account instead of to an expense account, the book value of the
fixed asset is overstated and the net income and owners' equity also
are overstated.

The proper treatment of some of the more common types of
expenditures is indicated on the following page.

Particulars	Revenue Expenditures	Capital Expenditures	
		Book Value of Assets Increased by Charges to	
	Charged to Expense Accounts	Asset Account	Accumulated Depreciation Account
Acquisition cost:			
A company purchased three second-hand machines; charge the fixed asset account.		$3,000	
Expenditures to make good depreciation which took place prior to acquisition:			
Before the machines were put into use, they were thoroughly overhauled. This was a capital expenditure..................		400	
Installation cost:			
This is a capital expenditure............		50	
Betterment:			
Additional accessories were purchased for use with the machines; this expenditure is chargeable to the asset account.......		75	
Ordinary repair:			
At the end of the first month of operations, a repair bill was paid; this was a revenue expenditure or expense...............	$18		
Extraordinary repair:			
After three years of use, the machines were again thoroughly reconditioned at a cost of $400. This was a capital expenditure because it made good some of the depreciation subsequent to acquisition and thus extended the use-life of the asset; it should not be recorded by a charge to the asset account because it is not an addition to cost; it should be recorded by a charge to the accumulated depreciation account because it is a reduction of accrued depreciation.................			$400

Reinstallation expense:

The first cost of installing machinery in a factory is a proper charge to the asset account. If machinery is rearranged in the factory for the purpose of improving the routing or otherwise reducing the time and cost of production, a question arises with respect to the proper treatment of the reinstallation expense. Presumably, the cost of one installation will already have been charged to the Machinery account. Theoretically, therefore, the cost, or the undepreciated remainder of the cost, of the first installation should be removed from the accounts (by crediting the fixed asset with the original cost and debiting the accumulated depreciation account with the accumulated depreciation thereon), and the reinstallation cost should be capitalized by charge to the Machinery account.

Disposal of fixed assets. If a fixed asset is disposed of during the year and it is the accounting policy to record depreciation for fractional periods, an entry is required debiting depreciation and crediting accumulated depreciation for depreciation from the date of the last preceding depreciation provision to the date of disposal.

To record the disposal, an entry should be made debiting Cash for the amount received, debiting the accumulated depreciation account with the depreciation provided against the asset, crediting the asset account with the cost of the asset, and debiting or crediting an account to show the loss or gain on the disposal.

Three illustrations follow; it is assumed that any required entries for fractional-period depreciation have been made.

(1) Price equal to book value:

Assume that, at the date of disposal of a machine, the asset and accumulated depreciation accounts had the following balances:

	Debit	Credit
Machinery.....................................	$2,500.00	
Accumulated depreciation—Machinery...........		$2,200.00

The asset had a net book value of $300 and was sold for $300. The entry to record the sale is:

Cash..	300.00	
Accumulated depreciation—Machinery...........	2,200.00	
Machinery................................		2,500.00
To record the sale of machinery, relieving the accounts of the cost and accumulated depreciation.		

(2) Price less than book value:

Assume that the accounts had the following balances:

	Debit	Credit
Machinery.....................................	$2,500.00	
Accumulated depreciation—Machinery...........		$1,760.00

The asset had a net book value of $740 and was sold for $400; hence, there was a loss of $340. The entry to record the sale is:

Cash..	400.00	
Loss on disposal of machinery.................	340.00	
Accumulated depreciation—Machinery...........	1,760.00	
Machinery................................		2,500.00
To record the sale of machinery.		

(3) Price more than book value:

Assume that the accounts had balances as shown on the following page.

	Debit	Credit
Machinery....................................	$2,500.00	
Accumulated depreciation—Machinery..........		$2,200.00

The asset had a net book value of $300 and was sold for $500; hence, there was a gain of $200. The entry to record the sale of the machinery at a gain of $200 is shown below:

Cash..	500.00	
Accumulated depreciation—Machinery..........	2,200.00	
Machinery..............................		2,500.00
Gain on disposal of machinery.............		200.00
To record the sale of machinery.		

Losses and gains on the disposal of fixed assets were formerly charged to the Earned Surplus (now often called Retained Earnings) account. In recent years, this procedure has been strongly opposed, and it is contended that such gains or losses should be reported in the income statement.

In this connection, the reader is referred to a discussion starting on page 103, under the caption "Unusual and non-recurring items," and concluding on page 106, which contains the following excerpt from Bulletin No. 43 of the Committee on Accounting Procedure of The American Institute of Certified Public Accountants:

"It is the opinion of the committee that there should be a general presumption that all items of profit and loss recognized during the period are to be used in determining the figure reported as net income. The only possible exception to this presumption relates to items which in the aggregate are material in relation to the company's net income and are clearly not identifiable with or do not result from the usual or typical business operations of the period."

What is "material" is a matter of opinion. Therefore, it seems desirable for purposes of this text to regard all losses or gains from the disposal of fixed assets as immaterial and hence not to be charged or credited to Retained Earnings.

Trade-ins. The preceding paragraphs dealt with disposals of fixed assets by sale. However, it is not uncommon for a business to dispose of fixed assets by trading them in on new assets. It is considered acceptable to account for trade-ins by treating the trade-in allowance as though it were the selling price of the old asset. Thus, the difference between the trade-in allowance and the book value of the asset being traded in, after recording depreciation to the date of disposal, is the gain or loss on disposal.

This approach to trade-ins is illustrated by using the data on the opposite page.

	Case A	Case B
Old asset:		
Cost..	$5,000	$5,000
Accumulated depreciation...........................	3,000	3,000
Book value...	2,000	2,000
Trade-in allowance.................................	2,300	1,800
List price of new asset.............................	6,000	6,000
Cash payment.......................................	3,700	4,200

Entries	Case A		Case B	
Asset account (new asset)...............	6,000		6,000	
Accumulated depreciation...............	3,000		3,000	
Loss on disposal of old asset.............			200	
Gain on disposal of old asset.........		300		
Asset account (old asset)............		5,000		5,000
Cash.............................		3,700		4,200
To record exchange of assets.				

Under this approach, the new asset is set up in the accounts at its list or advertised price. It seems relevant to inquire whether this practice will always satisfy the general rule that, initially, fixed assets should be recorded at their cost. As noted earlier, cost is equal to the cash value of the consideration parted with; that is, the cash paid and the amount that could be obtained by a sale of the old asset. Referring to the two preceding cases, and assuming that, in each case, the old asset could be disposed of for $1,750, the facts to be recorded would be:

	Case A	Case B
Cost of new asset:		
Cash payment.....................................	$3,700	$4,200
Cash value of old asset............................	1,750	1,750
Total...	$5,450	$5,950
Loss on disposal of old asset:		
Cost..	$5,000	$5,000
Accumulated depreciation..........................	3,000	3,000
Book value..	$2,000	$2,000
Cash value..	1,750	1,750
Loss on disposal of old asset....................	$ 250	$ 250

Entries	Case A		Case B	
Asset account (new asset)...............	5,450		5,950	
Accumulated depreciation...............	3,000		3,000	
Loss on disposal of old asset.............	250		250	
Asset account (old asset)............		5,000		5,000
Cash.............................		3,700		4,200

For income tax purposes, no recognition is given to gains or losses resulting from trading in one asset as part payment for another. Under the tax rule, the cost of the new asset, for purposes of computing depreciation and the gain or loss on subsequent disposal, is the sum of the book value of the old asset plus the additional expenditure made in acquiring the new asset. On this basis, the entry to record the exchange of assets in cases A and B would be as shown below.

	Case A	Case B
Asset account (new asset)............	5,700	6,200
Accumulated depreciation..............	3,000	3,000
Asset account (old asset)..............	5,000	5,000
Cash..............................	3,700	4,200

Many accountants, as a matter of convenience, prefer to follow the tax rule in the accounts.

Depreciation program revisions. After an asset has been in use for some time, it may be found that too much or too little depreciation has been provided. Such a condition may be due to an error in estimating the life of the asset or to an incorrect estimate of the residual value. In any event, it would be incorrect to continue with the existing depreciation program under such circumstances, unless, of course, the amount involved is so small that it can be ignored on practical grounds. If a change is warranted, either of the following alternatives is acceptable:

(1) Adjust the Accumulated Depreciation account to the amount which it would have contained if depreciation had originally been based on the estimates which now seem correct, and base subsequent depreciation charges on the revised estimates.

Data for example:

Asset cost..	$9,000
Estimated scrap value....................................	—0—
Estimated useful life.................................	10 years

Depreciation entries to date:

Year	
1...	$ 900
2...	900
3...	900
4...	900
5...	900
6...	900
Accumulated depreciation at the end of the sixth year.......	$5,400

During the seventh year, before recording any depreciation for the seventh year, it is established that the asset will probably last six more years (revised useful life = 12 years).

Computation of correction of accumulated depreciation:

Depreciation recorded during the first six years..........	$5,400
Revised annual charge for depreciation:	
$9,000 ÷ 12 = $750.	
Revised depreciation for the first six years:	
$750 × 6 =....................................	4,500
Amount of adjustment................................	$ 900

Entry to adjust the Accumulated Depreciation account:

```
Accumulated depreciation........................    900.00
    Correction of prior years' depreciation*........           900.00
    To adjust the Accumulated Depreciation account to
    conform to the revised estimate of useful life.
```

Entry for depreciation for seventh and subsequent years:

```
Depreciation expense...........................    750.00
    Accumulated depreciation....................           750.00
    Depreciation for the year.
```

(2) Spread the undepreciated amount over the remaining useful life of the asset by revised depreciation provisions, without changing the current balance in the Accumulated Depreciation account.

Data for example:

Same conditions as above.

Computation of depreciation provision for the seventh and subsequent years:

```
Undepreciated cost:
    Cost.................................... $9,000
    Accumulated depreciation..............  5,400  $3,600
Revised remaining useful life...................  6 years
Revised annual depreciation provision...........  $   600
```

Entry for depreciation for seventh and subsequent years:

```
Depreciation expense...........................    600.00
    Accumulated depreciation....................           600.00
    Depreciation for the year.
```

The above illustration dealt with overdepreciation. If underdepreciation is discovered, the changes will be as follows:

For alternative (1):

The Accumulated Depreciation account will be credited for the amount of the underdepreciation, and Correction of Prior Years' Depreciation will be debited.

The subsequent provisions for depreciation will be larger than the former annual provisions.

For alternative (2):

The subsequent provisions for depreciation will be larger than the former annual provisions.

The second alternative is found more commonly in practice, possibly for the reasons stated on the following page.

---

* But see quotation from Institute bulletin on page 296.

(a) One reason was well expressed by the Committee on Accounting Procedure in its Bulletin 27:

"Under most circumstances, costs once identified and absorbed through amortization or depreciation charges are not considered to be subject to further accounting, and corrections of estimates affecting the allocations are commonly reflected in revised charges during the remaining life of the property."

(b) Alternative (1) is not acceptable for federal income tax purposes.

(c) Particularly if the difference between the former annual depreciation provision and the new annual depreciation provision is not large in relation to average net income, accountants are inclined to avoid an adjustment for the accumulated error resulting from past depreciation entries, since their effect on reported net income was immaterial. The approximate character of depreciation accounting does not seem to require such a precise treatment.

Subsidiary records. The general ledger should contain an account with each class of fixed assets, such as Land, Buildings, Machinery, Furniture and Fixtures, and Delivery Equipment. It is also desirable to maintain a subsidiary plant ledger containing considerable information with respect to the cost, depreciation, repairs, and so forth, of each unit. Thus, the subsidiary machinery record might contain a card or page for each machine, showing the following data:

Name of asset.
Identification number.
Location.
Manufacturer.
From whom purchased.
Date of installation.
Purchase cost.
Other incidental costs.
Depreciation data:
   Estimated life.
   Estimated residual value.
   Depreciation rate.
   Periodic and accumulated provision for depreciation.
Ordinary and extraordinary repairs, with information as to date, nature, and cost.

Actual life, residual value, and gain or loss on disposal.
Information as to abnormal operating conditions, such as overtime work, affecting rapidity of depreciation.

Such records furnish a good control over the fixed assets, as
they are virtually a perpetual inventory showing all fixed assets
which should be in the company's possession. The information
regarding the cost and accumulated depreciation of each unit can
be used in making entries to relieve the asset and accumulated
depreciation accounts of the correct amounts when a unit is fully
depreciated. The subsidiary records are also useful in connection
with insurance claims.

Natural Resources

Valuation. Natural resources, such as timber tracts, mines,
and oil wells, should be carried in the asset accounts at cost. As
the resource is converted, a portion of its cost is removed from
the fixed asset account and assigned to other accounts, thereby
reducing the book value of the fixed asset. Such cost transfers
give recognition to depletion. Such assets are sometimes called
wasting assets.

Development expenditures, such as those made for the removal
of surface earth for strip mining operations, which do not result in
the acquisition of tangible fixed assets, may be charged to the
wasting asset account. Tangible fixed assets acquired for purposes
of developing or extracting the wasting asset should be recorded
in separate accounts; they should be depreciated in amounts proportionate to the depletion, if the developments will render service
throughout the entire life of the wasting asset; they should be
depreciated over a shorter period if their useful life will expire before
the wasting asset is completely depleted.

Depletion. A per-unit depletion charge usually is computed by
dividing the cost of the wasting asset by the estimated number of
units (tons, barrels, thousand feet, and so forth) in the asset. The
total depletion charge for each period is then computed by multiplying the unit charge by the number of units converted during
the period.

To illustrate, assume that $90,000 was paid for a mine which
was estimated to contain 300,000 tons of available deposit. The
unit depletion charge is $90,000 ÷ 300,000, or $.30. If 60,000 tons
are mined during a given year, the depletion charge for the year is
$.30 × 60,000, or $18,000.

The depletion charge will be recorded as follows:

Depletion....................................	18,000.00	
Accumulated depletion.....................		18,000.00

If some of the units converted remain unsold at year-end, the depletion charge relating to such units is assignable to an inventory account.   In other words, depletion is a charge against revenue when the units converted are sold, not when they are converted.

The credit balance in an accumulated depletion account should be deducted in the balance sheet from the debit balance in the asset account.

Intangible Fixed Assets Normally Subject to Amortization

Reason for amortization.   Some intangible fixed assets are subject to amortization because their lives are limited by law, regulation, contract, or the nature of the asset.   Examples are patents, copyrights, franchises for limited periods, leaseholds, and leasehold improvements.   It should be understood that the period fixed by law, regulation, or contract is the maximum period of life, and that the usefulness of such assets may cease prior to the expiration of that period; in such instances, the shorter useful life should be the period on which the amortization is based.

If the original estimate of useful life is subsequently regarded as incorrect, the accountant may either (1) adjust the book value of the asset to the amount which would be reflected by the accounts if amortization had originally been based on the estimates which now seem correct, and base the subsequent amortization on the revised useful life; or (2) spread the unamortized balance over the remaining useful life, as revised.   These are the same alternatives that were discussed in connection with depreciation revisions, on pages 298 to 300.

Patents.   If a patent is acquired by purchase, its cost is the purchase price.   If it is obtained by the inventor, its cost is the total of the experimental expense and costs of constructing working models and obtaining the patent, including drawings, attorney's fees, and filing costs.   Since a patent has no proven value until it has stood the test of an infringement suit, the cost of a successful suit may be charged to the Patents account.   If the suit is unsuccessful, and the patent is thereby proved to be valueless, the cost of the suit and the cost of the patent should be written off.

A patent is issued for 17 years, and its cost should be amortized over that period, unless it was acquired after the expiration of a portion of the 17-year period, in which case it should be written off over its remaining life.   If there is a probability that the patented device or the product of the device will become obsolete before the expiration of the patent, conservatism would suggest writing off the patent during a period shorter than its legal life.

A patent may give its owner a monopoly which enables him to

develop his business to a point where, after the expiration of the patent, competitors will find it extremely difficult to enter the field and overcome the handicap. When this happens, a goodwill is created during the life of the patent. Nevertheless, the patent should be amortized, and no goodwill should be set up.

Copyrights. A copyright gives its owner the exclusive right to produce and sell reading matter and works of art. The fee for obtaining a copyright is only a nominal amount, too small to justify an accounting procedure of capitalization and amortization. Costs sufficient in amount to justify such an accounting procedure may be incurred, however, when copyrights are purchased.

Copyrights are issued for 28 years with a possibility of renewal for an additional 28 years. However, publications rarely have an active market for a period as long as 28 years, and it usually is regarded as advisable to write off copyright costs over a much shorter period.

Franchises. Franchises should not be set up in the books unless a payment was made in obtaining them. Franchises are sometimes perpetual, in which case their cost need not be amortized; usually they are granted for a definite period of time, in which case their cost should be amortized over that period.

Leasehold improvements. Leases for long periods frequently provide that the lessee (the party who acquired the right to occupy the property) shall pay the cost of any alterations or improvements which he may desire, such as new fronts, partitions, and built-in shelving. Such alterations and improvements become a part of the real estate and revert to the owner of the real estate at the expiration of the lease; all that the lessee obtains by the expenditure is the intangible right to benefit by the improvements during the life of the lease. The lessee should therefore charge such expenditures to a Leasehold Improvements account; the cost should be amortized over the life of the lease or the expected useful life of the improvements, whichever is shorter, by journal entries charging Rent and crediting Leasehold Improvements. The Rent account is also charged with the cash payment for rent. Or the amortization may be debited to Amortization—Leasehold Improvements.

Intangible Fixed Assets Not Normally Subject to Amortization

Some intangible fixed assets are not normally subject to amortization because they are assumed to have an unlimited useful life. Examples are trademarks, trade names, secret processes and formulas, and goodwill.

Such assets may be carried indefinitely at cost if there is no reason to believe that their useful lives will terminate so long as the business continues to be a going concern. However, their amortization or complete write-off may be proper under several conditions. First, at the time of its acquisition there may be good reason to fear that the useful life of such an asset will terminate, even though there is no conclusive evidence to that effect; in such instances, periodic amortization charges may be made against revenue. Second, at some date subsequent to acquisition, the asset may be found to be valueless, in which case it should be written off; or conditions may have developed which indicate that the life of the asset will terminate, in which case its cost may be amortized over the estimated remaining life; or a portion of the cost may be charged off immediately (as representing amortization for prior periods) and the remainder may be amortized over the estimated remaining life.

Trademarks. The right to the use of a trademark may be protected by registry; the right does not terminate at the end of a definite period, and trademarks are, therefore, normally carried indefinitely in the accounts at cost, without amortization.

Goodwill. The following statement, intended to indicate the nature of goodwill, is quoted from a court decision:

"When an individual or a firm or a corporation has gone on for an unbroken series of years conducting a particular business, and has been so scrupulous in fulfilling every obligation, so careful in maintaining the standard of the goods dealt in, so absolutely fair and honest in all business dealings that customers of the concern have become convinced that their experience in the future will be as satisfactory as it has been in the past, while such customers' good report of their own experience tends continually to bring new customers to the concern, there has been produced an element of value quite as important as—in some cases, perhaps, far more important than—the plant or machinery with which the business is carried on. That it is property is abundantly settled by authority, and, indeed, is not disputed. That in some cases it may be very valuable property is manifest. The individual who has created it by years of hard work and fair business dealing usually experiences no difficulty in finding men willing to pay him for it if he be willing to sell it to them."

This quotation is interesting because it indicates some of the ways in which goodwill may be created. However, it does not adequately indicate the nature of goodwill for two reasons.

In the first place, it implies that goodwill is produced only by satisfactory customer relations; but since goodwill is dependent upon earnings, and since many things other than customer satisfaction contribute to earnings, there are many sources of goodwill. Some of these sources are: location; manufacturing efficiency; satisfactory relations between the employees and the management, which contribute to earnings through effective employee service and the reduction of losses from labor turnover; adequate sources of capital and a credit standing which is reflected in low money costs; advertising; monopolistic privileges; and, in general, good business management.

In the second place, in laying the emphasis on customer relations, the quotation fails to put the emphasis where it really belongs: on the relation between earnings and net assets. A company may be scrupulous, fair, and honest, and its good repute may tend continually to attract new customers, and yet the company may have no goodwill. The existence of goodwill depends upon the amount of the earnings.

The meanings of three terms, as used in the following discussion of goodwill, are stated below:

Investment—The net assets of a business exclusive of any goodwill.

Basic rate of income—The rate of net income on the investment which, for the particular industry, may be agreed upon by the purchaser and seller as the rate which a new enterprise entering the field might reasonably be expected to earn.

Excess earnings—The amount by which the actual earnings of a business exceed earnings on the investment at the basic rate of income.

Goodwill may be defined as the value of the excess earnings. Let us assume the following conditions:

	Company A	Company B
Investment	$100,000	$100,000
Basic rate of income	10%	10%
Net income earned	$ 10,000	$ 15,000
Income on investment at basic rate	10,000	10,000
Excess earnings	$ —	$ 5,000

The excess earnings of Company B indicate that it has a goodwill; Company A apparently has no goodwill because it has no excess earnings.

Methods of computing goodwill. The price to be paid for goodwill in connection with the sale of a business may be an amount arbitrarily agreed upon by the purchaser and seller, without formal computation. On the other hand, it may be computed on the basis of past or anticipated earnings of the business. Three goodwill valuation bases are illustrated on the following page.

(1) Some multiple of the average past annual earnings. For instance, assume that the average earnings for five years prior to the sale of the business have been $10,000, and that the goodwill is to be valued at twice the average earnings; the goodwill will be valued at $20,000. The price so computed is said to be "two years' purchase" of the average annual earnings.

This method is illogical because it fails to give recognition to the fact that goodwill is dependent upon the existence of excess earnings.

Recognition is given to this fact in the two following bases of goodwill valuation.

(2) Some multiple of the average past earnings in excess of a return at an agreed rate on the average investment. For instance, assume average annual earnings for five years of $10,000, an average investment of $100,000, and an agreement to pay for goodwill three years' purchase of the average earnings in excess of 8% on the average investment. The goodwill computation would be:

Average earnings..	$10,000
Less 8% on average investment.............................	8,000
Excess..	$ 2,000
Multiply by number of years' purchase.....................	3
Goodwill...	$ 6,000

(3) The capitalized value of excess earnings. For instance, assuming the same facts as in (2) with respect to average income and investment, and assuming an agreement to compute goodwill by capitalizing, at 10%, the average annual earnings in excess of 8% on the average investment, we would compute the goodwill as follows:

Average earnings..	$10,000
Less 8% on average investment.............................	8,000
Excess to be capitalized..................................	$ 2,000
Capitalized value..........................$2,000 ÷ .10 =	$20,000

Proper book value of goodwill. A Goodwill account can properly appear on the books only if the goodwill was specifically paid for. The management of a business may believe that it has created goodwill by advertising expenditures or otherwise, and may desire to charge such items to a Goodwill account. Accountants do not approve of such charges to Goodwill because of the practical impossibility of identifying specific expenditures as representing the cost of goodwill.

It is usually considered good accounting to carry goodwill as an asset indefinitely at its cost. However, since the price paid for goodwill is generally based on a belief that "excess earnings" will be realized, what should the accountant do with the Goodwill account if "excess earnings" fail to materialize?

As a general rule, accountants do not favor perpetuating an asset balance when there is no underlying value in support of the asset. And, where an accountant has convincing evidence that an asset is significantly overstated, such overstatement should be removed from the accounts, possibly by direct charge to Retained Earnings or to partners' or proprietor's capital accounts.

As a practical matter, there is no way of determining the "life" of goodwill. Many accountants believe that it is unlikely that goodwill will last over the entire life of an enterprise. For this reason, it is considered acceptable to amortize goodwill over a reasonable period of time. The Committee on Accounting Procedure has supported this practice in its Bulletin No. 43. The Committee's opinion is paraphrased below:

> Where a corporation decides that goodwill may not continue to have value during the entire life of the enterprise, it may amortize the cost of such intangible by systematic charges against income despite the fact that there are no present indications of limited existence . . .

Organization costs. The accounting treatment of organization costs, which may be regarded as an intangible fixed asset, was discussed on pages 177 and 178.

Fixed Assets in the Balance Sheet

It usually is considered desirable to show the total tangible fixed assets and the total intangible fixed assets separately in the balance sheet. One procedure is illustrated below:

Tangible fixed assets:

Land..		$ 20,000.00	
Buildings...........................	$150,000.00		
Less accumulated depreciation........	30,000.00	120,000.00	
Machinery and equipment..............	$ 90,000.00		
Less accumulated depreciation........	12,000.00	78,000.00	
Tools..............................	$ 15,000.00		
Less accumulated depreciation........	4,000.00	11,000.00	
Delivery equipment..................	$ 5,000.00		
Less accumulated depreciation........	2,000.00	3,000.00	
Furniture and fixtures................	$ 5,500.00		
Less accumulated depreciation........	2,200.00	3,300.00	
Total tangible fixed assets................................			$235,300.00

Intangible fixed assets:

Patents...........................	$ 8,000.00		
Less accumulated amortization........	2,000.00	$ 6,000.00	
Goodwill..		50,000.00	
Total intangible fixed assets...................	....	56,000.00	

If there are many fixed assets, space can be saved by a balance sheet presentation similar to the following:

	Cost	Accumulated Depreciation or Amortization	Cost Less Depreciation or Amortization
Tangible fixed assets:			
Land..................	$ 20,000.00		$ 20,000.00
Buildings...............	150,000.00	$30,000.00	120,000.00
Machinery and equipment	90,000.00	12,000.00	78,000.00
Tools..................	15,000.00	4,000.00	11,000.00
Delivery equipment......	5,000.00	2,000.00	3,000.00
Furniture and fixtures....	5,500.00	2,200.00	3,300.00
Total tangible fixed assets................	$285,500.00	$50,200.00	$235,300.00
Intangible fixed assets:			
Patents................	$ 8,000.00	$ 2,000.00	$ 6,000.00
Goodwill...............			50,000.00
Total intangible fixed assets................			56,000.00

CHAPTER 19
Liabilities

Classes of liabilities. Amounts shown in a balance sheet as liabilities may be classified as follows:

(1) Money obligations:
    (a) Long-term, such as bonds and mortgages payable.
    (b) Short-term, such as accounts and notes payable.
(2) Performance obligations, such as deferred revenue and provisions for future free service.

Accounts representing performance obligations usually arise in connection with a proper matching of revenue and expense for a period. The portion of revenue collected in advance that has not been earned at the end of the accounting period remains in an unearned revenue account, where it represents an obligation to be satisfied, not by the payment of money, but by the rendering of service.

A proper matching of revenue and expense requires that, in the period when revenues are reported in the income statement, the debits against such revenues include the costs already incurred and estimated applicable future costs such as those to be incurred in rendering free repair service or in the fulfillment of guarantees. The debits for future costs are offset by credits to allowance or provision accounts, such as Provision for Free Service Costs.

In this chapter we are concerned primarily with money obligations.

Long- and short-term liabilities. The accepted rules for distinguishing between long-term and short-term money obligations were stated in Chapter 8.

A special problem arises when long-term liabilities approach their maturity and are due within, say, a year. Should they be included among the current liabilities although in preceding balance sheets they have been classed as long-term liabilities? The proximity of the maturity date probably should not be the sole determining factor. If an issue of bonds is to be paid from the proceeds of another issue of long-term securities, it is proper to continue to classify it as a long-term liability.

Sources of corporate funds. When a corporation finds it necessary or desirable to raise additional funds, it may borrow them on a short-term note, on a long-term mortgage note, or on bonds, or it may issue additional stock.   It usually is regarded as good business management to borrow on short-term notes only in case the funds are needed for current operations and the current operations presumably will produce the cash with which to repay the loan.   If the funds are to be used for plant additions or permanent investments, they usually should be obtained by issuance of either stocks or bonds.

Stocks and bonds—advantages and disadvantages.   Bond issues have certain advantages over stock issues:

(1) Bondholders have no vote; therefore, the stockholders do not have to share the management with them.

(2) The money cost may be lower.   If common stock is issued, the contributors of new capital will share pro rata with the old common stockholders in dividends and retained earnings.   If preferred stock is issued, it may be participating, in which case the dividends may be greatly in excess of reasonable interest on bonds; or it may be nonparticipating, in which case it usually is necessary to give the preferred stock a dividend rate higher than the interest rate at which bonds could be sold, because bonds are a positive, and usually a secured, liability with a definite maturity, and also because bond interest is payable unconditionally, whereas the payment of preferred dividends is dependent upon earnings and the existence of retained earnings.

(3) The fact that bond interest is deductible as an expense in the computation of income taxes, whereas dividends are not, is frequently a deciding factor in the choice of securities to be issued and has sometimes even influenced corporations to convert preferred stock into bonds.

On the other hand, if interest and principal payments on a bond issue are not made when due, the bondholders may institute foreclosure proceedings and the borrowing company may lose fixed assets which are essential to its operations and may even be forced into liquidation, with a consequent loss which will leave a very small equity for the stockholders.

Long-Term Liabilities

Mortgage notes and bonds.   If all the desired long-term funds can be borrowed from one lender, the borrower may issue a note and a mortgage; the note will recite the terms of the obligation (date, maturity, interest rate, and so forth) and the mortgage will effect a pledge of certain property as security.   A mortgage originally was a conveyance of property from a debtor to a creditor or his representative, subject to the proviso that, if the debtor met his obligation, the conveyance would be nullified. In most states the form of the mortgage has been changed to give it the status of a lien instead of a conveyance or transfer of title.

If it is impossible to obtain the funds from one lender, an issue of bonds may be offered to the public. Since the bonds may be held by many people, who are not known at the time of arranging for the issue and who will change with each transfer of a bond from one holder to another, the lenders cannot be named in a mortgage. Therefore, the borrower selects a trustee, usually a bank or a trust company, to act as a representative of the bondholders; and a mortgage, or deed of trust, is executed conveying a conditional title to the pledged property to the trustee as agent for the bondholders. This trustee is called the *trustee under the mortgage.*

Since long-term borrowings by corporations are usually represented by bonds, this chapter deals specifically with bonds. However, except as indicated above, long-term mortgage notes are essentially of the same nature as secured bonds. Therefore, what is said with respect to secured bonds may be regarded as also applying generally to long-term mortgage notes.

Classes of bonds. It is impossible to discuss all the different kinds of bonds which have been devised for use in corporate financing. Some of the more common forms are:

(1) Secured bonds. These differ as to the nature of the property which is pledged as security. Three classes of secured bonds are in common use:
  (a) Real estate mortgage bonds. These are secured by mortgages on land, or on land and buildings.
  (b) Chattel mortgage bonds. These are secured by mortgages on tangible personal property, such as machinery and equipment of various kinds.
  (c) Collateral trust bonds. These are secured by a pledge of stocks, bonds, or other negotiable instruments.
(2) Unsecured bonds. Unsecured bonds are sometimes called *debentures.* Since they are not secured by a pledge of any specific property, their marketability depends upon the general credit of the borrower.

Bonds of any of the classes mentioned above may be convertible; that is, their holders may have the right to exchange them for the issuing company's stock—usually, common. The bond stipulates the terms on which the exchange can be made; that is, par for par; or par for the bonds and book value for the stock; or par and accrued interest for the bonds and par and "accrued" dividends for the stock; or any other arrangement.   Such bonds give the holder a more assured income during the development period of the issuing company than he might have as a stockholder, with a right to become a stockholder if the business proves to be successful.

First and second mortgages.   Bonds may be secured by first, second, or even third mortgages on the same property.   If the obligations are not met, and foreclosure ensues, the proceeds of the mortgaged property must go first to the satisfaction of the first-mortgage bondholders, any residue to the satisfaction of the second-mortgage bondholders, and so on.

Second-mortgage bonds are thus obviously a less desirable investment than first-mortgage bonds, because they are secured by a secondary lien on the pledged assets.   First-mortgage bonds are called *prior-lien* or *underlying* bonds; second-mortgage bonds are called *junior* bonds.

Registered and coupon bonds.   Bonds may be classified in three groups on the basis of registry, as follows:

(1) Registered as to both principal and interest.

> The name of the owner of the bond is recorded on the books of the issuing company or its fiscal agent, and the interest is paid by checks drawn to the order of the bondholders.   This method has the advantage of safeguarding the owner against loss or theft, but it has two disadvantages: First, a sale and transfer can be made only by assignment and registry, instead of merely by delivery; second, the check method of paying interest is burdensome.

(2) Registered as to principal only.

> By registering the bonds as to principal only, and attaching coupons for the interest, the owner is safeguarded against loss or theft of principal, and the debtor company is relieved of the burden of issuing numerous interest checks.

(3) Unregistered.

> Such a bond is transferable by mere delivery; the owner's endorsement is not required.   The danger from loss or theft is, of course, much greater than with a bond which is registered as to principal.   The interest is collected by clipping the interest coupons and presenting them to a bank for deposit or collection.

Recording the bond issue. A separate liability account should be kept with each bond issue. If there is more than one issue, the account title for each issue should contain a comprehensive description of the issue, such as "First Mortgage, 6%, Real Estate Bonds Payable, 1980," or "Collateral Trust, 7% Bonds Payable, 1985." The year is the year of maturity.

The mortgage, or trust deed, states the amount of bonds that can be issued. Each bond is signed by the trustee under the mortgage to indicate that it is secured by the mortgage; this is called *authentication by the trustee.*

Very frequently, the amount of bonds immediately authenticated by the trustee and issued by the borrowing company is less than the total issue provided for under the trust deed. The amount of bonds that can be issued may be shown by a memorandum notation in the bond account, and the par of the bonds issued is shown by a credit entry in the account. To illustrate, assume that a company's real estate is ample in value to secure an issue of $100,000 of first-mortgage bonds. Only $60,000 of funds are immediately required, but there may be future requirements for $40,000 more. If the trust deed were drawn to secure an issue of only $60,000, a subsequent loan of $40,000 could be secured only by a second mortgage; a second-mortgage issue, being less desirable, might require a higher interest rate and might be difficult to market. In anticipation of its future requirements, the company may authorize a total first-mortgage bond issue of $100,000, drawing a trust deed as security for a loan of that amount. If $100,000 of bonds are authenticated, but only $60,000 are issued, the entry for the issuance will be:

```
Cash.......................................... 60,000.00
     First mortgage, 6%, real estate bonds payable,
         1980......................................         60,000.00
     To record the issuance of $60,000 par value of
     bonds.
```

The ledger account will appear as follows:

First Mortgage, 6%, Real Estate Bonds Payable, 1980

	Authorized	issue, $100,000	
		Date	60,000.00

The facts with respect to authorized, unissued, and issued bonds should be shown in the balance sheet as follows:

```
Long-term liabilities:
    First-mortgage, 6%, real estate bonds pay-
        able, due March 1, 1980:
            Authorized........................ $100,000.00
            Less unissued.....................   40,000.00 $60,000.00
```

Or thus:

Long-term liabilities:
First-mortgage, 6%, real estate bonds payable, due
March 1, 1980; authorized, $100,000.00; issued......... $60,000.00

The amount of unissued bonds should be shown in the balance sheet, because the bondholders have a right to know that $40,000 of additional bonds can be issued under the same trust deed which secures their bonds. Thus, if the real estate is carried in the balance sheet at $150,000, the holders of the $60,000 of issued bonds would be interested in knowing that an additional $40,000 of bonds could be issued. On the basis of the issued bonds only, the ratio of security to debt is 150 to 60; but on the basis of the total authorized issue, the ratio of security is only 150 to 100.

If the bonds are registered as to principal or interest, or both, subsidiary records should be kept, showing the names and addresses of the holders.

Issuances between interest dates. Bonds are often issued between interest dates, in which case the purchaser is usually required to pay the accrued interest. To illustrate, assume that $10,000 of 6% bonds are issued two months after the interest date, at par and accrued interest; the entry will be:

Cash....................................... 10,100.00
    Bonds payable...........................   10,000.00
    Bond interest expense...................   100.00

Entry when the semiannual interest is paid four months later:

Bond interest expense........................ 300.00
    Cash....................................   300.00

The $300 debit to Bond Interest Expense made at the time of paying the interest, minus the $100 credit to Bond Interest Expense made at the time of selling the bonds, leaves the account with a $200 debit balance, which is the interest expense for four months.

Payment of interest. Most bonds provide for the payment of interest semiannually. The methods of paying bond interest depend upon whether the bonds are registered as to interest. Two conditions are illustrated:

(1) The bonds are registered as to interest. If there are a large number of bondholders, it is advisable to draw a check for the entire amount of the bond interest and deposit it in a special bond interest bank account. The entry will be:

The X Bank—Bond interest account.............. 6,000.00
    Cash...................................   6,000.00
    To record deposit of funds in the account for pay-
    ment of bond interest.

Such a procedure has the advantage of simplifying the reconciliation of the principal bank account; also, the chief disbursing officer can be relieved of the task of signing a large number of interest checks by delegating the work of signing interest checks to a subordinate.

Separate checks will then be drawn on the bond interest account, the total of these checks being debited to Bond Interest Expense and credited to The *X* Bank—Bond Interest Account.

(2) The bonds are not registered as to interest, but bear coupons which are clipped by the holders and presented for collection. The bondholder usually deposits the coupons in his own bank account, and the bank makes the collection. The coupons usually designate a bank at which collection can be made; when the semiannual interest is due, the company deposits the total amount of the interest in a special account at the bank where the coupons are payable; when coupons are presented for payment, the bank pays them and charges the amount to the company's account. The issuing company's entries are:

On or before the date when interest is payable:

The *X* Bank—Bond interest account.............	6,000.00	
Cash....................................		6,000.00
Transfer of funds to special bank account for payment of interest.		

On the date when interest is payable:

Bond interest expense...........................	6,000.00	
Accrued bond interest payable...............		6,000.00
To record the expense and liability for six months' interest.		

At the end of the month or at any other date when the bank reports the amount of coupons paid:

Accrued bond interest payable...................	5,700.00	
The *X* Bank—Bond interest account..........		5,700.00
To record the payment of interest coupons presented to the bank.		

Since some bondholders may be dilatory in presenting coupons for payment, balances may remain in the special bank account and in the Accrued Bond Interest Payable account. The balance sheet should show as an asset any balance in the special bank account, and should show as a liability any balance in the Accrued Bond Interest Payable account; the mere deposit of funds in a special bank account to be used for the payment of bond interest does not constitute payment of the liability.

Bond discount. If the bond interest rate is lower than the market rate for bonds of a similar nature (for instance, similar in the nature of the borrower's business and credit standing, in the nature of the borrower's security, and in the amount of its earnings), it may be impossible to obtain par for the bonds. Let us assume, by way of illustration, that a ten-year, 5% bond issue of $100,000 is disposed of for a net amount of $98,000. The issuance of these bonds will be recorded by the following entry:

```
Cash.......................................   98,000.00
Bond discount.............................    2,000.00
    Bonds payable.........................              100,000.00
    Issuance of bonds at 98.
```

Amortization of bond discount. In the preceding illustration, $98,000 was received, but $100,000 must be repaid. The $2,000 excess of the amount to be paid over the amount received is an expense to be spread over the life of the bonds. The total interest cost over the life of the bonds includes the discount as well as the semiannual interest payments.

The Bond Discount account should be written off to Bond Interest Expense in periodic installments. If an interest-payment date coincides with the close of the company's accounting year, the write-off usually is made in equal amounts each six months, at the semiannual interest-payment dates. Since there will be twenty semiannual interest payments during the ten-year life of the bonds, the discount will be written off in twenty equal installments of $100. The charges to Bond Interest Expense each six months will be as shown in the following entries:

```
Bond interest expense.....................   2,500.00
    Cash..................................               2,500.00
    Payment of semiannual interest.

Bond interest expense.....................    100.00
    Bond discount.........................                100.00
    To amortize 1/20 of the discount.
```

These semiannual amortizations will completely write off the Bond Discount account at the end of the tenth year, and will produce equal total semiannual charges to Bond Interest Expense.

If a semiannual interest-payment date does not coincide with the end of the issuing company's accounting period, an adjusting entry will be required for the accrued interest, and another entry will be required to amortize the portion of the discount applicable to the period between the last preceding interest date and the end of the accounting period. For example, referring to the preceding illustration, assume that interest was paid and an amortization entry was made on September 30, and that the issuing company's

accounting year ends on December 31. The following entries will
be required on December 31:

Bond interest expense.........................   1,250.00
    Accrued bond interest payable............   1,250.00
Accrued interest for three months.

Bond interest expense.........................   50.00
    Bond discount.........................   50.00
Amortization of discount for three months.

Bond premium. If bonds are issued at a premium, the premium reduces the interest charge. For instance, if the bonds
mentioned in the preceding illustration were sold for $102,000,
the $2,000 premium received when the bonds were sold would not
have to be repaid at their maturity, and should therefore be offset
against the interest payments to determine the net cost of the use
of the money.

The entry at the time of the issuance of the bonds would be as
follows:

Cash...................................... 102,000.00
    Bonds payable........................   100,000.00
    Bond premium.........................   2,000.00
Issuance of bonds at 102.

The payment of the bond interest and the amortization of the
bond premium in equal semiannual installments would be recorded
by the entries shown below:

Bond interest expense.........................   2,500.00
    Cash.................................   2,500.00
Payment of semiannual interest.

Bond premium..............................   100.00
    Bond interest expense..................   100.00
Amortization of bond premium.

If an interest-payment date does not coincide with the end of
the issuing company's accounting period, end-of-period entries
should be made for the accrued interest and for the amortization
of premium for the fractional period.

Bond premium and discount in the balance sheet. It has long
been regarded as correct accounting procedure to show unamortized
bond discount under a Deferred Charges caption at the bottom of
the asset side of the balance sheet, and unamortized bond premium
on the liability side under a caption of Deferred Credits, between the
long-term liabilities and the stockholders' equity. For instance,
assume that a trial balance contained the following balances:

First-mortgage, 6%, real estate bonds, 1980......   100,000.00
First-mortgage equipment bonds, 5½%, 1975....   50,000.00
Premium on first-mortgage real estate bonds.....   3,000.00
Discount on first-mortgage equipment bonds..... 1,800.00

The customary presentation of these facts in the balance sheet is:

Assets

Deferred charges:
Discount on first-mortgage equipment bonds.......................... $ 1,800.00

Liabilities and Stockholders' Equity

Long-term liabilities:
First-mortgage, 6%, real estate bonds, 1980.......... $100,000.00
First-mortgage equipment bonds, 5½%, 1975........   50,000.00
Total long-term liabilities....................................   150,000.00

Deferred credits:
Premium on first-mortgage real estate bonds.....................   3,000.00

There has been some agitation in favor of showing unamortized premium as an addition to, and unamortized discount as a deduction from, the par of the bonds, thus:

Liabilities and Stockholders' Equity

Long-term liabilities:
First-mortgage, 6%, real estate bonds, 1980.......... $100,000.00
Add unamortized premium.......................   3,000.00 $103,000.00
First-mortgage equipment bonds, 5½%, 1975........ $ 50,000.00
Deduct unamortized discount....................   1,800.00   48,200.00

This procedure has not been generally adopted by the accounting profession.

Retirement of bonds.   Bonds may be retired:

(1) In total at maturity, out of the borrowing company's general funds.   The payment of the bonds under such conditions is recorded by debiting Bonds Payable and crediting Cash.

(2) In a series.   Bonds retirable in this way are called *serial* bonds.

To illustrate, assume that $100,000 is borrowed; nothing is to be paid off during the first five years; at the end of the sixth year, and each year thereafter, $20,000 is to be paid, so that the bonds will be retired serially by the end of the tenth year.   Each retirement is recorded by a debit to Bonds Payable and a credit to Cash.

(3) In total at maturity out of a sinking fund created by periodic deposits with a sinking fund trustee.   This method is discussed below.

Sinking funds.   If bonds are to be retired at maturity through the operation of a sinking fund, the borrowing company agrees, as one of the terms of the trust indenture, to make periodic deposits with a sinking fund trustee, who invests the deposited funds in securities.   The sinking fund trustee may, or may not, be also the trustee under the mortgage.   Sinking fund deposit agreements take various forms, particularly with respect to the amounts of the periodic contributions.   As a simple illustration, we shall assume that a company borrows $100,000 which is repayable at the end of ten years.   It agrees to deposit $10,000 with the sinking fund trustee at the end of the first year; the trustee is to invest the fund in securities and add the income earned on these securities to the fund.   At the end of the second year, the company will deposit enough to bring the total fund up to $20,000.   At the end of the third year, the company will deposit enough to bring the total fund up to $30,000; and so on to the end of the tenth year.   The annual contributions by the company will decrease because the interest collected by the trustee on the accumulating fund will increase each year.

Assume that the trustee is able to earn 5% on the securities in the fund; the accumulation of the sinking fund may be tabulated in the manner illustrated below:

End of Year	Interest Earned	Deposit	Total Fund
1		$10,000.00	$ 10,000.00
2	$ 500.00	9,500.00	20,000.00
3	1,000.00	9,000.00	30,000.00
4	1,500.00	8,500.00	40,000.00
5	2,000.00	8,000.00	50,000.00
6	2,500.00	7,500.00	60,000.00
7	3,000.00	7,000.00	70,000.00
8	3,500.00	6,500.00	80,000.00
9	4,000.00	6,000.00	90,000.00
10	4,500.00	5,500.00	100,000.00
	$22,500.00	$77,500.00	

Annual entries for the deposit of funds with the trustee and the collection of interest by the trustee on sinking fund securities are indicated below:

End of first year:

```
Sinking fund cash............................ 10,000.00
    Cash....................................            10,000.00
    Deposit with sinking fund trustee.
```

End of second year:

```
Sinking fund cash............................   500.00
    Sinking fund income......................               500.00
    Income earned on sinking fund securities.  (The
    Sinking Fund Income account will be closed to
    Revenue and Expense.)

Sinking fund cash............................ 9,500.00
    Cash....................................             9,500.00
    Deposit with sinking fund trustee.
```

The trustee is expected to invest the sinking fund deposits in securities, but there usually will be some uninvested cash in the fund. The company's records should show what portion of the sinking fund is represented by cash and what portion is represented by securities. Therefore, when the trustee reports the purchase of securities, the company should make an entry debiting Sinking Fund Securities and crediting Sinking Fund Cash.

The sinking fund cash and securities may be shown in one total in the balance sheet, or they may be detailed as follows:

```
Sinking fund:
   Cash...................................... $   300.00
   Securities................................  19,700.00 $20,000.00
```

The sinking fund may be shown under the Sundry Assets caption or as a separate item.

When the bonds mature, the sinking fund securities will be disposed of by the trustee, who will pay the bonds from the cash in the sinking fund. Assuming that the entire $100,000 fund was invested in securities, that the securities were disposed of without loss, and that the bonds were paid, the trustee would report the facts to the debtor company, and the company would make entries as follows:

```
Sinking fund cash........................... 100,000.00
   Sinking fund securities..................            100,000.00
   Sale of sinking fund securities.

Bonds payable.............................. 100,000.00
   Sinking fund cash........................            100,000.00
   Retirement of the bonds.
```

If a loss is incurred in the disposal of the sinking fund securities, the company will be obliged to make another deposit with the trustee in an amount sufficient to bring the fund up to the required balance. Assume that the trustee loses $500 on the disposal of the securities; the company will be obliged to make up this loss by a deposit of $500, and its entries will be:

```
Sinking fund cash........................... 99,500.00
Loss on sale of sinking fund securities.........   500.00
   Sinking fund securities..................            100,000.00
   Sale of sinking fund securities at a loss.

Sinking fund cash...........................   500.00
   Cash.....................................               500.00
   Additional deposit with trustee to cover the
   loss from the disposal of the securities in the
   fund.

Bonds payable.............................. 100,000.00
   Sinking fund cash........................            100,000.00
   Retirement of bonds by sinking fund trustee.
```

On the other hand, if the trustee makes a gain of $540 on the disposal of the sinking fund securities, the residue of the fund will be returned to the company.   The company's entries will be:

```
Sinking fund cash...........................  100,540.00
    Sinking fund securities...................               100,000.00
    Gain on sale of sinking fund securities.....                   540.00
    Sale of sinking fund securities at a gain.

Bonds payable...........................  100,000.00
    Sinking fund cash......................               100,000.00
    Retirement of bonds by sinking fund trustee.

Cash...................................      540.00
    Sinking fund cash......................                   540.00
    Excess in sinking fund received from trustee.
```

Sinking fund expense.   The service fee charged by the sinking fund trustee may be paid from the sinking fund cash.   If this is done, the issuing company should debit Sinking Fund Expense and credit Sinking Fund Cash.   Or the trustee's fee may be paid from the issuing company's general cash; if so, the entry will be: debit Sinking Fund Expense and credit Cash.

Sinking fund reserves.   In addition to requiring sinking fund deposits, the terms of the bond issue may restrict the amount of dividends which the borrowing company may pay during the life of the bonds.   One way of making this restriction is by requiring the establishment of a sinking fund reserve by transfers from Retained Earnings.

The sinking fund reserve requirement is intended to prevent the impairment of the company's working capital.   Suppose, for instance, that the company which issued the bonds mentioned in the foregoing illustration had a working capital (current assets minus current liabilities) of $100,000 after issuing its bonds, and that this amount was considered no more than adequate to carry on operations.   Assume that, during the first year of the life of the bonds, the company had a net income of $20,000, which increased the working capital an equal amount; if the company paid dividends to the full extent of the $20,000 net income and also paid $10,000 to the sinking fund trustee, the working capital would be reduced $10,000.   If this took place year after year, the working capital might be so impaired that the company would not be able to carry on its operations profitably.   A year might soon come when the operations would be so unprofitable that the company would not be able to make its sinking fund deposit.

To restrict the payment of dividends, and thus to avoid a dangerous impairment of working capital, the terms of the bond issue may include a provision similar to the following: "In addition to increasing the sinking fund $10,000 each year, the company shall transfer $10,000 each year from its Retained Earnings account to a Sinking Fund Reserve account; the retained earnings set apart in this reserve shall not be available for dividends until the bonds have been paid."

Referring to the illustration in the section on sinking funds, and assuming that the company was obligated to set up a reserve in accordance with the provision just quoted, the following annual entries would be made:

End of first year:

Sinking Fund entry:

Sinking fund cash	10,000.00	
Cash		10,000.00
Deposit with the sinking fund trustee.		

Sinking Fund Reserve entry:

Retained earnings	10,000.00	
Sinking fund reserve		10,000.00
To transfer a portion of the retained earnings to a reserve.		

End of second year:

Sinking Fund entries:

Sinking fund cash	500.00	
Sinking fund income		500.00
Income collected by sinking fund trustee on securities in the fund.		
Sinking fund cash	9,500.00	
Cash		9,500.00
Deposit with the trustee.		

Sinking Fund Reserve entry:

Retained earnings	10,000.00	
Sinking fund reserve		10,000.00
To transfer a portion of the retained earnings to a reserve.		

A sinking fund reserve is really a part of the retained earnings; for the time being, dividends cannot be charged to it, but it is retained earnings nevertheless. Therefore, it should be shown in the balance sheet under the Stockholders' Equity caption, as illustrated below:

Stockholders' equity:			
Capital stock			$500,000.00
Retained earnings:			
Sinking fund reserve—Not available for dividends	$20,000.00		
Free—Available for dividends	15,000.00		
Total retained earnings		35,000.00	
Total stockholders' equity			$535,000.00

It is sometimes difficult to understand that a sinking fund reserve is really a part of the retained earnings. The nature of the sinking fund reserve would be more easily understood if it were called "Retained Earnings Appropriated for Sinking Fund," or "Retained Earnings Not Available for Dividends Until After the Bonds Have Been Paid."

After the bonds have matured and been paid, the bondholders have no further right to restrict the payment of dividends; therefore, an entry can be made debiting the Sinking Fund Reserve and crediting Retained Earnings. Thus the balance in the Sinking Fund Reserve is returned to Retained Earnings and is again free from any contractual limitations upon the payment of dividends. However, it might be expedient for the directors to refrain voluntarily from the payment of dividends from these retained earnings in order to protect the company's working capital position.

Other methods of restricting dividends. A sinking fund reserve requirement such as the one quoted on pages 321 and 322 may not be an adequate safeguard against an impairment of working capital as a result of dividend payments. If a company is required to deposit $10,000 in a sinking fund, it may not be sufficient to require that $10,000 also be transferred from Retained Earnings to a Sinking Fund Reserve; even though this requirement may be met, the borrowing company may still deplete its working capital by paying dividends out of retained earnings accumulated before the long-term debt was incurred. For this reason, other methods of restricting dividends have come into wide use. For instance, the issuing company may agree to refrain from paying dividends that will reduce the stockholders' equity below a stipulated amount, or that will reduce the working capital below the amount existing when the bonds were issued.

Dividend restrictions not reflected by a sinking fund reserve should be stated parenthetically in the balance sheet in the manner illustrated below:

```
Stockholders' equity:
  Capital stock.........................  $100,000.00
  Retained earnings (of which $40,000 is not
    available for cash dividends because of
    restrictions in the bond indenture)......   65,000.00  $165,000.00
```

Current Liabilities

Inclusion of all liabilities. The most important matter to be dealt with in connection with current liabilities is the importance of seeing that all such liabilities are included in the balance sheet. Some of the liabilities not infrequently omitted from balance sheets are mentioned on the following page.

(1) Accounts payable for purchases. There is normally some delay between the receipt of merchandise and the recording of the purchase. At the end of any period for which financial statements are prepared, it is highly important that all purchases of goods to which title has passed be recorded before the statements are prepared.

(2) Miscellaneous liabilities for services rendered the business before the close of the period but not billed until the succeeding period.

(3) Accrued liabilities for wages, interest, taxes, employees' bonuses, and so forth.

(4) Dividends which have been declared and therefore represent a liability, but which have not been recorded.

(5) Unearned revenues.

Recording purchase liabilities net. Under the method of recording purchase discounts previously explained in this text, purchases and the liabilities therefor were recorded gross, and any discounts taken were credited to Purchase Discounts.

For example, assume that goods are purchased at a list price of $1,000, and with terms of 2/10; n/30. The purchase would be recorded thus:

```
Purchases....................................... 1,000.00
    Accounts payable*.........................        1,000.00
```

If the bill was paid within the discount period, the payment would be recorded thus:

```
Accounts payable............................... 1,000.00
    Purchase discounts.........................          20.00
    Cash......................................         980.00
```

The foregoing procedure shows the amount of discount *taken*. The accounts do not show the amount of discount *lost* by failure to pay bills within the discount period. An alternative method of recording purchases and purchase discounts to disclose this important information is illustrated below:

The purchase is recorded at the *net* price:

```
Purchases....................................... 980.00
    Accounts payable..........................         980 00
```

If the bill is paid within the discount period, the payment is recorded thus:

```
Accounts payable............................... 980.00
    Cash......................................         980.00
```

---

*In this and subsequent entries in this illustration, an account in the subsidiary ledger should also be debited or credited.

If the bill is paid after the discount period has expired, the following entry is made:

Accounts payable.............................	980.00	
Discounts lost.................	20.00	
Cash.....................		1,000.00

At the end of each period for which statements are prepared, an adjusting entry debiting Discounts Lost and crediting Accounts Payable should be made for the discount on all invoices for which the discount period has expired.

Discussion of the method. The method of recording purchases and purchase discounts lost, just described, is commonly referred to as the "net price" procedure. Many accountants favor the net price procedure for three reasons: (1) it discloses very significant information—namely, the amount of discount lost; (2) it records purchases at the price which will secure the goods; and (3) it results in presenting liabilities more nearly in terms of the amounts that will be expended for their settlement; if most invoices are paid before the discount period expires, the recording of purchases and liabilities in terms of gross invoice price tends to overstate the liabilities by the amount of the purchase discounts on unpaid invoices. But since the net price procedure is unusual, if it is followed the balance sheet should indicate parenthetically that the liability on accounts payable is stated net of available discounts.

There is some difference of opinion regarding the proper position of the Discounts Lost account in the income statement. Many accountants believe that, as a matter of theory, the net price is the correct measure of cost. Following this theory, they would show the discounts lost in the income statement as an administrative expense, since, presumably, it is the responsibility of the administrative officers to see that obligations of the business are paid within the discount period.

Other accountants believe that cost is equal to the entire amount paid for an item. Under this theory, the balance of the Discounts Lost account is added to the purchases.

Contingent Liabilities

A contingent liability exists when there is no present debt but when a liability may develop as the result of an action or default by an outsider. For instance, if a note receivable is discounted, no immediate liability is created; however, a contingent liability exists because the maker of the note may default and the endorser may be required to make payment. Pending lawsuits in which the company is defendant and disputed claims for additional income tax payments are other illustrations.

If there is little probability that a liability and an accompanying loss or expense will develop, it is sufficient to disclose the contingent liability by a balance sheet footnote.   If a liability and an accompanying loss or expense are likely to develop, a liability account (for instance, Provision for Possible Additional Income Taxes) may be credited, with (usually) an offsetting debit to an expense account. As indicated on pages 103–106 (in the discussion of clean surplus and current operating concepts), circumstances might justify a charge to Retained Earnings.

CHAPTER 20
Manufacturing Operations

Purpose of chapter. In preceding chapters we have dealt with accounting procedures applicable to service organizations and merchandising enterprises. Manufacturing is another of the major areas of business operations, and therefore it seems desirable at this point to acquaint the student with some elementary features of accounting for manufacturing operations. More advanced material, dealing with cost accounting, is presented in the next chapter.

Manufacturing costs. A merchandising concern buys its goods ready for resale; its books, therefore, contain a Purchases account which shows the cost of merchandise purchased. A manufacturing concern also uses a Purchases account, but the goods purchased are raw materials which are not ready for resale. To change the raw materials to finished goods ready for sale requires expenditures for labor and for a great variety of other manufacturing costs. The books, therefore, must contain accounts in which to record all such costs.

Manufacturing costs are of three classes: materials (often called raw materials), direct labor, and manufacturing overhead.

Materials include only those things that enter into and become a part of the finished product; supplies used in the operation of the factory are not classified as materials because they do not become part of the finished product.

The nature of direct labor can best be shown by distinguishing it from indirect labor. Employees who work on the product with tools, or who operate machines in the process of production, are direct laborers; but superintendents and foremen, who supervise the work of production, and janitors and engineers, whose services are incidental to the process of production, are indirect laborers.

Manufacturing overhead, or manufacturing expense, includes all costs incurred in production that cannot be classified as material or direct labor. Manufacturing overhead includes, among other things, indirect labor, depreciation of the factory buildings and equipment, power, supplies used, taxes and expired insurance on the assets used in manufacture, and repairs and upkeep of the factory.

The cost of finished goods manufactured during a given period cannot be determined, however, merely by adding the costs incurred during the period for materials, direct labor, and manufacturing overhead. There may be unfinished goods, called *goods in process*, on hand at the end of the period, and the cost of these unfinished goods must be deducted to determine the cost of goods finished. Similarly, there may have been goods in process at the beginning of the period, and these must also be taken into consideration.

The following statement indicates the elements that enter into the computation of the cost of goods manufactured. Payroll taxes have been omitted to simplify the illustration.

THE *A B C* COMPANY   Exhibit D

Statement of Cost of Goods Manufactured
For the Year Ended December 31, 1958

Materials:			
Inventory, December 31, 1957			$ 12,000
Purchases		$94,000	
Deduct:			
Purchase returns and allowances	$1,500		
Purchase discounts	1,200	2,700	
Net purchases		$91,300	
Transportation in		800	
Total			92,100
Total inventory and purchases			$104,100
Deduct inventory, December 31, 1958			9,000
Cost of materials used			$ 95,100
Direct labor			80,750
Manufacturing overhead:			
Indirect labor		$ 9,125	
Heat, light, and power		3,000	
Building and machinery repairs		300	
Depreciation:			
Buildings		3,200	
Machinery and equipment		6,000	
Insurance expense		850	
Taxes		1,200	
Factory supplies used		3,500	
Miscellaneous factory expense		2,500	
Total manufacturing overhead			29,675
Total cost of manufacturing			$205,525
Add goods in process, December 31, 1957			15,000
Total			$220,525
Deduct goods in process, December 31, 1958			11,000
Cost of goods manufactured			$209,525

Income statement. The income statements of manufacturing companies do not necessarily differ from those of trading companies except in one particular: the statements of manufacturing companies show the cost of goods *manufactured* (as determined in the statement of cost of goods manufactured), whereas the statements of trading companies show the cost of goods *purchased*. The following statement is illustrative.

THE *A B C* COMPANY   Exhibit C

Income Statement

For the Year Ended December 31, 1958

Gross sales			$300,000
Deduct:			
Sales returns and allowances		$ 2,000	
Sales discounts		2,500	4,500
Net sales			$295,500
Deduct cost of goods sold:			
Finished goods inventory, December 31, 1957		$ 20,000	
Cost of goods manufactured—per Exhibit D		209,525	
Total		$229,525	
Deduct finished goods inventory, December 31, 1958		17,000	
Cost of goods sold			212,525
Gross profit on sales			$ 82,975
Deduct expenses:			
Selling expenses:			
Advertising	$ 9,000		
Salesmen's salaries	20,360		
Salesmen's traveling expenses	8,000		
Heat and light	150		
Miscellaneous selling expenses	2,500	$ 40,010	
General expenses:			
Officers' salaries	$18,000		
Office salaries	3,040		
Stationery and printing	400		
Office supplies used	300		
Depreciation:			
Building	300		
Furniture and fixtures	750		
Heat and light	350		
Insurance expense	100		
Taxes	200		
Bad debts expense	800		
Miscellaneous general expenses	700	24,940	
Total expenses			64,950
Net income before federal income tax			$ 18,025
Federal income tax			5,500
Net income			$ 12,525

Statement of retained earnings. There are no unusual features in the statement of retained earnings of a manufacturing company. The statement of The *A B C* Company appears below:

THE *A B C* COMPANY   Exhibit B

Statement of Retained Earnings

For the Year Ended December 31, 1958

Balance, December 31, 1957	$71,450
Net income for the year—per Exhibit C	12,525
Total	$83,975
Deduct dividends	6,000
Balance, December 31, 1958	$77,975

Balance sheet. The balance sheet of a manufacturing company will usually show three inventories—finished goods, goods in process, and materials—and certain factory fixed asset account balances.

Exhibit A

THE *A B C* COMPANY
Balance Sheet
December 31, 1958

Assets

Current assets:

Cash			$25,000
Accounts receivable	$40,000		
Deduct allowance for doubtful accounts	1,000		39,000
Inventories:			
Finished goods	$17,000		
Goods in process	11,000		
Materials	9,000		37,000
Unexpired insurance			300
Total current assets			$101,300

Fixed assets:

Land			$10,000
Buildings	$70,000		
Deduct accumulated depreciation	15,500		54,500
Machinery and equipment	$60,000		
Deduct accumulated depreciation	21,000		39,000
Furniture and fixtures	$ 5,000		
Deduct accumulated depreciation	2,250		2,750
Total fixed assets—cost less depreciation			106,250
			$207,550

Liabilities and Stockholders' Equity

Current liabilities:

Accounts payable	$ 22,800	
Accrued salaries and wages	1,275	
Federal income tax payable	5,500	
Total current liabilities		$ 29,575
Stockholders' equity:		
Capital stock	$100,000	
Retained earnings—per Exhibit B	77,975	
Total stockholders' equity		177,975
		$207,550

Working papers. The preceding illustrative statements were prepared from the working papers on pages 332 and 333. These working papers have a new pair of columns headed *Manufacturing;* they contain all of the amounts used in determining the cost of goods manufactured. To simplify the illustration, it is assumed that all adjusting entries were made before the trial balance was drawn off; therefore, a pair of Adjustments columns is not required.

Observe that the balance of the Heat, Light, and Power account is apportioned to manufacturing overhead, selling expense, and general expense, and that the balances of the Depreciation—Buildings account, the Insurance Expense account, and the Taxes account are apportioned to manufacturing overhead and general expense. The letters "S" and "G" in the Revenue and Expense debit column indicate the classification of the related amount as selling or general expense in the income statement. These letters may be used also if an account balance is not apportioned but the title of the account does not clearly indicate whether the item should be classified as selling or general.

Closing the books. The procedure for closing the books of a manufacturing concern involves setting up a Manufacturing account, debiting it with the total of all the items appearing in the debit Manufacturing column of the working papers, and crediting it with the total of all the items appearing in the credit Manufacturing column.

1958			
Dec. 31	Manufacturing.....................................	232,225.00	
	Goods in process inventory (12/31/57).......		15,000.00
	Materials inventory (12/31/57).............		12,000.00
	Purchases—Materials......................		94,000.00
	Transportation in.........................		800.00
	Direct labor..............................		80,750.00
	Indirect labor............................		9,125.00
	Heat, light, and power....................		3,000.00
	Building and machinery repairs............		300.00
	Depreciation—Buildings...................		3,200.00
	Depreciation—Machinery and equipment....		6,000.00
	Insurance expense.........................		850.00
	Taxes....................................		1,200.00
	Factory supplies used.....................		3,500.00
	Miscellaneous factory expenses.............		2,500.00
	To transfer manufacturing costs to Manufacturing account.		
31	Purchase returns and allowances.................	1,500.00	
	Purchase discounts............................	1,200.00	
	Goods in process inventory (12/31/58)...........	11,000.00	
	Materials inventory (12/31/58).................	9,000.00	
	Manufacturing............................		22,700.00
	To close manufacturing accounts with credit balances and record end-of-year inventories.		

THE *A B C* COMPANY
Working Papers
For the Year Ended December 31, 1958

Account	Trial Balance After Adjustments Dr	Cr	Manufacturing Dr	Cr	Revenue and Expense Dr	Cr	Retained Earnings Dr	Cr	Balance Sheet Dr	Cr
Cash	25,000								25,000	
Accounts receivable	40,000								40,000	
Allowance for doubtful accounts		1,000								1,000
Inventories—December 31, 1957:										
Finished goods	20,000				20,000					
Goods in process	15,000		15,000							
Materials	12,000		12,000							
Unexpired insurance	300								300	
Land	10,000								10,000	
Buildings	70,000								70,000	
Accumulated depreciation—Buildings		15,500								15,500
Machinery and equipment	60,000								60,000	
Accumulated depreciation—M. & E.		21,000								21,000
Furniture and fixtures—F. & F.	5,000								5,000	
Accumulated depreciation—F. & F.		2,250								2,250
Accounts payable		22,800								22,800
Accrued salaries and wages payable		1,275								1,275
Federal income tax payable		5,500								5,500
Capital stock		100,000								100,000
Retained earnings		71,450							71,450	
Dividends	6,000						6,000			
Sales		300,000				300,000				
Sales returns and allowances	2,000				2,000					
Sales discounts	2,500				2,500					
Purchases—Materials	94,000		94,000							
Purchase returns and allowances		1,500		1,500						
Purchase discounts		1,200		1,200						
Transportation in	800		800							
Direct labor	80,750		80,750							
Indirect labor	9,125		9,125							
Heat, light, and power	3,500		3,000		{150S / 350G}					
Building and machinery repairs	300		300							
Depreciation—Buildings	3,500		3,200		300G					
Depreciation—Machinery and equipment	6,000		6,000							
Insurance expense	950		850		100G					
Taxes	1,400		1,200		200G					
Factory supplies used	3,500		3,500							
Miscellaneous factory expenses	2,500		2,500							
Totals forward	474,125	543,475	232,225	2,700	25,600	300,000	6,000	71,450	210,300	169,325

THE *A B C* COMPANY
Working Papers (Concluded)
For the Year Ended December 31, 1958

	Trial Balance After Adjustments		Manufacturing		Revenue and Expense		Retained Earnings		Balance Sheet	
Totals brought forward	474,125	543,475	232,225	2,700	25,600	300,000	6,000	71,450	210,300	169,325
Advertising	9,000				9,000					
Salesmen's salaries	20,360				20,360					
Salesmen's traveling expenses	8,000				8,000					
Miscellaneous selling expenses	2,500				2,500					
Officers salaries	18,000				18,000					
Office salaries	3,040				3,040					
Stationery and printing	400				400					
Office supplies used	300				300					
Depreciation—Furniture & fixtures	750				750					
Bad debts expense	800				800					
Miscellaneous general expenses	700				700					
Federal income tax	5,500				5,500					
	543,475	543,475								
Inventories—December 31, 1958:										
Finished goods						17,000			17,000	
Goods in process				11,000					11,000	
Materials				9,000					9,000	
				22,700						
Cost of goods manufactured				209,525	209,525					
			232,225	232,225	304,475	317,000				
Net income					12,525			12,525		
					317,000	317,000		83,975		
								83,975		
Retained earnings							6,000	77,975		77,975
							83,975	83,975	247,300	247,300

The closing procedure is completed by debiting and crediting Revenue and Expense with all of the items appearing in the Revenue and Expense columns of the working papers and transferring the net income and the balance of the Dividends account to Retained Earnings. Observe that, although $150 of the Heat, Light, and Power account was shown in the income statement as a selling expense and $350 as a general expense, the two amounts are combined in the second following closing journal entry.

1958			
Dec. 31	Revenue and expense.........................	209,525.00	
	Manufacturing..........................		209,525.00
	To close the Manufacturing account.		
31	Revenue and expense.........................	94,950.00	
	Finished goods inventory (12/31/57)........		20,000.00
	Sales returns and allowances..............		2,000.00
	Sales discounts..........................		2,500.00
	Advertising..............................		9,000.00
	Salesmen's salaries......................		20,360.00
	Salesmen's traveling expenses..............		8,000.00
	Heat, light, and power...................		500.00
	Miscellaneous selling expenses..............		2,500.00
	Officers' salaries.........................		18,000.00
	Office salaries............................		3,040.00
	Stationery and printing...................		400.00
	Office supplies...........................		300.00
	Depreciation—Buildings..................		300.00
	Depreciation—Furniture and fixtures.......		750.00
	Taxes....................................		200.00
	Insurance expense.......................		100.00
	Bad debts expense.......................		800.00
	Miscellaneous general expenses............		700.00
	Federal income tax......................		5,500.00
	To close accounts with debit balances.		
31	Sales..	300,000.00	
	Finished goods inventory (12/31/58)............	17,000.00	
	Revenue and expense....................		317,000.00
	To close the Sales account and record end-of-year inventory of finished goods.		
31	Revenue and expense.......................	12,525.00	
	Retained earnings......................		12,525.00
	To transfer net income to Retained Earnings.		
31	Retained earnings...........................	6,000.00	
	Dividends..............................		6,000.00
	To close the Dividends account.		

Miscellaneous Matters

Use of account numbers. Space can be saved in the books of original entry by providing a narrow Account Number column instead of a wide Account Name column.

For example, a Sundry Accounts Debited section similar to the one at the left below could be included in any book of original entry in which it would be useful.

Since the bookkeeper has used account numbers to indicate the accounts to which the postings *are to be made*, it would be confusing to use account numbers also to show that postings have been made. Therefore, a check mark is used for that purpose. After the entries have been posted, the Sundry Accounts Debited section will appear as shown at the right.

Sundry Accounts Debited				Sundry Accounts Debited		
Acct. No.	√	Amount		Acct. No.	√	Amount
1321		1,000 00		1321	√	1,000 00
8235		25 00		8235	√	25 00

To facilitate posting, account numbers as well as names may appear at the head of special columns. For instance, the heading of a special column for sales in the cash receipts book might be at the right.

Sales (4001)

The fact that the total of this column has been posted could be evidenced by placing a check mark below the column total.

General journal entries may show account numbers as well as account names, thus:

```
3233—Dividends.....................................  xxx
    2133—Dividends payable.........................      xxx
```

Expense controls. In studying controlling accounts with customers and creditors, you learned that controlling accounts may be introduced into the accounting system when the work becomes so heavy that it must be divided.

Manufacturing Expense (5300)		
Acct. No.	√	Amount
5328		106 90

In a very large business, the controlling account procedure can also be applied to expense accounts, thus providing for further subdivision of the accounting work. For instance, the voucher register may contain a section for debits headed as shown at the left.

The column total will be posted to the Manufacturing Expense controlling account and the individual entries may be posted to a subsidiary manufacturing expense ledger or to a manufacturing expense analysis record similar to the one on page 336. This

Manufacturing Expense Analysis Record

Date	Vo. No.	Ref.	5301	5315	5328	5329	5338	5339	5380	5381	5384	5390
19— July 3	4				106 90							
5	7											141 75
10	21						376 60					
20	35			572 89								
24	42				65 39							
31		PR 1	3,609 80									
31		J 4				485 00						
31		J 4						219 60				
31		J 5							119 40			
31		J 5								204 25		
31		J 5									116 60	
			3,609 80	572 89	172 29	485 00	376 60	219 60	119 40	204 25	116 60	141 75

The "Ref." column shows the source of all entries not posted from the voucher register. These entries came from the payroll record and the general journal.

Credits in subsidiary expense record columns can be indicated by red ink or starred entries.

analysis record shows entries from the voucher register and other books of original entry.

The bookkeeper who posts to the subsidiary expense ledger or analysis record prepares a statement of the manufacturing expenses for the month in the following form:

Manufacturing Expenses—July, 19—

5301	Indirect labor	$3,609.80
5315	Heat, light, and power	572.89
5328	Repairs to buildings	172.29
5329	Depreciation—Buildings	485.00
5338	Repairs to machinery and equipment	376.60
5339	Depreciation—Machinery and equipment	219.60
5380	Taxes—General	119.40
5381	Factory supplies	204.25
5384	Insurance	116.60
5390	Miscellaneous	141.75
	Total	$6,018.18

This summary is prepared for two reasons: first, to prove that the subsidiary record is in agreement with the controlling account; second, for use in connection with the periodic statements.

CHAPTER 21

Cost Accounting

Purposes of cost accounting. One of the major objectives of cost accounting is the determination of the unit cost of products manufactured. Such information is valuable to management in various ways; for instance, it furnishes information that can be used for:

The pricing of inventories.

The determination of the reasons for variations in the cost of different batches of the same product. Such information may enable the management to reduce costs.

The computation of the rate of gross profit earned on each product. With such data, the management is in a position to deal intelligently with such questions as the following: With respect to high-profit goods, may it be advisable to reduce selling prices to put the company in a more favorable competitive position? With respect to low-profit goods, can costs be reduced; can selling prices be increased without pricing the product out of the market; or should the manufacture of the product be discontinued?

Another advantage of cost accounting arises from the fact that general ledger accounts may be kept to show the flow of costs through the factory and ultimately into the cost of goods sold. The chart on page 339 illustrates this feature.

The general ledger accounts kept in the manner described in the chart make it possible to prepare financial statements without the necessity of taking physical inventories.

The three inventory accounts in the general ledger may be supported by perpetual inventory records showing, on a continuous basis, the quantity and cost of each class of materials, goods in process, and finished goods. Such perpetual inventory records serve several useful purposes, of which the following may be mentioned: They show the quantities which *should be* on hand, and thus are useful in the detection of mysterious disappearances; they are useful to the purchasing department by furnishing information regarding purchase requirements, thus avoiding production delays that might result from failure to order materials with sufficient promptness and in sufficient quantities; and, as is shown later in the chapter, they supply the information about unit costs required

(1) Costs of materials, labor, and manufacturing overhead are accumulated.	(2) As materials, labor, and manufacturing overhead are utilized in production, the costs thereof are transferred to an "in process" account.	(3) When goods are finished, the costs applicable thereto are transferred to a finished goods account.	(4) When finished goods are sold, their costs are transferred to an account showing the cost of goods sold.

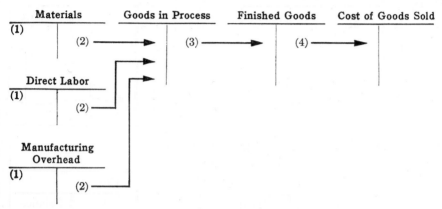

Chart Showing Flow of Costs

to make the general ledger transfers from Materials, to Goods in Process, to Finished Goods, to Cost of Goods Sold.

The fundamental procedures of cost accounting may be set forth by describing two types of cost accounting: specific order cost accounting, and process cost accounting.

Specific Order Cost Accounting

This method of cost accounting is suitable for use in a factory that makes a variety of products, either for stock or on special order. The procedures for recording the flow of material, labor, and overhead costs into goods in process, thence to finished goods, and finally to cost of sales are discussed below. It is assumed that perpetual inventories are kept.

Materials purchased. Let us assume that a company, at the beginning of its operations, purchased the following materials: 500 units of material A at $4 per unit, and 1,500 units of material B at $2 per unit.

General ledger entries. The general ledger accounts debited and credited will be:

```
Materials.....................................  5,000.00
    Accounts payable..........................            5,000.00
```

Entries in perpetual inventory of materials. The perpetual inventory of materials will contain a page or card for each kind of material. The invoice will be used by the perpetual inventory clerk to make entries as shown below:

					Material A			

Date		Quantity			Price		Cost		
		In	Out	Balance			In	Out	Balance
19-- Feb.	3	500		500	4	00	2,000 00		2,000 00

					Material B			

Date		Quantity			Price		Cost		
		In	Out	Balance			In	Out	Balance
19-- Feb.	3	1,500		1,500	2	00	3,000 00		3,000 00

Materials used. Materials should not be taken from the storeroom for use in the factory without a written order, called a *requisition,* approved by some person in authority. Let us assume that the two following material requisitions were issued in February:

Material Requisition			No. 1	
For Production Order No. 1		Date 2/5/19--		
Material	Number of Units	Cost per Unit		Amount
A	200	4	00	800 00
B	700	2	00	1,400 00
				2,200 00
Approved _J. H. T._				

Material Requisition			No. 2

For Production Order No. 2   Date 2/16/19--

Material	Number of Units	Cost per Unit	Amount
A	150	4 00	600 00
B	100	2 00	200 00
			800 00

Approved ___*Q.H.Z.*___

The unit costs and the extended amounts were entered on the requisitions by the perpetual inventory clerk.

Entries in perpetual inventory of materials. The material items shown by these requisitions were entered by the perpetual inventory clerk in the Out columns of the materials perpetual inventory records, and the balances were computed and entered on the cards by the perpetual inventory clerk, as shown below.

Material A

Date		Quantity			Price		Cost		
		In	Out	Balance			In	Out	Balance
19--Feb.	3	500		500	4 00	2,000 00			2,000 00
	5		200	300				800 00	1,200 00
	16		150	150				600 00	600 00

Material B

Date		Quantity			Price		Cost		
		In	Out	Balance			In	Out	Balance
19--Feb.	3	1,500		1,500	2 00	3,000 00			3,000 00
	5		700	800				1,400 00	1,600 00
	16		100	700				200 00	1,400 00

Entries in perpetual inventories of goods in process. The perpetual inventory records of goods in process are called *production orders.* A production order is kept for each job in the factory.

Let us assume that the company worked on two products during February: product X and product Y. Product X was started first, and its costs will be recorded on production order 1; the costs of product Y will be recorded on production order 2. The two production orders, after the material costs shown by the requisitions have been entered, are shown below:

		Production Order 1	
For 800 Product X		Date Completed	

Date	Materials	Direct Labor	Overhead
19-- Feb. 5	2,200 00		

		Production Order 2	
For 200 Product Y		Date Completed	

Date	Materials	Direct Labor	Overhead
19-- Feb. 16	800 00		

General ledger entries. The material requisitions are listed in a requisition register, as follows:

Requisition Register

Date	Requisition No.	Amount
19-- Feb. 5	1	2,200 00
16	2	800 00
		3,000 00

The requisition register is footed at the end of the month, and the following journal entry is made:

```
Goods in process.............................  3,000.00
    Materials...............................               3,000.00
    To transfer the cost of materials used during the
    month out of the Materials account and into Goods
    in Process.
```

Direct labor. Each factory workman keeps a record of the time spent on each production order. He uses a separate card each day for each production order on which he is engaged. When the card is turned in at the office, it shows the workman's number, the production order number, and the time worked. Clerks compute the elapsed time, enter the hourly wage rate, and compute the total labor cost. Following are two cards turned in by one workman.

Date	FEB 20		Date	FEB 20
Employee's number	21		Employee's number	21
Hour in	8 00		Hour in	1 00
Hour out	12 00		Hour out	4 00
Elapsed time	4:00		Elapsed time	3:00
Hourly rate	$2.25		Hourly rate	$2.25
Amount	$9.00		Amount	$6.75
Production order	1		Production order	2

These cards are used in making up the payroll. The cards are then sorted according to the production order numbers, and a summary is prepared showing the total direct labor cost applicable

Production Order Direct Labor Cost Summary				
Production Order	Payroll Periods			
	Feb. 1 to 15		Feb. 16 to 28	
1	1,000	00	200	00
2			800	00
	1,000	00	1,000	00

to each production order.　The summary shows the direct labor cost incurred during February on each production order.

Entries on production orders.　The direct labor costs shown by the labor cost summary were entered on the two production orders as shown below:

Production Order_____1

For _____800 Product X_____　Date Completed_____

Date	Materials		Direct Labor		Overhead	
19-- Feb.						
5	2,200	00				
15			1,000	00		
28			200	00		

Production Order_____2

For _____200 Product Y_____　Date Completed_____

Date	Materials		Direct Labor		Overhead	
19-- Feb						
16	800	00				
28			800	00		

Production order 1 was charged with $1,000 and $200 of direct labor.

Production order 2 was charged with $800 of direct labor.

General ledger entries.　The general ledger entries for payroll costs during February were:

```
Feb. 15   Direct labor.......................... 1,000.00
               Cash.............................            1,000.00
            Payment for first payroll period.
      28   Direct labor.......................... 1,000.00
               Cash.............................            1,000.00
            Payment for second payroll period.
      28   Goods in process...................... 2,000.00
               Direct labor.....................            2,000.00
            To charge Goods in Process with direct
            labor costs shown by production order
            direct labor cost summary.
```

Manufacturing overhead.   The material and labor costs applicable to each production order can be definitely determined by the methods just explained.   Overhead expenses must be estimated. This may be done as follows: If, in the past, the annual manufacturing overhead has been about 50 per cent of the annual direct labor cost, it may be assumed (unless conditions indicate otherwise) that this ratio will continue.   Therefore, when the labor cost is entered on the production orders, the manufacturing overhead may be estimated as 50 per cent of the labor cost.

Entries on production orders.   It is assumed that 50 per cent is a fair overhead rate for the concern under illustration.   Therefore, the cost clerk, after entering the direct labor cost on the production orders, enters overhead charges equal to 50% of the direct labor costs, as shown below:

		Production Order	1	
For 800 Product X		Date Completed _____		
Date	Materials	Direct Labor	Overhead	
19 - - Feb. 5	2,200 00			
15		1,000 00	500 00	
28		200 00	100 00	

		Production Order	2	
For 200 Product Y		Date Completed _____		
Date	Materials	Direct Labor	Overhead	
19-- Feb. 16	800 00			
28		800 00	400 00	

General ledger entries.   Overhead in the total amount of $1,000 was charged to the two production orders.   Therefore, the following journal entry affecting general ledger accounts was made at the end of February:

```
Goods in process.............................. 1,000.00
    Manufacturing overhead applied.............          1,000.00
    To charge Goods in Process with total overhead
    applied to production orders.
```

The credit is made to Manufacturing Overhead Applied to avoid making numerous small credits to the various manufacturing overhead accounts.

Completed production orders. Product X was completed and the production order was summarized to determine the total cost and the unit cost, as shown below:

			Production Order __1__
For __800 Product X__		Date Completed __2/20__	

Date		Materials		Direct Labor		Overhead	
19—— Feb.	5	2,200	00				
	15			1,000	00	500	00
	28			200	00	100	00
Total		2,200	00	1,200	00	600	00

Summary:		
Material	2,200	00
Direct labor	1,200	00
Overhead	600	00
Total	4,000	00
Unit cost (Quantity produced __800__)	5	00

Perpetual inventories. To indicate that product X is no longer in the status of goods in process, production order 1 is removed from the file of production orders in process.

The production order furnishes the information for the following entry on the finished goods perpetual inventory card for product X.

Date	Quantity			Unit Cost	Cost		
	In	Out	Balance		In	Out	Balance
19-- Feb. 20	800		800	5 00	4,000 00		4,000 00

Product __X__ (heading above table)

General ledger entries. The total cost shown by a production order is entered in a register of completed production orders, thus:

Register of Completed Production Orders

Date	Production Order Number	Total Cost
19-- Feb. 20	1	4,000 00

At the end of the month, the register is totaled, and the cost of goods finished during the month is transferred out of Goods in Process into Finished Goods by the following journal entry:

```
Finished goods.................................  4,000.00
     Goods in process...........................           4,000.00
     Total cost of goods completed during the month.
```

Sales and cost of goods sold. On February 27, a sale of 500 units of product X was made.

Perpetual inventories. The carbon copy of the invoice is provided with a Cost column at the right of the Amount (selling price) column. The carbon copy is sent to the perpetual inventory clerk, who performs the following operations:

(1) Looks up the unit price on the finished goods inventory card.

(2) Computes the total cost of the goods sold and enters this cost in the Cost column of the carbon copy of the invoice:

(Heading of the Invoice)				
Number	Description	Unit Price	Amount	Cost
500	Product X	7 00	3,500 00	2,500 00

(3) Makes entries in the Out columns of the inventory card, showing the number and the cost of the articles sold, and computes the new quantity and cost balances. (See below.)

(4) Sends the carbon copy of the invoice back to the office for entry in the sales book.

The inventory card for product *X* now appears as follows:

| Date | Quantity | | | Unit Cost | Cost | | |
	In	Out	Balance		In	Out	Balance
19-- Feb. 20	800		800	5 00	4,000 00		4,000 00
27		500	300			2,500 00	1,500 00

Product __X__

Since product X is the only article of finished goods on hand, this one card shows the total cost of the finished goods inventory at the end of February—$1,500.

General ledger entries. Invoices are recorded in the sales book in the manner shown below:

Sales Book

Date		Name	Invoice Number	Selling Price	Cost
19-- Feb 27	✓	Henderson & Riley	1	3,500 00	2,500 00

At the end of the month the two columns are totaled, and the totals are posted as follows:

Total of Selling Price column:
 Debit Accounts Receivable controlling account
 Credit Sales
Total of Cost column:
 Debit Cost of Sales
 Credit Finished Goods

Summary of general ledger accounts and perpetual inventories. After the completion of the accounting procedures discussed in the preceding portion of this chapter, the general ledger accounts and the perpetual inventory records will appear as follows:

General ledger accounts.

Materials

Purchased.................. 5,000.00	To Goods in Process.......... 3,000.00

Direct Labor

Cost....................... 2,000.00	To Goods in Process......... 2,000.00

Manufacturing Overhead (Control)

Costs incurred............. 1,020.00	

Manufacturing Overhead Applied

	To Goods in Process.......... 1,000.00

Goods in Process

Materials.................. 3,000.00	To Finished Goods........... 4,000.00
Direct labor............... 2,000.00	
Manufacturing overhead...... 1,000.00	

Finished Goods

Manufactured.............. 4,000.00	Sold....................... 2,500.00

Sales

	Selling price................ 3,500.00

Cost of Sales

From Finished Goods........ 2,500.00	

The Cost of Sales account makes it possible to compute the gross profit on sales without taking a physical inventory. The income statement will show the balances of the Sales and Cost of Sales accounts.

Perpetual inventories. The perpetual inventories of materials (page 341) show the following balances:

Material A............................	$ 600
Material B............................	1,400
Total—per Materials account.............	$2,000

The costs of the only goods in process are shown by production order 2—see page 345. They are:

Materials......	$ 800
Direct labor......	800
Manufacturing overhead..................	400
Total—per Goods in Process account.......	$2,000

The perpetual inventory card for product X (the only finished goods on hand) is on page 348. It shows a balance of $1,500, which agrees with the balance of the Finished Goods account.

Underabsorbed and overabsorbed overhead. To illustrate the various methods of dealing with underabsorbed and overabsorbed manufacturing overhead, let us assume that the manufacturing overhead accounts at the end of a period have the following balances:

```
Manufacturing overhead (Controlling account)......   $11,000
Manufacturing overhead applied.................                $10,500
```

The actual overhead costs were $11,000; the amount applied to production orders was only $10,500.

The $500 of unapplied burden may be treated in either of two ways, as follows:

(1) Theoretically, it should be apportioned to finished goods manufactured and sold during the period, finished goods on hand, and goods in process, on the basis of the actual or estimated direct labor in these three elements. The journal entry might be as follows:

```
Cost of sales....................................   425.00
Finished goods......................... ..........    60.00
Goods in process................................    15.00
    Manufacturing overhead applied.............           500.00
```

(2) If the greater portion of the finished goods manufactured during the period has been sold, it is reasonably correct to charge the entire unabsorbed overhead to Cost of Sales, thus:

```
Cost of sales....................................   500.00
    Manufacturing overhead applied..............           500.00
```

After one of the foregoing entries is made at the end of the period to bring the credit balance of the Manufacturing Overhead Applied account into agreement with the debit balance of the Manufacturing Overhead account, the two accounts are closed by the following entry:

```
Manufacturing overhead applied............... 11,000.00
    Manufacturing overhead..................           11,000.00
```

Adjustments for overabsorbed manufacturing overhead may be made similarly, that is:

(1) By credits to Cost of Sales, Finished Goods, and Goods in Process.

(2) By credit to Cost of Sales.

Process Cost Accounting

The simplest situation to which process cost accounting is suitable is found in a factory which makes a single, standardized product, each unit of which requires the same amount of material, direct labor, and utilization of plant facilities. The immediately following illustrations assume the existence of such a situation. The application of process cost accounting procedures to somewhat more complex situations is discussed later.

Illustration—No goods in process at beginning or end of period. Assume that, during January (the first month of its operations), a company produced 8,000 units of commodity X, and that there were no goods in process at the end of the month. The unit cost of the product could be determined by the preparation of a statistical statement similar to the following:

Materials......................................	$ 26,000.00
(This cost could be determined by totaling material requisitions.)	
Direct labor...................................	34,000.00
(Since all direct labor costs in the factory were incurred in the manufacture of commodity X, the entire direct labor payroll for January may be regarded as a cost of commodity X.)	
Manufacturing overhead........................	40,800.00
(The total manufacturing overhead for the month might be used; however, since it may be desired to compute the cost of each of several batches produced during a period, it is customary to apply an estimated overhead rate. In this illustration, the estimated overhead rate is 120% of direct labor.)	
Total......................................	$100,800.00

Unit Costs—January

Materials.........$26,000.00 ÷ 8,000.............	$ 3.25
Direct labor.......$34,000.00 ÷ 8,000.............	4.25
Overhead.........$40,800.00 ÷ 8,000.............	5.10
Total.......................................	$12.60

Illustration—Goods in process at end of period. Assume that, during February, the company completed 9,000 units of commodity X, and that 400 units were in process at the end of the month. The goods in process were in the following stage of completion:

Materials.................	75%
Direct labor..............	50%

The company's costs for the month were:

Materials.............................	$ 28,830.00
Direct labor..........................	37,720.00
Overhead—120% of direct labor.........	45,264.00
Total..............................	$111,814.00

The costs shown above cannot be divided by 9,000 (the number of units completed) to determine unit costs of completed goods because some of these costs were incurred on the goods in process at the end of the month. "Equivalent production" data must be compiled. This is done as follows:

Computation of Equivalent Production—February

	Material	Direct labor
Units completed..................................	9,000	9,000
Add goods in process at end of February—400 units:		
Material:		
75% of the material requirements have been placed in production. This is equivalent to the material requirements for 75% of 400 finished units, or...............	300	
Direct labor:		
50% of the total labor costs have been incurred. This is equivalent to the labor costs for 50% of 400 units, or....		200
Equivalent production................................	9,300	9,200

Unit Costs—February

Materials..................$28,830.00 ÷ 9,300......................	$ 3.10
Direct labor..................$37,720.00 ÷ 9,200......................	4.10
Overhead....................120% of direct labor....................	4.92
Total...	$12.12

Unit Costs—Goods in Process February 28

Materials....................75% of $3.10............................	$2.325
Direct labor..................50% of $4.10............................	2.050
Overhead....................120% of direct labor....................	2.460
Total...	$6.835

Distribution of Total Costs—February

Finished goods...............$12.12 × 9,000.....................	$109,080.00
Goods in process February 28 · ·$6.835 × 400.......................	2,734.00
Total...	$111,814.00

Illustration—Goods in process at beginning and end of period. Assume that the costs incurred by the company in March were as follows:

Materials..............................	$ 30,600.00
Direct labor...........................	40,400.00
Overhead—120% of direct labor.........	48,480.00
Total.................................	$119,480.00

The company completed 10,000 units in March. There were 500 units in process at the end of the month, in the following stage of completion:

Materials................	100%
Direct labor..............	60%

The computation of the equivalent production for March is shown on the opposite page.

Computation of Equivalent Production—March

	Material	Direct labor
Units completed during March..........................	10,000	10,000
Deduct goods in process at beginning of month—400 units:		
Material..... ....75% of 400....................	300	
Direct labor..........50% of 400.............		200
	9,700	9,800
Add goods in process at end of month—500 units:		
Material.............100% of 500	500	
Direct labor......... ...60% of 500....................		300
Equivalent production.	10,200	10,100

Unit Costs—March

Materials......................$30,600.00 ÷ 10,200.....................	$ 3.00
Direct labor..................$40,400.00 ÷ 10,100......................	4.00
Overhead.................... ....120% of direct labor.......................	4.80
Total...........................	$11.80

Unit Costs—Goods in Process February 28
After Completion

	Materials	Direct Labor	Overhead	Total
Costs incurred in February:				
Materials........75% of $3.10............	$2.325			$ 2.325
Direct labor......50% of $4.10............		$2.05		2.050
Overhead.......120% of direct labor.......			$2.46	2.460
Total February.......................				$ 6.835
Costs incurred in March:				
Materials........25% of $3.00............	.750			$ .750
Direct labor......50% of $4.00............		2.00		2.000
Overhead.......120% of direct labor.......			2.40	2.400
Total March...				$ 5.150
Total................................	$3.075	$4.05	$4.86	$11.985

Unit Costs—Goods in Process March 31

Materials...... ....100% of $3.00............................	$3.00
Direct labor......... ....60% of $4.00............................	2.40
Overhead....................120% of direct labor.......................	2.88
Total...........	$8.28

Distribution of Total Costs—March

Goods in process February 28....400 units at $5.15.................	$ 2,060.00
Other finished goods...........9,600 units at $11.80.................	113,280.00
Goods in process March 31 ·.....500 units at $8.28................	4,140.00
Total..	$119,480.00

Management statistics. Comparisons of unit costs, similar to those on the following page, can provide management with useful information regarding trends in costs.

		February		March	
			Per Cent of		Per Cent of
	January	Amount	January	Amount	January
Materials	$ 3.25	$ 3.10	95.4%	$ 3.00	92.3%
Direct labor	4.25	4.10	96.5	4.00	94.1
Overhead	5.10	4.92	96.5	4.80	94.1
Total	$12.60	$12.12	96.2	$11.80	93.7

Applicability of process cost procedure. At the beginning of this discussion, it was stated that the simplest situation to which process cost accounting is suitable is found in a factory which makes a single, standardized product. The process cost procedure is also applicable to less simple situations.

Assume, for instance, that a factory used all of its facilities for a period (days, weeks, or months) in the manufacture of a batch of commodity A and that, when that was finished, turned to the manufacture of commodity B. Process cost accounting procedures could be used to determine the unit cost of each commodity.

Or assume that a company manufactured several products which were processed in some or all of five departments. For instance, product A might be started in department 1, passed on to department 2 for further processing, thence to department 3, and finally to department 5. Unit costs could be determined for the processing of product A in departments 1, 2, 3, and 5; the total of these departmental unit costs would be the unit cost of product A. Product B might require processing in departments 1, 4, and 5, and product C might require processing in departments 1, 2, 3, 4, and 5; the unit cost of each product would be the sum of the unit costs incurred in the various processing departments.

When a factory is divided into departments, the overhead costs (and, consequently, the overhead rates) of the several departments may differ. For instance, department 1 may occupy a relatively large amount of floor space, use expensive machinery, and incur large power costs; department 2, on the other hand, may be a small department in which work is done at benches with inexpensive hand tools. Under such circumstances, an overhead rate should be determined for each department.

General ledger accounts and perpetual inventories. Process cost accounting may be tied in with the general ledger accounts by entries recording the flow of costs into goods in process and thence to finished goods and cost of goods sold, and perpetual inventories may be maintained. Or process cost procedures may be limited to the preparation of statements, of the nature of those illustrated, showing unit costs.

CHAPTER 22
Accounting Principles

Usefulness of accounting data. Accounting data serve the needs of businessmen and others who are interested in the operations and financial position of a business.

In order to conduct the routine operations of the business, management requires records showing the assets, liabilities, revenues, expenses, and the elements of the owners' equity. Supplementary detailed records are required for various purposes. For example, records are required for payroll tax purposes; property records enable the management to keep track of the location and condition of numerous fixed assets; records showing the names and addresses of stockholders are needed for the purpose of making dividend payments.

Accounting data are also useful to management in making policy decisions. Should the physical plant be expanded? If so, where should the new plant be located? Should a new product be introduced? Should selling prices be changed? Should an employee retirement program be started, or the old one revised? Decisions on such matters usually are not made without reference to accounting data. The more accounting information relevant to management problems that is available for management's use, the better the chances for excellent decisions.

Accounting data are of use also to grantors of credit, such as banks and suppliers. What are the earnings prospects? What is the debt-paying ability? What is the record of past performance in debt payment? These are pertinent questions. Although accounting data cannot be expected to be the only determining factor in the granting or refusal of credit in all cases, such information usually affects the decision.

In a similar fashion, accounting information may serve the needs of stockholders, governmental agencies, labor unions, and possible investors. These groups are often interested in the effectiveness of the operating activities of a business, as shown by earnings data, and in its financial position.

Need for accounting principles. It requires something more than clerical procedures, something more than journalizing, posting, taking trial balances, and closing the books, to satisfy such diverse and complex needs as those just described. The accountant

355

must have some "principles" or "guides to action" for a task of such dimensions.   Unless there exist some generally accepted concepts regarding the nature and measurement of assets, liabilities, revenues, and expenses, and some widely supported standards of disclosure and reporting, the usefulness of accounting will not be maximized.   There can be no widespread understanding of, and reliance on, accounting statements unless they have been prepared in conformity with generally accepted principles.   The necessity of some common agreement on accounting matters becomes apparent when we contemplate the chaotic condition that would prevail if every businessman or every accountant could follow his own definitions of revenue and expense.

The nature of accounting principles.   It would be incorrect to suggest that accounting principles are a body of basic laws like those found in physics or chemistry.   Accounting principles are more properly associated with such terms as *concepts, conventions,* and *standards.*   It is important to stress the fact that accounting principles are man-made, in contrast to natural law.

Accounting principles are constantly evolving, being influenced by business practices; the needs of statement users; legislation and governmental regulation; the opinions and actions of stockholders, creditors, labor unions, and management; and the logical reasoning of accountants.   The sum total of such influences finds its expression first in accounting theory.   Some theories are rejected; some are accepted.   General acceptance of an accounting theory is essential to raise it to the authoritative status of an accounting principle. The primary purpose of accounting theory is to develop common agreement on accounting matters and to narrow the area of alternatives.

Two basic assumptions.   If the accounting process is to be fully understood, the student must be aware of certain basic assumptions discussed below:

The going concern assumption.   In Chapter 1, a going concern was defined as an established business that is being conducted with the expectation of continuing indefinitely.   The generally accepted accounting principles that have been developed and that are applied in the process of accounting for the financial affairs of a business entity are, in many instances, appropriate only for a going concern.   If a business is failing and its assets are subject to forced sale, the conventional accounting approach, although acceptable for a going concern, would often result in inadequate financial information.

For instance, it is customary to show land used for business purposes at cost.   For a going concern that intends to continue using such property for business purposes, current market value is not particularly relevant. But if a business is winding up its affairs and must sell its assets to satisfy creditors' claims, the original cost of the land is no indicator of realizable value, which is the crucial question at such a time.

Somewhat similarly, many fixed assets are shown, in accordance with accepted accounting principles, at cost less depreciation. Again, market value is not relevant. The accepted balance sheet valuation is cost less accumulated depreciation computed at rates which presumably will charge the cost to expense over the useful life of the asset—a valuation that is based on the assumption that the business, as a going concern, will continue to use the asset during its useful life.

Prepaid expenses, although they may have no realizable value, have an asset status because, as a going concern, the business expects to derive future operating benefits from them.

The stable-dollar assumption. For accounting purposes, it is assumed that the monetary unit (the dollar) remains fixed; in other words, it is assumed that the purchasing power of the dollar remains unchanged. During certain periods this assumption has squared substantially with reality. But it is also true that, during other periods, the purchasing power of the dollar has changed. A case in point occurred after World War II, when the purchasing power of the dollar declined, with the result that it took more dollars to purchase a given quantity of assets or services. In other words, the level of prices increased. But during such periods of change in the value of the dollar, accounting has continued to treat all dollars as equal, whether the dollar amounts in the accounts represented 1932 dollars or 1949 dollars or current dollars. Such accounting could result in misleading financial statements. For example, assume that Company *A* paid $100,000 for land in 1932 and that Company *B* paid the same amount for land in 1956; the dollar amounts shown for land in the balance sheets of the two companies would be the same, but a reader of the two balance sheets might be misled into a false assumption that the two companies owned land of comparable present value.

Since the assumption of a stable dollar is an assumption contrary to fact, it probably would be more correct to say that accountants recognize the fact of the unstable dollar but choose to do nothing about it in the reported valuation of assets. For one reason, during most periods the changes in the value of money have been so gradual as not to materially undermine the validity of the assumption. For another, and more cogent, reason, cost is a determinable fact, whereas uncertainty would result from any attempt to adjust the asset accounts to show what the assets would cost at current prices.

Changes in the value of the dollar have a bearing not only on the balance sheet but also on the computation of net income. For instance, suppose that goods costing $10 are sold for $15. However, suppose that the purchasing power of the dollar has declined, with the result that it will cost the seller $12 to restock his inventory. Did the seller make $5 or $3 on the sale? A generally accepted answer is $5. But suppose that the seller (a corporation) followed the practice of paying out in dividends all such dollar profits. In the simple case assumed here, that would leave only $10 available to restock the inventory after the $5 dividend was paid. Considering the higher price that must be paid to replace the goods sold, sooner or later the seller would have to borrow funds or raise additional capital to avoid curtailing the activities of the business. Such a development would seem to suggest that the earnings had been incorrectly computed. The *lifo* inventory method is a means of eliminating, to some extent, the effect of the unstable dollar on the computation of net income.

Two basic principles. Two fundamental principles of accounting are discussed below:

Conservatism. Conservatism is particularly applicable when matters of opinion or estimate are involved, accountants believing that it is commendable, in instances of doubt, to understate net income and owners' equity rather than to overstate them. The doctrine of conservatism found expression in the oft-repeated tenet: "Anticipate no profit and provide for all possible losses."

Accountants can cite ample evidence that businessmen are inclined to be optimistic. Unless accounting conservatism was applied, assets would in many cases be overstated or liabilities understated, with the result that bankers, other creditors, and investors might be misled. As an example, take the matter of provisions for uncollectible accounts. This is a matter of estimate, and most accountants prefer leaning in the direction of possible overstatement, rather than understatement, of the allowance for doubtful accounts. The consequences of an understatement of assets and net income do not seem as serious as the opposite.

Balance sheet conservatism was once regarded as the accounting principle that outranked all other principles. But there is a growing tendency to question the time-honored beliefs that balance sheet conservatism outweighs all other considerations, that a conservative balance sheet is a good balance sheet for all purposes, and that balance sheet conservatism automatically produces a proper statement of operations. Accountants are becoming increasingly aware that adherence to the doctrine of balance sheet conservatism may result in income statements that are:

(a) Incorrect. .

> It may be conservative from the balance sheet stand-
> point to charge expense accounts with expenditures
> which would more properly be charged to fixed asset
> accounts, or to make excessive allowances for depre-
> ciation and bad debts, but the net income is misstated.

(b) And sometimes unconservative.

> For instance, assume that excessive depreciation allow-
> ances are made, with the result that certain fixed assets
> are fully depreciated before the end of their useful life.
> The periods in which the fixed assets are used after
> they have been fully depreciated are relieved of
> charges for depreciation expense; the net income for
> such periods is overstated and the income statements
> are unconservative.

Conservatism can scarcely be regarded as a virtue if, as its consequence, balance sheets and income statements do not fairly
present the financial position and the results of operations.

Consistency. Another important principle of accounting is consistency of method. Accounting is not composed of a set of rules
which prescribe the "one way" that things can be done. For
example, there are several methods of computing periodical depreciation. The accountant should seek to apply the method best
suited to each particular case, and it is of prime importance that
the method selected be applied consistently year after year. If
the accountant continually changed the method of accounting for
certain assets or expenses, each method might be acceptable but
successive periodical financial statements would not be comparable.
For example, by changing depreciation methods, the net income
could be altered, perhaps significantly. A statement user might
be misled and think that earnings had improved, whereas in reality
the increase was the result of a change in accounting method.
Changes in net income reported in successive statements should be
traceable to changes in business conditions or management effectiveness, and not merely to changes in accounting methods.
Therefore, consistency of method is an important element in the
accounting process.

The emphasis on consistency does not mean that accounting
methods, once adopted, can never be changed. If an accountant
believes that a change to another generally accepted method of
accounting would more fairly reflect the results of operations and
the financial position of the business, the change may be made.

However, adequate disclosure is required. For example, if the method of computing depreciation is changed at the beginning of 1958, the accountant would compute depreciation for 1958 by the old and new methods. The amount computed under the new method would be recorded in the books and reported in the statements. A footnote would be appended to the financial statements for 1958 describing the change in depreciation method; if the difference between the amounts computed by the two methods is significant, the effect on net income should be stated.

Current emphasis on net income determination. For many decades, accountants regarded the balance sheet as of primary importance and the income statement as of secondary importance—possibly a reflection of the attitude then held by bankers and other grantors of short-term credit. Grantors of credit were concerned with the margin of security for their loans; they were primarily interested in two questions: What assets does the applicant for credit own? What liabilities does he already owe? The answers to these questions were found in the balance sheet.

Over the years, a shift in emphasis—from the balance sheet to the income statement—has taken place. In part, this shift can be traced to a change in the point of view of credit grantors, their current approach placing more emphasis on the earnings potential as an indication of debt-paying ability. Another factor has been the increase in the number of investors in corporate securities. Investors and speculators are disposed to measure the attractiveness of securities by the earnings of the issuing company. As net income goes up, security values tend to increase; as net income goes down, security values tend to decrease.

With the increasing emphasis on the income statement, the determination and reporting of net income have become the central objectives of the accounting process. As a result, a significant portion of accounting theory is devoted to the development of concepts, standards, and criteria regarding net income determination, often described as a process of "matching" revenue and related expense. Matters affecting the determination of periodic revenues, related expenses, and the resulting net income are considered in the remainder of this chapter.

Revenues

The nature of revenue. Revenue is an inflow of assets in the form of cash, receivables, or other property from customers and clients, and is related primarily to the disposal of goods and the rendering of services. Although revenue is an inflow of assets, not all asset inflows are revenue. Obviously, an inflow of capital funds from stockholders is not revenue to a corporation, nor should a business regard as revenue an inflow of assets that is offset by an increase in liabilities.

How is revenue measured?   In a sense, revenue is measured in the market place.   The actions of buyers and sellers establish the dollar amounts of revenue transactions.   In typical situations, this means that the amounts are objectively determined, being a product of bargained transactions.

It is important to remember that the process of revenue measurement also results in measuring, initially, certain assets, namely, those arising from revenue-producing transactions.   In other words, the revenue figure is used not only as a revenue credit but also as an asset debit.   The assets most commonly acquired through revenue transactions are cash and accounts and notes receivable.   Occasionally, securities or even fixed assets are acquired from revenue transactions, in which case they are recorded initially in the accounts at the cash transaction price established for the goods or services sold in exchange by the business.   Thus, revenue measurement and asset valuation are not completely separate activities.   However, it should be recognized that not all asset balances are traceable to revenue transactions.   Many asset balances are the result of purchases by a business.   For example, this is typically the case for machinery and equipment.   This matter is discussed later under the caption, "Expenditures: Assets and Expenses."

When is revenue earned?   Revenue is earned when goods are disposed of or when services are rendered.   A transfer or exchange occurs.   The business gives up goods or renders services and acquires other assets in exchange.   There is a performance accompanied by a concurrent acquisition of an asset.   (In rare instances, the performance could result in a reduction of a liability instead of an acquisition of an asset.)

For retail, wholesale, and manufacturing businesses, the point of sale is generally regarded as the point when revenue is earned, because (1) it is the point at which a conversion takes place—an exchange of one asset for another—and conversion is regarded as evidence of realization; and (2) it is the point at which the amount of revenue is, in the normal case, objectively determinable from a sale price.

Revenue is earned by service-type businesses as services are performed.   In some cases—usually, when the rendering of services extends over a fairly long time period and involves more than one accounting period—estimates may be used in order that revenue may be recorded and reported during the periods when the

work is being performed.   Practical considerations may lead to the
adoption of a policy of postponing the reporting of any revenue
from services until the services are completed; the amount to be
charged for the entire service may not be determinable until completion, and as a consequence, the revenue applicable to services
rendered during the periods prior to completion may not be
determinable.

Expenditures : Assets and Expenses

Nature of expenditures.   The earning of income is the primary
objective of a business enterprise.   In carrying on the numerous
and varied activities aimed at "generating" income, a business
makes expenditures for a wide variety of articles and services.

An expenditure is a payment, in cash or otherwise, or the incurring of an obligation to make a future payment, for a benefit
received or to be received.

Expenditures are made in the belief that they will contribute
toward making the enterprise profitable (advertising, for example)
or because they cannot be avoided without curtailing the activities
of the business (taxes, for example).

Some terms used in the following discussion require definition.
The expression *cost outlay* will be used as synonymous with expenditure.   The term *cost transformation* refers to such changes as the
conversion of material, labor, and overhead costs into finished
goods cost.   *Expired costs* are costs which have no asset status;
they are expenses or losses.   A *cost residue* is the unexpired portion
of a cost outlay; it may properly appear on the asset side of the
balance sheet.

Classification of expenditures.   Expenditures are of two general
classes:

(1) Those chargeable to expense accounts.

> If it is known at the time of making an expenditure that
> the related benefit will not extend beyond the current
> accounting period (as when a month's rent is paid at
> the beginning of the month), it is customary and expe-
> dient to charge the cost immediately to an expense
> account.   Although such costs may not have expired
> *at the time of the expenditure,* the accounting entries are
> reduced by making an immediate charge to an expense
> account rather than charging an asset account and sub-
> sequently making a transfer from the asset account to
> an expense account.

(2) Those chargeable to asset accounts.

> Such cost amounts may either
> (a) remain indefinitely in the asset account, as would a cost outlay for land under normal circumstances;
> (b) be transferred to another asset account, as would raw materials when converted into finished goods by manufacturing operations; or
> (c) be assigned to expense at the appropriate time.

Accounting problems related to expenditures. The accounting problems related to expenditures for assets are of two kinds:

(1) Measuring initially, in dollars and cents, the cost of the assets acquired.
(2) Determining periodical expirations of costs.

Determination of asset costs. Cost is the measure used for accounting for assets acquired by purchase and, ultimately, for asset expirations chargeable to expense. Costs are a product of the actions of buyers and sellers and, therefore, costs are established objectively.

Incidental costs. The cost of an asset includes not only the basic, or purchase, price, but also related, incidental costs such as the following: costs of title searches and legal fees incurred in the acquisition of real estate; transportation, installation, and breaking-in costs incident to the acquisition of machinery; storage, taxes, and other costs incurred in aging certain kinds of inventories, such as wine; and expenditures made in the rehabilitation of a plant purchased in a run-down condition.

Assets acquired for noncash assets. Some difficulty may be encountered in determining cost if assets other than cash are used in payment. For instance, suppose that a new machine selling for a price listed at $1,500 is acquired by the payment of $1,000 cash and the trade-in of an old machine carried in the accounts at $400 (cost less depreciation). Assume that the old machine could have been sold by the owner for $250. Did the new machine cost $1,500 (the list price), or $1,400 (the sum of the cash payment and the carrying value of the old machine), or $1,250 (the sum of the cash payment and the cash value of the old machine)?

A figure of $1,500 for cost, although sometimes regarded as acceptable, is theoretically questionable because it involves the taking of a profit of $100 on the disposal of the old machine, although a loss of $150 ($400 carrying value minus $250 cash value) would have been incurred if the old machine had been sold. This $100 "profit," although nominally arising from the disposal of the old machine, is so related to the purchase transaction that its realization is debatable.

A figure of $1,400 for cost has some theoretical justification, since it is, in a sense, cost on a going-concern basis; that is, it is the total of an unexpired cost (the old machine) and an additional cost.

A figure of $1,250 appears most truly to represent cost, because it is the sum of the cash paid and the cash value of the old asset.

In the determination of cost, the general rule may be stated as follows: cost equals the cash value of the consideration parted with. This rule would apply when any noncash asset, such as investment securities, is used as part or full payment for the asset acquired.

Cost transformations. It is possible for cost amounts to be transferred from one asset account to another prior to being assigned to expense. Furthermore, the original form of the asset may be completely changed although the cost amount continues to be treated as an asset. For example, the cost of gasoline used in an engine that furnishes power for a factory becomes "transformed" into a part of the cost of finished goods.

Cost expirations. Cost expirations are of two classes: expenses and lost costs. Accountants recognize, in theory, a difference between expenses and losses, but both are deducted from revenue in determining the profitability of an enterprise.

Expenses. Expenses help generate revenue. The amounts of cost properly assignable to expense may be determined by any of the following approaches, the accountant using the one that he regards as the most suitable in the given circumstances.

(1) Identification with revenue transactions.

> Salesmen's commissions are an example. Such expenses would not exist if sales were not made; therefore, they are directly associated with the revenue from sales and should be charged to expense in the period in which the sales are reported as revenue.

(2) Identification with a period of time.

> Annual dues paid to a trade association are an example. Although there may be some connection between such expenses and revenue, the relationship is usually so indirect that it is impracticable to attempt to establish it. However, there is a clear identification with a period of time. Such expenses are sometimes called "period expenses."

(3) Apportioning cost outlays between cost expirations and cost residues.   This may be done in either of two ways:

(a) By making computations of cost expirations (expenses) and accepting the remainder as cost residues (assets).   This is the procedure normally applied to fixed assets.   The cost expiration (depreciation) is estimated and the cost residue is reported as an asset.

(b) By making computations of cost residues and accepting the remainders as cost expirations.   If the accountant can establish the portion of a cost outlay that is assignable to the future, he has, in effect, established the cost expiration.   This procedure is illustrated by the following apportionment of the cost outlay for office supplies.

On hand at beginning of period—at cost	$ 400
Purchased during the period	1,100
Total	$1,500
On hand at end of period—at cost	300
Expense	$1,200

(4) Estimating cost recoverability.

Costs should not be carried in the accounts as assets at amounts exceeding those that can be recovered through sales or utilization.   Thus, if merchandise costing $1,000 becomes out of style and only $700 can be expected from its sale, the accountant will regard as cost residue only an amount consistent with its recoverability prospects.

Lost costs.   Two examples of lost costs are given below:

A flood causes merchandise costing $50,000 to be unsalable. The business carries no insurance covering flood damage. There is a $50,000 lost cost.

A business obligates itself under a five-year lease for a warehouse at an annual rental of $4,000.   At the end of the third year, the business changes its location and, as a result, makes no further use of the warehouse.   The rental payments for the remaining two years of the lease do not help generate revenue and therefore are lost costs.

Interrelationship between assets and expenses.   One of the features of the accounting process that is commonly misunderstood or overlooked is the direct relationship between certain asset balances and the balances of accounts charged against revenue. For accounting purposes, asset valuation and expense determination are, in many instances, one and the same process. Cost amounts are either applicable to the future or are assignable as expenses or losses. If assets are misstated, it follows that cost expirations are misstated.

To illustrate, consider the relationship of fixed assets and depreciation expense. As depreciation is recorded, the carrying value of the asset decreases. If the depreciation is excessive, the related assets will be understated. On the other hand, insufficient depreciation leads to overstated assets.

Bases of asset valuations. The accepted bases for the balance sheet valuation of assets, including those usually acquired by expenditures and those usually acquired by revenue transactions, are stated below:

(A) Usually acquired by expenditures:

    (1) Applicable to operations—Inventories, prepaid expenses, and fixed assets.

        These are shown initially at cost, which, at the time of acquisition, will presumably closely approximate cash value. Subsequently, only the portion assignable to future operations is shown as the asset amount. The balances in these accounts represent unexpired costs, not cash values.

    (2) Long-term investments.

        These are shown initially at cost. If, subsequently, it appears probable that their cost will not be ultimately recovered, their carrying value should be reduced; market fluctuations that presumably are temporary can be ignored.

    (3) Short-term investments.

        These are current assets and should be shown at the lower of cost or market value at the balance sheet date.

(B) Usually acquired by revenue transactions:

    (1) Cash assets.

        These are automatically shown at cash value.

    (2) Receivables.

        These are money claims and are stated as nearly as possible at cash realizable amounts.

Income

Matching revenues and related expenses. The income determination process in accounting is a matter of matching, or associating, revenues with related expenses (and, occasionally, lost costs). Thus, revenue is a gross concept, whereas income is a net or resultant amount. If revenues exceed expenses, the business earns income, the dollar amount thereof being shown in the income statement usually as "net income." If expenses exceed revenues, a loss results.

In the determination of net income for a period, it is imperative that revenues and related expenses be reported in the same period. Two illustrations involving proper "matching" are presented.

Assume that commissions are paid to salesmen when orders are received for future delivery; to obtain a proper matching, the commissions should not be reported as an expense until the period in which the sales are reported as revenue. If the commissions were deducted from revenue in the period when paid, instead of being deferred until the period in which the sales are reported as revenue, there would not be a proper matching of revenue with related expense. The rule may be stated as follows:

> If revenue is deferred because it is regarded as not yet earned, all elements of revenue and expense related to such deferred revenue must be deferred also, in order to achieve a proper matching and a proper determination of income for the period.

Or assume that products are sold with agreements to provide service thereon for a period of time without additional cost to the purchaser. If expenses incurred in connection with the service agreements were deducted from revenue in a subsequent period when paid, net income for the period when such sales were made would be overstated because a portion of the expense associated with the revenue would not as yet have been deducted. The rule may be stated as follows:

> In cases where a "future" expense is associated with current revenue, provisions for such future outlays should be made by charges to expense in the period when the related revenue is earned.

Often the process of matching requires the use of judgment and estimates. Under such circumstances, conservatism and consistency, mentioned earlier, play important roles in the process of income determination.

Incidental transactions. As a general rule, accountants believe that informative reporting of the regular operations of the business requires showing in the income statement both revenues and related cost expirations, in appropriate detail, and not merely net amounts. Thus, it usually would be considered unacceptable to omit sales and cost of goods sold from the income statement and show merely the gross profit.

However, in the case of extraneous or incidental transactions, it is considered adequate to report only the gain or loss. For example, suppose that a manufacturing business sold, for $60,000, a parcel of land carried in the accounts at its cost, $50,000; only the $10,000 gain need be shown in the income statement.

Unrealized appreciation. The accounting principle that income should not be regarded as earned until an asset increment has been realized, or until its realization is reasonably assured, is violated if unrealized appreciation is regarded as income.

Let us assume that a company purchases marketable securities for $50,000 and that, at the end of the accounting period, these securities have a market value of $60,000. Has $10,000 of income been earned? No. The securities have not been sold, and the market price may decline before they are sold; therefore, no asset increment has been realized, and there is no reasonable assurance that an increment will be realized.

Income and savings. A saving, but not income, results from manufacturing a thing at a cost less than the price at which it could have been purchased. To regard such savings as income is a violation of the accounting principle relative to the realization of asset increments.

Companies which construct fixed assets for their own use at a cost less than the market purchase price sometimes desire to record the fixed assets at a theoretical purchase price and take up a "profit." The manufacture of fixed assets may increase the future income by reducing future depreciation charges, but a present saving with a prospect of increased future income should not be confused with realized income.

Ultimate income from sales of merchandise may be increased by manufacturing the goods instead of purchasing them; but no income should be regarded as realized until the goods are sold.

CHAPTER 23
The Analysis of Financial Statements

Why are financial statements analyzed? Financial statements are analyzed in an effort to find answers to a variety of practical and important questions, such as the following: What are the earnings record and prospects? What is the short-term debt-paying ability of the business? Are expenses under control? Is the investment in inventory excessive? Is there any danger of default on the long-term liabilities? Is the investment in fixed assets excessive? Is the amount of debt large in comparison to owners' equity?

As a general rule, accounting data will help answer most of such questions. The primary challenge is to discover which accounts reveal the changes, trends, and relationships that are relevant to the question or questions confronting the statement user. For example, the fixed asset account balances will provide little, if any, information relevant to the question of short-term debt-paying ability. Similarly, the net income figure for one year alone may offer no clue regarding the earnings prospects of a business.

Another problem facing the statement analyst is to develop a basis or norm for comparison in order to permit a conclusion that what is discovered about a business by an analysis of the financial statements is good, or bad, or typical. For instance, would it be particularly helpful to learn that the net income of a business amounted to 4 per cent of net sales, without knowing that the net income per cents for the three preceding years declined and were 7 per cent, 6 per cent, and 5 per cent, respectively, and that the industry average for the current year was 7 per cent?

It should be apparent that statement analysis requires experience and judgment. Whole volumes have been written on the subject; it is probably unnecessary to mention that, within the limitations of a single chapter of an introductory text, the treatment of the subject matter must be limited to fundamentals. It is the purpose of this chapter to discuss and illustrate some of the most widely adopted analytical procedures and to point out their usefulness as well as the limitations inherent in some of them.

Amounts, ratios, and per cents. A person analyzing financial statements soon realizes that the changes and relationships shown by account balances are more clearly disclosed if the dollar amounts are supplemented by ratios or per cents. For example, the relationship between current assets and current liabilities is important; assume that the amounts in a given case are as follows:

Current assets   = $221,000
Current liabilities = $ 93,000

Most analysts obtain a clearer picture if the relationship is also expressed as a ratio. In this example, the ratio of current assets to current liabilities is 2.38 to 1, computed by dividing $221,000 by $93,000.

Similarly, the significance of changes becomes more apparent if the dollar amounts are supplemented by per cents. Thus, if current assets have increased from $186,000 to $221,000 in one year, stating the change as an increase of 19 per cent (as well as $35,000) will be more informative for most individuals.

A good share of the mechanics of statement analysis consists of expressing the relationships of dollar amounts by the use of ratios or per cents. This is illustrated by the comparative balance sheet on pages 371 and 372.

The per cents in the first two columns to the right of the amount columns show what per cent each account balance is of the total; for instance, at the end of 1958, cash was 5.90 per cent of the total assets. This type of analysis is referred to as *vertical analysis*. It is so called because the per cents apply to related amounts usually shown in a statement column.

The amounts and per cents in the last columns reveal the increases and decreases that have occurred in one year's time. This type of analysis, referred to as *horizontal analysis*, is so called because the amounts used in the computations are usually shown on the same line of a statement.

Analysis of the balance sheet. The vertical analysis of the comparative balance sheet on pages 371 and 372 shows very little change in the per cents of the various assets and liabilities to the balance sheet totals. Probably the most significant change disclosed is the increase in current liabilities from 14.06 per cent to 17.72 per cent of the balance sheet totals.

The horizontal analysis shows increases and decreases in amounts and in per cents. Sales data are included so that the analyst can compare the per cent of increase in sales with the per cents of increase and decrease in the assets and liabilities. For instance, with a 25 per cent increase in net sales, are only a 14.81 per cent increase in cash and a 50 per cent increase in current liabilities matters for concern?

SPECIALTY PRODUCTS COMPANY   Exhibit A
Comparative Balance Sheet
December 31, 1958 and 1957

	Amounts		Per Cents of Total		Increase—Decrease*	
	1958	1957	1958	1957	Amount	Per Cent
Assets						
Current assets:						
Cash.................	$ 31,000	$ 27,000	5.90%	6.12%	$ 4,000	14.81%
Marketable securities..	$ 10,000	$ 8,000	1.91%	1.81%	$ 2,000	25.00
Accounts receivable...	$ 99,000	$ 80,000	18.86%	18.14%	$ 19,000	23.75
Allowance for doubtful accounts......	3,000	2,000	.57	.45	1,000	50.00
Net.................	$ 96,000	$ 78,000	18.29%	17.69%	$ 18,000	23.08
Inventories:						
Finished goods......	$ 38,000	$ 33,000	7.24%	7.48%	$ 5,000	15.15
Goods in process....	16,000	14,000	3.05	3.17	2,000	14.29
Raw materials......	26,000	23,000	4.95	5.22	3,000	13.04
Total...........	$ 80,000	$ 70,000	15.24%	15.87%	$ 10,000	14.29
Prepaid expenses......	$ 4,000	$ 3,000	.76%	.68%	$ 1,000	33.33
Total current assets	$221,000	$186,000	42.10%	42.17%	$ 35,000	18.82
Fixed assets:						
Land.................	$ 35,000	$ 40,000	6.67%	9.07%	$ 5,000*	12.50*
Buildings............	$250,000	$199,000	47.62%	45.12%	$ 51,000	25.63
Accumulated depreciation..........	61,000	53,000	11.62	12.01	8,000	15.09
Net.................	$189,000	$146,000	36.00%	33.11%	$ 43,000	29.45
Machinery and equipment............	$ 90,000	$ 75,000	17.14%	17.01%	$ 15,000	20.00
Accumulated depreciation..........	15,000	11,000	2.86	2.49	4,000	36.36
Net.................	$ 75,000	$ 64,000	14.28%	14.52%	$ 11,000	17.19
Furniture and fixtures.	$ 9,000	$ 8,000	1.71%	1.81%	$ 1,000	12.50
Accumulated depreciation..........	4,000	3,000	.76	.68	1,000	33.33
Net.....	$ 5,000	$ 5,000	.95%	1.13%	—	—
Total fixed assets..	$304,000	$255,000	57.90%	57.83%	$ 49,000	19.22
	$525,000	$441,000	100.00%	100.00%	$ 84,000	19.05
Net sales..............	$950,000	$760,000			$190,000	25.00

SPECIALTY PRODUCTS COMPANY
Comparative Balance Sheet (Concluded)
December 31, 1958 and 1957

Liabilities and Stockholders' Equity	Amounts		Per Cents of Total		Increase— Decrease*	
	1958	1957	1958	1957	Amount	Per Cent
Current liabilities:						
Accounts payable......	$ 18,000	$ 13,000	3.43%	2.95%	$ 5,000	38.46%
Notes payable—Bank..	40,000	25,000	7.62	5.67	15,000	60.00
Accrued taxes, wages, and other expenses.	35,000	24,000	6.67	5.44	11,000	45.83
Total current liabilities..............	$ 93,000	$ 62,000	17.72%	14.06%	$ 31,000	50.00
Long-term liabilities:						
Bonds payable—Secured by real estate....	100,000	100,000	19.04	22.67	—	—
Total liabilities....	$193,000	$162,000	36.76%	36.73%	$ 31,000	19.14
Stockholders' equity:						
Capital stock—$100 par value:						
Preferred—6%.......	$ 50,000	$ 50,000	9.52%	11.34%	—	—
Common...........	250,000	200,000	47.62	45.35	50,000	25.00
Retained earnings—Exhibit B............	32,000	29,000	6.10	6.58	3,000	10.34
Total stockholders' equity	$332,000	$279,000	63.24%	63.27%	$ 53,000	19.00
	$525,000	$441,000	100.00%	100.00%	$ 84,000	19.05
Net sales..............	$950,000	$760,000			$190,000	25.00

Analysis of the income statement. A comparative statement of income and retained earnings is shown below.

SPECIALTY PRODUCTS COMPANY Exhibit B
Comparative Statement of Income and Retained Earnings
For the Years Ended December 31, 1958 and 1957

	Amounts		Per Cents of Net Sales		Increase— Decrease*	Ratio 1958 to 1957
	1958	1957	1958	1957		
Gross sales............	$970,000	$787,000	102.11%	103.55%	$183,000	1.23
Sales returns and allowances...............	20,000	27,000	2.11	3.55	7,000*	.74
Net sales..............	$950,000	$760,000	100.00%	100.00%	$190,000	1.25
Cost of goods sold—Exhibit C..............	685,000	583,000	72.11	76.71	102,000	1.17
Gross profit on sales.....	$265,000	$177,000	27.89%	23.29%	$ 88,000	1.50
Expenses—Schedule 1:						
Selling..............	$146,000	$ 89,000	15.37%	11.71%	$ 57,000	1.64
Administrative........	71,000	47,000	7.47	6.18	24,000	1.51
Total.............	$217,000	$136,000	22.84%	17.89%	$ 81,000	1.60
Net income from operations................	$ 48,000	$ 41,000	5.05%	5.40%	$ 7,000	1.17
Net financial expense:						
Interest expenses:						
On notes payable...	$ 900	$ 700				
On bonds payable...	6,000	6,000				
Total...........	$ 6,900	$ 6,700				
Interest on securities..	500	400				
Net financial expense	$ 6,400	$ 6,300	.67	.83	100	1.02
Net income before federal income tax..........	$ 41,600	$ 34,700	4.38%	4.57%	$ 6,900	1.20
Federal income tax......	15,600	12,700	1.64	1.67	2,900	1.23
Net income............	$ 26,000	$ 22,000	2.74%	2.90%	$ 4,000	1.18
Retained earnings—Beginning of year........	29,000	26,000				
Total................	$ 55,000	$ 48,000				
Dividends:						
Preferred.............	$ 3,000	$ 3,000				
Common.............	20,000	16,000				
Total.............	$ 23,000	$ 19,000				
Retained earnings—End of year..............	$ 32,000	$ 29,000				

Vertical analysis of an income statement for a single period is not very informative; there is no basis for judging the acceptability of the various per cents. For instance, referring to the income statement for 1958, is a 27.89 per cent rate of gross profit good or bad for the industry?   Are 15.37 cents of selling expense per dollar of net sales too high?   Is a net income of 2.74 cents per sales dollar in line with the net income of other concerns in the same kind of business?

Vertical analysis takes on more meaning when applied to a comparative statement.   For instance:

> It is interesting to observe that the per cent of sales returns and allowances has decreased—from 3.55 per cent to 2.11 per cent of net sales.   Sales returns and allowances mean wasted sales effort and dissatisfied customers.
>
> It is encouraging to note that the rate of gross profit has increased from 23.29 per cent to 27.89 per cent of net sales.
>
> But it is disturbing to see that the selling and administrative expenses have increased from 17.89 per cent to 22.84 per cent of net sales.

The use of ratios of 1958 amounts to 1957 amounts (instead of per cents of increase and decrease) is illustrated in the horizontal analysis of the income statement.   The ratios are computed by dividing the amounts for the later period by the amounts for the earlier period.   Although such ratios are less commonly used than per cents of increase and decrease, they have some advantages.   In the first place, per cents of decrease must be shown in red ink or in some other manner to distinguish them from per cents of increase; this fact somewhat increases the work of preparing the statements and may cause some confusion in interpreting them.   In the second place, it probably is difficult for many persons to grasp the significance of large per cents, such as a 1,400 per cent increase; it is much easier to understand that one item is 15 times as large as another item.

The horizontal analysis of the income statement seems to be more informative than the vertical analysis.   It shows a number of interesting changes:

> The gross sales ratio is 1.23 (23 per cent increase) and the sales returns and allowances ratio is .74 (26 per cent decrease); as a consequence of these two factors, the net sales ratio is 1.25.
>
> The net sales ratio is 1.25 but the cost of goods sold ratio is only 1.17; as a result, the gross profit on sales ratio is 1.50.   We cannot tell from the statements what caused the gross profit ratio to be greater than the net sales ratio; it was, of course, due to a change in the relationship between unit selling prices and unit costs, or a shift in sales from low-profit merchandise to high-profit merchandise, or perhaps both.

Although the gross profit ratio is 1.50, the selling and administrative expense ratio is 1.60; as a consequence, the net income from operations ratio is only 1.17.

Analysis of expense schedules.   Following is a comparative schedule of selling and administrative expenses.   The Per Cents of Net Sales columns (vertical analysis) show material increases in the per cents of salesmen's salaries, salesmen's traveling expenses, advertising, officers' salaries, and bad debts.   The Ratio column (horizontal analysis) shows that many expenses increased out of proportion to the increase in net sales.

SPECIALTY PRODUCTS COMPANY   Exhibit B
Comparative Schedule of Selling and Administrative Expenses Schedule 1
For the Years Ended December 31, 1958 and 1957

	Amounts		Per Cents of Net Sales		Increase— Decrease*	Ratio 1958 to 1957
	1958	1957	1958	1957		
Selling expenses:						
Salesmen's salaries and payroll taxes..........	$ 29,000	$ 17,000	3.06%	2.24%	$ 12,000	1.71
Salesmen's traveling expenses...............	27,000	18,000	2.84	2.37	9,000	1.50
Advertising.............	80,000	45,000	8.42	5.92	35,000	1.78
Freight out.............	8,000	6,000	.84	.79	2,000	1.33
Miscellaneous....	2,000	3,000	.21	.39	1,000*	.67
Total...............	$146,000	$ 89,000	15.37%	11.71%	$ 57,000	1.64
Administrative expenses:						
Officers' salaries and payroll taxes.............	$ 24,000	$ 13,000	2.52%	1.71%	$ 11,000	1.85
Office salaries and payroll taxes.................	26,000	20,000	2.74	2.64	6,000	1.30
Stationery and supplies..	3,000	2,000	.32	.26	1,000	1.50
Postage, telephone, and telegraph.............	3,000	2,000	.32	.26	1,000	1.50
Depreciation of furniture and fixtures..........	1,000	1,000	.10	.13	—	1.00
Bad debts expense.......	13,000	7,000	1.37	.92	6,000	1.86
Miscellaneous..........	1,000	2,000	.10	.26	1,000*	.50
Total...............	$ 71,000	$ 47,000	7.47%	6.18%	$ 24,000	1.51
Net sales................	$950,000	$760,000			$190,000	1.25

Analysis of cost of goods manufactured.   Following is a comparative statement of cost of goods manufactured and sold.   The vertical analysis shows that the per cent of material cost to total cost of manufacturing decreased, and that the labor per cent increased.   The horizontal analysis shows the same information in a different way: the total cost of manufacturing increased 17.89 per cent; the material cost increased only 9.86 per cent; and the labor cost increased 24.90 per cent.

SPECIALTY PRODUCTS COMPANY   Exhibit C

Comparative Statement of Cost of Goods Manufactured and Sold
For the Years Ended December 31, 1958 and 1957

	Amounts		Per Cents of Cost of Goods Manufactured		Increase— Decrease*	
	1958	1957	1958	1957	Amount	Per Cent
Cost of goods manufactured:						
Raw materials:						
Inventory—Beginning of year............	$ 23,000	$ 21,000			$ 2,000	
Purchases............	237,000	215,000			22,000	
Total..............	$260,000	$236,000			$ 24,000	
Inventory—End of year..............	26,000	23,000			3,000	
Materials used.......	$234,000	$213,000	33.91%	36.35%	$ 21,000	9.86%
Direct labor...........	316,000	253,000	45.80	43.17	63,000	24.90
Manufacturing expenses	142,000	121,000	20.58	20.65	21,000	17.36
Cost of manufacturing..	$692,000	$587,000	100.29%	100.17%	$105,000	17.89
Variation in goods in process inventory:						
Beginning of year....	$ 14,000	$ 13,000				
End of year........ .	16,000	14,000				
Increase........... .	$ 2,000	$ 1,000	.29	.17	1,000	
Cost of goods manufactured........	$690,000	$586,000	100.00%	100.00%	$104,000	17.75
Finished goods—Beginning of year................	33,000	30,000				
Total..................	$723,000	$616,000				
Finished goods—End of year.................	38,000	33,000				
Cost of goods sold.......	$685,000	$583,000				

Comments on vertical analysis.   A word of caution is in order in connection with vertical analysis of a comparative statement. Per cents are computed by dividing one number, called the *percentage* (for instance, the administrative expenses) by another number, called the *base* (for instance, the net sales).   A change in a per cent can be caused by a change in the percentage, a change in the base, or changes in both.   Therefore, changes in vertical analysis per cents have to be carefully interpreted. For instance, the schedule of selling and administrative expenses shows that administrative expenses increased from 6.18 per cent to 7.47 per cent of net sales. This might be thoughtlessly interpreted as indicating an inconsequential increase; actually, the administrative expenses increased $24,000. This increase was nearly offset, percentagewise, by the increase in net sales. The vertical analysis per cents in the statement do not bring forcefully to the attention of the management this really significant question: Was the dollar increase in administrative expenses justified by the dollar increase in sales? Unless administrative expenses should normally increase in proportion to an increase in sales (an unusual situation), the per cent of administrative expenses to sales should have decreased in 1958.

Comments on horizontal analysis. Some comments on the computations incident to horizontal analysis are of importance.

Computation of per cents of increase and decrease. Following are illustrations of some problems which arise in the determination of per cents of increase and decrease; the asterisks indicate entries in red ink.

	This Year	Last Year	Increase—Decrease*	
			Amount	Per Cent
Cases in which there were positive amounts last year: *Statement item*				
A..........................	$1,500.00	$1,000.00	$ 500.00	50%
B..........................	500.00	1,000.00	500.00*	50*
C..........................	—	1,000.00	1,000.00*	100*
D..........................	500.00*	1,000.00	1,500.00*	150*
Cases in which there were no amounts last year: *Statement item*				
E..........................	1,500.00	—	1,500.00	—
F..........................	500.00*	—	500.00*	—
Cases in which there were negative amounts last year: *Statement item*				
G.......	1,500.00*	1,000.00*	500.00*	—
H..........................	500.00	1,000.00*	1,500.00	—
I..........................	—	1,000.00*	1,000.00	—

The computations of the per cents for items A, B, C, and D are obvious. No per cents can be computed for items E and F because, in each instance, there is no last-year amount to serve as a base; and none can be computed for items G, H, and I because the last-year amounts are negative.

Positive and negative (black and red) amounts sometimes appear on the same line (as in item H) in comparative statements which, for reasons of condensation, show only differences between certain debit and credit balances. For instance, assume that a complete income statement shows the following items:

	This Year	Last Year
Net income from operations	$31,500.00	$29,860.00
Add interest earned	3,700.00	3,000.00
Net income from operations and other income	$35,200.00	$32,860.00
Deduct interest expense	2,950.00	3,900.00
Net income	$32,250.00	$28,960.00

A condensed statement might show the net amounts of interest income and expense, thus:

	This Year	Last Year
Net income from operations	$31,500.00	$29,860.00
Interest income (expense*)—net	750.00	900.00*
Net income	$32,250.00	$28,960.00

Comparison of more than two statements. If comparative statements include data for more than two periods or as of more than two dates, there are two available bases for computing amounts of increases and decreases.

(1) Comparisons may be made with data for the immediately preceding period or date, thus:

	Year Ended December 31,			Increase—Decrease*	
	1958	1957	1956	1958 1957	1957 1956
Sales	$205,000	$180,000	$210,000	$25,000	$30,000*

(2) Or comparisons may be made with data for the earliest date or period, thus:

	Year Ended December 31,			Increase—Decrease*	
	1958	1957	1956	1958 1956	1957 1956
Sales	$205,000	$180,000	$210,000	$5,000*	$30,000*

It might seem that the same two bases of comparison could also be used to show per cents of increase and decrease. That is:

(1) The per cents might be based on data for the immediately preceding date or period, thus:

	Year Ended December 31,			Per Cent of Increase—Decrease*	
	1958	1957	1956	1958 1957	1957 1956
Sales..........	$205,000	$180,000	$210,000	14%	14%*

(2) Or the per cents might be based on data for the earliest date or period, thus:

	Year Ended December 31,			Per Cent of Increase—Decrease*	
	1958	1957	1956	1958 1956	1957 1956
Sales..........	$205,000	$180,000	$210,000	2%*	14%*

Per cents of increase and decrease based on the data for the immediately preceding date or period are likely to be misleading. For instance, the statement prepared by method 1 above shows that the sales decreased 14 per cent in 1957 and increased 14 per cent in 1958; if one considered only the per cents, he might jump to the incorrect conclusion that the increase in 1958 offset the decrease in 1957. The method 2 statement shows that, although some of the 1957 decrease was recovered in 1958, the sales for 1958 were still 2 per cent below those for 1956.

The confusion which may result from the use of method 1 arises, of course, from the fact that the per cents were computed on two bases: the per cent of decrease in 1957 was computed on a base of $210,000, whereas the per cent of increase in 1958 was computed on a base of $180,000.

The Results of Operations

In the analysis of the results of operations, horizontal and vertical analyses may be supplemented by other computations, as illustrated on the following page.

Ratio of net income to average stockholders' equity. Since capital is invested and business is conducted with the object of earning income, a basic measure of business success is the ratio of net income to the capital committed to the business. Because the amount of capital changes during the year, the ratio should be based on the average capital during the year. If the data were available, it would be desirable to compute the average capital by using the capital at the beginning of the year and the capital at each month-end during the year. Working with the available data, the computation of the ratios for Specialty Products Company is as follows:

Ratio of Net Income to Average
Stockholders' Equity

		1958	1957
Net income...................................	(a)	$ 26,000	$ 22,000
Average stockholders' equity:			
Equity at beginning of year....................		$279,000	$276,000
Equity at end of year.........................		332,000	279,000
Average...	(b)	$305,500	$277,500
Ratio (a ÷ b)...................................		8.51%	7.93%

The ratio shows an improvement (from 7.93 per cent to 8.51 per cent); but, like most ratios, the ratio of net income to owners' equity would be more meaningful if there were some standard for comparison. How do the ratios for this company compare with the ratios of other companies in the same line of business? Information for the answer to this question is sometimes available in the form of statistics furnished by trade associations, or published in reference books such as *Moody's Manual of Investments* and *Standard & Poor's Corporation Records*.

Number of times preferred dividend earned. The ratio of net income to owners' equity gives no recognition to different classes of stock. Preferred stockholders, particularly if their shares are non-participating, are primarily interested, so far as earnings are concerned, in the relation of the net income to the preferred dividend requirement, which is computed as follows:

Number of Times Preferred Dividends Earned

		1958	1957
Net income..	(a)	$26,000	$22,000
Preferred dividend requirement...................	(b)	3,000	3,000
Number of times preferred dividend earned (a ÷ b)...		8.67	7.33

Earnings per share of common stock. Common stockholders are less interested in the total net income than in the net income applicable to the common stock—that is, in the net income minus the preferred dividend requirements. Assuming that the preferred stock of Specialty Products Company is non-participating, the earnings per share of common stock are computed in the manner shown below:

Per-Share Earnings on Common Stock Outstanding at End of Year

	1958	1957
Earnings applicable to common stock:		
Net income	$26,000	$22,000
Amount required for dividend on 6% non-participating preferred stock	3,000	3,000
Earnings applicable to common stock...........(a)	$23,000	$19,000
Number of shares of common stock outstanding at end of year...........(b)	2,500	2,000
Earnings per share (a ÷ b)	$9.20	$9.50

In appraising the significance of the decrease in the earnings per share of common stock, it would be helpful to know how long the additional shares were outstanding during 1958.

It is, of course, understood that earnings per share are not always the same as dividends per share; but undistributed earnings increase the book value of the common stock and thus tend to increase the value of the common stockholders' investments.

Earnings per share are often compared with market values of stock as an indication of the advisability of making or retaining an investment in the shares. Assume, for example, that the common stock of Specialty Products Company is quoted on the market at $150; a common stockholder who is considering the advisability of retaining his holdings, or a person who is considering investing in the common stock, will probably ask himself the question: Is $9.20 a satisfactory return on an investment of $150?

Number of times bond interest earned. Bondholders are interested in the debtor company's earnings as well as in the mortgaged security, because current income is the normal source of funds required for the payment of bond interest. Since the bond interest is a claim against revenue which takes precedence over income taxes, and since the earnings available for bond interest are, of course, the earnings before bond interest, the computation of the number of times the bond interest is earned is made as follows:

Number of Times Bond Interest Earned

	1958	1957
Net income before bond interest and income tax:		
Net income before income tax	$41,600	$34,700
Bond interest	6,000	6,000
Income available for bond interest...........(a)	$47,600	$40,700
Bond interest...........(b)	$ 6,000	$ 6,000
Number of times bond interest earned (a ÷ b)........	7.93	6.78

Working Capital

In the analysis of the statements of a business, great stress is laid on the analysis of working capital. Some of the applicable analytical procedures are discussed below.

Amount of working capital. The working capital of a business is the excess of its current assets over its current liabilities. The following schedule shows the working capital of Specialty Products Company at two dates and the changes in the elements thereof in the interval.

Schedule of Working Capital

	December 31, 1958	December 31, 1957	Increase— Decrease*
Current assets:			
Cash	$ 31,000	$ 27,000	$ 4,000
Marketable securities	10,000	8,000	2,000
Accounts receivable	99,000	80,000	19,000
Allowance for doubtful accounts	3,000#	2,000#	1,000*
Inventories:			
Finished goods	38,000	33,000	5,000
Goods in process	16,000	14,000	2,000
Raw materials	26,000	23,000	3,000
Prepaid expenses	4,000	3,000	1,000
Total current assets........(a)	$221,000	$186,000	$35,000
Current liabilities:			
Accounts payable	$ 18,000	$ 13,000	$ 5,000
Notes payable—Bank	40,000	25,000	15,000
Accrued taxes, wages, and other expenses	35,000	24,000	11,000
Total current liabilities......(b)	$ 93,000	$ 62,000	$31,000
Working capital (a − b)	$128,000	$124,000	$ 4,000

Deduction.

The working capital is an indication of the ability of a business to pay its current liabilities as they mature. It is sometimes called a measure of short-term solvency. The schedule shows that the working capital increased slightly, but not significantly, during the year.

Working capital ratio. The working capital should be sufficient to provide for the payment of current liabilities as they mature and for the financing of current operations. But the *amount* of working capital is not an adequate measure of sufficiency; this fact can be demonstrated by comparing the working capital positions of two companies, as follows:

	Company A	Company B
Current assets	$10,000	$100,000
Current liabilities	5,000	95,000
Working capital	$ 5,000	$ 5,000

Both companies have the same amount of working capital, but their current positions differ radically. Any test of the adequacy of working capital must give consideration to the possibility of shrinkages in the realizable values of the current assets; in the event of forced liquidation, the inventory may have to be disposed of at a loss, and in the event of a general business recession, it may be difficult to dispose of the inventory and to collect the receivables. The current assets of Company *A*, even with a 50% shrinkage, are sufficient to pay the current liabilities; Company *B* can suffer only a 5% shrinkage.

For the reasons indicated above, it is important to know, not only the amount of the working capital, but also the ratio of current assets to current liabilities.   These ratios, for Specialty Products Company, are computed below:

Working Capital Ratio

		December 31,	
		1958	1957
Total current assets	(a)	$221,000	$186,000
Total current liabilities	(b)	93,000	62,000
Working capital ratio—Dollars of current assets per dollar of current liabilities (a ÷ b)		$2.38	$3.00

Although the amount of working capital increased slightly, the decrease in the ratio may be significant.

Window dressing. Since businessmen know that banks are interested in the working capital ratio, they sometimes conduct their affairs just prior to the statement date in such a manner as to increase the working capital ratio. To illustrate, assume that Specialty Products Company, late in December of each year, had:

(1) Sold the marketable securities at their carrying value and applied the proceeds to the reduction of the accounts payable.
(2) Used $10,000 of cash to reduce the bank loans.
(3) Postponed $10,000 of raw material purchases on account until the following January.

By these procedures, the current assets and current liabilities would have been reduced by equal amounts, as follows:

	December 31,	
	1958	1957
Reduction in current assets:		
Sale of marketable securities for payment of accounts payable	$10,000	$ 8,000
Use of cash to reduce bank loans	10,000	10,000
Postponement of raw material purchases	10,000	10,000
Offsetting reduction in liabilities	$30,000	$28,000

The effect of the window dressing is shown below; observe that the amounts of working capital are not affected, but that the working capital ratios are increased:

	December 31,	
	1958	1957
Current assets	$191,000	$158,000
Current liabilities	63,000	34,000
Working capital	$128,000	$124,000
Working capital ratio	3.03	4.65
Instead of	2.38	3.00

Effect of seasonal business. If business activities vary radically during different seasons of the year, the working capital ratio is likely to vary also. During a relatively active season, the inventories, accounts receivable, and accounts payable are apt to be large, and bank loans may be needed to finance the operations; during a relatively slack season, the inventory may be reduced, the accounts receivable should be relatively small, and there should be a corresponding reduction in the accounts payable and any bank loans.

The *amounts* of working capital may be approximately the same during both periods; but since, as we have seen, an equal increase in current assets and current liabilities reduces the working capital ratio, the *ratio* is likely to be smaller during the rush season than during the slack season. For this reason (and because it is easier to take a small inventory during the slack season than a large inventory during a busy season), many concerns close their books and prepare statements at the close of the slack season, which is known as *the close of the natural business year.*

Effect of good and bad times. Periods of boom and periods of depression affect the working capital ratio in the same manner that it is affected by seasonal activity. A boom period is a busy period, and the working capital ratio tends to be relatively low; a depression period, with slack business, tends to increase the ratio. Therefore, an increase in the working capital ratio of a given business is not necessarily a good sign; the increase may have been caused by a slump in business.

Distribution and movement of current assets. For many years the appraisal of the working capital position was pretty much limited to a rule of thumb: a working capital ratio of 2 to 1 was generally considered satisfactory. Reliance on this ratio as an adequate measure of short-term credit standing is rapidly disappearing. Analysts now recognize that the working capital ratio alone is not sufficiently informative; information is also needed with respect to the two matters mentioned on the following page.

The distribution of current assets—What kinds of current assets does the business own?

The movement of current assets—How rapidly are the current assets converted from raw materials to finished goods to accounts receivable to cash?

Distribution. Two computations which give consideration to the distribution of current assets are discussed below:

Acid-test ratio. In the computation of the acid-test ratio, only the quick current assets (cash, temporary investments in marketable securities, and accounts and notes receivable) are used. The acid-test ratios for Specialty Products Company are computed below. A ratio of at least 1 to 1 is considered desirable.

Acid-Test Ratio

	December 31, 1958	December 31, 1957	Increase— Decrease*
Quick current assets:			
Cash....................................	$ 31,000	$ 27,000	$ 4,000
Marketable securities................	10,000	8,000	2,000
Accounts receivable—Less allowance for doubtful accounts..............	96,000	78,000	18,000
Total quick current assets.....(a)	$137,000	$113,000	$24,000
Current liabilities..................(b)	93,000	62,000	31,000
Excess of quick current assets over current liabilities......................	$ 44,000	$ 51,000	$ 7,000*
Acid-test ratio—Dollars of quick current assets per dollar of current liabilities (a ÷ b)...........................	$1.47	$1.82	$ .35*

Distribution of current assets. The acid-test ratio is sometimes supplemented by a list of the current assets showing what per cent each current asset is of the total.

Distribution of Current Assets
December 31,

	1958 Amount	1958 Per Cent of Total	1957 Amount	1957 Per Cent of Total
Cash.......................	$ 31,000	14.03%	$ 27,000	14.52%
Marketable securities..........	10,000	4.53	8,000	4.30
Accounts receivable—Less allowance for doubtful accounts...	96,000	43.44	78,000	41.94
Finished goods...............	38,000	17.19	33,000	17.74
Goods in process.............	16,000	7.24	14,000	7.53
Raw materials...............	26,000	11.76	23,000	12.36
Prepaid expenses.............	4,000	1.81	3,000	1.61
	$221,000	100.00%	$186,000	100.00%

This schedule shows that there have been no shifts of material consequence in the *percentage* distribution of current assets. But the per cents, like all vertical analysis per cents, must be carefully interpreted to avoid unwarranted conclusions. The per cents applicable to the inventories have all decreased, and the per cent applicable to accounts receivable has increased. At first glance, this may be interpreted as an improvement in distribution. But we should remember that the change in a vertical-analysis per cent applicable to an item is the result of the change in that item and the change in the total of all items; and we should observe that the amounts of the inventory items have increased although the per cents have decreased, and that the total of the current assets was affected by the increase in the accounts receivable—an increase which may have been caused in part by a slowing up of collections.

An increase in inventories may be good or bad. It is good if the increased inventories are necessitated by an increase in sales volume or if larger-than-normal purchases have been made in expectation of price rises; it is bad if the increase is not justified by increased volume or if it is due to an accumulation of unsalable or obsolete items.

Movement. In the following sections we shall consider tests of the movement of accounts receivable, finished goods, and raw materials.

Accounts receivable. The question with which we are concerned here is: How rapidly are the accounts receivable collected, or how old are the accounts?

The ideal source of information for the answer to this question is found in an aging schedule of the accounts. Following is such a schedule for Specialty Products Company.

Age of Accounts Receivable

	December 31, 1958		December 31, 1957	
	Amount	Per Cent of Total	Amount	Per Cent of Total
30 days or less.................	$38,000	38.39%	$34,000	42.50%
31 to 60 days..................	27,000	27.27	25,000	31.25
61 to 90 days..................	16,000	16.16	14,000	17.50
91 to 120 days.................	15,000	15.15	6,000	7.50
Over 120 days.................	3,000	3.03	1,000	1.25
	$99,000	100.00%	$80,000	100.00%

This schedule shows that the accounts on December 31, 1958, were relatively older than those on December 31, 1957.

The preparation of an aging schedule requires access to the accounts. Outsiders, who do not have access to the accounts, sometimes compute the ratio of accounts receivable at the end of the year to the net sales during the year. The ratios for Specialty Products Company on the following page show that a slightly smaller per cent of the year's sales remained uncollected at the end of 1958 than at the end of 1957, *but they give no indication of the relative ages of the uncollected balances.*

Per Cent of Year's Sales Uncollected

		1958	1957
Accounts receivable at end of year............(a)		$ 99,000	$ 80,000
Net sales for the year........................(b)		950,000	760,000
Per cent of year's sales uncollected (a ÷ b)........		10.42%	10.53%

Theoretically, the ratio should be computed by dividing the accounts receivable by the charge sales, rather than by the aggregate sales, for the period. Usually this information is not available in published statements. The use of aggregate sales will still disclose trends, unless there is a shift in the relative amounts of charge sales and cash sales.

Finished goods. The movement of finished goods is measured by their turnover. The following computation for Specialty Products Company is illustrative of the procedure.

Finished Goods Turnovers

	1958	1957
Cost of goods sold...........................(a)	$685,000	$583,000
Average finished goods inventory:		
Inventory at beginning of year..................	$ 33,000	$ 30,000
Inventory at end of year......................	38,000	33,000
Average inventory.........................(b)	$ 35,500	$ 31,500
Turnovers (a ÷ b)...........................(c)	19.30	18.51
Average number of days per turnover (365 ÷ c)....	19	20

If there is a seasonal variation in inventories, a more accurate turnover computation can be made by the use of the average of the inventory at the beginning of the year and all month-end inventories during the year.

A high turnover of finished goods is desirable because it increases the liquidity of the inventory; moreover, given a certain per cent of gross profit, the total amount of gross profit earned during a year increases as the turnovers increase. However, increasing the turnover by reducing the inventory may ultimately have the disastrous effect of alienating customers who become dissatisfied with the assortment.

Raw materials. The movement of raw materials is measured by their turnover, as is illustrated by the computation for Specialty Products Company shown below.

Raw Materials Turnovers

	1958	1957
Raw materials used..........................(a)	$234,000	$213,000
Average raw materials inventory:		
Inventory at beginning of year..................	$ 23,000	$ 21,000
Inventory at end of year......................	26,000	23,000
Average inventory.........................(b)	$ 24,500	$ 22,000
Turnovers (a ÷ b)...........................(c)	9.55	9.68
Average number of days per turnover (365 ÷ c)....	38	38

What was said about the use of an average of monthly inventories of finished goods if there are seasonal variations in the inventories applies equally to the use of an average of monthly inventories of raw materials in the raw material turnover computations.

General Financial Condition

Some balance sheet analysis procedures in addition to those concerned with working capital are discussed in following sections of this chapter.

Ratio of owners' equity to debt. The ratios of the owners' equity of Specialty Products Company to the total of the company's current and long-term liabilities at the two year ends are computed below:

Ratio of Owners' Equity to Debt

	December 31,	
	1958	1957
Owners' equity.............................(a)	$332,000	$279,000
Total liabilities..................................(b)	193,000	162,000
Ratio of owners' equity to debt (a ÷ b)...........	1.72	1.72

From the creditors' standpoint, a high ratio of owners' equity to debt is desirable. Since, in the event of trouble, the stockholders stand to lose their investment before the creditors suffer any loss, a high ratio means a large capital cushion of protection to the creditors of the business.

From the stockholders' standpoint, a high ratio may not be desirable. Whenever borrowed funds generate income in excess of the interest cost, additional debt may be attractive.

While a low ratio of owners' equity to debt may be advantageous to stockholders from the standpoint of the rate of income on the investment, too low a ratio is hazardous; in a period of business recession, a shrinkage of assets and the pressure of creditors may be disastrous.

Analysis of equities. More detailed information about the equities of various classes of creditors and stockholders is furnished by a statement similar to the following:

Analysis of Equities

	December 31, –			
	1958		1957	
	Amount	Per Cent of Total	Amount	Per Cent of Total
Current liabilities.............	$ 93,000	17.72%	$ 62,000	14.06%
Long-term liabilities..........	100,000	19.05	100,000	22.67
Preferred stock...............	50,000	9.52	50,000	11.34
Common stock equity........	282,000	53.71	229,000	51.93
	$525,000	100.00%	$441,000	100.00%

The most significant changes disclosed by this statement are shown by the per cents of current liabilities and common stock equity. The common stock equity increased from 51.93 per cent to 53.71 per cent—an increase of 1.78 percentage points. However, the current liabilities increased from 14.06 per cent to 17.72 per cent—an increase of 3.66 percentage points.

Security for long-term debt. A measure of the security for a long-term debt is indicated by the ratio of pledged fixed assets to long-term debt. The ratio is computed in the manner illustrated below, using data of Specialty Products Company:

Ratio of Pledged Fixed Assets to Long-Term Debt

	December 31,	
	1958	1957
Pledged fixed assets—Book value:		
Land....................................	$ 35,000	$ 40,000
Buildings...............................	250,000	199,000
Accumulated depreciation.................	61,000*	53,000*
Total................................ (a)	$224,000	$186,000
Long-term debt......................... (b)	$100,000	$100,000
Ratio of pledged fixed assets to long-term debt (a ÷ b)................................	2.24	1.86

* Deduction.

The change in the ratio shows an increased degree of protection, but the ratio has no positive significance because the security is governed by market values rather than by book values.

Possible overinvestment in fixed assets. Investments in fixed assets impose upon a business fixed charges such as depreciation, insurance, and taxes. Although many expenses can be reduced in a period of business depression, fixed charges often cannot be reduced. Hence, the greater the amount of fixed expenses, the greater the danger that a business may not be able to ride out a business recession. This can be shown by an illustrative "break-even point" computation. Assume the facts stated below:

	Company A	Company B
Sales.....................................	$500,000	$500,000
Costs and expenses:		
Fixed expenses:		
Incident to ownership of fixed assets...	$ 60,000	$ 10,000
Other fixed expenses.................	20,000	20,000
Total...........................	$ 80,000	$ 30,000
Variable costs and expenses (Assumed to vary in direct proportion to sales):		
Merchandise costs....................	$350,000	$350,000
Other variable expenses...............	20,000	70,000
Total...........................	$370,000	$420,000
Per cent of variable expenses to sales.........	74%	84%

The sales points at which the companies will break even (have neither a net income nor a net loss) are computed below; S represents the sales at the break-even point.

For Company A:

$$S = \$80,000 + .74S$$
$$.26S = \$80,000$$
$$S = \$307,692$$

For Company B:

$$S = \$30,000 + .84S$$
$$.16S = \$30,000$$
$$S = \$187,500$$

Company A, in order to avoid a net loss, must keep its sales up to a level of \$307,692. Company B's sales can drop to \$187,500 before it will incur a loss.

An overinvestment in fixed assets is also dangerous because, in a period of depression, fixed assets are likely to become frozen assets.

Obviously there can be no standard per cent or ratio to mark the danger point in investments in fixed assets; the fixed asset requirements of different businesses vary. Two ratios which indicate trends are illustrated.

Ratio of owners' equity to fixed assets. The computation of this ratio is illustrated below:

Ratio of Owners' Equity to Fixed Assets

	December 31,	
	1958	1957
Owners' equity...............................(a)	\$332,000	\$279,000
Fixed assets—Cost less depreciation............(b)	304,000	255,000
Ratio of owners' equity to fixed assets ($a \div b$)......	1.09	1.09

Ratio of sales to fixed assets. Changes in the ratio of sales to fixed assets are an indication (but not a conclusive one) of whether sales are moving down toward or up from the break-even point.

Ratio of Sales to Fixed Assets

	1958	1957
Net sales...................................(a)	\$950,000	\$760,000
Fixed assets................................(b)	304,000	255,000
Ratio of sales to fixed assets ($a \div b$)...............	3.13	2.98

Conclusion

Several words of caution need to be expressed before closing the discussion of statement analysis:

(1) Avoid meaningless ratios. With the increasing interest in statement analysis during recent years, there has been a tendency to develop a multiplicity of ratios, some of which have little or no significance. If two dollar amounts have little or no significance

in relation to each other, a ratio expression of their relation is no more significant. For instance, it is claimed by some that the ratio of current assets to long-term debt is meaningful, but it is difficult to see any reason for regarding it as significant.

(2) Avoid ratios which may be misinterpreted. The turnover of working capital, often regarded as a very significant ratio, is a good example. It is computed by dividing the net sales by the working capital; an increase in the ratio is usually interpreted as desirable. But an increase in turnover may be caused by either an increase in the sales or a decrease in the working capital. An increase in working capital turnover caused by a decrease in working capital may be an undesirable trend.

(3) Appraise related ratios. For instance, the comparative balance sheet on page 371 shows that, with a 25 per cent increase in sales, the accounts receivable increased 24 per cent. Instead of jumping to the conclusion that the receivables have the same collectibility at the end of 1958 as they had at the end of 1957, observe that the schedule of administrative expenses (page 375) shows that the bad debt provisions were 1.37 per cent of net sales in 1958 as compared with .92 per cent in 1957. This suggests a greater degree of possible loss in the receivables at the end of 1958 than in the receivables at the end of 1957. Then observe that, although the bad debt provision nearly doubled in 1958 ($13,000 compared with $7,000), the Allowance for Doubtful Accounts shown in the balance sheet has not been increased proportionately.

(4) Be aware that undesirable business operations or conditions may account for apparently favorable ratios, and vice versa. For instance, it was pointed out earlier in the chapter that a higher working capital ratio is more likely to exist in a period of poor business than in a period of good business.

(5) Be aware that facts not disclosed by the statements might affect the interpretation placed on the statements. For instance, assume that the management informed you that the large bad debt provision in 1958 was principally the result of a serious impairment of the Allowance for Doubtful Accounts caused by the bankruptcy of one customer; the line of reasoning in (3) above would be affected.

(6) Bear constantly in mind the fact that changes in vertical-analysis per cents are affected by changes in the items being measured and changes in the base—for instance, changes in expense items and a change in net sales. Changes in vertical-analysis per cents cannot safely be interpreted without a constant awareness of this fact.

(7) Remember, also, that horizontal-analysis per cents and ratios must often be interpreted in the light of supplementary

information. For instance, if net sales increased 25 per cent, it does not necessarily follow that any expense increases of 25 per cent or less are satisfactory. The propriety of that conclusion depends on whether the expense is relatively fixed or relatively variable.

(8) Weigh the results of the analysis of a given business against the trends in the industry and in business in general. It may be that, although conditions in the specific business have worsened, they are better than the average.

(9) Give consideration to changes in price levels and in the purchasing power of the dollar. For instance, if sales have been uniform for two years and there has been no change in the dollar amount of the inventory, but there has been a 25 per cent increase in unit purchase costs, a 20 per cent decrease in inventory quantities is indicated. But before accepting such a conclusion, find out whether the business uses *fifo* or *lifo*.

CHAPTER 24

The Statement of Application of Funds

Change in working capital and causes thereof. Suppose that
you were given the following comparative balance sheet:

THE A COMPANY
Comparative Balance Sheet
December 31, 1958 and 1957

	December 31,	
	1958	1957
Assets		
Cash...	$ 4,700	$ 3,000
Accounts receivable..............................	11,500	12,000
Merchandise.....................................	9,000	8,000
Land...	6,600	5,000
	$31,800	$28,000
Liabilities and Stockholders' Equity		
Accounts payable................................	$ 4,500	$ 7,000
Capital stock....................................	25,000	20,000
Retained earnings................................	2,300	1,000
	$31,800	$28,000

If you were asked to prepare a statement detailing the changes
in the elements of working capital, you would use the balances in
the current asset and current liability accounts and would prepare
the following schedule.

THE A COMPANY
Schedule of Working Capital
December 31, 1958 and 1957

	December 31,		Changes in Working Capital	
	1958	1957	Increase	Decrease
Current assets:				
Cash.......................	$ 4,700	$ 3,000	$1,700	
Accounts receivable...........	11,500	12,000		$ 500
Merchandise.................	9,000	8,000	1,000	
Total current assets.........	$25,200	$23,000		
Current liabilities:				
Accounts payable.............	4,500	7,000	2,500	
Working capital.................	$20,700	$16,000		
Increase in working capital.				4,700
			$5,200	$5,200

This chapter deals with a statement which shows the *causes* of
the change in working capital; but, before the statement is illustrated, it will be helpful to look at the comparative balance sheet
on the following page, in which the changes in working capital

393

accounts are shown in one pair of columns and the changes in other accounts are shown in another pair of columns. Observe that the net debits in the working capital accounts and the net credits in the other accounts are equal.

THE *A* COMPANY

Comparative Balance Sheet

With Classification of Changes in Account Balances

December 31, 1958 and 1957

			Changes in Account Balances			
			In Working Capital Accounts		In Other (Non-Current) Accounts	
	December 31,					
	1958	1957	Debit	Credit	Debit	Credit
Assets						
Cash......................	$ 4,700	$ 3,000	$1,700			
Accounts receivable.........	11,500	12,000		$ 500		
Merchandise................	9,000	8,000	1,000			
Land......................	6,600	5,000			$1,600	
	$31,800	$28,000				
Liabilities and Stockholders' Equity						
Accounts payable............	$ 4,500	$ 7,000	2,500			
Capital stock...............	25,000	20,000				$5,000
Retained earnings...........	2,300	1,000				1,300
	$31,800	$28,000				
Net debits in working capital accounts.................				4,700		
Net credits in non-current accounts.................					4,700	
			$5,200	$5,200	$6,300	$6,300

By referring to the non-current accounts in the ledger and determining what caused the changes in them, we shall at the same time ascertain the causes of the change in working capital. The causes of the changes in the non-current accounts and the related effects on working capital are shown below:

	Changes in Non-Current Account Balances		Working Capital Result	
	Debit	Credit	Increase	Decrease
Land:				
Cause—Land purchased...................	$1,600			
Effect on working capital—Decrease........				$1,600
Capital stock:				
Cause—Additional stock issued............		$5,000		
Effect on working capital—Increase........			$5,000	
Retained earnings:				
Cause—Net income for the year...........		1,300		
Effect on working capital—Increase........			1,300	
	$1,600	$6,300	$6,300	$1,600
Net credits to non-current accounts and increase in working capital........................	4,700			4,700
	$6,300	$6,300	$6,300	$6,300

The credits in the non-current accounts indicate the sources of new funds that came into the business during the year; the non-current account debit reflects the use of funds for a purpose other than an increase in working capital; the excess of the credits over the debit is the amount of the increase in working capital, $4,700. This amount agrees with the increase in working capital shown in the schedule of working capital on page 393.

The causes of the increase in working capital are assembled in the following statement.

THE *A* COMPANY
Statement of Application of Funds
For the Year Ended December 31, 1958

Funds provided:
By operations... $1,300
By issuance of capital stock............................... 5,000
   Total funds provided.................................... $6,300
Funds applied:
To purchase of land.. 1,600
Increase in working capital—per schedule..................... $4,700

Purpose of the statement.   The primary purpose of the statement of application of funds is to show the causes of the change in working capital during a period.   It is of particular interest to bankers and other grantors of short-term credit.   A schedule of working capital, such as the one on page 393, shows the change in working capital but it does not answer the question: What caused this change?   The answer to this question may be very important.

Suppose that three prospective borrowers submitted reports to a banker showing working capital of $50,000 at the beginning of the year and $60,000 at the end of the year.   One submitted a statement of application of funds showing:

Funds provided:
By operations... $15,000
Funds applied:
To payment of dividends................................... 5,000
Increase in working capital............................... $10,000

This statement would probably create a favorable impression. Another submitted the statement appearing below:

Funds provided:
By operations... $ 8,000
By issuance of five-year notes............................ 25,000
   Total funds provided.................................. $33,000
Funds applied:
To purchase of land............................. $18,000
To payment of dividends......................... 5,000
   Total funds applied.................................. 23,000
Increase in working capital............................... $10,000

This statement would probably create a less favorable impression. The banker would observe the smaller amount of funds provided by operations and the greater proportion thereof paid out in dividends. He might want to ask the management why they thought the expenditure for land advisable. And he probably would be particularly interested in an answer to the following question: Unless they can increase the funds provided by operations or will reduce their dividends, how do they expect to pay off the $25,000 of notes in five years without impairing their working capital?

The third submitted a statement showing:

Funds provided:
By operations.. $ 2,000
By issuance of five-year notes............................ 20,000

Total funds provided............................... $22,000
Funds applied:
To payment of dividends............................... 12,000

Increase in working capital............................. $10,000

This statement would create a very unfavorable impression. It does not seem to be good financial management to borrow money in order to pay dividends equal to six times the small amount of funds provided by operations. And, with such results of operations and such a dividend policy, how does the management expect to pay the five-year notes, to say nothing of an additional bank loan?

Additional features illustrated. The following comparative balance sheet is the basis of this illustration.

THE *B* COMPANY
Comparative Balance Sheet
December 31, 1958 and 1957

	December 31, 1958	December 31, 1957	Increase— Decrease*
Assets			
Cash..................................	$ 6,600	$ 3,500	$3,100
Accounts receivable...................	5,900	6,200	300*
Merchandise..........................	19,000	16,500	2,500
Investment securities..................	7,000	9,000	2,000*
Goodwill..............................	—	2,500	2,500*
	$38,500	$37,700	$ 800
Liabilities and Stockholders' Equity			
Accounts payable......................	$ 1,500	$ 1,900	$ 400*
Long-term notes payable...............	—	5,000	5,000*
Capital stock.........................	34,500	30,000	4,500
Paid-in surplus........................	450	—	450
Retained earnings.....................	2,050	800	1,250
	$38,500	$37,700	$ 800

The first step is to prepare the schedule of working capital shown on page 398.

To determine the causes of the increase in working capital, the following analysis of the non-current accounts is prepared. The information required for the analysis was obtained from the non-current accounts in the ledger. (It might be necessary sometimes to go back to the books of original entry for information about the ledger entries. However, in many cases the causes of changes in the balances of non-current accounts are apparent, making it unnecessary to refer to the ledger accounts or the journals.)

THE *B* COMPANY

Analysis of Non-Current Accounts

For the Year Ended December 31, 1958

	Debit Credit*	Working Capital Result	
		Increase (Funds Provided)	Decrease (Funds Applied)
Investment securities:			
12/31/57............................	9,000		
Sale of securities at cost............	2,000*	2,000	
12/31/58............................	7,000		
Goodwill:			
12/31/57............................	2,500		
Write-off to Retained Earnings..N-1	2,500*		
12/31/58............................	—		
Long-term notes payable:			
12/31/57............................	5,000*		
Payment............................	5,000		5,000
12/31/58............................	—		
Capital stock:			
12/31/57............................	30,000*		
Par of stock issued.................	4,500*	4,500a	
12/31/58............................	34,500*		
Paid-in surplus:			
12/31/57............................	—		
Premium on stock issued............	450*	450a	
12/31/58............................	450*		
Retained earnings:			
12/31/57............................	800*		
Net income.........................	4,750*	4,750	
Dividends..........................	1,000		1,000
Goodwill write-off.............N-1	2,500		
12/31/58............................	2,050*		
		11,700	6,000
Increase in working capital................... ..			5,700
		11,700	11,700

N—The symbol N indicates that the entry had no relation to working capital accounts and therefore is not to be shown in the statement of application of funds. In this instance, the write-off of goodwill affected the Goodwill and Retained Earnings accounts only, neither being a working capital account. Since there may be several pairs of such non-fund entries, it is advisable, for cross-reference purposes, to give each pair a number.

a—The par value of the stock issued and the premium thereon are marked "a" to indicate that they are to be shown together in the statement of application of funds.

THE *B* COMPANY
Schedule of Working Capital
December 31, 1958 and 1957

	December 31,		Changes in Working Capital	
	1958	1957	Increase	Decrease
Current assets:				
Cash........................	$ 6,600	$ 3,500	$3,100	
Accounts receivable............	5,900	6,200		$ 300
Merchandise...................	19,000	16,500	2,500	
Total current assets..........	$31,500	$26,200		
Current liabilities:				
Accounts payable..............	1,500	1,900	400	
Working capital.................	$30,000	$24,300		
Increase in working capital.......................				5,700
			$6,000	$6,000

The increase in working capital shown in the analysis on page 397 agrees with the increase shown in the schedule of working capital, thus showing that the analysis of non-current accounts provides all of the information required for the preparation of the statement of application of funds.

THE *B* COMPANY
Statement of Application of Funds
For the Year Ended December 31, 1958

Funds provided:		
By operations....................................		$4,750
By issuance of capital stock:		
Par....................................	$4,500	
Premium.............................	450	4,950
By sale of investment securities...................		2,000
Total funds provided...............................		$11,700
Funds applied:		
To payment of long-term debt....................	$5,000	
To payment of dividends.........................	1,000	
Total funds applied................................		6,000
Increase in working capital...........................		$ 5,700

What goes into the statement of application of funds. The funds statement is a summary, covering a period of time, of the transactions that resulted in a change in the *amount* of working capital. To understand the funds statement, it is important to realize that some transactions and entries have no effect on the amount of working capital.

Transactions that affect current asset and/or current liability accounts *only* do not change the amount of working capital. For example, a purchase of securities to be held as short-term investments causes an increase in one current asset account (Investments) and an equal decrease in another current asset (Cash). Since transactions of this nature have no effect on the *amount* of working capital, they are not reflected in the statement of application of funds; they will, of course, affect the schedule of working capital.

Some transactions affect non-current accounts only. For instance, the issuance of $100,000 of common stock in retirement of an equal par value of preferred stock would have no effect on working capital. The resulting account changes would not appear in the statement of application of funds.

Some changes in non-current accounts result from mere book entries debiting one non-current account and crediting another. The write-off of goodwill in the preceding illustration is an example. Working capital was not affected.

The entries that are relevant for funds-statement purposes are those affecting one or more working capital accounts and one or more non-current accounts. Such entries reflect a change in the amount of working capital. The changes in the current accounts affect the schedule of working capital; the changes in the non-current accounts affect the statement of application of funds.

Funds provided by operations may be greater than net income. Some charges to expense accounts reduce the net income without having any bearing on the working capital. For instance, depreciation of fixed assets reduces the net income but has no effect on working capital.

Although depreciation is an expense, the charge for depreciation does not involve an expenditure of funds. Therefore, to determine the amount of funds provided by operations, it is necessary to add the net income for the period and the depreciation provisions made during the period.

To illustrate, assume that a man began business on January 1, and that his financial condition at that date was as follows:

```
Assets:
    Machine................. $500.00
    Cash....................   100.00
Owner's equity..............  $600.00
```

He did a cash business, selling all goods for cash and paying cash for all purchases and miscellaneous expenses. At the end of the year, he prepared the following summary Cash account and income statement:

Cash

Opening balance............	100.00	Purchases...................	800.00
Sales......................	2,000.00	Expenses....................	200.00
		Ending balance.............	1,100.00
	2,100.00		2,100.00

Income Statement

Sales...		$2,000.00
Deduct cost of goods sold...............................		800.00
Gross profit on sales...................................		$1,200.00
Deduct:		
Miscellaneous expenses........................	$200.00	
Depreciation................................	50.00	250.00
Net income...		$ 950.00

These statements show that, while the net income was $950, the working capital of the business was increased $1,000 by operations. Thus, to determine the increase in working capital resulting from operations, it is necessary to add the $950 net income and the $50 depreciation allowance.

The following comparative balance sheet is the basis of an illustration showing funds provided by operations in excess of net income.

THE C COMPANY
Comparative Balance Sheet
December 31, 1958 and 1957

	December 31, 1958	December 31, 1957	Increase— Decrease*
Assets			
Cash...	$ 11,200	$ 8,500	$ 2,700
Accounts receivable............................	21,300	23,500	2,200*
Allowance for doubtful accounts.................	(1,350)	(1,425)	75
Merchandise inventory.........................	35,000	30,600	4,400
Bond sinking fund.............................	16,000	12,000	4,000
Land..	10,000	10,000	—
Building.......................................	60,000	60,000	—
Accumulated depreciation—Building.............	(12,000)	(9,000)	3,000*
Furniture and fixtures.........................	8,000	7,000	1,000
Accumulated depreciation—Furniture and fixtures.	(3,200)	(2,400)	800*
	$144,950	$138,775	$ 6,175
Liabilities and Stockholders' Equity			
Accounts payable..............................	$ 15,000	$ 18,000	$ 3,000*
Notes payable.................................	10,000	7,500	2,500
Real estate mortgage payable...................	40,000	40,000	—
Capital stock..................................	50,000	45,000	5,000
Sinking fund reserve...........................	16,000	12,000	4,000
Retained earnings.............................	13,950	16,275	2,325*
	$144,950	$138,775	$ 6,175

( ) Deduction.

Again, the first step is to prepare the schedule of working capital. It is at the top of page 402.

The analysis of the non-current accounts is on the opposite page.

THE C COMPANY

Analysis of Non-Current Accounts

[For the Year Ended December 31, 1958

	Debit— Credit*	Working Capital Result	
		Increase (Funds Provided)	Decrease (Funds Applied)
Bond sinking fund:			
12/31/57......................	12,000		
Contribution...................	4,000		4,000
12/31/58......................	16,000		
Accumulated depreciation—Building:			
12/31/57......................	9,000*		
Depreciation for the year.........	3,000*	3,000a	
12/31/58......................	12,000*		
Furniture and fixtures:			
12/31/57......................	7,000		
Purchase......................	1,000		1,000
12/31/58......................	8,000		
Accumulated depreciation—Furniture and fixtures:			
12/31/57......................	2,400*		
Depreciation for the year.........	800*	800a	
12/31/58......................	3,200*		
Capital stock:			
12/31/57......................	45,000*		
Stock issued...................	5,000*	5,000	
12/31/58......................	50,000*		
Sinking fund reserve:			
12/31/57......................	12,000*		
Transfer from Retained Earnings... N-1	4,000*		
12/31/58......................	16,000*		
Retained earnings:			
12/31/57......................	16,275*		
Net income....................	6,675*	6,675a	
Dividend......................	5,000		5,000
Transfer to Sinking Fund Reserve.. N-1	4,000		
12/31/58......................	13,950*		
		15,475	10,000
Increase in working capital.......................			5,475
		15,475	15,475

Since the same increase in working capital is shown in the schedule of working capital and the analysis of non-current accounts, the statement on page 402 may be prepared.

THE *C* COMPANY

Schedule of Working Capital

December 31, 1958 and 1957

| | December 31, | | Changes in Working Capital | |
	1958	1957	Increase	Decrease
Current assets:				
Cash................................	$11,200	$ 8,500	$ 2,700	
Accounts receivable....................	21,300	23,500		$ 2,200
Allowance for doubtful accounts.......	1,350*	1,425*	75	
Merchandise inventory.................	35,000	30,600	4,400	
Total current assets.................	$66,150	$61,175		
Current liabilities:				
Accounts payable.....................	$15,000	$18,000	3,000	
Notes payable........................	10,000	7,500		2,500
Total current liabilities..............	$25,000	$25,500		
Working capital.........................	$41,150	$35,675		
Increase in working capital..............................				5,475
			$10,175	$10,175

* Deduction.

THE *C* COMPANY

Statement of Application of Funds

For the Year Ended December 31, 1958

Funds provided:
By operations:
Net income for the year.......................... $6,675
Add: Depreciation—Building...................... 3,000
Depreciation—Furniture and fixtures.......... 800 $10,475
By issuance of capital stock.............................. 5,000
Total funds provided... $15,475
Funds applied:
Contribution to sinking fund.............................. $ 4,000
Purchase of furniture and fixtures......................... 1,000
Payment of dividend....................................... 5,000
Total funds applied... 10,000
Increase in working capital...................................... $ 5,475

Decrease in working capital. The following comparative balance sheet is the basis of an illustration showing a decrease in working capital.

THE *D* COMPANY

Comparative Balance Sheet

December 31, 1958 and 1957

| | December 31, | | Increase— |
	1958	1957	Decrease*
Assets			
Cash.................................	$ 3,500	$ 4,000	$ 500*
Accounts receivable...............	6,000	5,000	1,000
Inventory.......................	18,000	20,000	2,000*
Furniture............................	13,500	6,000	7,500
Accumulated depreciation—Furniture....	(2,300)	(1,800)	500*
	$38,700	$33,200	$5,500

Liabilities and Stockholders' Equity

Accounts payable....................	$ 2,100	$ 2,300	$ 200*
Capital stock........................	25,000	20,000	5,000
Retained earnings...................	11,600	10,900	700
	$38,700	$33,200	$5,500

( ) Deduction.

Following is the schedule of working capital.

THE *D* COMPANY

Schedule of Working Capital
December 31, 1958 and 1957

	December 31,		Changes in Working Capital	
	1958	1957	Increase	Decrease
Current assets:				
Cash.........................	$ 3,500	$ 4,000		$ 500
Accounts receivable...........	6,000	5,000	$1,000	
Inventory............	18,000	20,000		2,000
Total current assets.........	$27,500	$29,000		
Current liabilities:				
Accounts payable...	2,100	2,300	200	
Working capital.................	$25,400	$26,700		
Decrease in working capital......................			1,300	
			$2,500	$2,500

The analysis of non-current accounts appears below:

THE *D* COMPANY

Analysis of Non-Current Accounts
For the Year Ended December 31, 1958

	Debit— Credit*	Working Capital Result	
		Increase (Funds Provided)	Decrease (Funds Applied)
Furniture:			
12/31/57......	6,000		
Purchase.......................	7,500		7,500
12/31/58................... . ..	13,500		
Accumulated depreciation—Furniture:			
12/31/57....	1,800*		
Depreciation for the year..........	500*	500a	
12/31/58......................	2,300*		
Capital stock:			
12/31/57........................	20,000*		
Stock dividend................N-1	2,000*		
Issued for cash..................	3,000*	3,000	
12/31/58......................	25,000*		
Retained earnings:			
12/31/57........................	10,900*		
Net income.................. ...	12,700*	12,700a	
Stock dividend.............. ..N-1	2,000		
Cash dividend......	10,000		10,000
12/31/58......................	11,600*		
		16,200	17,500
Decrease in working capital.........		1,300	
		17,500	17,500

A decrease in working capital is best shown in the statement of application of funds by reversing the sequence of the statement; that is, by showing the funds applied above the funds provided.

THE _D_ COMPANY

Statement of Application of Funds

For the Year Ended December 31, 1958

Funds applied:

    To purchase of furniture............................. $ 7,500

    To payment of dividend........................... 10,000

        Total funds applied... $17,500

Funds provided:

    By issuance of capital stock...................... $ 3,000

    By operations:

        Net income for the year............... $12,700

        Add operating charge not affecting funds

          —Depreciation of furniture........... 500   13,200

        Total funds provided.................................... 16,200

Decrease in working capital................................ $ 1,300

CHAPTER 25
Accounting Aids to Management

Introduction. Businessmen, of necessity, must make many decisions in the process of managing the operations of a business concern. Experience and judgment are important, but in many instances accounting data are a source of help in the decision-making process.

In using accounting information to assist in the management function, the first step is to define the particular problem and determine the kinds of factual information that would be helpful in reaching a decision. Of course, it is necessary to know the kinds of data available, and to use judgment and imagination in organizing the information so that the pertinent trends and relationships will be set forth.

Since business decisions cover such a wide variety of matters, it is difficult to state any general rules or procedures that apply to the assembly and use of accounting data for management purposes. Also, it is impossible to illustrate all of the problems that confront management. In the following pages several examples of managerial uses of accounting data are shown. They should serve to suggest the vast area of management application of accounting data. It seems appropriate to mention that an intelligent use of accounting data probably can result only if the basic features of the accounting process are understood by those charged with making business decisions.

Raw Material Inventories Out of Balance

It is desirable that, so far as practicable, raw material inventories of a factory be balanced; that is, the inventories of all classes of raw material should contain only sufficient units to make approximately the same number of units of finished product. Otherwise, funds are tied up in unbalanced inventories.

It may be impracticable, or even undesirable, to maintain even an approximate inventory balance. Among the reasons, the following may be mentioned: Certain materials may be available only seasonally, with the possible result that an entire year's supply must be purchased when the materials are available. Or, purchasing in large quantities may effect a price saving that more than offsets the disadvantage of tying up funds in unbalanced inventories.

A computation of an inventory imbalance is shown below:

Computation of Inventory Imbalance

	Materials			
	A	B	C	D
Units—December 31, 1958..................	2,500	5,250	3,500	1,800
Units required per unit of product..........	5	7	10	3
Units of product that can be made from materials in inventory..........	500	750	350	600
Deduct smallest number of units that can be made from materials in inventory...........	350	350	350	350
Imbalance in terms of product..............	150	400		250
Multiply by units of material per unit of product	5	7		3
Imbalance in terms of material units..........	750	2,800		750
Multiply by cost per unit of material......... $ 18	$ 27			$ 35
Funds tied up in unbalanced inventories......	$13,500	$75,600		$26,250

A somewhat different computation is suitable if the same class of raw material is used in the manufacture of several products. The procedure is illustrated below.

Computation of Inventory Imbalance When Same Raw Material Is Used in More Than One Product

	Units of Material per Unit of Product	Average Number of Units of Product per Month	Materials			
			1	2	3	4
Units in inventory, December 31, 1958........................			2,400	4,500	750	1,300
Units required for one month's average production:						
Product A:						
Material 1.................	10	30	300			
Material 2................	7	30		210		
Material 4................	5	30				150
Product B:						
Material 1.................	12	50	600			
Material 3................	8	50			400	
Product C:						
Material 2.................	15	60		900		
Material 4................	6	60				360
Total..................			900	1,110	400	510
Number of months' requirements in inventory.....................			2.67	4.05	1.88	2.55

Factory Employee Performance

As a measure of the relative efficiency of direct laborers in a factory, a tabulation similar to the one on the following page may be made.

Employee   Performance   May 15, 1958

Name	Operation No.	Pieces Finished	Minutes Actual Total	Actual Per Unit	Standard Per Unit	Per Cent Efficiency
Brown, Horace...........	1	25	480	19.20	20	104%
Harrison, James..........	1	22	480	21.82	20	92
Jones, William.............	1	18	360	20.00	20	100
	2	7	120	17.14	15	88
Martin, John.............	2	10	200	20.00	15	75
	3	30	280	9.33	10	107
Patterson, Daniel.........	3	50	480	9.60	10	104
Stephenson, Fred.........	1	6	150	25.00	20	80
	2	8	130	16.25	15	92
	3	18	200	11.11	10	90
Templeton, Irving.........	2	22	300	13.64	15	110
	3	19	180	9.47	10	106
Webster, Oliver...........	1	6	160	26.67	20	75
	2	10	180	18.00	15	83
	3	12	140	11.67	10	86

Summary

	Operation 1	Operation 2	Operation 3
Brown, Horace.......	104%		
Harrison, James.................................	92		
Jones, William...................................	100	88%	
Martin, John....................................		75	107%
Patterson, Daniel...............................			104
Stephenson, Fred............	80	92	90
Templeton, Irving...............................		110	106
Webster, Oliver.......................	75	83	86

Judging only from the data in the summary, it would seem advisable, to the extent possible, to have the several operations performed by the following persons:

Operation	Employee
1...................	Horace Brown
2.................	Irving Templeton
3.................	John Martin

However, some other factors should be given consideration, namely:

(a) Decisions should not be based on data for one day only.

(b) Differences in pay rates might offset low per cents of efficiency, but it must be remembered that the cost of an employee's services includes the factory overhead applicable to his operation as well as the wages paid to him.

Advisability of Fixed Asset Additions or Replacements

Additions. Baxter Company operates a factory and is considering adding a new product to its line. The company has no equipment that could be used in the production of this product; the new equipment would cost $9,000 and would have an estimated life of 15 years. It is believed that the new product would have the following effect on annual operations:

Sales of new product..		$40,000
Deduct:		
Cost of sales—except depreciation on new equipment	$30,000	
Depreciation on new equipment...................	600	
Additional selling and administrative expenses......	7,000	37,600
Net income before income tax.............................		$ 2,400
Income tax...		1,200
Net income...		$ 1,200

Two computations that may be of assistance in determining the advisability of making the expenditure for the equipment are illustrated.

Period of cost recovery. The purpose of this computation is to determine the number of years that will be required for the funds produced by the new product to equal the cost of the new equipment—that is, the number of years required for cost recovery. Since operations produce funds equal to the net income plus the depreciation, the annual cost recovery is estimated at $1,200 + $600, or $1,800. Then,

$$\$9,000 \div \$1,800 = 5, \text{ the years required to recover cost}$$

Rate of income on average investment. With an equipment cost of $9,000 and an estimated life of 15 years, the annual depreciation is $600. The average investment over the life of the equipment is computed by adding the original cost and the carrying value at the beginning of the last year of useful life and dividing by 2.

Original investment..............................	$9,000
Cost less depreciation—beginning of 15th year.......	600
Total..	$9,600
Divide by.......................................	2
Average...	$4,800

The rate of income on the average investment is:

$$\$1,200 \div \$4,800 = 25\%$$

Since the whole computation is based on estimates, it is sufficiently accurate to determine the average investment by dividing the cost by 2. The rate of income would then be computed thus:

$$\$1,200 \div \$4,500 = 26.7\%$$

From one viewpoint, a long estimated use-life is desirable because of the prospective income over a long period. On the other hand, there is more uncertainty in making long-period forecasts than in making short-period forecasts; for this reason, management usually is greatly interested in a short prospective cost-recovery period.

Replacements. Henderson Corporation is considering replacing one of its machines with a current model that will reduce its manufacturing costs. The new machine sells for $6,000; the manufacturer will allow $1,500 for the old machine (which has a book value of $3,000 and an estimated remaining use-life of ten years) and Henderson Corporation will pay $4,500 in cash. The main attraction is the prospective reduction in the cost of manufacturing. The new machine is expected to last for 15 years.

Period of investment recovery. In choosing between the alternatives of keeping the old machine or acquiring the new one, the management will be interested in knowing how long it will take to recover its $4,500 investment. This requires a comparison of the funds provided by operations under the alternatives. Such a comparison is facilitated by preparing data showing the expected results of operations, first, if the present machine is retained, and second, if the new machine is acquired as a replacement.

	Expected Operating Results With			
	Present Machine		New Machine	
Sales......................................		$10,000		$10,000
Deduct:				
Cost of goods sold—except depreciation.......	$6,000		$5,000	
Depreciation (see computation below).........	300		500	
Selling and administrative expenses...........	2,700		2,700	
Total.................................		9,000		8,200
Net income before income tax..................		$ 1,000		$ 1,800
Income tax (say, 50%).......................		500		900
Net income................................		$ 500		$ 900
Funds provided by operations:				
Net income.............................	$ 500		$ 900	
Add depreciation........................	300	$ 800	500	$ 1,400
Funds provided by operations with old machine..				800
Increase in funds provided by operations with new machine..................................				$ 600

The depreciation charges are computed as follows:

	Present Machine	New Machine
Remaining book value of old machine...............	$3,000	$3,000
Cash payment for new machine....................		4,500
Depreciation base...............................	$3,000	$7,500
Years of estimated use-life.......................	10	15
Annual depreciation.............................	$ 300	$ 500

As shown on page 409, it is estimated that the new machine will cause a $600 increase in the funds provided annually by operations. Under such circumstances, the $4,500 investment for the replacement of the old machine can be recovered in 7½ years. The computation is presented below:

$$\$4,500 \div \$600 = 7\frac{1}{2} \text{ years}$$

Rate of income on average additional investment. The increased net income produced by the new machine is estimated at $400. The average investment is $4,500 ÷ 2, or $2,250. The per cent of income on the average additional investment is computed as follows:

$$\$400 \div \$2,250 = 17.8\%$$

Relative Effectiveness of Salesmen

In January, 1958, the sales manager of Hamilton Company was giving consideration to recommendations he would make for salary increases for the salesmen. He looked first at the following tabulation.

Sales—By Salesmen
For the Years Ended December 31, 1957 and 1956
Sales

	1957		1956		Increase	
Salesmen	Amount	Per Cent of Total	Amount	Per Cent of Total	Amount	Per Cent
Abbott, Henry.........	$179,800	19.56%	$148,920	17.97%	$30,880	20.74%
Ferguson, George......	195,740	21.29	181,435	21.89	14,305	7.88
Jacobson, Irving.......	187,600	20.40	174,370	21.03	13,230	7.59
Luther, Bert..........	185,650	20.19	165,430	19.96	20,220	12.22
Sutherland, Oliver.....	170,620	18.56	158,745	19.15	11,875	7.48
Total..............	$919,410	100.00%	$828,900	100.00%	$90,510	10.92

He observed particularly the fact that the per cents of increase in the sales of Abbott and Luther, 20.74% and 12.22% respectively, were considerably above the 10.92% average for the business as a whole. He regarded the changes in the per cents of totals as less significant because the change in each salesman's per cent was affected not only by the change in his sales but also by the changes in the sales of all other salesmen.

Because the obtaining of new customers is an important factor in the effectiveness of a salesman, he had the data shown on the opposite page assembled.

He observed that Abbott's and Luther's per cents were again relatively high. He also observed that Sutherland's per cents were low.

Sales to New Customers—By Salesmen
For the Years Ended December 31, 1957 and 1956

Salesmen	1957			1956		
		Sales to New Customers			Sales to New Customers	
	Total Sales	Per Cent		Total Sales	Per Cent	
		Amount	of Total		Amount	of Total
Abbott, Henry..........	$179,800	$12,047	6.7%	$148,920	$ 8,640	5.8%
Ferguson, George.......	195,740	7,438	3.8	181,435	6,530	3.6
Jacobson, Irving........	187,600	11,068	5.9	174,370	8,370	4.8
Luther, Bert............	185,650	14,110	7.6	165,430	9,760	5.9
Sutherland, Oliver.......	170,620	5,289	3.1	158,745	4,440	2.8
Total...............	$919,410	$49,952	5.4	$828,900	$37,740	4.6

The amount of business a man brings in is not the whole measure of his value. It is also important to know what it costs to keep him in the field and the per cent of this cost to his sales.

Sales and Salaries and Traveling Expenses—By Salesmen
For the Years Ended December 31, 1957 and 1956

Salesmen	1957			1956		
		Salaries and Expenses			Salaries and Expenses	
	Sales	Amount	Per Cent of Sales	Sales	Amount	Per Cent of Sales
Abbott, Henry...	$179,800	$ 26,900	15.0%	$148,920	$ 24,420	16.4%
Ferguson, George.	195,740	27,840	14.2	181,435	28,485	15.7
Jacobson, Irving..	187,600	28,100	15.0	174,370	26,680	15.3
Luther, Bert......	185,650	27,645	14.9	165,430	26,300	15.9
Sutherland, Oliver	170,620	26,320	15.4	158,745	25,715	16.2
Total..........	$919,410	$136,805	14.9	$828,900	$131,600	15.9

The differences in salary and expense amounts were reasonably attributable to differences in salaries and in travel and subsistence costs in the various territories. The decreases in the per cents of sales were caused by the fact that the sales increases more than offset the salary and expense increases.

Because gross profits produced by salesmen are a good measure of efficiency, he had the following statement prepared.

Gross Profits and Salaries and Traveling Expenses—By Salesmen
For the Years Ended December 31, 1957 and 1956

Salesmen	1957			1956		
		Salaries and Expenses			Salaries and Expenses	
	Gross Profit	Amount	Per Cent of Gross Profit	Gross Profit	Amount	Per Cent of Gross Profit
Abbott, Henry...	$ 60,415	$ 26,900	44.5%	$ 49,740	$ 24,420	49.1%
Ferguson, George.	64,368	27,840	43.3	58,420	28,485	48.8
Jacobson, Irving..	69,785	28,100	40.3	64,168	26,680	41.6
Luther, Bert......	71,290	27,645	38.8	58,230	26,300	45.2
Sutherland, Oliver	54,770	26,320	48.1	48,735	25,715	52.8
Total..........	$320,628	$136,805	42.7	$279,293	$131,600	47.1

He realized that the differences in the per cents of salaries and expenses to gross profits were due in part to the differences in salaries and expenses, but he believed that the principal cause was the difference in gross profit; and he suspected that some of the salesmen (particularly Sutherland) were trying to make a good showing on sales volume by selling easier-to-market low-profit goods.   He therefore had the following study made.

Gross Profit Rates—By Salesmen
For the Years Ended December 31, 1957 and 1956

| | 1957 | | | 1956 | | |
| | | Gross Profit | | | Gross Profit | |
Salesmen	Sales	Amount	Per Cent of Sales	Sales	Amount	Per Cent of Sales
Abbott, Henry........	$179,800	$ 60,415	33.6%	$148,920	$ 49,740	33.4%
Ferguson, George.....	195,740	64,368	32.9	181,435	58,420	32.2
Jacobson, Irving......	187,600	69,785	37.2	174,370	64,168	36.8
Luther, Bert..........	185,650	71,290	38.4	165,430	58,230	35.2
Sutherland, Oliver....	170,620	54,770	32.1	158,745	48,735	30.7
Total..............	$919,410	$320,628	34.9	$828,900	$279,293	33.7

This statement confirmed the sales manager's suspicion that the salesmen were not making equal efforts to sell high-profit merchandise.

He took note of the fact that Jacobson's and Luther's rates of gross profit were above the average in both years, and that the other three were below the average in both years.   He also noted that Sutherland's rate was consistently the lowest.

Other things being equal, large sales are preferable to small ones, partly because it is reasonable to assume that the larger the sales, the larger the gross profit, and partly because the office expense of processing an order is not necessarily proportionate to its dollar amount.

Average Dollars Per Sale—By Salesmen
For the Years Ended December 31, 1957 and 1956

| | 1957 | | | 1956 | | |
Salesmen	Sales	Number of Sales	Average Sale	Sales	Number of Sales	Average Sale
Abbott, Henry............	$179,800	292	$616	$148,920	252	$591
Ferguson, George.........	195,740	321	610	181,435	291	624
Jacobson, Irving..........	187,600	330	569	174,370	301	579
Luther, Bert..............	185,650	290	640	165,430	275	602
Sutherland, Oliver........	170,620	340	502	158,745	329	483
Total.................	$919,410	1,573	585	$828,900	1,448	572

As a summary of the salesmen's rankings on the various factors of efficiency discussed above, the tabulation on the following page may be made.

Salesmen's Rankings

	Abbott		Ferguson		Jacobson		Luther		Sutherland	
	1957	*1956*	1957	*1956*	1957	*1956*	1957	*1956*	1957	*1956*
Per cent of total sales.....	4	*5*	1	*1*	2	*2*	3	*3*	5	*4*
Per cent of increase in sales	1		3		4		2		5	
Per cent of salesman's sales to new customers to his total sales..........	2	*2*	4	*4*	3	*3*	1	*1*	5	*5*
Per cent of salaries and expenses to sales.........	4	*5*	1	*2*	3	*1*	2	*3*	5	*4*
Per cent of salaries and expenses to gross profits...	4	*4*	3	*3*	2	*1*	1	*2*	5	*5*
Gross profit rates.........	3	*3*	4	*4*	2	*1*	1	*2*	5	*5*
Average dollars per sale...	2	*3*	3	*1*	4	*4*	1	*2*	5	*5*

Inventory Turnovers by Items

A computation of inventory turnovers by items of merchandise may be helpful to management in making decisions with respect to the discontinuance of an item or a reduction in its inventory.

Computation of Turnovers by Items of Merchandise

Article	Units in Inventory December 31, 1957	1958	Average	Sales	Turnover
A......................	18	20	19	76	4.00
B......................	100	90	95	1,120	11.79
C......................	70	60	65	215	3.31
D......................	300	320	310	1,560	5.00
E......................	40	45	43	375	8.72
F......................	90	76	83	965	11.63
G......................	140	132	136	150	1.10
H......................	74	85	80	410	5.13

The fact that a certain item of merchandise has a low rate of turnover is, of course, not a sufficient reason to warrant the discontinuance of the item.   It may be a large-profit item or an article that must be kept in stock to maintain a full line.   Nevertheless, a low rate of turnover may indicate the desirability of reducing the inventory, particularly if the cost per unit is large, if the item can be readily replaced, and if it is so bulky that considerable storage space is required.

Trends in Departmental Operations

The management of a store with departments may obtain very useful information from a tabulation of sales, gross profit, and direct departmental expense data similar to that shown on the following page.

Trends in Departmental Operations
1958 and 1957

		Amount		Ratio	Per Cent of Net Sales	
Department		1958	1957	1958 to 1957	1958	1957
Net sales:						
	A........	$247,500	$222,400	111%		
	B........	158,200	148,100	107		
	C........	99,000	88,800	111		
	D........	63,500	78,700	81		
	Total.....	$568,200	$538,000			
Gross profit on sales:						
	A........	$ 99,000	$ 84,500	117%	40.0%	38.0%
	B........	60,900	62,985	97	38.5	42.5
	C........	34,350	32,380	106	34.7	36.5
	D........	17,780	23,610	75	28.0	30.0
	Total.....	$212,030	$203,475			
Direct departmental expense:						
	A........	$ 54,000	$ 48,500	111%	21.8%	21.8%
	B........	40,250	40,325	100	25.4	27.2
	C........	27,200	20,770	131	27.5	23.4
	D........	15,875	17,315	92	25.0	22.0
	Total.....	$137,325	$126,910			
Gross profit minus direct departmental expense:						
	A........	$ 45,000	$ 36,000	125%	18.2%	16.2%
	B........	20,650	22,660	91	13.1	15.3
	C........	7,150	11,610	62	7.2	13.1
	D........	1,905	6,295	30	3.0	8.0
	Total.....	$ 74,705	$ 76,565			

Some of the analyses that can be made from these data are shown below:

Sales increased in all departments except Department D.

The sales in Department A increased 11% but the gross profit minus direct departmental expense increased 25%. The reasons were:

The sales increased 11%; as a result of this increase and an increase in the rate of gross profit from 38% to 40% the amount of gross profit increased 17%.

Although the direct departmental expense increased 11%, it remained at the same per cent of net sales—namely, 21.8%. This may not be entirely satisfactory, since part of the departmental expense is probably fixed, rather than variable with the volume of sales. It might be worth while to make an investigation of the variable expenses.

The 1958 sales in Department B were 107% of the sales of 1957, but the gross profit minus direct departmental expense dropped to 91%. The reasons were:

The rate of gross profit decreased from 42.5% to 38.5%, or a decrease of 4 percentage points.

The decrease in the rate of gross profit was partly offset by a decrease in the direct departmental expense; but only partly, because the decrease in expense was only from 27.2% of net sales to 25.4%, or 1.8 percentage points.

Sales in Department C in 1958 were 111% of those in 1957, but the gross profit minus direct departmental expense was only 62% of that in 1957. Reasons:

The rate of gross profit decreased from 36.5% of sales to 34.7%.

Direct departmental expense increased from 23.4% of sales to 27.5%.

Sales in Department D in 1958 were 81% of those in 1957, but the gross profit minus direct departmental expense was only 30% of that in 1957. Reasons in addition to the decrease in sales:

A decrease in the rate of gross profit from 30% to 28%.

An increase in the ratio of departmental expense from 22% to 25%.

These analytical methods may also be applied to data for branches.

Budgeted Planning

Dawson, Incorporated, had been operating a retail store for several years, selling merchandise from three departments in leased quarters. For some time the management of the company had been considering adding two departments, in which the rates of gross profit promised to be considerably higher than the store average, but had been unable to do so because of limited space. In the fall of 1957, the owner of the building informed Dawson, Incorporated, that additional space would be available on January 1, 1958; the management studied the sales potential of the two proposed additional departments and decided to lease the additional space.

Early in 1958, after the 1957 statements had been completed, the company management prepared an estimate of the 1958 operations and the prospective financial position at the end of that year. As a first step in the preparation of this budget,* the following estimate of sales and gross profits was made.

---

* The methods used in the preparation of this budget, while indicative of budget procedure, should not be assumed to include all of the techniques and refinements that have been developed for budgeting purposes. Such a coverage would require an entire book.

Sales and Gross Profits   Schedule 1
1957 Actual and Budget for 1958

Department	Sales	Gross Profit Amount	Per Cent	Cost of Sales
1957 Actual:				
1.........	$185,000	$ 64,750	35%	$120,250
2.........	150,000	45,000	30	105,000
3.........	150,000	42,000	28	108,000
Total.......	$485,000	$151,750	31	$333,250
1958 Budget:				
1.........	$200,000	$ 70,000	35	$130,000
2.........	175,000	52,500	30	122,500
3.........	160,000	44,800	28	115,200
4.........	125,000	47,500	38	77,500
5.........	120,000	48,000	40	72,000
	$780,000	$262,800	34	$517,200

This budget was prepared by estimating the sales in the five departments, determining the estimated gross profits by applying the 1957 rates to the budgeted sales of the first three departments and estimated rates to the budgeted sales of the two new departments. The estimated costs of sales were computed by deducting the budgeted gross profits from the budgeted sales.

The management then prepared the following estimates:

Selling and Administrative Expenses   Schedule 2
1957 Actual and Budget for 1958

	1957 Actual	1958 Budget
Selling expenses:		
Salesmen's salaries and payroll taxes.........	$25,000	$35,000
Advertising.............................	20,000	20,000
Rent....................................	9,500	14,500
Depreciation—Store fixtures...............	1,200	2,200
Miscellaneous..........................	19,100	22,300
Total..............................	$74,800	$94,000
Administrative expenses:		
Officers' salaries and payroll taxes...........	$30,000	$30,000
Office salaries and payroll taxes.............	9,000	12,000
Rent....................................	500	500
Depreciation—Office furniture and equipment	300	300
Bad debts expense........................	4,500	6,000
Miscellaneous............................	9,150	11,000
Total..............................	$53,450	$59,800

Increases were budgeted for salesmen's and office salaries and payroll taxes because additional employees would be needed.

The entire $5,000 rent for the additional space was included in selling expense because no additional office space would be required.

No increase in advertising expense was budgeted because the management believed that the newspaper space bought in 1957 would be sufficient for advertising for all departments.

Depreciation of store fixtures was increased because additional fixtures had been purchased, at a cost of $10,000.

Bad debts expense was increased because of the budgeted increase in sales, giving consideration to the expectation that proportionately more cash sales would be made in the new than in the old departments.

Miscellaneous expenses were increased on the basis of rather rough estimates.

The management next prepared the following statement of income and retained earnings.

Statement of Income and Retained Earnings   Exhibit B
1957 Actual and Budget for 1958

	1957 Actual	1958 Budget
Sales—Schedule 1	$485,000	$780,000
Cost of goods sold:		
Inventory—Beginning of year	$ 85,000	$ 90,000
Purchases	338,250	567,200
Total	$423,250	$657,200
Inventory—End of year	90,000	140,000
Cost of goods sold	$333,250	$517,200
Gross profit on sales	$151,750	$262,800
Expenses—Schedule 2:		
Selling	$ 74,800	$ 94,000
Administrative	53,450	59,800
Total	$128,250	$153,800
Net income before federal income tax	$ 23,500	$109,000
Federal income tax	7,050	51,180
Net income	$ 16,450	$ 57,820
Retained earnings—Beginning of year	35,950	46,400
Total	$ 52,400	$104,220
Dividends	6,000	7,500
Retained earnings—End of year	$ 46,400	$ 96,720
Per Cents		
Gross profit on sales	31.29%	33.69%
Net income on sales	3.39	7.41
Net income on stockholders' equity at beginning of year:		
Stockholders' equity:		
Capital stock	$ 60,000	$ 75,000
Retained earnings	35,950	46,400
Total	$ 95,950	$121,400
Net income	$ 16,450	$ 57,820
Per cent of net income on stockholders' equity at beginning of year	17.14%	47.63%

Estimated sales were taken from Schedule 1.
Estimated purchases were computed as follows:

Estimated cost of sales—Schedule 1	$517,200
Desired inventory—End of year	140,000
Total	$657,200
Inventory—Beginning of year	90,000
Estimated purchases	$567,200

Estimated selling and administrative expenses were taken from Schedule 2.

Estimated federal income tax was computed at the following rates: 30% of the first $25,000 of net income, 52% on the remainder.

The additional dividend was accounted for by the fact that $15,000 of additional stock was issued at the beginning of 1958 in the belief that this amount, together with the increased revenue, would be sufficient to finance the expanded operation.

The management next prepared the following 1957 actual and 1958 budgeted balance sheets.

Balance Sheets, December 31   Exhibit A
1957 Actual and 1958 Budgeted

	December 31,	
	1957 Actual	1958 Budget
Assets		
Current assets:		
Cash..	$ 17,500	$ 75,220
Accounts receivable.........................	$ 25,000	$ 39,000
Allowance for doubtful accounts..............	1,500	2,000
Net...	$ 23,500	$ 37,000
Merchandise inventory........................	$ 90,000	$140,000
Prepaid expenses.............................	$ 3,000	$ 4,000
Total current assets........................	$134,000	$256,220
Fixed assets:		
Store fixtures...............................	$ 12,000	$ 22,000
Accumulated depreciation.....................	4,800	7,000
Net...	$ 7,200	$ 15,000
Office furniture and equipment................	$ 3,000	$ 3,000
Accumulated depreciation.....................	1,200	1,500
Net...	$ 1,800	$ 1,500
Total fixed assets...........................	$ 9,000	$ 16,500
	$143,000	$272,720
Liabilities and Stockholders' Equity		
Current liabilities:		
Accounts payable.............................	$ 25,000	$ 40,000
Accrued taxes, wages, and other expenses........	11,600	61,000
Total current liabilities.....................	$ 36,600	$101,000
Stockholders' equity:		
Capital stock................................	$ 60,000	$ 75,000
Retained earnings............................	46,400	96,720
Total stockholders' equity...................	$106,400	$171,720
	$143,000	$272,720
Working capital ratio.........................	3.66 to 1	2.54 to 1
Acid-test ratio..............................	1.12 to 1	1.11 to 1
Ratio of worth to debt.......................	2.91 to 1	1.70 to 1

Estimates not previously mentioned were made as follows:

Accounts receivable: Since the receivables at the end of 1957 were approximately 5% of the 1957 sales, the same rate was applied to the budgeted 1958 sales to compute the estimated accounts receivable. There was an inconsistency in this procedure. In the computation of the provision for uncollectible accounts, it was assumed that proportionately more cash sales would be made in 1958 than in 1957; this assumption was ignored in making the estimate of end-of-1958 receivables.

Accounts payable: The accounts payable at the end of 1957 were about 7% of the purchases for the year. A similar rate was applied to the budgeted purchases for 1958 to estimate the accounts payable at the end of that year.

Cash: The estimated cash balance at the end of 1958 was computed on the basis of other estimates, as shown below:

Computation of Estimated Cash Balance
December 31, 1958

Balance—December 31, 1957				$ 17,500
Receipts:				
Issuance of capital stock				15,000
Accounts receivable and sales:				
Accounts receivable—Dec. 31, 1957		$ 25,000		
Sales		780,000		
Total		$805,000		
Deduct:				
Accounts receivable—Dec. 31, 1958		$ 39,000		
Accounts written off:				
Reserve balance—Dec. 31, 1957...	$ 1,500			
Provision during 1958	6,000			
Total	$ 7,500			
Reserve balance—Dec. 31, 1958...	2,000	5,500	44,500	760,500
Total				$793,000
Disbursements:				
Purchase of store fixtures		$ 10,000		
Accounts payable and purchases:				
Accounts payable—Dec. 31, 1957		$ 25,000		
Purchases		567,200		
Total		$592,200		
Deduct accounts payable—Dec. 31, 1958		40,000	552,200	
Expenses and prepaid expenses:				
Selling expenses		$ 94,000		
Administrative expenses		59,800		
Federal income tax		51,180		
Increase in prepaid expenses		1,000		
Total		$205,980		
Deduct:				
Depreciation	$ 2,500			
Provision for doubtful accounts	6,000			
Increase in accrued expenses	49,400	57,900	148,080	
Dividend			7,500	
Total disbursements				717,780
Balance—December 31, 1958				$ 75,220

The management was somewhat disturbed by the projected sharp decrease in the working capital ratio and the ratio of worth to debt, but felt safe because the working capital ratio was more than the traditional 2 to 1, and particularly because the acid-test ratio remained almost unchanged. The prospective large increase in net income pleased the management very much.

At the end of 1958 the following statements were prepared:

Statement of Income and Retained Earnings   Exhibit B
For the Year Ended December 31, 1958

	Budget	Actual	Actual Over—Under* Budget
Sales..	$780,000	$770,000	$10,000*
Cost of goods sold:			
Inventory—Beginning of year..............	$ 90,000	$ 90,000	$ —
Purchases..............................	567,200	615,750	48,550
Total...................................	$657,200	$705,750	$48,550
Inventory—End of year...................	140,000	165,000	25,000
Cost of goods sold......................	$517,200	$540,750	$23,550
Gross profit on sales........................	$262,800	$229,250	$33,550*
Expenses—Schedule 1:			
Selling...............................	$ 94,000	$119,300	$25,300
Administrative.........................	59,800	64,650	4,850
Total.................................	$153,800	$183,950	$30,150
Net income from operations.................	$109,000	$ 45,300	$63,700*
Interest expense—Note payable..............		500	500
Net income before federal income tax.........	$109,000	$ 44,800	$64,200*
Federal income tax........................	51,180	17,800	33,380*
Net income...............................	$ 57,820	$ 27,000	$30,820*
Retained earnings—Beginning of year........	46,400	46,400	—
Total....................................	$104,220	$ 73,400	$30,820*
Dividend.................................	7,500	—	7,500*
Retained earnings—End of year..............	$ 96,720	$ 73,400	$23,320*
Per Cents			
Gross profit on sales......................	33.69%	29.77%	3.92%*
Net income on sales.......................	7.41	3.51	3.90 *
Net income on stockholders' equity at beginning of year:			
Stockholders' equity:			
Capital stock.......................	$ 75,000	$ 75,000	—
Retained earnings...................	46,400	46,400	—
Total..............................	$121,400	$121,400	—
Per cent of net income on stockholders' equity............................	47.63%	22.24%	25.39%*

Selling and Administrative Expenses   Schedule 1
For the Year Ended December 31, 1958

	Budget	Actual	Actual Over—Under* Budget
Selling expenses:			
Salesmen's salaries and payroll taxes..........	$35,000	$ 35,000	$ —
Advertising...............................	20,000	42,000	22,000
Rent.....................................	14,500	14,500	—
Depreciation—Store fixtures.................	2,200	2,200	—
Miscellaneous.............................	22,300	25,600	3,300
Total.................................	$94,000	$119,300	$25,300
Administrative expenses:			
Officers' salaries and payroll taxes............	$30,000	$ 30,000	$ —
Office salaries and payroll taxes..............	12,000	14,000	2,000
Rent.....................................	500	500	—
Depreciation—Office furniture and equipment.	300	300	—
Bad debts expense.........................	6,000	7,500	1,500
Miscellaneous.............................	11,000	12,350	1,350
Total.................................	$59,800	$ 64,650	$ 4,850

Balance Sheet   Exhibit A
December 31, 1958

	Budget	Actual	Actual Over—Under* Budget
Assets			
Current assets:			
Cash..................................	$ 75,220	$ 25,400	$49,820*
Accounts receivable.......................	$ 39,000	$ 35,000	$ 4,000*
Allowance for doubtful accounts..........	2,000	2,000	—
Net..................................	$ 37,000	$ 33,000	$ 4,000*
Merchandise inventory.....................	$140,000	$165,000	$25,000
Prepaid expenses..........................	$ 4,000	$ 4,500	$ 500
Total current assets.....................	$256,220	$227,900	$28,320*
Fixed assets:			
Store fixtures.............................	$ 22,000	$ 22,000	$ —
Accumulated depreciation................	7,000	7,000	—
Net..................................	$ 15,000	$ 15,000	$ —
Office furniture and equipment..............	$ 3,000	$ 3,000	$ —
Accumulated depreciation................	1,500	1,500	—
Net..................................	$ 1,500	$ 1,500	$ —
Total fixed assets.....................	$ 16,500	$ 16,500	$ —
	$272,720	$244,400	$28,320*
Liabilities and Stockholders' Equity			
Current liabilities:			
Accounts payable.........................	$ 40,000	$ 48,000	$ 8,000
Note payable—Bank loan..................	—	25,000	25,000
Accrued taxes, wages, and other expenses....	61,000	23,000	38,000*
Total current liabilities.................	$101,000	$ 96,000	$ 5,000*
Stockholders' equity:			
Capital stock.............................	$ 75,000	$ 75,000	$ —
Retained earnings—Exhibit B..............	96,720	73,400	23,320*
Total stockholders' equity...............	$171,720	$148,400	$23,320*
	$272,720	$244,400	$28,320*

	Budget	Actual
Balance Sheet Ratios		
Working capital ratio.....................	2.54 to 1	2.37 to 1
Acid-test ratio...........................	1.11 to 1	.61 to 1
Ratio of worth to debt...................	1.70 to 1	1.55 to 1

The results of operations were disappointing; the net income from operations was $63,700 less than the budget estimate. The causes were:

Gross profit under budget...................	$33,550
Selling expenses over budget.................	25,300
Administrative expenses over budget.........	4,850
Total....................................	$63,700

The increase in selling expenses was caused principally by the fact that the management had increased the expenditure for advertising as soon as it became apparent that potential customers were slow in becoming aware that merchandise of the two new departments was available at the store.

The management was principally concerned with the fact that the gross profit was so much under the budget. Why, when actual sales were $770,000 compared with the $780,000 budget estimate, was the gross profit $33,550 less than the budget estimate? An investigation was undertaken.

The first thing the investigation disclosed was that the sales in the departments with high gross profit rates were smaller per cents of the total sales than the budget estimates.

Budgeted and Actual Sales by Departments

		Per Budget		Actual	
Department	Budgeted Gross Profit Rate	Amount	Per Cent of Total	Amount	Per Cent of Total
1......................	35%	$200,000	25.64%	$180,000	23.38%
2......................	30	175,000	22.44	185,000	24.03
3......................	28	160,000	20.51	230,000	29.87
4......................	38	125,000	16.03	80,000	10.39
5......................	40	120,000	15.38	95,000	12.33
		$780,000	100.00%	$770,000	100.00%

The point can be made somewhat more emphatic by the following tabulation, in which the departments are listed in the order of budgeted rates of gross profit.

		Per Cents of Total Sales	
Department	Budget Rate of Gross Profit	Per Budget	Actual
5................	40%	15.38%	12.33%
4................	38	16.03	10.39
1................	35	25.64	23.38
2................	30	22.44	24.03
3................	28	20.51	29.87
		100.00%	100.00%

The next thing disclosed by the investigation was the fact that, in all departments except No. 2, the actual rate of gross profit was less than the rate used in the budget.

Comparison of Budget and Actual Rates of Gross Profit

Department	Budget Rate	Actual Rate	Actual Over— Under* Budget
1	35%	32%	3%*
2	30	31	1
3	28	23	5 *
4	38	34	4 *
5	40	36	4 *

The failure to meet the operating budget with respect to gross profit and expenses not only affected the net income adversely; it also affected the cash position, resulting in an acid-test ratio of .61 instead of the budgeted 1.11—a matter of very material significance.

CHAPTER 26

Departmental Operations

Departmental profits. If a merchandising concern operates two or more departments, it is advisable for it to keep the accounts in such a way that an income statement can be prepared showing the results of operations by departments.

Determining gross profits by departments. To determine the gross profits by departments, as shown in the working papers on pages 425 and 426 and the income statement on page 427, the following departmental merchandise accounts were kept:

Inventory—Department *A*
Inventory—Department *B*
Sales—Department *A*
Sales—Department *B*
Sales Returns and Allowances—Department *A*
Sales Returns and Allowances—Department *B*
Sales Discounts—Department *A*
Sales Discounts—Department *B*
Purchases—Department *A*
Purchases—Department *B*
Purchase Returns and Allowances—Department *A*
Purchase Returns and Allowances—Department *B*
Purchase Discounts—Department *A*
Purchase Discounts—Department *B*

The trial balance in the working papers on pages 425 and 426 shows that only one Transportation In account was kept. If, in a business with departments, it is practicable to analyze the carriers' bills to determine the transportation costs applicable to each department, departmental Transportation In accounts may be kept. In the illustration in this chapter, it is assumed that the management prefers to make an approximate apportionment of the cost of transportation in, rather than to incur the expense of analyzing the carriers' bills. The apportionment was made on the basis of purchases.

Department	Purchases	Per Cent	Transportation In
A.............	$ 60,000	40%	$ 720
B.............	90,000	60	1,080
Total........	$150,000	100%	$1,800

To simplify the illustrative working papers, a trial balance after adjustments is used. If a trial balance before adjustments is used, a pair of Adjustments columns will be required.

THE RANDALIA COMPANY
Working Papers
Showing Gross Profit on Sales by Departments
For the Year Ended December 31, 1958

	Trial Balance (After Adjustments)		Department A		Department B		Unallocated	Retained Earnings		Balance Sheet	
Cash	8,030									8,030	
Accounts receivable	14,800									14,800	
Allowance for doubtful accounts		740									740
Notes receivable	3,000									3,000	
Accrued interest receivable	30									30	
Inventories—Dec. 31, 1957:											
Dept. A	17,000		17,000								
Dept. B	29,000				29,000						
Unexpired insurance	250									250	
Delivery equipment	4,000									4,000	
Accumulated depreciation—D. E.		2,000									2,000
Accounts payable		12,000									12,000
Notes payable		5,000									5,000
Federal income tax payable		1,000									1,000
Accrued salaries payable		90									90
Capital stock		50,000									50,000
Retained earnings—Dec. 31, 1957		5,995							5,995		
Dividends	5,000							5,000			
Sales:											
Dept. A		75,000		75,000							
Dept. B		125,000				125,000					
Sales returns and allowances:											
Dept. A	400		400								
Dept. B	900				900						
Sales discounts:											
Dept. A	600		600								
Dept. B	1,000				1,000						
Purchases:											
Dept. A	60,000		60,000								
Dept. B	90,000				90,000						
Purchase returns and allowances:											
Dept. A		600		600							
Dept. B		850				850					
Totals forward	234,010	278,275	78,000	75,600	120,900	125,850		5,000	5,995	30,110	70,830

Working Papers for Year Ended December 31, 1958
(Concluded)

	Trial Balance (After Adjustments)		REVENUE AND EXPENSE						Retained Earnings		Balance Sheet	
			Department A		Department B		Unallocated					
Totals brought forward	234,010	278,275	78,000	75,600	120,900	125,850			5,000	5,995	30,110	70,830
Purchase discounts:												
Dept. A		390		390								
Dept. B		810				810						
Transportation in	1,800		720		1,080							
Store rent	6,000						6,000					
Advertising	4,000						4,000					
Salesmen's salaries:												
Dept. A	6,000						6,000					
Dept. B	7,000						7,000					
Delivery expense	4,000						4,000					
Depreciation—Delivery equipment	1,000						1,000					
Officers' salaries	10,000						10,000					
Office salaries	2,400						2,400					
Insurance	600						600					
Bad debts expense	420						420					
Miscellaneous general expenses	1,200						1,200					
Interest expense	125						125					
Interest earned		80						80				
Federal income tax	1,000						1,000					
	279,555	279,555	78,720		121,980		43,745					
Inventories—Dec. 31, 1958:												
Dept. A				13,000							13,000	
Dept. B						31,000					31,000	
				88,990		157,660		45,950				
Gross profit on sales			10,270		35,680			46,030				
			88,990	88,990	157,660	157,660						
Net income—To Retained Earnings							2,285			2,285		
							46,030	46,030		8,280		
Retained earnings—Dec. 31, 1958									5,000			3,280
									3,280			
									8,280	8,280	74,110	74,110

Income Statement
Showing Gross Profit on Sales by Departments
For the Year Ended December 31, 1958

	Department A		Department B		Total	
Gross sales..........		$75,000		$125,000		$200,000
Deduct:						
Sales returns and allowances....	$ 400		$ 900		$ 1,300	
Sales discounts....	600	1,000	1,000	1,900	1,600	2,900
Net sales....		$74,000		$123,100		$197,100
Deduct cost of goods sold:						
Purchases....		$60,000		$90,000		$150,000
Deduct:						
Purchase returns and allowances....	$600		$850		$ 1,450	
Purchase discounts....	390	990	810	1,660	1,200	2,650
Net cost of purchases....		$59,010		$88,340		$147,350
Add transportation in....		720		1,080		1,800
Total....		$59,730		$89,420		$149,150
Add inventory— December 31, 1957....		17,000		29,000		46,000
Total cost of goods available for sale..		$76,730		$118,420		$195,150
Deduct inventory—December 31, 1958..		13,000		31,000		44,000
Cost of goods sold....		63,730		87,420		151,150
Gross profit on sales....		$10,270		$ 35,680		$ 45,950
Deduct expenses:						
Selling expenses:						
Store rent....					$ 6,000	
Advertising....					4,000	
Salesmen's salaries:						
Department A....					6,000	
Department B....					7,000	
Delivery expense....					4,000	
Depreciation—Delivery equipment....					1,000	
Total selling expenses....					$ 28,000	
General expenses:						
Officers' salaries....					$10,000	
Office salaries....					2,400	
Insurance....					600	
Bad debts expense....					420	
Miscellaneous general expenses....					1,200	
Total general expenses....					14,620	
Total operating expenses....						42,620
Net operating income....						$ 3,330
Deduct net interest expense:						
Interest expense....					$ 125	
Interest earned....					80	45
Net income before federal income tax..						$ 3,285
Deduct federal income tax....						1,000
Net income....						$ 2,285

Departmental inventories in the balance sheet. In the balance sheet of a business with departments, the inventories may be set out separately, thus:

```
Inventories:
    Department A...........................  $13,000.00
    Department B...........................   31,000.00
        Total..............................              $44,000.00
```

If there are very many departments, it is impracticable to detail the inventories; hence, they may be shown in total.

Gross profit less selling expenses by departments. If it is desired to have the income statement show gross profit less selling expenses by departments (as in the illustration on page 431), departmental selling expense accounts should be kept to the extent practicable. The trial balance in the working papers shows that, in this illustration, only the following departmental expense accounts were kept:

Salesmen's Salaries—Department A
Salesmen's Salaries—Department B

In many cases it is not practicable to identify selling expenses by departments at the time they are incurred; in such cases, one account is kept for each type of expense and some basis of apportionment for statement purposes is adopted. The balances of such accounts are frequently apportioned to departments in the ratio of sales by departments; but this is only a "rough and ready" method and is not likely to be very accurate because the departmental expenses are rarely, if ever, proportionate to the departmental sales.

If possible, some accurate basis of apportionment should be used for each expense. In the illustration, it is assumed that the store rent was apportioned by departments on the basis of floor space occupied, and that the advertising was apportioned on the basis of advertising space occupied. In some businesses it may be possible to apportion delivery expenses on the basis of the number of deliveries made for each department, with proper consideration of differences in weight and bulk of the merchandise of the various departments. In this illustration it is assumed that such a procedure is impracticable, and the apportionment was made on the basis of sales, as follows:

Department	Sales	Per Cent	Delivery Expense	Depreciation—Delivery Equipment
A..................	$ 75,000	37.5%	$1,500	$ 375
B..................	125,000	62.5	2,500	625
Total...........	$200,000	100.0%	$4,000	$1,000

THE RANDALIA COMPANY
Working Papers
Showing Gross Profit Less Selling Expenses by Departments
For the Year Ended December 31, 1958

	Trial Balance (After Adjustments)		Revenue and Expense — Department A		Department B		Unallocated	Retained Earnings		Balance Sheet	
Cash	8,030									8,030	
Accounts receivable	14,800									14,800	
Allowance for doubtful accounts		740									740
Notes receivable	3,000									3,000	
Accrued interest receivable	30									30	
Inventories—Dec. 31, 1957:											
Dept. A	17,000		17,000								
Dept. B	29,000				29,000						
Unexpired insurance	250									250	
Delivery equipment	4,000									4,000	
Accumulated depreciation—D. E.		2,000									2,000
Accounts payable		12,000									12,000
Notes payable		5,000									5,000
Federal income tax payable		1,000									1,000
Accrued salaries payable		90									90
Capital stock		50,000									50,000
Retained earnings—Dec. 31, 1957		5,995							5,995		
Dividends	5,000							5,000			
Sales:											
Dept. A		75,000		75,000							
Dept. B		125,000				125,000					
Sales returns and allowances:											
Dept. A	400		400								
Dept. B	900				900						
Sales discounts:											
Dept. A	600		600								
Dept. B	1,000				1,000						
Purchases:											
Dept. A	60,000		60,000								
Dept. B	90,000				90,000						
Purchase returns and allowances:											
Dept. A		600		600							
Dept. B		850				850					
Totals forward	234,010	278,275	78,000	75,600	120,900	125,850		5,000	5,995	30,110	70,830

Working Papers for the Year Ended December 31, 1958
(Concluded)

Account	Trial Balance (After Adjustments) Dr	Cr	Revenue and Expense — Dept. A Dr	Cr	Dept. B Dr	Cr	Unallocated Dr	Cr	Retained Earnings Dr	Cr	Balance Sheet Dr	Cr
Totals brought forward	234,010	278,275	78,000	75,600	120,900	125,850			5,000	5,995	30,110	70,830
Purchase discounts:												
Dept. A		390		390								
Dept. B		810				810						
Transportation in	1,800		720		1,080							
Store rent	6,000		2,400		3,600							
Advertising	4,000		1,600		2,400							
Salesmen's salaries:												
Dept. A	6,000		6,000									
Dept. B	7,000				7,000							
Delivery expense	4,000		1,500		2,500							
Depreciation—Delivery equipment	1,000		375		625							
Officers' salaries	10,000						10,000					
Office salaries	2,400						2,400					
Insurance	600						600					
Bad debts expense	420						420					
Miscellaneous general expenses	1,200						1,200					
Interest earned		80						80				
Interest expense	125						125					
Federal income tax	1,000						1,000					
	279,555	279,555										
Inventories—Dec. 31, 1958:												
Dept. A				13,000							13,000	
Dept. B						31,000					31,000	
Departmental income (loss*)			90,595	88,990	138,105	157,660	15,745	17,950				
			1,605*		19,555							
			88,990	88,990	157,660	157,660	18,030	18,030				
Net income—To Retained Earnings							2,285			2,285		
									5,000	8,280		
Retained earnings—Dec. 31, 1958									3,280			3,280
									8,280	8,280	74,110	74,110

THE RANDALIA COMPANY
Income Statement
Showing Gross Profit Less Selling Expenses by Departments
For the Year Ended December 31, 1958

	Department A	Department B	Total
Gross sales	$75,000	$125,000	$200,000
Deduct:			
Sales returns and allowances	$ 400	$ 900	$ 1,300
Sales discounts	600	1,000	1,600
	1,000	1,900	2,900
Net sales	$74,000	$123,100	$197,100
Deduct cost of goods sold:			
Purchases	$60,000	$90,000	$150,000
Deduct:			
Purchase returns and allowances	$600	$850	$1,450
Purchase discounts	390	810	1,200
	990	1,660	2,650
Net cost of purchases	$59,010	$88,340	$147,350
Add transportation in	720	1,080	1,800
Total	$59,730	$89,420	$149,150
Add inventory—December 31, 1957	17,000	29,000	46,000
Total cost of goods available for sale	$76,730	$118,420	$195,150
Deduct inventory—December 31, 1958	13,000	31,000	44,000
Cost of goods sold	63,730	87,420	151,150
Gross profit on sales	$10,270	$ 35,680	$ 45,950
Deduct selling expenses:			
Store rent	$ 2,400	$ 3,600	$ 6,000
Advertising	1,600	2,400	4,000
Salesmen's salaries	6,000	7,000	13,000
Delivery expense	1,500	2,500	4,000
Depreciation—Delivery equipment	375	625	1,000
Departmental income (loss*)	$ 1,605*	$ 19,555	$ 17,950
Deduct general expenses:			
Officers' salaries			$ 10,000
Office salaries			2,400
Insurance			600
Bad debts expense			420
Miscellaneous general expenses			1,200
			14,620
Net operating income			$ 3,330
Deduct net interest expense:			
Interest expense			125
Interest earned			80
			45
Net income before federal income tax			$ 3,285
Deduct federal income tax			1,000
Net income			$ 2,285

Dangers of approximations. To the extent that items of expense or income are allocated to departments by some method of approximation, the departmental income statement is affected by estimates and guesswork; unless management is constantly aware of this element of guesswork, unwise policies may be adopted.

Net income by departments. An income statement carried to the final point of net income or net loss is illustrated on page 433. It is assumed that:

(a) The bad debts expense by departments was determined by analyzing the accounts receivable.

(b) The office salaries, officers' salaries, and miscellaneous general expenses were apportioned to departments on the basis of sales, for want of a better basis.

Interest earned was apportioned on the basis of sales, on the assumption that the interest was earned on notes received from customers.

Interest expense was apportioned on the basis of purchases, on the assumption that funds were borrowed to finance purchases.

It is obvious that most of the foregoing assumptions are of doubtful validity and that the apportionments are subject to question. The computations are shown below:

Apportionments on Basis of Sales

	Total	Dept. A	Dept. B
Sales	$200,000	$75,000	$125,000
Per cent	100.0%	37.5%	62.5%
Office salaries	$ 2,400	$ 900	$ 1,500
Officers' salaries	10,000	3,750	6,250
Miscellaneous general expenses	1,200	450	750
Interest earned	80	30	50

Apportionment on Basis of Purchases

	Total	Dept. A	Dept. B
Purchases	$150,000	$60,000	$ 90,000
Per cent	100%	40%	60%
Interest expense	$ 125	$ 50	$ 75

(c) The insurance was apportioned to departments in the ratio of the average inventories, on the assumption that the premiums were paid for insurance on the merchandise. (Automobile insurance was charged to Delivery Expense.) The computation is shown below:

	Total	Dept. A	Dept. B
Inventories, December 31, 1957	$ 46,000	$17,000	$ 29,000
Inventories, December 31, 1958	44,000	13,000	31,000
Total	$ 90,000	$30,000	$ 60,000
Average inventories	$ 45,000	$15,000	$ 30,000
Fractions		$\frac{1}{3}$	$\frac{2}{3}$
Insurance	$ 600	$ 200	$ 400

THE RANDALIA COMPANY
Income Statement
Showing Net Income by Departments
For the Year Ended December 31, 1958

	Department A			Department B			Total		
Gross sales			$75,000			$125,000			$200,000
Deduct:									
Sales returns and allowances		$ 400			$ 900			$ 1,300	
Sales discounts		600	1,000		1,000	1,900		1,600	2,900
Net sales			$74,000			$123,100			$197,100
Deduct cost of goods sold:									
Purchases			$60,000			$ 90,000			$150,000
Deduct:									
Purchase returns and allowances	$ 600			$ 850			$ 1,450		
Purchase discounts	390	990		810	1,660		1,200	2,650	
Net cost of purchases		$59,010			$ 88,340			$147,350	
Add transportation in		720			1,080			1,800	
Total		$59,730			$ 89,420			$149,150	
Add inventory—December 31, 1957		17,000			29,000			46,000	
Total cost of goods available for sale		$76,730			$118,420			$195,150	
Deduct inventory—December 31, 1958		13,000			31,000			44,000	
Cost of goods sold			63,730			87,420			151,150
Gross profit on sales			$10,270			$ 35,680			$ 45,950
Deduct operating expenses:									
Selling expenses:									
Store rent	$2,400			$3,600			$ 6,000		
Advertising	1,600			2,400			4,000		
Salesmen's salaries	6,000			7,000			13,000		
Delivery expense	1,500			2,500			4,000		
Depreciation—Delivery equipment	375	$11,875		625	$ 16,125		1,000	$ 28,000	
General expenses:									
Officers' salaries	$3,750			$6,250			$10,000		
Office salaries	900			1,500			2,400		
Insurance	200			400			600		
Bad debts expense	150			270			420		
Miscellaneous general expenses	450	5,450		750	9,170		1,200	14,620	
Net operating income (loss*)		17,325	$ 7,055*		25,295	$ 10,385		42,620	$ 3,330
Deduct net interest expense:									
Interest expense		$ 50			$ 75			$ 125	
Interest earned		30	20		50	25		80	45
Net income (loss*) before federal income tax			$ 7,075*			$ 10,360			$ 3,285
Federal income tax (credit #)			2,000#			3,000			1,000
Net income (loss*)			$ 5,075*			$ 7,360			$ 2,285

Special attention is directed to the treatment of income tax in the income statement. On the assumption of the correctness of the expense and revenue apportionments to departments, Department A suffered a loss, which reduced the income tax. Although this assumption is of doubtful validity, consistency requires that Department B be charged with income tax in the amount which would have been payable on its net income, and that Department A be given credit for the tax reduction resulting from its net loss.

Significance of the statement. Because the apportionments of expenses are to such a large degree based on assumptions which may not be valid, complete reliance should not be placed on the amounts shown as net loss for Department A and net income for Department B.

Moreover, even if no assumptions had been made in the allocation of expenses to departments, the fact that Department A shows a loss should not be accepted as a conclusive reason for discontinuing the department. The discontinuance of Department A would result in eliminating all the gross profit resulting from its operations, but it would not result in eliminating all the expenses which were charged to it. Before reaching any decision with respect to the advisability of discontinuing Department A, the management should make a study of the expenses and the miscellaneous revenue for the purpose of determining the probable reductions which would result from such a discontinuance. The following statement is assumed to be the result of such a study.

Probable Reduction in Expenses and Miscellaneous Revenue Which Would Result from Discontinuance of Department A

	Charged to Department A	EFFECT OF DISCONTINUANCE OF DEPARTMENT A	
		Eliminated	Not Eliminated
Selling expenses:			
Store rent...................	$ 2,400.00		$2,400.00
Advertising..................	1,600.00	$1,600.00	
Salesmen's salaries..........	6,000.00	6,000.00	
Delivery expense............	1,500.00		1,500.00
Depreciation—Delivery equipment....	375.00		375.00
Total selling expenses......	$11,875.00	$7,600.00	$4,275.00
General expenses:			
Officers' salaries............	$ 3,750.00		$3,750.00
Office salaries..............	900.00		900.00
Insurance...................	200.00	$ 200.00	
Bad debts expense...........	150.00	150.00	
Miscellaneous general expenses.......	450.00	150.00	300.00
Total general expenses......	$ 5,450.00	$ 500.00	$4,950.00
Interest earned..............	$ 30.00	$ 30.00	
Interest expense.............	$ 50.00	$ 50.00	

The first column shows the items of expense and revenue which appear in the Department A columns of the income statement on page 433. The second column shows the items which, in the opinion of the management, would be eliminated if Department A were discontinued. The third column shows the items which the management believes would not be eliminated. The management's conclusions were reached as follows:

The store rent would not be reduced, because the entire space would have to be retained under the lease. The advertising and salesmen's salary charges could be eliminated. The delivery equipment and the driver would have to be retained to make deliveries for Department B. There is only one office employee, and no portion of her salary could be eliminated. The officers' salaries would not be reduced. Since the merchandise inventory of Department A would be eliminated, the insurance cost applicable to it would be eliminated. It is estimated that one-third of the miscellaneous general expenses apportioned to Department A could be eliminated. With the discontinuance of sales by Department A, there would be no bad debt losses in that department. Without Department A, the interest earned on receivables arising from Department A sales, and the interest expense incurred to make purchases for that department, would disappear.

The consequences of discontinuing Department A can now be estimated as follows:

Estimated Effect on Net Income Before Income Tax Which Would Result from Discontinuance of Department A

Net income of Departments A and B before income tax.........		$3,285.00
Net income which would be lost by discontinuing Department A:		
Income lost:		
Gross profit on sales.......................	$10,270.00	
Interest earned...........................	30.00	
Total income lost.......................	$10,300.00	
Expense reductions:		
Selling expenses.................. $7,600.00		
General expenses................. 500.00		
Interest expense................. 50.00		
Total expense reduction..................	8,150.00	
Net income lost....................................		2,150.00
Resulting net income before income tax......................		$1,135.00

This statement indicates that, although the statement on page 433 shows that Department A had a net loss of $7,075 before income tax adjustment, the elimination of that department would not increase the net income of the business but would reduce it from $3,285 to $1,135 before income taxes.

Contribution to overhead. Some accountants now prepare statements in which no attempt is made to show the net income,

THE RANDALIA COMPANY
Income Statement
For the Year Ended December 31, 1958

	Department A			Department B			Total		
Gross sales			$75,000			$125,000			$200,000
Deduct:									
Sales returns and allowances		$400			$900			$1,300	
Sales discounts		600	1,000		1,000	1,900		1,600	2,900
Net sales			$74,000			$123,100			$197,100
Deduct cost of goods sold:									
Purchases		$60,000			$90,000			$150,000	
Deduct:									
Purchase returns and allowances	$600			$850			$1,450		
Purchase discounts	390	990		810	1,660		1,200	2,650	
Net cost of purchases		$59,010			$88,340			$147,350	
Add transportation in		720			1,080			1,800	
Total		$59,730			$89,420			$149,150	
Add inventory—December 31, 1957		17,000			29,000			46,000	
Total cost of goods available for sale		$76,730			$118,420			$195,150	
Deduct inventory—December 31, 1958		13,000			31,000			44,000	
Cost of goods sold			63,730			87,420			151,150
Gross profit on sales			$10,270			$35,680			$45,950
Add interest and other income			30			50			80
Total gross profit and other income			$10,300			$35,730			$46,080
Deduct direct departmental expenses:									
Advertising		$1,600			$2,400			$4,000	
Salesmen's salaries		6,000			7,000			13,000	
Insurance		200			400			600	
Miscellaneous general expenses		150			250			400	
Bad debts expense		150			270			420	
Interest expense		50			75			125	
Total direct departmental expenses			8,150			10,395			18,545
Contribution to nondepartmental overhead			$2,150			$25,335			$27,485
Deduct nondepartmental overhead:									
Store rent								$6,000	
Delivery expense								4,000	
Depreciation—Delivery equipment								1,000	
Officers' salaries								10,000	
Office salaries								2,400	
Miscellaneous general expenses								800	
Total nondepartmental overhead									24,200
Net income before federal income tax									$3,285
Deduct federal income tax									1,000
Net income									$2,285

or even the gross profit less selling expenses, by departments. Instead, each department is credited with the revenue and charged with the expenses which, in the opinion of the management, would disappear if the department were discontinued. The excess of such revenue over the "direct" departmental expenses represents the contribution of the department to what may be called the overhead of the business as a whole, or nondepartmental overhead. Such a statement is illustrated on page 436.

CHAPTER 27

Consignments. Installment Sales. Branches

Consignments

Definitions. A *consignment* is a shipment of merchandise from the owner (called the *consignor*) to another party (called the *consignee*) who becomes the agent of the owner for the purpose of selling the goods. Each consignment is:

A consignment out from the standpoint of the consignor.
A consignment in from the standpoint of the consignee.

Why consignments are made. A person may be willing to accept goods on consignment although he would not be willing to purchase them, because of:

(1) Market fluctuations. In the produce field, for instance, market prices are subject to sudden and often unpredictable fluctuations. To avoid the risk of price declines that might occur between the purchase date and the date the goods are received and are available for resale, commission merchants take the produce on consignment and sell it for the consignor at the price obtainable.

(2) The risk of tying up capital in unsalable merchandise. If merchandise is purchased, it must be paid for in accordance with the credit terms, regardless of the length of time it may remain on the purchaser's shelves. But if the goods are accepted on consignment, there is no obligation to remit for them until they are sold.

The owner of the merchandise may:

(1) Prefer to ship goods on consignment rather than sell them, in order to avoid credit risks; goods consigned to a person who becomes insolvent can be recovered.

(2) Be forced to place goods on consignment to introduce a new product which distributors are unwilling to purchase.

Accounting for consignments. The consignor should not record consignments as sales, and the consignee should not record them as purchases, because there is no change in the ownership of the goods.

Since the consignor has not made a sale, he should not take up any profit at the time of making the consignment; the sales entry should not be made until a sale has been reported by the consignee.

Any unsold consigned goods in the hands of the consignee at the end of the accounting period should be included in the consignor's inventory.

Consignor's entries. There are various methods of keeping a record of consignments out. The following illustration shows one method of achieving the desired objectives.

Shipment of merchandise. Wallson Company shipped 10 radios to Lowry and Woodruff on November 18; these radios cost Wallson Company $40 each. Although this transaction is not a sale, some entry should be made so that the books will contain a record of the consignment. The following journal entry shows the cost of the goods shipped:

```
Nov. 18   Consignment out—Lowry and Woodruff......  400.00
               Consignment shipments.................          400.00
          Shipment of 10 radios.
```

A separate Consignment Out account is opened with each consignee, but one Consignment Shipments account is credited with the cost of all goods shipped.

Payment of freight. Wallson Company paid $20 freight on November 19. Since the goods were not sold, the freight should not be charged to Freight Out. The freight is a cost incurred on the consignment; to indicate this fact, the debit is made to the Consignment Out account.

```
Nov. 19   Consignment out—Lowry and Woodruff......   20.00
               Cash...............................           20.00
          Payment of freight.
```

Consignee's report of sales. On November 28 the consignor receives an *account sales* from the consignee (see top of page 440); it reports the sale of six of the ten radios consigned.

In recording the sale of the consigned goods, Wallson Company should:

(1) Reverse the memorandum entry for the cost of the six radios sold, thus:

```
Nov. 28   Consignment shipments....................  240.00
               Consignment out—Lowry and Woodruff..          240.00
          Reverse memo entry for cost of 6 consigned
          radios sold by consignee.
```

(2) Charge off the freight applicable to the six radios sold, thus:

```
Nov. 28   Freight out..............................   12.00
               Consignment out—Lowry and Woodruff..           12.00
          Freight applicable to 6 radios sold.
```

LOWRY AND WOODRUFF
Peoria, Illinois

November 28, 19—

Account sales of   6 Wallson radios

Sold for account and risk of

Wallson Company

Chicago, Illinois

Sales:
        6 radios at $82.50 $495.00

Charges:
        Advertising $60.00
        Commission—20% of $495.00   99.00   159.00
Proceeds—Check enclosed $336.00

Consigned merchandise unsold   4 radios

---

(3) Record the facts shown by the account sales.

Nov. 28	Advertising..............................	60.00	
	Commissions to consignee..................	99.00	
	Cash..................................	336.00	
	Sales...............................		495.00
	Sales, expense, and commission reported by		
	consignee.		

After these entries are posted, the Consignment Out and the Consignment Shipments accounts will appear as follows:

Consignment Out—Lowry and Woodruff

19—			19—		
Nov. 18	Cost of 10 radios con-		Nov. 28	Cost of 6 radios sold...	240.00
	signed.............	400.00	28	Freight on 6 radios sold	12.00
19	Freight paid.........	20.00			

(The account has a debit balance of $168.)

Consignment Shipments

19—			19—		
Nov. 28	Cost of 6 radios sold...	240.00	Nov. 18	Cost of 10 radios	
				shipped.............	400.00

(The account has a credit balance of $160.)

Assuming that the consignor's books are to be closed at the end of November, the working papers will contain the following items:

Working Papers

	Trial Balance		Adjustments and Eliminations		Income Statement	Statement of Retained Earnings	Balance Sheet
Consignment out— L. & W..........	168			160a			8
Consignment shipments..........		160	160a				
	Tot	als					
Inventories—November 30:							
On hand—Determined by taking an inventory.................................					5,000		5,000
On consignment—Determined by balance of Consignment Shipments account.........					160		160

The inventories may be shown in the balance sheet detailed as follows:

Inventories:
    On hand.................. $5,000
    On consignment............ 168

The $168 valuation of the inventory on consignment includes the $160 cost of the radios and the $8 freight cost incurred in getting them to the place where they are offered for sale.

Consignee's entries. The consignee's entries are illustrated below:

Receipt of the merchandise. Lowry and Woodruff (the consignees) will make no debit and credit entries for the receipt of the merchandise, but will make a memorandum entry in a Consignment In account, as illustrated in the account below.

Sales of consigned goods. As sales of the consigned goods are made, the consignee will debit Cash (or Accounts Receivable) and credit Consignment In—Wallson Company.

Payment of expenses. The $60 payment for advertising would be recorded by debiting Consignment In—Wallson Company and crediting Cash.

Charge for commission. The $99 charge for commission would be recorded by debiting Consignment In—Wallson Company and crediting Consignment Commissions Earned.

Cash remitted to consignor. The payment of cash to the consignor would be recorded by debiting Consignment In—Wallson Company and crediting Cash.

After these entries were made and posted, the Consignment In account would appear as follows:

Consignment In—Wallson Company

19—			19—		
Nov. 20	10 radios		Various		
21	Advertising............	60.00	dates	Sales (6 radios)........	495.00
28	Commission...........	99.00			
28	Cash remitted.........	336.00			

A consignment in account may have a credit balance by reason of the fact that debits for commissions, expenses, and remittances were less than the sales proceeds. Such a credit balance should be shown as a current liability in the balance sheet.

The account will have a debit balance if there are debits for expenses and no credits for sales, or if the debits for expenses and commissions exceed the credits for sales. A debit balance should be shown as a current asset in the balance sheet.

Installment Sales

Nature of installment sales. An installment sale is a sales arrangement whereby the selling price is collected in periodical installments. A down payment usually is required. The uncollected balance may or may not be subject to interest. By mortgage or otherwise, the seller usually has the right to recover the sold property if the installments are not collected in accordance with the sales agreement.

Accounting procedure. The installment accounting procedure consists of taking the gross profit on installment sales into income in installments on the basis of cash collections. Each collection is regarded as including gross profit and a return of cost in the same proportion that these elements are included in the selling price. For instance, if a sale price of $150 included $100 cost and $50 gross profit, a collection of $15 would be regarded as including a $10 return of cost and $5 of gross profit. There are several reasons why a better matching of revenue and expense by periods may be achieved by taking the gross profit into income in the periods when collections are received than by taking it into income in the period of sale.

In the first place, it is somewhat more difficult to estimate the allowance required for collection losses on installment sales than on ordinary sales. The opportunity to make payments in installments appeals to people who are not in a financial position to make immediate payment or to make payment on a short-term credit basis, and who, in many cases, prove to be unable or unwilling to make payment even in installments. The right of recovery is not always an adequate protection to the seller, because of the status of the property as second-hand merchandise.

In the second place, installment sales involve more expenses in periods subsequent to the period of sale than are usually incurred in connection with ordinary sales. There are more collection and accounting costs. Also, the seller may find it necessary to make repairs to the property before the sale price is completely collected because the purchaser may otherwise refuse to make additional payments or to protect the seller's equity in the property which serves as security. And, if the merchandise is repossessed, costs may be incurred in reconditioning it for resale.

A satisfactory matching of revenue and expense could theoretically be achieved by taking the gross profit into income in the period of sale and making provisions in the same period for subsequent losses and expenses; but from a practical standpoint, the difficulty of making reliable estimates of losses and expenses often makes such a procedure unsatisfactory.

Illustration of procedure—Single sale. As a simple illustration of the accounting procedure applied in taking up profits on the basis of the gross profit element included in each collection, let us assume the following facts:

```
Sale—July 15, 1957............................ $1,500
Cost.........................................  1,000
Gross profit.................................    500
Ratio of gross profit to selling price—33⅓%.

Collections during the year of sale:
  Down payment..............................  $  300
  Five monthly payments of $150 each........     750
```

The sale is recorded by the following entry:

```
1957
July 15   Accounts receivable—A customer.................. 1,500.00
            Cost of installment sales (Nature, purpose, and
              disposition of this account explained later).....          1,000.00
            Deferred gross profit on installment sales........            500.00

          Cash...........................................  300.00
            Accounts receivable—A customer..............            300.00
```

Assuming that installments are collected regularly on the first of each month, the customer's account at the end of the year will appear as follows:

A Customer

1957			1957		
July 15	Sale	1,500.00	July 15	Cash	300.00
			Aug. 1	Cash	150.00
			Sept. 1	Cash	150.00
			Oct. 1	Cash	150.00
			Nov. 1	Cash	150.00
			Dec. 1	Cash	150.00

Since $1,050 has been collected, and since the ratio of gross profit to selling price is 33⅓%, the gross profit regarded as realized during the year is one-third of $1,050, or $350. This realized portion of gross profit is taken into income for the year by the following entry:

```
1957
Dec. 31   Deferred gross profit on installment sales......  350.00
               Realized gross profit on installment sales..         350.00
               To take up the portion of the gross profit on
               installment sales realized by collections.
```

After this entry is posted, the two gross profit accounts will appear as follows:

Deferred Gross Profit on Installment Sales

1957	1957
Dec. 31 To Realized Gross Profit	July 15 Total gross profit...... 500.00
on Installment Sales. 350.00	

Realized Gross Profit on Installment Sales

	1957
	Dec. 31 From Deferred Gross
	Profit............. 350.00

The Realized Gross Profit account is closed to Revenue and Expense.

A subsequent section of this chapter contains a statement of the balance sheet presentation of any balance in the Deferred Gross Profit account.

If the remaining installments are collected in 1958, the remaining $150 of deferred gross profit will be transferred to the Realized Gross Profit account.

Disposition of Cost of Installment Sales account. Assume that the company which made this installment sale made other sales not collectible in installments, and that its accounts at the end of the year contained the following balances:

```
Inventory, December 31, 1956..................   5,000.00
Purchases.....................................  25,000.00
Cost of installment sales.....................          1,000.00
```

Also assume that the inventory on December 31, 1957, was $6,000. The closing entries would include the following:

```
1957
Dec. 31   Revenue and expense................. 30,000.00
               Inventory, December 31, 1956.....            5,000.00
               Purchases.......................           25,000.00

      31   Inventory, December 31, 1957.........  6,000.00
           Cost of installment sales............  1,000.00
               Revenue and expense.............            7,000.00
```

The net debit of $23,000 to Revenue and Expense is the cost of goods sold on regular terms.

Showing gross profits in the income statement. Assuming that sales on regular terms amounted to $30,000, the total gross profit realized in 1957 would be shown in the income statement as follows:

Partial Income Statement

Sales—Other than installment sales......................................			$30,000.00
Less cost thereof:			
Inventory, December 31, 1956.........................	$ 5,000.00		
Purchases..	25,000.00		
Total...	$30,000.00		
Deduct:			
Inventory, December 31, 1957.............	$6,000.00		
Cost of installment sales.................	1,000.00	7,000.00	23,000.00
Gross profit on regular sales...			$ 7,000.00
Realized gross profit on installment sales............................			350.00
Total gross profit...			$ 7,350.00

Illustration—Numerous sales. When numerous installment sales are made, it is impracticable to attempt to compute the rate of gross profit on each sale and to apply a separate rate of gross profit to the collections from each sale. Instead, an average rate of gross profit on all installment sales for a year may be applied to the collections on receivables resulting from installment sales of that year.

To assemble the required information, an installment sales register similar to the following may be kept.

Installment Sales Register

Date	Customer's Name	Address	Invoice Number	Sales	Cost
1958					
Jan. 2	Frank Henderson	1140 Inglewood, Chicago 17	1	350.00	250.00
3	D. O. Franklin	347 Oak Ave., Berwyn, Ill.	2	200.00	140.00

The individual entries would be posted daily, and the column totals would be posted monthly. Assuming that the column totals for January were $6,000 and $4,200, the entry for January would be:

1958			
Jan. 31	Accounts receivable...............................	6,000.00	
	Cost of installment sales......................		4,200.00
	Deferred gross profit on installment sales........		1,800.00

Assume that totals for the year were:

Installment sales....................	$75,000
Cost of installment sales............	51,000
Average rate of gross profit—32%	
Collections.......................	45,000

The accounts, after taking up the portion of the gross profit regarded as realized, and after closing the books, would have total entries as follows:

Accounts Receivable

Installment sales........... 75,000.00	Collections................ 45,000.00

Cost of Installment Sales

To Revenue and Expense.... 51,000.00	Total..................... 51,000.00

Deferred Gross Profit on Installment Sales

To Realized Gross Profit on Installment Sales—32% of $45,000................. 14,400.00	Total..................... 24,000.00

Realized Gross Profit on Installment Sales

	From Deferred Gross Profit on Installment Sales......... 14,400.00

Defaults and repossessions. If a customer defaults in the payment of installments, and if no further collections can be expected, both his account and the deferred gross profit applicable to the uncollectible installments should be written off.

A default by a customer usually results in the repossession of the merchandise by the seller. It should be recorded at its value at the time of repossession.

To illustrate, assume the following facts relative to a repossession from A. B. Harvey:

Balance of account receivable..............	$60
Applicable rate of gross profit..............	30%
Deferred gross profit applicable to uncollected balance—30% of $60..................	$18
Value of repossessed article................	$35

The entry to record the repossession would be:

Repossessed merchandise inventory.....................	35.00	
Deferred gross profit on installment sales................	18.00	
Loss on repossession...................................	7.00	
Accounts receivable—A. B. Harvey.................		60.00

The value of the repossessed merchandise may be sufficient to produce a gain on the repossession.

Balance sheet presentation. Installment receivables may be classified as current assets. This treatment is approved in Bulletin 43 of the American Institute's Committee on Accounting Procedure if the installment receivables "conform generally to normal trade practices and terms within the business."

With regard to the location of the balance of the Deferred Gross Profit on Installment Sales account in the balance sheet, the traditional and customary procedure is to show it immediately above the Owners' Equity section under a Deferred Income or Deferred Credits caption.

Home Office and Branch Accounting

Recording transactions between home office and branch. A company operating a store in the city of H decides to open a branch in the town of B. Books will be kept at the home office in H and at the branch in B. In addition to the usual purchase, sale, and expense transactions, it will be necessary to record transactions between the home office and the branch, such as:

Shipments of merchandise from the home office to the branch.
> Recorded on the home office books by debiting Branch Current and crediting Shipments to Branch.
> Recorded on the branch books by debiting Shipments from Home Office and crediting Home Office Current.

Remittances of cash from the home office to the branch.
> Recorded on the home office books by debiting Branch Current and crediting Cash.
> Recorded on the branch books by debiting Cash and crediting Home Office Current.

Remittances of cash from the branch to the home office.
> Recorded on the home office books by debiting Cash and crediting Branch Current.
> Recorded on the branch books by debiting Home Office Current and crediting Cash.

Assume that the branch was organized on January 1, 1958, and that the totals of the entries in the two current accounts during the year were as follows:

Branch Current

Cash sent to branch............	1,000	Cash received from branch.......	4,000
Merchandise sent to branch.....	15,000		

(This account has a debit balance of $12,000.)

Home Office Current

Cash sent to home office.........	4,000	Cash received from home office..	1,000
		Merchandise from home office...	15,000

(This account has a credit balance of $12,000.)

These two current accounts are reciprocal; that is, the debit balance in the Branch Current account (on the home office books) is equal to the credit balance in the Home Office Current account (on the branch books).

Trial balances. Following are the trial balances of the home office and branch books at the end of the year.

COMPANY *H*
Home Office and Branch Trial Balances After Adjustments
December 31, 1958

	Home Office		Branch	
Cash.................................	38,500		7,300	
Accounts receivable.................	5,000		1,000	
Allowance for doubtful accounts......		750		100
Inventory, December 31, 1957........	4,000			
Branch current.....................	12,000			
Home office current.................				12,000
Accounts payable...................		3,000		100
Common stock......................		50,000		
Retained earnings..................		7,500		
Shipments to branch.................		15,000		
Shipments from home office..........			15,000	
Sales.............................		25,000		12,000
Purchases.........................	40,000		300	
Expenses..........................	1,500		500	
Bad debts expense..................	250		100	
	101,250	101,250	24,200	24,200
Inventories, December 31, 1958.......	8,000		4,500	

Branch statements and closing entries. The branch income statement and balance sheet appear below:

BRANCH *B*
Income Statement
For the Year Ended December 31, 1958

Sales..			$12,000
Deduct cost of goods sold:			
Shipments from home office......................		$15,000	
Purchases......................................		300	
Total.......................................		$15,300	
Deduct inventory, December 31, 1958.............		4,500	
Remainder—Cost of goods sold.......................			10,800
Gross profit on sales......................................			$ 1,200
Deduct:			
Expenses.......................................	$	500	
Bad debts expense..............................		100	600
Net income—To Home Office Current......................		$	600

BRANCH *B*
Balance Sheet
December 31, 1958

Assets			Liabilities and Home Office	
Cash.......................		$ 7,300	Liabilities:	
Accounts receivable.... $1,000			Accounts payable........... $	100
Less allowance for doubtful accounts.. 100		900	Home office current..........	12,600
Inventory...................		4,500		
		$12,700		$12,700

The $12,600 credit balance in the Home Office Current account is the sum of the $12,000 balance resulting from home office-branch transactions during the year and the $600 net income.

The books of a branch are closed in exactly the same way that the books of a separate company would be closed, with one exception: there is no Retained Earnings account on the branch books; the Home Office Current account serves as the owner's equity account; therefore, the Revenue and Expense account is closed to the Home Office Current account.

```
Sales.............................................  12,000
Inventory, December 31, 1958......................   4,500
    Revenue and expense...........................          16,500
    To close the Sales account and record the end-of-year
    inventory.

Revenue and expense...............................  15,900
    Shipments from home office....................          15,000
    Purchases.....................................             300
    Expenses......................................             500
    Bad debts expense.............................             100
    To close operating accounts with debit balances.

Revenue and expense...............................     600
    Home office current...........................             600
    To close the Revenue and Expense account.
```

Home office statements and closing entries.   When the home office receives the branch's income statement, it makes this entry:

```
Branch current....................................  $ 600
    Income from branch operations.................            600
    To take up the net income of the branch.
```

The home office then prepares the following statements (income **tax** ignored):

COMPANY H

Income Statement
For the Year Ended December 31, 1958

```
Sales.............................................................  $25,000
Deduct cost of goods sold:
    Inventory, December 31, 1957...................  $ 4,000
    Purchases......................................   40,000
        Total......................................  $44,000
    Deduct:
        Shipments to branch...........  $15,000
        Inventory, December 31, 1958..    8,000   23,000
    Cost of goods sold.............................           21,000
Gross profit on sales.............................           $ 4,000
Deduct:
    Expenses.......................................  $ 1,500
    Bad debts expense..............................      250    1,750
Net income from home office operations............           $ 2,250
Add net income from branch operations.............              600
Net income........................................           $ 2,850
```

COMPANY *H*
Statement of Retained Earnings
For the Year Ended December 31, 1958

Balance, December 31, 1957	$ 7,500
Net income for year	2,850
Balance, December 31, 1958	$10,350

COMPANY *H*
Balance Sheet
December 31, 1958

Assets			Liabilities and Stockholders' Equity		
Cash		$38,500	Liabilities:		
Accounts receivable.... $5,000			Accounts payable		$ 3,000
Less allowance for doubtful accounts..	750	4,250	Stockholders' equity:		
Inventory		8,000	Common stock..... $50,000		
Investment in branch		12,600	Retained earnings...	10,350	60,350
		$63,350			$63,350

Following are the home office closing entries:

Sales	25,000	
Shipments to branch	15,000	
Income from branch operations	600	
Inventory, December 31, 1958	8,000	
Revenue and expense		48,600
To close operating accounts with credit balances and record the end-of-year inventory.		
Revenue and expense	45,750	
Inventory, December 31, 1957		4,000
Purchases		40,000
Expenses		1,500
Bad debts expense		250
To close operating accounts with debit balances.		
Revenue and expense	2,850	
Retained earnings		2,850
To close the Revenue and Expense account.		

Combined statements.   The separate statements for the home office and the branch do not show the total sales, purchases, expenses, assets, and liabilities of the company as a whole.   The working papers on page 451 assemble the information required for combined statements.   They were prepared by cross-adding the amounts in the two trial balances, with the exception of the two current accounts and the two shipments accounts; these reflect transactions and relations between the home office and the branch, and are eliminated because the combined statements should show only transactions and relations of the company with the outside world.

COMPANY H
Home Office and Branch
Combined Working Papers
For the Year Ended December 31, 1958

	Trial Balances				Eliminations		Income Statement		Statement of Retained Earnings		Balance Sheet	
	Home Office Dr	Home Office Cr	Branch Dr	Branch Cr	Dr	Cr	Dr	Cr	Dr	Cr	Dr	Cr
Cash	38,500		7,300								45,800	
Accounts receivable	5,000		1,000								6,000	
Allowance for doubtful accounts		750		100								850
Inventory, December 31, 1957	4,000						4,000					
Branch current	12,000					12,000A						
Home office current				12,000	12,000A							
Accounts payable		3,000		100								3,100
Common stock		50,000										50,000
Retained earnings		7,500								7,500		
Shipments to branch		15,000			15,000B							
Shipments from home office			15,000			15,000B						
Sales		25,000		12,000				37,000				
Purchases	40,000		300				40,300					
Expenses	1,500		500				2,000					
Bad debts expense	250		100				350					
	101,250	101,250	24,200	24,200	27,000	27,000	46,650	49,500				
Inventories, December 31, 1958	8,000		4,500					12,500			12,500	
Net income							2,850			2,850		
							49,500	49,500		10,350		
Retained earnings, December 31, 1958									10,350			10,350
									10,350	10,350	64,300	64,300

Following are the statements prepared from the foregoing working papers:

COMPANY *H*
Home Office and Branch
Income Statement
For the Year Ended December 31, 1958

Sales..		$37,000
Deduct cost of goods sold:		
Inventory, December 31, 1957....................	$ 4,000	
Purchases......................................	40,300	
Total.......................................	$44,300	
Deduct inventory, December 31, 1958.............	12,500	31,800
Gross profit on sales....................................		$ 5,200
Deduct:		
Expenses.......................................	$ 2,000	
Bad debts expense..............................	350	2,350
Net income...		$ 2,850

COMPANY *H*
Home Office and Branch
Statement of Retained Earnings
For the Year Ended December 31, 1958

Balance, December 31, 1957.............................	$ 7,500
Net income for the year................................	2,850
Balance, December 31, 1958.............................	$10,350

COMPANY *H*
Home Office and Branch
Balance Sheet
December 31, 1958

Assets			Liabilities and Stockholders' Equity		
Cash........................		$45,800	Liabilities:		
Accounts receivable....	$6,000		Accounts payable..........		$ 3,100
Less allowance for					
doubtful accounts..	850	5,150	Stockholders' equity:		
Inventory...................		12,500	Common stock.....	$50,000	
			Retained earnings...	10,350	60,350
		$63,450			$63,450

CHAPTER 28
Consolidated Statements

Parents and subsidiaries. If one company owns all of, or a controlling interest (more than fifty per cent) in, the voting stock of another company, a parent-and-subsidiary relationship exists. The company that owns the stock is the parent; the company whose stock is owned by the parent is the subsidiary. When a parent-and-subsidiary relationship exists, it may be desirable, for reasons to be stated later, to prepare consolidated statements.

Consolidated Balance Sheets

Balance sheet at date of organization of subsidiary. To show in a very simple way the nature of a consolidated balance sheet, let us assume that Company *P*, incorporated in Illinois, operated a branch in another state. The state in which the branch was located required Company *P* to pay a franchise tax for the privilege of operating in the state as a foreign corporation. It also levied a tax on the portion of the net income of Company *P* earned by the branch operations, and the management of Company *P* questioned the fairness of the method that it was required to use in computing the portion of its net income subject to this tax. To avoid the payment of the franchise tax and to establish definitely the amount of net income subject to tax, the management decided to organize a subsidiary in the state where the branch had operated.

On December 31, 1956, the date when the subsidiary was organized, the branch had the following assets and liabilities:

```
Assets:
  Cash.......................................... $13,000
  Accounts receivable...........................  15,000
  Merchandise inventory.........................  30,000
    Total assets......................................... $58,000
Liabilities:
  Accounts payable.......................................   8,000
Net assets............................................... $50,000
```

Company *P* transferred these assets and liabilities to the subsidiary, Company *S*, in exchange for the subsidiary's entire capital stock—$50,000.

After the transfer of assets and liabilities to the subsidiary, Company *P*'s balance sheet appeared as shown on page 454.

Although this balance sheet correctly reflects the financial position of Company *P*, it is not wholly satisfactory, for two reasons.

COMPANY *P*
Balance Sheet
December 31, 1956

Assets		Liabilities and Stockholders' Equity		
Cash	$ 30,000	Accounts payable		$ 27,000
Accounts receivable	25,000			
Merchandise inventory	65,000	Stockholders' equity:		
Investment in stock of Company *S*	50,000	Common stock	$100,000	
		Retained earnings	43,000	143,000
	$170,000			$170,000

First, although the investment in the subsidiary is nearly one-third of the total assets of the parent and is equal to more than one-third of its total stockholders' equity, no information is given about the underlying net assets which give it value. Second, it does not give a comprehensive picture of the financial position of the parent and subsidiary combined; this is important information because, although the parent and subsidiary are separate *legal* entities, they are essentially a unit from a *business* standpoint.

To show the financial position of a parent and its subsidiary as a single business enterprise, a consolidated balance sheet may be prepared. Following are the working papers in which the information for a consolidated balance sheet of the parent and its subsidiary is assembled, and the consolidated balance sheet.

COMPANY *P* AND SUBSIDIARY
Consolidated Balance Sheet Working Papers
December 31, 1956

	Balance Sheets		Intercompany Eliminations		Consolidated Balance Sheet
	Company *P*	Company *S*			
Assets					
Cash	30,000	13,000			43,000
Accounts receivable	25,000	15,000			40,000
Merchandise inventory	65,000	30,000			95,000
Investment in Company *S*	50,000			50,000	
	170,000	58,000			178,000
Liabilities and Stockholders' Equity					
Accounts payable	27,000	8,000			35,000
Common stock:					
Company *P*	100,000				100,000
Company *S*		50,000	50,000		
Retained earnings	43,000				43,000
	170,000	58,000	50,000	50,000	178,000

COMPANY *P* AND SUBSIDIARY
Consolidated Balance Sheet
December 31, 1956

Assets		Liabilities and Stockholders' Equity		
Cash	$ 43,000	Accounts payable		$ 35,000
Accounts receivable	40,000	Stockholders' equity:		
Merchandise inventory	95,000	Common stock	$100,000	
		Retained earnings	43,000	143,000
	$178,000			$178,000

Observe that the parent's Investment account and the subsidiary's Common Stock account are eliminated in the working papers and are not shown in the consolidated balance sheet. The reason for the elimination may be stated as follows: A consolidated balance sheet is a statement of the financial position of a group of affiliated companies in relation to the outside world, with all intercompany relationships eliminated. Company *P*'s Investment account reflects the intercompany relationship on the parent's books, and Company *S*'s Common Stock account reflects the intercompany relationship on the subsidiary's books.

Other eliminations are illustrated later in the chapter.

A parent's unconsolidated balance sheet and a consolidated balance sheet (see page 454) serve different purposes. An unconsolidated balance sheet should be used when it is desired to show the financial position of the parent company from a legal standpoint as a separate corporate entity. A consolidated balance sheet may be used when the legal reality of separate corporate entities can safely be ignored and it is desired to show, in a single statement, all of the assets that the parent company owns or controls through stock ownership, and all of the liabilities to which these assets are subject. To show the financial position from both points of view, parent companies sometimes publish both an unconsolidated balance sheet and a consolidated balance sheet.

Consolidated Income Statement, Consolidated Statement of Retained Earnings, and Consolidated Balance Sheet

Consolidated income statement. A parent company's unconsolidated income statement shows, as income, dividends received or receivable from the subsidiary as the result of dividend declarations by the subsidiary during the period. This is correct from a legal standpoint; since the parent and the subsidiary are separate corporate entities, the earnings of the subsidiary are not earnings of the parent until they are passed on to the parent in the form of dividends.

But the dividends paid or declared by a subsidiary during a year may bear little or no relation to the subsidiary's net income for the year. For instance, the subsidiary may have a net income of $25,000 and pay a $6,000 dividend; or it may have a net loss of $25,000 and pay a $6,000 dividend from earnings accumulated in prior years. Therefore, the sum of the parent's earnings from its own operations during a year and the dividends paid or payable to it as a result of dividend declarations by the subsidiary during the year is not an accurate measure of the parent's interest in the net income of the group of companies as a whole.

The consolidated net income of a parent and subsidiary is shown by a consolidated income statement. It is prepared by combining the revenue and expense accounts of the parent and subsidiary, after eliminating revenue and expense account balances, or portions thereof, resulting from intercompany transactions.

Dividends received by the parent from the subsidiary are not shown in the consolidated income statement; from the viewpoint of the combined entity, such dividends are not income but are merely transfers of assets. They are eliminated in the working papers by a debit to the parent's dividend income account and a credit to the subsidiary's account showing dividends paid.

Consolidated statement of retained earnings. The consolidated statement of retained earnings shows the consolidated retained earnings at the beginning of the period, the consolidated net income for the period, any dividends declared by the parent company during the period, and the consolidated retained earnings at the end of the period.

First illustration. Working papers for the preparation of a consolidated income statement and a consolidated statement of retained earnings of Company *P* and its subsidiary for the year ended December 31, 1957, and a consolidated balance sheet at the end of the year are shown on page 457. They were prepared as follows:

The trial balances of the two companies were entered in the first two columns.

Eliminations were made as follows:

A—Book value of subsidiary stock at date of acquisition, $50,000.

B—Intercompany receivable and payable, $5,000.

C—Intercompany sales and purchases, $40,000.

D—Intercompany dividend, $3,000.

The Eliminations columns were footed and ruled.

The account balances after eliminations were extended to the statement columns.

The combined inventory on December 31, 1957, after deduction of intercompany profit, was entered in the Income Statement credit column and in the Balance Sheet debit column.

Company *P* sold goods to Company *S* during the year, and goods on which Company *P* made a profit of $1,000 remained in Company *S*'s inventory at the end of the year. From a consolidated standpoint, intercompany sale-purchase transactions are similar to merchandise transfers between departments of the same business and are therefore eliminated in the working papers; and any intercompany profit on goods

COMPANY P AND SUBSIDIARY

Consolidated Working Papers
For the Year Ended December 31, 1957

	Trial Balances — Company P	Trial Balances — Company S	Eliminations	Income Statement	Statement of Retained Earnings	Balance Sheet
Debits						
Cash	31,000	15,000				46,000
Accounts receivable:						
Trade	24,000	17,000				41,000
Company S	5,000		5,000B			
Merchandise inventory—beginning of year	65,000	30,000		95,000		
Investment in stock of Company S (100%)—at cost	50,000		50,000A			
Purchases	120,000	75,000	40,000C	155,000		
Expenses	30,000	18,000		48,000		
Dividends:						
Company P	6,000				6,000	
Company S		3,000	3,000D			
	331,000	158,000				
Credits						
Accounts payable:						
Trade	30,000	6,000				36,000
Company P		5,000	5,000B			
Common stock:						
Company P	100,000					100,000
Company S		50,000	50,000A			
Retained earnings—beginning of year:						
Company P	43,000				43,000	
Company S						
Sales:						
Company P	155,000			212,000		
Company S		97,000	40,000C			
Dividend from subsidiary	3,000		3,000D			
	331,000	158,000	98,000 98,000			
Inventories, December 31, 1957:						
Company P 67,000						
Company S 32,000						
Total 99,000						
Intercompany profit 1,000						
Net 98,000				98,000		98,000
Consolidated net income				12,000	12,000	
				310,000 310,000		
Consolidated retained earnings					49,000	49,000
					55,000 55,000	185,000 185,000

Eliminations

A—Parent's 100% of subsidiary stockholders' equity at date of acquisition.
B—Intercompany account receivable and payable.
C—Intercompany sales.
D—**Intercompany dividend.**

remaining in inventory should be excluded from the inventory valuation and from the consolidated net income. This is accomplished by stating the inventory in the working papers net of intercompany profit.

The consolidated net income was entered as a balancing figure in the Income Statement debit column and extended to the Retained Earnings credit column. The Income Statement columns were footed and ruled.

The amount of the consolidated retained earnings on December 31, 1957, was entered as a balancing figure in the Retained Earnings debit column and extended to the Balance Sheet credit column. The Retained Earnings columns were footed and ruled.

The Balance Sheet columns were footed and ruled.

COMPANY *P* AND SUBSIDIARY   Exhibit C
Consolidated Income Statement
For the Year Ended December 31, 1957

Sales...		$212,000
Deduct cost of goods sold:		
Inventory, December 31, 1956..................	$ 95,000	
Purchases..................................	155,000	
Total....................................	$250,000	
Deduct inventory, December 31, 1957..........	98,000	152,000
Gross profit on sales.......................................		$ 60,000
Deduct expenses..		48,000
Net income..		$ 12,000

COMPANY *P* AND SUBSIDIARY   Exhibit B
Consolidated Statement of Retained Earnings
For the Year Ended December 31, 1957

Balance, December 31, 1956..............................	$43,000
Add net income—Exhibit C.............................	12,000
Total..	$55,000
Deduct dividends.......................................	6,000
Balance, December 31, 1957.............................	$49,000

COMPANY *P* AND SUBSIDIARY   Exhibit A
Consolidated Balance Sheet
December 31, 1957

Assets		Liabilities and Stockholders' Equity		
Cash......................	$ 46,000	Accounts payable...........		$ 36,000
Accounts receivable.........	41,000	Stockholders' equity:		
Merchandise inventory.......	98,000	Common stock...	$100,000	
		Retained earnings		
		—Exhibit B....	49,000	149,000
	$185,000			$185,000

Second illustration. Working papers for the preparation of consolidated statements of Company *P* and its subsidiary for the year ended December 31, 1958, are on page 459. The purpose is to illustrate two new features discussed on page 460.

COMPANY P AND SUBSIDIARY
Consolidated Working Papers
For the Year Ended December 31, 1958

	Trial Balances		Eliminations		Income Statement	Statement of Retained Earnings	Balance Sheet
	Company P	Company S					
Debits							
Cash	30,000	21,000					51,000
Accounts receivable—Trade	40,000	16,000					56,000
Merchandise inventory—beginning of year	67,000	32,000		1,000A	98,000		
Investment in stock of Company S (100%)—at cost	50,000			50,000B			
Purchases	130,000	95,000		45,000C	180,000		
Expenses	32,000	19,000			51,000		
Dividends:							
Company P	6,000					6,000	
Company S		2,000		2,000D			
	355,000	185,000					
Credits							
Accounts payable—Trade	33,000	10,000					43,000
Common stock:							
Company P	100,000						100,000
Company S		50,000	50,000B				
Retained earnings—beginning of year:							
Company P	47,000		1,000A			46,000	
Company S (all earned since acquisition)		3,000				3,000	
Sales	173,000	122,000	45,000C		250,000		
Dividend from subsidiary	2,000		2,000D				
	355,000	185,000	98,000	98,000			
					99,500		99,500
Consolidated net income					20,500	20,500	
					349,500		
					349,500		
Consolidated retained earnings						63,500	63,500
						69,500	206,500
						69,500	206,500

Inventories, December 31, 1958:

Company P	70,000
Company S	31,000
Total	101,000
Deduct intercompany profit	1,500
Net	99,500

Eliminations

A—Intercompany profit in beginning inventory.
B—Parent's 100% of subsidiary stockholders' equity at date of acquisition.
C—Intercompany sales.
D—Intercompany dividend.

Adjustment for intercompany profit in opening inventory. In the working papers for the year ended December 31, 1957, intercompany profit of $1,000 was deducted from the $99,000 gross amount of the end-of-year inventories, and the net amount, $98,000, was extended to the Income Statement and Balance Sheet columns and was shown in the consolidated statements. The same amount should be shown as the beginning-of-year inventory in the consolidated statements for 1958. The company trial balances in the working papers show beginning inventories of $67,000 and $32,000, or a total of $99,000; this total is reduced to $98,000 for consolidated statement purposes by a credit of $1,000 in the Eliminations columns.

The offsetting debit is made against the parent's retained earnings. The $47,000 balance in the parent's Retained Earnings account at the beginning of 1958 includes the profit on all of the parent's sales to the subsidiary during 1957; for 1958 consolidated statement purposes, the opening balance of retained earnings should not include the $1,000 intercompany profit on goods remaining in the inventory at the end of 1957.

Subsidiary's retained earnings at the beginning of the year. The $3,000 balance in the subsidiary's Retained Earnings account is the undistributed portion of the net income of the subsidiary for the period between the date of acquisition of its stock by Company *P* and the beginning of 1958, the year for which consolidated statements are now to be prepared. It is therefore part of the consolidated retained earnings at the beginning of 1958 and consequently is extended to the Retained Earnings credit column.

COMPANY *P* AND SUBSIDIARY   Exhibit C

Consolidated Income Statement
For the Year Ended December 31, 1958

Sales..		$250,000
Deduct cost of goods sold:		
Inventory, December 31, 1957............	$ 98,000	
Purchases............................	180,000	
Total................................	$278,000	
Deduct inventory, December 31, 1958...........	99,500	178,500
Gross profit on sales..................................		$ 71,500
Deduct expenses.......................................		51,000
Net income..		$ 20,500

COMPANY *P* AND SUBSIDIARY   Exhibit B

Consolidated Statement of Retained Earnings
For the Year Ended December 31, 1958

Balance, December 31, 1957............................	$49,000
Add net income—Exhibit C............................	20,500
Total..	$69,500
Deduct dividends.....................................	6,000
Balance, December 31, 1958...........................	$63,500

COMPANY *P* AND SUBSIDIARY   Exhibit A

Consolidated Balance Sheet

December 31, 1958

Assets		Liabilities and Stockholders' Equity		
Cash	$ 51,000	Accounts payable		$ 43,000
Accounts receivable	56,000			
Merchandise inventory	99,500	Stockholders' equity:		
		Common stock	$100,000	
		Retained earnings		
		—Exhibit B	63,500	163,500
	$206,500			$206,500

Subsidiary's Retained Earnings at Date of Acquisition

Introduction. Organizing a company is not the only way to acquire a subsidiary. A corporation may acquire a subsidiary by purchasing, from shareholders, the stock of an existing company. In such circumstances, the newly acquired subsidiary will usually have a balance in its Retained Earnings account.

The question arises whether such "purchased" retained earnings may be treated as part of the consolidated retained earnings. The answer is, No. If it were possible to combine the subsidiary's retained earnings existing at acquisition with the parent's retained earnings, a parent company could increase consolidated retained earnings merely by investing in a subsidiary with a credit balance in its Retained Earnings account. This is not defensible; a parent company cannot properly include in the consolidated retained earnings any earnings resulting from subsidiary operations prior to the date when the parent acquired its interest in the subsidiary.

The subsidiary's retained earnings at the date of acquisition are part of the book value of the stock at that date and must be eliminated, together with the subsidiary's capital stock, in the process of preparing consolidated financial statements.

Illustration. Assume that, on December 31, 1955, Hudson Company purchased, from the stockholders of Raleigh Company, the $50,000 par value of outstanding stock of the latter-named company. At that date, Raleigh Company had retained earnings of $20,000. The stock was purchased at book value, $70,000.

Consolidated statements are to be prepared for the year ended December 31, 1958, three years after the date of acquisition. At the beginning of 1958, Raleigh Company's retained earnings amounted to $30,000, which was an increase of $10,000 since the parent-subsidiary relationship was established. So long as the parent company retains its 100 per cent interest in the subsidiary, the entire amount of the subsidiary's retained earnings at the date of acquisition should be eliminated from the subsidiary's Retained Earnings account. The correct eliminations are shown in the partial working papers on page 462.

HUDSON COMPANY AND SUBSIDIARY
Partial Consolidated Working Papers
For the Year Ended December 31, 1958

	Trial Balances		Eliminations	Income Statement	Statement of Retained Earnings	Balance Sheet
	Hudson Company	Raleigh Company				
Debits						
Investment in stock of Raleigh Company (100%)—at cost..........	70,000		70,000A			
Credits						
Common stock:						
Raleigh Company..........		50,000	50,000A			
Retained earnings—December 31, 1957:						
Raleigh Company..........		30,000	20,000A		10,000	
At date of acquisition....20,000						
Increase to 12/31/57......10,000						

Minority Interest

Nature of minority interest. When a subsidiary is purchased, the parent may not desire to acquire all of the subsidiary's outstanding stock or may be unable to do so. The holders of the shares not acquired are called *minority stockholders,* and their percentage of the subsidiary's capital stock and retained earnings is called the *minority interest.*

Illustration. Referring to the preceding illustration, assume that, on December 31, 1955, Hudson Company had acquired only 90 per cent of the stock of Raleigh Company. The book value of all of the Raleigh Company stock and the book value of the 90 per cent interest acquired by Hudson Company are shown below:

	Total	90% Interest
Capital stock...............................	$50,000	$45,000
Retained earnings...........................	20,000	18,000
	$70,000	$63,000

Hudson Company paid book value for the shares acquired, $63,000. The amounts in the 90% Interest column are those which will be eliminated from the subsidiary's Common Stock and Retained Earnings accounts and from the parent's Investment account. The remaining amounts in these accounts, $5,000 and $2,000, respectively, constitute the minority interest as of the date of acquisition.

The illustration on pages 464 to 466 relates to 1958. The following additional information is required in order to complete the working papers: The inventories of the two companies on December 31, 1958 were: parent, $28,000; subsidiary, $19,000; total, $47,000. There were no intercompany profits in the inventories at either the beginning or the end of the year. The subsidiary's net income for the year 1958 was $8,000; the minority interest's share thereof was $800.

HUDSON COMPANY AND SUBSIDIARY
Consolidated Working Papers
For the Year Ended December 31, 1958

	Trial Balances		Eliminations		Income Statement	Minority Interest	Statement of Retained Earnings	Balance Sheet
Debits	Hudson Company	Raleigh Company						
Cash...........................	31,150	41,000						72,150
Accounts receivable..........	12,500	29,900						42,400
Allowance for doubtful accounts...............	600*	1,300*						1,900
Inventory—December 31, 1957..........................	30,000	18,000			48,000			
Store equipment.............	5,000	12,000						17,000
Accumulated depreciation—Store equipment...........	1,000*	2,000*						3,000
Investment in stock of Raleigh Company (90%)—at cost...........................	63,000			63,000A				
Purchases....................	165,000	78,000		50,000B	193,000			
Selling and general expenses	20,000	15,000			35,000			
Dividends:								
Hudson Company.........	6,000						6,000	
Raleigh Company.........		3,000		2,700C		300		
	331,050	193,600						
Credits								
Accounts payable...........	14,000	13,600						27,600
Common stock:								
Hudson Company.........	100,000							100,000
Raleigh Company.........		50,000	45,000A			5,000		
Retained earnings—December 31, 1957:								
Hudson Company.........	14,350						14,350	
Raleigh Company (See comments at foot of working papers)......		30,000						

At date of acquisition... 20,000			18,000A							
Increase to 12/31/57..... 10,000										
Sales.....	200,000	100,000		250,000		2,000				
Dividend from subsidiary....	2,700		50,000B 2,700C			1,000			9,000	
	331,050	193,600	115,700 115,700							
Inventories—December 31, 1958.									47,000	
Net income.....				47,000	21,000					
Apportionment:										
Minority—10% of subsidiary's $8,000 net income.....						800				
Consolidated—Remainder.....								20,200		
				297,000 297,000	297,000					
Minority interest.....						8,500 8,800 8,800		37,550		8,500
Consolidated retained earnings.....							37,550			37,550
						43,550	43,550	178,550	178,550	

* Deduction.

Eliminations

A—90% of subsidiary stockholders' equity at date of acquisition (eliminated for reason stated on page 463):

  Capital stock—90% of $50,000......... 45,000
  Retained earnings—90% of $20,000......... 18,000
    Total......... 63,000

B—Intercompany sales.
C—Intercompany dividend.

It is then apportioned as follows:

Retained earnings at date of acquisition—$20,000.
  90% of the $20,000 is eliminated because no portion of the subsidiary's retained earnings at the date of acquisition can properly be included in consolidated retained earnings.
  10% of the $20,000 is extended to the Minority Interest credit column.

Increase in retained earnings from date of acquisition to the beginning of 1958—$10,000.
  10% of the $10,000 increase is entered in the Minority Interest credit column.
  90% of the $10,000 increase is entered in the Statement of Retained Earnings credit column.

Observe the treatment of the subsidiary's retained earnings at the beginning of the year.   The $30,000 balance is entered in the subsidiary's Trial Balance column.

HUDSON COMPANY AND SUBSIDIARY · Exhibit C

Consolidated Income Statement

For the Year Ended December 31, 1958

Sales		$250,000
Deduct cost of goods sold:		
Inventory, December 31, 1957	$ 48,000	
Purchases	193,000	
Total	$241,000	
Deduct inventory, December 31, 1958	47,000	194,000
Gross profit on sales		$ 56,000
Deduct selling and general expenses		35,000
Total net income		$ 21,000
Minority interest		800
Consolidated net income		$ 20,200

HUDSON COMPANY AND SUBSIDIARY · Exhibit B

Consolidated Statement of Retained Earnings

For the Year Ended December 31, 1958

Balance, December 31, 1957	$ 23,350
Add consolidated net income—Exhibit C	20,200
Total	$ 43,550
Deduct dividends	6,000
Balance, December 31, 1958	$ 37,550

HUDSON COMPANY AND SUBSIDIARY · Exhibit A

Consolidated Balance Sheet

December 31, 1958

Assets

Current assets:		
Cash		$ 72,150
Accounts receivable	$42,400	
Less allowance for doubtful accounts	1,900	40,500
Inventory		47,000
Total current assets		$159,650
Fixed assets:		
Store equipment		$ 17,000
Less accumulated depreciation		3,000
		14,000
		$173,650

Liabilities and Stockholders' Equity

Current liabilities:		
Accounts payable		$ 27,600
Minority interest		8,500
Stockholders' equity:		
Common stock	$100,000	
Retained earnings	37,550	
Total stockholders' equity		137,550
		$173,650

Difference Between Cost of Subsidiary Stock
and Book Value at Acquisition

In all preceding illustrations, the parent paid exactly book value for its investment in the subsidiary stock.   We shall now consider the procedures to be followed if the cost of the stock exceeded its book value at acquisition, and vice versa.

Excess of cost over book value.   Assume that a parent had acquired all of the stock of a subsidiary whose stockholders' equity at the date of acquisition was as follows:

Common stock................	$100,000
Retained earnings..............	50,000
Total.......	$150,000

Suppose that the parent paid $160,000 for the subsidiary stock, or $10,000 more than book value.   In all subsequent working papers, so long as the parent's per cent of ownership remains unchanged, $100,000 will be eliminated from the subsidiary's Common Stock account and $50,000 will be eliminated from the subsidiary's Retained Earnings account.   The $150,000 total will be eliminated from the parent's Investment account and the $10,000 excess will be extended to the Balance Sheet debit column.   It may be shown as the last item on the asset side of the consolidated balance sheet, thus:

Cost of subsidiary stock in excess of book value at acquisition $10,000.00

Partial working papers illustrating the eliminations are shown on page 468, it being assumed that a consolidated balance sheet is being prepared at a date when the subsidiary's retained earnings have increased to $65,000.

Partial Consolidated Working Papers
For the Year Ended December 31, 1958

	Trial Balances		Eliminations	Income Statement	Statement of Retained Earnings	Balance Sheet
	Parent	Subsidiary				
Debits						
Investment in stock of subsidiary.....	160,000		150,000A			10,000
Eliminate book value at acquisition.						
Excess of cost over book value......						
Credits						
Common stock:						
Subsidiary...............		100,000	100,000A			
Retained earnings:						
Subsidiary...............		65,000	50,000A		15,000	
At date of acquisition... $50,000						
Increase to 12/31/58.... $15,000						

Book value in excess of cost. Referring to the preceding illustration, assume that the parent company had acquired only 90 per cent of the subsidiary's stock, and had paid $130,000 for it. The book value of the stock acquired was 90 per cent of $150,000, or $135,000, which was $5,000 in excess of the cost of the stock. The working papers are shown below. The excess of book value over cost may be shown in the consolidated balance sheet in the Stockholders' Equity section, thus:

Book value of subsidiary stock at acquisition in excess of cost.................. $5,000

Partial Consolidated Working Papers
For the Year Ended December 31, 1968

	Trial Balances Parent	Trial Balances Subsidiary	Eliminations	Income Statement	Minority Interest	Statement of Retained Earnings	Balance Sheet
Debits							
Investment in stock of subsidiary.............	130,000						
Eliminate book value at acquisition...........			135,000A				
Excess of book value over cost...............							5,000
Credits							
Common stock:							
Subsidiary..........		100,000	90,000A		10,000		
Retained earnings:							
Subsidiary.........		65,000					
At date of acquisition 50,000			45,000A		5,000		
Increase to 12/31/58 15,000					1,500	13,500	

When to consolidate. A parent-subsidiary relationship does not exist unless the intercompany stockholding is more than 50 per cent of the voting stock. Although the existence of voting control is a basic determinant of the propriety of including a company's accounts in consolidated statements, it does not follow that all controlled companies should be consolidated. If a parent owns 100 per cent of the voting stock of a subsidiary, it still has no legal ownership of the subsidiary's assets, but a condition exists which, for consolidated statement purposes, is *assumed* to represent effective ownership. If the parent owns 95 per cent of the voting stock of the subsidiary, there is a 5 per cent error in the assumption of effective ownership; this error is regarded as insignificant and is adequately disclosed by the inclusion of the minority interest in the consolidated statements. But if there is a 49 per cent minority interest, the degree of error in the assumption is so great that most accountants believe that the accounts of such a subsidiary should not be included in consolidated statements. Unfortunately, there is no well-accepted rule concerning the per cent of voting-stock control required to justify the inclusion of a subsidiary's accounts in consolidated statements. Some accountants believe that a 60 per cent interest is sufficient; others regard a 75 per cent or an 80 per cent interest as a minimum.

Summary and Review

Preceding chapters have been devoted to matters that must be given consideration if the income statement and the balance sheet are to reflect the results of operations and the financial position in accordance with generally accepted accounting principles. The purpose of this section is to review, and to emphasize the importance of, these accounting principles.

It is assumed that The $X Y Z$ Company's bookkeeper prepared the statements on pages 472 and 473. A certified public accountant audited the books before they were closed. He discovered that numerous errors of accounting principle had been committed during the year, and also that the statements prepared by the bookkeeper were not in the most acceptable form.

The importance of conforming to accepted accounting principles is demonstrated by the fact that the bookkeeper's statements, affected by many violations of accounting principles, reflect good operating results and a satisfactory financial position, whereas the auditor's statements (pages 483–486), conforming with accepted principles, present a far less satisfactory picture.

Auditor's adjustments. On pages 474–477 is a list of the various matters discovered by the auditor and his adjustments therefor.

These adjustments are applied to the bookkeeper's trial balance in the working papers on pages 478–481. Adjustments are shown for all of the matters discovered by the auditor, although some of them are of such small amounts that they might be regarded as immaterial and be ignored.

All of the adjustments except adjustment (b) were recorded in the books.

Adjustment (b) was made for statement purposes only.

The auditor made some changes in terminology,

Using	*Instead of*
Income statement	Profit and loss statement
Retained earnings	Earned surplus
Allowance for doubtful accounts	Reserve for bad debts
Accumulated depreciation	Reserve for depreciation
Stockholders' equity	Net worth

THE *X Y Z* COMPANY
Statement of Profit and Loss and Earned Surplus
For the Year Ended December 31, 1958

Sales..			$707,987
Deduct sales returns and allowances........................			9,620
Net sales..			$698,367
Deduct cost of goods sold:			
Inventory, December 31, 1957...................		$ 70,000	
Purchases...........................	$532,317		
Freight in...........................	7,400		
Total............................	$539,717		
Deduct purchase returns and allowances	8,500	531,217	
Total..		$601,217	
Deduct inventory, December 31, 1958...........		85,000	
Cost of goods sold...................................			516,217
Gross profit on sales..			$182,150
Deduct selling and general expenses:			
Rent of leased building........................		$ 1,800	
Salesmen's salaries............................		23,200	
Delivery expense..............................		13,200	
Officers' salaries..............................		32,000	
Office salaries................................		18,200	
Bad debts.....................................		3,200	
Insurance expense.............................		3,000	
Taxes—Other than federal income..............		3,600	
Miscellaneous general expenses.................		3,410	
Depreciation..................................		9,400	
Total selling and general expenses................			111,010
Net profit on operations....................................			$ 71,140
Deduct net financial expense:			
Bond interest.................................		$ 3,600	
Notes payable interest........................		900	
Discount on sales.............................		7,650	
Total.......................................		$ 12,150	
Deduct:			
Dividend income....................	$ 350		
Interest income....................	410		
Sinking fund income................	390		
Discount on purchases..............	4,310		
Miscellaneous income...............	1,000	6,460	5,690
Net income..			$ 65,450
Add:			
Earned surplus, December 31, 1957.....................			69,250
Write-up of goodwill..................................			20,000
Write-up of preferred treasury stock from cost to par.......			500
Total..			$155,200
Deduct write-off of discount on issuance of bonds...........			2,000
Earned surplus, December 31, 1958.............			$153,200

THE *X Y Z* COMPANY
Balance Sheet
December 31, 1958
Assets

Current assets:

Cash	$ 13,800	
Accounts receivable	94,233	
Notes receivable	10,000	
Merchandise inventory	85,000	
Investments in stocks and bonds	48,850	
Total current assets		$251,883

Fixed assets:

Land and building	$140,000	
Store fixtures	30,000	
Delivery equipment	10,000	
Office furniture and equipment	10,000	
Goodwill	50,000	
Total fixed assets		240,000

Deferred charges:

Discount on common stock	7,500
	$499,383

Liabilities and Net Worth

Current liabilities:

Accounts payable	$ 58,783	
Notes payable	30,000	
Total current liabilities		$ 88,783

Fixed liabilities:

Bonds payable	60,000

Reserves:

Reserve for bad debts	$ 8,000	
Reserve for depreciation	29,400	
Total reserves		37,400

Net worth:

Capital stock—Common	$100,000	
Capital stock—Preferred	50,000	
Earned surplus	153,200	
Capital surplus	10,000	
Total net worth		313,200
		$499,383

(a) In accordance with the requirements of the indenture, the company has established a sinking fund for the payment of the bonds payable. On December 31, 1958, cash in the amount of $150 was in the hands of the sinking fund trustee, but it is included in the $13,800 shown as cash. Since this $150 is not available for unrestricted disbursement, the following entry is required:

Sinking fund cash	150.00	
Cash		150.00

(b) The $94,233 shown in the bookkeeper's balance sheet as accounts receivable is the balance in the controlling account. The subsidiary ledger contains accounts with credit balances totaling $2,000. Since liabilities should not be offset in the balance sheet against assets, the following adjustment is made:

Accounts receivable	2,000.00	
Credit balances in customers' accounts		2,000.00

(c) The amount shown in the balance sheet as accounts receivable includes accounts with officers totaling $25,000. These accounts did not arise from sales made in accordance with the usual credit terms; therefore, the following entry is required:

Accounts receivable—Officers	25,000.00	
Accounts receivable		25,000.00

(d) The company ships some merchandise on consignment and has followed the practice of recording consignments as sales, thus anticipating profits. On December 31, 1958, the unsold goods consigned amounted to $15,000 at selling price; the entry recording these consignments as sales should be reversed.

Sales	15,000.00	
Accounts receivable		15,000.00

The unsold consigned goods cost $10,000; this amount should be added to the inventory shown in the bookkeeper's statements.

(e) After reviewing the accounts receivable with the credit manager, the auditor decided that $1,500 should be added to the allowance for doubtful accounts.

Bad debts	1,500.00	
Allowance for doubtful accounts		1,500.00

(f) The business was acquired as a going concern, and the purchase price included $30,000 in payment for goodwill. When the bookkeeper submitted his profit and loss statement for 1958, the directors thought that the net income for the year justified a goodwill valuation of $50,000. The bookkeeper was directed to write up the Goodwill account to that amount; and, since the goodwill valuation was based on the net income (which would go to the

Earned Surplus account), the bookkeeper was told to make the offsetting credit to Earned Surplus. To conform with the cost principle, a Goodwill account should not have a balance in excess of the amount paid for the goodwill; therefore, the following reversing entry should be made:

```
Retained earnings..............................  20,000.00
    Goodwill..................................              20,000.00
```

(g) Unexpired insurance premiums of $1,200 were not deferred.

```
Unexpired insurance...........................   1,200.00
    Insurance expense.........................               1,200.00
```

(h) The $48,850 shown in the balance sheet as investments in stocks and bonds contains diverse elements; they should be detailed by the following entry:

```
Investments in bonds.........................   18,500.00
Stock investments............................    7,000.00
Sinking fund securities......................   11,850.00
Treasury stock—Preferred.....................   11,500.00
    Investments in stocks and bonds...........              48,850.00
```

The bonds are short-term investments; the stocks are long-term investments.

(i) The investments in bonds are carried at their cost, $18,500; their market value on December 31, 1958, was $17,800. Because they will be shown in the balance sheet as current assets, their valuation should be reduced to market.

```
Market loss on short-term bond investments...     700.00
    Bond investment valuation allowance......                700.00
```

(j) The $140,000 shown in the bookkeeper's balance sheet as land and building should be detailed.

```
Land held for resale.........................   10,000.00
Land.........................................    7,000.00
Parking lot (Completed December 28, 1958)....    3,000.00
Store building...............................  100,000.00
Leasehold improvements.......................   20,000.00
    Land and building........................             140,000.00
```

The charge to Leasehold Improvements is the cost of alterations to a leased building used as a supplementary sales room.

(k) As of December 31, 1958, after the depreciation for the year had been recorded, the bookkeeper, in accordance with a resolution of the board of directors, made an entry writing up the building from $90,000 (its cost) to $100,000, with an offsetting credit to Capital Surplus. This entry violated the cost principle, and it should be reversed.

```
Capital surplus..............................   10,000.00
    Store building...........................              10,000.00
```

(l) During 1958, the company spent $2,000 to provide a customers' parking lot, hiring and supervising men to do the work. Since the lowest bid obtained from any contractor was $3,000, the company management took the position that a profit of $1,000 had been made. The bookkeeper was therefore directed to make an entry debiting Land and Building and crediting Miscellaneous Income $1,000. To maintain a proper distinction between profits and savings, the following entry should be made:

Miscellaneous income	1,000.00	
Parking lot		1,000.00

(m) The reserve for depreciation should be detailed by the following entry:

Reserve for depreciation	29,400.00	
Accumulated depreciation—Store building		10,800.00
Accumulated depreciation—Store fixtures		9,000.00
Accumulated depreciation—Delivery equipment		4,000.00
Accumulated depreciation—Office furniture and equipment		4,000.00
Leasehold improvements		1,600.00

(n) The bonds payable were issued four years ago at a discount of $2,000. No periodical amortization entries were made, but, with the idea of being conservative, the directors ordered the write-off of the entire $2,000 on December 31, 1958, by a debit to Earned Surplus. To conform with the accounting principle requiring a proper matching of revenue and expense, the discount should have been amortized over the 20-year life of the bonds. The following entry reverses the write-off:

Discount on bonds payable	2,000.00	
Retained earnings		2,000.00

(o) The annual amortization of the bond discount should have been one-twentieth of $2,000, or $100. Applying the clean-surplus theory, the amortization for the three preceding years should be shown in the income statement as a correction of the net income for those years, and the amortization for 1958 should be charged to Bond Interest Expense.

Correction of prior years' net income—Amortization of bond discount	300.00	
Bond interest expense	100.00	
Discount on bonds payable		400.00

(p) Prior to the close of the year, the company purchased $10,000 worth of merchandise that was in transit on December 31. Title had passed, but (because the goods had not been received) no entry was made to record the purchase and the liability. The following entry is required:

Purchases..	10,000.00	
Accounts payable............................		10,000.00

The goods were not included in the inventory. No adjusting entry is required, but $10,000 should be added to the inventory shown in the bookkeeper's statements.

(q) Merchandise costing $4,000 was received late in the afternoon of December 31 and was included in the inventory, but the purchase was not recorded.

Purchases..	4,000.00	
Accounts payable............................		4,000.00

(r) The following adjusting entry is required for expenses that were ignored:

Salesmen's salaries............................	1,800.00	
Taxes—Other than federal income..............	2,500.00	
Miscellaneous general expenses..................	1,200.00	
Notes payable interest expense..................	450.00	
Accrued expenses payable..................		5,950.00

(s) No provision was made by the bookkeeper for federal income taxes for 1958. The estimated amount was $19,500.

(t) A six per cent dividend on the preferred stock was declared December 31, 1958, but the declaration was not recorded. The par value of the outstanding preferred stock was $38,500 ($50,000 total minus $11,500 par value of treasury stock). The dividend was 6% of $38,500, or $2,310.

Dividends..	2,310.00	
Dividends payable—Preferred..............		2,310.00

(u) The treasury stock has a par value of $11,500. It was acquired in 1958 at a cost of $11,000, but the bookkeeper increased its carrying value to par, with an offsetting credit to Earned Surplus. Since treasury stock is normally carried at cost, the entry should be reversed.

Retained earnings............................	500.00	
Treasury stock—Preferred..................		500.00

(v) The $9,400 shown in the bookkeeper's profit and loss statement as depreciation should be detailed by the following entry:

Depreciation—Store building..................	3,600.00	
Depreciation—Store fixtures..................	3,000.00	
Depreciation—Delivery equipment..............	1,000.00	
Depreciation—Office furniture and equipment....	1,000.00	
Amortization—Leasehold improvements..........	800.00	
Depreciation............................		9,400.00

THE X Y Z COMPANY
Working Papers
For the Year Ended December 31, 1958

Assets	Trial Balance Before Adjustments Dr	Cr	Adjustments Dr	Cr	Revenue and Expense	Retained Earnings	Balance Sheet Dr	Cr
Cash	13,800			150a			13,650	
Accounts receivable	94,233		2,000b	25,000c 15,000d }			56,233	
Allowance for doubtful accounts		8,000		1,500e				9,500
Notes receivable	10,000						10,000	
Investments in stocks and bonds	48,850			48,850h				
Merchandise inventory—December 31, 1957	70,000				70,000			
Land and building	140,000			140,000j				
Store fixtures	30,000						30,000	
Delivery equipment	10,000						10,000	
Office furniture and equipment	10,000						10,000	
Reserve for depreciation		29,400	29,400m					
Goodwill	50,000			20,000f			30,000	
Sinking fund cash			150a				150	
Accounts receivable—Officers			25,000c				25,000	
Unexpired insurance			1,200g				1,200	
Investments in bonds			18,500h				18,500	
Stock investments			7,000h				7,000	
Sinking fund securities			11,850h				11,850	
Bond investment valuation allowance				700i				700
Land held for resale			10,000j				10,000	
Land			7,000j				7,000	
Parking lot			3,000j	1,000l			2,000	
Store building			100,000j	10,000k			90,000	
Leasehold improvements			20,000j	1,600m			18,400	
Accumulated depreciation—Store building				10,800m				10,800
Accumulated depreciation—Store fixtures				9,000m				9,000
Accumulated depreciation—Delivery equipment				4,000m				4,000
Accumulated depreciation—Office F. & E.				4,000m				4,000
Discount on bonds payable			2,000n	400o			1,600	
Totals forward	476,883	37,400	237,100	292,000	70,000		352,583	38,000

Adjustments

(a) Transfer to Sinking Fund Cash.
(b) Credit balances in customers' accounts.
(c) Transfer to Accounts Receivable—Officers.
(d) Reverse charge for unsold consignments.
(e) Additional allowance for doubtful accounts.
(f) Reverse goodwill write-up.
(g) Unexpired insurance.
(h) Detail Investments in Stocks and Bonds.
(i) Reduce bond investment from cost to market.
(j) Detail Land and Building account.
(k) Reverse write-up of building.
(l) Reverse entry for "profit" on parking lot.
(m) Detail Reserve for Depreciation.
(n) Restore discount on bonds payable—Written off.
(o) Amortization of bond discount to December 31, 1958.

THE *X Y Z* COMPANY
Working Papers (Continued)
For the Year Ended December 31, 1958

Liabilities	Trial Balance Before Adjustments (Dr)	Trial Balance Before Adjustments (Cr)	Adjustments (Dr)	Adjustments (Cr)	Revenue and Expense	Retained Earnings (Dr)	Retained Earnings (Cr)	Balance Sheet (Dr)	Balance Sheet (Cr)
Totals brought forward	476,883		237,100	292,000	70,000			352,583	
Accounts payable		37,400							38,000
Notes payable		58,783		10,000p} 4,000q}					72,783
Bonds payable		30,000							30,000
Credit balances in customers' accounts		60,000		2,000b					60,000
Accrued expenses payable				5,950r					5,950
Federal income tax payable				19,500s					19,500
Dividend payable—Preferred				2,310t					2,310
Stockholders' Equity									
Capital stock—Preferred		50,000							50,000
Capital stock—Common		100,000							100,000
Discount on common stock	7,500							7,500	
Retained earnings		87,750	20,000f} 500u}	2,000n			69,250		
Capital surplus		10,000	10,000k						
Treasury stock—Preferred			11,500h	500u				11,000	
Dividends			2,310t			2,310			
Totals forward	484,383	433,933	281,410	338,260	70,000	2,310	69,250	371,083	380,543

Adjustments

(b) Credit balances in customers' accounts.
(f) Reverse goodwill write-up.
(h) Transfer from Investments in Stocks and Bonds.
(k) Reverse write-up of store building.
(n) Reverse write-off of discount on issuance of bonds.
(p) Unrecorded purchase.
(q) Unrecorded purchase.
(r) Accrued expenses.
(s) Estimated federal income tax.
(t) Unrecorded declared dividend.
(u) Reverse write-off of discount on acquisition of treasury stock.

THE X Y Z COMPANY
Working Papers (Concluded)
For the Year Ended December 31, 1958

Revenue and Expense	Trial Balance Before Adjustments		Adjustments		Revenue and Expense		Retained Earnings		Balance Sheet	
Totals brought forward	484,383	433,933	281,410	338,260	70,000	692,987	2,310	69,250	371,083	380,543
Sales		707,987	15,000d			692,987				
Sales returns and allowances	9,620				9,620					
Sales discounts	7,650				7,650					
Purchases	532,317		10,000p / 4,000q		546,317					
Freight in	7,400				7,400					
Purchase returns and allowances		8,500				8,500				
Purchase discounts		4,310				4,310				
Rent of leased building	1,800				1,800					
Salesmen's salaries	23,200		1,800r		25,000					
Delivery expense	13,200				13,200					
Officers' salaries	32,000				32,000					
Office salaries	18,200				18,200					
Bad debts	3,200		1,500e		4,700					
Insurance expense	3,000			1,200g	1,800					
Taxes—Other than federal income	3,600		2,500r		6,100					
Depreciation	9,400			9,400v						
Miscellaneous general expenses	3,410		1,200r		4,610					
Dividend income		350				350				
Interest income		410				410				
Sinking fund income		390				390				
Miscellaneous income		1,000	1,000l							
Bond interest expense	3,600		100o		3,700					
Notes payable interest expense	900		450r		1,350					
Depreciation—Store building			3,600v		3,600					
Depreciation—Store fixtures			3,000v		3,000					
Depreciation—Delivery equipment			1,000v		1,000					

Depreciation—Office F. & E.		1,000v		1,000				
Amortization—Leasehold improvements		800v		800				
Market loss on short-term bond investments		700i		700				
Correction of prior years' net income—								
Amortization of bond discount		300o		300				
Federal income tax		19,500s		19,500				
Totals	1,156,880	1,156,880	348,860	348,860				
Inventory—December 31, 1958:								
Per company statements...... 85,000								
Omissions:								
On consignment........ 10,000								
In transit............ 10,000								
Total............ 105,000			105,000	105,000				
			783,347	811,947		2,310	97,850	95,540
Net income			28,600		28,600	97,850		
			811,947	811,947	95,540			105,000
Retained earnings					97,850	97,850	476,083	476,083 95,540

Adjustments

(d) Reverse credit for consignments unsold.
(e) Additional allowance for doubtful accounts.
(g) Unexpired insurance.
(p) Unrecorded purchase.
(q) Unrecorded purchase.
(o) Amortization of bond discount.
(r) Accrued expenses.
(s) Estimated federal income tax.
(v) Detail Depreciation account.

Statements. The statements prepared from the foregoing working papers are on pages 483 to 486. Attention is directed to the following matters:

Information given parenthetically. Since the investments in bonds are a current asset, their valuation was reduced to market; their cost is stated parenthetically in the balance sheet.

Since the stock investments are long-term holdings, their valuation for balance sheet purposes has not been reduced to market, but the market value is shown parenthetically.

Notes to financial statements. Some important matters requiring disclosure are mentioned in the "Notes to Financial Statements" because the disclosure requires a lengthier statement than can conveniently be made parenthetically in the statements and/or because they have a bearing on more than one statement.

Changes in statement organization. The following changes were made in the income statement:

Sales discounts are deducted from sales, and purchase discounts are deducted from purchases, instead of being shown as financial expense and income, respectively.

The operating expenses are classified as selling and general. (Incidentally, these expenses are shown in a separate schedule. This was done merely to reduce the length of the income statement.)

The federal income tax is shown in the auditor's statement.

The correction of prior periods' net income is shown in the income statement, in accordance with the clean-surplus theory.

A separate statement of retained earnings was prepared. The numerous items affecting retained earnings discovered by the auditor would have unduly encumbered a combined statement of income and retained earnings.

The following changes were made in the organization of the balance sheet:

The reserves for depreciation and for bad debts were shown on the liability side of the bookkeeper's balance sheet. In the auditor's balance sheet, they are deducted (with names changed) from the related assets.

In the auditor's balance sheet, the fixed assets and the accumulated depreciation are detailed.

Pertinent information about the bonds payable is given in the auditor's balance sheet.

In the auditor's balance sheet, the treasury stock and the discount on stock are shown as deductions in the Stockholders' Equity section instead of on the asset side.

THE X Y Z COMPANY

Exhibit C

Income Statement

Year Ended December 31, 1958

Sales...			$692,987
Deduct:			
Sales returns and allowances.........................		$ 9,620	
Sales discounts.......................................		7,650	17,270
Net sales..			$675,717
Deduct cost of goods sold:			
Inventory, December 31, 1957......................		$ 70,000	
Purchases....................................	$546,317		
Add freight in...............................	7,400		
Total..	$553,717		
Deduct:			
Purchase returns and allowances........ $8,500			
Purchase discounts.................... 4,310	12,810		
Net purchases...		540,907	
Total opening inventory and purchases.....................		$610,907	
Deduct inventory, December 31, 1958....................		105,000	
Cost of goods sold..			505,907
Gross profit on sales...................................			$169,810
Deduct selling and general expenses—Schedule 1.......................			116,810
Net operating income......................................			$ 53,000
Add other income:			
Dividend income.....................................		$ 350	
Interest income......................................		410	
Sinking fund income.................................		390	1,150
Net operating and other income............................			$ 54,150
Deduct other expenses:			
Bond interest, including discount amortization.............		$ 3,700	
Notes payable interest...............................		1,350	
Market loss on short-term bond investments...............		700	5,750
Net income before correction of net income of prior periods and federal income tax..			$ 48,400
Correction of net income of prior periods—Amortization of bond discount...			300
Net income before federal income tax...............................			$ 48,100
Federal income tax..			19,500
Net income..			$ 28,600

Note: Applicable notes in the accompanying Notes to Financial Statements are an integral part of this statement.

THE *X Y Z* COMPANY   Exhibit C

Selling and General Expenses   Schedule 1

Year Ended December 31, 1958

Selling expenses:

Rent of leased building.....................................		$ 1,800
Salesmen's salaries..		25,000
Delivery expense..		13,200
Depreciation:		
Store building...............................	$3,600	
Store fixtures................................	3,000	
Delivery equipment...........................	1,000	7,600
Amortization—Leasehold improvements....................		800
Total selling expenses...		$ 48,400
General expenses:		
Officers' salaries...	$32,000	
Office salaries..	18,200	
Bad debts..	4,700	
Insurance expense..	1,800	
Taxes—Other than federal income........................	6,100	
Depreciation—Office furniture and equipment..............	1,000	
Miscellaneous general expenses............................	4,610	
Total general expenses......................................		68,410
Total selling and general expenses................................		$116,810

THE *X Y Z* COMPANY   Exhibit B

Statement of Retained Earnings

Year Ended December 31, 1958

Balance, December 31, 1957:		
Balance per books, December 31, 1958.....................	$87,750	
Add (deduct*) reversal of improper 1958 entries:		
Write-off of discount on bonds payable...................	2,000	
Increase in treasury stock from cost to par...............	500*	
Write-up of goodwill...................................	20,000*	$69,250
Add net income for the year—Exhibit C............................		28,600
Total...		$97,850
Deduct dividend on preferred stock...................................		2,310
Balance, December 31, 1958..		$95,540

THE *X Y Z* COMPANY   Exhibit A

Balance Sheet
December 31, 1958

Assets

Current assets:

Cash...		$ 13,650
Investments in bonds (Cost, $18,500)—at market...........		17,800
Accounts receivable...........................	$56,233	
Less allowance for doubtful accounts............	9,500	46,733
Notes receivable.....................................		10,000
Merchandise inventory....		105,000
Unexpired insurance.................................		1,200
Total current assets......................................		$194,383

Sundry assets:

Stock investments (Market value, $6,200)—at cost..........	$ 7,000	
Land held for resale.................................	10,000	
Sinking fund:		
Securities.................................	$11,850	
Cash......................................	150	12,000
Accounts receivable—Officers...........................	25,000	
Total sundry assets...		54,000

Fixed assets:

Land..	$ 7,000	
Parking lot..	2,000	
Store building.................................	$90,000	
Less accumulated depreciation...................	10,800	79,200
Store fixtures..................................	$30,000	
Less accumulated depreciation...................	9,000	21,000
Delivery equipment............................	$10,000	
Less accumulated depreciation...................	4,000	6,000
Office furniture and equipment...................	$10,000	
Less accumulated depreciation...................	4,000	6,000
Total tangible fixed assets..................................		121,200
Goodwill..		30,000

Deferred charges:

Leasehold improvements—Unamortized balance.............	$ 18,400	
Discount on bonds payable—Unamortized balance..........	1,600	
Total deferred charges...		20,000
		$419,583

THE *X Y Z* COMPANY

Balance Sheet (Concluded)

December 31, 1958

Liabilities and Stockholders' Equity

Current liabilities:

Accounts payable	$ 72,783	
Notes payable	30,000	
Federal income tax payable	19,500	
Dividends payable—Preferred	2,310	
Credit balances in customers' accounts	2,000	
Accrued expenses payable	5,950	
Total current liabilities		$132,543

Real estate, sinking fund, 6% bonds payable; due
December 31, 1974 60,000

Stockholders' equity:

Capital stock:

Preferred—$100 par; authorized, 750 shares; issued (of which 115 shares are in the treasury), 500 shares	$ 50,000	
Common—$100 par; authorized, 2,000 shares; issued and outstanding, 1,000 shares	100,000	
Retained earnings	95,540	
Total	$245,540	

Deduct:

Treasury stock—Preferred (at cost)	$11,000	
Discount on common stock	7,500	18,500
Stockholders' equity		227,040
		$419,583

Note: Applicable notes in the accompanying Notes to Financial Statements are an
integral part of this statement.

Notes to Financial Statements

On December 31, 1958, the company changed its basis of inventory valuation from first-in, first-out to last-in, first-out, thus reducing the inventory at the end of the year and the net income for the year, before federal income tax, approximately $6,400.

The company's retained earnings are restricted, for dividend purposes, in the amount of $11,000, the cost of the treasury stock.

As a part of the indenture executed when the bonds were issued, the company agreed to refrain from the payment of any dividends on its common stock which would reduce the retained earnings to an amount less than $60,000, the par of the bonds.

Comparison of bookkeeper's and auditor's statements. Some of the important differences between the statements prepared by the bookkeeper and those prepared by the auditor are mentioned below:

	Bookkeeper's Statements	Auditor's Statements
Net income for the year	$ 65,450	$ 28,600
Stockholders' equity—End of year	313,200	227,040
Retained earnings—End of year	153,200	95,540
Working capital:		
Current assets	$251,883	$194,383
Current liabilities	88,783	132,543
Working capital	$163,100	$ 61,840
Working capital ratio	2.8	1.5
Ratio of worth to debt:		
Stockholders' equity	$313,200	$227,040
Current and long-term debt	148,783	192,543
Ratio of worth to debt	2.1	1.2

APPENDIX 1
Matters Related to Payrolls

Federal old age benefits taxes. The Social Security Act of 1935, as amended, provides for federal government disbursements called variously "old age benefits," "old age and survivors' benefits," "old age insurance," and "old age annuities." These payments include monthly benefits to retired workers, supplementary benefits to their wives, husbands, and dependent children, benefits for survivors of deceased wage earners, "disability benefits," and lump-sum payments in some cases.

The funds required for these disbursements are obtained from taxes (often called "O.A.B. taxes") levied under the Federal Insurance Contributions Act on employers and employees, in amounts based on wage payments for services performed in the United States, Alaska, Hawaii, Virgin Islands, and Puerto Rico, and on American vessels and aircraft. Certain services are excepted. Payments made to an independent contractor for services are not wages.

The taxes levied on employees are withheld by the employers from wage payments; these tax withholdings, as well as the taxes levied on the employers, are remitted by the employers to the District Director of Internal Revenue for the district in which the principal place of business of the employer is located. At the time of this writing, the rate is $2\frac{1}{4}\%$, to increase to $2\frac{3}{4}\%$ in 1960, to $3\frac{1}{4}\%$ in 1965, to $3\frac{3}{4}\%$ in 1970, and to $4\frac{1}{4}\%$ in 1975 and thereafter. Because of possible revisions in the law, you should ascertain the rate currently in effect.

The tax is not levied on wages in excess of $4,200 paid to a worker by one employer during a calendar year. However, if an individual works for two or more employers during a calendar year, each employer is required to pay the tax on his wage payments to the employee up to $4,200, and to make similar deductions from the employee's wages. The employee can obtain a refund from the government for deducted taxes on his aggregate wages for the year in excess of $4,200; the employers cannot obtain a refund.

Each employer must apply to the Social Security Administration for an "identification number," to be shown on his tax return. Each worker must apply to the Administration for an "account number"—often referred to as his *social security number;* the employer must be informed of the account number of each of his employees, for use in his records and reports.

The law specifies that every employer withholding taxes must furnish the employee with an annual statement on or before January 31 of the succeeding year which shows the total social security tax withheld.

If employment is terminated, the employer must give a final statement to the employee not later than 30 days after the final wage payment. Many employers find it convenient to report the tax deduction at the time of making each wage payment; methods of making such reports to employees are illustrated on pages 497 and 499.

The employer is required to maintain records which show, as to each employee, his name, address, and social security number; the total compensation due him at each pay date; any portion thereof not subject to tax; the period covered by the payment; and the amount of the employee's tax deducted. The employer must also keep copies of all returns and reports filed by him with government authorities.

Self-employed persons. Self-employed persons other than doctors of medicine are covered by the old age and survivors' insurance program. The tax on self-employment income is handled in all particulars as an integral part of the federal income tax. The rate is 1½ times the social security withholding rate for employees; it is applied to the first $4,200 of net earnings.

Federal unemployment insurance taxes. Taxes are levied against employers (but not against employees) under the Federal Unemployment Tax Act to obtain funds required to meet the provisions of the Social Security Act relative to unemployment insurance, sometimes called *unemployment compensation.* Unemployment compensation payments are not made by the federal government directly to unemployed persons; the funds obtained by the collection of federal unemployment insurance taxes are used to make grants to the various states to assist them in carrying out their own unemployment compensation programs. Laws providing for unemployment compensation payments have been enacted by all the states and territories.

Unlike the federal old age benefit tax, which is assessed against an employer with one or more employees in covered employment, the federal unemployment insurance taxes are assessed against only certain employers, as defined in the law, as follows:

"The term 'employer' does not include any person unless on each day of some twenty days during the taxable year, each day being in a different calendar week, the total number of individuals who were employed by him in employment for some portion of the day (whether or not at the same moment of time) was four or more."

The expression "employed by him in employment" has the significance of *employed by him in covered employment,* or, in other words, not employed in the performance of exempt services. A person is not subject to the federal unemployment insurance tax unless he has employed at least four individuals for the performance of nonexempt services on at least one day during at least twenty different weeks of the calendar year; and an employer who is subject to the tax is assessed on the basis of wages paid to only those employees who are engaged in the performance of nonexempt services.

The federal unemployment insurance tax rate is 3%; wages in excess of $3,000 paid to any one individual during the taxable year are not subject to the tax. Although the tax rate is 3%, the employer is entitled to a credit for taxes paid to the states and territories under their unemployment compensation laws. This credit cannot be more than 90% of the tax assessed by the federal government at the 3% rate. Because of this provision in the federal law, the states have generally established a 2.7% unemployment compensation tax rate. Since taxable wages are generally (though subject to some minor exceptions) computed in the same manner for both federal and state taxes, the tax rates are usually considered to be as follows:

Federal tax............... .3%
State tax................ 2.7
Total................. 3.0%

Although the basic rate for state taxes is 2.7%, the tax actually payable to a state may be computed at a lower rate. Since one of the purposes of state unemployment legislation is to stabilize employment, the state laws contain provisions for merit-rating plans; under these provisions, an employer who establishes a good record for stable employment (thus reducing the claims upon state funds for unemployment compensation) may obtain the benefit of a state tax rate much lower than 2.7%. In order to assure the employer of the enjoyment of the tax saving resulting from the reduced state rate, the federal law provides that an employer paying a state tax at a rate less than 2.7%, as a result of the state's merit-rating plan, may deduct as a credit an amount computed at the 2.7% rate or at the highest rate applicable to any taxpayer in the state, whichever is lower; the amount of the credit cannot, of course, be more than 90% of the federal tax.

The employer must file his federal unemployment tax return with the District Director of Internal Revenue on or before January 31 following the taxable calendar year. To assure himself of obtaining the credit for state taxes, he should pay these taxes not later than January 31.

The employer's records should contain all information required to support his tax return.

State unemployment compensation taxes. Stimulated by the enactment of the federal unemployment insurance legislation, all the states and territories have passed laws which have, in general, the following principal objectives:

(1) The payment of compensation, of limited amounts and for limited periods, to unemployed workers.

(2) The operation of facilities to assist employers in obtaining employees, and to help workers obtain employment.

(3) The encouragement of employers to stabilize employment; the inducement offered is a reduction in the tax rate, through the operation of merit-rating systems.

Since the laws of the several states differ in many particulars, it is possible here to give only a general discussion. All the states levy a tax on employers; a very few also levy a tax on employees (in most cases, for payment of benefits in non-occupational disability cases). The list of exempt services in the federal law is rather closely followed in most of the state laws. Whereas the federal unemployment insurance tax is assessed against only those employers who have four or more employees, many of the states assess taxes on employers of a smaller number of individuals—even as few as one. In most states the tax is not assessed on salaries in excess of $3,000. In general, the state tax rate is basically 2.7%, but provision is made in some of the laws for increased rates if they are essential to meet disbursement requirements. All state laws include a merit-rating plan of some kind; these plans are intended to effect lower taxes by a reduction of the tax rate or by a credit against taxes for employers who have established (during an experience period, usually of three years) a favorable record of stable employment. The *reserve ratio* plan is typical; in principle it operates as follows:

Assume that an employer's average annual payroll for three years has been $100,000.

Assume, also, that the balance in the state's reserve account with this employer is $5,000; this is the excess of the taxes paid by this employer over the amounts of benefits paid by the state to his former employees.

The reserve ratio ($5,000 ÷ $100,000) is 5%.

The higher the reserve ratio, the lower the tax rate.

Most states require employers to file returns quarterly and to pay the tax by the end of the month following the close of the quarter. Since the amount of taxable wages paid to an individual is usually one of the factors determining the amounts of benefits payable to him when he is unemployed, employers are required to file information returns showing the amount of compensation paid to each employee during the period.

The states require employers to maintain a compensation record for each employee, showing, among other things, the period of employment, the reason for termination of employment, the cause of lost time, and the amounts of periodical payments of compensation to him during the period of employment. The specific requirements of each state are shown in its published regulations.

Federal income tax withholding. Employers of one or more employees are required to withhold federal income taxes from the wages of employees, except certain exempt wage payments.

The amount withheld from an employee's wages is affected by his income and the number of exemptions ($600 each).

An individual is entitled to:

(1) An exemption for himself.
(2) An additional exemption if he is over 65 or will become 65 on or before January 1 of the following year.
(3) An additional exemption if he is blind.

If the employee is married, he can claim any of the above exemptions which his spouse could claim if she were employed—unless, of course, she is employed and claims them herself.

(4) An exemption for each dependent. No *additional* exemptions are allowed for aged or blind *dependents*.

A dependent is a person who is closely related to the taxpayer, has a gross income of less than $600 for the year, and received more than half of his support for the year from the taxpayer.

In order to determine the amount of tax which he should withhold from an employee's compensation, the employer must know the number of exemptions claimed by the employee. Therefore, the employee is required to furnish an Employee's Withholding Exemption Certificate to his employer.

If the employee's status as to exemptions changes during the year, he should give his employer an amended certificate; he is required to do so if the number of exemptions decreases, and he is permitted to do so if the number of exemptions increases.

The employer's report and payment procedures are summarized as follows:

Each employer must file a quarterly combined return for F. I.

C. A. taxes and withheld income taxes. Except as noted in the following paragraph, the return and taxes are due and payable on or before the last day of the month following the calendar quarter covered by the return.

If the combined F. I. C. A. taxes and withheld income taxes of any employer exceed $100 in any month other than the last month of a quarter (March, June, September, or December), the employer is required to deposit them in an authorized depositary bank by the 15th of the following month. For March, June, September, or December, the employer may deposit the taxes in an authorized bank on or before the end of the following month. If all these monthly deposits have been made on time, the due date for the quarterly return is extended to the 10th day of the second month following the calendar quarter covered.

On or before January 31, the employer should give each of his employees a withholding statement showing the employee's total wages for the preceding year and the amount of income tax and social security tax withheld therefrom. If an employee's employment is terminated, the employer should give him, at the time of the last wage payment, a withholding statement covering the portion of the year during which he was employed.

With the return for the last calendar quarter, each employer must file the carbon copies of all withholding statements given to employees. These must be accompanied by a listing of the amounts of withheld taxes as shown by the copies of the withholding statements.

Other payroll deductions. Employers may make other deductions from payrolls, such as the following: deductions for premiums for group hospital insurance, deductions for purchases of government bonds for the employees, and deductions for payment of union dues.

Requirements of Federal Fair Labor Standards Act. This act establishes a minimum hourly wage rate and maximum hours of work per week for certain classes of employees engaged directly or indirectly in interstate commerce, and provides that payment for overtime hours in excess of 40 hours during any work week shall be at the rate of $1\frac{1}{2}$ times the regular hourly wage. The act also requires that employers subject to it shall maintain a record for each subject employee showing his name, address, date of birth (if under 19), occupation, work week, regular rate of pay per hour, basis of wage payment (hour, week, month, piecework, and so on), hours worked per day and per work week, daily or weekly wages at his regular rate, weekly excess compensation for overtime worked, miscellaneous additions to or deductions from wages, total periodical wage payments, and date of payment.

Following are some illustrations of the application of the requirement for the payment of wages at $1\frac{1}{2}$ times the regular hourly rate for hours of work in excess of 40 hours during any work week:

(1) A's regular hourly rate is $2.00. He works 45 hours during one week. His wages are computed as follows:

```
45 hours at $2.00............................ $90.00
 5 hours at  1.00............................   5.00
    Total...................................  $95.00
```

(2) B's wages are $58.50 a week for a regular work week of 39 hours (7 hours a day for 5 days, and 4 hours on Saturday). He works 45 hours during one week.

```
$58.50 ÷ 39 = $1.50 regular hourly rate.
45 hours at $1.50 = $67.50
 5 hours at   .75 =   3.75 (Excess payment for hours over 40)
    Total            $71.25
```

(3) C accepts a position with the understanding that he is to work 7 hours per day during each of the 6 days of his work week, and is to receive a weekly wage of $86; that the weekly wage includes overtime at time and one-half for the 2 hours over 40; and that if he works less than 42 hours, a corresponding deduction will be made. He works 50 hours during one week. To determine his regular hourly rate, we must remember that his regular work week consists of 42 hours, and that for 2 of these hours he is being paid $1\frac{1}{2}$ times the regular hourly rate; in other words, for the 2 hours regularly worked in addition to 40 hours, he is given the equivalent of 3 hours' pay. Therefore,

```
$86.00 ÷ 43 = $2.00, the regular hourly rate.
```

If he works the regular 42 hours, his wage is (theoretically) computed as follows:

```
42 hours at $2.00 = $84.00
 2 hours at  1.00 =   2.00 (Excess for hours over 40)
    Total            $86.00
```

For the week that he works 50 hours, his wage is:

```
50 hours at $2.00 = $100.00
10 hours at  1.00 =   10.00 (Excess for hours over 40)
    Total            $110.00
```

If wages are paid monthly or semimonthly, recognition must be given to the fact that the time-and-one-half requirement applies to each work week separately. To illustrate, assume that an employee whose regular hourly rate is $2.00 was paid for the half-month ended Wednesday, July 15, and that he was entitled to no overtime payment for that period. We are now to compute his wage payment for the last half of July; we require the following information as to hours worked:

In prior payroll period:

Monday,	July 13	8
Tuesday,	" 14	8
Wednesday,	" 15	8

In current payroll period:

Thursday,	July 16	8
Friday,	" 17	7
Saturday,	" 18	5
Monday,	" 20	6
Tuesday,	" 21	7
Wednesday,	" 22	7
Thursday,	" 23	8
Friday,	" 24	6
Saturday,	" 25	7
Monday,	" 27	8
Tuesday,	" 28	8
Wednesday,	" 29	8
Thursday,	" 30	8
Friday,	" 31	8

His total wage payment for the semimonthly period is computed as follows:

(a) For the portion of the work week ended July 18:
   Considering that work week as a whole, he worked 44 hours. Since, at the time of making the payment for the period ended July 15, it was not known whether he would work over 40 hours during the entire week, he was paid for the first 3 days at the regular rate. We now find that he worked 44 hours during that week, 20 of them during the current payroll period. Therefore, the payment to him now should be:

$$20 \text{ hours at } \$2.00 = \$40.00$$
$$4 \text{ hours at } 1.00 = \underline{4.00}$$
$$\text{Total} \qquad \$44.00$$

(b) For the work week ended July 25:
   During this week he worked 41 hours. For it he should be paid:

$$41 \text{ hours at } \$2.00 = \$82.00$$
$$1 \text{ hour at } 1.00 = \underline{1.00}$$
$$\text{Total} \qquad \$83.00$$

(c) For the portion of the work week ended July 31:
Although he had already worked 40 hours during the week, there was no certainty on Friday night that he would work on Saturday. Therefore, he should be paid an amount computed as follows:

40 hours at $2.00 = $80.00

His total wage payment for the semimonthly period is the total of the items shown below:

For partial work week ended July 18	$ 44.00
For work week ended July 25	83.00
For partial work week ended July 31	80.00
Total	$207.00

Payroll procedures. The payroll summary on page 498 furnishes information required for the entries in the ledger accounts applicable to wages and payroll deductions. Postings of column totals may be made directly from the payroll summary to the ledger; the debits and credits are shown below.

Wages (If it is desired to debit various accounts for amounts of wages payable for different services, an analysis must be made to obtain the information for this purpose)	3,265.20	
F. I. C. A. tax liability		68.78
Income tax withholding liability		419.90
Accrued payroll		2,776.52

One account, "Withholding and F. I. C. A. Tax Liabilities," may be used for both the social security and the income tax withholdings since such withheld amounts are combined and reported, with the employer's share of the F. I. C. A. tax, on the same form to the same agency of the federal government.

The amount shown in the payroll summary for F. I. C. A. withholdings is not exactly $2\frac{1}{4}\%$ of the payroll; this is presumably because some of the wage payments represented excesses over $4,200, which therefore were not subject to the social security taxes.

The employer should compute his own liability for social security taxes in the manner shown below.

Total wages	$3,265.20	$3,265.20
Wages (in excess of $4,200) not subject to F. I. C. A. taxes	208.10	
Wages (in excess of $3,000) not subject to unemployment taxes		608.10
Wages subject to taxes	$3,057.10	$2,657.10
Taxes:		
F. I. C. A.—$2\frac{1}{4}\%$ of $3,057.10		$ 68.78
Federal unemployment—0.3% of $2,657.10		7.97
State unemployment—2.7% of $2,657.10		71.74
		$ 148.49

The entry to record the expense and the liabilities for these taxes may be as follows:

```
Payroll taxes expense (separate expense accounts may be
   used if desired).....................................  148.49
   F. I. C. A. tax liability............................           68.78
   Federal unemployment tax liability.................            7.97
   State unemployment tax liability...................           71.74
```

To meet the requirements of the social security legislation, it is also desirable to keep, for each employee, an individual employment and compensation record, similar to that illustrated on page 498.

To comply with legal requirements, payroll records, with supporting data, should be retained for four years.

Wage payment reports to employees. As previously stated, many employers make reports to employees of payroll deductions at the time of each wage payment.

If wages are paid by check, a stub may be attached to the check and the data may be shown on the stub, as illustrated on page 499.

If wages are paid in cash, the pay envelope may be printed as illustrated below:

```
┌───────────────────────────────────────────────────┐
│           THE BROWN COMPANY                        │
│                                                     │
│      Employee's                                     │
│         name_____               │
│                                                     │
│      Employee's number_____               │
│                                                     │
│      Date paid_____19____                │
│                        Hours     Wages             │
│      Regular          _____   _____            │
│      Overtime         _____   _____            │
│        Total          _____   _____            │
│      Deductions:                                    │
│        F. I. C. A. tax _____                      │
│        Fed. Inc. tax   _____                      │
│        Savings bonds  _____                       │
│        Insurance       _____                      │
│                       _____   _____            │
│                                                     │
│                       _____   _____            │
│           Total deductions     _____             │
│      Cash enclosed             _____             │
└───────────────────────────────────────────────────┘
```

PAYROLL SUMMARY

For the Week Ended ___ August 7, 195—   Date of Payment ___ August 9, 195—

Employee No.	Income Tax Exemptions	Name	Day of Month — Hours Worked						Total Hours	Hours Over 40	Hourly Wage Rates		Wages			Deductions			Net	Check No.
			1	2	3	4	5	6 7			Regular	Excess	Regular	Excess	Total	F.I.C.A.	Income Tax	Hospital Insurance		
35	1	John Jones	7	8	6	8	7	7	43	3	1 95	975	83 85	2 93	86 78	1 95	13 40		71 43	5216
36	3	Frank Brown	7	7	7	7	7	7	42	2	2 15	1 075	90 30	2 15	92 45	2 08	9 80		80 57	5217
													3,128 40	136 80	3,265 20	68 78	419 90		2,776 52	

INDIVIDUAL EMPLOYMENT AND COMPENSATION RECORD

Name ___ John Jones   Employee No. ___ 35

Address ___ 2913 So. Burns Ave.,   Social Security Acct. No. ___ 325-10-0876

___ Chicago   Date of Birth ___ 8-17-28

Phone ___ BA 9-4631

Date Employed ___ 8-1-5—

Date of Severance ___

Cause ___

For Week In 195– Ended	Income Tax Exemptions	Lost Time		Hours Worked		Regular Hourly Rate	Total Wages	F.I.C.A.	Deductions		Net	Check No.
		Hours	Cause	Total	Over-time				Income Tax	Hospital Insurance		
Aug. 7	1	1	V	43	3	1 95	86 78	1 95	13 40		71 43	5216
14				42	2		83 85	1 89	12 60		69 86	5273

V—Voluntary time off.

PAY ROLL CHECK

HUDSON & DUTTON
210 SOUTH LA SALLE STREET

No. A 210

CHICAGO 4, _____ 19____

PAY
TO THE
ORDER OF _____

$ _____

_____ DOLLARS

PAY ROLL

FIDELITY NATIONAL BANK
OF CHICAGO

HUDSON & DUTTON

BY _____

DETACH BEFORE CASHING CHECK

STATEMENT OF EARNINGS AND DEDUCTIONS
FOR EMPLOYEE'S RECORD COVERING PAY
PERIOD TO AND INCLUDING DATE
SHOWN BELOW

HUDSON & DUTTON
210 S. LA SALLE ST.
CHICAGO, ILL.

DATE _____ 19____

TO _____

TOTAL WAGES	
OLD AGE BENEFIT	
WITHHOLDING FED. INCOME TAX	
SAVINGS BONDS	
INSURANCE	
TOTAL DEDUCTIONS	
AMOUNT THIS CHECK	

APPENDIX 2

Locating Errors

It is impracticable to attempt to state a procedure which can invariably be followed, step by step, in locating errors in the general ledger or in the subsidiary records. Experience is the best guide, but the following suggestions may be helpful.

Checking the general ledger. It is usually advisable to locate any errors in the general ledger before looking for errors in the subsidiary records. Until the general ledger is in balance, there can be no assurance that the controlling accounts are correct. Suppose, for instance, that the general ledger is out of balance and that the accounts receivable ledger is not in agreement with its control; it may be that the Accounts Receivable controlling account is incorrect and that, after the error in that account has been located, the subsidiary ledger and the controlling account will be in agreement.

If the general ledger is out of balance, the following procedure may be followed by the bookkeeper:

(1) Refoot the general ledger trial balance.
(2) See that the ledger balances have been correctly transcribed to the trial balance, watching for errors in amounts, for debit balances entered on the credit side of the trial balance or vice versa, and for ledger balances omitted from the trial balance.
(3) Recompute the ledger balances and refoot the debit and credit sides of the accounts.
(4) Check the postings from the books of original entry to the ledger, watching for errors in amounts and for postings to the wrong side of an account. As mentioned in Chapter 10, entries affecting controlling accounts are sometimes made in books of original entry which do not contain special columns for the controlling accounts affected; the amounts are entered in the General Ledger column and are posted twice: to the controlling account and to the subsidiary ledger. In checking the postings, give special attention to such items to be sure that they have been properly posted.

As each item in a book of original entry is traced to the ledger, place a check mark beside the amount in the book

500

of original entry and also beside the amount in the ledger. After this work has been completed, look for unchecked items in the books of original entry (indicating items which have not been posted), and for unchecked items in the ledger (indicating entries which have been posted twice, or which, for some other reason, do not belong in the ledger).

(5) Refoot the books of original entry from which column totals have been posted.   (Of course, if a column total is posted as a debit to one account and a credit to another account, the general ledger will not be thrown out of balance, even though the column was incorrectly footed.)

If a book of original entry contains debit and credit columns, cross-foot the column totals to see that the sum of the debit column totals is equal to the sum of the credit column totals.

Posting to work sheets.   If the procedure described above does not result in locating the error, it may be necessary to post all the entries to work sheets.   Using sheets as large as can easily be handled, head up skeleton accounts, thus:

Cash	Accounts Receivable	Notes Receivable

Provide skeleton accounts for all the accounts in the ledger, putting as many accounts as possible on one page, and allowing only as much space as is necessary in each account.   Copy into the skeleton accounts all the ledger balances at the beginning of the period; take a trial balance of the skeleton accounts, thus proving that the accounts were in balance at the beginning of the month or the year.   Post all the entries from the books of original entry, entering only the reference to the book of original entry and the amount, thus:

Accounts Receivable	
Bal........ 10,000	RS........ 1,000
S.......... 30,000	CR........ 27,000
	J.......... 1,500

After completing the posting to the work sheets, compute the balance of each work sheet account and compare it with the balance of the corresponding ledger account.   If the balance of a work sheet account does not agree with the balance of the corresponding ledger account, compare the entries in the ledger account with the entries in the work sheet account.

This procedure is called *abstracting the books of original entry,* and will often locate an error after all other methods have failed.

Checking the subsidiary ledgers. After the general ledger has been balanced, if a subsidiary ledger does not agree with its control:

(1) It may be tentatively assumed that the general ledger is correct and that the error lies in the subsidiary ledger.

   (a) Refoot the schedule of the subsidiary ledger.
   (b) See that the balances of the subsidiary ledger accounts have been correctly transcribed from the ledger to the schedule, watching for errors in amounts and for balances omitted from the schedule. In some cases, subsidiary ledgers which normally contain only debit balances (as the accounts receivable ledger) have a few credit balances, and ledgers which normally contain only credit balances (as the accounts payable ledger) have a few debit balances; such exceptional balances should be watched for.
   (c) Recompute the ledger balances.
   (d) Trace all postings from the books of original entry to the subsidiary ledgers, place check marks beside the entries in the books of original entry and the accounts, and look for unchecked items.

(2) The assumption that the error is in the subsidiary ledger may be incorrect. Suppose, for instance, that a sales book appears as follows:

Sales Book

Date		Name	√	Amount
19—				
July	3	John Smith.....................	√	500 00
	15	William Brown.................	√	600 00
	29	Fred White...........	√	300 00
				1,500 00
				(10) (501)

This sales book has been incorrectly footed; the total should be $1,400 instead of $1,500. The error in footing resulted in an excess debit to Accounts Receivable control and a similar excess credit to Sales, and left the general ledger in balance—but incorrect. The subsidiary accounts receivable ledger will not agree with its control; but the error is in the general ledger, notwithstanding the fact that the general ledger is in balance.

Because of such possibilities, all column totals posted to controlling accounts should be refooted.

Checking other subsidiary records. The voucher register is a subsidiary record, but postings are not made to it as they are to a subsidiary accounts receivable or accounts payable ledger. The open or unpaid items consist of those entries which have no notations in the Date Paid column. If the schedule of open items in the voucher register does not agree with the balance of the Vouchers Payable account:

(1) Refoot the Vouchers Payable columns in all books of original entry to see that the totals posted to the controlling account are correct.

(2) See whether there are any debits to Vouchers Payable in any of the books of original entry, recording cancellations of vouchers because installment payments are to be made or for any other reasons; if any such debits to Vouchers Payable are found, see that they have been correctly posted.

(3) The check register shows the numbers of all paid vouchers; working from the check register, see that notations have been made in the Date Paid column for all paid vouchers.

(4) Vouchers are sometimes canceled by the issuance of notes; in such cases, suitable notations should be made in the voucher register. See that all such notations have been made.

(5) Other journal entries, such as for purchase returns and allowances, may affect the balance of the Vouchers Payable account; be sure that they were given proper recognition when the schedule of open vouchers was prepared.

The note registers may be subsidiary records; if so, the open items should agree with the balances in the Notes Receivable and Notes Payable accounts. If the notes receivable register is out of agreement with the controlling account:

(1) See that there is an entry in the register for each note received and recorded in the journal (notes received on account) or in the cash disbursements book or voucher register (notes received for money loaned).

(2) See that a notation in the Date Paid column of the register has been made for each note collected (recorded in the cash receipts book) or otherwise canceled (recorded in the journal or elsewhere).

If the notes payable register is out of agreement with its control, similar procedures may be followed.

Expense ledgers or analysis records are also subsidiary records. If they do not agree with their controls:

(1) Refoot the summaries prepared at the end of the month, or recompute the balances if subsidiary ledgers are kept.
(2) Check all postings from the voucher register (or from the vouchers, if postings are made from the vouchers) and watch particularly for charges or credits to expense controls from other books, seeing that entries have also been made in the subsidiary records. For instance, depreciation charges will be recorded in the journal, expense adjustments may also be made in the journal, and refunds credited to expense accounts may be recorded in the cash receipts book.

Special tests. Certain special tests may be applied in locating errors in the general ledger or in finding differences between the subsidiary ledgers and the controls. These tests, stated below, may be applied before beginning the routine already described.

(1) Determine the exact difference to be located; for instance, assume that the debit total of the general ledger trial balance is $50,200 and that the credit total is $50,000; the difference is $200—too little credit or too much debit.

(a) Look for a credit balance of $200 in the ledger; it may have been omitted from the trial balance.
(b) Look for a $200 error in transcribing the balances from the ledger accounts; for instance, a debit balance of $2,000 entered in the trial balance as $2,200, or a credit balance of $2,200 entered in the trial balance as $2,000.
(c) Look for an entry of $200 in the books of original entry; if it is a credit, it may not have been posted; if it is a debit, it may have been posted twice.

(2) Treating a debit as a credit (or vice versa) either in posting or in transferring balances to the trial balance will produce a trial balance difference of twice the amount of the item incorrectly treated. Therefore, divide the trial balance difference by two; in the foregoing illustration, the quotient will be $100. Since we have too much debit (or too little credit):

(a) Look for a credit balance of $100 in the ledger and see whether it may have been entered on the debit side of the trial balance.

(b) Look for a credit entry of $100 in the books of original entry and see if it may have been posted to the debit side of the ledger.

(3) Transpositions of figures (for instance, $78.50 posted as $75.80) are errors frequently and easily made; they should be constantly guarded against and may be sought for if the books are out of balance. A transposition of two figures will produce an error of an amount exactly divisible by nine; if the transposed figures are in adjacent decimal positions, the significant figure of the quotient after dividing by nine will be the difference between the figures transposed; and the decimal position of this significant figure will be that of the right of the two numbers transposed.

As an illustration:

An entry of......	$78.50
Posted as......	75.80
Will cause a difference of......	$ 2.70
Dividing this difference by 9 will produce a quotient of......	.30

Since the difference ($2.70) is exactly divisible by 9, a transposition is indicated; the difference between the figures transposed appears to be 3; and these figures appear to be in the dimes column and the column at its left. Hence we may look for items (ledger balances or entries) where the difference between the two figures in the dimes and dollars places is 3, as in the number $78.50.

As another illustration:

An entry of......	$613.50
Posted as......	163.50
Will produce a difference of......	$450.00
The quotient after dividing by 9 is......	50.00

Suggesting a transposition (in the tens and hundreds columns) of two figures with a difference of 5.

These special tests for transpositions are sometimes helpful in locating errors, but the other methods described are more likely to be effective.

Correcting errors. Erasures in accounting books should be avoided, since they tend to discredit the records. Corrections should be made by drawing a line through the incorrect entry and making the correct entry above it, or by a journal entry, thus:

Machinery and equipment......	500.00	
Buildings......		500.00

To correct improper posting of voucher register entry of June 15. Debit was posted to Buildings account; should have been posted to Machinery and Equipment.

APPENDIX 3

Preparation of Monthly Statements When Books Are Closed Annually

On pages 508 and 509 are working papers prepared at the end of January, 1958. The books of the company were closed on the preceding December 31. They were not closed on January 31. Therefore, in the February 28, 1958 working papers (pages 510 and 511),

The Inventory account balance shows the amount of the inventory on December 31.

The Retained Earnings account balance shows the balance on December 31.

The balances of the revenue and expense accounts show results of operations for the two months ended February 28.

The asset and liability account balances show assets (other than inventory) and liabilities at the end of February.

If it is desired to prepare statements for the two months ended February 28, the working papers can be prepared in the manner with which you are already familiar.

However, if it is desired to prepare operating statements for February, the account balances will not show operating results for that month, and it will be necessary to deduct January 31 balances of operating accounts from February 28 balances to determine the changes in the account balances during February. Refer to the working papers on pages 510 and 511 and observe the following:

The trial balances after adjustment, on January 31 and February 28, are entered in the first two pairs of columns.

The balances in the revenue and expense accounts (beginning with Sales and ending with Federal Income Tax) on January 31 are deducted from the balances on February 28, and the differences (resulting from February transactions) are extended to the February Income Statement columns.

The inventory on December 31 is not extended to any column.

The inventory at the end of January (which was shown in the January working papers) is entered in the Income Statement debit column; and the inventory at the end of February is entered in the Income Statement credit and the Balance Sheet debit columns.

The balance in the Income Statement columns then shows the net income for February. This is entered as a balancing figure in the Income Statement debit column and is extended to the Retained Earnings credit column.

The balance of the Retained Earnings account as of December 31 is entered in the Retained Earnings credit column. The net income for January, shown by the working papers for that month, is also entered in the Retained Earnings credit column. The balance of the Retained Earnings columns then shows the retained earnings at the end of February; the amount is entered in the Retained Earnings debit column as a balancing figure and is extended to the Balance Sheet credit column.

The February 28 balances in the asset, liability, and capital stock accounts are extended to the Balance Sheet columns, and these columns are footed.

The statements for January and February are not shown; they would be prepared from the working papers in the usual manner.

THE BAILEY COMPANY
Working Papers
For the Month of January, 1958

	Trial Balance January 31, 1958 After Adjustments	Income Statement	Retained Earnings Statement	Balance Sheet
Cash	3,417.00			3,417.00
Accounts receivable	8,956.00			8,956.00
Allowance for doubtful accounts	460.00			460.00
Notes receivable	3,000.00			3,000.00
Accrued interest receivable	21.00			21.00
Inventory (December 31, 1957)	23,650.00	23,650.00		
Unexpired insurance	180.00			180.00
Land	10,000.00			10,000.00
Buildings	25,000.00			25,000.00
Accumulated depreciation—Buildings	3,083.00			3,083.00
Furniture and fixtures	6,000.00			6,000.00
Accumulated depreciation—F. & F.	1,050.00			1,050.00
Accounts payable	5,860.00			5,860.00
Notes payable	6,000.00			6,000.00
Accrued interest payable	18.00			18.00
Federal income tax payable	800.00			800.00
Capital stock	50,000.00			50,000.00
Retained earnings (December 31, 1957)	10,308.00		10,308.00	

Sales		11,975.00		11,975.00		11,918.00
Sales returns and allowances	212.00		212.00			
Sales discounts	207.00		207.00			
Purchases	6,730.00		6,730.00			
Purchase returns and allowances	115.00		115.00		115.00	
Purchase discounts	58.00		58.00		58.00	
Freight in	196.00		196.00			
Selling expense (Control)	862.00		862.00			
General expense (Control)	493.00		493.00			
Interest earned	15.00		15.00		15.00	
Interest expense	18.00		18.00			
Federal income tax	800.00		800.00			
	89,742.00	89,742.00				
Inventory, January 31, 1958					11,918.00	11,918.00
Net income for January		22,615.00	1,610.00	22,615.00	1,610.00	
			34,778.00	34,778.00	11,918.00	79,189.00
Retained earnings, January 31, 1958					11,918.00	79,189.00

THE BAILEY COMPANY
Working Papers
For the Month of February, 1958

	Adjusted Trial Balances		Income Statement	Retained Earnings Statement	Balance Sheet
	January 31, 1958	February 28, 1958			
Cash............................	3,417.00	5,095.00			5,095.00
Accounts receivable..........	8,956.00	9,329.00			9,329.00
Allowance for doubtful accounts...............	460.00	525.00			525.00
Notes receivable..............	3,000.00	3,000.00			3,000.00
Accrued interest receivable.	21.00	36.00			36.00
Inventory (December 31, 1957).....................	23,650.00	23,650.00			
Unexpired insurance........	180.00	165.00			165.00
Land..........................	10,000.00	10,000.00			10,000.00
Buildings.....................	25,000.00	25,000.00			25,000.00
Accumulated depreciation—Buildings...............	3,083.00	3,166.00			3,166.00
Furniture and fixtures.....	6,000.00	6,000.00			6,000.00
Accumulated depreciation—F. & F...............	1,050.00	1,100.00			1,100.00
Accounts payable............	5,860.00	5,320.00			5,320.00
Notes payable................	6,000.00	6,000.00			6,000.00
Accrued interest payable...	18.00	46.00			46.00
Federal income tax payable	800.00	1,520.00			1,520.00

	Dr.	Cr.	Dr.	Cr.	Dr.	Cr.	Dr.	Cr.
Capital stock		50,000.00		50,000.00				50,000.00
Retained earnings (December 31, 1957)		10,308.00		10,308.00				10,308.00
Sales		11,975.00		21,840.00		9,865.00		
Sales returns and allowances	212.00		387.00		175.00			
Sales discounts	207.00		394.00		187.00			
Purchases	6,730.00		12,570.00		5,840.00			
Purchase returns and allowances		115.00		207.00		92.00		
Purchase discounts		58.00		109.00		51.00		
Freight in	196.00		307.00		111.00			
Selling expense (Control)	862.00		1,709.00		847.00			
General expense (Control)	493.00		963.00		470.00			
Interest earned		15.00		30.00		15.00		
Interest expense	18.00		46.00		28.00			
Federal income tax	800.00		1,520.00		720.00			
	89,742.00	89,742.00	100,171.00	100,171.00				
Inventories:								
January 31					22,615.00		22,400.00	
February 28						22,400.00		1,430.00
Net income for February					1,430.00			
					32,423.00	32,423.00		
Net income for January								13,348.00
Retained earnings, February 28, 1958							13,348.00	81,025.00
							13,348.00	81,025.00

ASSIGNMENT MATERIAL

ASSIGNMENT MATERIAL

Ruled forms especially adapted to the solutions of all Group A problems are provided in the envelopes of laboratory material accompanying the text.

Journal, ledger, and analysis paper is suitable for solutions to most of the Group B problems. A pad of such paper, as well as some ruled forms more specifically adapted to the solutions of some problems, is available.

If no year is stated in the questions, problems, and practice sets, use the current year.

ASSIGNMENT MATERIAL FOR CHAPTER 1
Questions

1. Describe the work performed by accountants.

2. What are the three common forms of business organization?

3. What is a balance sheet?

4. What is the primary purpose of a balance sheet?

5. Define assets. Prepare a list of ten assets.

6. What is the balance sheet equation?

7. Discuss some of the characteristics of assets that make them valuable.

8. Mention transactions that would cause the conditions set forth below:

(a) Assets increased; owners' equity increased.
(b) Assets increased; liabilities increased.
(c) Assets decreased; liabilities decreased.
(d) Asset total unchanged; liabilities and owners' equity total unchanged.

Problems—Group A

Problem A 1-1. Using the following data, prepare the balance sheet of State Service Enterprises as of December 31, 1958.

Cash	$3,200
Capital stock	5,000
Accounts payable	2,500
Land	2,300
Accounts receivable	1,300
Repair supplies	700

Problem A 1-2. Prepare the balance sheet of Local Service Company as of June 30, 1958.

Capital stock	$8,000
Accounts receivable	1,100
Accounts payable	?
Installation parts	900
Office supplies	400
Cash	3,000
Land	4,000

Problem A 1-3. Prepare a balance sheet for Ames Corporation after each of the following transactions.

1958

June 1—The corporation was organized and $10,000 par value capital stock was issued for cash.

4—Office supplies were purchased for $500 cash.

7—The corporation issued $2,000 additional par value stock for cash.

9—The corporation acquired a tract of land for $6,000, paying $3,000 in cash and promising to pay the remaining $3,000 within thirty days.

515

Problem A 1-4. The following balance sheet is incorrect. Prepare a corrected balance sheet.

THE DAY CORPORATION
Balance Sheet
November 30, 1957

Cash	$2,500.00	Capital stock	$5,500.00
Accounts payable	1,215.00	Repair parts	480.00
Land	3,000.00	Accounts receivable	735.00
	$6,715.00		$6,715.00

Problem A 1-5. Prepare a balance sheet as of December 31, 1958, for *MO* Corporation.

December 10—*MO* Corporation was organized with $5,000 of par value capital stock issued for cash.
    15—Purchased land for $3,000 cash.
    21—Purchased $350 of office supplies on account.
    31—Paid $200 on account.

Problem A 1-6. The following transactions relate to the affairs of Block Corporation, a newly organized corporation.

May 1—$8,000 par value capital stock was issued for cash.
    13—Paid $800 to American Supply Company for service supplies.
    19—Purchased land for $5,000 cash.
    24—Service supplies costing $600 were purchased on account from McVee Corporation.
    27—The land was sold for $5,000 cash.
    29—Additional capital stock in the amount of $7,000 was issued for cash.
    31—A larger tract of land was acquired for $9,000 cash.
    31—Paid $300 on account to McVee Corporation.

Prepare the balance sheet as of May 31, 1958.

Problems—Group B

Problem B 1-1. Using the following data, prepare the balance sheet of Price Company as of December 31, 1958.

Cash	$1,500
Land	3,500
Capital stock	4,000
Accounts payable	850
Accounts receivable	725
Notes payable	1,200
Supplies	325

Problem B 1-2. Using the following data, prepare the balance sheet of Clinton Corporation as of June 30, 1959.

CLINTON CORPORATION
June 30, 1959
Balance Sheet

Cash	$3,000.00	Capital stock	$ 6,000.00
Accounts payable	500.00	Notes payable	3,000.00
Land	5,000.00	Repair parts	1,500.00
	$8,500.00		$10,500.00

Problem B 1-3. A balance sheet has been prepared for Austin Company after each transaction. From an analysis of the balance sheets, prepare a list of the transactions that occurred.

AUSTIN COMPANY
Balance Sheet
December 3, 1958

Assets		Stockholders' Equity	
Cash....................	$20,000.00	Capital stock.............	$20,000.00
	$20,000.00		$20,000.00

AUSTIN COMPANY
Balance Sheet
December 7, 1958

Assets		Stockholders' Equity	
Cash....................	$17,000.00	Capital stock.............	$20,000.00
Patent........	3,000.00		
	$20,000.00		$20,000.00

AUSTIN COMPANY
Balance Sheet
December 12, 1958

Assets		Liabilities and Stockholders' Equity	
Cash....................	$17,000.00	Liabilities:	
Parts and supplies........	2,500.00	Accounts payable........	$ 2,500.00
Patent....................	3,000.00	Stockholders' equity:	
		Capital stock............	20,000.00
	$22,500.00		$22,500.00

AUSTIN COMPANY
Balance Sheet
December 20, 1958

Assets		Liabilities and Stockholders' Equity	
Cash....................	$12,500.00	Liabilities:	
Parts and supplies........	2,500.00	Accounts payable........	$ 2,500.00
Land....................	4,500.00	Stockholders' equity:	
Patent....................	3,000.00	Capital stock............	20,000.00
	$22,500.00		$22,500.00

AUSTIN COMPANY
Balance Sheet
December 24, 1958

Assets		Liabilities and Stockholders' Equity	
Cash....................	$11,000.00	Liabilities:	
Parts and supplies........	2,500.00	Accounts payable........	$ 1,000.00
Land....................	4,500.00	Stockholders' equity:	
Patent....................	3,000.00	Capital stock............	20,000.00
	$21,000.00		$21,000.00

AUSTIN COMPANY
Balance Sheet
December 31, 1958

Assets		Liabilties and Stockholders' Equity	
Cash	$10,000.00	Liabilities:	
Parts and supplies	2,500.00	Accounts payable	$ 1,000.00
Land	10,500.00	Notes payable	5,000.00
Patent	3,000.00	Stockholders' equity:	
		Capital stock	20,000.00
	$26,000.00		$26,000.00

Problem B 1-4.   Prepare the March 31, 1958 balance sheet of *XYZ* Company.

1958
March 20—J. B. Webster and A. O. Snyder completed the organization of *XYZ*
Company, and each invested $12,500 cash; $25,000 of capital stock
was issued.

23—Purchased land for $4,000 cash.

24—Issued additional capital stock to J. R. Derby for $5,000 cash.

25—Service supplies costing $2,000 were purchased from Dunham Company on account.

30—$5,000 cash was invested in U. S. Treasury notes.

31—Building and land were acquired for $20,000.   A cash payment of
$16,000 was made and a mortgage payable was given for the
remainder.   The land was valued at $5,000.

31—Land acquired on March 23 was exchanged for service equipment
costing $4,000.

31—Paid Dunham Company $1,200 on account.

31—Additional service supplies were acquired for $800 cash.

Problem B 1-5.   Florida Company was organized on November 1, 1958.   The
following balance sheet was prepared after the fourth transaction was completed.
Analyze the balance sheet and prepare a list of the four transactions you believe
occurred.

FLORIDA COMPANY
Balance Sheet
November 3, 1958

Assets		Liabilities and Stockholders' Equity	
Cash	$2,000.00	Liabilities:	
Repair parts	1,000.00	Accounts payable	$1,000.00
Land	5,000.00	Notes payable	3,000.00
		Stockholders' equity:	
		Capital stock	4,000.00
	$8,000.00		$8,000.00

ASSIGNMENT MATERIAL FOR CHAPTER 2
Questions

1. In what way or ways is a trial balance useful?

2. What is a T-account?

3. Describe posting.

4. What does the word "double" mean in the phrase "double-entry bookkeeping"?

5. What is a compound journal entry?

6. State the use of dollar signs in accounting records and statements.

7. Distinguish between a ledger and a journal.

8. Is it customary to prepare a balance sheet after each business transaction?

Problems—Group A

Problem A 2-1. The following transactions relate to the affairs of The Fix-it Company, a newly organized corporation.

1958
January   2—$10,000 par value capital stock was issued for cash.
          5—Service parts costing $300 were purchased for cash.
          7—A $2,000 U. S. Government bond was purchased for cash.
          9—Service parts costing $400 were purchased on account.
          12—Acquired land for a building site, paying $2,000 in cash and giving a note payable for $8,000.
          15—Paid for the service parts purchased on January 9.
          20—Sold half of the land for $5,000 cash.

Required:

Record the above transactions in T-accounts, showing dates and amounts.

Problem A 2-2. Using the following data, prepare the trial balance of Apex Corporation as of December 31, 1958.

Accounts payable	$ 727.13
Accounts receivable	626.72
Building	8,500.00
Capital stock	25,000.00
Cash	1,542.47
Equipment	4,251.14
Land	3,355.00
Machinery	6,789.00
Mortgage payable	2,500.00
Notes payable	1,000.00
Notes receivable	500.00
Patents	1,215.00
Repair parts	329.37
Supplies	118.43
U.S. Government bonds	2,000.00

Problem A 2-3. The transactions listed below are those of Cross Service Company, which was organized on June 1, 1959. Journalize these transactions and post to ledger accounts. Take a trial balance.

1959
June 1—$30,000 cash was received for capital stock.
    5—A building was acquired for $24,000 cash. The land on which the building was located was purchased for an additional $2,500 cash.
    9—Service equipment was purchased from Imperial Manufacturing Co. on account at a cost of $6,350.
    14—Borrowed $12,500 from the City National Bank, giving a note payable in that amount.
    20—Paid $4,000 to Imperial Manufacturing Co. as part payment on the purchase of June 9.
    26—Additional capital stock was issued for $5,000 cash.
    30—Repair parts with a wholesale list price of $15,700 were purchased from Good Housekeeping Supply Company for $14,400 cash. Good Housekeeping Supply Company, currently short on storage space, was offering cut-rate prices in order to move existing inventories.

Problem A 2-4. David Smith and John Hutchins completed the organization of Community Service Company on September 15, 1958. Record the following transactions occurring during the latter part of September, 1958, in a journal; post to ledger accounts; and take a trial balance.

1958
September 15—Capital stock of $25,000 in total was issued to Smith and Hutchins for cash.
    17—Service equipment costing $5,000 was purchased on account from Iowa Suppliers Company.
    20—Office supplies costing $700 and repair supplies costing $800 were purchased on account from Universal Supply Co.
    24—Land was acquired under the following terms: $7,000 cash and $3,000 note payable.
    27—Iowa Suppliers Company agreed to accept $5,000 of capital stock in payment for the service equipment purchased September 17.
    29—Paid $500 on account to Universal Supply Co.
    30—Purchased a U. S. Government bond for $1,000.

Problem A 2-5. The following chart of accounts is planned for Arborview Company.

	Account Number
Assets:	
Cash	1
Parts and supplies	10
Land	15
Patent	20
Liabilities:	
Accounts payable	31
Notes payable	35
Stockholders' equity:	
Capital stock	50

Perform the following: (a) Journalize the transactions, (b) post to ledger accounts; (c) take a trial balance; and (d) prepare a balance sheet as of June 30, 1958.

1958
June 5—The company issued capital stock for $15,000.
      7—Parts and supplies costing $2,817.28 were purchased on account from Chicago Supply Corporation.
      10—The company paid $2,750 to an inventor for a patent.
      13—Purchased parts and supplies for cash, $927.78.
      18—Purchased land for $6,250, paying $2,250 in cash and giving a $4,000 note payable for the balance.
      22—Parts and supplies costing $1,128.59 were purchased on account from Midwest Wholesale Company.
      25—The company paid for the parts and supplies purchased on June 7.
      27—The company located a parcel of land more suited to its needs and purchased it at a cost of $7,800, paying $1,550 in cash plus the land acquired on June 18.
      30—Paid $500 on account to Midwest Wholesale Company.

Problems—Group B

Problem B 2-1. Record the following transactions in T-accounts, showing dates and amounts.

1958
July 1—The Trailer Company was incorporated and $70,000 of par value stock was issued for cash.
      2—Land was purchased as a trailer sales lot for $15,000, paid in cash.
      3—A small frame building was purchased and moved to the lot to serve as an office building; cost, $3,500, paid in cash.
      5—Trailers were purchased at auction for $40,000 cash.
      7—Three trailers costing $3,000 each were traded for service equipment worth $9,000.
      9—Additional service equipment costing $3,000 was purchased from A. B. White. White agreed to accept $3,000 par value capital stock in settlement.

Problem B 2-2. Describe each of the transactions that are recorded in the following journal of Ginger Company.

1959				
Aug.	1	Cash..	10 000 00	
		Capital stock............................		10 000 00
	3	Land...	3 000 00	
		Cash.......................................		3 000 00
	5	Repair parts................................	900 00	
		Accounts payable........................		900 00
	8	Land...	4 000 00	
		Cash.......................................		4 000 00

Aug.	14	Accounts receivable..........................			3	000	00			
		Land....................................						3	000	00
	18	Accounts payable...........................				900	00			
		Cash....................................							900	00
	21	Cash.......................................			3	000	00			
		Accounts receivable......................						3	000	00
	27	Repair parts...............................				600	00			
		Cash....................................							600	00
	31	U. S. Government bonds....................			2	000	00			
		Cash....................................						2	000	00

Problem B 2-3.   The following transactions relate to the affairs of Moon Corporation.

1959
December 16—Capital stock was issued for $10,000 cash.
    18—Land costing $5,000 was purchased from J. T. Rains, who agreed to accept capital stock for the selling price of the land.
    21—Repair parts costing $1,200 were purchased on account from Michigan Wholesale Supply.
    23—$2,000 cash was invested in U. S. Treasury notes.
    26—To comply with a request from Michigan Wholesale Supply, $500 was paid on account and a $700 note payable was given to cover the balance of the December 21 transaction.
    29—Repair parts were purchased for cash, $325.
    31—Land acquired on December 18 was exchanged for a patent costing $5,000.

Required:

(a) Journalize the transactions.
(b) Post to ledger accounts.
(c) Take a trial balance.

Problem B 2-4.   The following transactions are those of Interlaken Dredging Company.

1959
June 1—The corporate charter was received and capital stock was issued for $30,000 cash.
   3—Pipe costing $3,117.28 was purchased from Steel Supply Company under the following terms: $1,117.28 in cash and $2,000 in capital stock of Interlaken Dredging Company.
   7—Land costing $5,000 was purchased. The company assumed a mortgage payable of $2,000 which was on the property and paid the balance of $3,000 in cash.
  10—The company ordered a dredge from Eastern Manufacturing Corporation.
  12—Pipe costing $1,623.46 was purchased on account from Pipe Wholesalers, Inc.
  16—A patent relating to dredging operations was acquired for $2,500 cash.

June 22—One half of the amount owing to Pipe Wholesalers, Inc. was paid.

    25—Additional capital stock was issued for $10,000.

    28—The dredge ordered on June 10 was delivered. The total cost was $29,724.30. The company paid 90 per cent in cash and agreed to pay the balance in 60 days.

    30—The company purchased $317.75 of operating supplies for cash.

Required:

  (a) Journalize the transactions for June.

  (b) Post and take a trial balance.

  (c) Prepare a balance sheet as of June 30, 1959.

Problem B 2-5. The trial balance below is that of a newly organized corporation after five transactions have been completed. From an analysis of the account balances, submit journal entries, omitting dates, for the five completed transactions.

SERVICE DEVELOPMENT COMPANY
Trial Balance
October 31, 1959

Cash	7,250.00	
Municipal bonds	2,000.00	
Service parts	1,500.00	
Service equipment	3,000.00	
Accounts payable		750.00
Notes payable		3,000.00
Capital stock		10,000.00
	13,750.00	13,750.00

ASSIGNMENT MATERIAL FOR CHAPTER 3
Questions

1. Define revenue.

2. Distinguish between revenue and income.

3. Distinguish between expenses and dividends.

4. Describe the debit-credit procedure as it relates to transactions recorded in revenue and expense accounts.

5. How many revenue accounts and expense accounts will a business use?

6. How does the trial balance differ from the balance sheet?

7. What is meant by "closing the books"?

8. Describe the nature and purpose of the Revenue and Expense Summary account.

9. What is achieved by taking an after-closing trial balance?

10. After the books have been closed, what types of accounts have balances?

11. Describe the usual sequence of accounting procedures.

Problems—Group A

Problem A 3-1. The transactions listed below are those of a newly organized corporation. Journalize the transactions.

1959
July 1—Smith and Hepworth each invested $4,000 for capital stock in Campus Auto Laundry Company.

1—An agreement was made whereby car-washing equipment and facilities were rented on a monthly basis. Rent of $1,125 was paid for July. Campus Auto Laundry assumed responsibility for repairs.

2—Paid $75 for a newspaper advertisement announcing the nature of the company's business, namely, the washing of automobiles and trucks owned and operated by businesses.

5—Signed an agreement with Regional Car Rentals, Inc., to keep its fleet of rental cars washed.

15—Billed Regional Car Rentals, Inc., for car-washing services performed during the last ten days, $810.

17—Received a bill for $19 from Mechanical Fixit Shop for repairs to equipment.

19—Received $810 from Regional Car Rentals, Inc.

20—Signed an agreement with Airport Cab Company to keep its fleet of cabs washed.

22—Paid miscellaneous expenses of $35.

25—Paid bill owed to Mechanical Fixit Shop.

31—Billed Regional Car Rentals, Inc., $1,120 and Airport Cab Company $680 for car-washing services performed during last half of month.

31—Salaries and wages were paid, $925.

Problem A 3-2. The following trial balance is that of Blank Corporation at the end of the first month of operations. Journalize the closing entries.

BLANK CORPORATION
Trial Balance
January 31, 1958

Cash..	3,202.50	
Municipal bonds.............................	1,000.00	
Accounts receivable..........................	632.20	
Service parts................................	672.25	
Land..	3,000.00	
Notes payable...............................		1,220.00
Capital stock................................		7,000.00
Dividends...................................	35.00	
Fees earned.................................		1,132.35
Advertising expense..........................	185.30	
Office expense...............................	175.10	
Wages expense...............................	450.00	
	9,352.35	9,352.35

Problem A 3-3. Design Corporation was organized on July 1, 1958. The corporation is a service enterprise, prepared to help clients design packages and containers for their products. The corporation's primary source of revenue will be from fees. The following transactions occurred during the month of July.

1958
July 1—Capital stock in the amount of $7,000 was issued for cash.
2—Office facilities were rented. Rent for July was paid, $215.
7—A bill for $475 was mailed to Circle Food Company for work performed on a package design for a new product.
11—The Basement Appliance Co., another client, was billed $885 for work performed on a container for one of its products.
15—Salaries for the first half of July were paid, $1,000.
17—$475 was collected from Circle Food Company.
20—The plans for an extensive revision of package designs for Tri-State Supply Company were completed. According to the terms of the agreement, the bill, amounting to $1,800, was to be paid within thirty days from the date of the completion of the plans.
22—Paid $225 for advertising in a trade magazine.
24—Received the amount owed by The Basement Appliance Co.
26—Paid miscellaneous expenses in the amount of $44.
29—Submitted a bill to Midwest Manufacturing Co. for work performed, $815.
31—Salaries for the last half of July were paid, $1,000.
31—Paid miscellaneous expenses in the amount of $53.

Required:

(a) Journalize the above transactions.
(b) Post to ledger accounts.
(c) Take a trial balance.

Problem A 3-4. Black Corporation was organized on January 5, 1959. The data at the top of the following page show all but two of the accounts and balances appearing in the January 31, 1959 trial balance.

Accounts receivable		335.25
Repair parts on hand		925.50
Land		4,350.00
Accounts payable		548.00
Dividends (1%)		80.00
Commissions earned		1,900.00
Miscellaneous expense		312.25
Rent expense		280.00
Wages expense		1,100.00

Required:

(a) Present the complete January 31, 1959 trial balance.

(b) Prepare the income statement, the statement of retained earnings, and the balance sheet.

(c) Journalize the closing entries.

Problem A 3-5. The following transactions are those of Tops Company, a newly organized business, during its first month of operations.

1959

June 1—$3,000 of par value stock was issued to the organizers for cash.

2—Paid office rent for June, $225.

10—Received $750 in commissions.

12—Paid miscellaneous expenses of $35.65.

20—Received $600 in commissions.

30—Paid salaries for the month, $900.

30—Billed Acme Brokers per agreement for commissions earned during last ten days of June, $650.

30—Paid a dividend, $60.

30—Received a bill for $61.72 from State Supply Co. for miscellaneous expenses.

Required:

(a) Journalize the transactions.

(b) Post.

(c) Take a trial balance.

(d) Prepare the income statement, the statement of retained earnings, and the balance sheet.

(e) Make and post the journal entries necessary to close the books. Rule the accounts.

(f) Take an after-closing trial balance.

Problems—Group B

Problem B 3-1. Journalize the following transactions of Rapid Service Company.

1959

May 1—Received $300 in cash as commissions on sales made today.

3—Paid office rent for May, $130.

5—Received a bill from Local Supply Co. for miscellaneous expenses, $17.

6—Received $50 rent for the balance of the month of May on land owned by the company.

9—Paid traveling expenses incurred by employees, $38.

May 10—Paid the bill owed to Local Supply Co. in the amount of $17.
    15—Paid salaries for first half of May, $750.
    16—Received $800 in commissions.
    19—Invested $1,000 in municipal bonds.
    23—Paid miscellaneous expenses, $12.
    25—Received a bill for advertising from City Herald, $21.
    26—Paid repair expense in the amount of $24.
    27—Purchased additional land worth $2,500 by issuing capital stock with a par value of $2,000 and paying $500 in cash.
    29—Paid the bill received on May 25 from City Herald.
    31—Paid salaries for the last half of May, $750.
    31—Paid dividends of $150 to stockholders.
    31—Billed Metropolitan Realtors for $1,800 of commissions earned during May but remaining uncollected as of May 31.

Problem B 3-2. The transactions occurring during June, 1958, in the business of Bridge Repair Company, organized June 1, are given below:

1958
June 1—Issued capital stock for cash, $8,000.
    5—Paid $100 for two days' rental of a bulldozer used on a repair job.
    10—Paid $200 for repair materials used on a job.
    17—Collected $1,100 upon completion of repair work.
    22—Purchased repair materials costing $180 on account from O. P. Adams. These materials were used immediately on a job.
    24—Paid cash dividend of $125 to stockholders.
    25—Collected $2,000 for bridge repair work completed on this date.
    30—Paid salaries and wages of $2,300.

Required:

(a) Journalize the transactions.
(b) Post to ledger accounts.
(c) Prepare a trial balance.
(d) Prepare an income statement, a statement of retained earnings, and a balance sheet.
(e) Journalize and post closing entries.
(f) Rule the accounts having no balances.
(g) Take an after-closing trial balance.

Suggested account titles are:

    1—Cash
    21—Accounts Payable
    41—Capital Stock
    42—Retained Earnings
    43—Dividends
    44—Revenue and Expense Summary
    50—Repair Service Revenue
    60—Salaries and Wages Expense
    61—Repair Materials Expense
    62—Rental Expense

Problem B 3-3. Using the following data, prepare the January 31, 1958 trial balance of Scott Company.

SCOTT COMPANY
Balance Sheet
January 31, 1958

Assets		Liabilities and Stockholders' Equity		
Cash....................	$1,100.00	Liabilities:		
Repair parts...............	480.00	Accounts payable........		$ 300.00
Land.....................	1,500.00	Stockholders' equity:		
Patents..................	1,000.00	Capital stock..	$3,000.00	
		Retained		
		earnings.....	780.00	3,780.00
	$4,080.00			$4,080.00

Closing Entries
(Explanations Omitted)

1958

Jan. 31	Revenue from services..................	2,395.00		
	Revenue and expense summary.......		2,395.00	
31	Revenue and expense summary...........	210.00		
	Office rent expense.................		210.00	
31	Revenue and expense summary...........	330.00		
	Miscellaneous expense...............		330.00	
31	Revenue and expense summary..........	1,000.00		
	Salaries expense...................		1,000.00	
31	Revenue and expense summary..........	855.00		
	Retained earnings..................		855.00	
31	Retained earnings......................	75.00		
	Dividends.........................		75.00	

Problem B 3-4. The after-closing trial balances of Special Service Company as of July 31, 1958, and August 31, 1958, are given below.

The company has only one source of revenue, that being from the performance of services. Its expenses for the month of August consisted of salaries and wages of $2,400, office rent of $210, and advertising expense of $75. A cash dividend of $300 was paid in August.

SPECIAL SERVICE COMPANY
After-Closing Trial Balance
July 31, 1958

Cash..	4,500.00	
Accounts receivable.........................	7,225.00	
Land..	4,000.00	
Accounts payable............................		1,275.00
Capital stock...............................		10,000.00
Retained earnings...........................		4,450.00
	15,725.00	15,725.00

SPECIAL SERVICE COMPANY
After-Closing Trial Balance
August 31, 1958

Cash	4,720.00	
Accounts receivable	6,240.00	
Land	4,000.00	
Patents	1,000.00	
Accounts payable		810.00
Capital stock		10,000.00
Retained earnings		5,150.00
	15,960.00	15,960.00

Prepare the income statement for the month of August.

Problem B 3-5. The transactions listed below are those of Architectural Consultants, Incorporated, which was organized on April 1, 1959. Journalize, post, take a trial balance, and journalize and post the closing entries. Rule the closed accounts.

1959

April 1—Capital stock of a par value of $8,000 was issued for cash.

2—$125 was paid for the use of office facilities for April.

5—A consulting job was finished today and a fee of $300 was collected.

6—Paid traveling expenses in the amount of $45.

10—A bill was delivered to David Doyen in the amount of $625 for consulting work completed today. Doyen agreed to pay within ten days.

11—Paid $32 to Stenographic Aids Company for office expense.

15—Paid $380 for salaries.

18—Purchased land as a future building site, issuing $4,000 of capital stock in payment.

19—Received $625 from David Doyen for work completed on April 10.

23—A consulting job was finished today; the bill was $850. The customer, School Architects, promised to pay the bill within thirty days.

24—Paid traveling expenses in the amount of $49.

26—Paid $19 for local advertising.

30—Paid $380 for salaries.

30—Paid a $60 dividend to stockholders.

30—Received a bill from Stenographic Aids Company for office expense, $47.

ASSIGNMENT MATERIAL FOR CHAPTER 4
Questions

1. Discuss the validity of the following statement: If a company has earned revenue for which no cash has been received, an adjusting entry is required.

2. Is the following statement correct? "Adjusting entries, since they do not record transactions, are entered directly in the ledger accounts without being journalized."

3. On September 30, Community Televisions sent a bill to Sloan in the amount of $1,000 for commissions earned on sales made during the last half of September. On the same day, the following entry was made.

Accounts receivable..............................	1,000.00	
Commissions earned...........................		1,000.00

Suppose that Community Televisions had neglected to send the bill and make the above entry. Could the entry have been made as an adjusting entry?

4. Do accounts with the word "accrued" in their titles appear in both the income statement and the balance sheet?

5. Is it always desirable to prepare working papers before preparing the financial statements?

6. Describe the steps in the preparation of working papers.

7. Is it possible to prepare the financial statements by reference only to completed working papers?

8. After completing the Adjusted Trial Balance columns of the working papers, to what column or columns would you extend the balance of each of the following accounts?

Accounts Receivable	Dividends
Capital Stock	Salaries Expense
Accrued Rent Expense	Accrued Commissions Earned

9. Give the sequence of procedures for the accounting cycle.

Problems—Group A

Problem A 4-1. Drive-in Theatre, Inc., at the end of September, 1958, had the trial balance shown on the following page. Adjustments were required as follows:

    (1) Film rental expense equals 62% of gross admissions. No payments had been made for film rental on September admissions.

    (2) Accrued revenue from commissions on the refreshment concession amounted to $88.50 for the month.

    (3) Accrued equipment rental expense for September, $375.

    (4) Accrued maintenance expense, $11.67.

Required:

    (a) Adjusting entries.

    (b) Closing entries.

DRIVE-IN THEATRE, INC.
Trial Balance
September 30, 1958

Cash..	10,727.17	
Land.......................................	4,800.00	
Capital stock..............................		5,000.00
Retained earnings, August 31, 1958..............		1,316.55
Dividends..................................	50.00	
Admissions revenue...........................		12,150.00
Taxes expense..............................	87.25	
Advertising expense.........................	62.35	
Maintenance expense.........................	188.33	
Salaries expense.............................	2,551.45	
	18,466.55	18,466.55

Problem A 4-2. Prepare adjusting entries from the following information pertaining to the accounts of Motor Service Company at the end of May, 1959:

(1) Accrued wages payable, $225.
(2) Accrued interest on U. S. Government bonds owned, $75.
(3) A tow truck was rented during May from Transport Rental Company at the rate of fifteen cents a mile. This truck was driven 1,200 miles during the month and no rental had been paid as of May 31.
(4) Accrued interest payable, $18.
(5) Accrued service revenue, $110.
(6) Accrued taxes, $35.
(7) Accrued rent receivable, $90.
(8) On May 31 the company is notified by Transport Rental Company that, effective June 1, the tow truck rental will be revised. The revised terms are: $50 per month minimum charge; twelve cents per mile.

Problem A 4-3. Using the trial balance and the data for adjustments given below, prepare the working papers for Consulting Corporation for the month of July.

CONSULTING CORPORATION
Trial Balance
July 31, 1959

Cash..	4,713.00	
Notes receivable.............................	2,600.00	
Capital stock................................		6,000.00
Retained earnings............................		548.00
Dividends...................................	60.00	
Fees..		3,950.00
Salaries expense..............................	3,000.00	
Advertising expense..........................	125.00	
	10,498.00	10,498.00

Data for adjustments:

(a) Accrued interest receivable, $13.
(b) Accrued office rent for July, $215.
(c) Accrued advertising expense, $25.

Problem A 4-4. The trial balance of Promotion Company at the end of January is shown on the following page.

PROMOTION COMPANY
Trial Balance
January 31, 1958

Cash...	2,270.39	
Municipal bonds.............................	2,000.00	
Land..	6,000.00	
Notes payable................................		1,000.00
Capital stock.................................		5,000.00
Retained earnings...........................		1,875.65
Dividends.....................................	100.00	
Commissions earned.........................		4,910.00
Taxes expense................................	37.54	
Advertising expense.........................	877.72	
Salaries expense.............................	1,500.00	
	12,785.65	12,785.65

Data for adjustments as of January 31, 1958:

(a) Commissions earned but not billed or received, $90.
(b) Interest earned on the municipal bonds, $10.
(c) Interest accrued on the notes payable, $5.
(d) Accrued salaries for the last half of January, $1,525.
(e) Accrued car rentals for January, $371.23.

Required:

(1) Working papers.
(2) Closing entries.
(3) Statement of retained earnings.

Problem A 4-5. The after-closing trial balance of Tad Company at the end of May, 1958, was as follows:

TAD COMPANY
After-Closing Trial Balance
May 31, 1958

Cash...	1,310.00	
Land..	4,000.00	
Accounts payable............................		425.00
Capital stock.................................		4,500.00
Retained earnings...........................		385.00
	5,310.00	5,310.00

Transactions during June were as follows:

1958
June 1—Collected $50 for rent of land for June.
    5—Paid advertising expense of $60 in cash.
    8—Collected $400 for commissions earned.
    12—Paid $300 of the accounts payable.
    18—Collected $375 for commissions earned.
    23—Paid dividend of $90 in cash.
    28—Paid office expense, $78.
    30—Paid salaries for June, $600.

The following data were available for adjustments at the end of June:

(1) Accrued commissions, $200.
(2) Accrued property taxes on the land owned, $15.
(3) Office expense incurred during June but not paid amounted to $12.

Required: (See note below.)

(a) Journalize the June transactions and post.
(b) Prepare working papers.
(c) Prepare an income statement, a statement of retained earnings, and a balance sheet.
(d) Journalize and post adjusting entries.
(e) Journalize and post closing entries.
(f) Rule ledger accounts having no balances.
(g) Take an after-closing trial balance.

Note. Students using the forms prepared for the solution of the "A" problems will find the after-closing balances as of May 31, 1958, entered in the appropriate ledger accounts.

For those students not using the prepared forms, it will be necessary to enter the after-closing balances as of May 31, 1958, in appropriate ledger accounts. An example showing how this should be accomplished is given below:

		Cash			(1)
1958					
May 31	Balance	1,310 00			

Problems—Group B

Problem B 4-1. Supply the missing explanations for the following journal entries of Sum Company.

1958	(1)		
June 29	Accounts receivable......................	1,000.00	
	Commissions earned................		1,000.00
	(2)		
30	Wages and salaries expense..............	650.00	
	Cash...............................		650.00
	(3)		
30	Accrued interest receivable.............	15.00	
	Interest earned.....................		15.00
	(4)		
30	Car rentals.............................	160.00	
	Accrued car rentals payable..........		160.00
	(5)		
30	Tax expense............................	35.00	
	Accrued taxes......................		35.00
	(6)		
30	Accrued rent...........................	110.00	
	Rent earned.......................		110.00

Identify the entries which are probably adjusting entries.

Problem B 4-2. Using the trial balance and the data for adjustments on the following page, prepare adjusting and closing entries for Johnson Company for the month of August.

JOHNSON COMPANY
Trial Balance
August 31, 1959

Cash...................................	1,995.00	
Bonds..................................	5,000.00	
Land...................................	4,500.00	
Notes payable..........................		1,000.00
Capital stock..........................		8,000.00
Retained earnings......................		1,765.00
Dividends..............................	160.00	
Fees...................................		3,270.00
Interest earned........................		20.00
Travel expense.........................	379.00	
Advertising expense....................	221.00	
Salaries expense.......................	1,800.00	
	14,055.00	14,055.00

Data for adjustments:

(1) Fees earned but unbilled as of August 31, $130.
(2) Accrued interest on the bonds, $10.
(3) Accrued rent on the land owned, $20.
(4) Accrued salaries, $200.
(5) Accrued interest on the notes payable, $5.

Problem B 4-3. Certain data relating to Inman Corporation are presented below:

Trial balance data as of June 30, 1958:

Accounts receivable....................	810.00
Advertising expense....................	75.00
Capital stock..........................	2,500.00
Cash...................................	895.00
Commissions earned.....................	1,900.00
Interest earned........................	5.00
Land...................................	2,000.00
Notes payable..........................	700.00
Office rent............................	80.00
Retained earnings......................	555.00
Salaries expense.......................	800.00
Overstreet Company bonds...............	1,000.00

Data for adjustments:

(1) As of June 30, 1958, the earned, but unbilled, commissions amount to $60.
(2) As of June 30, 1958, the interest accrual on the bond investment amounts to $5.
(3) Accrued salaries amount to $100.
(4) Accrued rent on the land owned equals $55.
(5) Accrued interest on the notes payable amounts to $7.

Prepare a schedule listing the assets, with amounts, that would appear in the June 30, 1958 balance sheet of Inman Corporation.

Problem B 4-4.   The following trial balance is that of Zero Corporation.

ZERO CORPORATION
Trial Balance
January 31, 1958

Cash	4,302.50	
Municipal bonds	1,000.00	
Accounts receivable	731.20	
Service parts on hand	573.25	
Land	3,000.00	
Notes payable		1,220.00
Capital stock		7,000.00
Retained earnings, December 31, 1957		1,100.00
Dividends	35.00	
Fees earned		1,102.35
Rent earned		30.00
Advertising expense	185.20	
Office expense	170.20	
Wages expense	455.00	
	10,452.35	10,452.35

Data for adjustments:

(a) Accrued fees, $47.65.
(b) Accrued interest on the municipal bonds, $4.
(c) Accrued office expense, $14.60.
(d) Accrued interest on the notes payable, $6.10.

Prepare working papers and financial statements.

Problem B 4-5.   A trial balance after the journal entries for the September transactions had been posted was as follows:

NORMAL CORPORATION
Trial Balance
September 30, 1958

Cash	2,939.09	
Corporate bonds	3,000.00	
Accounts receivable	480.17	
Bank loans		1,500.00
Capital stock		4,000.00
Retained earnings		675.28
Revenue from services		3,121.42
Miscellaneous expense	727.44	
Salaries expense	2,150.00	
	9,296.70	9,296.70

Adjustments were required as follows:

(a) Accrued salaries, $200.
(b) Accrued office rent for September, $90.
(c) Accrued interest on the bonds owned, $15.
(d) Unbilled service revenue, $250.
(e) Accrued interest on the bank loans, $5.

Required:

Working papers.
Adjusting and closing entries.

Problem B 4-6. Below is an income statement which is incorrect because it was prepared without taking into consideration year-end adjustments.

AMOS CORPORATION
Income Statement
For the Year Ended December 31, 1958

Revenues:
Commissions earned................................		$14,720.00
Rent earned..		1,100.00
Total..		$15,820.00

Deduct expenses:
Salaries expense..........................	$12,000.00	
Office expense............................	975.00	
Car rent expense..........................	671.00	
Total..		13,646.00
Net income..		$ 2,174.00

The following income statement was prepared after the proper adjusting entries had been made.

AMOS CORPORATION
Income Statement
For the Year Ended December 31, 1958

Revenues:
Commissions earned................................		$14,720.00
Rent earned..		1,200.00
Interest earned....................................		15.00
Total..		$15,935.00

Deduct expenses:
Salaries expense..........................	$12,500.00	
Office expense............................	975.00	
Car rent expense..........................	701.00	
Tax expense..............................	40.00	
Total..		14,216.00
Net income..		$ 1,719.00

Compare the two income statements and submit the adjusting journal entries made by Amos Corporation as of December 31, 1958. Also prepare the correct closing entries as of December 31, 1958. (No dividends were paid during 1958.)

ASSIGNMENT MATERIAL FOR CHAPTER 5
Questions

1. Is it possible for a corporation to have a large cash balance and a large deficit?

2. Give an example of a transaction that results in a debit to an accrued expense payable account.

3. Will the depreciation expense account balance always equal the balance in the accumulated depreciation account?

4. Under what circumstances will the accountant not credit a revenue account when recording a revenue-producing transaction?

5. Will the totals appearing in the balance sheet always equal the column totals of the after-closing trial balance for the same date?

6. How does the accountant proceed in developing adjusting journal entries?

7. Under what circumstances might a corporation reporting an annual net income also show a decrease in retained earnings for the year?

8. Contrast the accrual and cash bases of accounting.

Problems—Group A

Problem A 5-1. The trial balance of the ledger of Duplex Decorators, Inc., on June 30, 1959, was as follows:

DUPLEX DECORATORS, INC.
Trial Balance
June 30, 1959

Cash.....................................	1,417.81	
Municipal bonds...........................	5,000.00	
Decorating supplies.......................	321.72	
Prepaid insurance.........................	300.00	
Land.....................................	3,000.00	
Building.................................	12,000.00	
Accumulated depreciation—Building..........		1,500.00
Capital stock............................		15,000.00
Retained earnings.........................		4,327.45
Revenue from services.....................		4,362.93
Wages expense............................	2,917.35	
Equipment rental expense..................	200.00	
Advertising expense.......................	33.50	
	25,190.38	25,190.38

Prepare adjusting entries for the following matters:

(1) The bonds were acquired on June 1 as an investment, and interest in the amount of $7 accrued in June.

(2) The $300 insurance premium was paid on June 1 for a one-year policy.

(3) The inventory of decorating supplies taken on June 30 was $101.31.

(4) Depreciation for the month of June was $50.

(5) Accrued wages payable amounted to $67.

(6) On June 30, $125 cash was collected for work to be performed in July. This amount was erroneously credited to the Revenue from Services account.

Problem A 5-2. Modern Electrical Company, engaged in inspection and repair work only, has been in business since 1950. It closes its books on December 31. The company's trial balance at the end of 1958 was:

MODERN ELECTRICAL COMPANY
Trial Balance
December 31, 1958

Cash..	2,100.00	
Notes receivable.............................	1,000.00	
Electrical supplies...........................	800.00	
Unexpired insurance.........................	240.00	
Land..	6,200.00	
Building....................................	18,800.00	
Accumulated depreciation—Building............		5,264.00
Equipment..................................	5,000.00	
Accumulated depreciation—Equipment..........		1,500.00
Accounts payable............................		350.00
Inspection fees received in advance.............		1,200.00
Capital stock...............................		25,000.00
Retained earnings...........................	1,124.00	
Repair service revenue.......................		13,250.00
Inspection fees earned.......................		3,100.00
Salaries and wages expense....................	12,500.00	
Miscellaneous expense........................	1,900.00	
	49,664.00	49,664.00

The building had an expected useful life of 25 years when new, and the equipment an expected life of five years when new. The accrued interest on the notes receivable amounted to $20 as of December 31, 1958. The insurance coverage was acquired on January 1, 1957, and the policy covered a three-year term. One-third of the inspection fees received in advance have been earned as of December 31, 1958. The year-end inventory of electrical supplies amounted to $150. Prepare adjusting entries and closing entries.

Problem A 5-3. Bond Cleaners had the following trial balance at the close of its fiscal year.

BOND CLEANERS
Trial Balance
July 31, 1959

Cash..	1,520.00	
Corporate bonds.............................	2,000.00	
Cleaning supplies...........................	2,660.00	
Land..	9,000.00	
Building....................................	20,000.00	
Accumulated depreciation—Building............		12,000.00
Cleaning equipment.........................	42,000.00	
Accounts payable............................		5,100.00
Capital stock...............................		60,000.00
Retained earnings...........................	2,658.00	
Cleaning service............................		19,125.00
Interest earned.............................		70.00
Salaries expense............................	16,317.00	
Advertising expense.........................	140.00	
	96,295.00	96,295.00

Data for adjustments:

(1) The bonds have been held for several years and they are the only source of interest earnings of the corporation. They earn $100 interest annually; interest

checks in the amount of $50 are received semiannually by the corporation.

(2) Cleaning supplies costing $615 were on hand July 31, 1959.

(3) The building depreciates $1,000 per year.

(4) The cleaning equipment is new; it was purchased on May 1.   Depreciation will be based on a useful life of ten years.

(5) Until July 20, Bond Cleaners had always operated on a cash-and-carry basis.   On July 20, City Delivery Service was engaged at the rate of $20 per day used.   Such service was used seven days in July and no payments were made.

Required:

(a) Working papers, omitting Adjusted Trial Balance columns.

(b) Income statement and balance sheet.

(c) Closing entries.

Problem A 5-4.   The data below relate to Ocean Company.   Use the data to reconstruct the June 30, 1958 trial balance of the ledger of Ocean Company before adjusting entries were made.

OCEAN COMPANY
Income Statement
For the Month of June, 1958

Revenues:

Commissions earned		$7,200.00
Service revenue		1,600.00
Total		$8,800.00

Deduct expenses:

Salaries expense	$6,700.00	
Supplies expense	800.00	
Rent expense	150.00	
Depreciation expense—Service equipment	174.00	
Total		7,824.00
Net income		$ 976.00

OCEAN COMPANY
After-Closing Trial Balance
June 30, 1958

Cash	1,100.00	
Supplies	100.00	
Service equipment	16,000.00	
Accumulated depreciation—Service equipment		4,174.00
Accrued salaries		310.00
Accrued rent payable		150.00
Service revenue received in advance		1,200.00
Capital stock		10,000.00
Retained earnings		1,366.00
	17,200.00	17,200.00

Data for June 30 adjusting entries:

(1) Depreciation of service equipment, $174.

(2) Salaries earned by employees but unpaid on June 30, $310.

(3) Rent payable for use of building during June, $150.

(4) Supplies used during June, $800.

(5) Of the service revenue received in advance, $1,600 was earned during June.

During June, $150 in dividends was paid to stockholders.

Problem A 5-5. Rough Grading Corporation was formed on April 1, 1958. The following transactions occurred during the first month of operations:

April 1—Issued $80,000 par value capital stock to R. S. Cole and A. R. Howes for cash.

        1—Equipment costing $60,000 was purchased for cash. The equipment has an expected useful life of five years.

      11—Rented temporary quarters for 30 days ending May 10; paid $600.

      14—Paid $161.35 for repairs to equipment. The repairs were necessitated by an accident on April 10.

      21—Received bill from State Supply Co. for supplies which had been used on a grading job, $197.32.

      27—Paid salaries and wages of $5,110.22.

      29—Paid dividend of $400.

      30—Completed a large grading project for Central Corporation, earning $9,041.25 from the job. Of this amount, $5,000 was collected in cash and the customer has agreed to pay the balance within 60 days.

Adjustments were required, in addition to those indicated above, as follows:

(1) Accrued salaries and wages, $188.40.

(2) An officer of Rough Grading Corporation, while negotiating the contract with Central Corporation, paid $83.50 of traveling expenses with his own funds. The officer will be reimbursed by the corporation.

Required:

(a) Journalize transactions and post to ledger accounts.
(b) Prepare working papers.
(c) Prepare statements.
(d) Make and post journal entries for adjustments.
(e) Make and post journal entries to close the books.
(f) Rule the closed accounts.
(g) Take an after-closing trial balance.

Problem A 5-6. The after-closing trial balance of Suburban Television Antenna Company is presented below. The company is located in an area where typical domestic TV antennas do not receive sufficient signal strength to permit good television reception. The company owns a large TV antenna tower. Customers connect their TV sets with the antenna tower and pay an installation fee, which varies depending on location, and a rental charge of $4.50 per quarter, in advance, for the use of the antenna.

SUBURBAN TELEVISION ANTENNA COMPANY
After-Closing Trial Balance
December 31, 1958

Cash	3,749.18	
Installation supplies	479.26	
Unexpired insurance	12.00	
Land	400.00	
Antenna tower	6,000.00	
Accumulated depreciation—Antenna tower		1,200.00
Accrued wages payable		80.00
Customer rentals received in advance		2,273.00
Capital stock		6,000.00
Retained earnings		1,087.44
	10,640.44	10,640.44

1959

January   3—Collected $65 in installation fees for work completed today.

5—Paid $79.16 in cash for installation supplies.

10—Paid semi-monthly wages, $250.   (Wages are paid on the tenth and twenty-fifth of each month.)

15—Collected $619 from customers for quarterly rentals.

15—The insurance policy expired today.   The policy was renewed for twelve months by the payment of a premium of $288.

24—Collected $174 in installation fees for work completed today.

25—Paid $17 for local advertising.

25—Paid semi-monthly wages, $260.

31—Collected $733 from customers for quarterly rentals.

Adjustments were required as follows:

(1) Customer rentals earned during January, $1,119.

(2) Accrued wages payable, $85.

(3) Installation supplies on hand, January 31, $422.50.

(4) $12 of the premium of the new insurance policy is assigned to expense covering the last half of January.

(5) The equipment is being depreciated over a five-year useful life.

Required:

(a) Journalize transactions and post.

(b) Prepare 10-column working papers.

(c) Prepare statements.

(d) Journalize and post adjusting entries.

(e) Journalize and post closing entries.

(f) Rule the closed accounts.

(The after-closing trial balance is omitted.)

Problem A 5-7.   The after-closing trial balance of Blend Corporation appears below.

BLEND CORPORATION
After-Closing Trial Balance
December 31, 1958

Cash..	6,100.00	
Accrued rent receivable—Land.................	100.00	
Repair supplies on hand.......................	200.00	
Land..	3,000.00	
Equipment.............................	8,000.00	
Accumulated depreciation—Equipment..........		4,000.00
Accrued salaries payable......................		500.00
Accrued taxes...............................		85.00
Capital stock................................		12,000.00
Retained earnings............................		815.00
	17,400.00	17,400.00

The corporation closes its books monthly.   Journalize the following transactions and all adjustments required for January, 1959 financial statements.

1959

January   3—The corporation rents out some of its land as a parking lot for $50 per month.   Today the corporation received $200 from the renter covering the four months ending February 28, 1959.

January 10—Paid salaries for the month ending January 10, 1959, $750.

17—Received $800 cash for repair services completed today.

19—Paid $75 for special supplies used on repair work completed January 17.

21—The corporation rented some of its equipment for the next 30 days ending February 20, receiving the $360 rental charge in advance.

31—Additional data required for adjustments:

> Depreciation, 6% per annum of cost of equipment.
> Accrued taxes, $100.
> Accrued salaries, $510.
> Repair supplies on hand, $175.
> Repair services performed, not billed, $340.

Problems—Group B

Problem B 5-1. The trial balance given below was taken from the ledger of Dome Company before adjusting entries were posted at the end of operations for the year 1959.

DOME COMPANY
Trial Balance
December 31, 1959

Cash	800.00	
Notes receivable	2,500.00	
Prepaid insurance	750.00	
Land	3,000.00	
Building	18,000.00	
Accumulated depreciation—Building		2,160.00
Service revenue received in advance		3,500.00
Mortgage payable		5,000.00
Capital stock		10,000.00
Retained earnings		2,590.00
Commissions earned		9,000.00
Salaries expense*	6,500.00	
Miscellaneous expense	700.00	
	32,250.00	32,250.00

* Salaries are paid on the 25th of each month.

Analyze the trial balance to determine likely adjusting entries. Prepare a list of such probable adjusting entries, stating in addition the accounts that would be debited and credited for each entry.

Problem B 5-2. From the trial balance and other data provided below, prepare 10-column working papers for College Company for the three months ended September 30, 1959. The books were last closed on June 30, 1959.

COLLEGE COMPANY
Trial Balance
September 30, 1959

Cash	2,571.07	
Parts	1,410.60	
Prepaid rent	900.00	
Equipment	15,000.00	
Accumulated depreciation—Equipment		5,400.00
Accounts payable		1,925.25
Fees received in advance		2,600.00

Capital stock..................................		8,000.00
Retained earnings.............................		1,675.03
Dividends.....................................	120.00	
Commissions earned...........................		4,925.00
Fees earned...................................		1,110.00
Wages and salaries expense....................	5,315.75	
Miscellaneous expense........................	317.86	
	25,635.28	25,635.28

Data for adjustments:

(1) Parts on hand at the end of September totaled $840.20.

(2) According to the terms of the lease, the annual rental of $1,200 is to be paid in advance on April 1 of each year.

(3) The equipment had an expected useful life of six years when purchased new.

(4) Wages and salaries earned by employees but not paid amounted to $211.

(5) Of the balance in the Fees Received in Advance account, $2,100 had not been earned as of September 30.

(6) On September 1, 1959, College Company rented some equipment to Alpha Fraternity under the following terms: $75 per month payable on the first day of each month following the start of the rental arrangement.

Problem B 5-3. Prepare adjusting entries relating to the accounts of Area Trailer Rental Company at the end of its business year, December 31, 1958. It is the policy of the company, which was organized on January 1, 1956, to prepare adjusting entries only at year end.

(1) Accrued interest on corporate bonds held as an investment, $35.

(2) The company depreciates its equipment over a five-year useful life. The Equipment account shows the following information:

> Balance, January 1, 1958................. $18,500
> July 1, 1958—new trailer................. 2,100
> Balance, December 31, 1958............. $20,600

(3) When the company was organized, it purchased a three-year fire insurance policy on its equipment for $93.

(4) All trailer rentals are collected in advance. The collections during 1958 were of two classes:

> $19,200 When these collections were received, it was known that the entire amount would be earned during 1958.
>
> 4,800 When these collections were received, it was known that the entire amount would not be earned during 1958.

As of December 31, 1958, $2,100 of trailer rentals were unearned, in comparison with $1,800 which was the unearned amount as of December 31, 1957.

(5) Supplies used during 1958 amounted to $375.

(6) Accrued wages as of December 31, 1958 amounted to $181.

(7) The company rents a plot of ground on which it parks its trailers. The monthly rental of $40 is paid in advance on the first of each month and is charged to Parking Lot Rent Expense. On December 30, 1958, the company paid the rent for the month of January, 1959, and the bookkeeper debited the amount to Parking Lot Rent Expense; the December 31, 1958 trial balance shows a balance of $520 for this account.

Problem B 5-4. Following is the after-closing trial balance of The Otto Company. The company closes its books annually.

THE OTTO COMPANY
After-Closing Trial Balance
December 31, 1958

Cash	2,710.00	
Note receivable	600.00	
Accrued interest receivable	5.00	
Equipment	6,000.00	
Accumulated depreciation—Equipment		1,500.00
Accounts payable		47.00
Accrued rent payable		90.00
Fees received in advance		450.00
Capital stock		7,000.00
Retained earnings		228.00
	9,315.00	9,315.00

Journalize the following transactions.

1959

January   2—Paid $36 for a two-year fire insurance policy on the equipment.

3—Paid the December, 1958 and the January, 1959 rent, in the total amount of $180.

8—Paid the $47 account payable, the bill involved covering supplies used during December, 1958.

10—Collected the note receivable, which matured today, principal and interest amounting to $606.

18—Collected $450 in fees for services completed today.

25—Paid $1,500 for new equipment.

28—Purchased supplies on account, $85. This quantity of supplies will cover the needs of the company for approximately three months.

Problem B 5-5. Trench Contracting Company was formed June 1 to engage in the specialty of digging trenches for municipalities and public utilities. The company planned to use the following chart of accounts.

Assets

1—Cash
3—Accounts receivable
6—Prepaid rent
10—Equipment
11—Accumulated depreciation—Equipment

Liabilities

21—Accounts payable
22—Traveling expense payable
24—Accrued salaries and wages payable

Stockholders' Equity

30—Capital stock
31—Retained earnings
35—Revenue and expense summary
38—Dividends

Revenue

40—Service revenue

Expenses

45—Salaries and wages expense
46—Repairs expense
47—Supplies expense
48—Traveling expense
49—Depreciation expense—Equipment
50—Rent expense

The transactions for June are set forth below.

1958
June 1—$60,000 par value capital stock was issued to the incorporators for cash.
      1—Rent was paid for the use of land and building for the next 12 months, $1,500.
    15—Equipment with an expected useful life of five years and costing $45,000 was purchased. The company paid $40,000 in cash and agreed to pay the balance within 30 days.
    19—Received a bill from Mechanical Skills Corporation for machinery repairs, $89.22.
    25—Paid $97.64 for supplies which had been used on a large contract.
    27—Received a bill from an officer of the company for traveling expense, $115.45.
    28—Paid salaries and wages, $4,371.50. (The salaries and wages for June 29 and 30 will amount to $122; however, they will be paid during July.)
    29—Paid a dividend, $300.
    30—Completed a contract for X City. The city was billed in full for $7,141, pursuant to the terms of the agreement.

Required:

(a) Journalize transactions and post to ledger accounts. (Plan for six lines in the ledger for each account except Cash; allow nine lines for the Cash account.)
(b) Prepare working papers (using either 10 or 12 columns).
(c) Prepare statements.
(d) Make and post journal entries for any necessary adjustments.
(e) Make and post journal entries to close the books.
(f) Rule the closed accounts.
(g) Take an after-closing trial balance.

Problem B 5-6. The following adjusted trial balance was taken from the ledger after adjusting entries had been posted but before the year-end closing entries were recorded.

BOOTH COMPANY
Adjusted Trial Balance
December 31, 1959

Cash	1,300.00	
State bonds	2,000.00	
Accrued rent receivable	60.00	
Prepaid insurance	320.00	
Installation parts	168.00	
Land	3,500.00	
Equipment	10,000.00	
Accumulated depreciation—Equipment		6,000.00
Accounts payable		714.00
Accrued wages payable		210.00
Installation fees received in advance		220.00
Capital stock		10,000.00
Retained earnings	3,169.00	
Commissions earned		11,500.00
Installation fees		2,100.00
Interest earned		500.00

Rent earned....................................		720.00
Wages expense................................	9,310.00	
Miscellaneous expense.........................	380.00	
Insurance expense.............................	242.00	
Installation parts expense.....................	515.00	
Depreciation expense—Equipment..............	1,000.00	
	31,964.00	31,964.00

The company closes its books annually.

During 1959, the company collected $2,220 in installation fees, 80 per cent of which were properly credited immediately to the Installation Fees account. These credits and the year-end adjusting entry were the only entries made in the Installation Fees account during the year.

The 1959 cash disbursements for insurance premiums included one premium of $24 paid on July 1 for 60-day coverage on the installation parts; all other premium payments were for policies with either two-year or three-year terms.

Submit the adjusting entries which you believe were entered in the journal of Booth Company at the end of 1959.

ASSIGNMENT MATERIAL FOR CHAPTER 6
Questions

1. How is the gross profit computed?

2. Describe how a sale of merchandise is recorded.

3. Describe the entries normally appearing in the Inventory account.

4. How is the cost of goods sold computed for the first accounting period of a newly organized business that started operations without a beginning inventory of merchandise?

5. If a merchandising business has two principal sources of revenue, where is the revenue from services shown in the financial statements?

6. If the following statement is inaccurate or misleading, correct it. "The Purchases account is used to record all purchases."

7. How are the beginning and ending inventories handled in the working papers?

8. What is meant by "internal control"?

9. The terms of an invoice are: 1/10; n/30. What does this mean?

10. What uses are made of purchase orders?

Problems—Group A

Problem A 6-1. Journalize the following transactions of Value Company. The company closes its books monthly.

1959

March 1—Paid rent for the month, $110.

2—Purchased merchandise on account from State Supply Co., $275.

3—Purchased additional store fixtures for $1,240, cash.

5—Cash sale, $78.

8—Issued a note to State Supply Co. for $275 to cover the purchase of March 2.

10—Purchased merchandise on account from Midwest Company at a cost of $171.

12—Sold merchandise on account to A. J. Boon, $128.

17—Cash purchase, $39.

19—Paid Midwest Company for merchandise that was purchased on March 10.

21—Renewed a fire insurance policy for two years; the premium was paid, $72.

25—Collected $128 from A. J. Boon for sale of March 12.

Problem A 6-2. The adjusted trial balance of Thin Corporation is submitted on the following page with the accounts listed in alphabetical order. Prepare closing entries and compute the cost of goods sold.

THIN CORPORATION
Adjusted Trial Balance
December 31, 1958

Accounts receivable........................	5,351.20	
Accrued wages payable.....................		192.63
Accumulated depreciation—Building..........		5,600.00
Accumulated depreciation—Equipment........		6,080.00
Advertising expense........................	3,120.00	
Building...................................	40,000.00	
Capital stock..............................		30,000.00
Cash......................................	4,592.40	
Depreciation expense—Building..............	1,600.00	
Depreciation expense—Equipment............	1,520.00	
Equipment.................................	15,200.00	
Interest expense...........................	600.00	
Inventory, December 31, 19 ?...............	7,849.00	
Land......................................	3,500.00	
Mortgage payable..........................		10,000.00
Purchases.................................	27,219.42	
Retained earnings..........................		2,566.18
Sales.....................................		68,863.22
Supplies..................................	355.00	
Supplies used.............................	2,245.00	
Taxes....................................	264.20	
Wages and salaries........................	9,885.81	
	123,302.03	123,302.03

Inventory, December 31, 19 ?............. $7,231.50

Problem A 6-3. Journalize the July, 1959 transactions of Air Overhaul Company. The company is organized to perform maintenance and repair services on aircraft. There will be two sources of earnings, one from the sale of parts and the other from the performance of maintenance and repair service. The company plans to close its books monthly.

July 1—Issued $8,000 par value stock for $5,000 cash and equipment valued at $3,000.

2—Paid July rent, $180.

5—Purchased airplane spare parts on account from Curtis Company, $1,817.

7—Purchased shop supplies for $410, cash.

9—Billed Charter Airline $287 for parts and $470 for labor used in making a periodic check of one of its aircraft.

11—Purchased additional airplane parts from Wright Corporation, paying $421 cash.

12—Collected $45 for repair of landing gear on a private plane. No parts were used.

14—Paid the Curtis Company bill.

15—Billed World Air Flights $417 for parts and $614 for labor used in rebuilding a tail assembly.

15—Paid wages of $800 for first half of July.

18—Collected $100 for periodic overhaul of a private plane; this amount included $20 for parts.

20—Received $757 from Charter Airline.

Signed an agreement with XYZ Company to perform all required labor for maintenance on its company plane for $600 per quarter, starting today. All parts used will be extra.

July 21—Collected $600 in advance from *XYZ* Company.

    23—Purchased a one-year fire insurance policy for cash, $30.

    25—Received $1,031 from World Air Flights.

    26—Billed Charter Airline $311 for parts and $580 for labor used in making a periodic check of one of its aircraft.

    27—Purchased airplane parts on account from Curtis Company, $622.

    29—Completed rebuilding landing gear on plane belonging to A. Y. Junior. The total bill amounted to $690, of which $200 was for parts. Junior gave his check for the entire bill when he called today for his plane.

    30—Purchased shop supplies on account from Modern Supply Co., $84.

    31—Paid wages for last half of July, $825.

    31—Billed *XYZ* Company, pursuant to agreement of July 20, for parts used in maintenance of company plane, $72.

Problem A 6-4. Using the following data, prepare working papers for the year ended December 31, 1958.

THEME CORPORATION
Trial Balance
December 31, 1958

Cash	1,327.00	
Accounts receivable	4,450.00	
Notes receivable	2,000.00	
Inventory, December 31, 1957	6,000.00	
Supplies	1,570.00	
Furniture and fixtures	3,500.00	
Accumulated depreciation—Furniture and fixtures		700.00
Accounts payable		2,114.00
Notes payable		3,000.00
Capital stock		7,000.00
Retained earnings		246.00
Sales		53,000.00
Purchases	34,702.00	
Wages	8,627.00	
Rent	2,600.00	
Taxes	1,214.00	
Interest on notes payable	90.00	
Interest on notes receivable		20.00
	66,080.00	66,080.00

Closing Entries—December 31, 1958
(Explanations Omitted)

Sales	53,000.00	
Interest on notes receivable	40.00	
Inventory	6,245.00	
Revenue and expense		59,285.00
Revenue and expense	56,212.00	
Inventory		6,000.00
Purchases		34,702.00
Wages		8,852.00
Rent		2,600.00
Taxes		2,476.00
Interest on notes payable		180.00
Supplies used		1,140.00
Depreciation expense—Furniture and fixtures		262.00
Revenue and expense	3,073.00	
Retained earnings		3,073.00

Problem A 6-5. The balance sheet of Sea Togs Company as of December 31, 1958, is presented below:

SEA TOGS COMPANY
Balance Sheet
December 31, 1958

Assets			Liabilities and Stockholders' Equity			
Cash		$ 1,100	Liabilities:			
Municipal bonds		3,000	Accounts payable...	$ 2,120		
Accounts receivable		2,300	Accrued taxes	380	$ 2,500	
Accrued interest receivable		20				
Inventory		4,710	Stockholders' equity:			
Prepaid insurance		108	Capital stock	$10,000		
Equipment	$6,000		Retained earnings..	2,938	12,938	
Less accumulated depreciation	1,800	4,200				
		$15,438			$15,438	

1959
January 2—Paid month's rent, $125.
4—Cash sale, $310.
7—Paid $250 on account.
10—Sale on account to D. W. Company, $750.
12—Paid half of the accrued taxes.
14—Purchased merchandise for cash, $170.
17—Collected $600 on account.
22—Purchased a two-year public liability policy for $50 cash.
25—Cash sale, $420.
27—Purchased merchandise on account from Boot Company, $812.
30—Sale on account to Sweeney and Sons, $515.
31—Paid selling commissions for January, $410.

Additional information:

(1) Interest earned during January on municipal bonds, $10.
(2) Prepaid insurance as of January 31, $130.
(3) Depreciation for January, $100.
(4) January taxes accrued, $35.
(5) January 31 inventory, $4,290.

Required:

(a) Journalize and post all transactions and adjustments.
(b) Prepare working papers.
(c) Prepare the income statement and the balance sheet.
(d) Close the books.

Problem A 6-6. Helicopter Sales Company was organized on August 1, 1959. The company plans to close its books annually on July 31.
(a) Journalize the August transactions.

1959
August 1—Issued at par for cash $50,000 of capital stock.
2—Paid rent on hangar space for August, $400.
4—Took delivery on two helicopters, paying $10,000 in cash and signing a note payable in the amount of $22,000 for the balance of the total purchase price.

August 6—Paid $190 for selling expenses to demonstrate the feasibility of helicopters for wealthy commuters.

9—A salesman sold one of the helicopters. He collected $20,000 from the customer. He deducted his commission on this sale and turned in $19,000 to the company.

10—When the company was organized, it ordered a one-year public liability policy. The policy was delivered today and the company paid the premium, $480.

15—Purchased another helicopter under the same terms as established by the August 4 transaction. The total purchase price was $16,000.

21—Sold a helicopter on account to Hi-Fi Company for $20,000. The salesman's commission of five per cent is withheld until the receivable is collected in full.

22—Paid $110 to deliver the helicopter to Hi-Fi Company, whose business office is in another city.

27—Received $4,000 from the helicopter manufacturer. A customer of Helicopter Sales Company took delivery of his helicopter at the factory. The factory collected the retail sales price of $20,000 and remitted to Helicopter Sales Company the difference between the factory price to dealers and the retail price.

(b) Post the August journal entries to T-accounts, omitting dates and posting references in the T-accounts.

(c) As noted above, the company will close its books annually on July 31. However, the management desires to know the net income (or loss) for August, 1959. Therefore, prepare working papers for August, 1959.

Additional information:

(1) The salesman making the sale described on August 27 is entitled to a commission of $1,000.

(2) The insurance policy dated August 1 covers a one-year term.

(3) Office salaries for August have not been paid, $800.

(4) Accrued interest on the notes payable, $120.

(5) August 31, 1959 inventory, $16,000.

Problems—Group B

Problem B 6-1. Journalize the following transactions of Wholesale Furniture Company.

1959
August 1—Paid $38 for repairs to building.

3—Purchased merchandise on account from Furniture Manufacturing Co., $478.

5—Purchased furniture for use in the office, $410 cash.

8—Cash sale, $112.

10—Paid $67 for property taxes.

12—Purchased furniture for resale from Style Company, $696; terms, 30 days.

15—Paid $478 to Furniture Manufacturing Company.

18—Sold furniture on account to Home Furniture Co., $2,585.

22—Made a special purchase of lawn furniture to hold for next season. The furniture normally is priced by the manufacturer (Lawn Furniture Company) at $1,500. Considering the season of the year, the price to Wholesale Furniture Company is $1,100; terms, 60-day note payable.

August 26—Purchased shipping supplies for $47 cash.

28—Collected $2,585 for sale made earlier to Home Furniture Co.

31—Paid wages and salaries for August, $680.

Problem B 6-2. Journalize the following transactions of Commercial Refrigerator Sales Company, a newly organized corporation. The company will close its books annually on June 30.

1958

July 1—Issued $10,000 par value stock for cash.

2—Paid rent for July, $110.

3—Purchased from Wholesale Supply Company, on account, five refrigerators for $200 each.

7—Sold one refrigerator for $300 cash.

8—Paid $40 as commission to the salesman.

9—As an advertising feature, the company has agreed to place a new refrigerator in the local Girl Scout Home each July. According to the plan, when the new refrigerator is delivered each year, the Girl Scouts may sell the old refrigerator and keep the proceeds. A refrigerator is delivered to the Girl Scout Home today.

10—Sold a refrigerator for $300 to R. S. Brown on account.

15—Paid $1,000 to Wholesale Supply Company.

18—Purchased for cash four refrigerators for $200 each.

20—Paid $30 for newspaper advertising.

24—Collected $300 from R. S. Brown.

24—Paid $40 commission to the salesman.

28—Cash sale of three refrigerators to Local Hospital for $860.

30—Paid $50 in dividends to stockholders.

Problem B 6-3. Using the data below, (a) prepare ten-column working papers, (b) prepare closing entries, and (c) compute the gross profit.

HOLLOW CORPORATION
Trial Balance
June 30, 1959

Cash	2,621.43	
Bonds	2,000.00	
Accounts receivable	819.27	
Inventory, June 30, 1958	5,417.50	
Supplies	875.15	
Prepaid insurance	183.30	
Equipment	4,717.10	
Accumulated depreciation—Equipment		1,834.21
Notes payable		700.00
Service revenue received in advance		1,925.50
Capital stock		15,000.00
Retained earnings	3,761.58	
Sales		47,919.74
Purchases	34,783.39	
Wages and salaries	9,876.23	
Rent	1,500.00	
Taxes	817.50	
Interest expense	7.00	
	67,379.45	67,379.45

Additional information:

(1) Accrued interest on the bonds, $35.
(2) Supplies on hand, $312.25.
(3) Insurance expired, $61.10.
(4) Depreciation of equipment, 10% per year.
(5) Accrued interest payable, $3.50.
(6) Service revenue earned, $1,417.20.
(7) Accrued taxes, $18.
(8) June 30, 1959 inventory, $5,271.10.

Problem B 6-4. The following adjusted trial balance was prepared at the end of the company's fiscal year.

TEE COMPANY
Adjusted Trial Balance
June 30, 1959

Cash	4,438.00	
Accounts receivable	12,720.00	
Inventory	5,500.00	
Office supplies	460.00	
Prepaid insurance	162.00	
Land	5,000.00	
Building	50,000.00	
Equipment	60,000.00	
Accounts payable		5,540.00
Notes payable		16,000.00
Capital stock		70,000.00
Retained earnings	4,578.00	
Service revenue		2,100.00
Sales		138,440.00
Purchases	84,410.00	
Selling commissions	7,132.00	
Delivery expense	2,170.00	
Salaries	34,160.00	
Property taxes	2,452.00	
Office supplies expense	1,910.00	
Insurance expired	108.00	
Depreciation expense—Building	2,000.00	
Depreciation expense—Equipment	12,000.00	
Interest expense	800.00	
Accrued property taxes		1,520.00
Accrued interest payable		400.00
Accumulated depreciation—Building		12,000.00
Accumulated depreciation—Equipment		44,000.00
	290,000.00	290,000.00

Additional information:

Inventory, June 30, 1959.............. $4,950.00

Required:

(a) Income statement, statement of retained earnings, and balance sheet.
(b) Journal entries to close the books.

Problem B 6-5. Partially completed working papers for The Tire Company appear below. Prepare completed working papers. Essential data, in addition to the information given below, are as follows:

(1) Inventory, December 31, 1958, $5,000.
(2) Retained earnings, after adjusting and closing entries, $420.

THE TIRE COMPANY
Working Papers
For the Six Months Ended December 31, 1958

	Trial Balance	Adjustments	Income Statement	Retained Earnings Statement	Balance Sheet
Cash.................	200.00				200.00
Accounts receivable......	4,800.00				
Inventory, June 30, 1958.....	800.00				570.00
Supplies on hand........	20,000.00				20,000.00
Fixtures............					
Accumulated depreciation—					
Fixtures.........	5,000.00				
Notes payable.......	6,000.00				5,500.00
Capital stock.......	15,000.00				6,000.00
Retained earnings......	1,120.00				15,000.00
Dividends........	300.00				
Sales............	30,000.00				
Purchases........	5,120.00				
Sales commissions......	500.00		600.00		
Rent expense........	120.00		150.00		
Interest expense.......					
	57,120.00				

ASSIGNMENT MATERIAL FOR CHAPTER 7
Questions

1. Distinguish between the following terms: F. o. b. destination and f. o. b. shipping point.

2. The following entry records the payment of transportation charges:

Accounts receivable................................. .... 11.00
    Cash... 11.00

Describe the transportation terms that would cause the above entry.

3. Considering the following data, what is the cost of goods available for sale during June?

Inventory, June 1............................. ..... $7,000
Inventory, June 30............................ $8,000
Purchases during June......................... $4,200
During June, the purchase returns and allowances exceeded
    the charges for transportation in by $80.

4. Distinguish between trade discounts and cash discounts.

5. How should depreciation and bad debt charges be classified in the income statement?

6. After all year-end adjustments were made, the ledger of a certain company contained the following data:

Accounts receivable............................ 68,000.00
Allowance for doubtful accounts................. 2,100.00
Bad debts expense............................. 1,700.00

Why is the credit balance of the allowance account greater than the debit balance in the Bad Debts Expense account? Of the above accounts, identify those closed periodically to Revenue and Expense.

7. Submit an explanation for the following entry:

Allowance for doubtful accounts....................... 58.00
    Accounts receivable............................. 58.00

8. Give an example of a "contra" account. How are such accounts shown in financial statements?

9. Of the several payroll taxes, which ones are expenses from the point of view of the employer?

10. Describe a procedure of accounting for sales taxes.

Problems—Group A

Problem A 7-1. The trial balance of The Plymouth Corporation as of December 31, 1959, is presented on the following page. Using the data given, prepare (a) working papers and (b) closing entries.

THE PLYMOUTH CORPORATION
Trial Balance
December 31, 1959

Cash	5,296.18	
Accounts receivable	27,545.22	
Allowance for doubtful accounts		397.12
Inventory, December 31, 1958	5,649.14	
Equipment	35,906.89	
Accumulated depreciation—Equipment		12,415.32
Accounts payable		7,991.26
Capital stock		35,000.00
Retained earnings		5,901.86
Dividends	2,000.00	
Sales		185,239.08
Sales returns and allowances	6,846.13	
Sales discounts	1,182.15	
Purchases	119,654.06	
Purchase returns and allowances		2,268.14
Purchase discounts		3,165.11
Transportation in	6,592.22	
Freight out	1,685.02	
Salesmen's salaries	22,619.17	
Advertising expense	1,048.36	
Rent expense	3,840.00	
Office salaries	9,200.47	
Property taxes	2,315.55	
Miscellaneous expense	997.33	
	252,377.89	252,377.89

(a) For probable bad debts, the company provides annually an amount equal to 1% of its sales less returns and allowances and discounts.

(b) Equipment is depreciated at a rate of 12% per annum. On September 30, 1959, the company purchased a machine costing $7,200.

(c) Income tax payable by the corporation is $2,900 for 1959.

(d) An advertising bill in the amount of $490 is not recorded.

(e) The property tax expense for the year is $2,517.49.

(f) The inventory at year-end is $8,317.62.

Problem A 7-2. The following information relates to some of the financial activities of Metropolitan Corporation during a particular month.

Purchased a piece of equipment from Alden Company on account. The list price was $3,000, with a 20% discount.

The customer to whom the corporation sold goods for $1,000 cash returned half of the shipment and was reimbursed.

R. L. Smith's account was deemed to be uncollectible, $20,000.

Received a check from a customer who took the corporation's usual 3% cash discount on an invoice of $3,200.

Returned to Henry Company merchandise which cost $2,500.

$175 was received on an order of merchandise to be delivered when available.

Total payroll accrued, $1,350.24. All salaries and wages were subject to social security (2¼%) and unemployment insurance. The income tax payable by employees amounted to $63.95. The state unemployment insurance rate is 2.7%.

Paid the above payroll and recorded the liability for payroll taxes thereon.

Paid transportation on shipment of merchandise received today; the amount was $68 and the goods were shipped f. o. b. destination.

Required: Journal entries, omitting dates.

Problem A 7-3. Apex Corporation's payroll summary for the period from August 15, 1958, to September 15, 1958, appears below.

	Salaries and Wages	F. I. C. A. Taxes Withheld	Income Tax Withheld	Net Payroll
Drivers' wages........	$ 9,418.63	$211.92	$1,006.32	$ 8,200.39
Office salaries.........	6,000.00	135.00	842.15	5,022.85
Totals............	$15,418.63	$346.92	$1,848.47	$13,223.24

Required: Ledger entries to record:

   (a) the accrual of the payroll as above on September 15;

   (b) the accrual of all employer tax expenses, assuming a state unemployment tax of 2.7% and that all the above earnings are subject to such taxes; and

   (c) the payment of salaries and wages to the employees on September 22, 1958, and all tax liabilities on October 15, 1958, except the federal unemployment insurance, which is payable annually.

Problem A 7-4. The information below relates to Stanton Corporation at year-end, December 31, 1959.

Debits	Trial Balance	Adjusted Trial Balance
Cash..................................	2,428.19	2,428.19
Accrued interest receivable...............	50.00	75.00
Accounts receivable......................	17,342.80	16,747.80
Notes receivable........................	1,800.00	1,800.00
Inventory, December 31, 1958.............	6,924.16	6,924.16
Prepaid insurance.......................	1,563.00	377.83
Supplies................................	2,714.27	912.13
Office equipment........................	15,000.00	15,000.00
Retained earnings.......................	12,847.27	12,847.27
Dividends..............................	500.00	500.00
Purchases..............................	72,356.19	72,356.19
Store salaries...........................	33,549.10	33,918.10
Payroll taxes expense....................	1,165.23	1,184.60
Advertising.............................	1,764.33	1,764.33
Store supplies expense...................	—	1,802.14
Depreciation expense—Office equipment....	—	2,250.00
Bad debts expense.......................	—	184.00
Insurance expense.......................	—	1,185.17
Sales discounts.........................	5,396.18	5,396.18
	175,400.72	177,653.09

Credits		
Allowance for doubtful accounts..........	1,562.00	1,151.00
Accumulated depreciation—Office equipment	7,200.00	9,450.00
Accrued salaries payable.................	—	369.00
Revenue received in advance.............	1,412.00	720.00
Withholding and F. I. C. A. tax liabilities...	492.18	500.48
Federal unemployment tax liability........	62.45	63.56
State unemployment tax liability..........	145.14	155.10
Sales..................................	113,492.36	113,492.36
Service revenue earned..................	10,250.00	10,942.00
Interest earned.........................	156.42	181.42
Purchase returns and allowances..........	628.17	628.17
Capital stock...........................	40,000.00	40,000.00
	175,400.72	177,653.09

The inventory on December 31, 1959, was $5,629.11.

Required:

  (a) Journal entries for the adjustments that have been put through the books for 1959.

  (b) Financial statements for the year 1959.

Problems—Group B

Problem B 7-1. From the following information relating to Starwick Corporation, compute the inventory on December 31, 1958.

Data for 1959

Sales..................................	$6,000
Store rent.............................	355
Depreciation expense—Equipment.........	500
Inventory, December 31, 1959............	1,749
Sales discounts........................	319
Purchases.............................	4,217
Trade discounts on sales................	1,250
Gross profit on sales...................	1,611

Problem B 7-2. The Accounts Receivable account in the trial balance of Hobart Company shows a balance of $62,927.43 on December 31, 1958, while the Allowance for Doubtful Accounts equals $1,906.20.

In reviewing the accounts, the management decides that the account of A. L. Green, amounting to $425.40, will be uncollectible.

  (a) Present the journal entry to write off the account.

  (b) Show the relevant section of the balance sheet after the write-off.

Problem B 7-3. The data below relate to the 1958 activities of Barton Company. Compute the purchase discounts and sales discounts for the year.

Bad debts expense......................	$ 300
Closing inventory......................	11,800
Purchases.............................	32,000
Salesmen's salaries.....................	1,700
Sales.................................	42,000
Opening inventory.....................	6,500
Cost of goods available for sale..........	37,000
Gross profit on sales...................	16,400

There were no returns and allowances.

Problem B 7-4. During the month of April, Allison Corporation had the following transactions, among others, in its operations:

Received notice that K. Jones, a customer, had gone into bankruptcy. His account, showing a debit balance of $2,745.80, was written off.

Paid freight of $36 on merchandise delivered to a customer.

Remitted 2% sales tax to the state on March sales of $3,560.

A customer returned merchandise damaged in transit, and credit was given for $500.

Purchased merchandise for $5,000, less trade discount of 30%; terms, 5/10; n/30.

A memorandum was received from the bank stating that it had collected a note receivable in the amount of $4,500, together with $62 interest, and that the amount had been added to the corporation's bank account.

Remitted to the federal government the income taxes withheld from employees, $692.54.

Paid for merchandise purchased above within the discount period.

Issued additional capital stock of $10,000 par value; payment was received half in cash and half in merchandise.

Paid $27 cartage on a shipment to O. A. Smith, which was sent f. o. b. shipping point.

Received a freight bill in the amount of $76 on a recent purchase of merchandise. The corporation did not have sufficient cash on hand to pay the bill immediately.

Required:

Omitting dates, submit the journal entries.

Problem B 7-5. The following balances were taken from the adjusted trial balance of Colonial Corporation, the accounts being kept in alphabetical order. The information pertains to the year ended December 31, 1959. On that date the inventory was $7,492.

Accounts payable	34,000
Accounts receivable	39,265
Accumulated depreciation—Store building	5,000
Accumulated depreciation—Store equipment	1,800
Advertising expense	4,280
Allowance for doubtful accounts	3,519
Bad debts expense	546
Building	29,000
Capital stock	28,000
Cash	9,248
Depreciation expense—Store building	1,000
Depreciation expense—Store equipment	450
Dividends	1,200
Freight out	465
Insurance expense	628
Inventory, December 31, 1958	5,246
Land	2,500
Liability for sales taxes	564
Office supplies expense	496
Payroll taxes expense (salesmen)	176
Purchases	49,546
Purchase returns and allowances	1,712
Retained earnings	10,238
Sales	75,457
Sales discounts	237
Salesmen's salaries	5,243
Sales returns and allowances	1,969
Store equipment	5,500
Store supplies expense	356
Taxes	744
Transportation in	2,414
Withholding and F. I. C. A. tax liabilities	219

Required:

(a) Income statement
(b) Closing entries.

Problem B 7-6. The Pontiac Corporation is a retail establishment operating in a state that has a 3% sales tax on all sales. The tax is collected by the merchants. Total receipts per cash registers for the month of April were $3,347.50. Submit the journal entry to record the above information.

Give the entry to record the remittance of the tax to the state.

Problem B 7-7. Worthmore Stores, Incorporated, operates several retail establishments. It employs a total of 75 salesmen at a rate of $1.25 per hour. They work a total of 40 hours per week and are paid weekly.

In addition to the hourly sales help, the company employs five department heads, called buyers, one general sales manager, eight office clerks, and an office manager. This group is paid monthly, as follows:

Buyers.....................	$450 per month
General Manager............	650 per month
Office Clerks...............	240 per month
Office Manager.............	425 per month

The store is subject to a state unemployment tax rate of 2.7%. Assume that there is no turnover in salaried personnel during the year.

Required:

(a) For the first weekly payroll, compute the total F. I. C. A. tax withheld from employees and the liabilities for unemployment insurance taxes.

(b) Compute the total unemployment insurance tax liability for the salaried personnel (separate federal and state) for the months of January, July, and December.

(c) Compute the total F. I. C. A. tax withheld from salaried personnel for January, July, and December.

Problem B 7-8. Below, in T-account form, is the Allowance for Doubtful Accounts ledger account of Bridgeport Corporation, containing entries from December 31, 1957 through 1959, the balances having been omitted.

Allowance for Doubtful Accounts

1958		1957	
Jan. 10	596.00	Dec. 31	3,000.00
Mar. 17	317.00	1958	
Aug. 28	417.00	Dec. 31	2,649.00
1959		1959	
Jan. 4	175.00	Dec. 31	3,618.00
April 10	262.00		
Nov. 17	198.00		

Required:

(a) The bad debts expense for 1958.

(b) The balance of the Allowance for Doubtful Accounts at the end of 1958.

(c) The account credited for the 1959 debit entries.

(d) The company provides ¾ of 1% of net sales each year. What were the net sales for the years 1957, 1958, and 1959?

ASSIGNMENT MATERIAL FOR CHAPTER 8
Questions

1. Define current assets.

2. What is an operating cycle?

3. Distinguish between current liabilities and long-term liabilities.

4. Why are short-term expense prepayments regarded as current assets?

5. Give some examples of incidental revenues. How may such items be shown in the income statement?

6. Why are exhibit letters used in financial statements?

7. Explain the all-inclusive concept and give some of the arguments that have been developed in support of the concept.

8. Contrast the current operating concept and the all-inclusive concept.

9. Cite some examples of how account numbers may indicate account classifications and account relationships.

10. Give two synonyms for each of the following terms: allowance for uncollectible accounts, accumulated depreciation, stockholders' equity, retained earnings.

Problems—Group A

Problem A 8-1. Prepare a classified balance sheet for Banner Company as of June 30, 1959. Select the accounts applicable from the following list.

Cash	$ 5,725.10
Sales	61,000.00
Retained earnings, June 30, 1959	5,544.00
Accounts payable	7,000.00
Purchase discounts	658.00
Land	13,750.00
Interest earned	170.00
Allowance for doubtful accounts	305.00
Wages and salaries payable	250.00
Taxes expense	9,222.10
Service revenue earned	1,000.00
Purchases	30,000.00
Inventory	14,600.00
Mortgage payable, due June 30, 1964	15,000.00
Buildings	47,000.00
Notes receivable	2,000.00
Accumulated depreciation—Buildings	9,000.00
Capital stock	45,000.00
Accrued rent receivable	654.20
Accrued taxes	5,326.30
Office expense	1,045.00
Accounts receivable	7,050.00
Wages and salaries expense	3,655.00
Prepaid insurance	180.00
Notes payable	2,000.00
Service revenue received in advance	1,534.00

Problem A 8-2. Statements of retained earnings for Elbow Company are given below:

ELBOW COMPANY
Statement of Retained Earnings
For the Year Ended December 31, 1958

Retained earnings, December 31, 1957		$57,850.00
Add:		
Net income for the year—Per income statement	$32,154.00	
Gain on disposal of equipment	4,222.00	36,376.00
Total		$94,226.00
Deduct:		
Dividends	$10,800.00	
Correction for underdepreciation of building during 1956 and 1957	3,000.00	13,800.00
Retained earnings, December 31, 1958		$80,426.00

ELBOW COMPANY
Statement of Retained Earnings
For the Year Ended December 31, 1959

Retained earnings, December 31, 1958		$ 80,426.00
Add:		
Net income for the year—Per income statement	$25,460.00	
Gain on sale of long-term investments	1,365.00	26,825.00
Total		$107,251.00
Deduct:		
Dividends	$20,400.00	
Payment of legal suit lost	8,800.00	29,200.00
Retained earnings, December 31, 1959		$ 78,051.00

Additional data:

(1) Rentals earned but unrecorded on December 31, 1959, amounted to $1,500.

(2) Interest expense accrued but unrecorded on December 31, 1959, amounted to $960.

Prepare corrected statements of retained earnings for the years 1958 and 1959, as they would have appeared if the company had followed the all-inclusive concept.

Problem A 8-3. From the accounts given below, (a) prepare an income statement under the clean surplus concept, and (b) compute net income under the current operating concept for the Mao Corporation for the year ending December 31, 1959.

Sales	$50,200.00
Inventory, December 31, 1958	4,680.00
Inventory, December 31, 1959	5,675.00
Salesmen's wages	6,500.00
Administrative salaries	7,000.00
Purchases	28,815.00
Delivery expense	680.00
Office supplies inventory, December 31, 1959	750.00
Office supplies used	1,550.00
Estimated income tax payable	4,200.00
Income taxes	3,100.00
Payment of assessment for additional income taxes for the years 1956 and 1957	1,250.00

Depreciation expense—Furniture............................	400.00
Gain on sale of marketable securities.........................	1,570.00
Land (held for future use)..............................	1,600.00
Interest earned.......................................	560.00
Dividends...	600.00

Problem A 8-4. The following data are available regarding K. & K., Inc., as of June 30, 1959:

(1) Cash on hand, $1,400.
(2) Capital stock issued, 6,000 shares, par $10.
(3) Cost of merchandise on hand, $40,300.
(4) Wages and salaries accrued, $150.
(5) Amounts owed to creditors, $4,300.
(6) Store building: value, $25,000; cost, $30,000; accumulated depreciation, $8,000.
(7) Store equipment: value, $10,000; cost, $10,000; accumulated depreciation, $3,000.
(8) Face amount of 60-day note, dated June 15, 1959, and payable to City Bank, with interest at 5%, $480. (Interest accrued thereon, $1.)
(9) Amounts owed by customers, $12,500; allowance for doubtful accounts, $600.
(10) Cost of U. S. Savings Bonds, $1,000; interest amounting to $12.50 for six months is collectible July 1, 1959. (Bonds are held as a temporary investment.)
(11) Cost of land, $5,000; value, $4,000.
(12) Mortgage on land and store building due January 1, 1964, $10,000.
(13) Interest accrued on mortgage, $200.
(14) Retained earnings amount to the excess of assets over the sum of the liabilities and the par value of the capital stock.

Prepare a classified balance sheet.

Problem A 8-5. Morrison Retailers, Inc., had the following trial balance at the end of December, 1958.

MORRISON RETAILERS, INC.
Trial Balance
December 31, 1958

Cash..	8,547.25	
Accounts receivable...........................	12,326.40	
Allowance for doubtful accounts................		410.50
Inventory, December 31, 1957..................	6,848.75	
Unexpired insurance..........................	300.00	
Land..	3,000.00	
Building.....................................	20,000.00	
Accumulated depreciation—Building............		6,000.00
Accounts payable.............................		14,600.00
Notes payable................................		2,000.00
Liability for sales taxes.......................		456.00
Withholding and F. I. C. A. tax liabilities........		151.80
Federal unemployment tax liability..............		45.00
State unemployment tax liability................		70.75
Capital stock.................................		14,000.00
Retained earnings............................		5,962.05
Sales..		52,500.00
Sales returns and allowances...................	490.00	

Purchases....................................	25,056.00	
Purchase discounts...........................		125.50
Transportation in............................	530.00	
Salesmen's salaries..........................	8,640.00	
Fixture rental expense.......................	1,200.00	
Office salaries...............................	7,005.00	
Payroll tax expense..........................	630.00	
Insurance expense...........................	200.00	
Miscellaneous office expenses..................	1,548.20	
	96,321.60	96,321.60

Other data:

(a) Accounts receivable previously considered doubtful and now deemed fully uncollectible amount to $180.

(b) Experience shows that ½ of 1% of sales, less returns and allowances, result in bad debts. No provision for such expected losses has been made for this year.

(c) The premium of $300 for the existing insurance policy was paid four months ago and covers a one-year period.

(d) The building is depreciated at the rate of 5% per annum.

(e) There is $10 accrued interest on the notes payable.

(f) Salaries for the last half of December have not been recorded. Salesmen's salaries were $355 and office salaries were $300 for this period.

(g) Payroll taxes have not been recorded for December. The employer's liability is:

F. I. C. A. taxes......................	$26.20
Federal unemployment tax............	3.90
State unemployment tax..............	35.10

(h) The inventory on December 31, 1958, is $5,854.50.

Required:

(a) Working papers.
(b) Classified income statement.
(c) Classified balance sheet.

Problems—Group B

Problem B 8-1. From the following accounting information taken from the records of *XYO* Company, compute total current assets. Show the details of your computation in the customary sequence.

Equipment....................................	$5,000.00
Inventory....................................	8,565.90
Sales discounts..............................	47.00
Land (held for future use).....................	2,550.00
Cash..	1,304.60
Purchase discounts...........................	88.00
Rent of land.................................	106.00
Temporary investments.......................	866.60
Supplies expense.............................	267.00
Accounts receivable..........................	4,655.20
Transportation in............................	205.00
Advertising.................................	465.00
Office salaries...............................	850.50
Allowance for doubtful accounts...............	87.50
Supplies on hand.............................	71.20

Problem B 8-2. From the following, prepare a classified balance sheet of A. L. Brown Corporation as of September 30, 1958.

Cash	$ 2,345.35
Interest expense	60.00
Accumulated depreciation—Buildings	1,500.00
Sales	16,000.00
Prepaid rent	65.00
Depreciation expense—Equipment	400.00
Accounts payable	3,210.45
Temporary investments	900.00
Capital stock	8,000.00
Mortgage payable—due March 31, 1963	1,500.00
Land	500.00
Withholding and F. I. C. A. tax liabilities	86.00
Allowance for doubtful accounts	80.00
Accumulated depreciation—Equipment	800.00
Purchases	8,455.00
Wages and salaries expense	5,450.00
Wages and salaries payable	65.00
Inventory	2,850.00
Buildings	5,000.00
Unemployment taxes payable	9.50
Retained earnings, September 30, 1958	2,339.00
Accounts receivable	1,985.60
Supplies expense	565.00
Land (Held for future use)	2,000.00
Equipment	2,400.00
Rent expense	675.00
Depreciation expense—Buildings	500.00
Estimated income tax payable	456.00

Problem B 8-3.

AROLD ALUMINUM COMPANY
Adjusted Trial Balance—December 31, 1959

Cash	5,256.00	
Accounts receivable	12,444.00	
Inventory, December 31, 1958	20,650.00	
Prepaid rent	200.00	
Equipment	24,000.00	
Accumulated depreciation—Equipment		7,200.00
Accounts payable		5,785.00
Accrued salaries and wages		680.00
Estimated income tax liability		3,450.00
Capital stock		35,000.00
Retained earnings, December 31, 1958		7,938.00
Sales		64,400.00
Purchases	27,450.00	
Salaries and wages	18,000.00	
Depreciation expense—Equipment	2,400.00	
Supplies expense	1,568.00	
Payroll taxes	980.00	
Income taxes	3,450.00	
Dividends	2,000.00	
Correction for overdepreciation of equipment during 1957 and 1958		5,595.00
Rent expense	2,400.00	
Storm loss in November, 1959	9,250.00	
	130,048.00	130,048.00

Prepare a statement of retained earnings on the assumption that the income statement was prepared under the current operating concept. The inventory on December 31, 1959 was $19,245.

Problem B 8-4. Incorrect financial statements for Lindsay Company are given below. Prepare revised statements in good form, substituting different accounting terminology where you believe it will improve understandability. Assume that the figure for income taxes is correct.

LINDSAY COMPANY
Balance Sheet—December 31, 1959
Assets

Cash..		$ 9,568.00
Inventory................................	$14,002.00	
Less purchase discounts....................	983.00	13,019.00
Building...................................	$10,000.00	
Less reserve for depreciation...............	2,500.00	7,500.00
Land...		1,500.00
Accounts receivable........................	$10,000.00	
Less reserve for bad debts..................	450.00	9,550.00
Unexpired insurance...............		50.00
		$41,187.00

Equities

Current liabilities:		
Accounts payable.........................	$ 4,565.00	
Mortgage payable, due January 1, 1962......	7,000.00	
Interest expense..........................	420.00	
Salaries and wages payable................	550.00	
Income taxes............................	1,600.00	$14,165.00
Net worth:		
Capital stock............................	$20,000.00	
Earned surplus...........................	7,022.00	27,022.00
		$41,187.00

LINDSAY COMPANY
Profit and Loss—December 31, 1959

Sales.....................................	$55,000.00	
Less sales discounts........................	900.00	$54,100.00

Cost of goods sold:			
Inventory, December 31, 1958...	$12,445.00		
Purchases....................	39,465.00		
Total......................	$51,910.00		
Inventory, December 31, 1959...	14,002.00	37,908.00	
General expenses:			
Salesmen's salaries.............	$ 4,500.00		
Office salaries.................	1,750.00		
Store supplies expense.........	1,250.00		
Office expense.................	1,580.00		
Depreciation expense—Building..	500.00		
Insurance expense.............	150.00		
Accrued interest..............	35.00		
Estimated income taxes payable.	1,600.00		
Miscellaneous selling expenses...	560.00	11,825.00	49,733.00
			$ 4,367.00

LINDSAY COMPANY
Statement of Earned Surplus—December 31, 1959

Balance, December 31, 1958............................	$5,555.00
Net income—Per profit and loss statement.................	3,467.00
Total..	$9,022.00
Deduct dividends.....................................	2,000.00
Earned surplus, December 31, 1959.....................	$7,022.00

Problem B 8-5. A. B. Carr Company completed its first month of business on January 31, 1958. The data below show the dollar total of the debits and the dollar total of the credits in each account as of January 31, 1958. Analyze the data and prepare journal entries showing the transactions and adjustments that occurred during January. For purposes of this exercise, you may omit dates from the journal entries.

A. B. CARR COMPANY
Account Data
January 31, 1958

Cash..	8,500.00	3,220.00
Accounts receivable..........................	6,000.00	3,000.00
Allowance for doubtful accounts...............		50.00
Inventory, January 1, 1958....................	4,500.00	
Unexpired insurance..........................	120.00	10.00
Land..	1,200.00	
Building.....................................	7,200.00	
Accumulated depreciation—Building............		40.00
Accounts payable.............................	2,040.00	5,100.00
Accrued interest payable......................		35.00
Mortgage payable, due 1/1/68.................		8,400.00
Capital stock (Issued in part for inventory)......		10,000.00
Sales.......................................		6,000.00
Purchases...................................	5,100.00	
Purchase discounts...........................		40.00
Salaries and wages...........................	1,100.00	
Bad debts expense............................	50.00	
Insurance expense............................	10.00	
Depreciation expense—Building................	40.00	
Interest expense.............................	35.00	
	35,895.00	35,895.00

ASSIGNMENT MATERIAL FOR CHAPTER 9
Questions

1. What is the maturity of a note dated December 31, 1958, due

    (a) four months after date?

    (b) 90 days after date?

2. Describe the accounting procedure to be followed when a renewal note is received.

3. We purchased goods from State Supply Company and issued a note therefor; the bookkeeper recorded the transaction as follows:

```
Purchases.........................................  410.00
    Notes payable...............................           410.00
```

State how you think the transaction should have been recorded, and give your reason.

4. Describe the accounting procedure to be followed in the event we dishonor our note payable.

5. Answer the following questions regarding the Loss from Discounting Notes Receivable account:

    (a) Under what circumstances will the account be debited?

    (b) Under what circumstances will the account be credited?

    (c) Where is the account shown in the financial statements?

6. What is a "protest" fee? Who must bear the cost of this fee?

7. What is the purpose of the Notes Receivable Discounted account?

8. What transactions are recorded in the following accounts? How should the facts shown by these accounts appear in the balance sheet?

Notes Receivable

19—				19—			
July	1	A. Smith	1,230 00	Aug.	12	A. Clark	300 00
	9	J. Brown	750 00		21	J. Brown	750 00
	28	A. Clark	300 00				
Aug.	4	J. P. Austin	100 00				

Notes Receivable Discounted

19—				19—			
Aug.	21	J. Brown	750 00	Aug.	12	J. Brown	750 00
					14	J. P. Austin	100 00

9. Describe the circumstances that would justify the following entry:

```
Notes receivable discounted..............................  xxx
    Notes receivable.....................................        xxx
```

10. Give the sequence of entries on the books of the seller and the purchaser when the terms of sale require the purchaser to accept a time draft for the amount of the invoice.

11. Compute the proceeds of the following $6,000 notes:

Date of Note	Time of Note	Rate of Interest	Date Discounted	Rate of Discount Charged by Bank
(a) May 9, 1958	60 days		May 15	6%
(b) June 19, 1958	60 days	5%	June 25	6%
(c) July 9, 1958	2 months		July 16	6%
(d) Aug. 29, 1958	2 months	4%	Sept. 4	6%

Problems—Group A

Problem A 9-1. Journalize the following transactions of B. & L. Company in the order in which they are presented. In all interest computations, use 360 days as a year. B. & L. Company closes its books annually on December 31.

(1a)   July   1—Borrowed $3,000 from Johnson and Company on a 30-day, non-interest-bearing note.

(1b)   July   31—Paid the above note.

(2a)   July   5—Borrowed $3,000 from K. L. Moore on a 30-day, 6% note.

(2b)   Aug.   4—Paid the above note.

(3a)   July   8—Borrowed $3,000 from City Bank by giving it our 30-day, non-interest-bearing note. The bank discounted the note at 6%.

(3b)   Aug.   7—Paid the above note.

(4a)   July   11—Loaned $2,000 to Bill Williams on a 60-day, 6% note.

(4b)   Sept.   9—Williams paid his note today.

(5a)   July   13—Loaned $2,000 to Henry Smith on a 60-day, non-interest-bearing note.

(5b)   Sept.   11—Smith paid his note today.

(6a)   July   15—Loaned A. B. Cole $2,000 on a 60-day note. We deducted discount at 6%.

(6b)   Sept.   13—Cole paid his note due today.

(7a)   July   17—Sold merchandise to E. F. George on account, $1,200.

(7b)   July   19—George gave us a 30-day, 6% note for the amount of the sale to him on July 17.

(7c)   Aug.   18—George paid his note due today.

(8a)   July   18—Purchased merchandise on account from Cronkhite & Sons, Inc., $1,500.

(8b)   July   18—Gave Cronkhite & Sons, Inc., a 60-day, 6% note for the amount of today's purchase.

(8c)   Sept.   16—Paid the above note.

(9a)   July   21—Received a 30-day, non-interest-bearing note for $600 from Henry Ward to apply on account.

(9b)   Aug.   20—Ward dishonored the note due today.

(10a)   Sept.   10—Received a 30-day, 6% note for $400 to apply on the account of B. B. Blue.

(10b)   Oct.   10—Blue dishonored the note due today.

(11a)   Jan.   3—Gave Danner's Company a 30-day, non-interest-bearing note for $800 to apply on account.

(11b)   Feb.   2—Dishonored the note due today to Danner's Company.

(12a)   Mar.   8—Gave Keller & Sons a 30-day, 6% note for $700 to apply on account.

(12b)   Apr.   7—Dishonored the note due today to Keller & Sons.

(13a)   May   10—Received a 30-day, non-interest-bearing note for $1,700 from Joe Blow to apply on account.

(13b) June   9—Received a 30-day, non-interest-bearing note from Joe Blow in renewal of the note due today.

(14a) June 18—Gave Jim Bertram a 30-day, non-interest-bearing note for $2,500 to apply on account.

(14b) July 18—Gave Bertram a 30-day, non-interest-bearing note in renewal of the note due him today.

(15a) Aug. 10—Received a 30-day, 5% note for $720 from Harvey Greenfield to apply on account.

(15b) Sept. 9—Greenfield dishonored his note due today.

(16a) Oct.   8—Gave M. E. Norberg a 30-day, 4% note for $600 to apply on account.

(16b) Nov.   7—Dishonored the Norberg note due today.

(17a) Dec. 21—Received a 45-day, 5% note for $1,600 from Blaine Larsen to apply on account.

(17b) Feb.   4—Collected the interest on the Larsen note, collected $400 on the principal of the note, and received a 45-day, 5% note for the balance.

(18a) Feb.   6—Gave a 20-day, 4% note for $720 to Norm Crandell to apply on account.

(18b) Feb. 26—Paid the interest on the Crandell note and $220 of the principal, and gave him a new 20-day, 4% note for the balance.

(19a) July   5—Purchased $1,800 worth of merchandise from Aris Company; terms, acceptance due 30 days after sight. The merchandise was received, and the draft was accepted.

(19b) Aug.   4—Dishonored the draft due today.

(19c) Aug.   8—Gave a 4%, 30-day note dated August 4 to cover the dishonored acceptance.

(19d) Sept. 3—Paid the note to Aris Company.

(20a) July 10—Sold merchandise to A. J. Burns in the amount of $400; terms, 10-day sight draft.

(20b) July 12—Received accepted draft from A. J. Burns, dated July 11.

(20c) July 21—Received $400 from A. J. Burns.

Problem A 9-2. The L. M. North Company closes its books annually as of December 31. Make journal entries to record the following transactions, and make supplementary entries in note registers.

1959
Jan. 5—Sold merchandise in the amount of $3,000 to Henry Johns on account.

     6—Purchased $1,600 worth of merchandise from Elco Company; terms, acceptance due 30 days after sight. The merchandise was received and the draft was accepted.

     8—Discounted our $6,000, 60-day note payable at Local Bank. Discount rate, 6%.

    15—Received from Henry Johns $1,200 cash and a 45-day, 5% note for the remainder of his account opened January 5.

    20—Sold merchandise to A. B. Cooke in the amount of $2,400; terms, 10-day sight draft.

    22—Received the draft accepted by A. B. Cooke on January 21.

    23—Sold merchandise in the amount of $1,800 to D. E. Fedder; terms, 30-day, 4% note.

    24—Received the $1,800 note from D. E. Fedder dated January 23.

    31—A. B. Cooke dishonored his acceptance.

Feb. 2—Received a 30-day, 3% note, dated January 31, for $2,400 from A. B. Cooke to cover the dishonored acceptance.

Feb. 5—Gave Elco Company a 30-day, 6% note to cover the 30-day acceptance due today.

    14—Received payment from Henry Johns for interest to date and principal on his note issued January 15.

    16—We drew an $800, 30-day sight draft on O. B. Dodge and mailed it today. Dodge's account is past due.

    22—D. E. Fedder paid his 30-day note in full today.

    23—Received $800 from O. B. Dodge.

    25—Our bank notified us that it held a $500, 20-day sight draft drawn on us by Smith Company, with bill of lading attached. We accepted the draft and received the bill of lading from the bank. We presented the bill of lading to the railroad and received the merchandise.

Problem A 9-3. Journalize the January, 1959 transactions, make adjusting entries, and post to ledger accounts, using the information given. The company closes its books monthly.

ACME LOAN COMPANY
After-Closing Trial Balance
December 31, 1958

Cash...................................	25,585.67	
Notes receivable.........................	100,800.00	
Notes receivable discounted.................		24,000.00
Accrued interest receivable..................	214.33	
Prepaid rent (6 months)....................	480.00	
Office equipment (10-year life)...............	2,400.00	
Accumulated depreciation—Office equipment...		720.00
Accounts payable.........................		1,748.00
Capital stock.............................		100,000.00
Retained earnings........................		3,012.00
	129,480.00	129,480.00

Details of certain accounts show the following as of December 31, 1958:

Notes receivable:

G. I. Hoad, 30-day, 6% note dated December 16, 1958.............	$ 18,000.00
J. K. Loey, 60-day, 5% note dated November 26, 1958............	24,000.00
M. N. Ovid, 45-day, 4% note dated November 21, 1958..........	30,000.00
P. Q. Rogers, 50-day, 5% note dated December 22, 1958..........	28,800.00
	$100,800.00

Notes receivable discounted:

J. K. Loey, at the bank......................................	$ 24,000.00

Accrued interest receivable:

On Hoad note..	$ 45.00
On Ovid note..	133.33
On Rogers note..	36.00
	$ 214.33

Transactions for the month of January, 1959, were:

Jan. 1—Received a 40-day, 6% note from D. E. Fade, for which we gave him $1,000 cash.

    5—Ovid paid his note plus interest today.

    6—Loaned $23,040 to A. B. Chase in exchange for a 40-day, 5% note.

    9—Loaned D. E. Fade $10,000; terms, 20-day, 6% note.

    11—Gave A. J. Fox $21,600 for his 60-day, 5% note.

Jan. 15—G. I. Hoad was unable to pay his note due today. To meet this obligation, he offered to transfer to the company a note receivable he was holding, and the accrued interest thereon, plus $3,687.40 in cash. The note was a 60-day, 6% note for $14,400 signed by B. J. Williams and dated January 5, 1959. The company accepted the offer and the transaction was completed.

16—Discounted our $24,000, 60-day note at the bank. Discount rate, 5%.

16—Loaned $15,600 to K. B. North on his 45-day, 6% note.

18—Purchased office supplies on account from Acres Supply Co., $45. The company expects to use these supplies before the end of the month.

20—Paid $1,250 on accounts payable.

25—Loey dishonored his note due today, and we paid the bank. We collected $14,200 from Loey on his note.

26—Received from Loey a 30-day, 6% note, dated January 25, for $10,000 in renewal of the balance of his note due yesterday.

28—Paid January salaries, $340.

29—D. E. Fade dishonored his note due today.

Problem A 9-4. The balance sheet of A. J. Reynolds Company as of December 31, 1958, follows:

A. J. REYNOLDS COMPANY
Balance Sheet
December 31, 1958
Assets

Cash..	$ 1,650.00
Accounts receivable................................	3,950.00
Inventory...	9,480.00
	$15,080.00

Liabilities and Stockholders' Equity

Liabilities:		
Accounts payable........................	$ 2,500.00	
Notes payable...........................	2,000.00	
Accrued interest payable..................	12.00	$ 4,512.00
Stockholders' equity:		
Capital stock...........................	$10,000.00	
Retained earnings.......................	568.00	10,568.00
		$15,080.00

Other data:

(1) The note payable was a 60-day, 6%, $2,000 note issued November 25, 1958, to Able Loan Company.

(2) On January 10, 1959, merchandise amounting to $2,400 was sold to Tom Lovejoy; terms, a 30-day, 6% note for $900 and the balance in cash.

(3) A. J. Reynolds Company paid its note and interest to Able Loan Company when it became due.

(4) The Lovejoy note was discounted at City Bank, January 25. Discount rate, 7%.

(5) Additional merchandise costing $1,800 was purchased from Regional Supply Co. on February 6, on account.

(6) A 30-day, 5% note for $1,200 and $600 cash were given on February 8 to cover the account owed to Regional Supply Co.

(7) Tom Lovejoy dishonored his note of January 10. City Bank collected the $900 note and interest from A. J. Reynolds Company on the due date.

(8) On February 15, A. J. Reynolds Company received a 40-day, 5% note for $720 from D. L. Knapp on his account, which was overdue.

(9) A. J. Reynolds Company discounted the Knapp note at City Bank, February 25. Discount rate, 6%.

(10) Other transactions for January and February summarized as of February 28 were:

Sales on account	$4,500
Cash sales	1,100
Salaries and wages paid	1,500
Purchases on account	4,500
Rent expense paid	200
Collections of accounts receivable	4,700
Payments on accounts payable	4,300

(11) Inventory, February 28, was $9,880.

Required:

(a) Journal entries for transaction data.
(b) Adjusting and closing entries as of February 28, 1959.
(c) Balance sheet as of February 28, 1959.

Problems—Group B

Problem B 9-1. Prepare journal entries, including adjustments at the close of each company's fiscal year, (a) for Black Company, and (b) for White Company according to the transaction data given.

1958
Dec. 6—Black Company sold merchandise to White Company in the amount of $540. White Company gave Black Company a 60-day, 4% note.
  11—White Company sold merchandise to Black Company for $3,960. The terms of sale were bill of lading attached to 10-day sight draft. The goods were shipped today.
  13—Black Company received the merchandise and the draft; accepted and returned the draft to White Company.
  15—White Company received the accepted draft.
  23—Black Company dishonored the acceptance and wrote White Company that it would be willing to cover the dishonored acceptance with a 30-day, 5% note.
  24—White Company received the Black Company letter and telephoned Black Company that the terms offered were satisfactory.
  26—Black Company mailed the 30-day, 5% note, dated December 23, for $3,960.
  28—White Company received the above note.
  31—Black Company completed its fiscal year today.
1959
Jan. 22—Black Company mailed a check covering both interest and principal to White Company today.
  23—The check from Black Company was received today by White Company.
  31—White Company ended its fiscal year today.

Feb. 4—White Company mailed a check covering the note of December 6, 1958.
6—Black Company received the check, dated February 4, from White Company.

Problem B 9-2. Journalize the following transactions on the books of Jackson Co. and Jacob Co.

May 14—Jackson Co. sold merchandise to Jacob Co. for $1,800, and received a 30-day, non-interest-bearing note from Jacob Co. for the selling price.
20—Jackson Co. discounted the note at a bank that charged discount at 6%.
June 13—Jacob Co. paid the note at the bank. Jackson Co. was informed of this.

Problem B 9-3. Certain accounts from Hailwood Company's ledger appear below. State the transactions for the three-month period beginning October 1, 1959, and compute the interest accrual as of December 31, 1959. The accounts receivable on December 31 show no amounts resulting from notes dishonored.

Notes Receivable

1959					1959					
Oct.	1	Jones	30-day	a	5,000 00	Oct.	31	Jones	a	5,000 00
	15	Black	40-day, 5%	b	7,200 00	Nov.	24	Black	b	7,200 00
Nov.	10	George	30-day, 6%	c	6,000 00		30	George	c	6,000 00
	24	Black	30-day, 6%	b	7,240 00	Dec.	24	Black	b	7,240 00
	26	Brown	60-day, 4%	d	1,440 00					
Dec.	11	Cornell	50-day, 5%	e	3,600 00					

Notes Receivable Discounted

1959					1959				
Nov.	24	Black	b	7,200 00	Oct.	25	Black	b	7,200 00
	30	George	c	6,000 00	Nov.	25	George	c	6,000 00
					Dec.	31	Cornell	e	3,600 00

Problem B 9-4. Make journal entries to record the following transactions on the books of Rogers, Inc., and Smith Co.

July 16—Rogers, Inc., sold merchandise to Smith Co., $2,160, and received a 60-day, 5% note for the purchase price.
26—Taylor Corp. sold merchandise to Rogers, Inc., for $6,000, and received (1) the Smith Co. note, which was accepted on a discounted basis, at a discount rate of 6%; and (2) a 30-day, 6% note for $3,000; and (3) cash for the balance.
Aug. 25—Rogers, Inc., paid the $3,000 note, plus interest.
Sept. 14—Smith Co. dishonored its note and Taylor Corp. collected it from Rogers, Inc. Rogers, Inc., collected $1,100 from Smith Co.

Problem B 9-5. The details of certain ledger accounts of Stanfield Corporation as of December 31, 1958, are given below.

Accounts receivable:
O. K. Baker.. $ 600.00
D. G. Cooke..   760.00
S. K. Drown..   1,020.00
Total.. $ 2,380.00

Notes receivable:

M. B. Fisher, 30-day, 5% note due 1/6/59.............	$ 1,440.00
B. N. Gang, 45-day, 6% note due 1/15/59.............	2,400.00
K. L. Hiss, 60-day, 6% note due 1/24/59.............	1,800.00
B. M. Idleman, 45-day, 6% note due 2/4/59...........	900.00
Total.......................................	$ 6,540.00

Notes receivable discounted:

B. N. Gang.......................................	$ 2,400.00
Accrued interest receivable............................	$ 17.10

Accounts payable:

Able Supply Co.....................................	$ 2,500.00
Best Buy Corporation...............................	3,636.00
Cooke Sales, Inc...................................	5,400.00
Total.......................................	$11,536.00

Notes payable:

City Bank, 60-day, 5% note due 1/20/59.............	$ 5,400.00
Office Wholesalers, Inc., 50-day, 4% note due 2/4/59.....	7,200.00
Total.......................................	$12,600.00
Accrued interest payable............................	$ 42.00

Transactions for January, 1959:

Jan. 2—Sold merchandise to R. B. Ring, $1,000; terms, 10-day sight draft.

4—Received the draft accepted by R. B. Ring on January 3.

6—M. B. Fisher sent us a 40-day, 6% note to cover his previous note and interest, which were due today.

9—Purchased merchandise from O. N. Sloan on account, $4,880.

11—S. K. Drown paid $300 on his account and gave us a 30-day, 5% note for the balance.

13—R. B. Ring dishonored his acceptance.

15—B. N. Gang dishonored his note, and we paid the amount owing as endorser. We recovered $1,418 cash from Gang, and he said that he would be willing to give us a 30-day, 6% note for the balance.

17—Received a 60-day, 4% note, dated January 13, from R. B. Ring to cover his dishonored acceptance.

19—Sold merchandise to F. I. Brown, $1,100, on account.

20—Dishonored the note due today to City Bank.

21—Received a 30-day, 6% note, dated January 15, from B. N. Gang to cover the balance of the dishonored note.

24—K. L. Hiss paid his note due today.

25—Sold merchandise worth $2,400 to A. C. Dickery for which we received a 60-day, 6% note.

31—Discounted the Dickery note at the bank; rate, 7%.

31—Paid City Bank note and interest which were due January 20, but which we dishonored at that time, plus interest on the principal for the additional days.

Required:

(a) Journal entries for January, 1959, including adjusting entries for accrued interest.

(b) Post applicable amounts to the ledger accounts mentioned on the following page.

Account Number		Account Number	
1	Accounts receivable	6	Notes payable
2	Notes receivable	7	Accrued interest payable
3	Notes receivable discounted	8	Interest earned
4	Accrued interest receivable	9	Interest expense
5	Accounts payable		

Problem B 9-6. Jennings Company had the following transactions involving notes. Prepare journal entries, including year-end adjustments, and a partial balance sheet as of December 31, 1958, showing notes receivable, accrued interest receivable, notes payable, and accrued interest payable.

1958

Oct. 10—Received a 40-day, 4% note for $4,500 from T. F. Sands on account.

15—Discounted our $5,000, 60-day note payable at the bank. Discount rate, 6%.

30—Transferred the Sands note of October 10 to A. B. Cole to apply on account. Discount rate, 5%.

Nov. 6—D. Bloan sent us, to apply on account, a 30-day, non-interest-bearing note, signed by T. Elliot, dated October 27, for $5,400. The note was taken at discounted value; rate, 6%.

16—Sold merchandise to B. Johnson for $900; terms, 50-day, 5% note. The merchandise was delivered and the note was received today.

19—T. F. Sands dishonored his note and we made payment to A. B. Cole, including a protest fee of $4.

21—Received a 60-day, 6% note dated today from T. F. Sands to cover the previously dishonored note, interest, and protest fee.

26—T. Elliot dishonored his 30-day note due today. D. Bloan covered the note by giving us a 45-day, 5% note for $5,400.

Dec. 1—Purchased merchandise, $6,000, from Acme Supply Co. for which we gave a 40-day, 4% note.

6—Received from E. J. Bertram $1,000 cash and a 30-day, 6% note for $2,000 for merchandise sold to him today.

14—Paid our 60-day note of October 15 which was due today.

16—Bill Sherman sent $5,000 cash and a 30-day, 6% note for $6,000, signed by John Boyles, dated December 1, to apply on account. The note was taken at face value plus accrued interest.

31—Boyles dishonored the note and we collected it from the endorser, Bill Sherman.

ASSIGNMENT MATERIAL FOR CHAPTER 10

Questions

1. Why is a check mark used in place of an account number to designate that a posting has been made to a subsidiary ledger?

2. What is the procedure for proving subsidiary ledgers?

3. Give two reasons why controlling accounts are maintained.

4. If controlling accounts are kept, why is it desirable to have special columns for them in the books of original entry?

5. When special books of original entry are used, what entries are made in the general journal?

6. Assume that a cash disbursements book contains a special Accounts Payable controlling account column; state the procedure for making postings from it.

7. If the journal is not provided with special controlling account columns for Accounts Payable, and you debit *ABC* Company, a creditor, for a note given to apply on our account, how should the debit entry be posted?

8. Under what circumstances would you suggest having a Notes Receivable debit column in the cash disbursements book?

9. Is it correct to describe a cash receipts book as a journal consisting of five money columns?

10. Which closing entries are journalized in the special journals?

Problems—Group A

Problem A 10-1. During the latter part of 1957, Goodhart Corporation was organized for the purpose of wholesaling electrical supplies. Operations began early in 1958, the first month's transactions appearing below. The corporation maintains subsidiary ledgers for accounts receivable and accounts payable. The books will be closed quarterly.

Journalize the data in a 10-column journal, post to ledger accounts as provided, and prepare a trial balance and schedules of subsidiary ledgers.

1958
Jan. 2—Capital stock issued for cash, $7,500.
Purchased goods from Acme Supply Company on account, $2,000. Terms, n/30.
3—Sold goods to Thomas Kellert on account, $427. Invoice No. 100; terms, n/30.
4—Paid four months' rent at $125 per month.
Cash sales, $39.
7—Sold goods to John Stanton on credit, $750. Invoice No. 101; terms, 2/15; n/30.
8—John Stanton returned goods worth $140.
Received merchandise ordered from Acme Supply Company, $1,635. Invoice was dated January 3; terms, n/30.
Paid for rental of delivery truck, $8.
Sold goods to Thomas Kellert, $933. Invoice No. 102; terms, n/30.

Jan. 10—Bought a job lot of goods from Retail Supply Corporation on account, $1,570. Terms, 5/10; n/30.

11—Paid Acme Supply Company for bill of January 2.

Purchased goods for cash, $550.

Shipped damaged goods back to Retail Supply Corporation, for which that company has agreed to send a credit memorandum for $430.

Sales salaries paid, $440. (Ignore withholding and payroll taxes.)

13—John Stanton settled his account of January 7.

Sold goods to Martin Fulton on account, $550. Invoice No. 103; terms, 5/10; n/30.

Thomas Kellert paid half the amount he owed as of this day.

15—Drivers' salaries paid, $275. (Ignore withholding and payroll taxes.)

16—Paid for rental of delivery truck, $22.

17—Sold goods to Thomas Kellert, $400. Invoice No. 104; terms, n/30.

18—Paid Retail Supply Corporation the balance of their account.

19—Paid cash for a delivery truck, $2,750.

21—Sold goods to Martin Fulton on account, $400. Invoice No. 105; terms, 5/10; n/30.

23—Received a shipment from Superior Trading Corp. Invoice was dated January 20. Amount, $1,900; terms, 2/10; n/30.

24—Martin Fulton paid for his purchase of the 21st.

25—Superior Trading Corp. account was paid in full.

Returned to Superior Trading Corp. goods which were found to be unsatisfactory after paying the bill. Credit of $500 was agreed upon.

27—Martin Fulton paid for his purchase of the 13th.

30—Sales salaries to date paid in cash, $360. (Ignore withholding and payroll taxes.)

31—Borrowed money from the bank on a 30-day note for $2,000; the discount rate was 6%.

Problem A 10-2. The trial balance of The Kane Corporation as of June 30, 1957, is given below. All postings have been completed for June. You are also given the totals and details for July from the various books used by the company.

Post the items into the given accounts, using correct references. Prepare a trial balance and schedules of accounts receivable and accounts payable as of July 31, 1957.

THE KANE CORPORATION
Trial Balance
June 30, 1957

Cash	46,240.00	
Temporary investments	17,000.00	
Accounts receivable	4,955.00	
Notes receivable	7,000.00	
Inventory	12,262.00	
Equipment	35,800.00	
Accumulated depreciation—Equipment		929.00
Accounts payable		3,650.00
Notes payable		5,000.00
Capital stock		50,000.00
Retained earnings		2,912.00
Dividends	550.00	
Sales		124,000.00
Sales returns	3,540.00	
Sales discounts	1,877.00	

Purchases...................................	62,450.00	
Purchase returns............................		8,720.00
Purchase discounts.........................		593.00
Rent......................................	975.00	
Salaries...................................	2,450.00	
Interest expense............................	783.00	
Interest earned............................		78.00
	195,882.00	195,882.00

The accounts receivable balances consist of:

Paul Henry.........................	1,612.00
M. P. Lawson.....................	3,343.00
Total..........................	4,955.00

There is only one account payable:

Peerless Supply Company...........	3,650.00

Data for July

Sales Book (Page 11):

Column total...............................		$ 8,399.00

Details:

July	5	C. W. Tanberg...............	$ 1,540.00
	11	M. P. Lawson................	2,162.00
	17	T. F. Millman................	750.00
	22	M. P. Lawson................	2,000.00
	26	T. F. Millman................	155.00
	30	Paul Henry..................	1,792.00

Purchases Book (Page 7):

Column total.....................................		$36,556.00

Details:

July	2	Kileel Wholesale Corp.........	$ 8,943.00
	12	Atlas Trading Corporation.....	15,176.00
	15	Kileel Wholesale Corp.........	5,922.00
	22	Peerless Supply Company.....	6,515.00

General Journal (Page 7) (6-column type):

Column totals:

Accounts Receivable................Debit...........	$	—
Accounts Payable..................Debit...........		10,945.00
Sundry...........................Debit...........		6,593.00
Sundry...........................Credit...........		13,445.00
Accounts Payable..................Credit...........		—
Accounts Receivable................Credit...... ...		4,093.00

Details:

Accounts Payable debits:

July	8	Peerless Supply Company....	$3,650.00
	18	Atlas Trading Corporation....	7,295.00

Sundry debits:

July	5	Notes receivable.............	$3,343.00
	25	Notes receivable.............	750.00
	27	Equipment..................	2,500.00

Sundry credits:

July	8	Notes payable...............	$3,650.00
	18	Purchase returns.............	7,295.00
	27	Notes payable...............	2,500.00

Accounts Receivable credits:

July	5	M. P. Lawson...............	$3,343.00
	25	T. F. Millman...............	750.00

Cash Receipts Book (Page 7):
Column totals:

Cash... $13,434.80
Sales Discounts.................................. 106.20
Accounts Receivable............................. 6,152.00
Sales... 1,695.00
Sundry.. 5,694.00

Details:
Accounts Receivable:

July	2	Paul Henry.................	$1,612.00
	17	C. W. Tanberg..............	1,540.00
	27	M. P. Lawson...............	1,000.00
	29	M. P. Lawson...............	2,000.00

Sundry:

July	5	Notes receivable.............	$5,000.00
	10	Interest earned..............	75.00
	19	Investments (sold)..........	619.00

Cash Disbursements Book (Page 11):
Column totals:

Cash... $32,452.25
Purchase Discounts.............................. 398.75
Accounts Payable................................ 23,339.00
Purchases....................................... 662.00
Sundry.. 8,850.00

Details:
Accounts Payable:

July	14	Kileel Wholesale Corp........	$8,943.00
	20	Atlas Trading Corporation....	7,881.00
	25	Peerless Supply Company....	6,515.00

Sundry:

July	1	Rent......................	$ 250.00
	15	Investments (temporary).....	2,500.00
	27	Equipment..................	500.00
	30	Dividends..................	600.00
	30	Notes payable..............	5,000.00

Problem A 10-3.   Below is presented a series of transactions relating to the cash activities of Perfection Services Company.   In addition to its regular operations, the company owns an office building, space in which is rented to several individuals.

Enter the following transactions for the month of March, 1958, in cash receipts and disbursements books.   The company's cash receipts book has a special column for Rent Earned; the cash disbursements book has a special column for Truck Expense.   Rule and balance these books.

1958

March   1—Received $200 rent from L. Callahan for part of the month.

Sold a parcel of land costing $2,750 for $3,500.

3—J. Weber paid his account of $1,700, less 1% discount.

Truck expenses for the week, $72.

4—Paid Ball Sales, Inc., invoice for $700, less 2%.

5—Received payment on note receivable, $846 face value, plus interest of $26.95.

6—Cash received for services performed, $590.

7—Purchased supplies for cash, $22.   (Treat as an expense.)

8—R. Loring paid his rent, $162.

Paid amount due on a non-interest-bearing note, $2,000.

March 10—Paid account of White Distribution Co., $950 less 2%.
  12—Paid $15 for gas and oil for truck.
  15—L. Callahan paid remainder of monthly rental, $240.
     Salary liability recorded in February paid today, $162.
     Purchased goods for cash, $103.
     Paid withholding and F. I. C. A. tax liabilities, $63.60.
  18—Cash sales made today, $214.
  19—Received cash from L. Shill in settlement of $1,440 invoice. A
     discount of 1% is allowed.
  20—Equipment bought for cash, $374.50.
     B. Lenhart paid his rent today, $434.
  24—Truck expenses paid, $62.
  25—Received interest on investments, $47.
  26—Walker Corp. account payable paid today, $450 less 2%.
  27—Cash sales, $106.
  28—R. Goss paid rent of $131.
     Paid bill for truck repairs, $110.
  31—J. Weber paid his bill, $500 less 1%.
     Garage rent paid, $45.

Problem A 10-4.   Ronald Company was organized at the end of June, 1959, and was ready to commence operations July 1. During July the company used the following accounts.

Chart of Accounts

1 Cash	40 Sales
2 Temporary investments	41 Sales discounts
3 Accounts receivable	45 Purchases
(Controlling account)	46 Purchase discounts
4 Notes receivable	47 Transportation in
6 Prepaid interest expense	50 Salaries
7 Unexpired insurance	51 Payroll taxes
10 Land	52 Supplies expense
11 Buildings	53 Interest expense
15 Accounts payable	60 Gain on sale of investments
(Controlling account)	
16 Notes payable	
17 Accrued payroll	
18 Withholding and F. I. C. A.	
tax liabilities	
25 Mortgage payable	
30 Capital stock	

All transactions for July are presented below.

1959
July 1—Issued capital stock for cash, $40,000.
   2—Goods were purchased on account from Scio Corporation, $17,200. The
     invoice was dated June 28; terms, 5/10; n/30.
     Signed a $40,000 agreement for the purchase of land and buildings,
     paying $20,000 in cash and giving a mortgage for the balance. The
     land is estimated to have a value of $5,000.
   5—Sold goods to Carl Peterson on credit, $6,000. Invoice No. 1; terms,
     2/10; n/30.

July 5—Purchased securities as a short-term investment, $700 cash.
Supplies were bought for use in the store, $172 cash.
  7—Sold goods for cash, $1,745.
  8—Paid for the goods bought on the 2nd.
Carl Peterson paid his bill.
  9—Paid $550 for a three-year fire insurance policy.
Sold goods to Wilfred Littleton on account, $7,200. Invoice No. 2;
terms, 2/10; n/30.
 12—Paid freight charges on Scio Corporation purchase, $520.
Goods bought from Brownell Suppliers, Inc., on account. Invoice
amount, $14,522; terms, 3/10; n/30.
 13—Wilfred Littleton paid his account in full.
Sold goods to William Prowter on credit, $4,675. Invoice No. 3; terms,
2/10; n/30.
 14—Sold goods to Wilfred Littleton on account, $1,362. Invoice No. 4;
terms, 2/10; n/30.
 15—Payroll was computed and recorded as of today. Earnings were $350;
employee withholdings were $42. The company is not subject to
unemployment insurance taxes. The 2¼% F. I. C. A. payroll tax
is recorded at this time, $7.88.
 16—Paid the employees today.
 18—Sold goods to Peter Gibson on account, $5,540. Invoice No. 5; terms,
2/10; n/30.
Discounted note with the bank for $14,000 at 5% discount rate. The
note is due one year from date.
Cash purchase, $927.
 20—Bought and received goods from Ellsworth Company for $5,620.
Terms, 2/10; n/60.
 22—Sold goods to James Stevens on account, $1,128. Invoice No. 6; terms,
2/10; n/30.
 23—Peter Gibson made a partial payment of $980. Sales discounts are
granted by the company on partial payments within the discount
period.
 25—Received goods from Brownell Suppliers, Inc. The invoice was dated
July 23; terms, 3/10; n/30; amount, $4,352.
Received a 30-day note from William Prowter in settlement of his
account.
 26—Sold the securities purchased July 5 for $900.
 27—Paid Brownell Suppliers, Inc., half of their invoice of July 12.
 29—Bought securities for $1,700, cash.
Sold goods to Peter Gibson on account, $4,254. Invoice No. 7; terms,
2/10; n/30.
 31—Cash sales, $542.
Paid mortgage installment of $500, of which $114.45 was interest
expense.
Recorded and paid the semi-monthly payroll. Earnings were $400;
employee withholdings were $58. Record the 2¼% payroll tax
thereon.

Required:

(a) Record the July transactions in the following journals:
1. Journal—2-column.
2. Sales book—1-column.

3. Purchases book—1-column.
4. Cash receipts book—5-column, like the illustration on page 143.
5. Cash disbursements book—5-column, like the illustration on page 145.

(b) Indicate how postings would be made from the above journals by placing all needed posting references in the journals.

(c) Journalize the cash transactions a second time by using expanded cash journals having both debit and credit columns for sundry accounts. Insert posting references in these journals.

Problem A 10-5. Paramount Sales, Inc., is a small organization engaged in trading operations. The company also engages in some real estate speculation in land. Owing to its varied activities, the company decided to use a monthly accounting cycle in its bookkeeping. The books are closed and statements are prepared soon after the end of each month.

Below is the trial balance at the end of August, 1959, after all of the accounts have been closed for the month.

PARAMOUNT SALES, INC.
After-Closing Trial Balance
August 31, 1959

Cash	10,907.00	
Accounts receivable	1,212.00	
Allowance for doubtful accounts		812.00
Notes receivable	7,200.00	
Accrued interest receivable	142.00	
Prepaid interest expense	26.58	
Inventory	1,157.00	
Land (Investment)	50,000.00	
Equipment	16,428.00	
Accumulated depreciation—Equipment		1,948.00
Accounts payable		2,375.00
Notes payable		7,500.00
Accrued interest payable		13.14
Accrued payroll		490.29
Withholding and F. I. C. A. tax liabilities		156.43
Mortgage payable		10,000.00
Capital stock		45,000.00
Retained earnings		18,777.72
	87,072.58	87,072.58

Accounts receivable:

Milton Jones	972.00
Henry Druhan	240.00
Total	1,212.00

Accounts payable:

Mart Wholesaling Corp	2,375.00

Following is the information necessary for September entries:

1959
Sept. 1—Additional capital stock issued, $5,000 cash.
      2—Paid Mart Wholesaling Corp. $375 and gave a note payable for the balance.

Sept. 3—Received payment for a 60-day, 6%, $3,000 note receivable. (Interest had been accrued to August 31.)

4—Sold goods to Peter Swanson on account, $327.   Invoice No. 1017; terms, 3/10; n/30.

5—Shipment arrived from Mart Wholesaling Corp.   Invoice date, September 3; amount, $1,559; terms, 5/10; n/60.

6—The company was notified that Milton Jones's account was not fully collectible.   The trustee estimates that payment will be on the basis of 33⅓¢ on the dollar.

Purchased merchandise for cash, $378.

7—Bi-weekly payroll was made up, covering the period from August 24 to date.

Amount earned .(salesmen's salaries), $943; withholdings for income and F. I. C. A. taxes, $105.86.   The company was not subject to unemployment insurance taxes.

Record the $9.05 payroll tax expense on the portion of the payroll applicable to September.   The payroll tax applicable to the payroll accrual as of August 31 was recorded by an adjusting entry for $9.81 as of that date.

9—Peter Swanson remitted a check to settle his account.

Cash sales were made in the amount of $264.17.

10—Paid bi-weekly payroll.

Selling expenses paid in cash, $428.

Issued credit memo to Henry Druhan for goods returned, $42.11.

Paid withholding and F. I. C. A. tax liabilities, $271.34.

11—Sold merchandise to Peter Swanson on account, $960.   Invoice No. 1018; terms, 3/10; n/60.

12—Ralph Foster gave the company a deposit of $375 for services to be rendered during November and December.

13—Paid Mart Wholesaling Corp. invoice of the 5th.

15—Goods purchased from Bernard Supply Company received today. Invoice date, September 12; amount, $2,217; terms, n/60.

16—Sold parcel of land costing $6,250 for $7,500, cash.

17—Paid $2,000 note payable due today and interest at 5½% for 60 days.

19—Received payment from Peter Swanson in full.

20—Sold goods on account to Henry Druhan, $1,129.   Invoice No. 1019; terms, n/30.

Gave a non-interest-bearing note to Bernard Supply Company to settle account.

21—Purchased goods from Mart Wholesaling Corp., $3,500.   Terms, 2/10; n/30.

22—Paid city taxes for city's fiscal year commencing September 1, 1959, $282.

Bi-weekly payroll was prepared.   Sales salaries earned, $1,015; withholdings for income and F. I. C. A. taxes, $119.12.   Record the $20.30 payroll tax expense.

23—Received payment from Henry Druhan, $240.

24—Received credit memo from Mart Wholesaling Corp. accepting our claim for damaged goods, $472.

Paid Mart Wholesaling Corp. the balance of the account.

25—Paid bi-weekly payroll.

26—Cash sales, $929.35.

Purchased inventory of bankrupt store for cash, $142.11.

Sept. 29—Paid selling expenses amounting to $43.60.

Paid $5,500 non-interest-bearing note payable discounted at bank on August 31, 1959. (Proceeds, $5,473.42.)

Made cash purchases of $74.92.

Sale of merchandise to Samuel Dodge, $626. Invoice No. 1020; terms, 2/10; n/60.

30—Discounted one-year note at bank at 6%, $3,500 face.

Received cash from Peter Swanson for half of the purchase of September 11. His bookkeeper was in error, as this amount had already been paid. However, the check was deposited before the error was discovered.

Monthly mortgage payment made, $250. Interest expense included therein, $77.11.

Sold goods on account to Hyde and Smith, $1,524. Invoice No. 1021; terms, 2/10; n/30.

Bought a parcel of land as an investment. Price, $22,500. Terms, $15,000 in cash and a mortgage of $7,500.

Data for adjustments:

A provision for bad debts is to be made, computed at 2% of sales less returns and allowances and discounts.

Depreciation is to be computed on the equipment at the rate of 8% per annum.

Total accrued interest receivable on notes amounts to $134.50 as of September 30, 1959.

Accrued interest on notes payable amounts to $9.44.

Taxes paid this month are to be apportioned on a monthly basis.

Salaries accrued at month-end amount to $370. Payroll tax expense of $7.40 is to be recorded on this amount.

Review your work to determine whether an adjustment is required as a result of the payment of the note on September 29.

The inventory on September 30, 1959, amounts to $4,429.

Required:

Journal entries in the appropriate books for all transactions.

Journal entries for the adjustments as given above.

Ledger accounts posted through the adjusting entries.

An adjusted trial balance.

Closing entries. (Do not post the closing entries.)

Problems—Group B

Problem B 10-1. Portions of the general journal and cash receipts book of White Corporation are presented on the following pages. Set up the necessary ledgers and post for the month. No detailed postings have been made during the month.

(Page 9)

Journal

	DEBITS					CREDITS		
Accounts Receivable	Accounts Payable	Sundry	Date	L.F.		Sundry	Accounts Payable	Accounts Receivable
			1958 May 5		Sales returns and allowances			
		615 00			Robert Bower..........			615 00
					Goods returned May 3.			
	2,000 00		10		Atlas Trading Co.			
					Notes payable.........	2,000 00		
					60-day note to settle account.			
		6,800 00	14		Cash			
		800 00			Loss on sale of equipment			
					Equipment............	7,600 00		
					Sale of equipment for cash.			
		492 00	19		Allowance for doubtful accounts			
					Louis Mahon..........			492 00
					To write off bad account.			
	740 00		23		Richmond Distributors			
					Purchase returns and allowances......	740 00		
					Goods returned May 20.			
		3,880 00	27		Cash			
		120 00			Interest expense			
					Notes payable........	4,000 00		
					Discounted 6% note for 6 months.			
3,549 00	6,210 00	15,338 00				18,433 00	5,097 00	1,567 00

Cash Receipts Book

(Page 24)

Date	Account Credited	Explanation	Cash	Sales Discounts	Accounts Receivable		Sales	Sundry		
					✓	Amount		L.F.	Amount	
1958										
May 7	Interest earned.............	Investments	62 00						62 00	
13	Robert Bower..............	Invoice less 2%	1,215 20	24 80		1,240 00				
16	Note receivable...........	Collected note	5,025 00						5,000 00	
	Interest earned...........	Interest at 6% for 30 days							25 00	
29	Rent earned..............	Jones' May rent	450 00						450 00	
			32,732 58	465 90		5,946 00	757 33		26,495 15	

Problem B 10-2. The following information has been extracted from the records of Wood Company.

Credit given customers for goods returned................	$ 5,766.65
Adjusting entry to provide for doubtful accounts..........	3,487.50
Merchandise purchased on credit from suppliers..........	128,937.26
Notes received from customers to settle bills.............	40,350.00
Cash paid to suppliers..............................	35,291.17
Discounts allowed by suppliers for prompt payment.......	3,560.11
An account was determined to be bad and was written off..	219.36
The company permitted customers to take discounts......	3,619.11
Total sales of merchandise on credit....................	140,306.92
Accounts of suppliers settled by notes and drafts..........	62,440.00
Cash receipts from sales of goods on credit..............	72,594.11
Goods returned to suppliers as unsatisfactory............	17,415.29

Set up controlling accounts for accounts receivable and accounts payable and enter therein the relevant amounts selected from the above data.

Problem B 10-3. In the interest of brevity, only selected cash transactions for the year 1958 are presented below. Journalize the transactions, assuming (1) that the company, Charm Company, uses cash books in the form illustrated on pages 143 and 145, and (2) that the company uses expanded cash books in the form illustrated on pages 148 to 151.

1958

Feb. 15—Purchased for cash 200 shares of the common stock of Millroad Corporation for $10 per share as a short-term investment.

Mar. 29—Purchased merchandise for cash, $6,300.

May 30—Purchased office equipment for $10,000. Paid $1,000 in cash and gave a one-year, 6% note for the balance.

June 25—Discounted at City Bank a $20,000 one-year note at 6%.

Sept. 25—Sold 100 shares of Millroad stock for $12 per share, cash.

Oct. 9—Collected the Patrick Bell $1,000 note, plus interest of $15.

Dec. 7—Paid William Seely in full, less 1% discount, $297.

Dec. 10—Sold 100 shares of Millroad stock for $9 per share. Received half of the selling price in cash and half in notes due in 30 days without interest.

Problem B 10-4. Starting February 1, 1959, Tollard Corporation adopted a 10-column journal as its only book of original entry. Below are summarized the transactions from page one of this journal for the month of February, 1959.

Using three-column paper for subsidiary accounts, present all ledger accounts with proper posting references for the month. Take a trial balance and prove the subsidiary ledgers.

Debits:

Column totals:

Purchases..	$62,867.00
Accounts Receivable.	20,468.00
Accounts Payable................................	25,217.00
Cash..	23,366.00
Sundry...	6,419.00

Details:

Accounts Receivable:

Feb.	2	B. A. Jones...................	$ 1,675.00
	4	W. S. Roth..................	5,400.00
	12	L. S. Moon..................	7,243.00
	20	W. S. Roth..................	6,150.00

Accounts Payable:
Feb. 20 Somers Wholesale............. $ 5,000.00
     26 Arbor Suppliers.............. 19,265.00
     26 Freemont Wholesalers......... 952.00
Sundry:
Feb. 2 Rent........................ $ 250.00
      7 Office salaries..............   562.00
     15 Taxes expense...............   340.00
     26 Notes receivable.............   4,250.00
     28 Advertising.................   1,017.00

Credits:
Column totals:
Sundry.. $ 7,202.00
Cash.. 22,958.00
Accounts Receivable........................... 13,225.00
Accounts Payable.............................. 61,443.00
Sales... 33,509.00
Details:
Accounts Receivable:
Feb. 16 W. S. Roth.................. $ 5,400.00
     19 B. A. Jones.................   1,675.00
     25 W. S. Roth.................   1,900.00
     26 W. S. Roth.................   4,250.00
Accounts Payable:
Feb. 3 Arbor Suppliers............. $19,265.00
     13 Freemont Wholesalers........ 10,540.00
     17 Somers Wholesale............ 16,293.00
     20 Arbor Suppliers.............   3,500.00
     28 Arbor Suppliers............. 11,845.00
Sundry:
Feb. 20 Notes payable............... $ 5,000.00
     24 Notes receivable.............   1,250.00
     26 Purchase returns............   952.00

Problem B 10-5. Set up a complete set of books for Brewster Enterprises, Inc., using the following books of original entry:

Journal—2 columns
Sales book—1 column
Purchases book—1 column
Cash receipts book—6 columns (including 2 Sundry columns)
Cash disbursements book—6 columns (including 2 Sundry columns)

Journalize, post, take a trial balance, and prepare subsidiary account schedules for the month of October. Allow five lines per ledger account, using three-column paper for subsidiary ledgers. The company plans to close its books monthly.

1958
Oct. 1—Issued $5,000 worth of capital stock for cash.
      2—Purchased goods from Ross Brothers, $2,243. Invoice date, October 1; terms, 3/10; n/30.
      3—Paid three months' rent, $1,050.
         Sold merchandise to Samuel Jackson on account, $240. Invoice No. 1; terms, 2/10; n/30.
      4—Cash sales, $590.
      5—Borrowed cash from C. Gregory and gave a note for $1,030, due January 1, 1959, with interest at 4%.

Oct. 6—Paid $75 to a customer for damaged goods sold on October 4.

     7—Sold goods to Paul Trotter on account, $198. Invoice No. 2; terms, 2/10; n/30.

       Bought $4,000 of municipal bonds as a temporary investment.

     8—Paid freight bill on goods shipped, $55.

       Cash purchases, $162.

       Received shipment from Wayland, Incorporated. The invoice was dated today; amount, $1,763; terms, 2/10; n/45.

   10—Paul Trotter paid his account, taking a discount of $3.96.

       Purchased equipment for cash, $4,290.

   12—Samuel Jackson returned goods for credit, $100.

       Sold merchandise to Samuel Jackson on account, $562. Invoice No. 3; terms, 2/10; n/30.

   14—Received shipment from Arrow Corporation, $1,145. Invoice dated October 12; terms, 1/10; n/30.

       Gave Arrow Corporation a 60-day, non-interest-bearing note for the above purchase.

       Salaries were recorded; gross earnings, $550; withheld for income and F. I. C. A. taxes, $75. (The company is not subject to unemployment insurance taxes.)

       Recorded the employer's 2¼% F. I. C. A. payroll tax.

   15—Paid the salaries accrued on October 14.

       Paid the amount due Ross Brothers.

       A $10,000, 45-day note was discounted at the bank today; discount rate, 5%.

       Sold goods to Arthur Parker on account, $629. Invoice No. 4; terms, 2/10; n/30.

       Received cash for interest on investments, $5.

   16—Bought a delivery truck from Local Dealer Co. for $3,500. Paid one-half in cash and gave a 90-day, non-interest-bearing note for the balance.

   17—Cash purchases, $475.

   20—Samuel Jackson paid his invoice of October 3.

   24—Sold goods to John Fraser, on account, $544. Invoice No. 5; terms, 3/10; n/60.

   25—Received shipment from Wayland, Incorporated. The invoice was dated October 22; amount, $1,950; terms, 2/10; n/45.

   28—Sold merchandise to Paul Trotter for $215. Invoice No. 6; terms, 2/10; n/30.

       Arthur Parker settled his account with a 60-day, non-interest-bearing note.

   29—Paid Wayland, Incorporated, for the shipment received October 25.

       Cash sales, $492.

   31—A bill for office supplies for the month was paid, $162. There were no supplies on hand.

       John Fraser made a partial payment, leaving a balance of $244 in his account, to be paid November 10. Discount is allowed on partial payments.

ASSIGNMENT MATERIAL FOR CHAPTER 11

Questions

1. Describe the entries that may be found in the drawing account of an individual proprietorship.

2. State the differences in procedure of closing the books of an individual proprietorship, a partnership, and a corporation.

3. In what way or ways will the balance sheet of an individual proprietorship differ from a balance sheet of a corporation?

4. How may a Goodwill account arise on the books of a partnership?

5. If partners make an agreement regarding the division of income, without any mention of losses, how are losses divided?

6. How is the federal income tax treated in the financial statements of a partnership?

7. One of the partners, C. A. Thomas, takes merchandise from the store for his personal use. The merchandise cost the partnership $75 and was marked to sell for $100. What entry should be made?

8. Mention some of the things which should be given consideration in the determination of an equitable division of partnership earnings.

9. Is a salary allowance to a partner agreed upon by the partners an expense of the business?

10. If partners' salaries and interest on their capitals are agreed upon, must allowances therefor be made even though the operations of the business result in a loss? Devise an example to illustrate the procedure which conforms with your answer.

11. If a new partnership is being formed and some of the partners invest fixed assets, is it acceptable to record such assets on the partnership books at their cost (less depreciation) to the individual partners?

12. A partnership's books show the following liabilities and partners' capitals:

Accounts payable...............	$12,000.00
R. J. Oliver, loan................	5,000.00
F. R. Todd, capital..............	18,000.00
R. J. Oliver, capital.............	24,000.00
Total......................	$59,000.00

All the assets have been sold for $43,000, and this amount is on hand in cash. Losses on the disposal of the assets have not been charged to the partners. How should the cash be paid out?

Problems—Group A

Problem A 11-1. On the following page is the trial balance as of December 31, 1959, for John Dowd. The proprietor's capital account is also given. Assuming that all adjustments have been made and that the closing inventory is $17,316, prepare working papers, the balance sheet, the statement of proprietor's capital, and the closing entries.

JOHN DOWD
Trial Balance
December 31, 1959

Cash..	10,700	
Accounts receivable...............................	17,690	
Inventory, December 31, 1958......................	28,440	
Building...	50,000	
Accumulated depreciation—Building.................		1,360
Accounts payable..................................		5,124
Notes payable.....................................		3,000
John Dowd, capital................................		75,000
John Dowd, drawings..............................	9,400	
Sales..		162,000
Purchases...	118,635	
Purchase returns and allowances...................		7,559
Operating expenses................................	19,628	
Interest earned....................................		450
	254,493	254,493

John Dowd, Capital

1958		
Dec. 31	Balance..............	60,000
1959		
Mar. 10	Additional investment.	15,000

Problem A 11-2. Smart and Watson have been in partnership for several years and share net income in the ratio of 60 per cent and 40 per cent. The inventory on June 30, 1958, was $42,633. It is expected that Watson's loan will not be repaid next year.

Using the information supplied, prepare working papers for the year, a balance sheet and a statement of partners' capitals, and the closing journal entries.

SMART AND WATSON
Trial Balance
June 30, 1958

Cash..	25,781	
Accounts receivable...............................	34,000	
Inventory, June 30, 1957..........................	46,274	
Loans receivable—C. L. Watson....................	3,500	
Land..	15,000	
Accounts payable..................................		27,930
Loans payable—J. S. Smart.......................		10,000
J. S. Smart, capital...............................		35,000
C. L. Watson, capital.............................		54,400
J. S. Smart, drawings.............................	5,400	
C. L. Watson, drawings...........................	4,600	
Sales..		104,293
Purchases...	92,450	
Expenses..	4,618	
	231,623	231,623

J. S. Smart, Capital

1957		
June 30	Balance..............	30,000
Nov. 17	Additional investment.	5,000

C. L. Watson, Capital

1958		1957	
Apr. 10	600	June 30 Balance.............. 55,000	

Problem A 11-3. The December 31, 1957 adjusted trial balance of Wilson and Lang, a partnership, is presented below. Using the following data, prepare working papers and a statement of partners' capitals.

(a) Lang invested $3,000 on June 10, 1957.
(b) A salary of $2,000 is to be given Wilson for 1957.
(c) Interest is to be allowed the partners at the rate of 4%, computed on the beginning capitals.
(d) Earnings are to be divided as follows: Wilson, 70%; Lang, 30%.
(e) The end-of-year inventory was $42,565.

WILSON AND LANG
Trial Balance
December 31, 1957

Cash...	10,590	
Accounts receivable.............................	17,390	
Inventory, December 31, 1956....................	33,740	
Equipment......................................	119,000	
Accumulated depreciation—Equipment..............		65,400
Goodwill.......................................	30,000	
Accounts payable................................		60,450
Notes payable...................................		5,000
Loans payable—N. Lang..........................		27,000
R. Wilson, capital...............................		40,000
N. Lang, capital.................................		28,000
R. Wilson, drawings.............................	5,200	
N. Lang, drawings...............................	5,900	
Sales..		298,910
Sales returns and allowances......................	3,620	
Purchases......................................	278,340	
Selling expenses................................	17,150	
Office expenses.................................	3,280	
Insurance expense...............................	550	
	524,760	524,760

Problem A 11-4. Capital accounts for the partners A, B, and C are presented below. The accounts show the investments and drawings in excess of agreed amounts for the year 1959.

A, Capital

1959		1958	
Mar. 31	600	Dec. 31 Balance.............. 27,000	

B, Capital

1959		1958	
Aug. 31	250	Dec. 31 Balance.............. 40,000	
Sept. 30	150	1959	
		May 15 Additional investment.	5,000

C, Capital

	1958
	Dec. 31 Balance.............. 26,000
	1959
	Sept. 4 Additional investment. 3,000

The net income for the year was $13,700.

Submit journal entries to close the Revenue and Expense account under each of the conditions outlined below:

(1) The first $6,600 to be divided equally, the remainder 1:2:1.
(2) Each partner to be allowed a salary of $4,200, the remainder divided equally.
(3) The net income to be divided in the ratio of partners' capitals at year-end.
(4) Salaries to be allowed as follows: *A*, $5,000; *B*, $4,500; and *C*, $6,000; the remainder to be divided equally.
(5) Interest at 4% to be allowed on capitals at beginning of the year, salaries of $3,000 each to be paid, and the remainder divided 3:2:1.

Problem A 11-5. Jason and Radford decide to liquidate their partnership on August 15, 1959. On this day, Hamilton Corp. decides to take over certain assets of the business on the following basis:

Inventory...................... $28,000
Land.......................... 3,600
Accounts receivable............ 38,500

Jason and Radford are to keep the cash and pay all debts.

JASON AND RADFORD
After-Closing Trial Balance
August 15, 1959

Cash......................................	3,000	
Accounts receivable.......................	42,000	
Inventory.................................	20,000	
Land......................................	4,000	
Accounts payable..........................		7,000
Loans payable—M. Radford..................		10,000
H. Jason, capital.........................		35,000
M. Radford, capital.......................		17,000
	69,000	69,000

Submit the journal entries necessary to close the books of the partnership, assuming that cash is received from Hamilton Corp. and that all cash is finally distributed.

Problems—Group B

Problem B 11-1. Martin Desmond, an individual proprietor, keeps his ledger accounts in alphabetical order. On the following page are data from the trial balance on June 30, 1958, and Mr. Desmond's capital account.

Using the information given, and assuming an end-of-year inventory of $33,374, prepare financial statements for the year ended June 30, 1958, and entries to close the books on that date.

Accounts payable	$ 45,759
Accounts receivable	35,912
Accrued interest payable	792
Accumulated depreciation—Equipment	12,440
Allowance for doubtful accounts	1,763
Cash	16,888
Equipment	61,319
General expenses	7,932
Interest expense	1,395
Inventory	41,371
Martin Desmond, capital	80,000
Martin Desmond, drawings	10,400
Notes payable	25,000
Prepaid taxes	2,450
Purchases	155,427
Purchase discounts	3,420
Sales	221,670
Sales returns and allowances	21,510
Selling expenses	36,240

Martin Desmond, Capital

	1957		
	June 30	Balance	54,500
	1958		
	Mar. 17	Additional investment	10,000
	Apr. 10	Additional investment	15,500

Problem B 11-2.   Information from the trial balance of Rogers and Sloan as of May 31, 1959, is presented below:

Accounts payable	$25,450
Accumulated depreciation—Equipment	6,600
Cash	11,800
Equipment	27,000
General expenses	6,240
Inventory, May 31, 1958	13,410
Loan receivable—Harry Sloan	7,500
Notes receivable	15,500
Purchases	45,960
Rent earned	290
Leon Rogers, capital	28,500
Leon Rogers, drawings	6,200
Sales	67,990
Sales returns and allowances	2,200
Selling expenses	10,240
Harry Sloan, capital	24,800
Harry Sloan, drawings	5,800
Transportation in	1,780

The loan is to be repaid within the year.   The end-of-year inventory is $10,540. The partners' capital accounts appear as follows:

Leon Rogers, Capital

	1958		
	May 31	Balance	25,000
	1959		
	Feb. 4	Additional investment	3,500

Harry Sloan, Capital

1958			1958		
July 20		200	May 31	Balance..............	20,000
			1959		
			Mar. 9	Additional investment.	5,000

Required:

Income statement.
Statement of partners' capitals.
Balance sheet.
Closing entries.

Problem B 11-3. S. L. Rand had been in business for several years. The balances in his balance sheet accounts as of September 30, 1957, appear below:

Cash...	$ 5,000	
Accounts receivable...........................	14,000	
Inventory.....................................	35,000	
Patent..	7,000	
Accounts payable..............................		$29,000
Notes payable.................................		10,000
S. L. Rand, capital...........................		22,000

On September 30, 1957, G. Porter offered to join Rand in a partnership. Porter agreed to invest the following:

Goodwill..............	$ 7,000
Land.................	3,000
Building..............	25,000

Rand, in agreeing to the formation of the partnership, approved the assumption by the partnership of Porter's current liabilities, $3,000. Thus, Porter's opening capital was $32,000. The building had an estimated use-life of 50 years, as of September 30, 1957.

During the first year of operations, Rand and Porter made a net income of $39,000, which was divided equally; they each withdrew $7,500 in cash, which left a cash balance of $12,500 in the partnership bank account as of September 30, 1958. Changes other than in cash were as follows:

$ 4,000 increase in inventory
19,000 increase in accounts receivable
6,000 increase in accounts payable

Rand and Porter then approached L. Rogers to join the partnership, and Rogers agreed under the following terms:

Inventory is to be valued at..............	$52,000
Patent is to be restated at............	10,000
Rogers is to invest cash of............ ..	53,000

Required:

(a) Journal entries to show the formation of the partnership, September 30, 1957.
(b) The balance sheet of Rand and Porter as of September 30, 1958.
(c) Journal entries to show the addition of Rogers to the partnership on September 30, 1958.
(d) The Partners' Equity section of the balance sheet of Rand, Porter, and Rogers as of September 30, 1958.

Problem B 11-4. The income statement of X, Y, and Z, a partnership, showed a net loss of $3,400 for the year ended June 30, 1957.

X had a capital account balance of $26,000, which had not changed since June 30, 1956. Y had invested additional capital in the amount of $3,000 on January 10, 1957. Z had withdrawn $1,500 more than the agreed amount in March, 1957. Y's and Z's capital accounts had balances of $14,000 and $8,500, respectively, on June 30, 1956.

Submit journal entries to close the Revenue and Expense account under each of the following conditions:

(1) X is to be allowed a salary of $5,000; the remainder is to be divided: X, 70%; Y, 20%; and Z, 10%.

(2) Interest at 6% is to be allowed Y on his capital at the beginning of the period; the remainder is to be divided in the ratio of capitals at the end of the period before the above interest allowance.

(3) Interest at 5% is to be allowed all partners on capital balances at the beginning of the period; the remainder is to be divided 7-4-4.

(4) A $4,000 salary is to be allowed Z; interest at 4% is to be allowed X and Y on their capital account balances at the end of the period; and the remainder is to be divided equally.

(5) Salaries of $2,500 are to be given each partner; interest at 4% is to be allowed on capitals at the beginning of the year; and the remainder is to be divided in the ratio of 1-3-1.

Problem B 11-5. Krans, Larson, and Moore decided to liquidate their business. All assets have been sold with the exception of the merchandise inventory, and no cash has as yet been paid out.

The balance sheet accounts at this time are as follows:

Cash..	$20,000	
Inventory.......................................	35,000	
Accounts payable..............................		$11,000
A. Larson, loan................................		3,000
G. Krans, capital..............................		16,000
A. Larson, capital.............................		7,000
T. Moore, capital..............................		18,000

Show how the cash will be distributed under each of the following conditions:

(1) The inventory is successfully sold on the market for $44,000.

(2) The inventory has little value and nets $5,000.

(3) The inventory is sold as scrap for only $2,000.

Problem B 11-6. Make journal entries for the distribution of cash in liquidation in the following cases.

Case 1:

Cash..	15,000	
Accounts payable..............................		3,000
Z, capital......................................		14,000
Y, capital......................................	2,000	
	17,000	17,000

Case 2:

Cash..	18,000	
X, loan..		3,000
X, capital......................................	2,000	
W, capital.....................................		17,000
	20,000	20,000

Case 3:

Cash..	18,000	
Notes payable...................................		12,000
Accrued interest payable.........................		1,000
V, loan..		5,000
V, capital.....................................	2,000	
U, capital.....................................	4,000	
T, capital.....................................		6,000
	24,000	24,000

Case 4:

Cash..	21,000	
Taxes payable..................................		3,000
S, loan..		3,000
S, capital.....................................	4,000	
R, capital.....................................		7,000
Q, capital.....................................		12,000
	25,000	25,000

Partnership Practice Set

Evans and Fuller, a partnership, sells the self-service, food-vending machines of Universal Company. The partnership has been in operation for about four years.

The firm uses the books of original entry shown below.

Cash Receipts Book

Date	Account Credited	Explanation	DEBIT Cash	CREDITS Accounts Receivable √ Amount	Sales	Sundry L.F. Amount

Cash Disbursements Book

Date	Account Debited	Explanation	DEBITS Universal Company	Transportation In	Sundry L.F. Amount	CREDITS Cash	Purchase Discounts

Purchases Book

Date	Name	Invoice Date	Amount

Sales Book

Date	Name √	Invoice No.	Amount

General Journal

Date	Account and Explanation	L.F.	DEBITS Universal Company	Sundry	CREDITS Sundry	Accounts Receivable

The firm uses a general ledger and an accounts receivable ledger. All purchases on account are made from Universal Company, and therefore no subsidiary ledger is needed for accounts payable. The accounts used by the firm, with their May 31, 1958 balances, are presented below:

Acct. No.	Account Title	May 31, 1958 Balances	
1110	Cash......	3,348.44	
1130	Accounts receivable......	2,891.00	
1139	Allowance for doubtful accounts......		55.70
1140	Notes receivable......	2,010.00	
1154	Accrued interest receivable......	4.09	
1170	Inventory......	2,616.00	
1190	Unexpired insurance......	282.50	
1191	Prepaid advertising......		
1192	Shipping supplies......	39.00	
1193	Office supplies......	21.50	
1320	Store fixtures......	10,800.00	
1329	Accumulated depreciation—Store fixtures......		2,700.00
1330	Office fixtures......	2,016.00	
1339	Accumulated depreciation—Office fixtures......		756.00
2130	Universal Company......		663.50
2155	Accrued payroll......		
2180	F. I. C. A. tax liability......		40.56
2181	Income tax withholding liability......		77.44
3110	C. D. Evans, capital......		8,747.68
3119	C. D. Evans, drawings......		
3210	D. E. Fuller, capital......		10,987.65
3219	D. E. Fuller, drawings......		
4000	Sales......		
4008	Sales returns and allowances......		
5170	Purchases......		
5178	Purchase returns and allowances......		
5179	Purchase discounts......		
5200	Transportation in......		
6001	Store rent......		
6002	Delivery truck rent......		
6029	Depreciation expense—Store fixtures......		
6055	Delivery salaries......		
6155	Sales salaries......		
6191	Advertising expense......		
6192	Shipping and delivery expense......		
6200	Miscellaneous selling expenses......		
7039	Depreciation expense—Office fixtures......		
7049	Bad debts expense......		
7055	Office salaries......		
7080	Payroll tax expense......		
7090	Insurance expense......		
7093	Office expense......		
7200	Miscellaneous general expenses......		
8054	Interest earned......		
9000	Revenue and expense......		

The accounts receivable to be used will be:

Name	May 31, 1958 Balance
City Insurance Company	$372
County of X	832
Courtland and Sparks	—
De Witt Supply Co	—
Low Wholesale Grocery	—
Mound Corporation	375
Outboard Manufacturing	226
Trench Building Co	730
Welliston Electric Co	356
Wilson Company	—

The notes receivable held by the partnership are listed below:

Date 1958	Maker	Time	Int. Rate	Due Date	Amount
May 16	Supply Corporation	60 days	6%	July 15	$1,500
May 27	Hook Company	30 days	6%	June 26	510

The firm hires three employees, who are paid on the 15th and last day of each month. The payroll data, effective June 1, 1958, are scheduled below:

Name	Position	Pay Period	Semimonthly Gross Salary	Withholding F. I. C. A.	Income Tax	Net Pay
John Jones	Office clerk	Semi-monthly	$150.00	$3.38	$16.62	$130.00
Donald Smith	Store salesman	Semi-monthly	170.00	3.83	20.17	146.00
Robert Vines	Truck driver	Semi-monthly	130.00	2.93	3.07	124.00

The books of Evans and Fuller are closed monthly, and this practice set will cover the operations of the firm for the month of June, 1958.

Instructions

(1) Journalize the transactions for the month of June, 1958.
(2) Post the journal entries to the ledgers.
(3) Prepare the June 30, 1958 trial balance. (Use the Trial Balance columns of the working papers.) Schedule the accounts receivable as of June 30, 1958, and compare with the controlling account.
(4) Complete the working papers.
(5) Prepare the following monthly statements:

> Income statement.
> Statement of partners' capitals.
> Balance sheet.

(6) Journalize the adjusting and closing entries.
(7) Post.

Transactions for the Month of June, 1958

1958

June 1—Store rent for June is paid, $225.

Sale of vending machines is made on account to Low Wholesale Grocery, $217. (Start with invoice number 601.)

An invoice dated May 31 is received from Universal Company for the purchase of vending machines, $3,100; terms, 2/10; n/30.

Freight on above shipment is paid to the carrier, $68.

2—Collection is received from Mound Corporation, $375.

Cash sale, $225.

5—Shipping supplies are purchased for cash, $59.

A sales agreement is completed with Wilson Company whereby, during the next 15 days, Wilson Company will purchase on account coffee vending machines for the convenience of employees at all of its retail stores. If all of the Wilson Company stores are equipped with Universal machines within the 15-day period, a special 4% price reduction covering all of the sales will be granted to Wilson Company. On the fifteenth day, Wilson Company will sign a note for one-half of the amount owing and will pay the balance in cash within five days thereafter. The first sale under this agreement is completed today, $1,200.

6—An invoice from Universal Company dated May 29, in the amount of $663.50, is paid. The terms are 2/10; n/30.

Vending machines are sold to Low Wholesale Grocery, $630.

7—Collections are received from:

Outboard Manufacturing............ $226

Welliston Electric Co............... 356

Sale of coffee vending machines to Wilson Company, $1,235.

8—Gas and oil for the delivery truck are purchased for cash, at a cost of $8.35.

Low Wholesale Grocery returns one of the machines purchased on June 6 to replace it with a fully automatic model, which is placed on order. A credit memorandum is issued for $152.

9—The Universal Company invoice dated May 31 is paid.

The withholding and F. I. C. A. tax liabilities of $118 are settled by sending a check to the District Director of Internal Revenue.

Newspaper advertising is purchased for cash, $27.25.

Cash sale, $215.

12—Sale of coffee vending machines to Wilson Company, $963.

An invoice dated June 11 is received from Universal Company, $2,222; terms, 2/10; n/30. Freight is paid to the carrier, $39.20.

The fully automatic model ordered for Low Wholesale Grocery is received in today's shipment from Universal Company. It is delivered to the customer, $225.50.

Premium on a three-year insurance policy is paid, $180. The policy is dated June 15.

13—A new coffee vending machine is removed from the inventory and placed in the store for the use of the employees of Evans and Fuller; cost, $138.24.

Evans withdraws cash for his personal use, $200.

Paid miscellaneous selling expenses, $11.65.

June 14—Sales of vending machines on account:

> De Witt Supply Co................ $722
> Wilson Company.................... 435

County of X check, covering its May 31 balance, is received.
Office supplies are purchased for cash, $31.65.
15—Semimonthly salaries for the first half of June are journalized and paid.
The accrual for the F. I. C. A. payroll tax is recorded at this time.
Paid miscellaneous general expenses, $9.23.
16—An invoice for $2,800 dated June 15 is received from Universal Company; terms, 2/10; n/30, f.o.b. destination.
Fuller withdraws cash for his personal use, $425.
19—Collections are received from:

> City Insurance Company........... $272
> De Witt Supply Co................ 722

A defective machine received in the latest shipment is returned to Universal Company. Full credit is taken in line with an agreement with the supplier. The amount is $119.
Sales of vending machines on account:

> Courtland and Sparks........... $1,250
> Wilson Company................. 1,167

With the above order, all of the Wilson Company stores are equipped with Universal machines.
Pursuant to the agreement of June 5, a credit memorandum is issued to Wilson Company in the amount of 4% of the total sales to Wilson Company covering the period from June 5 to date.
20—A 6%, 60-day note dated today is received from Wilson Company for $2,400.
Advertising supplies to be used for the next several months are purchased for cash, $235.
Cash sale, $200.
21—Paid miscellaneous selling expenses, $7.78.
Sale is made on account to Trench Building Co., $465.
22—Paid office expenses, $6.66.
Newspaper advertising is purchased for cash, $23.45.
The machine sold for cash on June 20 was dented during delivery. The customer accepts $25 in full settlement for the damage.
23—Received $2,400 from Wilson Company.
Gas and oil for the delivery truck are purchased for cash, $7.35.
26—Paid $1,400 on account to Universal Company.
Telephone bill is paid, $7.75. (Charge Office Expense.)
Sales of vending machines on account:

> De Witt Supply Co................ $815
> Trench Building Co............... 333

Hook Company's note dated May 27 is collected.
27—Received $60 from City Insurance Company with a letter stating that this was the final payment on its bill, since the company was going out of business. Since the company is insolvent and is going out of business, the balance of the account is written off as uncollectible.

June 27—Janitor services for the month are paid, $36. (Charge Miscellaneous General Expenses.)

28—Received $688 from Low Wholesale Grocery.

The monthly delivery truck rental is paid to Argo Mobil Equipment Co., $80.

Sale is made on account to Welliston Electric Co., $543.

29—Utilities for June are paid, $26.30. The firm charges half of each monthly utility bill to Miscellaneous Selling Expenses and half to Miscellaneous General Expenses.

30—Semimonthly salaries for the last half of June are journalized and paid. The accrual for the F. I. C. A. payroll tax is recorded at this time.

Shipping supplies are purchased for cash, $57.68.

Required Adjustments

(a) The insurance policies are:

Date Purchased	Protection	Term	Total Premium
June 15, 1955	Fire on merchandise	3 years	$180
February 1, 1957	Public liability	3 years	108
February 1, 1958	Fire and theft on fixtures	2 years	264
June 15, 1958	Fire on merchandise	3 years	180

(b) Accrued interest on the notes receivable outstanding at the end of the month.

(c) The annual depreciation rates are:

Asset	Annual Rate
Office fixtures..	10%
Store fixtures...	12½%

Vending machine transferred to store during June should be depreciated for one-half month.

(d) It is estimated that the monthly provision for uncollectible accounts should be $\frac{3}{10}$ths of 1% of the net credit sales (total credit sales less returns and allowances applicable to credit sales).

(e) Inventories of supplies, as of June 30, 1958, are as follows:

Advertising supplies.............	$195.00
Shipping supplies................	45.34
Office supplies..................	16.15

Other Data

The ending inventory of merchandise is $3,573.22.

The partners share earnings as follows: C. D. Evans, 40%; D. E. Fuller, 60%.

ASSIGNMENT MATERIAL FOR CHAPTER 12
Questions

1. List several advantages accruing to stockholders because corporate shares are transferable that are not available to partners.

2. Explain what is meant by the phrase "double taxation" when used in reference to taxes on corporate income.

3. What makes a corporation a *foreign* corporation?

4. What is discount liability?

5. Illustrate how premium and discount on capital stock are presented in the financial statements.

6. Explain why the issuance of no-par stock is not recorded the same way in all cases.

7. Express an opinion on the following statement: "A stock selling for less than its par value is a bargain."

8. What kind of an account is Subscriptions Receivable?

9. Does a capital stock subscribed account normally have a debit or a credit balance? Where does such an account appear in the financial statements? What does its balance show?

10. When capital stock is issued for property other than cash, a valuation problem may arise. Discuss this problem and some possible solutions.

11. What is a minute book? What is found in such a book?

12. What is the recommended practice regarding the disposition of the balance appearing in stock premium accounts?

Problems—Group A

Problem A 12-1. Brighton Company, a newly organized corporation, obtained authorization for 5,000 shares of no-par common stock. In conformance with the state laws, the directors have assigned a stated value of $25 a share to the no-par stock.

On December 15, 1958, the company issued 1,000 shares for $25 per share.

On December 17, a patent was purchased at a cost of $8,000.

An additional 800 shares were issued for cash on December 23 at $27 per share.

By the end of the month, prospects for the company had greatly improved, and on December 30 a subscription was received for 1,500 shares at $30 each.

Give journal entries for the above transactions. Also show how the Common Stock account would appear in the general ledger and prepare a partial balance sheet, as of December 31, 1958, for Brighton Company, showing the Stockholders' Equity section.

Problem A 12-2. Nelson Corporation was organized in early February, 1959, and was authorized to issue 1,000 shares of no-par stock. The company was organized in a state in which the laws require that the entire amount received for no-par shares shall be regarded as legal capital.

On February 5, J. K. Nelson transferred certain assets and liabilities to the corporation in exchange for 500 shares of common stock. These items included: accounts receivable, $2,000, of which $150 were deemed worthless; notes receivable, $5,000; inventory worth $4,500 according to reliable indicators, but for which Mr. Nelson had paid $5,000; supplies valued at $650; land appraised at $5,000; a building valued at $15,000 for which Mr. Nelson had paid $24,000 and had accumulated depreciation thereon to the extent of $12,000; and accounts payable, $2,000.

Subscriptions were received on February 6 from D. E. Frederick and L. M. Norge for 100 shares each at $62 per share. Frederick paid for his subscription in full on February 12, and a stock certificate for 100 shares was issued to him on that date.

Ten shares were issued on February 17 to an attorney in payment of $615 of costs incurred in the organization of the corporation.

Journalize the transactions involving the subscription and issuance of shares of stock as indicated above.

Problem A 12-3. Give journal entries for the following transactions of Gardner Corporation, and show how the Common Stock ledger account would appear after the entries were posted, assuming three different conditions as follows:

(a) Authorization was obtained for the issuance of 5,000 shares of no-par stock.
(b) Authorization was obtained for the issuance of 5,000 shares of no-par stock, with the directors voting to assign a stated value of $20 a share to the stock.
(c) Authorization was obtained for the issuance of 5,000 shares of $20 par value stock.

1959
Jan. 10—Cash subscriptions were received for 1,500 shares at $20 per share. The cash was collected and stock certificates were issued.
    16—Subscriptions were received for 1,000 shares at $21 per share.
    31—The subscriptions of January 16 were collected in full. Stock certificates were issued at this time.

Problem A 12-4. Eastern Corp. was organized early in January, 1959. Authorization was obtained to issue 10,000 shares of common stock, par value $10.

Jan. 10—Subscriptions were received for 3,000 shares at $10 per share.
    13—The subscriptions received January 10 were collected in full and stock certificates were issued.
    20—Subscriptions were received for 2,000 shares at $12 per share.
    23—The subscriptions received January 20 were collected in full and stock certificates were issued.
    26—Subscriptions were taken for 1,000 shares at $12 per share.
    30—Subscriptions received January 26 for 500 shares were collected in full and $4,500 cash was received from other subscribers of that date.

Required:

(a) Journal entries.
(b) Postings to: 1. Subscriptions Receivable
                  2. Common Stock
                  3. Common Stock Subscribed
                  4. Premium on Common Stock
(c) Balance sheet presentation of stockholders' equity, January 31, 1959.

Problem A 12-5. Fred Mumby, George Booth, and John Logan organized Mum-Bo-Lo Corporation on June 1, 1959, with authorization to issue 5,000 shares of $100 par common stock.

On June 1, subscriptions were taken from Fred Mumby for 1,200 shares, from George Booth for 1,300 shares, and from John Logan for 800 shares, all at $110 per share.

On June 5, Fred Mumby transferred the following assets and liabilities to the newly formed corporation in partial payment of his subscription:

Accounts receivable	$34,650
Notes receivable	7,000
Inventory	63,820
Accounts payable	6,060

On June 6, George Booth transferred the following assets to the corporation in partial payment of his subscription:

Land	$15,000
Building	87,000

The corporation received a bill on June 10 in the amount of $5,000 from a local attorney for legal fees for organizational services rendered. The attorney accepted 50 shares of stock in full payment, and the certificate was issued.

A subscription for 100 shares at $112 per share was taken from Paul Jones on June 11.

On June 12, Mumby, Booth, and Logan paid the remainder of their subscriptions.

On June 14, Jones paid $70 per share on his 100-share subscription.

On June 14, certificates were issued to Mumby, Booth, and Logan for 1,200, 1,300, and 800 shares, respectively.

Make journal entries to record the above transactions, post the same to ledger accounts, and prepare a classified balance sheet for Mum-Bo-Lo Corporation as of June 15, 1959.

Problems—Group B

Problem B 12-1. Bean Corporation was organized on July 1, 1959, and was authorized to issue 2,000 shares of $100 par common stock. On July 1, D. B. Frank and F. D. George paid $90 cash per share for 200 shares each. The company's officers obtained several contracts beneficial to the company during the early part of July, and on July 15, 300 shares were issued at par for cash to L. K. Moore. As the month progressed, the earnings outlook became more favorable, and, being in need of additional funds, the company secured $110 a share cash for the issuance of 250 shares to R. S. Timkey on July 30.

Journalize the above transactions involving the issuance of shares of capital stock.

Problem B 12-2. Best Services, Inc., was organized on May 1, 1959, and its entire authorized issue of 1,000 shares of common stock was sold for cash at $90 per share on the date of organization.

Journalize this initial transaction under the following conditions:

(a) Authorization had been obtained for 1,000 shares of no-par stock, and the company was organized in a state in which the laws require that the entire amount received for no-par shares shall be legal capital.

(b) Authorization had been obtained for 1,000 shares of no-par stock. The company was organized in a state in which the laws permit the crediting of a surplus account with a portion of the proceeds from the sale of no-par shares. The directors have voted to assign a stated value of $80 a share to the no-par stock.

(c) Authorization has been obtained for 1,000 shares of $100 par stock.

Problem B 12-3.   Major Corporation was organized on May 1, 1959, and was authorized to issue 6,000 shares of no-par common stock. The laws in the state of incorporation require a minimum stated value of $5 per share for such stock. However, the directors did not pass any resolution concerning stated value.

During May, the company issued shares as follows:

May 1—2,000 shares at $9 per share, for cash.
      10—1,500 shares at $10 per share for land worth $3,000, buildings valued at $8,000, and cash of $4,000.
      21—1,200 shares at $12 per share, for cash.

The company paid $3,500 for organization fees on May 5.

Assuming earnings of $1,500 for May and the payment of no dividends, prepare the Stockholders' Equity section of the balance sheet of Major Corporation as of May 31, 1959.

Problem B 12-4.   Hartford Corporation was organized on June 1, 1959, and was authorized to issue 1,000 shares of $50 par value common stock.

(a) Give entries in general journal form for the following transactions.
(b) Show how the Common Stock and Common Stock Subscribed accounts would appear in the general ledger after the entries were posted.
(c) Prepare the Stockholders' Equity section of Hartford Corporation's balance sheet as of June 30, 1959.

1959
June 1—A subscription for 400 shares at $45 per share was received from H. M. Hadler.
      3—Hadler transferred land worth $8,000 to the company in partial payment of his subscription and paid cash for the balance. A stock certificate was issued.
    15—B. J. Wilson paid in $50 per share cash for 300 shares.
    23—Subscriptions were received from several small subscribers for 200 shares at $50 per share.
    28—Subscriptions of June 23 for 150 shares were collected in full, and $1,000 cash was collected from the other subscribers.

Problem B 12-5.   Westwood Company was organized on March 1, 1959, and was authorized to issue 2,000 common shares of $50 par stock.

Land worth $4,000 and a building thereon valued at $21,000 were acquired on the date of organization for 500 shares of common stock.

Machinery, valued at $12,000, was acquired on March 4 for 150 shares of stock and a $5,250, 40-day, non-interest-bearing note.

On March 5, subscriptions for 50 shares at $45 were received.

To protect the manufacturing process, an existing patent was purchased. The previous owner wanted $4,500 cash, but he accepted 100 shares of stock, which were issued on March 6.

Having the patent, the officers of the company were able to obtain several contracts which were advantageous to the company, and on March 10, 200 shares were issued to several persons for cash, at par.

Collections in full were received on March 12 for 30 shares subscribed March 5, and $400 was received from other March 5 subscribers.

Give journal entries to record the transactions for the first half of March, 1959, as indicated above.

Problem B 12-6. R. J. Hammer and B. C. Moore organized H. & M. Company on March 1, 1959. The state in which the company was incorporated allows a portion of the proceeds of the sale of stock to be credited to a surplus account. Authorization was obtained to issue 5,000 shares of no-par value common stock, and a stated value of $20 per share was assigned to the stock by the directors.

Hammer subscribed for 1,000 shares and Moore subscribed for 1,500 shares at $25 per share on the date of organization, and stock certificates were issued.

On March 8, Hammer transferred to the company land worth $10,000 in part payment of his subscription and paid cash for the balance. Moore paid for his entire subscription on the same date by paying cash and transferring to the company delivery equipment worth $14,400 and supplies valued at $600.

Attorneys' costs of $1,050 incurred in connection with the organization of the company were paid March 18 by issuing 42 shares of stock.

On March 30, B. T. Vance paid $30 per share cash for 150 shares.

Required:

(a) Give entries in journal form to record the above transactions.
(b) Assuming earnings of $1,950 for March and the payment of no dividends, prepare the Stockholders' Equity section of the balance sheet of H. & M. Company as of March 31, 1959.

Problem B 12-7. Mid-West Company was organized on February 1, 1959, and was authorized to issue 2,000 shares of no-par common stock. In conformance with the laws of the state of organization, the directors passed a resolution stipulating that a stated value of $50 a share would be assigned to the no-par stock.

(a) Prepare entries in journal form to record the following transactions.
(b) Show how the following accounts would appear in the ledger:

1. Subscriptions Receivable   3. Common Stock Subscribed
2. Common Stock   4. Paid-in Surplus

(c) Prepare a balance sheet as of February 15, 1959.

1959
Feb. 1—Issued 1,000 shares at $52 per share for cash.
      3—Received subscriptions for 200 shares at $52.
      4—20 shares of stock issued in payment of land acquired.
      7—Purchased merchandise from Basil Company on account, $20,560.
     10—Received full payment for half of the shares subscribed for on February 3, and $2,600 in partial payment for the rest of the shares subscribed for on that date.
     12—Issued 10 shares to an attorney in payment of $530 organization costs.

ASSIGNMENT MATERIAL FOR CHAPTER 13
Questions

1. What basic rights does the ownership of shares of stock confer upon a stockholder? Are these rights always enjoyed proportionately by all classes of stockholders?

2. What is meant by the words "cumulative" and "participating" as applied to preferred stock?

3. Discuss the following statement: Common stockholders have no right to dividends unless the directors declare them, but in the case of preferred stockholders, their right to dividends is essentially the same as a note holder's right to interest.

4. In your opinion, is book value a meaningful figure?

5. Describe several transactions that produce an increase in paid-in surplus.

6. Are all declared dividends liabilities?

7. What is appropriated surplus? Give some examples.

8. What is the primary purpose of a surplus appropriation?

9. When are dividends "in arrears"?

10. What is the net result of a stock dividend?

11. Define treasury stock.

12. Tell how retained earnings and paid-in surplus are affected by the following:

    (a) Payment of a previously declared cash dividend.
    (b) Declaration of a stock dividend.
    (c) Acquisition of treasury shares.
    (d) Reissuance of treasury shares.

Problems—Group A

Problem A 13-1. Prepare journal entries, omitting explanations, to reflect the information given below. Bi-Way Company has 5,000 shares of $20 par value common stock outstanding.

(1) Established a reserve for contingencies in the amount of $15,000.
(2) Declared a cash dividend of $.50 a share.
(3) Declared an 8% stock dividend. Fair value at the time, $21 per share.
(4) A tract of land worth $5,000 was donated to the company.
(5) Paid the cash dividend previously declared.
(6) Established a reserve for plant extension in the amount of $30,000.
(7) Issued the stock dividend previously declared.
(8) Purchased equipment for $15,000, on account.
(9) Received a donation of 600 shares of Bi-Way Company common stock.
(10) Increased the reserve for plant extension by $12,000.
(11) Acquired 500 shares of treasury stock for $11,500. (The company records treasury stock acquisitions at cost.)

(12) Eliminated the reserve for contingencies.
(13) Sold 200 shares of treasury stock acquired in (11) for $24 per share.
(14) Sold 300 shares of treasury stock acquired in (11) for $7,500.
(15) Sold the donated treasury stock for $27 per share.

Problem A 13-2.   The Stockholders' Equity section of Garrison Corporation's balance sheet on May 31, 1959, appeared as follows:

GARRISON CORPORATION
Partial Balance Sheet
May 31, 1959

Stockholders' equity:

4% preferred stock—1,000 shares authorized at $100 per share; issued, 800 shares..........................	$85,500.00	
No-par common stock—2,000 shares authorized; stated value, $50; issued, 1,500 shares.....................	87,500.00	
4% preferred stock—to be issued June 15, as a 10% common stock dividend—75 shares.................	8,250.00	
Surplus...	54,297.00	$235,547.00

An analysis showed that the above surplus amount was derived as follows:

Retained earnings....................................	$26,497.00
Donated surplus.....................................	5,000.00
Appraisal surplus....................................	10,000.00
Reserve for doubtful accounts.........................	800.00
Reserve for possible declines in inventory prices...........	4,000.00
Reserve for plant extensions...........................	8,000.00
	$54,297.00

Other so-called "reserves" found in the ledger included:

Reserve for depreciation..............................	$ 7,600.00
Reserve for bond sinking fund.........................	8,400.00
Reserve for general contingencies.......................	9,000.00

Restate the Stockholders' Equity section of the balance sheet in more acceptable form.

Problem A 13-3.   Barnnett Corporation presented the Stockholders' Equity section of its June 30, 1959 balance sheet in the following form:

Stockholders' equity:
Capital stock:

5% cumulative preferred—3,000 shares authorized; 2,000 shares issued; par value, $100......................................	$190,000.00
No-par common—20,000 shares issued; 3,000 shares held in treasury; 25,000 shares authorized; stated value, $20..........	331,000.00

Retained earnings:

Premium on common stock.................................	55,000.00
Operating surplus (see Note A).............................	86,000.00
	$662,000.00

Note A—In view of a planned future purchase to reduce the number of preferred shares outstanding, the directors have earmarked $50,000 of accumulated earnings as not available for dividend purposes.

The common stock has been issued at various dates.   Collections from shares issued have been: 15,000 shares at $22 per share and 5,000 shares at $25 each. There are no subscriptions receivable as of June 30.   The 3,000 shares of common stock held in the treasury were recently purchased at $23 per share. The corporation is organized in a state where treasury stock acquisitions must not impair the stated capital.

The preferred stock was issued on July 1, 1956. To date, no dividends have been declared on this stock.

Prepare the Stockholders' Equity section of the balance sheet in good form.

Problem A 13-4. On March 31, 1959, the ledger accounts of Tooele Company had the following balances:

Cash...	$ 9,485.00
Accounts receivable.....................................	28,543.00
Land..	23,000.00
Building...	150,000.00
Treasury stock—Preferred.............................	8,800.00
Treasury stock—Common..............................	5,700.00
Organization costs.......................................	2,980.00
Premium on common stock............................	12,260.00
Common stock subscribed..............................	10,000.00
Subscriptions receivable—Common....................	8,000.00
Common stock..	90,000.00
Dividends payable—Common...........................	1,700.00
Preferred stock...	60,000.00
Subscriptions receivable—Preferred....................	12,500.00
Preferred stock subscribed.............................	20,000.00
Reserve for retirement of preferred stock..............	15,000.00
Allowance for doubtful accounts.......................	1,200.00
Accumulated depreciation—Building...................	15,000.00
Retained earnings..	18,868.00
Paid-in surplus—From treasury stock transactions........	5,800.00
Inventory..	16,500.00
Accounts payable..	15,680.00

The company was authorized to issue 1,000 shares of 5% cumulative participating preferred stock with a par value of $100, and 3,000 shares of $50 par value common stock. It has issued 600 shares of preferred and 1,800 shares of common. Shares subscribed for but not issued consist of 200 shares of preferred and 200 shares of common, and the subscriptions are due in the near future. The company holds 80 shares of preferred and 100 shares of common in the treasury—both classes being carried at cost. The company is organized in a state where treasury stock acquisitions must not impair the stated capital.

Prepare a classified balance sheet for Tooele Company as of March 31, 1959.

Problems—Group B

Problem B 13-1. Using the cost basis, journalize the following treasury stock transactions of Allman Corporation. The company was authorized to issue 6,000 shares of no-par value stock, and the directors voted to assign a stated value of $40 per share to this stock.

1959
Feb. 1—Purchased 200 shares of its stock at $45 per share. These shares were originally issued at $42 per share.

5—Received a donation of 500 shares of the company's stock.

11—Sold, for $48 per share, 120 shares of the treasury stock purchased February 1.

Feb. 21—Reissued the remaining 80 shares of the February 1 purchase at $43 per share.

28—Sold the donated treasury stock for $47 per share.

Problem B 13-2.   On November 30, 1958, Kahn Corporation had 4,000 shares of common stock issued and outstanding.   The company was organized with authorization to issue 8,000 shares of common stock with a par value of $40. Balances showing at the above date included Premium on Common Stock, $20,000, and Retained Earnings, $20,000.   Earnings from operations after taxes but before dividends amounted to $1,000 per month throughout the succeeding year.   The company did not buy or sell any treasury shares during this period.

Prepare journal entries to record the following dividend transactions and any related closing entries.   Assume that the books are closed monthly.

On December 20, 1958, the directors declared a dividend of $.50 per share, to be paid in cash on January 10, 1959, to stockholders of record on December 28, 1958.

The directors declared a dividend on March 20, 1959, to distribute on April 10 inventory items, costing $4,000, to stockholders of record on March 28.

A 5% stock dividend on shares held on June 28, 1959, was declared by the directors on June 20 to be issued on July 10.   Fair value of the shares was regarded to be $50.

Another cash dividend of $.50 per share was declared by the directors on September 20, 1959, to be paid on October 10, to stockholders of record on September 28; one-third of the dividend was to be charged to paid-in surplus, which was permissible under the laws of the state in which the company was incorporated.

Problem B 13-3.   The following facts are available concerning the capital structure of Kinsteel Company as of December 31, 1958.

Preferred stock dividends in arrears.....................	$ 18,000.00
Preferred stock—6% cumulative; par value, $100; 1,500 shares authorized...................................	150,000.00
Common stock—Par value, $10; 20,000 shares authorized..	200,000.00
Retained earnings....................................	20,000.00
Paid-in surplus—From treasury stock transactions........	5,000.00
Donated surplus......................................	20,000.00
Common stock, 15,000 shares issued....................	150,000.00
Premium on common stock............................	15,000.00
Preferred stock, 1,000 shares issued....................	100,000.00

Prepare the Stockholders' Equity section of the balance sheet as of December 31, 1958, and compute the book value per share of common stock.

Problem B 13-4.   Zoom Company has 2,000 shares of $50 par value 5% preferred stock and 2,000 shares of $50 stated-value common stock outstanding.

With the understanding that the directors declare all dividends possible each year, show how earnings of $4,000 in 1957, $11,000 in 1958, and $16,000 in 1959 will be distributed to each class of stockholders if the preferred stock is:

(a) Non-cumulative and non-participating.
(b) Cumulative and non-participating.
(c) Cumulative and fully participating.

Problem B 13-5.   Stanfield Corporation has authorization for 10,000 shares of no-par common stock to which the directors have assigned a stated value of

$20 per share, and 1,000 shares of 5% cumulative preferred stock of $100 par value. Current market values according to the stock exchanges are: common, $25 and preferred, $110.

Preferred stock has been issued as follows:

> July 1, 1957—800 shares for $100 per share.
> July 1, 1958—100 shares for $105 per share.
> June 30, 1959—100 shares for $110 per share.

Common stock has been issued as follows:

> July 1, 1957—5,000 shares for $100,000.
> June 1, 1958—1,000 shares for $22,000.
> Oct. 15, 1958—1,000 shares for $23,000.
> June 15, 1959—1,000 shares for $25,000.

Subscriptions were secured for 1,000 additional common shares at $25 per share on June 20, 1959. Collections have been made in full for 500 of these shares, and $6,000 has been received from other subscribers. No stock certificates have been issued.

Although the prospects for the future are bright, the company, as of June 30, 1959, has preferred dividends in arrears totaling $8,500.

Reserves and allowances which appear in the ledger accounts include the following:

Plant extensions	$10,000
Building depreciation	7,000
Bond sinking fund	25,000
Doubtful accounts	2,500

Total retained earnings amount to $48,500.

Prepare the Stockholders' Equity section of the balance sheet for Stanfield Corporation as of June 30, 1959.

Problem B 13-6. Van Dyke Company is seeking a bank loan. The company's accountant has come to you for advice concerning the desirability of presenting the bank with the balance sheet in the present form. A portion of the company's balance sheet is reproduced below:

VAN DYKE COMPANY
Partial Balance Sheet
March 31, 1959

Stockholders' equity:

Common stock—$10 par value; 5,000 shares authorized; 3,000 shares issued and outstanding	$30,000.00	
Surplus	25,823.00	$55,823.00

An analysis of the accounting records of the company showed the following facts relating to surplus:

Net income for certain years	$70,669.00
Dividends declared and paid	24,000.00
Discount on the issuance of stock	8,000.00
Proceeds from the sale of donated shares	12,000.00
Net losses for certain years	25,446.00
Excess of cost of purchased treasury stock over proceeds from sale thereof	2,400.00
Premium on issuance of capital stock	3,000.00

The minutes of the March meeting of the board of directors reveals the fact that approval has been given for the establishment of a $10,000 reserve for plant extensions.

Prepare a revised partial balance sheet showing the Stockholders' Equity section in more acceptable form.

Problem B 13-7. Give journal entries to reflect the apparent transactions that gave rise to the changes in the stockholders' equity of Orson Company as indicated by the two partial balance sheets given below. The company follows a policy of accepting subscriptions only if they are paid immediately in cash.

ORSON COMPANY
Partial Balance Sheet
December 31, 1958

Stockholders' equity:
Common stock—No-par; stated value, $20; authorized,
6,000 shares; issued, 4,000 shares............................ $ 80,000.00
Surplus:
Paid-in surplus—Common......................... $16,000.00
Retained earnings............................... 34,000.00   50,000.00
                                                            $130,000.00

ORSON COMPANY
Partial Balance Sheet
December 31, 1959

Stockholders' equity:
Common stock—No-par; stated value, $20; authorized,
6,000 shares; issued, 5,000 shares, of which 120 shares
are in the treasury............................. $100,000.00
To be issued January 20, as a stock dividend—488
shares.. 9,760.00 $109,760.00
Surplus:
Paid-in surplus:
Paid-in surplus—Common...................... $ 21,000.00
Retained earnings capitalized in connection with a
stock dividend............................ 2,440.00   23,440.00
Retained earnings:
Reserve for plant expansion.................. $ 15,000.00
Not available for dividends—Equal to cost of
treasury stock........................... 2,880.00
Free................................... 31,200.00   49,080.00
        Total... $182,280.00
Deduct cost of treasury stock................................. 2,880.00
                                                            $179,400.00

ASSIGNMENT MATERIAL FOR CHAPTER 14
Questions

1. If a business purchases a delivery truck for cash and records the transaction by debiting Delivery Equipment and crediting Cash, is the company using a voucher system?

2. If a voucher register is in use, will the business be likely to use a purchases book also?

3. Point out the contrasting features between a check register and a cash disbursements book.

4. Describe how postings are made from a voucher register.

5. How does a voucher system permit the elimination of the accounts payable subsidiary ledger?

6. When a voucher system is used, what is the procedure:

(a) When merchandise is purchased on account?
(b) When merchandise is purchased for cash?
(c) When merchandise is purchased and a note is issued therefor?

7. If at the time when a liability is incurred it is known that it will be paid in installments, what is the accounting procedure with a voucher system?

8. When a voucher system is in use, describe three ways in which the total owing on open account may be determined.

9. What is the purpose of the Deductions columns in the voucher register?

10. Is the voucher system applicable only to large businesses?

Problems—Group A

Problem A 14-1. Show how the voucher register of Arrow Corporation would appear after the following transactions had been journalized.

1958
Jan. 4—Merchandise is received on account from H. Moon, $4,000. Terms, 2/10; n/30.
5—Received a bill for the January rent, $125. It is paid today to Central Rental Agency by check number 1.
7—Paid $2,000 for land purchased today from A. B. Miles.
9—Merchandise is received on account from Star Company, $3,100. Terms, $1,000 in cash and the balance in 30 days. Issued a check for $1,000.
12—Paid for the merchandise purchased January 4.
14—Received a bill from City Printers for office supplies, $37.
17—Merchandise is received on account from Black Supply Co., $1,700. Terms, 2/10; n/30.
21—A 30-day, non-interest-bearing note to Sam White matures and is paid today, $900.
22—Returned some of the merchandise purchased from Black Supply Co. on January 17. Received a credit memo for $50.

Problem A 14-2. The following are selected transactions of Moot Corporation during July, 1958. Record these transactions in a voucher register, check register, and journal, using appropriate voucher and check numbers.

1958

July 5—Merchandise costing $4,000 is received from A. Cranston. Terms, 2/10; n/30.

     6—Merchandise is purchased on account from X. Henry, $3,600.

     8—A 5%, 20-day note is given in payment of the purchase of July 6.

   10—A bookkeeping machine is purchased for $5,000 from Lee Co. A down payment of $2,000 is made, and the balance is to be payable in monthly installments of $1,000 each.

   11—Half of the merchandise purchased from A. Cranston on July 5 is returned.

   13—A credit memo (No. 124) is received from A. Cranston for $2,000.

   14—A. Cranston is paid for one-half of the merchandise received on July 5, less 2% discount.

   18—Freight bills amounting to $26 are paid in cash to Williams Truckers, Inc., for delivery service on goods purchased.

   25—Rent for July is paid to B. Hoffman, $600.

   28—The X. Henry note of July 8, due today, is paid, including interest.

Problem A 14-3. Hicks-Ponder, a partnership, uses the voucher system. Record the following selected transactions for the month of March, 1959, in the books of original entry, using appropriate voucher and check numbers.

1959

March 3—Office supplies are purchased from Universal Suppliers, $100. Terms, n/20.

     6—Merchandise is received from Dale Bros. on account, $3,000. Terms, 2/10; n/30.

     9—A machine costing $7,000 is purchased from Johnson Equipment Co. A cash payment of $2,500 is made and the balance will be paid in three equal monthly installments.

   13—Supplementary equipment costing $1,000, and additional office supplies costing $400, are purchased from Universal Suppliers. Terms, n/10.

   14—Merchandise is received from John Wallace on account, $2,000. Terms, 1/10; n/30.

   16—A check for $940 and a 6%, 10-day note for $2,000 are sent to Dale Bros. in full payment of the March 6 purchase.

   18—Merchandise costing $800 is returned to John Wallace and a credit memo (No. 524) for that amount is received.

   21—Richard Ponder, a partner, withdraws $750 cash.

   23—A check for $1,500 is written to Universal Suppliers to cover invoices of March 3 and 13.

   24—John Wallace is paid the appropriate amount for the balance due on the March 14 purchase.

   26—Note and interest due today are paid to Dale Bros. (See March 16.)

Problem A 14-4. Bill Lindsay and John Lang formed a partnership on June 15, 1959, to be operated under the name of L. & L. Wholesalers and to have a fiscal year ending May 31. Record the transactions for the first half-month's operations as indicated below in the books of original entry, post to ledger accounts, and prepare a trial balance and a schedule of vouchers payable as of

June 30, 1959.   The books of original entry used to record the stated transactions are:

Journal   Check register
Voucher register   Cash receipts book

1959

June 15—Bill Lindsay invests $40,000 cash.

John Lang invests $20,000 cash and $20,000 in merchandise.

A three-year fire insurance policy is purchased from Farrell Insurance Co. for cash, $1,200.

Six months' rent is paid in advance to Hill Housing, $1,500.

16—Cash sales, $1,580.

18—Merchandise costing $8,500 is purchased as follows:

> D. B. Darnett, cash................................. $1,700
> James Black, on account.   Terms, 2/10; n/30........ $2,800
> Martin Co.   Terms, 30-day, 6% note, issued today.... $4,000

19—Supplies are purchased from Ace Supply for cash, $400.   These are expected to be used during the current fiscal year.

Merchandise is received from W. W. Wilber on account, $2,200. Terms, 3/10; n/30.   Invoice date, June 18.

20—Equipment is purchased from Sims Outfitters, $8,400.   Terms, $3,000 down (payment made) and three equal monthly installments of $1,800.

21—Merchandise is returned to James Black and a credit memo for $460 is received (see June 18).

23—Cash sales for the week, $8,980.

25—Transportation in amounting to $850 is paid to Cabot Delivery.

26—Merchandise is received as follows:

> Peter Davis, on account.   Terms, 2/10; n/30......... $1,650
> Henry Born, on account.   Terms, 1/10; n/30.......... $ 890

27—Cash refund is made to John Baker, who returned merchandise in the amount of $750.

Payments for merchandise previously purchased on account are made as follows:

> James Black (June 18).............. $1,500 less 2% discount
> W. W. Wilber (June 19)............. $2,200 less 3% discount

29—Bill Lindsay and John Lang each withdraw $550 cash.

30—Cash sales for the week, $6,850.

Additional equipment is purchased from Hawkins Co., $10,000. Terms, $4,000 down and four monthly installments of $1,500 each.

$1,960 is borrowed from the bank on a six-month, 6% note.

The $4,000 down payment is made to Hawkins Co.

Problems—Group B

Problem B 14-1.   The books of original entry for Adams and Cass Company are as follows:

Journal   Voucher register (with "Deductions" section)
Cash receipts book   Check register
Sales book

Indicate the books in which entries for the following selected transactions would be made. Include a statement of any additional notations that would normally be required and name the book in which each would be recorded.

Example: Purchased merchandise for cash.
Answer: Entered in voucher register and check register.
           Notation in voucher register.

1. Returned merchandise to a vendor and received a credit memo.
2. Purchased equipment on the installment basis and paid the initial installment.
3. Made a sale to a customer, receiving partial payment in cash and the remaining balance in the form of a promissory note.
4. Borrowed money by discounting a note at the bank.
5. Purchased merchandise and five days later gave a note to the creditor for the full amount of the purchase.
6. Received merchandise returned as unsatisfactory by a cash customer.
7. Paid a note at the bank. (Note bore no interest and had been discounted.)
8. Made a partial payment to a creditor for a purchase previously recorded.
9. Paid a note to a creditor, plus interest.
10. Paid salaries for the month.
11. Collected a customer's note, plus interest.
12. Purchased merchandise from a creditor. Terms, 2/10; n/30.
13. Wrote off an uncollectible account.
14. Declared a cash dividend.

Problem B 14-2. After all June, 1959 postings had been completed, Commander Company had the following trial balance.

COMMANDER COMPANY
Trial Balance
June 30, 1959

Cash...	10,000.00	
Securities...................................	5,000.00	
Accounts receivable..........................	8,000.00	
Allowance for doubtful accounts..............		980.00
Notes receivable.............................	2,000.00	
Inventory....................................	20,155.00	
Prepaid interest.............................	45.00	
Prepaid rent.................................	200.00	
Sales equipment..............................	18,000.00	
Accumulated depreciation—Sales equipment....		6,300.00
Vouchers payable.............................		6,000.00
Notes payable................................		3,000.00
Capital stock................................		25,000.00
Retained earnings............................		19,045.00
Sales..		60,000.00
Purchases....................................	35,260.00	
Transportation in............................	1,000.00	
Purchase discounts...........................		700.00
Delivery expense.............................	4,000.00	
Depreciation expense—Sales equipment........	900.00	
Rent...	1,200.00	
Salaries.....................................	15,000.00	
Payroll taxes................................	225.00	
Interest expense.............................	90.00	
Interest earned..............................		50.00
	121,075.00	121,075.00

Additional accounts utilized during the month of July were:

Office equipment
Accumulated depreciation—Office
  equipment
Accrued payroll
Withholding and F. I. C. A. tax liabilities

State unemployment tax liability
Federal unemployment tax liability
Purchase returns and allowances
Depreciation expense—Office equipment
Gain on sale of securities

No general ledger postings have been made from the books of original entry for July, which are presented in summary form below. Set up the necessary general ledger accounts, post, and prepare a general ledger trial balance as of July 31, 1959.

Journal: (Page 10)
  Debit column details:
    Vouchers payable......................(July 5).... $1,800.00
    Notes receivable......................(July 11)....   900.00
    Vouchers payable......................(July 18)....   740.00
    Salaries..............................(July 30).... 1,700.00
    Payroll taxes.........................(July 30)....   70.60
    Interest expense......................(July 31)....   15.00
    Rent..................................(July 31)....   200.00
    Depreciation expense—Office equipment..(July 31)....   50.00
    Depreciation expense—Sales equipment...(July 31)....   150.00

      Column total................................... $5,625.60

  Credit column details:
    Notes payable.........................(July 5).... $1,800.00
    Accounts receivable...................(July 11)....   900.00
    Purchase returns and allowances.......(July 18)....   740.00
    Withholding and F. I. C. A. tax liabilities..(July 30)....   340.00
    Accrued payroll.......................(July 30).... 1,360.00
    Withholding and F. I. C. A. tax liabilities..(July 30)....   30.60
    State unemployment tax liability......(July 30)....   36.00
    Federal unemployment tax liability.....(July 30)....   4.00
    Prepaid interest......................(July 31)....   15.00
    Prepaid rent..........................(July 31)....   200.00
    Accumulated depreciation—Office
      equipment...........................(July 31)....   50.00
    Accumulated depreciation—Sales
      equipment...........................(July 31)....   150.00

      Column total................................... $5,625.60

Voucher register: (Page 21)
  Column totals:
    Vouchers payable... $17,436.00

    Purchases.. $ 6,580.00
  Sundry accounts:
    Details: Office equipment.............(July 1).... $6,000.00
             Delivery expense.............(July 5)....   850.00
             Transportation in............(July 7)....   240.00
             Prepaid rent.................(July 20)....   600.00
             Notes payable................(July 25).... 1,800.00
             Interest expense.............(July 25)....   6.00
             Accrued payroll..............(July 30).... 1,360.00

      Column total...................................   10,856.00
                                                        $17,436.00

Check register: (Page 18)
Column totals:

Vouchers payable	$12,430.00
Purchase discounts	$ 175.00
Cash	12,255.00
	$12,430.00

Cash receipts book: (Page 14)
Column totals:

Cash	$14,560.00
Accounts receivable	$ 8,980.00

Sundry accounts:

Details: Securities	(July 14)....	$5,000.00
Gain on sale of securities	(July 14)....	580.00
Column total		5,580.00
		$14,560.00

Sales book: (Page 11)

Column total	$11,300.00

Problem B 14-3. The books of original entry used by Hobson Company are: journal, check register, cash receipts book, sales book, and voucher register. Assuming appropriate voucher, check, and page numbers, construct a voucher register for Hobson Company and record therein the necessary entries and notations for the selected transactions given below. The voucher register includes columns providing for deductions, vouchers payable, purchases, and sundry accounts.

1959
March 5—Purchased merchandise from Rockwell Co. on account, $3,000. Terms, 2/10; n/30.

       7—Paid P. Savage $6,030 for note due today. The face amount of the note was $6,000; interest previously recorded amounted to $23.

      8—Received merchandise from Mills & Sons, $8,000.

    10—Purchased office supplies from Utility Forms on account, $500. Terms, n/30.

          Mailed a check for $2,600 and a 5% note payable for $5,400 to Mills & Sons to cover the purchase of March 8.

    12—Refunded $850 to J. Meade, a customer, who had purchased merchandise for cash.

    13—Received merchandise from Bess Co. on account, $4,000. Terms, 1/10; n/30.

    14—Made a partial payment to Rockwell Co., $1,800 less 2% discount (see March 5).

    15—Returned merchandise costing $1,500 to Bess Co. and received a credit memo for that amount.

    16—Purchased delivery equipment from Safety Transit Co., $10,000. Terms were as follows: $4,000 down (payment made) and three equal monthly installments of $2,000.

    17—Received from J. P. Miles merchandise worth $1,200 previously sold to him on account. Credit is given to him for this amount on his present account.

    20—Paid Kelly Bros. $300 cash for March rent.

    22—Paid Bess Co. $2,500 less 1% discount (see March 13).

    24—Received merchandise from Marbury Corporation, $4,200, on account. Terms, 3/10; n/30, Invoice date, March 23.

March 28—Paid to Mills & Sons the 20-day, 5% note plus interest which was due today.

31—Paid office salaries, $450, and salesmen's salaries, $650, less withholding and F. I. C. A. taxes of $310. Employers' taxes on this payroll were: F. I. C. A. taxes, $24.75; state unemployment taxes, $29.70; federal unemployment taxes, $3.30.

Problem B 14-4. Set up the books of original entry for Three-J Corporation, record the July transactions given below, post to general ledger accounts, and prepare a trial balance and a schedule of vouchers payable as of July 31, 1958.

The company uses the following books of original entry, with money columns therein as indicated:

Journal: Debit, Credit.
Voucher register: Deductions, Vouchers Payable, Purchases, and Sundry Accounts.
Check register: Vouchers Payable, Purchase Discounts, and Cash.
Cash receipts book: Cash, Sales Discounts, Accounts Receivable, Sales, and Sundry Accounts.

1958
July 3—Capital stock was issued as follows: $10,000 to George Johnson for cash; $25,000 to Clare Jones for inventory; and $15,000 to Roy Joliet for equipment worth $7,800 and a 15-day, 6% note for $7,200.

5—Office supplies are purchased from Office Wholesalers, Inc., on account, $400. Terms, n/10.

7—Rent is paid for the month of July to Howard Walker, $250.

8—A four-year fire insurance policy is purchased from Welch Mutual for cash, $800.

10—Merchandise is purchased: $5,000 from Hatch Co., cash; $3,000 from Iceman Corp., on account (terms, 2/10; n/30).

12—Additional equipment costing $6,000 is purchased from Equipment Suppliers, Inc. A $1,600 down payment is made, with the balance payable in monthly installments of $1,100 each.

13—Cash sale, $2,000. 1% sales discount is allowed for cash.

14—Office Wholesalers, Inc., is paid $400 for the purchase of July 5.

15—Merchandise is received from Ralton Co., $3,700. Terms, 1/10; n/30.

17—Transportation charges on various incoming orders are paid to the L. A. Truck Co., $325.

18—Joliet's note of July 3 is collected in full, plus interest.
Merchandise costing $1,100 is returned to Ralton Co. and a credit memorandum is received.

20—Merchandise is received from B. B. Cast on account, $4,150. Terms, 1/10; n/30. Invoice date, July 19.
A 30-day, 5% note is given to Iceman Corp. for the net amount of their July 10 invoice.

22—Cash of $550 is refunded to B. Willard, a customer, who had purchased for cash.

24—A check is sent to Ralton Co. for the amount due. (See July 15.)

27—Cash sales, $6,560.

28—Partial payment is made on the July 19 invoice of B. B. Cast by issuing a check in the amount of $1,980. Cast's policy is to allow discounts on partial payments.

30—Merchandise is received from K. L. Prince on account, $4,750. Terms, 2/10; n/30.

July 31—Salaries for the month are paid: $800 less withholding and F. I. C. A. taxes of $180.   Employers' taxes are: F. I. C. A., $18; state unemployment, $21.60; and federal unemployment, $2.40.

ASSIGNMENT MATERIAL FOR CHAPTER 15

Questions

1. What is the purpose of a petty cash fund? Describe the procedure of setting up and operating a petty cash fund.

2. A company has been using a petty cash fund for many years. On June 1 of the current year, you notice the following debits and credits in the journals.

Debit: Petty cash.................................... 50.00
Credit: Vouchers payable............................ 50.00

Debit: Vouchers payable............................ 50.00
Credit: State Savings Bank.......................... 50.00

Provide suitable explanations for the above entries.

3. List several basic requirements for a good system of internal control with regard to cash.

4. Describe a suitable procedure for handling cash received through the mail.

5. Describe the operation of the Cash Over and Short account.

6. Explain the meaning of the following symbols found on a bank statement: *N.S.F.*, *S.C.*, and *P.S.*

7. A bank reconciliation will show the amounts of any "deposits in transit." How are such amounts computed?

8. How are certified checks handled when a bank reconciliation is being prepared?

9. How are bank overdrafts shown in the balance sheet?

Problems—Group A

Problem A 15-1. Excerpts from the cash records of Murchison-Smith Corporation are presented on the opposite page.

Required:

    (a) The corporation's bank reconciliation, showing the adjusted balances as of May 31, 1958.

    (b) Any necessary journal entries, assuming that the cash journals have been ruled and posted for the month of May.

Cash Receipts Book		Cash Disbursements Book		
Date	Debit Cash	Check No.	Date	Credit Cash
1958			1958	
May 1	29.18	605	May 1	259.12
1	250.00	606	2	418.35
2	163.12	607	2	262.19
3	195.18	608	3	110.03
3	26.62	609	4	111.55
3	186.60	610	4	2.69
4	78.12	611	6	100.35
5	90.02	612	7	120.39
8	112.95	613	10	142.18
8	31.91	614	11	210.29
10	419.89	615	13	124.15
12	265.03	616	17	69.80
12	19.18	617	18	135.14
12	100.28	618	20	109.02
15	273.19	619	26	147.18
17	42.12	620	27	216.08
19	86.03	621	29	57.33
19	4.12			2,595.84
21	29.30			
24	162.27			
24	110.17			
26	503.85			
28	90.49			
29	12.65			
30	102.87			
	3,385.14			

A bank account is held with Surety State Bank, whose statement for the month of May is presented below. All cash receipts are deposited. There were no outstanding checks or deposits in transit on April 30, 1958.

SURETY STATE BANK

Checks		Deposits	Date	Balance
Vouchers Returned 16		Balance from last statement Apr. 30, 1958		7,280.14
259.12		279.18	May 2, 1958	7,300.20
42.30 N.S.F.		163.12	May 3, 1958	7,421.02
418.35		408.40	May 4, 1958	7,411.07
.75 Ex.		78.12	May 5, 1958	7,488.44
2.69		90.02	May 6, 1958	7,575.77
2.82 Col.		144.86	May 9, 1958	7,717.81
262.19	111.55	419.89	May 11, 1958	7,763.96
120.39		384.49	May 14, 1958	8,028.06
142.18		273.19	May 16, 1958	8,159.07
210.29		42.12	May 18, 1958	7,990.90
109.02	1.25 Ex.	90.15	May 20, 1958	7,970.78
69.80		29.30	May 22, 1958	7,930.28
135.14		272.44	May 25, 1958	8,067.58
		503.85	May 27, 1958	8,571.43
216.08			May 29, 1958	8,355.35

Problem A 15-2. Below and on the following pages are presented the cash receipts and disbursements books of Murchison-Smith Corporation, as well as two bank statements for the month of June, 1958. The company opened an account with Union Trust Company on June 1.

From the information given, and the material in Problem A 15-1, prepare reconciliations of the two accounts and the necessary journal entries, assuming that the company's fiscal year ends June 30.

Cash Receipts Book

		DEBITS			CREDITS			
Date	Account Credited	Surety State Bank	Union Trust Company	Sales Discounts	Sundry Accounts		Accounts Receivable	
					L.F.	Amount	✓	Amount
1958								
June 2	Pure Distributing Co.		152 10				✓	152 10
4	Sales	490 08			50	490 08		
4	Apex Corporation	75 19					✓	75 19
6	Notes receivable	750 00			6	750 00		
7	General Manufacturing Co.		36 20	80			✓	37 00
9	Sales		120 53		50	120 53		
10	Interest earned		4 90		91	4 90		
10	Pure Distributing Co.		219 30	4 48			✓	223 78
12	Harry Moore	15 30					✓	15 30
15	Gordon & Roberts	111 59		3 50			✓	115 09
16	Sales	265 18			50	265 18		
18	Notes receivable		1,200 00		6	1,200 00		
20	General Manufacturing Co.		214 56				✓	214 56
22	Pure Distributing Co.	61 10		1 24			✓	62 34
24	Notes receivable	800 00			6	800 00		
27	Sales		56 20		50	56 20		
29	Harry Moore		110 03	3 40			✓	113 43
30	Gordon & Roberts	211 56		4 32			✓	215 88
		2,780 00	2,113 82	17 74		3,686 89	✓	1,224 67
		(1)	(2)	(59)				(4)

Cash Disbursements Book

Date	Payee	CREDITS — Cash — Surety State Bank Check No.	Amount	CREDITS — Cash — Union Trust Company Check No.	Amount	Purchase Discounts	Vo. No.	Debit Vouchers Payable
1958 June								
2	Grenfell Bros	622	120 06			6 00	1012	126 06
4	Simon Stewart	623	62 10				1040	62 10
4	City Telephone			624	40 87		1018	40 87
5	County Gas Co	625	102 83				1020	102 83
7	Payroll			101	590 37		1022	590 37
8	Stationery Supply Co	626	14 43				1015	14 43
9	Equipment Mfg. Co.	627	116 60			3 60	1019	120 20
9	Carl Gibson			102	291 32		1025	291 32
10	Burgess, Inc.			103	65 80		1017	65 80
12	Grenfell Bros.	628	2 53				1024	2 53
14	Carl Gibson			104	45 80	95	1016	46 75
16	Pierce Industries	629	135 11			2 76	1021	137 87
16	Palisades Supply			105	190 82		1030	190 82
19	Payroll			106	640 09		1031	640 09
23	District Director of Internal Revenue	630	21 93				1028	21 93
24	Burgess, Inc.	631	210 40			11 10	1026	221 50
28	Corliss-White, Inc.			107	85 33		1032	85 33
29	Frank Cyril	632	19 40				1029	19 40
30	Palisades Supply	633	180 44			3 70	1027	184 14
			985 83		1,950 40	28 11		2,964 34
			(1)		(2)	(69)		(31)

SURETY STATE BANK

Checks		Deposits	Date	Balances
Vouchers Returned __13__		Balance from last statement➝ May 31, 1958		8,355.35
		103.14	June 1, 1958	8,458.49
		102.87	June 2, 1958	8,561.36
110.03	120.06		June 3, 1958	8,331.27
40.87		565.27	June 5, 1958	8,855.67
147.18		750.00	June 7, 1958	9,458.49
5.40 Col.			June 9, 1958	9,453.09
57.33			June 11, 1958	9,395.76
2.53		15.30	June 13, 1958	9,408.53
100.35		376.77	June 16, 1958	9,684.95
135.11			June 19, 1958	9,549.84
102.83			June 21, 1958	9,447.01
		800.00	June 24, 1958	10,247.01
210.40			June 28, 1958	10,036.61
21.93	14.43	148.00	June 30, 1958	10,148.25

Checks and memos returned by Surety State Bank were as follows:

Checks			Memos	
No. 608	110.03	June 9	Collection charge........	5.40
619	147.18	30	Non-interest-bearing note	
622	120.06		collected..............	148.00
621	57.33			
624	40.87			
628	2.53			
611	100.35			
629	135.11			
625	102.83			
631	210.40			
630	21.93			
626	14.43			

UNION TRUST COMPANY

Checks		Deposits	Date	Balances
		Balance from last statement➝ May 31, 1958		—0—
		152.10	June 3, 1958	152.10
590.37			June 7, 1958	dr 438.27
		156.73	June 8, 1958	dr 281.54
36.20 P.S.			June 10, 1958	dr 317.74
		224.20	June 11, 1958	dr 93.54
45.80			June 15, 1958	dr 139.34
219.32	640.09	1,200.00	June 19, 1958	201.25
1.95 Col.		214.56	June 21, 1958	413.86
		61.10	June 23, 1958	474.96
		110.03	June 29, 1958	584.99

Returned checks and debit memos were as follows:

Checks		Memos		
No. 101	590.37	June 21	Collection charge.............	1.95
104	45.80	10	Payment stopped	
102	219.32		(General Manufacturing Co.)...	36.20
106	640.09			

Problem A 15-3. Howard Corp. uses the voucher system but decides to pay small expenses out of a petty cash fund. Following are the transactions of the fund for the month of February, 1957. The numbers at the extreme left indicate petty cash voucher numbers.

Prepare a petty cash record similar to the illustration in the text, with special columns for Transportation In, Cleaning, and Meals. Submit, in journal form, the entries that would result from the facts given, indicating the book of original entry in which each entry would be recorded.

     1957

     Feb. 5—A petty cash fund of $45 was established.

100   6—Paid the H. & O. Railroad for freight on merchandise purchased, $12.95, and for freight on goods sold, $4.32.

101   Bought advertising posters from Ace Printing Co., $8.69.

102   7—Paid for office cleaning, $4.50.

103   8—Gave Jim Jones $3.25 for carfare.

104   10—Paid telegraph company messenger $5.95 for telegrams.

105   11—Meals for overtime work paid, $2.90.

            12—The fund was replenished today. Owing to the apparent inadequacy of the amount, it was decided to increase it to $70.

106   13—Paid the H. & O. Railroad $11.62 for freight on merchandise purchased.

107   Purchased postage stamps, $1.65.

108   17—Paid for office cleaning, $6.90.

109   18—Paid Tom Dolby for delivery of advertising circulars, $7.50.

110   19—Drury Trucking was paid $4.90 for delivery of goods purchased to the company warehouse, and $2.40 for delivery of goods to a customer.

111   Had sign painted on door, $12.

112   Paid for meals due to overtime work, $6.

            The fund was replenished.

113   22—Paid for office cleaning, $3.50.

114   23—Purchased a gift for Tom Smith for his help in stock-taking, $2.50.

          28—Since the fiscal period ends on February 28, the fund was replenished.

The auditors have verified the cash on February 28 as being correct.

Problem A 15-4. Lawner Corporation uses a bank register in its books of account, and has an account with Fidelity Bank. Using the data on the following page relating to its banking operations, prepare the bank register for the month of February, 1959.

Bank Reconciliation—January 31, 1959

Balance, per books....................................		$1,610.02
Deduct deposit in transit..............................		260.18
		$1,349.84

Add outstanding checks:

#110	Dec. 16..............................	$195.90	
150	Jan. 29..............................	62.10	
151	30..............................	11.33	269.33
Balance, per bank....................................			$1,619.17

Bank Reconciliation—February 28, 1959

Balance, per books....................................		$ 311.83
Deduct deposit in transit..............................		124.46
		$ 187.37

Add outstanding checks:

#110	Dec. 16..............................	$195.90	
218	Feb. 28..............................	130.32	
219	28..............................	375.81	702.03
Balance, per bank....................................			$ 889.40

A list of the returned checks, as they appear on the bank statement for February, is presented below. The bookkeeper has put the date each check was written to the right of the amounts.

Date Paid	Amount	Date Written
Feb. 4	$ 62.10	Jan. 29
5	11.33	29
6	31.40	Feb. 4
6	59.14	4
9	8.75	7
9	29.20	7
10	157.59	7
12	254.30	10
17	219.06	15
17	100.80	15
19	80.17	15
22	413.27	17
23	241.86	20
25	30.46	24
28	427.92	26
28	3.95	28
28	629.03	17
28	62.80	26
	$2,823.13	

The deposits shown by the bank statement are given below. Occasionally cash is held over and two days' receipts are combined; these are indicated by (2). Otherwise, cash is deposited on the day following its receipt.

Date	Deposit	
Feb. 2	$ 260.18	
4	337.20	
7	129.12	
15	695.13	(2)*
17	410.75	
20	20.65	
26	240.33	(2)*
	$2,093.36	

*The register balances prior to these deposits were:

Feb. 10	$2,155.99
24	1,100.14

Problems—Group B

Problem B 15-1. From the following information relating to the banking activities of Scott Corp., prepare a bank reconciliation showing the adjusted bank balances as of February 28, 1957. The account is kept with Pacific Bank.

(1) The balance per ledger on February 1, 1957, is $11,395.18.
(2) Cash receipts for February, per the cash book, are $45,634.92; checks written during the month total $52,911.34.
(3) The statement from the bank shows a balance of $6,841.13 at the end of the month.
(4) Included in the returned checks is a memo stating that the check of M. Price has been returned marked N.S.F.; the amount is $842.17.
(5) An examination of the checks reveals that the following are still outstanding: No. 1593, $30.50; No. 1812, $110.38; No. 1962, $69.12; No. 2008, $117.39; No. 2009, $4.82; and No. 2010, $29.11.
(6) The bank has deducted from the account, in error, a check of Sprott, Inc.; the amount is $614.32.
(7) There is a deposit in transit at the end of February in the amount of $1,843.20.
(8) The bookkeeper made an error in recording a check received from R. Mason; the amount recorded was $94.76; it should have been $947.60.
(9) A debit memo shows that service charges amount to $42.10.
(10) During the month, the corporation borrowed $5,000 from the bank on a note discounted at 6% for six months. This item has not been entered in the books.

Problem B 15-2. From the following information, prepare a bank reconciliation of Morgan's, Inc., as of July 31, 1959.

1. The ledger shows a balance of $1,760.22 on July 31, 1959.
2. The bank statement shows a balance of $2,031.55 on July 31, 1959.
3. Cash on hand amounting to $419.83 has not been deposited in the bank.
4. An examination of the returned checks reveals that the following have not cleared: No. 197, $13.65; No. 198, $111.42; No. 210, $86.10; No. 213, $3.95; and No. 214, $440.83.
5. The bank statement shows $40.80 as the amount deducted for a certain check, while the check was made out for $40.08.
6. During July, R. D. Ellis, a customer, stopped payment of his check for $92.14.
7. The bank collected a non-interest-bearing note for the company's account; the face was $155; collection charges were $2.90.
8. Interest charges on outstanding loans, deducted by the bank, amounted to $15.03.
9. The bookkeeper recorded one of our checks made out for $321.92 as $312.92; the account was the Putnam Supply Co.
10. A certified check of $134.39, payable to Sells Company, is included among the checks returned.

Give the journal entries necessary to bring the ledger account up to date. The company closes its books on July 31.

Problem B 15-3. Mellow Distributors Company uses a voucher system. The company's fiscal year ends September 30. Prepare entries in general journal form to record the facts stated on the following page.

1958

Aug. 10—An imprest cash fund of $75 was established.

30—The composition of the fund was as follows:

Cash on hand:
Currency.............................	$29.00
Coin.................................	7.70

Receipts and vouchers for:
Office expense.........................	5.20
Express charges.......................	10.83
Tips (Charge Miscellaneous Expense)....	6.29
Overtime suppers.....................	16.40
Carfare..............................	1.50

Because the cash on hand is too large, the fund was reduced to $50 on this date.

Sept. 30—The composition of the fund was as follows:

Cash on hand:
Currency.............................	$ 3.00
Coin.................................	1.29

Receipts and vouchers for:
Office expense.........................	6.19
Express charges.......................	4.20
Tips.................................	19.11
Overtime suppers.....................	3.95
Carfare..............................	7.40
Flowers..............................	4.28

The fund was not replenished as of September 30, 1958, but a voucher to do so was prepared.

Problem B 15-4. Marchant Corporation, which uses the voucher system, has the following payroll for the week ending December 5, 1957:

Delivery salaries............	$422.00
Office salaries..............	124.00
Officers' salaries............	750.00

All employees are subject to the 2¼% F. I. C. A. tax and the 2.7% state unemployment insurance tax. The income tax withheld amounts to $185.17.

The company maintains a payroll bank account with Unity Trust Co.

Prepare entries to record the payroll for the week, including the payroll taxes.

Problem B 15-5. From the following information pertaining to Alden Realties, prepare bank reconciliations as of April 30, 1957, using the two methods shown in the text.

(1) The balance per ledger March 31, 1957, is $1,406.08.

(2) Total receipts for the month amount to $4,423.03.

(3) Disbursements for the month are $6,210.14.

(4) The bank statement shows a balance of $1,807.09 on April 30, 1957.

(5) The collection by the bank of a note in the amount of $400 has not been recorded.

(6) Checks outstanding on April 30, 1957, are: No. 2510, $965.08; No. 2815, $519.62; No. 2903, $408.11; No. 2904, $37.50; No. 2906, $2,003.19; and No. 2907, $993.79.

There were no outstanding checks on March 31, 1957.

(7) A deposit of $1,139.17 has been mailed to the bank but does not appear on the April statement. There were no deposits in transit on March 31, 1957.

(8) During April the bank charged the account of Alden Realties $2,000 for the face amount of a maturing bank loan. This charge has not been recorded on the books.

Problem B 15-6. Ellsworth Corp. was organized in 1957. During 1958, 3,000 shares of its capital stock were issued. On December 12, 1958, the directors declared a dividend of $1.50 per share, payable to stockholders of record December 21, 1958. The dividend was payable on January 15, 1959.

Submit entries in journal form arising from the above facts, assuming that the corporation uses a voucher system and maintains a special bank account for the dividend payments.

ASSIGNMENT MATERIAL FOR CHAPTER 16
Questions

1. How are accounts receivable from employees shown in the balance sheet?

2. Is it acceptable to offset accounts receivable and accounts payable if the same individual or business is involved?

3. Describe an acceptable procedure for accounting for C. O. D. sales.

4. What is a red balance in a subsidiary ledger? How are such balances presented in financial statements?

5. Describe the accounting procedure for bad debt recoveries.

6. Explain the nature and operation of an allowance for merchandise returns account.

7. What considerations determine whether an investment should or should not be classified as a current asset?

8. How are gains and losses arising from the sale of investments shown in financial statements?

9. Explain the nature of the following entry:

Investment in bonds.................................... 3.68	
Bond interest earned..............................	3.68

10. How should long-term investments be valued for balance sheet purposes?

Problems—Group A

Problem A 16-1. The following relates to the activities of Pearson Company for the month of March, 1958.

1958

March   5—Sold goods to Roger Parker on account, $2,150. Invoice No. 506.

      7—Sold goods to Smith and White, Paris, Ohio, for $340. Invoice No. 507. Terms, C. O. D.

        Bought goods from Lane Trading Co. on account, $12,465.

      8—Collected $340 from Smith and White for C. O. D. sale.

      9—Sold goods to L. Martin, Rome, N. Y., for $962. Invoice No. 508. Terms, C. O. D.

    10—Sold goods to S. Babcock on account, $1,143. Invoice No. 509. Received payment from Roger Parker, $2,150.

    11—Collected $962 from L. Martin for C. O. D. sale.

    12—Sold goods to Warner and Darrow on account, $575. Invoice No. 510.

    14—Issued a credit memo for goods returned by S. Babcock, $160.

    15—Bought goods from Dobson's, Inc., on account, $14,450. Sold goods to R. Malm, London, Ill., for $247. Invoice No. 511. Terms, C. O. D.

    16—Sold goods to J. Lecava, Boston, Mass., for $196. Invoice No. 512. Terms, C. O. D.

March 18—Received a check from S. Babcock for $993.
    20—Bought goods from Roger Parker on account, $840.
        Received a check from Warner and Darrow for $575.
    21—Collections were received covering the C. O. D. sales to R. Malm and J. Lecava.
    22—Bought goods from Dobson's, Inc., on account, $985.
    23—Sold goods to Roger Parker on account, $629.   Invoice No. 513.
    25—Sold goods to A. Moore, Carson, Nev., for $257.   Invoice No. 514. Terms, C. O. D.
    26—Paid Roger Parker $840.
        Bought goods from Lane Trading Co. on account, $9,975.
    27—Received a credit memo for goods returned to Roger Parker, $75.
    28—Paid Dobson's, Inc., $15,535.
    29—Bought goods from Roger Parker on account, $1,012.
    30—Issued a credit memo for goods returned by Roger Parker, $127.
        Issued a credit memo for goods returned by Warner and Darrow, $210.
        Paid Lane Trading Co. $12,465.
    31—Paid Roger Parker's account in full.

Required:

Subsidiary ledger accounts (omitting posting references).
C. O. D. register.
Schedules of accounts receivable and accounts payable as of March 31, 1958.
Relevant portions of the March 31, 1958 balance sheet showing the receivables and payables.

Problem A 16-2. Rialto Corporation had idle funds during its "slow" season and decided to invest in some securities. The following events occurred.

1959
June 10—A deposit of $3,000 was given to a stockbroker for contemplated purchase of securities.
    17—Bought 52 shares of Krispy stock at 65¼; the brokerage fee amounted to 1%. In addition, stamps costing 20 cents per share and incidental expenses of $1.42 were billed by the broker.
        Paid the stockbroker in full, after deducting the deposit.
July   1—Bought, through the same stockbroker, 38 Magnus Corp. $1,000 bonds at par, plus accrued interest at 4%. Interest dates are May 1 and November 1. The brokerage fee was $5 per bond.
     6—Sent check to stockbroker to cover bond purchase in full.
Aug.   4—Bought 106 shares of Purcel stock. This stock was purchased by the corporation as a long-term investment. The price was 11½, plus a brokerage fee of 1%. Additional charges were: stamps, 20 cents per share and incidental expenses, $.93. A dividend of $1.50 per share had been declared July 20, payable on August 15, to stockholders of record August 8. The same stockbroker handled the purchase.
    10—Sent check to stockbroker to cover purchase of August 4.
    15—Received dividend check on Purcel stock.
Sept. 30—The company's fiscal year ends September 30. Securities are quoted on the market on this day as follows: Krispy, 63½; Magnus, 98; Purcel, 10¾.

Required:

(a) Entries in general journal form to record the above.
(b) Relevant sections of the balance sheet on September 30, 1959.

Problem A 16-3.   The following was taken from the books of account of The Mason Corporation as of February 28, 1957.

ACCOUNTS RECEIVABLE SUBSIDIARY LEDGER
B. Armen

1956						
Dec.	4		S10	320.00		320.00
	20	Note	J 6		100.00	220.00
1957						
Feb.	10		S12	400.00		620.00

R. Dawson

1956						
Nov.	3		S 9	75.00		75.00
	15		CR20		75.00	—
Dec.	8		S10	212.00		212.00
	10	Return	J 6		40.00	172.00
	12		S10	89.00		261.00
	15		CR21		172.00	89.00
1957						
Jan.	9		S11	62.00		151.00
	15		CR22		62.00	89.00
	20		S11	214.00		303.00
	31		CR22		107.00	196.00

J. Masten

1956						
July	8		S 5	246.00		246.00
Oct.	8		S 8	317.00		563.00
	12		S 8	490.00		1,053.00
Nov.	9		CR20		807.00	246.00
Dec.	8		S10	517.00		763.00
1957						
Jan.	3		CR22		517.00	246.00
	11		S11	203.00		449.00
	15	Return on 1/11 sale	J 7		45.00	404.00
Feb.	1		S12	710.00		1,114.00

S. Porter

1956						
May	5		S 3	95.00		95.00
Sept.	15		S 7	212.00		307.00
Oct.	3		S 8	614.00		921.00
Nov.	1		CR20		614.00	307.00
Dec.	10		S10	530.00		837.00
	15	Return on 12/10 sale	J 6		57.00	780.00
1957						
Jan.	5	Note, applicable to 12/10 sale	J 7		400.00	380.00

R. Thomas

1957								
Jan.	10		S11	472.00				472.00
	20	Note receivable	J 7			200.00		272.00
	29		S11	409.00				681.00
Feb.	10		CR23			409.00		272.00
	15		S12	950.00				1,222.00
	22	Partial collection on 2/15 sale	CR23			650.00		572.00

J. Walker

1956								
Nov.	3		S 9	1,218.00				1,218.00
Dec.	4		CR21		1,218.00			—
1957								
Jan.	8		S11	550.00				550.00
	15		CR22			200.00		350.00
Feb.	10	Return	J 8			462.00	CR	112.00

The company decided to provide for doubtful accounts as follows:

1–30 days...............	2%
31–60 days...............	5%
61–90 days...............	15%
91 days to 6 months........	40%
Over 6 months............	70%

In addition, the management wishes to provide for various amounts that probably will not be collected as a result of expected returns, discounts, and freight, as follows:

Total expected returns are estimated to be 8% of sales for the year; there are returns of $4,218.93 to date on the sales of the current fiscal year.

Total expected discounts are estimated to be 3% of sales for the year; there are discounts of $1,901.40 to date on the sales of the current fiscal year.

An analysis of the freight charges reveals that an additional $577.60 should be provided for expected deductions.

Sales for the fiscal year ended February 28, 1957, were $73,490. The balance in the Allowance for Doubtful Accounts as of February 28, 1957, is $172.18.

Required:

An aging schedule.

Computation of the requirements for doubtful accounts.

Computation of the current provisions for doubtful accounts, expected returns, discounts, and freight deductions.

The related adjusting journal entries.

Problem A 16-4. Sunset Industries Company, which closes its books each December 31, had purchased the following bonds in 1958:

Three Series **X** Bonds of Georgian Corporation, $1,000 face; price, 102¾; purchased on February 1, 1958; maturity date, August 1, 1960.

Two State of Ashton Bonds, $500 face; price, 96⅛; purchased on June 1, 1958; maturity date, December 1, 1960.

Interest payment dates of the Series X Bonds: February 1 and August 1.
Interest payment dates of the Ashton Bonds: June 1 and December 1.

Rate of interest on the Series X Bonds, $3\frac{1}{2}\%$.
Rate of interest on the Ashton Bonds, 4%.

Required:

Schedules of amortization for the above bonds.
Journal entries on August 1, 1958, and December 1, 1958.

Problem A 16-5. Hall and Sons Company had the following transactions relating to purchases and sales of temporary investments in 1958:

1958
Jan. 10—Bought 40 shares of *X* stock for $152.50 per share.
Feb. 15—Bought 20 bonds of *B*, due January 1, 1960, for 100 plus accrued interest at 3%. The bonds have a face value of $1,000, with interest payable January 1 and July 1.
      19—Bought 1,000 shares of *Y* stock for $7.95 per share; a dividend had been declared payable March 1 to stockholders of record February 25. The dividend was 75¢ per share.
Mar. 1—The dividend was received.
      10—Sold 24 shares of *X* stock for $158 per share.
May   4—Bought 75 shares of *Z* stock for $40.10 per share.
June 1—Sold 20 bonds of *B* for 98 plus accrued interest.
      30—The company's fiscal year ends on June 30. Stock quotations, as of June 30, were:

$$X............. \$138.00$$
$$Y.............   7.20$$
$$Z.............   35.00$$

Sept. 6—Sold 60 shares of *Z* stock for $33 per share.

Prepare journal entries resulting from the above transactions and whatever entry is required as of June 30, considering the stock quotations.

Problems—Group B

Problem B 16-1. The March 31, 1958 balance sheet of Merson Corporation shows the following item under current assets: Accounts receivable, $160,419.83. The amount is composed of the following:

Regular customers—controlling account balance..	$157,295.39	
Less amount owing to customers—recorded in accounts payable ledger...................	4,451.80	$152,843.59
Subscriptions receivable (collected in April, 1958)............		1,500.00
Advances to employees................................		492.00
Accrued interest receivable..............................		167.48
C. O. D. customers..		2,145.63
Discount on preferred stock.............................		3,000.00
Red balances in accounts payable.............. $	692.18	
Less red balances in accounts receivable........	421.05	271.13
		$160,419.83

What amount should be reported in the balance sheet as accounts receivable?

Problem B 16-2. Parsons Sales Corporation has the following securities in its portfolio on December 31, 1958.

Stocks	Quantity	Par	Purchase Date	Cost	Dividend Declared	Rate	Dividend Date
Anpar Corp..........	27	No-par	9/10/58	83⅛	11/ 1/58	$1 share	Paid 12/17/58
Lektro Sales..........	135	$50	6/ 6/58	55½	12/23/58	6 %	Payable 1/10/59

Bonds	Quantity	Par	Purchase Date	Cost Per Bond	Interest Dates	Rate	Maturity
Government of Smilan..	10	$1,000	7/20/58	$1,000	Oct. 1 & Apr. 1	3 %	Oct. 1970
City of Dennis.........	44	$ 500	3/10/58	$ 500	Feb. 1 & Aug. 1	3½ %	Aug. 1968
Giant Supermarket.....	16	$1,000	9/18/58	$1,000	June 1 & Dec. 1	4 %	June 1972

The only accounts relating to the investments appearing in the trial balance (unadjusted) as of December 31, 1958, were as follows:

Investments in bonds   Dividends earned
Investments in stocks   Bond interest earned

Required:

Adjusting entries as of December 31, 1958, the fiscal year-end.
Entries in general journal form during the year 1959, relating to the investments.

Problem B 16-3. The following accounts were on the books of Potsdam Company on February 28, 1959.

ACCOUNTS RECEIVABLE SUBSIDIARY LEDGER
R. Furness

1958							
Sept.	16			S 3	1,780.00		1,780.00
Oct.	9			S 4	4,920.00		6,700.00
	22			CR 9		1,780.00	4,920.00
Dec.	3			S 6	2,015.00		6,935.00
	16			S 6	2,609.00		9,544.00
1959							
Jan.	6			CR12		2,609.00	6,935.00
Feb.	10			S 8	595.00		7,530.00
	22	Return on 2/10 sale		J 5		63.00	7,467.00

L. Mace

1958							
Aug.	8			S 2	850.00		850.00
Dec.	14	Return		J 3		124.00	726.00
1959							
Jan.	10			S 7	485.00		1,211.00
	17			S 7	211.00		1,422.00
Feb.	10			CR13		696.00	726.00

G. White

1958							
Oct.	17			S 4	880.00		880.00
	24			CR 9		75.00	805.00
Dec.	3			S 6	591.00		1,396.00
1959							
Jan.	17			S 7	283.00		1,679.00
Feb.	21	Note		J 5		591.00	1,088.00

C. Zaab

1958							
June	8		S50	1,450.00			1,450.00
Sept.	12		S 3	314.00			1,764.00
	19		CR 8		1,250.00		514.00
	28		CR 8		314.00		200.00
Dec.	4		S 6	1,076.00			1,276.00
	6		CR11			538.00	738.00
1959							
Feb.	10		S 8	619.00			1,357.00

The company provides for doubtful accounts on the basis of the age of the receivables, as follows:

1–30 days	1%
31–60 days	5%
61–90 days	10%
91 days to 6 months	35%
Over 6 months	42%

There is a balance of $2,132.03 in the allowance account on February 28, 1959.

Required:

An aging schedule.
Computation of the allowance requirements.
The related adjusting entry.

Problem B 16-4. Walton Corporation bought a $1,000 bond of X Company as a long-term investment on July 1, 1958. The price paid was 104⅞. Interest at 3¾% is payable on January 1 and July 1. The maturity date is January 1, 1966.

On November 17, 1958, the company bought ten shares of M stock, at 112½, as a short-term investment. The company closes its books on December 31, and on that date in 1958, the market value of M stock was 109. On January 10, 1959, the investment was sold for 102¼.

Give all entries in journal form, starting July 1, 1958, and ending January 10, 1959, that would be made as a result of the above facts. Also prepare an amortization schedule for the bond.

Problem B 16-5. Stoller Corporation had the following transactions relating to its accounts receivable during June and July of 1958.

1958
June 20—Sold goods to Alan Smith for $740; freight charges to be paid by customer. Terms, 3/10; n/30; f.o.b. destination.
　　23—Sold goods to Calvin Rinder for $453. Terms, 3/10; n/30.
　　25—Sold goods to Stan Morton for $1,230. Terms, 3/10; n/30.
　　26—Calvin Rinder returned goods with an invoice price of $85. We issued a credit memo.
　　27—Received a check from Alan Smith, accompanied by a paid freight bill for $42.50, in payment of the goods purchased by him on June 20.
July　3—Received a check from Stan Morton for $800 to apply on his account. It is the company's policy to allow discounts on customers' partial payments.
　　7—Received a check from Calvin Rinder for payment in full.

July 10—Sold goods to Joshua Moll for $380. Terms, 3/10; n/30.

12—A non-interest-bearing note receivable for $590 from M. Shore, a customer, is dishonored and is written off as uncollectible.

17—Received a check from Joshua Moll in settlement of the July 10 transaction.

19—Received $400 cash from the trustee of the estate of R. Logan, a customer whose account had been written off. A notification enclosed stated that the entire amount originally due, $620, is collectible.

20—Joshua Moll returned one-fourth of the shipment of July 10. We issued a credit memo.

22—Since the entry for the return by Joshua Moll created a credit balance in his account, the corporation issued a check covering the return.

Prepare entries in general journal form to record the above transactions.

ASSIGNMENT MATERIAL FOR CHAPTER 17
Questions

1. Describe the basic contrasting features of the periodical and perpetual inventory methods.

2. Is it ever acceptable to include in a physical inventory goods not on hand?

3. Devise an illustration to show how inventory errors affect net income.

4. What elements are properly included in cost for inventory-pricing purposes?

5. Describe the operation of the last-in, first-out inventory method.

6. Define the term "market" as it is used in applying the cost-or-market basis of inventory valuation.

7. Describe the acceptable ways of applying the cost-or-market method.

8. How is obsolete merchandise priced for inventory purposes?

9. Devise an illustration showing how inventories may be estimated by the gross profit method.

10. Is it acceptable to show inventories at retail in the financial statements, provided the retail inventory method is followed?

11. Will an inventory pricing method have any effect on the financial statements? Explain.

Problems—Group A

Problem A 17-1. The inventory on December 1, 1958, of a particular class of merchandise of Bentley Corporation consisted of 180 units priced at a unit cost of $2. Purchases during the month of December were made as follows:

Date	Quantity	Unit Cost
December 6	50	$2.00
12	100	1.96
14	70	2.10
18	40	2.20
23	110	2.30

On December 31, 1958, 200 units were on hand, as determined by count.

Compute the closing inventory, using each of the following methods of determining cost: (a) weighted average; (b) first-in, first-out; and (c) last-in, first-out.

Problem A 17-2. Lake Suppliers, Inc., was organized on January 1, 1958. A summary of the purchases and sales during 1958, for the two categories of merchandise handled, is presented below:

	Quantity		Unit Price		
	Purchased	Sold	Cost	Market	Retail
Boats:					
Rowboats....................	15	11	$100	$105	$ 125
Canoes..	10	7	160	150	200
Outboard runabouts..........	20	14	325	310	400
Inboards....................	5	2	950	940	1,200

	Quantity		Unit Price		
	Purchased	Sold	Cost	Market	Retail
Outboard motors:					
5HP........................	30	24	95	100	125
10HP........................	33	22	180	175	220
15HP........................	25	15	250	250	300
25HP........................	10	5	290	300	375

(a) Compute the ending inventory at the lower of cost or market, applying the method to: (1) each item in the inventory; (2) the inventory in each category; and (3) the entire inventory.

(b) Show how each application of the cost-or-market rule affects the gross profit.

Problem A 17-3. The following information relating to the merchandise transactions of Hanson Company is available for the month of September 1959:

	Date	Article Code	Quantity	Price	Amount
Inventory......	Sept. 1	CDF	250	$10	$2,500
		KKL	500	12	6,000
		RSU	425	8	3,400
Purchases......	5	KKL	100	11	1,100
		RSU	80	9	720
	10	CDF	75	9	675
		KKL	80	12	960
		RSU	90	10	900
	20	CDF	100	11	1,100
	25	CDF	50	12	600
		KKL	120	10	1,200
		RSU	130	9	1,170
Purchase returns	12	KKL (Sept. 5)	10	11	110
	18	RSU (Sept. 10)	20	10	200
Sales for the month		CDF*	210	15	3,150
		KKL	240	18	4,320
		RSU	305	14	4,270

* Details of sales of CDF:

Sept. 4................	100
15................	30
28................	80

(a) Compute the gross profit for September, using (1) the *lifo* inventory method and (2) the *fifo* inventory method, at cost.

(b) Prepare a perpetual inventory card for article CDF, assuming that the company uses the *fifo* inventory method.

Problem A 17-4. Brighton Brothers operates a retail store and a fountain‧ A summary of various inventory data for the month of January, 1959, is as follows:

	Regular		Fountain	
	Cost	Retail	Cost	Retail
Inventory, December 31, 1958.......	$45,000	$67,860	$2,500	$4,200
Inventory, January 31 (physical count, at retail)........................	—	72,000	—	4,750
Purchases........................	13,775	20,500	780	1,400
Sales............................	—	16,000	—	1,000
Transportation in..................	125	—	80	—
Purchase returns..................	300	460	—	—
Sales returns.....................	—	550	—	—
Sales discounts...................	—	450	—	—

From the foregoing information, compute by the retail inventory method the inventory amounts which would be used for balance sheet purposes as of January 31, 1959.

Problems—Group B

Problem B 17-1. Burr Company's inventory of fuel oil on December 31, 1958, was 10,000 gallons, which cost $.23 per gallon. The inventory on June 30, 1959, was 14,000 gallons. All sales during the six-month period were made at $.30 per gallon, and purchases for the period were as follows:

Date	Quantity (Gallons)	Cost
January 15	7,000	$1,540
March 1	9,000	2,090
April 15	5,000	1,200
May 5	8,000	1,920
May 26	5,000	1,250
June 20	6,000	1,440
Totals	40,000	$9,440

Using (a) weighted-average; (b) first-in, first-out; and (c) last-in, first-out methods of determining cost, prepare partial income statements showing the gross profit on sales. You are to assume that the perpetual inventory procedure was used and that no fuel oil was lost by evaporation or leakage.

Problem B 17-2. Universal Appliance Store maintains two departments— main salesroom and bargain basement.

On December 31, 1958, the inventory was composed of the items shown below:

		Unit Price	
	Quantity	Cost	Market
Main salesroom:			
Refrigerators	75	$170	$173
Dryers	120	85	85
Dishwashers	50	60	65
Automatic washers	30	160	150
Bargain basement:			
Refrigerators	15	140	142
Dryers	25	50	50
Dishwashers	40	40	42
Automatic washers	60	100	90

Compute the closing inventory at the lower of cost or market, applying the method to: (a) each item in the inventory; (b) the inventory in each department; (c) the entire inventory.

Problem B 17-3. Lynn Company, a department store, has a fiscal year ending January 31 and uses the retail inventory method. The management suspected Mrs. *A*, a sales clerk with exclusive control of Department *M*, of theft, and hence took a surprise inventory of her department on March 15, 1959. Valuation of the inventory at this time was $4,400, retail.

Investigation of company records reveals the following information relevant to Department *M* for the six-week period:

Inventory, January 31, at retail	$4,950
Inventory, January 31, at cost	3,400
Purchases, at retail	1,650
Purchases, at cost	1,170

Sales..................................	$1,600
Transportation in.......................	80
Purchase allowances.....................	30

In past years the company has experienced shrinkage losses due to customer theft, breakage, and the like, but the costs thereof, in total, have never exceeded ten per cent of total sales.

Compute the minimum apparent loss to the company, at cost, due to theft during the six-week period ending March 15, 1959.

Problem B 17-4. The Corner Store lost its entire stock of merchandise as a result of a fire which occurred during the night of April 10, 1959. Most of the accounting records were destroyed. However, the company's accountant was able to recover assorted documents and schedules which permitted him to compute several account balances, as follows:

As of January 31, 1959, the company's fiscal-year end:

Inventory.............................	$11,300
Cash.................................	3,875
Retained earnings.....................	17,800

As of April 10, 1959:

Purchases.............................	$ 8,470
Purchase returns and allowances..........	83
Transportation in......................	137
Sales................................	17,370
Salesmen's commissions..................	868
Store rent expense......................	320
Cash.................................	4,122
Retained earnings......................	17,800

The president of the company had placed a condensed income statement for the preceding year in his safe-deposit box. This is shown below:

THE CORNER STORE
Condensed Income Statement
For the Year Ended January 31, 1959

Sales..		$88,000.00
Cost of goods sold.....................................		52,800.00
Gross profit..		$35,200.00
Deduct:		
Selling expenses..........................	$18,440.00	
Administrative expenses...................	8,560.00	27,000.00
Net income before income taxes.........................		$ 8,200.00
Income taxes...		3,800.00
Net income...		$ 4,400.00

Estimate the cost of the inventory destroyed by the fire.

Problem B 17-5. The after-closing trial balance of MacDonald Corporation as of December 31, 1959, included the following:

Account	Amount
Inventory—Product A...............	$ 9,000
Inventory—Product B...............	7,100
Retained earnings..................	10,000

An audit of the inventory accounts and procedures of the company reveals the following data:

(1) Purchases of 200 units of product A costing $8 each (November 30) in transit on December 31, 1959, were not included in the closing inventory, although the invoice from the vendor had been entered in the purchases journal. The goods were shipped f.o.b. MacDonald Corporation's plant.

(2) 100 units of product A were sold to Hawk Company, and the sale was recorded. Hawk Company requested that delivery be postponed until January 15, 1960. The cost of these goods was included in the product A inventory on December 31, 1959, although title had passed to Hawk Company.

(3) The purchases journal also included a purchase of 30 units of product B at $18 each which was in transit on December 31, 1959, and not included in the closing inventory. These goods had been shipped f.o.b. shipping point.

(4) Another group of 80 units of product B had also been excluded from the ending inventory because they were not on hand when the inventory count was made. These units were shipped to Davies Wholesalers on consignment, and, as of December 31, had not been sold by the consignee.

(5) The company uses the *fifo* inventory valuation method. The accountant had computed the ending inventory, using the following data:

Product A				Product B			
Date	Quantity	Price	Total	Date	Quantity	Price	Total
1959				1959			
Jan. 1 Inventory....	1,000	$10	$10,000	Jan. 1 Inventory.....	400	$14	$ 5,600
Feb. 15 Purchase.....	300	11	3,300	Jan. 20 Purchase......	100	15	1,500
Apr. 1 Purchase.....	200	12	2,400	Mar. 25 Purchase......	120	16	1,920
Apr. 28 Purchase.....	200	12	2,400	May 30 Purchase......	150	16	2,400
June 5 Purchase.....	250	11	2,750	July 15 Purchase......	110	17	1,870
Aug. 1 Purchase.....	350	9	3,150	Sept. 10 Purchase......	90	18	1,620
Oct. 1 Purchase.....	300	8	2,400	Nov. 1 Purchase......	130	17	2,210
Nov. 30 Purchase.....	400	8	3,200	Dec. 15 Purchase......	80	19	1,520
Totals..............	3,000		$29,600		1,180		$18,640
Dec. 31 Inventory....	900			Dec. 31 Inventory.....	500		

His computations were as follows:

Product A: 900 × $10 = $9,000   Product B: 400 × $14 = $5,600
                                            100 × $15 = 1,500
                                   Total... 500 $7,100

(a) Compute the correct inventory balances as of December 31, 1959, for MacDonald Corporation.

(b) Prepare a schedule showing how retained earnings would be affected by your corrections. Ignore any income tax adjustments which might be necessary.

ASSIGNMENT MATERIAL FOR CHAPTER 18
Questions

1. How are fixed assets valued for accounting purposes?

2. Is it ever acceptable accounting to charge the cost of a building to the Land account?

3. Suppose that a company can construct a particular fixed asset for less than it costs to purchase it, but elects to purchase the fixed asset anyway. Is it acceptable to record such an asset at the construction cost figure, since it is below the purchase price?

4. Is it ever acceptable to value land at the lower of cost or market?

5. Contrast depreciation and depletion.

6. Describe two methods of accounting for depreciation program revisions.

7. What use does the accountant make of scrap value?

8. What charges may be made to an accumulated depreciation account?

9. Describe two methods of accounting for trade-ins.

10. Is it ever considered acceptable to depreciate an asset over a period shorter than its useful life?

11. Does amortization accounting apply to all intangible assets?

12. Should the following be charged to the asset account, to the related accumulated depreciation account, or to expense?

    (a) Broker's commission in connection with the purchase of real estate.
    (b) Property taxes accrued at the date of purchase.
    (c) Property taxes after purchase.
    (d) Cost of remodeling a section of the building to convert it into an office.
    (e) Annual painting and decorating costs.

Problems—Group A

Problem A 18-1. Given below are facts relating to the purchase of three machines by Molten Corporation on January 1, 1958. Prepare a schedule of depreciation data showing total cost of the machines, annual depreciation charge for each machine, accumulated total depreciation for all machines, and the carrying value of the group for the eight-year period ending December 31, 1965, assuming that depreciation was computed by (a) the straight-line method and (b) the sum-of-years'-digits method.

	Machine A	Machine B	Machine C
Cost....................	$7,500	$7,500	$7,500
Scrap value.............	None	1,200	300
Estimated life...........	5 years	6 years	8 years

Problem A 18-2. Pilmont Company was organized on January 1, 1958. At the end of 1958, its ledger contained a Land and Buildings account with debits

647

and credits as shown below. According to the bookkeeper, the entries had been made in accordance with the accounting principle that all costs during the construction period should be capitalized. Analyze and reclassify the items charged to this account, indicating the proper account to which each item should have been charged.

Debits:

Cost of land and old buildings (Appraised values at time of purchase: Building A, $15,000; Building B, $20,000; Building C, $25,000; Land, $40,000. Building B was to be retained and Buildings A and C were being demolished.)	$ 90,000.00
Broker's commission on above purchase	900.00
Attorney's fees for the year:	
Incorporating the company	500.00
Patent investigation	300.00
Examination of real estate title	150.00
Cost of demolishing Buildings A and C	7,000.00
Contract cost of new building completed June 30, 1958	260,000.00
Cost of rehabilitation of Building B, completed June 30, 1958	19,200.00
Landscaping:	
1957	300.00
1958	300.00
Interest on $260,000 for six months at 5% (The new building was paid for with the funds obtained from the sale of preferred stock.)	6,500.00
Material, labor, and overhead costs of partitions and other interior items installed by company employees	11,600.00
Saving on interior work. A contractor bid $14,100 to do the work done by company employees for $11,600	2,500.00
Salary of Bill Johns for the first six months of the year (Johns supervised the building construction; after July 1 he became maintenance director.)	2,000.00
Real estate taxes for 1958	4,000.00
Discount on $360,000 of preferred stock issued for cash to obtain funds for purchase of land and old buildings and construction of new building	10,800.00
Par value of preferred stock given to a contractor for his services in grading, landscaping, laying sidewalks, etc. (This stock was issued on the same date as the preferred stock mentioned immediately above.)	20,000.00
Cost of building a fence around the property	3,000.00
Plumbing repairs made in November and December	300.00
Repairs necessitated by a severe windstorm in October	4,000.00
Total debits	$443,350.00

Credits:

Proceeds from sale of salvage from buildings demolished	$ 5,000.00
Proceeds from sale of portion of land	9,000.00
Recovery from insurance company for windstorm damages	3,000.00
Total credits	$ 17,000.00
Balance	$426,350.00

Problem A 18-3. For each item of equipment listed on the following page, give journal entries for the following:

(1) The purchase of the asset by Satellite Company.
(2) The depreciation at the end of each of the first two accounting periods. (The company is on a calendar-year basis.)
(3) The disposal of the asset, following the income tax rule.

Date Acquired	Cost	Estimated Scrap Value	Estimated Useful Life	Depreciation Method	Disposal Date	Disposal Details
(a) 7/ 1/56	$1,150	$150	5 years	Straight-line	12/31/57	Traded in on (b)
(b) 12/31/57	$600 plus trade-in	$250	6 years	Straight-line	1/ 3/62	Sold for $525
(c) 1/ 2/57	$900	—0—	5 years	Sum-of-years'-digits	10/ 1/59	Traded in on (d)
(d) 10/ 1/59	$875 plus trade-in	$140	4 years	Straight-line	12/31/63	Sold as scrap for $150

Problem A 18-4. W. W. Walker Company started business on January 1, 1955, taking over the operations of the UVW partnership. Included in the assets purchased for cash were the following:

Machine A, $5,000; estimated remaining life, 5 years; scrap value, $500.
Machine B, $5,800; estimated remaining life, 8 years; scrap value, $400.
Machine C, $5,500; estimated remaining life, 10 years; scrap value, none.
Patents, $4,200; expiration date, January 1, 1958.
Goodwill, $3,000.

On October 1, 1955, Machine D (estimated life, 7 years; scrap value, $280) was purchased from White Efficiency Company for $6,000; terms, 2/10; n/30. Payment for this machine was made on October 8, 1955.

By the end of the first year of operations, it became apparent that the goodwill purchased from the old partnership had little significant value, and therefore it was completely written off.

Machine A was thoroughly reconditioned early in 1957. Payment for these improvements was made January 15, 1957, in the amount of $1,200 (estimated life extended two years; scrap value, $500).

On April 1, 1957, Machine C was sold for $3,500. On July 1, 1957, Machine E (estimated life, 5 years; scrap value, none) and Machine F (estimated life, 7 years; scrap value, $100) were purchased from Ellis Corporation for $8,100, cash. Machine E was appraised at $5,000 and Machine F at $4,000.

The patents were written off when they became fully amortized.

On January 1, 1958, Machine B was traded in for Machine G, which had a list price of $6,000. Although Machine B was actually worth only $2,500, an allowance of $2,800 was received for it; the balance of the list price was paid in cash. The life of Machine G was estimated as ten years, with a scrap value of $200. (Do not follow the income tax procedure.)

During the fall of 1959, it became apparent that Machine D would become obsolete by the end of 1960, and that the undepreciated cost should be written off over the newly estimated remaining life. However, it appeared that $160 would be received as scrap at the end of this time.

(A) Prepare journal entries for all of the transactions above, including the proper depreciation (sum-of-years'-digits method) and amortization (straight-line method) entries made at the end of each year through 1959.

(B) Post the above entries where applicable to the Machinery or Accumulated Depreciation—Machinery accounts, showing their balances as of December 31, 1959.

(C) Prepare a schedule showing (1) the cost of the machines on hand on December 31, 1959, and (2) the depreciation accumulated to date on those machines.

Problems—Group B

Problem B 18-1. The Fixed Assets section of the balance sheet of Carroll Company as of December 31, 1958, is on the following page.

CARROLL COMPANY
Partial Balance Sheet
December 31, 1958

Fixed assets:

Land, buildings, and equipment...........	$153,100.00	
Less accumulated depreciation..........	46,500.00	$106,600.00
Intangibles..		30,000.00

Amounts taken from ledger accounts which supported this portion of the balance sheet were:

Land.	$15,000.00	
Patents.............................	5,100.00	
Delivery equipment........................	18,000.00	
Buildings.................................	80,000.00	
Machinery..............................	35,000.00	$153,100.00
Less accumulated depreciation or amortization:		
Patents............................	$ 1,500.00	
Delivery equipment.................	6,000.00	
Buildings...........................	24,000.00	
Machinery.........................	15,000.00	46,500.00
Land, buildings, and equipment.........................		$106,600.00
Goodwill...		30,000.00

Required:

Two alternative balance sheet presentations of the fixed assets in more acceptable form.

Problem B 18-2. In 1956, Cool Ore Corporation paid $86,000 for a mine which was estimated to contain 400,000 tons of ore. Early in 1959, another deposit, estimated at 85,000 tons in total, was discovered adjacent to the mine, but the vein also extended to other property not owned at that time. The company paid $10,900 for the additional property. Ore was mined in the following quantities during the four-year period:

1956..............	35,000 tons
1957..............	68,000 tons
1958..............	87,000 tons
1959..............	90,000 tons

Make the proper journal entry recording the depletion charge for 1959. (Show your computations.)

Problem B 18-3. On April 1, 1956, Barton Company purchased a used machine at a cost of $5,400. This piece of equipment was overhauled at a cost of $480, and accessories costing $120 were added for use with the machine. An electrician was paid $210 to check the wiring in the machine and for his services in connection with the installation, which was completed on May 1, 1956. On September 1, 1956, the same electrician performed additional electrical repair work, for which the company paid $80. It is considered unlikely that the machine will have any scrap value.

The company's balance sheet as of December 31, 1959, contained the following account balances:

Machinery....................................	$5,400.00	
Less accumulated depreciation..............	2,200.00	$3,200.00

The income statements show the following amounts of net income:

1956.............	$3,568.00	1958.............	$4,650.00
1957.............	4,234.00	1959.............	4,728.00

Compute the correct amount of depreciation for each year, assuming that the straight-line method of depreciation was used; show the effect of the above errors on the reported earnings, and show what the annual net income figures would have been if the above-stated expenditures had been given the proper accounting treatment.

Problem B 18-4. The partnership agreement of KIM and Company provides: "In case of death or dissolution, the goodwill of the firm shall be computed as twice the average earnings for the preceding five full years in excess of 7½% on the average investment of all partners during the five-year period." Elsewhere in the articles of partnership, provision was made for the sharing of profits and losses as follows: Karn, 30%; Ireland, 45%; and Melcori, 25%. The partners decided to sell their business outright, and later Teller Corporation agreed to purchase the business as of March 31, 1959.

Analysis of the partnership accounts revealed the following information:

	Annual	Capital Account Balances, December 31		
Year	Earnings	Karn	Ireland	Melcori
1954...............	$ 7,850	$24,000	$36,000	$20,000
1955...............	9,160	29,000	43,000	20,000
1956...............	10,300	37,000	47,000	21,000
1957...............	10,940	37,000	51,000	22,000
1958...............	11,750	38,000	53,000	22,000

Because the partnership will be dissolved as a result of the sale, you are asked to compute the value of the goodwill in accordance with the partnership agreement and to present the required entry to record goodwill on the partnership books.

Problem B 18-5. Medium Company owns three machines. The machines have no scrap value. On different dates during 1959, the machines are traded in on new machines.

Machinery

1955		
July 1	Machine A	3,000.00
1956		
Jan. 2	Machine B	4,000.00
1957		
May 1	Machine C	4,800.00

Accumulated Depreciation—Machinery

1955	
Dec. 31	250.00
1956	
Dec. 31	1,500.00
1957	
Dec. 31	2,300.00
1958	
Dec. 31	2,700.00

Data on trade-ins:

Machine Traded In	Date of Trade-in	List Price of New Machine	Allowance on Old Machine	Cash Value of Old Machine	Accounting Method to Be Followed
A.........	1/ 2/59	$3,200	$1,400	$1,200	Income tax rule
B.........	10/ 1/59	4,175	525	450	Recognize cash value of old asset
C.........	12/30/59	5,000	1,450	1,425	Treat trade-in allowance as selling price of old asset

(a) Give the entries required at the time of each trade-in.
(b) Set up a schedule to show the depreciation that would have been taken on each of the three machines during the four years ended December 31, 1958, if the sum-of-years'-digits method had been used by Medium Company.

Problem B 18-6. An audit of the books of Polk Company in early January, 1960, reveals some peculiarities in accounting for equipment, as indicated by the following data:

Schedule of Depreciation
Machine #123

Cost: $8,000   Estimated scrap value: $1,000   Depreciation rate: 10%

Year	Debit Depreciation	Credit Accumulated Depreciation	Total Accumulated Depreciation	Carrying Value
				$8,000
1955.........	$800	$800	$ 800	7,200
1956.........	720	720	1,520	6,480
1957.........	324	324	1,844	6,156
Trade-in for machine #124			(1,844)	(6,156)
			—0—	—0—

Schedule of Depreciation
Machine #124

Cost: $10,000   Estimated scrap value: $2,000   Depreciation rate: 10%

Year	Debit Depreciation	Credit Accumulated Depreciation	Total Accumulated Depreciation	Carrying Value
				$10,000
1957.........	$500	$500	$ 500	9,500
1958.........	950	950	1,450	8,550
1959.........	855	855	2,305	7,695

The following entry was recorded in the journal on July 1, 1957:

```
July 1  Equipment (Machine #124)....................  10,000
          Accumulated depreciation—Equipment..........   1,844
            Gain on disposal of equipment..............            1,344
            Cash..................................            2,500
            Equipment (Machine #123)...............            8,000
          Trade-in of Machine #123 for Machine #124 plus
          cash.  (Cash value of Machine #123, $6,500;
          list price of Machine #124, $10,000.)
```

Further analysis and discussion bring out the fact that the company uses the straight-line method of depreciation and normally records new assets from trade-ins at cash plus actual cash value of old assets.   The former accountant is no longer an employee of the company, and hence no ready explanation of the errors is available.

Prepare schedules of depreciation for machines #123 and #124 as they should have been prepared under the circumstances, and submit the entry necessary to correct the accounts as of December 31, 1959.

ASSIGNMENT MATERIAL FOR CHAPTER 19
Questions

1. Cite one example of a performance obligation account and explain the debit-credit operation of the account.

2. When long-term liabilities approach maturity, should they be classified as current liabilities in all situations? Explain.

3. Unissued bonds of a face value of $10,000, bearing 6% interest, are sold for $10,200 two months after the interest payment date. Give the entry or entries required to record this transaction.

4. What reasons would you give in favor of setting up a separate bank account for the payment of bond interest?

5. Would you consider it acceptable to offset for balance sheet purposes the undisbursed balance in a bond interest bank account and the liability representing the unpresented bond interest coupons?

6. Would you consider it acceptable to deduct the balance in a bond discount account from the balance in a bond premium account and show the net amount as a deferred credit in the balance sheet?

7. What is the difference in the nature of a sinking fund and a sinking fund reserve?

8. Under what circumstances would the bond interest cost exceed the interest rate printed on the bonds?

9. Give an appraisal of the effectiveness of a sinking fund reserve in achieving the objective for which it is established.

10. Describe a method of accounting by which discounts lost by failure to pay bills within the discount period may be shown in the financial statements.

11. What is a contingent liability? Where are contingent liabilities shown in the financial statements?

Problems—Group A

Problem A 19-1. Midwest Company is authorized to issue $100,000 of 3%, 7-year debentures dated March 1, 1958. Interest is to be paid semiannually on February 28 and August 31. On July 1, 1958, all of the debentures are issued at 96 plus accrued interest.

Prepare all entries through December 31, 1958, the close of the company's accounting period.

Problem A 19-2. On April 1, 1958, Coaster Corporation issued at par plus accrued interest $200,000 of bonds dated February 1, 1958. 6% interest on the 20-year bonds was to be paid semiannually on January 31 and July 31.

Interest was to be paid by means of interest coupons, the first of which came due July 31, 1958. A deposit, against which interest coupons will be charged, is to be made with City Bank each interest date.

Prepare journal entries to record the issuance of the bonds, the July 31, 1958 interest payment to City Bank, the payment by City Bank of $5,600 in honoring interest coupons, and the entries necessary to adjust the books as of November 30, 1958, the close of Coaster Corporation's accounting period.

Problem A 19-3.   Hollow Corporation has a fiscal year ending November 30. The corporation maintains an account to show purchase discounts lost.   Prepare entries required during November in general journal form for the following transactions.

1958

November   3—Merchandise is purchased from Style Company with a billed price of $600 and with terms of 3/10; n/30.

7—Merchandise is purchased from Fancy Corporation for cash. The merchandise has a list price of $500, but a discount of 1% is granted for all cash transactions.

10—Paid Style Company for the purchase of November 3.

12—Merchandise is purchased from Zero Company with a billed price of $200 and with terms of 2/10; n/30.

15—Store supplies are purchased from Ace Supply Company.   The invoice for the supplies totals $50.   The following terms are printed on the bottom of the invoice: "Add 2% of bill if not paid by first of following month."

17—Merchandise is purchased from White Company with a billed price of $620 and with terms of 2/10; n/30.

22—The store supplies are paid for.

29—Paid $200 to Zero Company for the purchase of November 12.

Problem A 19-4.   Swallow Corporation has a 5%, five-year bond issue maturing December 31, 1960.   Under the terms of the bond issue, $5,000 must be deposited annually in a special savings account under the control of a trustee. The account earns 3% interest annually, the interest being added to the account. At maturity, the trustee is to retire the bond issue and return any remaining balance in the special savings account to the corporation.

Selected accounts from the ledger of Swallow Corporation relating to the years prior to 1959 are presented below in T-account form.

Bonds Payable

	12/31/55	25,000.00

Bond Retirement Fund

12/31/56	5,000.00	
12/31/57	150.00	
12/31/57	5,000.00	
12/31/58	304.50	
12/31/58	5,000.00	

Reserve for Bond Retirement Fund

	12/31/56	5,000.00
	12/31/57	5,000.00
	12/31/58	5,000.00

Bond Discount

12/31/55	800.00	12/31/56	160.00
		12/31/57	160.00
		12/31/58	160.00

Required:

All journal entries, except closing entries, affecting the above accounts during the years 1959 and 1960.

Problem A 19-5. Using the trial balance and supplementary information, present all required adjusting entries as of December 31, 1958. (Ignore income taxes.)

HART COMPANY
Trial Balance
December 31, 1958

Cash..	3,170.00	
Inventory...	43,400.00	
Sinking fund securities, as of September 30, 1958	44,000.00	
Land..	76,000.00	
Accounts payable, all at net of discount		14,720.00
Bond premium.......................................		1,200.00
Bonds payable, 6%, due September 30, 1961...		50,000.00
Common stock......................................		50,000.00
Retained earnings.................................		35,795.00
Sales..		198,500.90
Purchases...	123,720.00	
Selling expenses..................................	30,630.00	
Discounts lost....................................	180.00	
Administrative expenses...........................	28,110.00	
Bond interest expense.............................	1,950.00	
Sinking fund income...............................		945.00
	351,160.00	351,160.00

Supplementary information:

(1) When the semiannual bond interest was paid on September 30, 1958, the Bond Premium account was correctly debited for $200. There have been no entries to the account during October, November, or December, 1958.

(2) The sinking fund is fully invested in interest-bearing securities; all of the securities in the fund bear the same interest rate. Each September 30, the company transfers sufficient cash to the fund so that, with the interest which is collected annually on September 30 and the cash transfer, the fund increases by $2,000 each year. The trustee immediately invests such additional funds in securities. On September 30, 1958, pursuant to the above terms, the company transferred $740 to the trustee.

(3) 2% discount has been lost on accounts payable being carried net at $2,156.

Problems—Group B

Problem B 19-1. Common Corporation closes its books annually on December 31. On April 1, 1958, the corporation issued $800,000 of 4% first-mortgage bonds. The bonds mature in 15 years, and interest is payable semiannually.

Prepare the journal entries (except closing entries) required during 1958 to account for the bonds described above, assuming that the bonds were issued at:

(a) 98½.
(b) 103.

Problem B 19-2. Prepare the balance sheet of Regional Corporation. The corporation is organized in a state where treasury stock acquisitions must not impair the stated capital.

REGIONAL CORPORATION
After-Closing Trial Balance
December 31, 1958

Cash...	15,400	
State Bank—Bond interest account.................	800	
Sinking fund cash...............................	500	
Notes receivable...............................	8,000	
Inventory.......................................	25,000	
Investments (non-current).......................	15,000	
Land (for future building site).................	20,000	
Bond discount—4% first-mortgage bonds...........	1,000	
Sinking fund securities.........................	6,000	
Equipment.......................................	90,000	
Accumulated depreciation........................		20,000
Accrued interest payable........................		800
Provision for service inspections...............		3,000
Accounts payable................................		17,000
Accrued taxes...................................		9,000
Estimated liability from six months' guaranty.......		5,000
Reserve for sinking fund........................		6,500
Bond premium—Sinking fund debentures...........		500
4% first-mortgage bonds payable—1970.............		40,000
5% sinking fund debentures payable—1972..........		25,000
Preferred stock, $10 par, 6%.....................		15,000
Common stock, no-par; 20,000 shares authorized; 17,500 shares issued............................		23,000
Treasury stock—Common, 500 shares, at cost........	1,100	
Retained earnings......		18,000
	182,800	182,800

Problem B 19-3. On July 1, 1950, Rose Corporation issued $100,000 of 4%, 10-year sinking fund bonds at 101. Interest on the bonds is payable annually on June 30, the close of the corporation's fiscal year. The bond indenture provides for a sinking fund to enable the trustee thereof to pay for the bonds at maturity. The trustee is required to keep the sinking fund fully invested.

During the latter part of June, 1960, just prior to maturity, the trustee of the sinking fund disposes of all of the sinking fund securities, carried at $100,000, and incurs a loss of $800.

Give all entries, omitting dates, relating to the bond issue and the sinking fund during June, 1960. The bond obligation is settled by the trustee at the end of that month.

Problem B 19-4. Tiger Corporation was organized on July 1, 1958. Its adjusted trial balance as of July 31, 1958, is as follows:

TIGER CORPORATION
Adjusted Trial Balance
July 31, 1958

Cash	11,850.00	
Accounts receivable	9,700.00	
Store equipment	9,600.00	
Accumulated depreciation		80.00
Accounts payable		7,000.00
Common stock		15,000.00
Sales		58,500.00
Purchases	47,000.00	
Purchase returns		2,000.00
Purchase discounts		700.00
Selling expenses	2,300.00	
General expenses	2,750.00	
Depreciation expense	80.00	
	83,280.00	83,280.00

Additional data:

(1) All merchandise is purchased under terms of 2/10; n/30.
(2) All merchandise returned by Tiger Corporation is returned within five days of purchase.
(3) As of July 31, 1958, the discount period had lapsed on $1,000 of outstanding accounts payable.

Required:

The July 31, 1958 adjusted trial balance as it would have appeared if the corporation had used the net price procedure for recording purchases.

Problem B 19-5. Selected accounts from three trial balances of Dynamic Corporation are presented in comparative form.

DYNAMIC CORPORATION
Trial Balances

	12/31/57		12/31/58
Debits	Unadjusted	Adjusted	Unadjusted
Cash	18,000	16,000	12,250
Sinking fund	—	—	2,800
Bond discount	595	590	540
Bond interest expense	150*	155	1,550
Credits			
Bonds payable, 6%, due 10/31/67	30,000	30,000	30,000
Retained earnings	6,000	7,500	9,800
Sinking fund reserve	—	—	—
Accrued bond interest payable	—	300	—

* Credit.

The bonds are ten-year bonds, with interest payable semiannually. The corporation received $29,555 when the bonds were issued. Each October 31 during the life of the bond issue, $3,000 of retained earnings are to be transferred to a "restricted" account.

Using the information given, prepare adjusting entries as of December 31, 1958.

ASSIGNMENT MATERIAL FOR CHAPTER 20

Questions

1. What are the three elements of manufacturing cost?

2. Distinguish between direct labor and indirect labor.

3. Tell in which element of manufacturing cost the following would be classified:

    (a) Floor-sweeping material.
    (b) Wages paid the factory timekeeper.
    (c) A machine operator's wages.
    (d) Sheet metal to be used in making filing cabinets to be sold.
    (e) Sheet metal to be used in making filing cabinets for the office.
    (f) First-aid kit for the factory.
    (g) Towels for the factory office.
    (h) Parts to be used in a machine to be sold.

4. How do the working papers of a manufacturing business and those of a trading business differ?

5. If you were given the amount for the cost of goods sold, what would you do to compute the cost of goods manufactured?

6. If an expense account balance is to be apportioned, how is such apportionment handled in the working papers?

7. Explain how space can be saved in books of original entry by the use of account numbers.

8. Describe the operation of expense controlling accounts.

Problems—Group A

Problem A 20-1. The adjusted trial balance of The Wells Corporation is presented on page 660, covering the year ended June 30, 1959.

The following allocations are to be made on June 30, 1959:

	Manufacturing	Selling	General
Heat, light, and power...................	62%	17%	21%
Depreciation—Furniture and fixtures.......	—	72%	28%
Taxes..................................	65%	20%	15%

(Carry all computations to the nearest dollar.)

Inventories—June 30, 1959:
Finished goods...........................	$15,300
Goods in process.........................	8,640
Raw materials...........................	4,805

Required:

Working papers for the year ended June 30, 1959.
Statement of cost of goods manufactured.
Entries to close the books, as of June 30, 1959.

THE WELLS CORPORATION
Adjusted Trial Balance
June 30, 1959

Cash..	7,152	
Accounts receivable..............................	17,000	
Allowance for doubtful accounts...................		3,410
Inventories—June 30, 1958:		
Finished goods................................	3,600	
Goods in process........	9,210	
Raw materials................................	5,790	
Machinery and equipment.........................	25,730	
Accumulated depreciation—Machinery and equipment		12,836
Furniture and fixtures............................	6,528	
Accumulated depreciation—Furniture and fixtures....		2,162
Accounts payable.................................		12,455
Capital stock....................................		40,000
Retained earnings................................		12,104
Dividends.......................................	1,500	
Sales..		108,450
Sales discounts..................................	791	
Purchases—Raw materials........................	61,132	
Purchase returns and allowances...................		1,544
Transportation in...............................	1,007	
Direct labor.....................................	9,066	
Indirect labor...................................	10,476	
Factory rent....................................	2,100	
Heat, light, and power...........................	1,983	
Machinery repairs	612	
Taxes...	300	
Depreciation—Machinery and equipment............	1,901	
Advertising......................................	3,250	
Salesmen's salaries........	6,353	
Selling expenses.................................	1,275	
Officers' salaries................................	7,000	
Office salaries...................................	2,783	
Depreciation—Furniture and fixtures..............	1,175	
Bad debts expense...............................	1,560	
Federal income tax........	3,687	
	192,961	192,961

Problem A 20-2. The adjusted trial balance of Crest Manufacturing Company, as of April 30, 1958, is presented on page 661. Prepare working papers and statement of cost of goods manufactured, using the following additional data:

Inventories—April 30, 1958:
Finished goods.........................	$13,449.00
Goods in process.......................	68,611.00
Raw materials.........................	21,440.00

Apportionments:	Manufacturing	Selling	General
Heat, light, and power..............	90%	7%	3%
Telephone.......................	10%	80%	10%
Depreciation of furniture and fixtures.	—	75%	25%
Insurance—Merchandise...........	37%	63%	
It is deemed advisable to distribute the expenses of the buildings, i.e., insurance, depreciation, and repairs, as follows......................	72%	16%	12%

CREST MANUFACTURING COMPANY
Adjusted Trial Balance
April 30, 1958

Cash	15,593.00	
Inventories—April 30, 1957:		
Finished goods	17,420.00	
Goods in process	61,317.00	
Raw materials	25,903.00	
Unexpired insurance	1,620.00	
Land	20,000.00	
Buildings	95,000.00	
Accumulated depreciation—Buildings		8,900.00
Machinery and equipment	161,450.00	
Accumulated depreciation—M. & E.		107,307.25
Furniture and fixtures	10,440.00	
Accumulated depreciation—F. & F.		7,746.20
Accounts payable		19,557.00
Capital stock		200,000.00
Retained earnings		69,993.00
Sales		535,420.00
Purchases—Raw materials	190,425.00	
Purchase returns and allowances		22,118.00
Transportation in	11,140.00	
Direct labor	171,668.00	
Indirect labor	43,060.00	
Heat, light, and power	40,560.00	
Building repairs	3,980.00	
Machinery repairs	1,920.00	
Depreciation expense—Buildings	2,850.00	
Depreciation expense—Machinery and equipment	20,181.25	
Insurance—Buildings	1,385.10	
Insurance—Machinery and equipment	850.50	
Factory supplies used	10,833.00	
Salesmen's commissions	38,411.00	
Insurance—Inventories	194.40	
Office salaries	22,500.00	
Telephone	1,505.00	
Depreciation expense—Furniture and fixtures	835.20	
	971,041.45	971,041.45

Problem A 20-3. Using the data below, prepare a statement of cost of goods manufactured for Fern Corporation for the month of June, 1958.

June manufacturing overhead:	
Indirect labor	$14,280.10
Heat, light, and power	3,120.45
Building and equipment repairs	879.92
Depreciation expense—Building and equipment	5,700.00
Insurance expense	1,400.00
Miscellaneous factory expense	4,721.33
Inventories—June 1, 1958:	
Finished goods	$13,111.80
Goods in process	4,250.00
Raw materials	15,570.00
Inventories—June 30, 1958:	
Finished goods	$14,202.70
Goods in process	4,840.00
Raw materials	13,140.00

The manufacturing overhead amounts to 50 per cent of the direct labor, and the direct labor and manufacturing overhead combined equal 50 per cent of the total cost of manufacturing. All materials are purchased f.o.b. receiving point. There were no purchase returns and allowances in June, but the corporation took discounts on its purchase obligations in the amount of $891.60.

Problem A 20-4. The trial balance of Wall Corporation, as of December 31, 1959, is presented below:

WALL CORPORATION
Trial Balance
December 31, 1959

Cash..	15,973.06	
Accounts receivable.........................	71,391.69	
Allowance for doubtful accounts.............		2,011.86
Inventories—December 31, 1958:		
Finished goods...........................	4,015.83	
Goods in process.........................	3,411.18	
Raw materials...........................	1,655.08	
Unexpired insurance........................	1,410.00	
Land.......................................	5,000.00	
Buildings..................................	12,200.00	
Accumulated depreciation—Buildings..........		1,859.92
Machinery and equipment....................	8,349.95	
Accumulated depreciation—M. & E...........		2,735.14
Delivery equipment.........................	1,345.32	
Accumulated depreciation—Delivery equipment		671.35
Furniture and fixtures......................	3,938.99	
Accumulated depreciation—F. & F............		2,610.77
Accounts payable...........................		10,692.22
Capital stock..............................		75,000.00
Retained earnings..........................		4,015.75
Dividends..................................	1,050.00	
Sales......................................		198,562.39
Sales returns and allowances................	3,529.85	
Sales discounts............................	2,416.83	
Purchases—Raw materials...................	97,019.36	
Purchase returns and allowances.............		1,642.81
Purchase discounts.........................		415.14
Transportation in..........................	2,919.22	
Direct labor...............................	33,911.01	
Indirect labor.............................	7,062.10	
Taxes—Real estate.........................	925.86	
Heat, light, and power.....................	2,116.44	
Repairs—Buildings.........................	354.41	
Repairs—Machinery and equipment...........	192.96	
Factory supplies used......................	1,244.13	
Miscellaneous factory expense...............	722.84	
Salesmen's salaries........................	5,312.56	
Advertising................................	2,063.18	
Repairs—Delivery equipment.................	429.90	
Delivery expense...........................	806.10	
Officers' salaries..........................	4,000.00	
Office salaries.............................	3,114.62	
Postage and stationery......................	1,927.92	
Miscellaneous general expense...............	319.12	
Interest expense...........................	448.22	
Interest earned............................		360.38
	300,577.73	300,577.73

Additional data:
Depreciation:
Buildings—2% per annum
Machinery and equipment—8½% per annum
Delivery equipment—25% per annum
Furniture and fixtures—12½% per annum

Insurance:
An examination of the insurance policies reveals that the following policies were in effect throughout 1959:

	Term	Premium
Buildings.............................	4 years	$ 300
Machinery and equipment..............	3 years	840
Delivery equipment...................	3 years	270
Merchandise (finished)................	5 years	410
		$1,820

Accrued wages and salaries:

Factory line workers...........................	$1,150
Plant foremen................................	126
Salesmen......................................	280
Drivers.......................................	162
Office clerks..................................	195
	$1,913

(Ignore payroll taxes in this problem.)

The following apportionments are to be made as of December 31, 1959:

	Manufacturing	Selling	General
Building expenses (repairs, depreciation, and insurance)....................	65%	—	35%
Real estate taxes....................	80%	15%	5%
Heat, light, and power..............	70%	20%	10%
Postage and stationery..............	5%	20%	75%
Depreciation—Furniture and fixtures...	—	60%	40%
Insurance (See schedule above.)			

Inventories—December 31, 1959:
Finished goods................. $4,329.91
Goods in process............... 2,941.73
Raw materials................. 2,091.47

Required:

Working papers.
Statement of cost of goods manufactured.
Income statement.

Problem A 20-5. The January, 1959 voucher register of *XYZ* Manufacturing Company is presented on the following page. A portion of the company's chart of accounts is shown on page 665.
Make all postings from the voucher register to the manufacturing expense analysis record and to the several general ledger accounts involved in the January transactions recorded in the voucher register.

Voucher Register

Line No.	Voucher No.	Date	Payee	Paid Date	Check No.	Vouchers Payable 2120	Purchases Raw Material 5171	Freight In 5172	Mfg Expense 5300 Acct. No.	✓	Amount	Sundry Accounts Debit Acct. No.	✓	Amount
1	1-1	1959 Jan. 2	Public Utility Co.	4	1	178 20			5315		178 20			
2	1-2	Jan. 3	Equipment Company	12	4	8,000 00						1331		8,000 00
3	1-3	Jan. 5	Clinton Service Co.	11	3	212 50			5328		212 50			
4	1-4	Jan. 6	King Corporation	15	6	3,200 00	3,200 00							
5	1-5	Jan. 8	Regional Truckers	9	2	37 30		37 30						
6	1-6	Jan. 9	Supply, Inc.	13	5	133 70			5381		133 70			
7	1-7	Jan. 11	State Insurance Co.			81 80			5384		81 80			
8	1-8	Jan. 14	Supply, Inc.	22	8	27 35			5381		27 35			
9	1-9	Jan. 16	National Corporation			4,128 00	4,128 00							
10	1-10	Jan. 19	Rapid Railway	20	7	57 16		57 16						
11	1-11	Jan. 22	General Technics			101 00			5338		101 00			
12	1-12	Jan. 23	Mountain Suppliers	25	9	31 11			5390		31 11			
13	1-13	Jan. 24	Kooler Co.			17 05			5390		17 05			
14	1-14	Jan. 26	Bond interest	27	10	1,000 00						7091		1,000 00
15			account											
16	1-15	Jan. 28	General Service Co.			51 00			5338		51 00			
17	1-16	Jan. 30	Clean Corporation			62 00			5381		62 00			
18	1-17	Jan. 31	Paymaster			2,710 00			5301		2,710 00			
						20,028 17	7,328 00	94 46			3,605 71			9,000 00

Number	Account
1331	Machinery and Equipment
2120	Vouchers Payable
5171	Purchases—Raw Material
5172	Freight In
5300	Manufacturing Expense—Control
	5301—Indirect Labor
	5315—Heat, Light, and Power
	5328—Repairs to Buildings
	5329—Depreciation—Buildings
	5338—Repairs to Machinery and Equipment
	5339—Depreciation—Machinery and Equipment
	5349—Depreciation—Tools
	5381—Factory Supplies
	5384—Insurance
	5390—Miscellaneous
7091	Bond Interest Expense

Problems—Group B

Problem B 20-1. From the information below, which pertains to the fiscal year ending September 30, 1959, prepare a statement of cost of goods manufactured for Kroll Manufacturing Company. All adjustments have been made.

Depreciation expense—Machinery	$ 5,400.00
Direct labor	17,927.17
Factory supplies used	1,003.90
Freight out	693.01
Heat, light, and power (factory)	1,639.61
Indirect labor	865.98
Insurance on factory	441.79
Inventories, September 30, 1958:	
Finished goods	6,530.19
Goods in process	1,538.72
Raw materials	15,478.10
Machinery repairs	511.69
Purchases—Raw materials	47,589.19
Purchase returns and allowances	1,980.02
Purchase discounts	495.20
Sales	73,814.28
Sales discounts	1,419.87
Salesmen's commissions	2,128.74
Transportation in	3,516.08

The ending inventories were determined to be as follows:

Finished goods	$ 7,290.12
Goods in process	1,307.20
Raw materials	12,648.93

Problem B 20-2. Using the information given in Problem A 20-4, prepare adjusting and closing entries.

Problem B 20-3. The following data pertain to the operations of L. L. Harris Company from May 1, 1957, to April 30, 1958.

Changes in inventories:	
Finished goods decreased by	$ 19,453
Goods in process decreased by	3,410
Raw materials increased by	10,541

Purchases—Raw materials..................	$ 92,596
Purchase returns and allowances............	1,380
Purchase discounts.......................	2,631
Direct labor costs........................	129,667
Manufacturing overhead incurred...........	56,619

From the above information, compute the following:

(a) Cost of manufacturing.
(b) Cost of goods manufactured.
(c) Cost of goods sold.

Problem B 20-4. The adjusted trial balance as of May 31, 1957, of Maron Corporation is given below.

MARON CORPORATION
Adjusted Trial Balance
May 31, 1957

Cash...	8,450	
Notes receivable.................................	6,600	
Finished goods inventory..........................	45,000	
Goods in process inventory........................	8,900	
Raw materials inventory...........................	62,400	
Prepaid taxes.....................................	1,270	
Machinery..	83,000	
Accumulated depreciation—Machinery...............		36,600
Accounts payable.................................		47,980
Accrued salaries and wages payable.................		240
Loans payable....................................		27,000
Capital stock....................................		60,000
Retained earnings.................................		12,680
Dividends..	3,000	
Sales..		198,520
Sales returns and allowances.......................	5,720	
Sales discounts...................................	1,690	
Purchases—Raw materials.........................	52,600	
Purchase returns and allowances...................		4,540
Purchase discounts................................		1,990
Transportation in................................	3,450	
Direct labor.....................................	31,630	
Indirect labor....................................	9,210	
Heat, light, and power............................	3,800	
Factory rent.....................................	5,000	
Factory insurance................................	1,740	
Depreciation—Machinery..........................	8,300	
Miscellaneous factory expenses.....................	11,450	
Advertising......................................	7,200	
Salesmen's salaries...............................	9,500	
Delivery expense.................................	3,410	
Miscellaneous selling expenses.....................	880	
Officers' salaries.................................	7,500	
Office salaries....................................	3,000	
Stationery.......................................	540	
Bad debts expense................................	1,780	
Interest expense..................................	440	
Interest earned...................................		1,160
Federal income tax...............................	3,250	
	390,710	390,710

May 31, 1957 inventories:

Finished goods...................	$61,150
Goods in process................	7,360
Raw materials...................	42,710

Heat, light, and power is allocated as follows:

Factory..........................	80%
Warehouse.......................	15%
Office...........................	5%

Required:

   (a) Working papers.
   (b) Closing entries.

Corporation Practice Set

This practice set is based on the transactions of Baker Corporation for the month of August. The current year should be used in all dates.

Charts of the general ledger accounts and the subsidiary expense accounts appear on the inside covers of the general ledger and the books of original entry. The general ledger contains the following controlling accounts:

1120—ACCOUNTS RECEIVABLE.
This account controls an accounts receivable subsidiary ledger.
2120—VOUCHERS PAYABLE.
5300—MANUFACTURING EXPENSE—CONTROL.
6000—SELLING EXPENSE—CONTROL.
7000—GENERAL EXPENSE—CONTROL.
Accounts 5300, 6000, and 7000 control expense analysis records, or distribution sheets, containing columns for the subsidiary accounts. You will make postings to the manufacturing expense analysis record. It is assumed that your assistant makes the postings to the other analysis records.

You will record transactions in the following books of original entry:

General journal.
Sales book.
Cash receipts book.
Voucher register.
Cash disbursements book (Check register).

Payroll summaries will be prepared by an assistant; postings from the summaries will be made by you. At some time before payroll entries are posted, you should read the material in Chapter 7 and in the appendix dealing with payroll deductions and taxes.

Postings, except column totals, should be made daily from all books of original entry.

Expenses and revenues wholly applicable to August should be recorded directly in expense and revenue accounts. Expense and revenue items not wholly applicable to August should be recorded in prepaid expense and deferred revenue accounts. Transfers from these accounts to expense and revenue accounts will be made by adjusting entries at the end of the month.

TRANSACTIONS

(The numbers in parentheses are transaction numbers; they are not to be entered in the records.)

August 1:
(1) Baker Corporation is organized with an authorized capitalization of 5,000 shares of capital stock, all of which is issued for cash at its par value of $100.

(2) Purchase the following assets of Douglas Brothers:

Accounts receivable	$10,850.75	
Less allowance for doubtful accounts	350.00	$ 10,500.75
Finished goods		75,926.35
Goods in process		35,286.40
Raw materials		57,942.67
Land		60,000.00
Buildings		140,000.00
Machinery and equipment		155,000.00
Tools		3,600.00
Delivery equipment		6,000.00
Furniture and fixtures		4,800.00
Patents		9,000.00
		$558,056.17

Record the purchase by a journal entry.

The accounts receivable acquired are detailed below:

George Booth	$10,513.60
J. H. Fowler	195.80
G. E. Nicholson	141.35
	$10,850.75

Enter these balances in the accounts receivable subsidiary ledger.

(3) Baker Corporation has authorized the issuance of $120,000 par value of 10-year, 5% real estate mortgage bonds. In part payment for the assets acquired from them, Douglas Brothers take the entire issue at a two per cent premium.

(4) Pay Douglas Brothers cash for the balance of the indebtedness to them.

August 2:

(5) Pay Daily News $23.45 for want ads for factory labor. (Account 5390)

(6) Issue a check for $1,000 to sales manager T. R. Price as an advance for salesmen's traveling expenses.

August 3:

(7) Give a 30-day, 6% note for $30,000 to Oliver Wharton for a purchase of machinery.

(8) Draw a check for $200 to the order of the petty cashier to establish a petty cash fund.

August 4:

(9) Purchase from Estee Company (terms, 2/10; n/30):

Raw materials	$53,412.45
Factory supplies	3,105.25
	$56,517.70

It is expected that the supplies will last several months.

August 5:

(10) Receive a 10-day, non-interest note from George Booth, dated today, for $10,513.60. (In order to compress within the limits of one month the transactions which it is desired to include in this practice set, the time periods of notes are unusually short.)

August 6:

(11) Sale to Arthur King, $46,500; terms, 2/10; n/30.

(12) Insurance policies expiring one year from August 1 are received today from Scott Insurance Agency, together with their bill for $4,920. The bill is paid.

August 8:

(13) Sale to Howard Tyrone, $22,000; terms, 2/10; n/30.

August 9:

(14) Write off J. H. Fowler's $195.80 account as uncollectible.

(15) Sale to Frank Anderson, $25,000; terms, 2/10; n/30. F.o.b. shipping point.

August 10:

(16) Pay Oliver Stevenson, attorney, $200 for examination of title to the land acquired from Douglas Brothers. The examination was made in July.

August 11:

(17) Purchase raw materials from Davis & Brown, $22,070; terms, 10-day acceptance for amount of invoice less 2% discount. We accept the draft today.

August 12:

(18) On August 5, G. E. Nicholson's account, $141.35, was placed in the hands of an attorney for collection. The attorney collected the account. The proceeds are received today, less $25 attorney's fee.

(19) Sale to Fred Nathan, $12,000; terms, 10-day sight draft less 2% cash discount. The acceptance is received today and is discounted at First State Bank; proceeds, $11,740.40.

August 13:

(20) Sale to William Camp, $15,950; terms, 2/10; n/30.

(21) Pay East and West Railroad freight bill, which is detailed below:

$335.00 On sale to Frank Anderson on August 9. Since the terms of this sale required that Anderson bear the expense of the freight, the $335 should be charged to him. (The charge should be entered in the Sundry Debits section of the voucher register; the customer's name should be written in the Remarks column to indicate the account in the subsidiary ledger to which the item should be posted.)
295.80 On sales.
275.00 On raw materials purchased.
$905.80

(22) Pay Estee Company voucher No. 5 for $56,517.70, less a credit memorandum for $600 received today and less 2% cash discount. Record all of these facts in the cash disbursements book.

August 15:

(23) Collect from George Booth the $10,513.60 non-interest note received from him on August 5.

(24) Sale to David Edwards, $8,000; terms, 10-day sight draft less 2% discount. Receive the acceptance in the face amount of $7,840

August 16:

(25) Sale to G. E. Gaines, $24,000; terms, 30-day, 6% note. The note is received.

(26) Collect from Arthur King the $46,500 invoice of August 6, less 2% discount.

(27) The payroll clerk has prepared the payroll summary for the first half of August, included in the pamphlet of books of original entry.

Your work in connection with the payroll consists of the following:

(a) Post to the general ledger accounts and to the manufacturing expense analysis record. (It is assumed that your assistant posts to the selling and general expense analysis records.) The accounts to be debited and credited are indicated on the payroll summary.

(b) Record a voucher and check payable to Payroll for the net payroll amount shown by the payroll summary.

August 17:

(28) Sale to Oscar Lewis, $32,000; terms, 2/10; n/30.

(29) Receive a check for $24,828.30 from Frank Anderson for the sale of August 9 and the $335 freight charge of August 13. In computing the amount of his remittance, Anderson erroneously took discount on the freight charge as well as on the amount of the sale. He is allowed discount on the sale price and is informed that he did not pay his account in full.

August 18:

(30) Sale to Robertson & Company, $15,300; terms, 2/10; n/30.

(31) Receive a bill from Paine's Print Shop, terms, 15 days, detailed as follows:

Sales forms (account 6090) . . . . $ 75.20
Office forms (account 7012) 68.40
                                                 $143.60

August 19:

(32) A credit memorandum is issued to Robertson & Company to correct a $500 error in overfooting their invoice of August 18. Since this credit memorandum was not issued for either a return or an allowance, but to correct an error in the billed amount, the record of the credit memorandum should not involve a debit to Sales Returns and Allowances.

August 20:

(33) Pay Davis & Brown acceptance.

(34) Effective today, part of one of our buildings has been rented to Millen Hardware Company for one year, at $300 per month. The first month's rent is collected today.

August 22:

(35) Machinery is purchased for $39,750 from Franklin Machine Co. Half of the purchase price is paid today; the remainder is payable September 22.

August 23:

(36) Issue credit memorandum for $800 to Oscar Lewis because of defective goods sold him on August 17.

(37) Purchase raw materials from R. C. Mather, $26,948. Terms, 2/10; n/30.

(38) Upon inquiry we are informed that Fred Nathan paid his $11,760 acceptance which we discounted at the bank on August 12.

August 24:

(39) Sale of merchandise to Daniel Norton, $24,500; terms, 2/10; n/30.

(40) Purchase raw materials from Walton and Morgan, $33,260; terms, 1/10; n/30.

August 25:

(41) Merchandise in the amount of $8,000 was sold to David Edwards on August 15, and a 10-day acceptance was received from him for the amount of the invoice less 2% discount. Edwards dishonored the acceptance today, and thereby forfeited the discount.

(42) Pay Albert & Co. $425 for installing the machinery purchased from Franklin Machine Co.

August 26:

(43) Collect from Oscar Lewis the amount of the invoice of August 17, less the credit memorandum issued on August 23, and less 2% cash discount.

August 27:

(44) On August 18 a sale was made to Robertson & Company in the billed amount of $15,300. On August 19 a credit memorandum for $500 was issued to correct an overfooting of the invoice. A check for $14,994 is received from Robertson & Company today. They apparently overlooked the credit memorandum, took too much discount, and overpaid their account. They are notified.

August 29:

(45) Collect from Howard Tyrone the amount of the invoice of August 8, $22,000. The discount period has expired.

(46) Pay Benson Corporation for the following:

Crane for delivery truck...............	$1,200
Tires—to replace tires worn out........	140
	$1,340

August 30:

(47) Pay East and West Railroad freight bill, which is detailed as follows:

$325.65	On machinery purchased from Franklin Machine Co.
419.50	On raw materials purchased.
116.29	On sales.
$861.44	

August 31:

(48) City Garage bills us for the following items, payable September 10:

Repairs...........................	$ 93.40
Gas and oil.......................	108.56
	$201.96

(49) Issue a check for $449.65 to the petty cashier to increase the fund to $500 after replenishing it for the following disbursements:

6075	Sales circulars..............	$ 73.15
7011	Typewriter supplies.........	26.50
1182	Postage....................	50.00
		$149.65

(50) The August bill received from Central Power Co., payable September 10, is analyzed as follows:

Factory light and power	$825.00
Office light	31.65
	$856.65

(51) A check for $1,000, the regular monthly sinking fund deposit for the bonds, is given to Midland Trust Company, the sinking fund trustee.

(52) Midland Trust Company informs us that it has purchased securities for the sinking fund at a cost of $950.

(53) Post from the August 16–31 payroll summary to the general ledger and the manufacturing expense analysis record.

Record a voucher and check payable to Payroll for the net payroll amount shown by the payroll summary.

(54) The directors declare a 1% cash dividend, payable September 10 to stockholders of record August 31.

(55) Foot and complete the posting of all of the books of original entry.

(56) Take a trial balance of the general ledger. Enter the account balances in the Trial Balance Before Adjustments columns of the working papers provided in the laboratory material.

(57) Apply the following adjustments in the working papers:
    (a) Expired insurance, chargeable as follows:

Account	Amount
5384	$300
6084	100
7084	10
	$410

    (b) Postage used, $37.15.
    (c) Salesmen's traveling expenses for the month amounted to $863.50.
    (d) Factory supplies used, $709.57.
    (e) Provision for bad debts—1% of gross sales.
    (f) Accrued interest on notes receivable, $60.
    (g) Accrued interest on notes payable, $140.
    (h) Depreciation, computed for a full month on August 1 balances and for one-half month on increases during the month, at the following annual rates:

Asset	Rate	Amount
Buildings	3%	$ 350.00
Machinery and equipment	12	1,902.50
Tools	24	72.00
Delivery equipment	18	99.00
Furniture and fixtures	12	48.00

    (i) The patents had a life of 15 years from August 1.
    (j) Accrued property taxes: factory, $325; general, $40.
    (k) Of the rent collected in advance, $100 has been earned.
    (l) Accrued bond interest, $500.
    (m) Amortization of bond premium.

(58) Complete the working papers.

The following schedules of subsidiary records, assumed to have been prepared by your assistant, will be found in the practice set envelope:

Accounts receivable
Vouchers payable

See that they are in agreement with the related controlling accounts.

Observe that the accounts receivable schedule shows that one account has a credit balance. Instead of entering the balance of the controlling account in the Balance Sheet debit column of the working papers, enter the total debit balances of the subsidiary ledger in the debit column and the credit balance in the credit column.

The inventories on August 31 were:

Finished goods	....	$63,275.22
Goods in process	...	40,374.65
Raw materials	...	36,928.70

The working papers should show a net income of $14,128.47 before income tax. Assume that the income tax provision should be $6,900; enter this provision in the working papers as follows:

	Income Statement Debit Column	Balance Sheet Credit Column
Federal income tax expense and liability	6,900.00	6,900.00

(59) Make and post (to the general ledger and the manufacturing expense analysis record) adjusting journal entries for the matters mentioned in (57) and for the estimated provision for income tax. Use the journal form provided for adjusting entries.

(60) The following schedules of subsidiary records, assumed to have been prepared by your assistant, will be found in the practice set envelope: Selling expenses; General expenses. See that they are in agreement with the related controlling accounts.

Prepare a schedule of the manufacturing expenses, and see that it is in agreement with the controlling account.

(61) Prepare the following statements:

Statement of cost of goods manufactured.
Income statement.
Statement of retained earnings.
Balance sheet.
(In accordance with the terms of the bond indenture, retained earnings are restricted and not available for dividends in an amount equal to the balance in the sinking fund.)

(62) Close the books. Use the journal pages allotted to closing entries.

(63) Take an after-closing trial balance.

ASSIGNMENT MATERIAL FOR CHAPTER 21
Questions

1. Name some uses of data on unit costs.

2. Demonstrate, by the use of T-accounts, how costs may be accumulated and transferred to follow the flow of goods through a factory.

3. Name some useful purposes served by perpetual inventory records.

4. Discuss two methods of disposing of underabsorbed and overabsorbed overhead.

5. Describe the functions of:

    (a) Materials perpetual inventory cards.
    (b) Material requisitions.
    (c) Production orders.
    (d) Register of completed production orders.

6. Is manufacturing overhead assigned to production orders in the same manner as material and direct labor?

7. Design a production order.

8. Illustrate the computation of equivalent production by using an assumed set of facts.

9. Under what circumstances might there be two different amounts for equivalent production for the same manufacturing process for the same period of time?

Problems—Group A

Problem A 21-1. Twin Rivers Manufacturing Co. produces wheels for power mowers. As an aid in controlling costs and production, the company uses the specific order method of cost accounting and assigns a production order number for each 1,000 wheels placed in production.

Using the data below, you are to prepare production order 1122 and present individual journal entries showing the accumulation of costs for production order 1122 and their ultimate transfer to Finished Goods. The company uses the perpetual inventory method for all of its inventories.

Dates	Events

1959
July 7—Materials are requisitioned covering estimated requirements for 1,000 wheels; cost, $625.

    10—Direct labor for the pay period ending today, $160.

    16—Supplementary requisition for materials needed to complete production order 1122; cost, $55.

    17—Direct labor to complete production order 1122, $410.
        Overhead is applied to completed production orders at the rate of 60% of materials and direct labor.

    18—The completed wheels are placed in the finished goods warehouse.

Problem A 21-2. Mono Manufacturing Company manufactures one product which passes through two manufacturing departments. Production and manufacturing costs for the month of October, 1957, were as follows:

	Department 1	Department 2
Production:		
Units in process, beginning of month......	—0—	—0—
Units started.........................	10,000	9,400
Units completed and transferred..........	9,400	9,400
Units in process, end of month—½ complete as to materials, direct labor, and manufacturing overhead..............	600	—0—
Manufacturing costs:		
Materials..	$19,400	$ 5,640
Direct labor...........................	24,250	42,300
Manufacturing overhead................	14,550	28,200
Total.............................	$58,200	$76,140

Required:

(1) Equivalent production for departments 1 and 2 for October, 1957.
(2) Unit costs for departments 1 and 2 for October, 1957.
(3) Distribution of total costs for departments 1 and 2 for October, 1957.

Problem A 21-3. Following is the trial balance of East Manufacturing Company on July 1, 1959. Prepare journal entries for the July transactions, post to general ledger accounts, prepare adjusting and closing entries for July 31, post, and prepare financial statements for the month of July.

EAST MANUFACTURING COMPANY
Trial Balance—July 1, 1959

Cash...	10,000	
Accounts receivable............................	25,000	
Finished goods.................................	30,000	
Goods in process...............................	12,000	
Materials......................................	11,000	
Equipment.....................................	40,000	
Accumulated depreciation—Equipment..............		14,000
Accounts payable...............................		31,000
Common stock.................................		60,000
Retained earnings.............................		23,000
	128,000	128,000

Summarized transactions during July were as follows:

(1) Materials were purchased on account, $36,000.
(2) Payments were made for: direct labor, $16,000; indirect labor, $2,000; other manufacturing overhead costs, $5,900; selling expense, $3,800; general expense, $2,250.
(3) Payments on account for material purchases, $32,000.
(4) Materials requisitioned for production, $30,000.
(5) Direct labor applied to production, $16,000.
(6) Estimated overhead assigned to production, $8,500.
(7) Production orders completed, $62,000.
(8) Sales were made on account, $59,000. The goods sold cost $42,000 to manufacture.
(9) Collections on account were $61,500.

Additional data as of July 31, 1959:

(a) Depreciation of equipment for July, $400.   Depreciation is considered to be chargeable 80% to manufacturing overhead and 10% each to general expense and selling expense.

(b) Underabsorbed or overabsorbed manufacturing overhead is treated as an adjustment of cost of sales.

Problem A 21-4.   Selected accounts from the ledger of Nod Company appear below in T-account form.   The amounts shown in the accounts are either beginning-of-year balances or postings from the books of original entry for the month of January.

Cash			Sales	
10,000	72,000			75,000
67,500				

Accounts Receivable			Cost of Sales	
20,000	67,500		55,000	
75,000			100	

Finished Goods			Direct Labor	
22,000	55,000		22,500	22,500
66,000				
65				

Goods in Process			Manufacturing Overhead	
12,000	66,000		17,200	
22,500			1,000	
29,700				
18,000				
35				

Materials			Manufacturing Overhead Applied	
15,000	29,700			18,000
27,000				200

Accumulated Depreciation—Machinery			Selling Expense	
	10,000		2,700	
	1,000			

Vouchers Payable			General Expense	
72,000	15,000		4,500	
	73,900			

The special journals and cost records maintained by the company are described below and on the following page.   From the data in the T-accounts, compute the January total for each of the columns mentioned.

Check register with columns for: Cash
                                 Vouchers Payable

Voucher register with columns for: Materials
Manufacturing Overhead
Direct Labor
Selling Expense
General Expense
Vouchers Payable

Sales book with columns for: Selling Price
Cost

Cash receipts book with columns for: Cash
Accounts Receivable

Production order direct labor cost summary with a column for: Monthly Payroll

Requisition register with a column for: Amount

Register of completed production orders with a column for: Total Cost

Also, reproduce the entries that appeared in the general journal during January and give the monthly closing entries. Omit all dates in the journal entries.

Problem A 21-5. The Doaker Corporation began operations on March 1, 1958. It manufactured one product in a single process. The following data relate to operations for the month of March, 1958.

Manufacturing costs:
Materials...................................... $ 64,050
Direct labor................................... 84,000
Manufacturing overhead—130% of direct labor...... 109,200

Production:
14,500 units completed and transferred to finished goods.
In addition to the units completed, there were 1,000 units in process, partially completed on March 31, 1958.

Unit costs of production for March, 1958:
Materials...................................... $ 4.20
Direct labor................................... 5.60
Manufacturing overhead......................... 7.28
Total...................................... $17.08

(1) Prepare a schedule showing the computation of equivalent production for March, 1958.
(2) Compute the cost of product completed and transferred to finished goods.
(3) Compute the cost of goods in process on March 31, 1958.

Problems—Group B

Problem B 21-1. Aero Foundry manufactures castings on special order from customers in the aircraft industry. When a contract is received, a production order is filled out on which cost data are accumulated. Since Aero Foundry produces only on order and delivers immediately upon the completion of production, no inventory of finished goods is maintained.

On April 15, 1959, an order is received for 200 feathering-mechanism housings from United Company. The specified sales price to apply to the order is $18 per unit.

On April 18, production is begun, with number 4321 assigned to the production order. Aluminum costing $600 is sent, upon requisition, to the furnace for melting. Other materials costing $76 for making molds (not reused) are requisitioned on April 19. Direct labor in melting, pouring, and cleaning for this order amounts to $800. It is assumed that overhead amounts to 125% of direct labor.

On April 28, the order is completed and delivered, and an invoice is prepared for $3,600 and sent to United Company.

Required:

    (a) The completed production order 4321, designed on plain paper, as it would appear after reflecting all of the information above.

    (b) Journal entries which would be made to reflect the production and delivery of these castings, assuming that perpetual inventory accounts are maintained by the company for materials and goods in process.

    Problem B 21-2. Boom Machine Company uses the following books of original entry:

    1. Journal
    2. Voucher register
    3. Sales book
    4. Cash receipts book
    5. Check register

In addition, the company keeps the following records upon which journal entries are based:

    1. Two-column materials requisition register, one column for materials requisitioned for production and one column for materials requisitioned for general use in the factory
    2. Production order direct labor cost summary
    3. Register of completed production orders

    Below are selected transactions of Boom Machine Company during June, 1958. For each transaction, indicate the book of original entry or other record in which the transaction would be recorded, and indicate the final debit-credit effect that each transaction would have on the general ledger accounts.

    Example: Creditors are paid for outstanding invoices, $700.
    Enter in check register.

               Debit: Vouchers payable.......... $700
               Credit: Cash...................... $700

    (1) Invoices representing manufacturing expense items are received from creditors, $1,950.
    (2) Direct labor payroll is paid, $4,800.
    (3) Materials are purchased on account, $950.
    (4) Sales are made on account, $3,000. These goods cost $2,000 to manufacture.
    (5) Manufacturing operations are completed on goods costing $880.
    (6) Materials are requisitioned for production, $900.
    (7) Direct labor cost is assigned to production orders, $3,200.
    (8) Materials are requisitioned for general use in the factory, $22.
    (9) Manufacturing overhead is estimated to be 50% of direct labor costs and is assigned to production orders at the same time as is direct labor cost. A summary entry reflecting the application of manufacturing expense to production orders is made at the end of each month. Total direct labor assigned to production orders during June, 1958, is $19,000.
    (10) Overabsorbed manufacturing overhead of $800 is assigned as follows: cost of sales, 80%; finished goods, 15%; and goods in process, 5%.

Problem B 21-3. The Trans-World Company manufactures one product in a single process. On March 31, 1957, there were no goods in process in the plant. During April, 1957, the following manufacturing costs were incurred:

Materials	$7,678
Direct labor	5,797
Manufacturing overhead	3,751

Production records, for April, 1957, were summarized as follows:

Units completed and transferred to finished goods	6,500
Units in process on April 30, 1957	800
Stage of completion:	
Materials	60%
Direct labor and manufacturing overhead	40%

Required:

(1) A schedule showing the equivalent production for April, 1957, in terms of materials, direct labor, and manufacturing overhead.
(2) Unit costs for April, 1957.
(3) A schedule showing the distribution of April, 1957 manufacturing costs.

Problem B 21-4. The Goods in Process account in the general ledger of Mart Manufacturing Company had a debit balance of $3,850 on June 30, 1957. This amount represented the cost of 1,000 units of the single product which were partially completed on June 30, 1957. The June 30, 1957 goods in process inventory included the following manufacturing costs:

Cost	Stage of Completion	Amount
Materials	80%	$1,600
Direct labor	60%	900
Manufacturing overhead		
(150% of direct labor)		1,350
Total		$3,850

The following manufacturing costs were charged to Work in Process during July, 1957:

Materials	$24,436
Direct labor	17,226
Manufacturing overhead	
(150% of direct labor)	25,839
Total	$67,501

During July, 1957, 12,000 units of product were completed (including the units in process on June 30, 1957); and on July 31, 1957, 1,200 units were in process at the following stages of completion:

Materials	60%
Direct labor	40%

Required:

(1) Equivalent production for July, 1957.
(2) Unit costs of production for July, 1957, including the unit costs of goods in process at the beginning and end of the month.

(3) Journal entries to record the charging of materials, direct labor, and applied manufacturing overhead to the Goods in Process account and to transfer the cost of completed production to the Finished Goods account.

(4) Reconciliation of the July 31, 1957 balance of the Goods in Process account with the unit costs of the goods in process on July 31 1957.

ASSIGNMENT MATERIAL FOR CHAPTER 22
Questions

1. Discuss the nature of accounting principles.

2. What is the "going concern" assumption as it relates to accounting theory?

3. Why is the accountant interested in consistency in relation to the application of accounting procedures?

4. What is revenue? How does the accountant *measure* revenue?

5. A wholesale company on a calendar-year basis received a $2,000 order on December 31. It had the goods in its warehouse to fill the order; they were purchased in November for $1,600; however, they had not been paid for. Since the order was routine in character and the goods would be shipped as soon as the order was processed (which normally required two days), the office manager treated the $2,000 as a sale as of December 31 and excluded the ordered goods from the December 31 inventory. Would you approve of this procedure?

6. A printer received an order for 10,000 textbooks, which he completed and had ready for delivery before the end of the year. As an accommodation to the publisher, the printer agreed to hold these books in his warehouse and make shipments to schools as directed to do so by the publisher. The printer desired to include the results of this work in his operating statement for the year. Would you approve?

7. How is cost computed when a noncash asset is acquired for noncash assets?

8. A company has its fixed assets appraised at each year-end and adjusts its accounts to show the values disclosed by the appraisal; the adjustments of the asset valuations are shown in the operating statement as revenue or expense. What comment do you have to make on this procedure?

9. A manufacturing company has expended a total of $3,000 worth of its material, labor, and expense in constructing a machine for its own use. This machine, if bought in the open market, would have cost $4,000. Is it sound accounting to capitalize this machine at the market price?

10. Distinguish between expenses and lost costs.

11. Describe the methods or approaches used by accountants in determining the amounts of cost properly assignable to expense.

12. Comment on the following statement: "If assets are misstated, it follows that cost expirations are misstated."

13. Is it true that all assets are shown in the balance sheet at cost or cost less depreciation or amortization?

Problems—Group A

Problem A 22-1. During 1957, Acme Company acquired two fixed assets, as described on the following page.

(1) On April 1, 1957, a machine was purchased for cash. The invoice price was $2,600 and a discount of 2% was allowed for the payment of cash, which was treated as other income by the company. In addition to the payment to the vendor of the machine, $150 was paid for freight on the shipment of the machine from the seller's plant and $350 was paid to install the machine. In an effort to be conservative, Acme Company charged the freight and installation costs to Maintenance Expense in 1957. This machine had an estimated service life of ten years; the depreciation recorded in 1957 amounted to $195.

(2) On July 1, 1957, a building was acquired in exchange for 1,000 shares of Acme Company $10 par value common stock. Acme Company recorded the building in its records at the aggregate par value of the stock issued for it. On July 1, 1957, Acme Company common stock was being traded on the market for $18 per share. The estimated service life of the building was 20 years.

(a) Compute the amount at which the two assets described above should have been initially recorded in the accounts of Acme Company.

(b) Compute the net error in net income for 1957 and 1958 caused by the procedures employed by Acme Company.

Problem A 22-2. The Gardner Corporation reported net income for 1956, 1957, and 1958, in the following amounts:

1956	$24,800
1957	32,100
1958	16,900

An examination of the records of The Gardner Corporation for the years 1956 and 1957 disclosed the following information:

(1) In 1956, a machine was constructed by The Gardner Corporation in its own plant. The total cost of construction was $10,400. The Gardner Corporation estimated that a similar machine, if purchased through the usual trade sources, would have cost $14,000, and it used this amount in recording the machine in its accounts. The excess of the recorded cost over the cost of construction was credited to Gain on Construction of Machinery. The Gardner Corporation has recorded depreciation on this machine at an annual rate of 10% since July 1, 1956, the date the machine was placed in service.

(2) In 1957, The Gardner Corporation increased the balance of the Land account by $12,000, representing the excess of the estimated replacement cost of the corporation's plant site over the original cost thereof. The amount of $12,000 was credited to Miscellaneous Income.

Prepare a schedule showing the computation of the correct net income for 1956, 1957, and 1958.

Problem A 22-3. David Smith, who operates a small retail store, has followed the practice of recording sales revenue when cash is collected from customers and merchandise purchases and expenses (other than depreciation) when cash is disbursed. He has prepared the following income statement for 1958.

DAVID SMITH

Income Statement

For the Year Ended December 31, 1958

Cash received from customers		$46,100.00
Cash paid for merchandise		31,800.00
Gross profit on sales		$14,300.00
Expenses paid	$10,600.00	
Depreciation	2,000.00	12,600.00
Net income		$ 1,700.00

Using the following additional information, prepare a corrected income statement for David Smith for 1958.   Show computation of sales, cost of goods sold, and expenses.

(1) Merchandise inventories:
    December 31, 1957.................. $6,800
    December 31, 1958................ 4,700
(2) Accounts payable—Merchandise:
    December 31, 1957.................. $3,600
    December 31, 1958................. 4,100
(3) Accrued expenses:
    December 31, 1957................. .... $1,600
    December 31, 1958................. 1,900
(4) Accounts receivable (all collectible):
    December 31, 1957.................. $5,200
    December 31, 1958................. 4,800

Problem A 22-4.   In the course of your examination of the records of Shadford Company for the years ended December 31, 1956, 1957, and 1958, you discover the following errors:

(1) The merchandise inventory on December 31, 1956, was understated in the amount of $1,600 as a result of errors in the extensions on inventory sheets.

(2) Unexpired insurance of $850, applicable to 1958, was ignored on December 31, 1957.

(3) Premium of $3,000 on the issuance of $200,000 par amount of ten-year bonds, dated July 1, 1956, was treated as current revenue on that date.

(4) A customer's order for merchandise in the amount of $3,400 was treated as a credit sale when received on December 18, 1958, although the related goods were not shipped until January, 1959, and were included in the December 31, 1958 inventory.

(5) On January 1, 1957, an item of equipment costing $2,600, with accumulated depreciation thereon of $1,200, was sold for $1,600, cash.   The amount received was recorded as Miscellaneous Income and depreciation on the asset was taken for 1957 and 1958 at an annual rate of 10% of cost.

(6) Accrued interest receivable, in the amount of $420, was not recorded on December 31, 1957.

The amounts of net income for the years ended December 31, 1956, 1957, and 1958, as determined by Shadford Company, were as follows:

    1956............... $18,900
    1957............... 16,200
    1958............... 6,800

(a) Compute the correct net income for Shadford Company for the years ended December 31, 1956, 1957, and 1958.

(b) Prepare the necessary correcting entry or entries as of December 31, 1958, assuming that the books have not been closed for 1958 and that Shadford Company desires to record corrections of prior years' net income in the Retained Earnings account.

Problem A 22-5.   The balance sheet on the following page was prepared by the accountant for Henry Corporation.

HENRY CORPORATION
Balance Sheet
For the Year Ended December 31, 1958
Assets

Current assets:

Cash	$ 6,400.00	
Accounts receivable	12,100.00	
Merchandise inventory	16,500.00	$35,000.00
Investments		15,000.00
Fixed assets		41,800.00
Deferred charges		2,900.00
		$94,700.00

Liabilities and Net Worth

Current liabilities:

Accounts payable	$ 1,900.00	
Bonds payable—Due July 1, 1962	10,000.00	$11,900.00
Reserves:		
Reserve for depreciation	$16,200.00	
Reserve for bad debts	1,000.00	
Reserve for contingencies	10,000.00	27,200.00
Net worth:		
Common stock—$50 par value	$25,000.00	
Surplus	30,600.00	55,600.00
		$94,700.00

The following information is made available to you:

(1) Included in Accounts Receivable is $2,200 representing the selling price of merchandise consigned to Granger Company. This merchandise cost Henry Corporation $1,500 and none had been sold by Granger Company on December 31, 1958.

(2) The Investments account represents 2,000 shares of common stock of R. Haun, Inc. This stock was acquired by Henry Corporation at a cost of $10,500 and is stated on the balance sheet at market value on December 31, 1958. Henry Corporation intends to hold this stock indefinitely.

(3) Fixed assets include the following:

Land acquired in 1950 at a cost of $5,000—At estimated December 31, 1958 market value	$ 7,500
Land acquired in 1958—At cost	3,000
Cost of building	20,400
Cost of equipment	10,900
Total	$41,800

You determine that attorney fees and sales commissions applicable to the purchase of the land in 1958, amounting to $800, were recorded as current expense.

(4) Deferred charges include unexpired insurance premiums of $1,800, the cost of store supplies on hand of $400, and unamortized discount on bonds payable of $700.

(5) Included in Surplus is $5,000, representing the excess received on the issuance of 500 shares of common stock over the par value thereof.

Prepare a revised balance sheet for Henry Corporation, making any desirable changes in amounts, classification, or terminology.

Problems—Group B

Problem B 22-1. The Goddard Corporation sells its product f.o.b. its plant and employs the perpetual inventory procedure. In examining the accounts of The Goddard Corporation for its fiscal year ended September 30, 1958, you discovered the following:

(1) An order, accompanied by the remittance of cash in the amount of the sales price of $880, was recorded as a cash sale and the $600 cost of the related product was transferred from Finished Goods to Cost of Goods Sold on September 15, 1958. You determine that this order was not shipped until October 10, 1958.

(2) A shipment of product on September 26, 1958, was properly credited to the Finished Goods account in the amount of $1,240, but no entry was made in the sales journal until October 4, 1958. The selling price of this lot of goods was $1,500.

(3) The $420 sales price of a shipment of product made on September 29, 1958, was properly recorded in the sales journal on that date, but no entry was made for the $320 cost of this shipment until October 2, 1958.

(4) A shipment of product on consignment to Schuler Company on September 10, 1958, was recorded as a credit sale. The selling price of this shipment was $4,500 and the cost (which was removed from the Finished Goods account) was $3,780. Schuler Company reported that it had not sold any of the goods in this shipment by September 30, 1958.

The following account balances appeared in the ledger of The Goddard Corporation on September 30, 1958:

$$\text{Sales}\dots\dots\dots\dots\dots\dots\dots\ \$214,800$$
$$\text{Cost of goods sold}\dots\dots\dots\ \ 178,500$$

(a) Compute the correct amounts for sales and cost of goods sold for the year ended September 30, 1958, assuming that all transactions, other than those described, were properly recorded.

(b) Prepare the necessary adjusting journal entries on September 30, 1958, assuming that the books have not been closed.

Problem B 22-2. Westminster, Inc., purchased a truck for $3,000 cash on October 1, 1956. An annual rate of 20% was adopted to compute depreciation on this truck. On July 1, 1957, a refrigeration system was added to the truck at a cost of $850, which was charged to Maintenance Expense. This system was expected to be of service during the remaining life of the truck.

On October 1, 1958, the truck was traded on a new truck with a list price of $4,200. An allowance of $1,200 was received for the old truck and the balance was paid in cash. The new truck was recorded in the books at list price, although the cash value of the old truck was known to be $1,000. The service life of the new truck was estimated to be four years.

(1) Compute the amount by which the net income of Westminster, Inc., was over- or under-stated for the calendar years 1957 and 1958 as a result of the procedures described above.

(2) Prepare the adjusting entry or entries, as of January 1, 1959, to correct the accounts of Westminster, Inc., assuming that the books have been closed for 1958, and that Westminster, Inc., desires to follow the "clean surplus" concept.

Problem B 22-3. The Monarch Company undertakes large construction projects under fixed-price contracts. The following data relate to one contract which was in progress during 1956, 1957, and 1958:

Contract price........... $4,500,000
Costs incurred:
1956................. 800,000
1957................. 2,800,000
1958................. 400,000

The construction was 20 per cent complete at the end of 1956, 90 per cent complete at the end of 1957, and finished on April 1, 1958.

Prepare schedules showing two ways by which you believe an accountant might compute net income for this construction contract, indicating the year or years in which the net income would be reported.

Problem B 22-4. You have been requested to prepare an income statement for the year ended September 30, 1958, and a balance sheet as of September 30, 1958, for Warren Cook, proprietor of a merchandising business. You discover that Cook does not maintain formal double-entry accounting records, but the following information is made available to you.

(a) Cook's balance sheet as of September 30, 1957, appeared as follows:

WARREN COOK
Balance Sheet
September 30, 1957
Assets

Cash..		$ 1,000.00
Accounts receivable...........................	$6,700.00	
Less allowance for doubtful accounts..........	500.00	6,200.00
Merchandise inventory.................................		8,100.00
Unexpired insurance.....................................		400.00
Store fixtures and equipment.................	$8,500.00	
Less accumulated depreciation...............	4,300.00	4,200.00
		$19,900.00

Liabilities and Proprietor's Equity

Accounts payable......................................	$ 4,300.00
Warren Cook, capital.................................	15,600.00
	$19,900.00

(b) All cash received by Cook has been deposited and all disbursements have been made by check.

(c) Total bank deposits for the year ended September 30, 1958, were $50,850. Included in this amount was $4,000 representing the proceeds of a six-month note payable dated July 1, 1958, with interest at 4% payable at maturity. The remainder represented amounts collected from customers after allowing cash discounts of $750.

(d) Checks written during the year ended September 30, 1958, were summarized as follows:

Rent..............................	$ 2,200
Insurance premiums.................	600
Store supplies......................	250
Wages..............................	3,800
Withdrawals by Cook...............	6,000
Purchase of store fixtures...........	2,400
Merchandise creditors..............	31,500
	$46,750

(e) Accounts receivable on September 30, 1958, totaled $8,400. Accounts receivable as of September 30, 1957, were collected with the exception of an account with a balance of $400 which was determined to be worthless. Accounts arising from sales of the current year estimated to be uncollectible amounted to $600.

(f) Accounts payable for merchandise purchased amounted to $5,100 on September 30, 1958. Cook took cash discounts of $580 on payments to merchandise creditors during the year.

(g) The cost of merchandise on hand on September 30, 1958, was $9,400.

(h) Unexpired insurance on September 30, 1958, was $560.

(i) Depreciation for the year ended September 30, 1958, was $900.

(j) Rent for September, 1958, in the amount of $200, was paid in October, 1958.

Problem B 22-5. Wire Company reported the following net income figures:

$$
\begin{array}{lr}
1956\ldots\ldots\ldots\ldots\ldots & \$18,000 \\
1957\ldots\ldots\ldots\ldots\ldots & 20,000 \\
1958\ldots\ldots\ldots\ldots\ldots & 17,500 \\
1959\ldots\ldots\ldots\ldots\ldots & 19,000 \\
\end{array}
$$

Two accounts from the ledger of Wire Company, kept to agree with income tax rules, are presented below.

Machinery				Accumulated Depreciation			
7/ 1/56 A	5,000	12/31/57 A	5,000	12/31/57	1,500	12/31/56	500
12/31/57 B	6,500	9/30/59 B	6,500	9/30/59	2,275	12/31/57	1,000
9/30/59 C	7,700					12/31/58	1,300
						9/30/59	975
						12/31/59	385

Machine A was traded in on B, and B was traded in on C. For depreciation purposes, machines of this type are assumed to have useful lives of five years. Data regarding the trade-ins are shown below:

Machine	List Price	Trade-in Allowance	Cash Paid	Market Value of Trade-in	Gain or Loss on Disposal Shown in Accounts	
B	$6,000	$3,000	$3,000	$2,500	For A	—0—
C	8,000	4,525	3,475	4,400	For B	—0—

Compute two other initial valuations for machines B and C. Also show how the net income figures reported would have been affected if the company had followed each of these alternatives.

ASSIGNMENT MATERIAL FOR CHAPTER 23
Questions

1. Why are financial statements analyzed?

2. How is it customary to compute the ratio showing the number of times bond interest has been earned?

3. Why may comparisons of analytical per cents be misleading?

4. Assume that two companies have the same amount of working capital and the same working capital ratio. Why may one company be in a better working capital position than the other?

5. List five ratios which you believe would indicate an improvement if the ratio showed an increase when compared to the same ratio for the previous year.

6. Discuss several weaknesses of financial statement analysis.

7. Distinguish between the working capital ratio and the acid-test ratio.

8. What is meant by the term "window dressing"?

9. What is meant by the term "break-even point"? Develop an example to illustrate the determination of the break-even point.

10. What is meant by the expression "natural business year"?

11. In the process of comparing two companies, suppose a statement analyst finds that the accounting data shown in the financial statements of one of the companies need adjusting in certain respects. Does this mean that accounting errors have been made by the company?

Problems—Group A

Problem A 23-1. A comparative income statement and a comparative balance sheet for Near Company are given below and on the following page.

Apply the horizontal-analysis technique, using these statements. For the income statement, express the changes as ratios; use per cents in analyzing the balance sheet.

NEAR COMPANY
Comparative Income Statement
For the Years Ended December 31, 1958 and 1957

	1958	1957
Sales	$329,500.00	$310,400.00
Deduct cost of goods sold	242,400.00	223,600.00
Gross profit on sales	$ 87,100.00	$ 86,800.00
Deduct:		
Selling expenses	$ 35,714.00	$ 32,513.00
General expenses	31,184.00	27,404.00
Total expenses	$ 66,898.00	$ 59,917.00
Net income	$ 20,202.00	$ 26,883.00

NEAR COMPANY
Comparative Balance Sheets
December 31, 1958 and 1957
Assets

	December 31,	
	1958	1957
Current assets:		
Cash.................................	$ 12,600.00	$ 10,540.00
Accounts receivable—net................	64,270.00	58,750.00
Inventory............................	82,570.00	94,885.00
Prepaid expenses......................	7,685.00	7,120.00
Total current assets...................	$167,125.00	$171,295.00
Fixed assets:		
Land.................................	$ 14,000.00	$ 14,000.00
Buildings—net.........................	89,790.00	92,415.00
Machinery—net........................	31,350.00	24,625.00
Total fixed assets.....................	$135,140.00	$131,040.00
	$302,265.00	$302,335.00

Liabilities and Stockholders' Equity

Current liabilities:		
Accounts payable......................	$ 46,835.00	$ 60,038.00
Accrued taxes.........................	20,000.00	14,000.00
Total current liabilities................	$ 66,835.00	$ 74,038.00
Stockholders' equity:		
Capital stock..........................	$200,000.00	$200,000.00
Retained earnings......................	35,430.00	28,297.00
Total stockholders' equity.............	$235,430.00	$228,297.00
	$302,265.00	$302,335.00

Problem A 23-2. Apply the vertical-analysis technique to the following statements.

MODE COMPANY
Balance Sheet
December 31, 1958
Assets

Current assets:		
Cash.................................	$ 25,400.00	
Accounts receivable—net................	65,000.00	
Inventory............................	40,800.00	$131,200.00
Fixed assets:		
Land.................................	$ 15,000.00	
Plant—net............................	48,700.00	
Store equipment—net...................	70,800.00	134,500.00
		$265,700.00

Liabilities and Stockholders' Equity

Current liabilities:		
Accounts payable......................	$ 31,900.00	
Notes payable.........................	10,000.00	$ 41,900.00
Stockholders' equity:		
Capital stock..........................	$150,000.00	
Retained earnings......................	73,800.00	223,800.00
		$265,700.00

MODE COMPANY
Income Statement
For the Year Ended December 31, 1958

Net sales.................................	$208,000.00	
Deduct cost of goods sold.................	132,600.00	
Gross profit on sales......................		$ 75,400.00
Deduct:		
Selling expenses.........................	$ 23,200.00	
Administrative expenses.................	17,400.00	40,600.00
Net income..............................		$ 34,800.00

Problem A 23-3. The following are statements of Brown Company as prepared at the end of 1958.

BROWN COMPANY
Income Statement
For the Year Ended December 31, 1958

Gross sales...	$600,000.00	
Returned sales and allowances.........................	15,000.00	
Net sales....	$585,000.00	
Cost of goods sold....	395,000.00	
Gross profit on sales....	$190,000.00	
Expenses:		
Selling expenses.........	$73,000.00	
General expenses.........	52,000.00	125,000.00
Net income from operations...........................		$ 65,000.00
Income from sinking fund securities....................		240.00
Gain on disposal of equipment.........................		1,000.00
Net income before interest expense and federal		
income tax.......................................		$ 66,240.00
Interest on mortgage payable...........................		3,600.00
Net income before federal income tax...................		$ 62,640.00
Federal income tax...................................		25,540.00
Net income...		$ 37,100.00

BROWN COMPANY
Balance Sheet
December 31, 1958
Assets

Current assets:			
Cash...		$ 25,000.00	
Accounts receivable...................	$208,000.00		
Less allowance for doubtful accounts..	8,000.00	200,000.00	
Inventory.......................................		140,000.00	
Prepaid expenses................................		15,000.00	
Total current assets..................................			$380,000.00
Sundry assets:			
Investment in sinking fund securities........................			10,000.00
Fixed assets:			
Land.......................................		$ 18,000.00	
Buildings.............................	$100,000.00		
Less accumulated depreciation........	20,000.00	80,000.00	
Equipment............................	$ 15,000.00		
Less accumulated depreciation........	3,000.00	12,000.00	
Total fixed assets..			110,000.00
			$500,000.00

Liabilities and Stockholders' Equity

Current liabilities:
Accounts payable............................... $109,700.00
Notes payable.................................   12,000.00
    Total current liabilities.................................. $121,700.00

Long-term liabilities:
Mortgage payable (secured by land and buildings)...............   60,000.00
    Total liabilities... $181,700.00

Stockholders' equity:
Preferred stock—5%, par value, $100................ $ 50,000.00
Common stock—Par value, $100...................   200,000.00
Retained earnings................................   68,300.00
    Total stockholders' equity...............................   318,300.00
                                        $500,000.00

At the end of 1957, the inventory was $80,000 and the total stockholders' equity was $300,960.

Compute the following: (Carry computation to two decimal places; for example, 6.78%.)

Working capital ratio.
Acid-test ratio.
Inventory turnover.
Per cent of year's net sales uncollected.
Ratio of owners' equity to debt.
Ratio of owners' equity to net fixed assets.
Ratio of net sales to net fixed assets.
Ratio of pledged fixed assets to long-term debt.
Earnings per share of common stock.
Ratio of net income to average owners' equity.
Number of times preferred dividends earned.
Number of times mortgage interest earned.

Problem A 23-4.   During the year 1958, Bramble Corporation operated at a loss.   The accountant prepared the following data relating to 1958:

Fixed expenses............. $100,000
Variable expenses.......... 150,000
Net sales... 200,000

The advertising manager wishes to undertake an extensive campaign which would cost $18,000.

(1) What amount of sales would be necessary to break even:
    a. If the advertising plan is discarded?
    b. If the advertising plan is undertaken?

(2) The management has indicated that in order to continue operations, annual net income should be at least $15,000.   What amount of sales would provide this net income, assuming that the advertising campaign is authorized?

Problem A 23-5.   The amounts shown on the following page were taken from the comparative income statement of Gear Corporation for the years ended December 31, 1958 and 1957.

	1958	1957
Purchases	$22,800	$25,090
Postage	920	1,300
Bonuses—Salesmen	1,360	1,240
Bonuses—Officers	1,200	—0—
Patents	—0—	880
Sales returns and allowances	310	760
Gain (loss*) on disposal of equipment	540	120*

Compute the amount and (when possible) the per cent of change for each of the items above.

Compute the per cents to two decimal places; for example, 4.87%.

Problem A 23-6. French Corporation has issued convertible bonds under an agreement to maintain net assets, defined in the agreement as assets minus all liabilities except the convertible bonds, at an amount not less than 230% of the convertible bonds outstanding, to maintain current assets at not less than 200% of the current liabilities, and to maintain working capital at not less than 100% of the convertible bonds outstanding.

On December 31, 1958, the corporation's adjusted trial balance was as follows:

FRENCH CORPORATION
Adjusted Trial Balance
December 31, 1958

Cash	10,000.00	
Accounts receivable	43,000.00	
Allowance for doubtful accounts		1,000.00
Inventory	46,000.00	
Prepaid expenses	2,000.00	
Land	6,000.00	
Building	52,000.00	
Accumulated depreciation—Building		7,000.00
Equipment	88,000.00	
Accumulated depreciation—Equipment		14,000.00
Accounts payable		23,000.00
Notes payable—due 1963		25,000.00
Accrued expenses		2,000.00
Convertible bonds payable		75,000.00
Common stock		50,000.00
Retained earnings		50,000.00
	247,000.00	247,000.00

As an accountant, you discover that the notes payable were issued on December 29, 1958, that the proceeds were used to settle current accounts payable, and that, on December 31, 1958, $25,000 cash was disbursed to settle a tax liability. A batch of goods costing $7,000 was recorded as sold for $10,000, although, according to the order, title was to pass to the buyer on January 15, 1959, the date the goods were to be shipped. The goods were excluded from the inventory.

Contrast, by means of comparative ratios, the reported conditions with those that would have existed if the transactions discovered had not occurred, so far as they relate to the ratios mentioned in the agreement with the bondholders.

Comment briefly on your findings.

Problems—Group B

Problem B 23-1. The following data are from the accounts of Tara Corporation on December 31, 1958.

Cash.....................................	$25,000
Accounts receivable—net....................	12,000
Inventory................................	8,000
Prepaid expenses..........................	2,000
Accounts payable..........................	12,000
Notes payable—due in six months............	3,000
Sales....................................	53,000
Purchases................................	34,000
Purchase returns and allowances.............	750

On the basis of the information presented above, compute the following:

    a. Working capital ratio.
    b. Acid-test ratio.
    c. Inventory turnover. (Inventory on December 31, 1957, was $7,000.)

Problem B 23-2. Trend Company's working capital ratio was 2 to 1 on December 31, 1958. Assume that the following additional transactions had occurred on that date, and indicate whether each transaction would have increased, decreased, or not affected the working capital ratio.

    1. Wrote off uncollectible account.
    2. Purchased inventory for cash.
    3. Paid for a three-year insurance policy in advance.
    4. Sold merchandise for cash.
    5. Paid cash for machinery.
    6. Paid a short-term creditor in full.
    7. Purchased inventory on account.
    8. Returned merchandise, for which no payment had been made to creditor.
    9. Sold fully depreciated fixed asset for cash at a gain.
   10. Discounted a non-interest-bearing note receivable at the bank.

Problem B 23-3. Statements for Ramar Company follow:

RAMAR COMPANY
Income Statement
For the Year Ended December 31, 1958

Gross sales...		$255,800.00
Sales returns and allowances..........................		4,500.00
Net sales...		$251,300.00
Cost of goods sold...................................		180,000.00
Gross profit on sales.................................		$ 71,300.00
Expenses...		57,300.00
Net income from operations...........................		$ 14,000.00
Interest on mortgage payable..........................		800.00
Net income before federal income tax........		$ 13,200.00
Federal income tax...................................		6,200.00
Net income..........................		$ 7,000.00

RAMAR COMPANY
Balance Sheet
December 31, 1958
Assets

Current assets:

Cash..		$ 10,000.00	
Accounts receivable...................	$95,000.00		
Less allowance for doubtful accounts...	6,000.00	89,000.00	
Inventory......................................		100,000.00	
Total current assets................................			$199,000.00

Fixed assets:

Land...		$ 12,000.00	
Buildings..............................	$60,000.00		
Less accumulated depreciation.........	12,000.00	48,000.00	
Store equipment.......................	$15,000.00		
Less accumulated depreciation.........	7,000.00	8,000.00	
Total fixed assets..			68,000.00
			$267,000.00

Liabilities and Stockholders' Equity

Current liabilities:

Accounts payable................................	$ 94,600.00	
Accrued expenses payable.........................	29,000.00	
Total current liabilities....................................		$123,600.00

Long-term liabilities:

Mortgage payable (secured by land and buildings)...............	20,000.00	
Total liabilities...		$143,600.00

Stockholders' equity:

Preferred stock, 6%—Par value, $100.................	$ 20,000.00	
Common stock—Par value, $100....................	90,000.00	
Retained earnings................................	13,400.00	
Total stockholders' equity................................		123,400.00
		$267,000.00

On December 31, 1957, the inventory was $80,000 and the total stockholders' equity was $120,000.

Compute the following (carry computations to two decimal places; for example, 14.71%):

Working capital ratio.
Acid-test ratio.
Inventory turnover.
Per cent of year's net sales uncollected.
Ratio of owners' equity to debt.
Ratio of owners' equity to net fixed assets.
Ratio of net sales to net fixed assets.
Ratio of pledged fixed assets to long-term debt.
Earnings per share of common stock.
Ratio of net income to average owners' equity.
Number of times preferred dividends earned.
Number of times mortgage interest earned.

Problem B 23-4. Determine the break-even point for the following cases:

	(1)	(2)	(3)
Fixed expenses............................	$90,000	$84,000	$30,000
Per cent of variable expenses to sales........	80%	30%	75%

Problem B 23-5. You are engaged by an investor holding the $30,000 of bonds payable of Harding Corporation to determine the following:

(a) The distribution of current assets.
(b) Working capital ratio.
(c) Acid-test ratio.
(d) Inventory turnover.
(e) Per cent of sales uncollected.
(f) Earnings per share.

Carry computations to two decimal places; for example, 7.18%.
Harding Corporation submitted the following financial statements.

HARDING CORPORATION
Balance Sheet
December 31, 1958
Assets

Cash..	$ 18,000.00
Marketable securities................................	20,000.00
Accounts receivable..................................	18,000.00
Inventory...	16,000.00
Goodwill..	1,200.00
Machinery...	50,000.00
Sinking fund securities..............................	1,400.00
	$124,600.00

Liabilities and Stockholders' Equity

6% bonds payable—due 1960..........................	$ 30,000.00
Accounts payable....................................	18,000.00
Accrued income taxes................................	4,900.00
Accrued expenses....................................	1,800.00
Accumulated depreciation—Machinery..................	8,000.00
Allowance for doubtful accounts......................	800.00
Reserve for contingencies............................	12,000.00
Capital stock, $10 par value.........................	40,000.00
Retained earnings...................................	9,100.00
	$124,600.00

HARDING CORPORATION
Income Statement
For the Year Ended December 31, 1958

Net sales..		$280,000.00
Cost of sales:		
Inventory, December 31, 1957.............	$ 17,000.00	
Purchases—Net of returns and allowances..	178,000.00	
Transportation in	800.00	
Total	$195,800.00	
Inventory, December 31, 1958.............	16,000.00	179,800.00
Gross profit on sales...............................		$100,200.00
Selling expense...........................	$ 19,000.00	
General expense...........................	68,500.00	87,500.00
Net operating income................................		$ 12,700.00
Interest expense....................................		1,950.00
Net income before income taxes......................		$ 10,750.00
Federal income taxes................................		4,750.00
Net income...		$ 6,000.00

In connection with these statements, you discover the following. The cash amount included $590 of sinking fund cash. Also, the corporation kept open the cash receipts book, the check register, and the voucher register until the middle of January, 1959. As a result, checks for $20,000 received in January in payment of merchandise purchased by customers during November and December were recorded as December receipts; checks for $15,000 issued in January in payment of vendors' December invoices were entered in the check register as December disbursements; and $8,000 of vendors' invoices received in January for goods delivered and services rendered in December were recorded in the voucher register. Of the latter amount, $5,000 represented goods included in the ending inventory and $3,000 was for selling expense items.

The corporation used the periodical inventory method. On December 30, 1958, a customer returned merchandise which had been sold to him for $600. The following entry was made on December 30:

Purchase returns and allowances...................... 600.00
Accounts receivable............................   600.00

The merchandise returned was included in the ending inventory at its cost, $400.

Problem B 23-6. The following ratios and other data are based on the 1958 financial statements of Roadster Corporation. The corporation does not use a perpetual inventory system.

Working capital ratio: $19,800 ÷ $7,800 = 2.54
Acid-test ratio: $9,800 ÷ $7,800 = 1.26
Inventory turnover: $40,000 ÷ $9,000 = 4.44
Number of times bond interest earned: $1,800 ÷ $300 = 6.0
Gross profit rate: $11,000 ÷ $51,000 = 21.57%

A review of the records of the corporation discloses that the following entries were made as of December 31, 1958, the last day of the accounting period.

1958
Dec. 31   Cash................................. 1,000.00
             Sales...........................   1,000.00
             Cash sales for today. (However, the
             goods were not delivered until January 2,
             1959, because the delivery truck was
             being repaired. Consequently, the goods
             were included in the ending inventory.)

      31   Cash................................. 1,600.00
             Notes receivable..................   1,600.00
             Collections received on January 2, 1959,
             on non-interest-bearing notes.

      31   Accrued payroll....................... 2,000.00
             Cash............................   2,000.00
             Checks issued January 2, 1959, dated
             December 31, 1958.

      31   Purchases........................... 800.00
             Accounts payable..................   800.00
             To record invoices received January 2,
             1959. (The merchandise covered by the
             invoices was received on December 30,
             1958, and was included in the December
             31, 1958 inventory.)

31	Insurance expense	1,500.00	
	Cash		1,500.00
	Five-year fire policy dated today.		

Recompute any of the above ratios that were affected by the entries. Ignore income taxes.

ASSIGNMENT MATERIAL FOR CHAPTER 24
Questions

1. What is the primary purpose of the statement of application of funds?

2. If you were given comparative data regarding all ledger accounts except the current assets and current liabilities, would it be possible to prepare a statement of application of funds?

3. Under what circumstances is it customary to show funds applied above the sources of funds in the statement of application of funds?

4. If, on October 15, a business borrows $5,000 from a bank by issuing a six-month interest-bearing note, will that transaction be shown as a source of funds in the statement of application of funds for the calendar year?

5. Would it be possible for a statement of application of funds to show an increase in working capital if the business operated at a loss?

6. Explain the use of the symbol N in the schedule analyzing the non-current accounts. List four examples of transactions where the use of symbol N would be appropriate.

7. A company declares a cash dividend in 1957 payable in 1958. Will this action have any effect on the statement of application of funds for 1957? For 1958?

Problems—Group A

Problem A 24-1. Following is the comparative balance sheet of South Turn Company:

SOUTH TURN COMPANY
Comparative Balance Sheet
December 31, 1959 and 1958
Assets

	December 31, 1959	December 31, 1958
Cash...	$ 5,000	$ 8,000
Accounts receivable.............................	18,000	13,500
Land..	6,200	5,000
Trademarks.......................................	900	800
	$30,100	$27,300

Liabilities and Stockholders' Equity

Accounts payable................................	$ 7,600	$ 6,400
Common stock....................................	19,000	18,000
Retained earnings...............................	3,500	2,900
	$30,100	$27,300

Asset acquisitions during the year included land for $1,200 and trademarks for $100. Stock was issued at par for $1,000. Net income for the year was $600.

Required:

(a) A schedule of working capital.
(b) An analysis of non-current accounts.
(c) A statement of application of funds.

Problem A 24-2.   Following are comparative balance sheet data of March Company.

| | December 31, | |
Debits	1959	1958
Cash..	$ 3,900	$ 4,500
Accounts receivable................................	8,850	7,450
Merchandise..	21,350	24,600
Land...	15,000	10,000
Goodwill...	2,500	5,000
	$51,600	$51,550

Credits		
Accounts payable..................................	$ 5,920	$ 5,180
Allowance for doubtful accounts...................	400	350
Bonds payable.....................................	3,000	6,000
Capital stock.....................................	37,000	35,000
Retained earnings.................................	5,280	5,020
	$51,600	$51,550

Some of the information regarding the non-current accounts is given below. Net income for the year amounted to $4,510.   Dividends were paid totaling $1,750.   Goodwill was written off against retained earnings to the extent of $2,500.   Land was purchased for $5,000.   One-half of the bonds outstanding at the beginning of the year were retired.

Prepare: (a) A schedule of 'working capital; (b) an analysis of non-current accounts; and (c) a statement of application of funds.

Problem A 24-3.

JARGON CORPORATION
Comparative Balance Sheet
March 31, 1959 and 1958
Assets

| | March 31, | |
	1959	1958
Cash...	$ 8,800	$ 6,600
Accounts receivable..............................	38,850	41,350
Allowance for doubtful accounts..............	930*	1,110*
Merchandise inventory...........................	34,800	28,700
Prepaid expenses................................	720	800
Land...	10,000	9,000
Buildings..	55,000	50,000
Accumulated depreciation—Buildings..........	15,125*	12,500*
Furniture and fixtures...........................	6,000	5,000
Accumulated depreciation—Furniture and fixtures................................	3,050*	2,500*
	$135,065	$125,340

#### Liabilities and Stockholders' Equity		
Accounts payable................................	$ 11,700	$ 15,000
Notes payable...................................	10,000	8,000
Accrued interest payable........................	600	500
Bonds payable, due 1965........................	30,000	25,000
Capital stock...................................	46,200	42,000
Reserve for contingencies.......................	15,000	10,000
Retained earnings..............................	21,565	24,840
	$135,065	$125,340

* Deduction.

Purchases during the year included land, $1,000; building, $5,000; and furniture and fixtures, $1,000. Total depreciation on old and new assets amounted to $2,625 on buildings and $550 on furniture and fixtures. Prepaid expenses as of March 31, 1958, were utilized during the next fiscal year, and payment was made for additional prepaid expenses of $720 applicable to the period after March 31, 1959. Additional short-term notes of $2,000 and bonds of $5,000 were given to the local bank to provide funds to meet additional obligations incurred during the fiscal year. Net income for the year was $8,125. A 10% stock dividend and a $2,200 cash dividend were paid during the year. The directors also appropriated an additional $5,000 of retained earnings to the reserve for contingencies.

From the above data, prepare:

(a) A schedule of working capital;
(b) An analysis of non-current accounts; and
(c) A statement of application of funds.

Problem A 24-4. From the following financial statements relating to Triangle Company, prepare: (a) schedule of working capital; (b) analysis of non-current accounts; and (c) statement of application of funds. In cases in which information is not given with respect to the causes of the changes in non-current accounts, use your best judgment regarding the probable causes.

TRIANGLE COMPANY
Comparative Balance Sheet
December 31, 1959 and 1958

Assets

	December 31,	
	1959	1958
Cash..	$11,570	$ 9,240
Accounts receivable...............................	13,200	14,810
Merchandise..	34,930	30,650
Prepaid rent.......................................	600	600
Long-term investments.............................	18,000	21,000
Land...	10,000	8,000
	$88,300	$84,300

Liabilities and Stockholders' Equity

Accounts payable...................................	$12,810	$12,740
Current installment due on bonds payable...........	2,000	2,000
Bonds payable......................................	10,000	12,000
Capital stock......................................	57,000	50,000
Retained earnings..................................	6,490	7,560
	$88,300	$84,300

TRIANGLE COMPANY
Statement of Retained Earnings
For the Year Ended December 31, 1959

Balance, December 31, 1958...............................		$ 7,560
Add:		
Net income.......................................	$5,430	
Gain on sale of long-term investments..............	600	6,030
Total..		$13,590
Deduct:		
Stock dividend...................................	$5,000	
Cash dividend...................................	2,100	7,100
Balance, December 31, 1959...............................		$ 6,490

Problem A 24-5.

FRISCO CORPORATION
Trial Balances
March 31, 1959 and 1958

	March 31,			
	1959		1958	
	Before Closing		After Closing	
	Debit	Credit	Debit	Credit
Cash..	8,100		10,200	
Accounts receivable.........................	18,200		16,100	
Allowance for doubtful accounts.............		1,050		820
Inventories.................................	25,700		19,600	
Long-term investments......................	9,500		8,000	
Land.......................................	10,000		10,000	
Buildings..................................	80,000		70,000	
Accumulated depreciation—Buildings.........		14,250		10,500
Equipment.................................	10,000		13,000	
Accumulated depreciation—Equipment........		4,000		3,900
Organization costs.........................	7,000		8,000	
Accounts payable..........................		9,250		11,560
Accrued wages.............................		720		640
Mortgage payable..........................		10,000		25,000
Capital stock..............................		100,000		80,000
Premium on capital stock...................		10,500		8,000
Reserve for contingencies...................		8,600		6,500
Retained earnings..........................		4,880		7,980
Sales......................................		241,150		
Cost of goods sold.........................	192,000			
Selling expense............................	20,000			
General expense............................	14,000			
Depreciation expense—Buildings (5% per year).	3,750			
Depreciation expense—Equipment (10% per year)...................................	1,150			
Interest expense...........................	1,000			
Dividends paid.............................	4,000			
	404,400	404,400	154,900	154,900

During the year, the company sold some of its equipment for $1,950. The equipment cost $3,000 and had been depreciated for 3½ years.

At the March 5, 1959 meeting of the board of directors, the board voted to write off $1,000 of the organization costs to Retained Earnings.

Prepare an analysis of the non-current accounts. Also compute the total funds provided during the year ended March 31, 1959.

Problems—Group B

Problem B 24-1.   From the following balance sheet accounts and supplementary data relating to Bailor Company, prepare a schedule of working capital, an analysis of non-current accounts, and a statement of application of funds.

| | December 31, | |
Debits	1959	1958
Cash......................................	$10,400	$ 8,600
Accounts receivable.......................	12,560	16,400
Merchandise..............................	26,300	19,000
Long-term investments....................	10,000	12,000
	$59,260	$56,000

Credits

Accounts payable	$ 3,300	$ 8,230
Allowance for doubtful accounts	490	650
Common stock	46,000	40,000
Paid-in surplus	5,200	4,000
Retained earnings	4,270	3,120
	$59,260	$56,000

Net income for the year amounted to $1,750. Investments, costing $2,000, were sold for $2,000. 600 shares of common stock, stated value, $10, were issued at $12 per share. Dividends of $600 were paid during the year.

Problem B 24-2.

MASON CORPORATION
Comparative Balance Sheet
January 31, 1959 and 1958
Assets

	January 31,	
	1959	1958
Cash	$10,420	$ 8,990
Accounts receivable	10,680	12,600
Merchandise	13,600	10,000
Patents	1,000	500
Goodwill	—0—	2,000
	$35,700	$34,090

Liabilities and Stockholders' Equity

Accounts payable	$ 7,890	$ 9,680
Long-term notes payable	4,000	3,000
Common stock	22,000	20,000
Retained earnings	1,810	1,410
	$35,700	$34,090

Additional patents were purchased during the year for $600. The Patents account was credited $100 for amortization. Goodwill was written off against Retained Earnings. A long-term loan for $1,000 was obtained from the bank. Net income for the year amounted to $2,400.

Prepare: (a) schedule of working capital; (b) analysis of non-current accounts; and (c) statement of application of funds.

Problem B 24-3.

LESLIE PRODUCTS, INC.
Balance Sheet Accounts
June 30, 1959 and 1958

Debits	June 30,	
	1959	1958
Cash	$ 10,650	$ 13,800
Accounts receivable	31,990	22,860
Inventories	50,740	47,600
Bond sinking fund	12,500	10,000
Land	10,000	15,000
Buildings	75,000	75,000
Equipment	12,000	10,000
Patents	5,000	6,000
	$207,880	$200,260

Credits

Accounts payable..........................	$ 19,000	$ 15,000
Accrued salaries and wages...................	9,250	8,750
Bonds payable, 1966.........................	18,000	18,000
Allowance for doubtful accounts...............	1,940	1,120
Accumulated depreciation—Buildings...........	20,000	15,000
Accumulated depreciation—Equipment.........	4,400	3,000
Capital stock...............................	105,000	100,000
Sinking fund reserve........................	12,500	10,000
Retained earnings...........................	17,790	29,390
	$207,880	$200,260

For the year ended June 30, 1959, the company suffered a net loss of $3,300 exclusive of the gain on the sale of land. The charges for depreciation were $5,000 for buildings and $1,400 for equipment; amortization of patents totaled $1,000. Land which had an original cost of $5,000 was sold for $6,200. Additional equipment was purchased for $2,000. A contribution of $2,500 was made to the bond sinking fund, and a transfer of $2,500 was made from Retained Earnings to the sinking fund reserve. Dividends paid during the year were: cash dividend, $2,000; stock dividend, $5,000.

From the above data, prepare an analysis of non-current accounts that could be used in preparing a statement of application of funds.

Problem B 24-4.

ZIMMER CORPORATION
Comparative Balance Sheet
June 30, 1959 and 1958
Assets

	June 30,	
	1959	1958
Cash...	$ 12,570	$ 10,680
U. S. Securities—Short-term.....................	27,430	32,970
Accounts receivable............................	16,140	18,350
Inventories....................................	28,600	27,400
Land...	18,300	10,800
Goodwill......................................	11,000	12,000
	$114,040	$112,200

Liabilities and Stockholders' Equity		
Accounts payable..............................	$ 8,690	$ 12,600
Accrued wages.................................	2,650	2,140
5% cumulative preferred stock—$100 par..........	18,000	15,000
Premium on preferred stock.....................	1,800	1,650
Common stock—No par.........................	66,000	60,000
Reserve for contingencies.......................	11,000	8,000
Retained earnings..............................	5,900	12,810
	$114,040	$112,200

The company declared and paid the following dividends: $750 cash dividends on preferred stock; $4,350 cash dividends on common stock. The corporation issued an additional 30 shares of preferred stock for $105 per share. The goodwill is being amortized; annual charges therefor, in the amount of $1,000, are shown in the income statements. All other changes in non-current accounts are the result of transactions typically recorded in such accounts.

Required:

(a) Schedule of working capital.
(b) Analysis of non-current accounts.
(c) Statement of application of funds.

ASSIGNMENT MATERIAL FOR CHAPTER 25
Questions

1. Give some reasons why it might be impracticable or undesirable to maintain balanced inventories.

2. Describe a procedure that would indicate inventory imbalance in a case where the same raw materials are used in the manufacture of several finished products.

3. Discuss two considerations that management might evaluate when deciding whether to replace a usable machine with a new model.

4. Refer to the tabulation of Salesmen's Rankings in Chapter 25. Rank the five salesmen in the order in which you would rank them for salary purposes, showing first the salesman you would recommend for the highest salary. Give reasons to support your decisions.

5. Name some analytical uses you might make of gross profit per cents if you were the manager of a retail store with four departments.

6. Describe two business problems (other than those referred to in Chapter 25) where accounting data could be useful to management in reaching solutions.

7. Does a low rate of inventory turnover always suggest an unprofitable merchandising activity?

8. Describe the procedure followed to determine the length of time required to recover the cost of an additional investment in machinery.

9. In Chapter 25, the actual 1958 financial statements of Dawson, Incorporated, were compared with a budget covering the same period. Make one suggestion to the management of Dawson, Incorporated, that, if followed, could lead to an improvement in operating results or financial position for 1959.

Problems—Group A

Problem A 25-1. The December 31, 1958 materials inventory of Noon Company is presented below:

Materials Inventory
December 31, 1958

Item	Units	Cost	Amount
Zip	2,900	$2.50	$ 7,250.00
Zoom	3,600	1.10	3,960.00
Yip	2,800	2.40	6,720.00
Boom	1,232	2.00	2,464.00
			$20,394.00

The company manufactures a single product which requires the following combination of materials: 10 units of Zip, 8 units of Zoom, 7 units of Yip, and 4 units of Boom.

Prepare a schedule which will show whether any funds are tied up in unbalanced materials inventory.

Problem A 25-2. Venture Corporation is planning on marketing two types of coal stokers. The corporation will purchase the component parts ready for assembly. Data regarding the component parts and contemplated production are set forth below:

Stokers	Unit Cost of Parts	Number of Parts per Stoker	Planned Daily Production of Stokers
Type AA:			10
Part No. 1...........	$5	1	
Part No. 2...........	3	4	
Part No. 3...........	6	5	
Part No. 5...........	2	2	
Type M:			15
Part No. 1...........	5	1	
Part No. 3...........	6	5	
Part No. 4...........	8	5	
Part No. 5...........	2	4	
Total daily production			25

Determine the investment in parts required to support ten days of assembly operations.

Problem A 25-3. From the following data relating to County-Wide Company, compute the 1958 inventory turnover for each article on hand.

		Inventory, at Cost December 31,		Sales	
Article	Unit Cost	1957	1958	Dollars	Units
L..............	$12.00	$360.00	$408.00	$ 2,160.00	144
N..............	8.00	688.00	624.00	7,413.00	706
E..............	7.25	848.25	920.75	10,980.00	1,220
O..............	6.80	802.40	897.60	9,901.20	1,110
R..............	4.00	812.00	788.00	12,120.00	2,424

Problem A 25-4. Topper Manufacturing Co. is considering adding a new product to its line. The company will need to purchase $20,000 of new equipment to manufacture the product. Its accountant estimates that the new product will create the following items of revenue and expense, on the average, each year for the useful life of the new equipment.

Sales of new product.......................................		$33,500
Deduct:		
Cost of sales—including $2,000 depreciation on the new equipment..............................	$25,400	
Additional selling and administrative expenses......	7,100	32,500
Net income before income tax.............................		$ 1,000
Income tax...		500
Net income from new product.............................		$ 500

(a) Prepare an estimate of the length of time required to recover the investment in the new equipment.

(b) Prepare an estimate of the rate of income that will be earned on the average investment in the new equipment.

Problem A 25-5. Fly Company is preparing a budget for 1958. One of the items to be budgeted is the amount of cash disbursements for direct operating expense. The company's accountant believes that such cash disbursements will be ten per cent more than the cash disbursed during 1957 for materials and services associated with this category of expense.

Using the data given, estimate the 1958 cash requirements.

	December 31,		Year
	1957	1956	1957
Prepaid operating expenses	$ 9,000	$11,000	
Accrued operating expenses	14,350	13,740	
Direct operating expense:			
Flying operations			$219,892
Flight equipment—Maintenance			93,328
Depreciation of flight equipment			61,700

Problem A 25-6. Dexter Company must expand its output. This can be achieved by either of the following alternatives: (a) buy an additional machine of the type now on hand; (b) trade in an old machine on a new one with greater capacity. Both new machines have an estimated useful life of ten years. If alternative (a) is selected, the new machine will cost $20,000. If alternative (b) is selected, an old machine with a remaining useful life of six years and a book value of $9,000 will be traded in for $3,000, leaving $22,000 to be paid in cash for the new machine with greater capacity.

Last year's results of operations are summarized below:

Sales		$100,000
Deduct:		
Cost of goods sold—except depreciation	$60,000	
Depreciation—on all machines	5,000	
Selling and administrative expenses	19,000	84,000
Net income before income tax		$ 16,000
Income tax		8,000
Net income		$ 8,000

Under either alternative, sales will increase 20 per cent; the cost of goods sold, except depreciation, will increase $11,000; and the selling and administrative expenses will increase 10 per cent.

Decide which alternative is more attractive, considering only the information given, and support your decision with suitable computations.

Problems—Group B

Problem B 25-1. Dusty Corporation has the following materials inventory:

Materials Inventory
June 30, 1958

Item	Units	Cost
Pica	3,300	$ 5
Mica	3,750	12
Beta	1,200	10

The corporation manufactures a single product which requires three units each of Pica and Mica and one unit of Beta. The president of the corporation considers it desirable to maintain a materials inventory that will produce 1,000 units of finished product.

Determine the amount invested in the materials inventory in excess of the limit set by the president.

Problem B 25-2. Vital Company manufactures three models of a household appliance. Five parts are used in the manufacturing operations, and the company's management attempts to maintain a balanced inventory of these parts in sufficient quantity to support 20 days of manufacturing operations. Data regarding parts requirements and average daily production are presented below:

Model and Component Parts	Parts Required	Daily Appliance Production
Custom:		100
Part 1..........................	4	
Part 3..........................	1	
Part 4..........................	2	
Special:		70
Part 1..........................	4	
Part 2..........................	2	
Part 4..........................	2	
Super:		50
Part 1..........................	4	
Part 3..........................	2	
Part 5..........................	8	

Compute the number of days' production that can be supplied by the following inventory of parts:

Parts Inventory
June 30, 1958

Part No.	Units	Cost	Amount
1................	18,480	$4	$ 73,920
2................	3,360	6	20,160
3................	10,000	5	50,000
4................	6,460	7	45,220
5................	8,800	8	70,400
			$259,700

Problem B 25-3. From the following data, prepare whatever analyses are possible that will show the relative effectiveness of the three salesmen of Huntwork Company. (Carry money amounts to the nearest dollar and per cents to two places; for example, 27.14%.)

	1958				1957			
	Sales		Salaries and Traveling	Number of	Sales		Salaries and Traveling	Number of
	Product A	Product B	Expenses	Sales	Product A	Product B	Expenses	Sales
Green, H. R...	$100,000	$ 79,800	$17,500	300	$90,000	$ 58,920	$15,800	270
Johnson, J. O..	79,354	110,000	18,100	290	72,140	100,000	16,600	285
Smith, R. R...	90,000	91,350	14,700	280	80,000	81,200	12,300	260

	Gross Profit Rates	
Product	1958	1957
A....................	40%	40%
B....................	30	30

Problem B 25-4. Northwest Company is considering replacing one of its machines, which has a book value of $1,600 and a remaining use life of eight years, with a new model that will reduce its cost of goods sold, exclusive of depreciation on the old machine, by $1,100 per year. The new machine sells for $12,000, less a trade-in allowance of $1,000, and has an estimated useful life of twelve years.

The expected operating results with the old machine are shown on the following page.

Sales		$60,000
Deduct:		
Cost of goods sold—except depreciation on old machine	$45,800	
Depreciation	200	
Selling and administrative expenses	10,000	56,000
Net income before income tax		$ 4,000
Income tax		2,000
Net income		$ 2,000

Compute the period of investment recovery and the income rate on the average additional investment, assuming that the old machine is traded in on the new machine.

Problem B 25-5.   Mark Corporation is considering adding a new product to its line.   Studies of accounting data indicate that the cost of sales, excluding depreciation on special equipment needed to manufacture the new product, will amount to 75 cents for each dollar of sales of the new product.   Additional selling and administrative expenses will amount to 18 cents for each sales dollar, and depreciation, based on a 10-year use-life for the special equipment needed to produce the new product, will amount to 2 cents per sales dollar.   The sales manager believes that sales of the new product will amount to $40,000 annually.

If the corporation is willing to undertake the manufacture and sale of the new product only if it can recover the investment in the special equipment in six years, how much can be invested in new equipment under the conditions described above?   What will be the rate of income on the average investment in the special equipment?   You may assume that income taxes will equal 50% of the net income before income taxes.

Problem B 25-6.   The Cash account page in the general ledger of Lang Corporation has been temporarily misplaced.   Using the data below, compute the cash received from customers during the year 1958.

	December 31,	
	1958	1957
Accounts receivable—Trade	$ 43,400	$29,400
Allowance for doubtful accounts	3,800	1,700
Sales	422,200	
Sales discounts	5,610	

During 1958, $1,650 of accounts receivable were written off as uncollectible and one account of $110, written off in 1956, was collected and credited to Allowance for Doubtful Accounts.

ASSIGNMENT MATERIAL FOR CHAPTER 26

Questions

1. What departmental accounts should be kept if it is desired to determine the gross profit by departments?

2. Do you think that departmental income statements based on apportionments are very reliable? Explain why.

3. Do you think it is good accounting to charge one department with an income tax amount larger than the liability for such tax for the business?

4. How is the contribution to overhead computed?

5. Suggest a basis for apportioning each of the following expenses to departments, and state your reason for selecting the basis used:

> Delivery expense
> Rent expense
> Advertising expense
> Transportation in

6. If the operations of a department result, year after year, in a net loss, after charging the department with reasonable amounts of selling and general expenses, could there by any possible reason for continuing its operations?

Problems—Group A

Problem A 26-1. Below is presented the adjusted trial balance of Allen Corporation. Prepare working papers showing the gross profit on sales by departments. The transportation-in charge is to be apportioned on the basis of gross purchases.

ALLEN CORPORATION
Adjusted Trial Balance
December 31, 1959

Cash..	7,280	
Accounts receivable.............................	34,300	
Allowance for doubtful accounts...................		1,430
Inventories—December 31, 1958:		
Dept. *X*.....................................	12,900	
Dept. *Y*.....................................	46,200	
Building.......................................	150,000	
Accumulated depreciation—Building................		67,500
Accounts payable................................		52,600
Accrued salaries payable.........................		920
Capital stock...................................		95,000
Retained earnings...............................		6,380
Dividends......................................	2,000	
Sales:		
Dept. *X*.....................................		56,000
Dept. *Y*.....................................		236,000
Sales returns and allowances:		
Dept. *X*.....................................	1,900	
Dept. *Y*.....................................	2,600	

Sales discounts:
    Dept. X...................................... 1,580
    Dept. Y...................................... 3,910
Purchases:
    Dept. X...................................... 40,000
    Dept. Y...................................... 160,000
Purchase returns and allowances:
    Dept. X......................................   4,200
    Dept. Y......................................   1,290
Purchase discounts:
    Dept. X......................................   2,600
    Dept. Y......................................   1,980
Transportation in................................ 6,500
Equipment rent.................................. 5,900
Advertising....................................... 2,700
Salesmen's salaries:
    Dept. X...................................... 8,000
    Dept. Y...................................... 14,000
Delivery expense................................. 3,800
Depreciation expense—Building.................... 3,000
Office salaries................................... 12,450
Insurance.. 490
Bad debt expense................................. 1,750
Interest expense.................................. 540
Federal income tax............................... 4,100
                              525,900   525,900

Inventories—December 31, 1959:

    Dept. X.............................. $17,320
    Dept. Y........ 49,900

Problem A 26-2.   Granger Corporation keeps its general ledger accounts in alphabetical order.   The adjusted trial balance as of December 31, 1958, is given below.   Prepare an income statement showing gross profit less selling expenses by departments, using the following bases for apportionment:

Transportation in on the basis of gross purchases.
Store rent on the basis of area; department A occupies 600 square feet, while department B occupies 400 square feet.
Advertising on the basis of an analysis of space occupied, which reveals that $590 should be allocated to department A.
Selling commissions on the basis of gross sales in each department.
Delivery expense and depreciation on the basis of the number of packages delivered. Supplementary records show twice as many deliveries for department A as for department B.

GRANGER CORPORATION
Adjusted Trial Balance
December 31, 1958

Accounts payable.................................   5,290
Accounts receivable.............................. 4,830
Accumulated depreciation—Delivery equipment........   930
Advertising...................................... 1,100
Allowance for doubtful accounts.....................   370
Bad debts expense................................ 610
Capital stock....................................   20,000
Cash.. 18,200
Delivery equipment............................... 2,500

Delivery expenses.	690	
Depreciation—Delivery equipment.	540	
Federal income tax.	200	
Federal income tax liability.		200
Insurance.	350	
Interest earned.		270
Inventories—December 31, 1957:		
Dept. *A*.	3,800	
Dept. *B*.	2,270	
Miscellaneous general expenses.	420	
Officers' salaries.	1,000	
Office salaries.	750	
Purchases:		
Dept. *A*.	16,500	
Dept. *B*.	13,500	
Purchase returns and allowances:		
Dept. *A*.		280
Dept. *B*.		820
Purchase discounts:		
Dept. *A*.		500
Dept. *B*.		720
Retained earnings.		5,060
Sales:		
Dept. *A*.		27,000
Dept. *B*.		18,000
Sales returns and allowances:		
Dept. *A*.	320	
Dept. *B*.	1,740	
Sales discounts:		
Dept. *A*.	640	
Dept. *B*.	1,270	
Salesmen's salaries:		
Dept. *A*.	2,200	
Dept. *B*.	1,600	
Selling commissions.	840	
Store rent.	1,200	
Taxes.	200	
Transportation in.	1,540	
Unexpired insurance.	630	
	79,440	79,440

Inventories—December 31, 1958:

Dept. *A*.	$4,270	
Dept. *B*.	1,960	

Problem A 26-3. The unadjusted trial balance of Williams Corporation is given on the following page. The following adjustments are to be made:

Store rent of $2,500 has not been paid for the year. (The owner of the property is a major stockholder in the corporation.)

The balance in the Notes Receivable account represents a one-year note received on May 1, 1958, with interest at 5%.

Depreciation is computed at 8% per annum.

Accrued salaries at year-end are:

Salesmen in Department *A*.	$ 950
Salesmen in Department *B*.	1,070
Delivery truck drivers.	265
Office clerks.	480

The Notes Payable account balance represents a long-term debt at 4%; no interest has been paid on this obligation for one year.

The unexpired insurance is a three-year premium on a policy dated January 1, 1958.

The charge for bad debts is to be computed on the basis of 1% of sales less returns and allowances and discounts.

Federal income taxes payable for the year are estimated at $500.

WILLIAMS CORPORATION
Trial Balance
December 31, 1958

Cash	27,150.37	
Accounts receivable	31,411.55	
Allowance for doubtful accounts		1,296.02
Notes receivable	6,000.00	
Accrued interest receivable	—	
Inventories—December 31, 1957:		
Dept. A	17,314.42	
Dept. B	8,903.12	
Unexpired insurance	1,800.00	
Delivery equipment	16,975.00	
Accumulated depreciation—Delivery equipment		2,620.00
Accounts payable		12,420.02
Notes payable		12,000.00
Federal income tax payable		—
Accrued salaries payable		—
Accrued interest payable		—
Capital stock		75,000.00
Retained earnings		5,424.03
Dividends	2,500.00	
Sales:		
Dept. A		140,262.17
Dept. B		63,290.11
Sales returns and allowances:		
Dept. A	3,512.10	
Dept. B	1,295.26	
Sales discounts:		
Dept. A	792.39	
Dept. B	420.17	
Purchases:		
Dept. A	96,649.19	
Dept. B	50,426.78	
Purchase returns and allowances:		
Dept. A		1,925.36
Dept. B		510.92
Purchase discounts:		
Dept. A		2,014.52
Dept. B		910.18
Freight in	3,610.29	
Advertising	6,317.40	
Salesmen's salaries:		
Dept. A	12,420.00	
Dept. B	8,295.00	
Delivery expense	2,840.12	
Depreciation—Delivery equipment	—	
Officers' salaries	10,150.00	
Office salaries	7,070.00	
Insurance	—	

Bad debts expense...........................	—	
Miscellaneous general expenses...............	1,924.17	
Interest earned.............................		302.00
Interest expense............................	198.00	
Federal income tax.........................	—	
	317,975.33	317,975.33

Inventories on December 31, 1958:

Dept. A......................	$25,429.18
Dept. B......................	8,045.10

The company insists on complete departmental allocation of expenses and income, and has schedules for such distributions. The following was taken from the accounting files:

Sales are to be used in apportioning the following:

Advertising	Office salaries
Delivery expense	Miscellaneous general expenses
Depreciation	Interest earned
Officers' salaries	

Purchases are to be used in apportioning the following:

Freight in
Interest expense

Average inventories are to be used to apportion the insurance.
Floor space is to be used to apportion the rent; department *A* occupies 22,000 square feet, while department *B* occupies 8,000 square feet.
Net sales (gross sales less returns and allowances and discounts) are to be used to allocate the bad debts expense.
The income tax estimated to be chargeable to department *A* is $5,000.
The income tax for the corporation is $500.

Required:

(a) A schedule of apportionments.
(b) Working papers showing the net income by departments.

Note: In the schedule of apportionments, carry the percentage figures to the nearest third place; for example, 55.7%.
    In allocations, carry the figures to the nearest cent; for example, consider $3,549.637 as $3,549.64.

Problem A 26-4. Using Problem A 26-3 and the following information, prepare:

(a) A schedule showing the probable reduction in expenses and miscellaneous revenue which would result from the discontinuance of department *B*.
(b) A schedule showing the increase or decrease in net income before income taxes resulting from the elimination of department *B*.

Data:

1. If department *B* were eliminated, the space released could be sublet for an annual rental of $500.

2. The total advertising bill would be reduced from $6,317.40 to $5,210.80.
3. The salesmen in department *B* would be dismissed.
4. $400 worth of gas and oil would be eliminated from the delivery expense.
5. There would be no effect on depreciation.
6. Officers' salaries would be unchanged.
7. The office payroll would be reduced by $480.
8. The insurance applicable to department *B* would not be needed.
9. There would be no bad debts charged to department *B*.
10. 20% of the miscellaneous general expenses would disappear.
11. All interest charges and earnings apportioned to department *B* would disappear.

Problem A 26-5. Below is presented the adjusted trial balance of Sands Corporation as of December 31, 1959. Prepare an income statement showing the departmental contribution to general overhead.

SANDS CORPORATION
Adjusted Trial Balance
December 31, 1959

Accounts payable		27,060
Accounts receivable	26,350	
Advertising expense	940	
Bad debts expense	720	
Capital stock		35,000
Cash	30,650	
Insurance expense	500	
Inventories—December 31, 1958:		
Dept. 100	4,910	
Dept. 200	9,250	
Interest earned:		
Dept. 100		160
Dept. 200		190
Miscellaneous general expenses:		
Dept. 100	920	
Dept. 200	340	
Officers' salaries	15,000	
Office salaries	3,800	
Purchases:		
Dept. 100	34,000	
Dept. 200	58,000	
Purchase returns and allowances:		
Dept. 100		1,270
Dept. 200		595
Purchase discounts:		
Dept. 100		1,930
Dept. 200		215
Retained earnings		9,140
Sales:		
Dept. 100		50,000
Dept. 200		80,000
Sales returns and allowances:		
Dept. 100	420	
Dept. 200	190	
Sales discounts:		
Dept. 100	300	
Dept. 200	275	
Salesmen's salaries:		
Dept. 100	3,100	
Dept. 200	4,200	

Selling expenses...................................	4,830	
Store rent..	5,000	
Taxes:		
Dept. 100......................................	180	
Dept. 200......	120	
Transportation in:		
Dept. 100......................................	945	
Dept. 200......................................	620	
	205,560	205,560

Inventories—December 31, 1959:

Dept. 100.............................	$5,030
Dept. 200.............................	8,475

Problems—Group B

Problem B 26-1.   The adjusted trial balance of Batten, Inc., is given below.

BATTEN, INC.
Adjusted Trial Balance
December 31, 1959

Cash...	36,630	
Accounts receivable..............................	22,000	
Allowance for doubtful accounts...................		720
Inventories—December 31, 1958:		
Dept. *L*......................................	26,300	
Dept. *M*.....................................	22,600	
Delivery equipment.............................	7,500	
Accumulated depreciation—Delivery equipment......		3,120
Accounts payable................................		17,140
Federal income tax payable.......................		3,800
Capital stock....................................		65,000
Retained earnings................................		5,450
Dividends.......................................	2,000	
Sales:		
Dept. *L*......................................		210,000
Dept. *M*.....................................		90,000
Purchases:		
Dept. *L*......................................	180,000	
Dept. *M*.....................................	60,000	
Purchase returns and allowances:		
Dept. *L*......................................		8,450
Dept. *M*.....................................		680
Purchase discounts:		
Dept. *L*......................................		4,600
Dept. *M*.....................................		980
Transportation in...............................	5,440	
Store rent......................................	12,000	
Advertising.....................................	3,500	
Salesmen's salaries..............................	16,350	
Delivery expense................................	920	
Depreciation expense—Delivery equipment...........	1,100	
Office salaries..................................	4,800	
Insurance.......................................	1,520	
Bad debts expense...............................	880	
Miscellaneous general expense.....................	2,600	
Federal income tax............................. ...	3,800	
	409,940	409,940

Inventories—December 31, 1959:

Dept. *L* $13,700
Dept. *M* 17,400

Prepare working papers showing net income by departments, using the following information:

The following are to be allocated on the basis of departmental gross sales:

Office salaries   Delivery expense
Miscellaneous general expense   Depreciation

The gross purchases are to be used in allocating transportation in.

The insurance is to be allocated on the basis of average inventories.

Bad debt losses have been analyzed, and it has been decided that $600 of the current charge is applicable to department *L*.

Store rent is to be apportioned on an area basis; department *L* occupies 800 square feet, while department *M* occupies 200 square feet.

Advertising deemed applicable to department *L* is $2,500.

Salesmen's salaries have been analyzed, and it was found that employees in department *L* earned $10,240.

Federal income tax payable on the income for the year is $3,800, as shown. However, it is appropriate to consider that the tax payable on department *M* profits would have been higher were it not for the loss in department *L*. It is assumed that the tax on department *M* would have been $5,700.

Problem B 26-2. On page 719 is presented the departmental income statement of Jarvis Company. The management is considering the elimination of department 1 and requests that a study be made of this matter.

Some of the expenses of the company are fixed and would not change as a result of the elimination of a department. These are: store rent, officers' salaries, office salaries, and depreciation of delivery equipment.

Some of the expenses are fully variable; that is, the portion applicable to a department would disappear if the department were shut down. These are: advertising, salesmen's salaries, bad debts expense, and interest earned.

Some of the expenses are semi-variable; that is, they would be partly eliminated with the discontinuance of a department. The management estimates that the following would be reduced to the extent of one-half the amount allocated to the department in 1959: insurance, miscellaneous general expense, and interest expense.

On the basis of the above information, prepare a schedule showing the effect on expenses if department 1 were discontinued.

Submit a schedule showing the net income before income taxes if department 1 were discontinued.

JARVIS COMPANY
Income Statement
For the Year Ended December 31, 1959

	Department 1			Department 2			Total		
Gross sales			$40,000			$30,000			$70,000
Deduct:									
Sales returns and allowances	$ 300			$ 190			$ 490		
Sales discounts	75	375		120	310		195	685	
Net sales			$39,625			$29,690			$69,315
Deduct cost of goods sold:									
Purchases			$27,000			$18,000			$45,000
Deduct:									
Purchase returns and allowances	$ 250			$ 110			$ 360		
Purchase discounts	300	550		92	202		392	752	
Net cost of purchases		$26,450			$17,798			$44,248	
Add transportation in		1,140			657			1,797	
Total		$27,590			$18,455			$46,045	
Add inventory—December 31, 1958		12,360			10,351			22,711	
Total cost of goods available for sale		$39,950			$28,806			$68,756	
Deduct inventory—December 31, 1959		8,517	31,433		6,211	22,595		14,728	54,028
Gross profit on sales			$ 8,192			$ 7,095			$15,287
Deduct operating expenses:									
Selling expenses:									
Store rent	$ 900			$ 600			$1,500		
Advertising	640			1,020			1,660		
Salesmen's salaries	1,200			760			1,960		
Depreciation of delivery equipment	400	$ 3,140		250	$ 2,630		650	$ 5,770	
General expenses:									
Officers' salaries	$3,500			$1,700			$5,200		
Office salaries	1,100			900			2,000		
Insurance	400			240			640		
Bad debts expense	175			317			492		
Miscellaneous general expenses	110	5,285	8,425	204	3,361	5,991	314	8,646	14,416
Net operating income (loss*)			$ 233*			$ 1,104			$ 871
Add net interest earned:									
Interest earned	$ 40			$ 210			$ 250		
Interest expense	120	80		45	165		165	85	
Net income (loss*) before federal income tax			$ 313*			$ 1,269			$ 956
Federal income tax (credit#)		80#			420			340	
Net income (loss*)			$ 233*			$ 849			$ 616

Problem B 26-3. Using the data in the statement shown in Problem B 26-2, prepare an income statement for Jarvis Company showing each department's contribution to non-departmental overhead. The following expenses may be regarded as non-departmental overhead: store rent, depreciation of delivery equipment, officers' salaries, and office salaries.

Problem B 26-4. The following has been extracted from the financial statements of Austin Corporation. The company is considering eliminating department P, and submits the necessary data for a study on this matter.

	Dept. P	Dept. Q	Total
Gross profit on sales....................	$65,230	$82,310	$147,540
Selling expenses:			
Store rent...........................	$12,000	$11,200	$ 23,200
Miscellaneous selling expenses..........	18,000	7,300	25,300
Commissions........................	8,570	3,980	12,550
Advertising.........................	3,600	4,900	8,500
Delivery expense.....................	1,960	1,040	3,000
Depreciation on truck.................	1,800	750	2,550
Total.............................	$45,930	$29,170	$ 75,100
General expenses:			
Officers' salaries.....................	$15,000	$12,000	$ 27,000
Office salaries.......................	3,200	1,800	5,000
Insurance expense....................	710	880	1,590
Bad debts...........................	1,220	440	1,660
Taxes..............................	1,550	650	2,200
Total.............................	$21,680	$15,770	$ 37,450
Interest expense.......................	$ 650	$ 290	$ 940
Total expenses........................	$68,260	$45,230	$113,490
Net income (loss*) before income taxes....	$ 3,030*	$37,080	$ 34,050

(a) There would be no change in the rental charge.
(b) Of the miscellaneous selling expenses, 25% would be eliminated.
(c) Advertising and commissions would no longer have to be paid.
(d) There would be no reduction in the delivery expenses or in the depreciation on the delivery truck.
(e) Officers' salaries would not be affected.
(f) Office salaries would be reduced to the extent of $750.
(g) Insurance charges would no longer be necessary for department P.
(h) Bad debts would be eliminated.
(i) Taxes would not be affected.
(j) The interest expense apportioned to department P would not be incurred.

Required:

A schedule showing the probable reduction in expenses as a result of discontinuing department P.

A schedule showing the estimated effect on net income, before income taxes, of the company as a result of eliminating department P.

ASSIGNMENT MATERIAL FOR CHAPTER 27

Questions

1. What is a consignment? Why are consignments made?

2. If there are unsold consigned goods in the hands of the consignee at the end of the accounting period, are they properly included in the inventory of the consignor or the consignee?

3. What is an "account sales"?

4. Under what circumstances might a Consignment In account have a debit balance? Where is such a balance shown in the financial statements?

5. Describe the entries you believe the consignor might have to make if unsold goods are returned by the consignee, thus terminating the consignment.

6. Do you believe there is any theoretical merit to the installment accounting procedure?

7. Describe the debit-credit operation and the financial statement location of the following accounts: Deferred Gross Profit on Installment Sales, Realized Gross Profit on Installment Sales.

8. Describe the accounting procedures required if an installment-sales customer defaults on his payments and the seller repossesses the merchandise.

9. Is it true that the net income shown in the income statement of a home office should equal the net income shown in the combined income statement of a home office and its branches?

10. Suppose a home office treated its shipments to branches as consignments. Would that accounting practice have any effect on the combined statements?

11. Identify the accounts that are eliminated when combined financial statements are prepared for a home office and its branch.

12. Suppose the home office ordered and paid for an item of equipment and directed that it be shipped to its branch. Also assume that the home office accountant directed the branch accountant to record the fixed asset on the books of the branch. Describe the entries that might be made on each set of books.

Problems—Group A

Problem A 27-1. On October 10, 1957, Williams Company consigned 100 television sets to Phillips, Inc. These sets cost Williams Company $140 each. Freight of $250 on this shipment to Phillips, Inc., was paid by Williams Company on October 18, 1957.

A report was received from Phillips, Inc., on January 3, 1958, showing the status of the consigned units on December 31, 1957, the close of Williams Company's accounting period. This report showed that 48 sets had been sold for $220 each. The consignee had paid the following expenses applicable to the consigned units sold: Advertising, $120; installation, $144; delivery, $90.

In addition to the preceding items, the consignee retained a commission of 15% of the selling price of consigned units sold and remitted the balance to the consignor.

(1) Prepare journal entries to record the preceding information in the records of Williams Company, including adjustments as of December 31, 1957.

(2) Compute the amount which will be shown in the December 31, 1957 balance sheet of Williams Company as inventory on consignment.

Problem A 27-2. Prepare journal entries in parallel columns to record the following transactions on the books of Rainier Company and its Tacoma branch.

(1) Cash in the amount of $3,000 was sent by the home office to the branch.

(2) The branch purchased merchandise on account at a cost of $2,100.

(3) Merchandise which cost $6,400 was sent by the home office to the branch.

(4) Wages were paid by the branch in the amount of $300.

(5) Sales were made by the branch as follows:

Cash.............. $2,100
Credit............. 7,400

(6) Branch collections on accounts receivable were $6,300.

(7) Estimated uncollectible branch accounts receivable amounted to $140.

(8) Branch accounts payable of $1,800 were paid.

(9) Cash in the amount of $7,000 was remitted by the branch to the home office.

Problem A 27-3. Clinton Company opened a branch store in De Witt on July 1, 1957, by sending the branch manager $2,000 to open a bank account for the branch. The only other transactions between the home office and branch in the year ended June 30, 1958, were the shipment of merchandise from the home office to the branch and the remittance of $1,500 in cash from the branch to the home office.

The income statement for the De Witt branch for the year ended June 30, 1958, appeared as follows:

DE WITT BRANCH
Income Statement
For the Year Ended June 30, 1958

Sales..		$18,200.00
Deduct cost of goods sold:		
Shipments from home office................	$12,850.00	
Purchases................................	1,200.00	
Total.....................................	$14,050.00	
Deduct inventory, June 30, 1958...........	2,600.00	
Remainder—Cost of goods sold....................		11,450.00
Gross profit on sales...............................		$ 6,750.00
Expenses...		4,800.00
Net income..		$ 1,950.00

Required:

(1) Closing entries for the De Witt branch on June 30, 1958.

(2) The journal entry to record the net income of the De Witt branch on Clinton Company's books.

(3) In journal entry form, the eliminations that would be made in combined working papers for Clinton Company and its De Witt branch.

Problem A 27-4.   The following account balances were taken from the records of Monroe Merchandising Corporation on March 31, 1958, the close of its fiscal year.

Cost of installment sales......................	$ 43,750
Installment accounts receivable................	41,400
Merchandise inventory, March 31, 1957..........	38,100
Deferred gross profit on installment sales.........	18,750
Administrative and general expense..............	61,400
Purchases....................................	191,200
Selling expense...............................	68,900
Sales..	216,500

The corporation has not treated any gross profit on installment sales as realized during the year ended March 31, 1958, which was the first year in which merchandise was sold on the installment basis.   The sales price of merchandise sold on the installment basis in the year ended March 31, 1958, was $62,500.   There were no defaults on installment accounts receivable in the year ended March 31, 1958.

Required:

(1) The journal entry to record realized gross profit on installment sales for the year ended March 31, 1958.
(2) Closing journal entries on March 31, 1958.   The merchandise inventory on March 31, 1958, was $36,400.

Problem A 27-5.   The December 31, 1958 trial balance of Tappan Corporation appeared as follows:

TAPPAN CORPORATION
Trial Balance
December 31, 1958

Cash...	31,620	
Accounts receivable...............................	64,800	
Allowance for doubtful accounts...................		2,200
Installment contracts receivable....................	42,400	
Merchandise inventory, December 31, 1958..........	72,500	
Land..	40,000	
Building...	88,200	
Accumulated depreciation—Building................		36,400
Furniture and equipment...........................	51,900	
Accumulated depreciation—Furniture and equipment..		32,500
Prepaid expenses..................................	2,400	
Accounts payable..................................		78,600
Note payable......................................		20,000
Interest payable...................................		300
Capital stock......................................		100,000
Retained earnings, December 31, 1957..............		76,400
Deferred gross profit on installment sales............		37,420
Sales..		416,800
Cost of goods sold.................................	265,400	
Selling expense....................................	61,600	
Administrative and general expense.................	79,200	
Interest expense...................................	600	
	800,620	800,620

Your examination of the accounts of Tappan Corporation discloses the following:

(1) During 1958, merchandise shipped on consignment has been recorded as a completed sale on the date of shipment, with the expected selling price being debited to Accounts Receivable and the cost transferred to Cost of Goods Sold. On December 31, 1958, there was unsold merchandise in the hands of consignees with a cost of $2,640 and an expected selling price of $3,400. Freight paid by Tappan Corporation on this merchandise and included in selling expense amounted to $160. Consignees had remitted to Tappan Corporation for all merchandise sold during 1958.

You determine that consignment transactions had been properly recorded in 1957 and prior years.

(2) An analysis of the balance of the Installment Contracts Receivable account on December 31, 1958, shows the following:

Year of Sale	Amount
1957	$11,800
1958	30,600
	$42,400

The total installment sales made in 1958 were $82,500. The cost of merchandise sold on the installment basis was $57,750. The deferred gross profit on installment sales was properly recorded at the time of the sale. Tappan Corporation first sold merchandise on the installment basis in 1957, and the rate of gross profit on installment sales in that year was 35%. On December 31, 1957, $36,200 of installment contracts receivable were uncollected.

Required:

(1) Adjusting journal entries indicated by the preceding data on December 31, 1958.

(2) Working papers for the year ended December 31, 1958.

(3) An income statement for the year ended December 31, 1958, and a balance sheet as of December 31, 1958.

Problem A 27-6. The December 31, 1957 trial balances of Monarch Sales Company and its Marshall branch are presented below.

MONARCH SALES COMPANY
Home Office Trial Balance
December 31, 1957

Cash	27,200	
Accounts receivable	36,600	
Inventory, December 31, 1956	8,500	
Fixtures and equipment	41,400	
Accumulated depreciation—Fixtures and equipment		15,200
Accounts payable		10,750
Common stock		75,000
Retained earnings		10,550
Sales		90,400
Purchases	114,600	
Shipments to branch		51,600
Operating expenses	19,800	
Branch current	5,400	
	253,500	253,500

MONARCH SALES COMPANY
Marshall Branch Trial Balance
December 31, 1957

Cash	5,600	
Shipments from home office	51,600	
Accounts receivable	9,600	
Inventory, December 31, 1956	2,400	
Accounts payable		3,400
Sales		72,900
Operating expenses	12,500	
Home office current		5,400
	81,700	81,700

Inventories on December 31, 1957, were:

Home office	$10,200
Marshall branch	3,800

Required:

(1) Working papers combining the accounts of the home office and branch.

(2) Combined income statement for the year ended December 31, 1957.

(3) Combined balance sheet as of December 31, 1957.

Problems—Group B

Problem B 27-1.　Boise Company receives merchandise from Burley Corporation to sell on consignment.　On December 31, 1957, Boise Company did not have any unsold consigned goods and had remitted in full to Burley Corporation for consigned goods sold in 1957.

During 1958, Boise Company received 180 units on consignment from Burley Corporation.　These units were to be sold for $150 each, and Boise Company was entitled to retain 20% of the selling price as its commission and to be reimbursed for all expenses incurred in connection with the consigned merchandise.　By June 30, 1958, 120 units had been sold for cash and Boise Company had paid the following expenses:

Advertising	$240
Delivery and installation of units sold	720

On June 30, 1958, Boise Company submitted an account sales to the consignor, together with payment in full of the amount due.

Required:

(1) Journal entries in the records of Boise Company, omitting dates, to record the transactions summarized above.

(2) The account sales submitted by Boise Company on June 30, 1958.

Problem B 27-2.　The following account balances were taken from the ledger of Miles, Inc., on December 31, 1957, after the recording of all adjusting entries on that date.

Installment accounts receivable—1957 sales	$62,500
Deferred gross profit on installment sales—1957 sales	20,000

During the year ended December 31, 1958, the transactions stated on the following page occurred:

Sales:
On installment basis.................................... $240,000
Cash and 30-day credit............................... 116,500
Cost of sales:
Installment sales...................................... 168,000
Cash and 30-day credit sales........................... 87,500
Collections on installment accounts receivable:
1957 sales... 55,000
1958 sales... 210,000
Operating expenses incurred:
Selling expenses...................................... 32,400
Administrative and general expenses.................... 41,800

Prepare an income statement for Miles, Inc., for the year ended December 31, 1958, using the installment accounting procedure.

Problem B 27-3. Seattle Company established a branch in Tacoma on July 1, 1957. The following information summarizes the transactions of the Tacoma branch for the year ended June 30, 1958.

(1) Cash received from the home office, $1,000.
(2) Merchandise received from home office, $8,200.
(3) Merchandise purchased by branch for cash, $540.
(4) Sales:

> For cash............... $2,400
> On account............. 7,200

(5) Expenses paid:

> Wages.................. $ 850
> Advertising............ 400
> Rent.................. 600
> Other................. 340

(6) Collections on accounts receivable from customers, $6,070.
(7) Cash remitted to home office, $5,000.
(8) Estimated uncollectible accounts receivable, $150.
(9) Merchandise inventory, June 30, 1958, $1,550.

Required:

(a) Entries to record the above information in the books of the home office and the branch.
(b) Closing entries for the branch on June 30, 1958.
(c) The entry to record the branch net income or loss in the home office books.

Problem B 27-4. Beaver Company was organized on July 1, 1957, to sell radios and television sets on the installment basis. However, during the fiscal year ended June 30, 1958, the company treated the revenue from sales as earned at the time merchandise was sold, and employed the perpetual inventory method of recording the cost of merchandise sold. The following data are available, applicable to the year ended June 30, 1958:

> Sales—all on the installment basis............ $118,500
> Cost of goods sold........................... 80,580
> Selling expense.............................. 12,410
> Administrative expense....................... 9,600
> Accounts receivable—June 30, 1958.......... 34,500

Required:

(1) Adjusting journal entries on June 30, 1958, to convert the accounts to the installment accounting basis.
(2) An income statement on the installment basis for the year ended June 30, 1958.

Problem B 27-5. Modern Appliance Company began business on July 1, 1956. On June 30, 1957, its balance sheet included the following accounts:

Installment contracts receivable....................	$62,400
Deferred gross profit on installment sales...........	26,208

During the year ended June 30, 1958, the company made sales on the installment basis totaling $188,500. The cost of merchandise sold on the installment basis was $113,100.

The following amounts were collected on installment contracts during the year ended June 30, 1958:

Year of sale	Amount Collected
Year ended June 30, 1957................	$50,200
Year ended June 30, 1958................	96,400

Installment contracts originating in the year ended June 30, 1957, with balances totaling $6,600, were determined to be uncollectible and the merchandise was repossessed. At the date of repossession, this merchandise had an estimated value of $3,250.

Prepare journal entries to record all transactions, and adjusting entries, related to installment sales during the year ended June 30, 1958.

ASSIGNMENT MATERIAL FOR CHAPTER 28
Questions

1. What is a subsidiary company?

2. Is the capital stock of a fully owned subsidiary shown in the consolidated balance sheet? Explain your answer.

3. If a parent-subsidiary relationship exists, would there ever be any reason to prepare an unconsolidated balance sheet for the parent corporation? Explain.

4. Give one reason why a consolidated income statement may be more truly indicative of the results of operations of the affiliated companies than would an income statement for the parent corporation only.

5. If an income statement shows the dividends received from subsidiary companies, is the income statement consolidated or unconsolidated?

6. Why are the inventories of affiliated companies reduced by the amount of any intercompany profit therein?

7. Describe the working paper procedure for eliminating the intercompany profit in a beginning inventory.

8. What is a minority interest?

9. Suppose that the consolidated balance sheet shows retained earnings as $40,000 and that the unconsolidated balance sheet of the parent for the same date shows retained earnings as $32,000. What does the difference of $8,000 represent, provided the affiliated companies never purchase or sell merchandise to each other?

10. If a parent acquires its interest in a subsidiary for less than book value, where is such difference between cost and book value shown in the consolidated statements?

Problems—Group A

Problem A 28-1. The condensed balance sheets of Jervis Corporation and Mountview Company appeared as follows on June 30, 1957:

	Jervis Corporation	Mountview Company
Assets		
Cash	$ 31,500	$ 8,400
Accounts receivable	72,600	10,600
Inventory	101,000	16,200
Property, plant, and equipment—Net of accumulated depreciation	121,400	28,900
Investment in Mountview Company	55,000	
	$381,500	$64,100
Liabilities and Stockholders' Equity		
Accounts payable	$ 26,300	$ 9,100
Bonds payable	100,000	
Capital stock	200,000	50,000
Retained earnings	55,200	5,000
	$381,500	$64,100

The Investment in Mountview Company account in the balance sheet of Jervis Corporation represents the cost of all of the capital stock of Mountview Company, acquired by Jervis Corporation on June 30, 1957.

Required:

Consolidated balance sheet working papers for Jervis Corporation and Mountview Company.

Problem A 28-2. The condensed balance sheets of Alpha Corporation and Beta Company on December 31, 1958, are presented below:

	Alpha Corporation	Beta Company
Assets		
Current assets..............................	$ 20,600	$ 10,100
Investment in Beta Company..................	112,000	
Other assets...............................	139,500	122,400
	$272,100	$132,500
Liabilities and Stockholders' Equity		
Current liabilities...........................	$ 46,800	$ 18,200
Capital stock...............................	150,000	100,000
Retained earnings...........................	75,300	14,300
	$272,100	$132,500

On December 31, 1953, Alpha Corporation acquired 90% of the capital stock of Beta Company at a cost of $112,000. On this date the balances of the Retained Earnings accounts of the two companies were:

Alpha Corporation.............. $48,900
Beta Company................. 30,000

Required:

(1) The amount of minority interest which would be included in the December 31, 1958 consolidated balance sheet.
(2) The Stockholders' Equity section of the December 31, 1958 consolidated balance sheet.

Problem A 28-3. The trial balances presented below were taken from the records of Bryce Company and its subsidiary, Zion Company, as of the end of their fiscal years.

BRYCE COMPANY AND ZION COMPANY
Trial Balances
April 30, 1958

Debits	Bryce Company	Zion Company
Cash...	76,800	18,600
Accounts receivable.............................	99,700	22,200
Inventory, April 30, 1957.......................	120,200	
Investment in Zion Company....................	40,000	
Equipment....................................	172,100	58,700
Purchases....................................	290,700	78,400
Operating expenses............................	90,600	26,600
Dividends....................................	40,000	10,000
	930,100	214,500

Credits

Accounts payable..............................	82,100	14,200
Allowance for doubtful accounts.................	5,600	4,000
Accumulated depreciation—Equipment............	131,600	5,600
Capital stock..................................	300,000	50,000
Retained earnings, April 30, 1957................	26,300	
Sales...	376,500	140,700
Dividends from subsidiary......................	8,000	
	930,100	214,500

Bryce Company acquired 80% of the capital stock of Zion Company on May 1, 1957, the date of organization of the latter company.

During the year ended April 30, 1958, Bryce Company purchased merchandise from Zion Company at a billed price of $85,000, which was the cost of this merchandise to the seller. On April 30, 1958, Bryce Company had not paid for $8,200 of the billed price of this merchandise.

The merchandise inventories on April 30, 1958, were: Bryce Company, $116,400; Zion Company, $10,800.

Prepare consolidated working papers for Bryce Company and Zion Company for the year ended April 30, 1958.

Problem A 28-4. The trial balances presented below were taken from the books of Boswell, Inc., and its subsidiary, Jewell Corporation, on December 31, 1957. Boswell, Inc., acquired 90% of the capital stock of Jewell Corporation on December 31, 1952, on which date Jewell Corporation's Retained Earnings account showed a credit balance of $6,400.

BOSWELL, INC., AND JEWELL CORPORATION
Trial Balances—December 31, 1957

Debits	Boswell, Inc.	Jewell Corporation
Cash...	32,400	21,500
Accounts receivable..........................	51,600	33,100
Inventories, December 31, 1956...............	72,500	37,400
Prepaid expenses.............................	3,800	1,800
Investment in Jewell Corporation.............	50,000	
Land...	22,400	15,400
Buildings....................................	128,600	39,100
Equipment...................................	180,700	61,400
Purchases....................................	416,200	218,300
Selling expense..............................	68,400	26,900
Administrative expense.......................	76,500	30,500
Income taxes.................................	74,800	43,500
Dividends paid...............................	35,000	10,000
	1,212,900	538,900

Credits		
Allowance for doubtful accounts..............	3,200	2,000
Accumulated depreciation—Buildings.........	14,700	8,600
Accumulated depreciation—Equipment........	72,900	24,200
Accounts payable............................	63,200	14,200
Income tax payable..........................	74,800	43,500
Capital stock...............................	200,000	60,000
Retained earnings, December 31, 1956.........	64,800	26,400
Sales..	710,300	360,000
Dividend from subsidiary....................	9,000	
	1,212,900	538,900
Inventories, December 31, 1957...............	78,800	34,000

During the year ended December 31, 1957, Jewell Corporation purchased merchandise from Boswell, Inc., for $152,000. This merchandise had cost Boswell, Inc., $128,000.

The December 31, 1957 inventory of the subsidiary included one-fourth of the merchandise purchased from the parent during the year. The December 31, 1956 inventory of Jewell Corporation included merchandise purchased from Boswell, Inc., on which there was intercompany profit of $4,500.

(1) Prepare consolidated working papers for the year ended December 31, 1957.

(2) Prepare a consolidated income statement and a consolidated statement of retained earnings for the year ended December 31, 1957, and a consolidated balance sheet as of December 31, 1957.

Problem A 28-5. The June 30, 1958 balance sheets of Randolph Company and Wilson Corporation are presented below.

RANDOLPH COMPANY AND WILSON CORPORATION
Balance Sheets
June 30, 1958

	Randolph Company	Wilson Corporation
Assets		
Cash...............................	$ 28,400.00	$ 6,800.00
Accounts receivable, net of allowance for doubtful accounts......................	46,100.00	10,200.00
Advance to Wilson Corporation.............	25,000.00	
Inventory..............................	83,500.00	18,500.00
Prepaid expenses.........................	6,400.00	2,600.00
Investment in Wilson Corporation..........	30,000.00	
Land..................................	15,000.00	6,400.00
Buildings, net of accumulated depreciation...	108,600.00	20,100.00
Furniture and equipment, net of accumulated depreciation..........................	138,900.00	12,300.00
	$481,900.00	$76,900.00
Liabilities and Stockholders' Equity		
Accounts payable.........................	$ 18,900.00	$14,200.00
Income tax payable.......................	62,400.00	4,300.00
Advance from Randolph Company..........		25,000.00
Capital stock............................	300,000.00	25,000.00
Retained earnings........................	100,600.00	8,400.00
	$481,900.00	$76,900.00

Randolph Company acquired its 90% investment in Wilson Corporation on July 1, 1954, on which date the balance of retained earnings of Wilson Corporation was $2,400.

On June 30, 1958, the inventory of Wilson Corporation included merchandise purchased from Randolph Company for $6,400, which was $800 above cost to Randolph Company.

Required:

(1) Consolidated balance sheet working papers as of June 30, 1958.

(2) A consolidated balance sheet as of June 30, 1958.

Problems—Group B

Problem B 28-1. From the following balance sheet data and supplementary information, prepare consolidated balance sheet working papers on October 31, 1957.

	Kramer Company	Barr Company
Assets		
Cash	$ 21,270.00	$ 7,800.00
Accounts receivable	36,800.00	16,200.00
Allowance for doubtful accounts	1,200.00*	800.00*
Inventory	46,500.00	26,600.00
Investment in Barr Company	53,130.00	
Furniture and fixtures	32,100.00	29,400.00
Accumulated depreciation—Furniture and fixtures	14,200.00*	8,600.00*
	$174,400.00	$70,600.00
Liabilities and Stockholders' Equity		
Accounts payable	$ 18,400.00	$ 6,200.00
Income tax payable	12,500.00	7,100.00
Capital stock	100,000.00	50,000.00
Retained earnings	43,500.00	7,300.00
	$174,400.00	$70,600.00

* Deduction.

Kramer Company acquired 100% of the capital stock of Barr Company on October 31, 1953, on which date the stockholders' equity of Barr Company was $51,300.

Problem B 28-2. The Stockholders' Equity sections of the December 31, 1957 balance sheets of Ann Company and its subsidiary, Arbor Corporation, are presented below:

	Ann Company	Arbor Corporation
Stockholders' equity:		
Capital stock	$300,000.00	$100,000.00
Retained earnings	78,000.00	24,300.00

Ann Company acquired 95% of the capital stock of Arbor Corporation on December 31, 1954, for $104,985, when the total stockholders' equity of Arbor Corporation was $106,300.

Determine the amounts at which the following items would be shown in the December 31, 1957 consolidated balance sheet. Show all pertinent computations.

(1) Difference between the cost of the subsidiary stock and the book value thereof.
(2) Minority interest.
(3) Consolidated retained earnings.

Problem B 28-3. The trial balances on the following page were taken from the records of Maxwell Company and its subsidiary, Tuttle Industries, on October 31, 1957.

MAXWELL COMPANY AND TUTTLE INDUSTRIES
Trial Balances
October 31, 1957

Debits	Maxwell Company	Tuttle Industries
Cash.......................................	78,600	22,800
Accounts receivable.........................	69,400	74,500
Inventories, October 31, 1956.................	62,400	25,200
Investment in Tuttle Industries—85%...........	100,000	
Furniture and fixtures.......................	101,800	46,600
Purchases..................................	480,200	305,600
Operating expenses..........................	96,800	34,500
Dividends..................................	20,000	10,000
	1,009,200	519,200
Credits		
Accumulated depreciation—Furniture and fixtures	20,100	14,600
Accounts payable............................	23,200	17,100
Wages payable...............................		1,100
Capital stock...............................	300,000	100,000
Retained earnings, October 31, 1956............	87,300	36,300
Sales......................................	570,100	350,100
Dividends received..........................	8,500	
	1,009,200	519,200
Inventories, October 31, 1957.................	72,800	38,600

On the date on which Maxwell Company acquired its investment in Tuttle Industries, the stockholders' equity of Tuttle Industries was $108,400.

(1) Prepare consolidated working papers for the year ended October 31, 1957.
(2) Prepare consolidated statements for the year ended October 31, 1957.

Problem B 28-4. The following selected account balances were taken from the records of Ace Company and its subsidiary, Deuce Company, on June 30, 1958:

	Ace Company	Deuce Company
Inventory, June 30, 1957.................	$ 42,100	$ 18,400
Sales.....................................	482,300	212,600
Administrative expenses...................	48,200	18,700
Retained earnings, June 30, 1957...........	61,800	24,900
Purchases.................................	286,900	146,700
Selling expenses...........................	42,100	16,700
Dividends declared.........................	30,000	10,000
Dividends received.........................	8,000	

Ace Company acquired 80% of the capital stock of Deuce Company on June 30, 1950, when Deuce Company had retained earnings of $6,900.

The June 30, 1958 inventories were:

Ace Company..............	$37,200
Deuce Company...........	20,600

Deuce Company purchased merchandise from Ace Company for $60,400 during the year ended June 30, 1958.

There was intercompany profit included in the inventories of Deuce Company in the amounts shown on the following page.

June 30, 1957................ $3,800
June 30, 1958................ 1,600

Required:

(1) Consolidated income statement for the year ended June 30, 1958.
(2) Consolidated statement of retained earnings for the year ended June 30, 1958.

Problem B 28-5. Lindsay Company acquired 90% of the capital stock of Howe Company on July 1, 1953, on which date the Retained Earnings account of Howe Company had a credit balance of $16,200.

The following trial balance data were taken from the records of the affiliated companies on June 30, 1958.

Debits	Lindsay Company	Howe Company
Cash......................................	37,640	19,810
Accounts receivable.........................	62,500	35,160
Allowance for doubtful accounts..............	1,800*	1,000*
Inventories, June 30, 1958...................	62,800	41,640
Investment in Howe Company.................	100,000	
Land......................................	50,000	15,640
Buildings..................................	68,450	39,250
Accumulated depreciation—Buildings...........	21,600*	14,160*
Fixtures and equipment......................	74,500	32,640
Accumulated depreciation—Fixtures and equipment....................................	31,200*	18,500*
Cost of goods sold...........................	478,800	220,560
Selling expenses.............................	42,460	21,300
Administrative expenses......................	57,310	30,650
Income taxes...............................	54,110	22,150
Dividends.................................	30,000	10,000
	1,063,970	455,140
Credits		
Accounts payable...........................	29,650	14,190
Wages payable..............................	4,200	
Income taxes payable........................	54,110	22,150
Capital stock...............................	250,000	100,000
Retained earnings, June 30, 1957..............	32,660	2,400
Sales......................................	684,350	316,400
Dividends received.........................	9,000	
	1,063,970	455,140

* Deduction.

During the year ended June 30, 1958, Lindsay Company sold Howe Company merchandise for $182,500. The inventories of Howe Company included intercompany profit in the following amounts:

June 30, 1957................ $4,100
June 30, 1958................ 2,200

Prepare consolidated working papers for the year ended June 30, 1958.

Index